A Study of the Soviet Economy

Volume 1

INTERNATIONAL MONETARY FUND

***

THE WORLD BANK

***

**ORGANISATION FOR ECONOMIC
CO-OPERATION AND DEVELOPMENT**

***

**EUROPEAN BANK FOR RECONSTRUCTION
AND DEVELOPMENT**

February 1991

Applications for permission to reproduce or translate
all or part of this publication should be made to:
Head of Publications Service, OECD
2, rue André-Pascal, 75775 PARIS CEDEX 16, France

Table of Contents

Volume 1

List of Tables

List of Tables (Continued)

C. Fixed Investment and Stockbuilding

D. Incomes and Sources and Uses of Funds

E. Prices, Wages and Labor Productivity

F. Labor Force and Employment

List of Tables (Continued)

List of Tables (Continued)

List of Tables (Continued)

List of Tables (Continued)

List of Tables (Concluded)

List of Charts

List of Charts (Concluded)

Part I

Introduction

Chapter I

Introduction

At the Houston Economic Summit in July 1990, the Heads of State and Government of the seven major industrial democracies and the President of the Commission of the European Communities requested that by the end of the year the IMF, the World Bank, the OECD and the designated president of the EBRD, in close consultation with the Commission of the European Communities, undertake a detailed study of the Soviet economy, make recommendations for its reform, and establish the criteria under which Western economic assistance could effectively support such reforms. The main findings and recommendations were incorporated in *The Economy of the USSR: Summary and Recommendations*, transmitted in December 1990 to the participants in the Houston Summit and published in January 1991. A series of background papers, pulling together the substantial amount of material that was collected and which underpins the views expressed in the summary report, are contained in these three volumes.

Members of the four organizations met with a wide variety of interlocutors at both the union and republican levels, and were received with much courtesy and helpfulness. The staffs of the Ministry of Foreign Affairs and the State Foreign Economic Commission of the Council of Ministers organized most of the discussions. The Gosbank, Goskomobrazovaniye, Goskomstat, Goskomtrud, Goskomtsen, Gossnab, Gosplan, Ministry of Finance, Ministry of Foreign Economic Relations, the State Commission for Economic Reform of the Council of Ministers, Vneshekonombank and many other organizations and individuals provided, at an already exceptionally busy time, unstinting assistance.

These background papers are based on discussions with Soviet officials and material obtained by the teams of the four organizations during visits to the USSR between August and December 1990 as well as sources available in the West. Economic policies are being rapidly modified in the USSR and it is possible that in some areas the situation as described in these papers may have already been overtaken by events. "Estimates" or "projections" refer to those made by the teams unless they are clearly noted as official estimates or projections.

3

The evaluation of economic developments is of necessity conditioned by the availability and quality of economic statistics. Soviet statistics are subject to well-known methodological problems, uncertainties of interpretation and systemic biases which may overstate economic performance. These limitations need to be kept in mind when reading these background papers. Nevertheless, it is the view of the four organizations that the statistical base was generally adequate to support the policy analysis and recommendations made in this study.

The background papers are divided into three volumes. The first volume contains chapters on general economic and reform developments (Part II) and macroeconomic policies and reform (Part III). Volume 2 deals with systemic reforms, including of prices, enterprises, foreign trade, foreign direct investment, the financial sector, labor market and social policies, and the legal system (Part IV). The third volume includes chapters on sectoral issues, including the environment, distribution, transport, telecommunications, agriculture, energy, metals and mining, manufacturing and housing (Part V), as well as a chapter on medium-term economic prospects (Part VI) and a bibliography (Part VII).

Part II

Economic Developments and Reform

The Traditional System And Developments Through 1985[1]

1. BACKGROUND

The USSR, spanning eleven time zones and covering one-sixth of the world's land surface, is geographically by far the largest country in the world. About one quarter of its territory falls in Europe and the remainder in Asia. The northern-most part of the country is arctic desert and tundra; south of the tundra stretch enormous forests, then the steppes and finally the deserts of Central Asia. Some 20 percent of the land is suitable for agricultural cultivation, of which about two thirds—including the famous black soil zone—is in the steppes. However, un-favorable weather conditions make full exploitation of this natural resource dif-ficult.

Within its territories, the USSR has enormous reserves of mineral and raw material wealth. It is estimated to contain around 40 percent of the world's reser-ves of natural gas and almost 6 percent of oil. In addition, it is the leading country in reserves of timber, iron ore, manganese, copper, zinc, nickel, lead and various precious metals. The distribution of unexploited reserves is uneven, and has generally shifted eastward over time: 90 percent of oil production and 75 percent of gas output are concentrated in the Russian republic (RSFSR).[2]

The USSR is divided into fifteen constituent republics (within which are twenty so-called autonomous republics and also some further ethnically-based territorial governments). Of the overall population of more than 288 million, some 51 percent live in the RSFSR, and a further 18 percent in the Ukraine. The popula-tion is growing most rapidly in the five predominantly Moslem republics of Central Asia (currently accounting for some 17 percent of the total). Per capita incomes,[3] which averaged rub 2,210 in 1988 for the USSR as a whole, ranged from rub 993 in Tadzhikistan to rub 2,624 in the RSFSR. Overall, there are more than 170 distinct ethnic groups, and at least 18 different languages having more than 1 million speakers.[4]

2. THE PLANNED ECONOMY

The strategy for economic growth in the USSR was established in the first Five Year Plan of 1928, and remained fundamentally unchanged for the next 50 years. At the time of the 1917 revolution, and despite a drive for industrialization in the late 19th century, economic development in Russia had continued to lag well behind that of the major European countries and the United States. By the late 1920s, following enormous losses incurred during World War I and the subsequent civil war, and in part due to the perceptions of an increasing threat of further military conflict, the objective of catching up with the West became the dominant influence on economic policy. The relatively liberal New Economic Policy of 1921-28 had mixed results and was seen as inadequate to the task of achieving the desired "dash for growth". The new approach, centered on accelerated industrialization, required the rapid mobilization of capital, labor and material inputs, with lesser emphasis being placed on their efficient use (so-called extensive development). This, in turn, implied the need to raise substantially the share of investment in national income, to increase labor force participation rates and to redeploy labor from agriculture to industry. The introduction of a full-scale command economy—including nationalization of almost the entire capital stock and the collectivization of agriculture—was seen as the only way to achieve these shifts in resources at the required pace.

The system that evolved was composed of a set of all-union ministries and state committees (such as Gosplan—the central planning agency—and the state committees on prices, labor and material supply) whose heads comprised the Council of Ministers, the chief executive body of the Government. The Communist Party of the Soviet Union (CPSU), however, was the dominant force, with virtually all the principal economic policymakers belonging to its Central Committee, which in turn formally elected the ruling Politburo.

With over 90 percent of production brought under direct state control, and with the coordinating role of markets almost entirely suppressed, the implementation of the broad economic objectives required detailed, centrally-determined, plans for the inputs and outputs of all branches of the economy. To facilitate the monitoring and processing of information between the central planning authorities and state enterprises, branch ministries were established, typically along sectoral lines. Annual plans, in principle consistent with the strategic Five Year Plans, generated sets of targets for the ministries, which in turn distributed these amongst the individual enterprises under their control. In general, the primary target was specified in terms of the physical volume of production, and rewards for managers and ministers were tied closely to plan fulfillment. Financial or efficiency objectives were, at best, of secondary importance and loss-making enterprises were rarely if ever shut down (the losses being absorbed by the state budget, the extension of credit, or through cross-subsidization within ministries). Direct competition between enterprises was typically suppressed, being viewed as a drain on

8

planning resources and a sacrifice of economies of scale. Consequently, production tended to be highly concentrated, with, in many cases, only one or two producers of a particular good in the entire country.

Under the command economy, the distribution priorities of the ruling Communist Party were directly enforced. The traditional top priority was investment in heavy industry, viewed by Marxist-Leninist political economists as the key to rapid economic growth, but also by the leadership as the basis for large scale weapons production, which was seen both as an essential guarantee of national security and as a means of projecting Soviet influence abroad. The high rate of capital formation and rapid expansion of heavy industry were accompanied by relatively slow growth of consumer goods production. As the result of an unfavorable relative price structure and a general lack of incentives and inputs, agriculture also became a neglected sector of the economy.[5]

The planning authorities controlled most investment at the enterprise level. The bulk of enterprise profits and depreciation allowances fell under the direction of the branch ministries, which reallocated funds for investment between their enterprises according to the requirements of the plan. The residual accrued to the state budget and was used partly to finance some investment directly from the center. Basic inputs were included in the so-called material balances, which the planners formulated to balance the production, stockbuilding and usage of hundreds and even thousands of products considered critical to fulfillment of the national economic plan.

The combination of gross output targets and soft budget constraints meant that demand for labor was consistently high—even though, once employed, workers could not normally be laid off without their consent. Enterprises were entrusted with the provision of many social benefits to their employees, including health care, recreation and vacation facilities and, in some cases, accommodation. Thus, despite strict controls on wages, there was some scope for enterprises to bid for extra labor by offering improved working conditions. As forced labor and various administrative restrictions on mobility declined significantly in importance after the mid-1950s, workers were increasingly able to respond to the demands for their services, and a labor market (albeit heavily regulated) developed.[6] The tying of most social benefits to employment, the lack of any system of unemployment benefits, and the inherent bias towards excess demand for labor are thought to have kept unemployment artificially low and essentially frictional in nature.

The substantial information flows connected with the planning and evaluation process took place mainly in a vertical, bureaucratic setting rather than in a market context. The potential information content of prices was largely ignored; indeed, it was deliberately suppressed as the planners were intent on maintaining the stability both of producer prices, to facilitate the planning process, and of retail prices (particularly for staple goods and services). Household goods and services were allocated mainly through (highly regulated) market means, however, since

9

formal rationing schemes were viewed as unpopular or too cumbersome. Fixity of prices inevitably led to periodic (in some cases chronic) shortages, which were generally resolved through queuing or by resort to the black market.

With the main allocations determined administratively, and with production and distribution effectively monopolized, price formation was a major challenge. The favored method was to peg wholesale prices at average cost plus a percentage mark-up, which prevented excess profits but discouraged cost saving. The structure of relative prices, though largely arbitrary and fixed, could nevertheless affect the output mix to the extent that enterprises had some scope for changing the composition of their inputs and outputs so as to boost the overall value of their production and their profits relative to the plan.

Private economic activity was strictly circumscribed by law. Households were allowed to hold some "personal" property with income-generating potential—such as small private plots, livestock, automobiles and housing— but resale was restricted and private citizens had little recourse against state-led harassment and confiscation campaigns. Other capital was banned, as was employment of hired labor, and supplies were difficult to obtain through legal channels. The main legally-sanctioned private activity was crop production on the household plots of collective farm members, which typically contributed a disproportionate share of total agricultural output.

In its economic relations with the rest of the world, the Soviet economy became relatively autarkic; for most of the period up to the late 1940s, only a very small share of domestic output was traded internationally. Thereafter, trade volumes rose rapidly, with the majority of this trade being carried out with the East European members of the CMEA, an organization formed in 1949 as a trading bloc for the newly emergent centrally planned economies. Despite a growing role for foreign trade, the authorities attempted to limit the influence of external conditions on the economy; first, by conducting virtually all trade through a state monopoly composed of noncompeting foreign trade organizations, whose function was to export only enough to pay for the imports required under the plan; and, second, by ensuring that changes in world prices were fully offset by implicit variable taxes and subsidies (so-called "price equalization"), with domestic prices remaining fixed. Thus, both enterprises and households were largely insulated from the world economy.[7]

Monetary and fiscal policy had no active, independent, role to play in the planned economy. The monetary system consisted of a monolithic state bank (Gosbank) whose primary functions were to grant credit to enterprises in whatever amounts were necessary to fulfill the plan for output and investment, to take deposits from households (there was little consumer credit), and to issue currency. Interest rates were generally low, in some cases negative in real terms, and capital charges for enterprises were not introduced until the 1960s. Consequently, from the enterprise's point of view, capital was virtually a free good. Enterprise deposits were strictly earmarked for planned expenditures and could not be converted into cash, except to make authorized payments, mainly wages. The accumulation of money by households was kept under control largely by ensuring that their incomes grew no faster than the availability of consumer goods and services. Thus, the avoidance of excess purchasing power in the economy was essentially an administrative matter.[8]

Similarly, fiscal policy was entirely subordinate to the plan's specific objectives for output, prices, defense, and social spending. At an operational level, budgetary preparation and execution, as well as extrabudgetary activities, were simply a part of the planning process. Thus, the state budget and extrabudgetary centralized funds were used to achieve a significant redistribution of resources among state enterprises. Enterprise surpluses were typically transferred to the budget and the centralized funds, and reallocated—often on a discretionary case-by-case basis—for enterprise investment and other uses. Likewise, through product-specific turnover taxes and subsidies—which were, in fact, variable wedges between retail and wholesale or producer prices—the budget fulfilled a redistributive function among households. Adherence to the plan—with full control over incomes, prices and quantities—combined with *ad* hoc direct intervention in enterprise finances, helped ensure approximate balance in the state budget.

3. ECONOMIC PERFORMANCE THROUGH 1985

a. Economic growth

After achieving high rates of growth by world standards in the 1930s and in the years following World War II, the Soviet economy entered a period of secular decline in output growth. When this decline began is a subject of continued debate; official statistics indicate it started only in the 1970s, whereas other sources—both Soviet and non-Soviet—suggest that it was already apparent in the 1960s. It is now generally accepted that official statistics have tended to exaggerate growth by the failure, for example, to adjust adequately for so-called hidden inflation.[9] There is little agreement, however, on the extent of overstatement.[10] According to official statistics, the average annual rate of growth of net material product (NMP)[11] fell from 7.8 percent in the second half of the 1960s to 5.6 percent in 1971-75, 4.3 percent in 1976-80, and 3.2 percent by the first half of the 1980s (Table A.1, Appendix II-1).

The slowdown in Soviet growth has been attributed to many factors. The relative contributions of these are difficult to assess, but it is useful in establishing a context for the reform efforts of the 1980s to distinguish between two sets of factors. The first relates to the choice of growth strategy. By relying on the rapid mobilization of capital, labor and raw materials to generate economic growth, the USSR was bound sooner or later to run into constraints on the availability of resources. It can be argued that, by the 1970s, these constraints were beginning

11

to bite, and that there was little that policy could do to relax them. A second set of factors, by contrast, points to inherent deficiencies in the planning system itself, and it was on these problems that reforms were primarily to focus.

The "extensive" nature of Soviet growth—that is, its dependence on increases in the quantity rather than the productivity of inputs—has been well-documented. Rapid growth in the labor supply was achieved mainly through a progressive rise in the proportion of the population engaged in the active work force, with policies aimed, in particular, at raising the participation rate of women. Fixed capital was accumulated at a rate generally well in excess of output growth, by devoting a much greater share of national income to investment than most market economies could sustain. And full use was made of the USSR's vast reserves of fossil fuels and other raw materials.

Clearly, the labor participation rate could not continue to rise indefinitely, and in the early 1970s it finally peaked at over 85 percent, considerably above the rates prevailing in Western Europe and the United States. Growth in the population of working age slowed, and the largest additions to the working age population were taking place in the predominantly Muslim republics of Central Asia, where the fall in participation rates in the 1980s was several times as great as in the rest of the union (Appendix Table F.1). Moreover, migration from this region to other areas of the USSR with shortages of labor was limited, partly for cultural reasons. As a result, the growth rate of employment began to decline by the early 1980s; indeed, in 1981-85, employment was growing at only one-half the rate of the late 1970s (Appendix Table A.1).

The scope for increasing investment growth was similarly bounded, as the share of income available for consumption had fallen towards the limit of what was considered politically sustainable. The decline in the growth rate of the fixed capital stock is thought to have begun in the late 1960s. By 1981-85, the fixed "productive" capital stock was still growing quite rapidly—at 6.4 percent annually—but at a rate that was only two thirds as great as that in the early 1960s (Appendix Table A.1). This picture is reinforced by the secular trends in investment over the same period. Both gross fixed investment and net fixed investment showed sharp declines in growth between 1970 and 1985, with recorded net fixed investment—in so-called comparable prices[12] —actually falling on average in the early 1980s (Appendix Table C.2).

As far as natural resources were concerned, there had been a tendency to exploit the more accessible reserves first. Costs of extraction and transportation therefore rose as production (of oil and gas in particular) was forced to shift from Europe and Central Asia to harsher and more remote regions in Siberia and the Far East.

Having approached these resource constraints, the Soviet economy could have maintained its rapid expansion only through accelerating productivity growth. However, some studies have estimated that total factor productivity

12

growth also slowed—and perhaps even turned negative—in this period, although this remains a highly controversial issue.[13] It seems likely that the efficiency with which the central planners were able to balance physical inputs and outputs branch-by-branch and enterprise-by-enterprise would have declined as the economy grew and became increasingly complex.[14] It is also possible that, as economic growth slowed, the traditional diversion of higher quality inputs to the defense sector would have put an increasing burden on the other, "productive", sectors of the economy.

At the same time, the incentives for enterprise managers to innovate, increase efficiency or improve the quality of their output were inadequate or even perverse. This stemmed in large part from the overriding emphasis in the plan on gross production targets. Innovation and the search for lower-cost techniques generally involve some short-term disruption to output, as new machinery is installed, employees are retrained and different work practices are tested and developed. But the planning system, which motivated higher production primarily by imposing increasingly ambitious targets, could not afford to allow temporarily lower output from one enterprise to jeopardize the inputs to others. Moreover, the typical rewards to innovation and efficiency in a market economy—lower prices, higher market-share, increased profits—were generally of little or no interest to a Soviet enterprise for which prices were typically set on a cost-plus basis, particularly if they came at the expense of missing the annual production target (to which all bonuses were tied). Even if improved techniques were successful in raising output within the year, the payoff to the enterprise would be extremely limited, since its target for the subsequent year would simply be raised accordingly (the so-called ratchet effect).

Similarly, an enterprise faced with the objective of delivering a certain volume of output had little reason to be concerned about the quality of its products, or whether they would meet the needs of the ultimate customer. While there were provisions in the system for enterprises to raise prices on the grounds of improved quality, no mechanism existed to distinguish genuine from spurious improvements. The artificial deadlines imposed by the planning system tended to aggravate the problem, since enterprises frequently found themselves having to rush production as the end of the year approached. Soviet goods were consequently of notoriously poor quality and low reliability, and, to the extent that this was true of intermediate and capital goods, productivity of the economy as a whole is likely to have suffered.

Despite a fairly elaborate system of wage bonuses, mostly dependent on production performance at the enterprise level, the motivation and morale of the work force were also consistently poor. This was partly a function of the preeminence of investment in the growth strategy, which resulted in a correspondingly limited supply of consumer goods, and implied an almost total neglect of the consumer services sector. But it also reflected some of the frustrations imposed

13

by the planning system: the limitations on private enterprise; the sporadic shortages and associated queuing; and the meager selection and poor quality of those consumer goods that were available.

The infrastructure and environment were further casualties of the preoccupation with growth and meeting the yearly plan objectives. The installation of new capacity was typically given precedence over expenditures on maintenance, transportation, distribution and storage facilities. The roads, the rail networks and the oil and gas pipeline systems, in particular, became increasingly overstretched and dilapidated. Similarly, risks of environmental damage were not allowed to obstruct the resource requirements of rapid industrialization, and would eventually impose enormous costs on the Soviet economy.

Whatever the role of productivity trends in this period, it would appear that the slowdown in output growth—in a generally supply-constrained system—was at least somewhat cushioned by the significant terms of trade gain accruing to the USSR as the result of successive increases in world oil prices after 1973. As the world's largest producer and exporter of petroleum, the USSR benefitted from an overall net barter terms of trade gain in the period 1971-85 that averaged over 3 percent annually (Appendix Table G.4). This enabled it to improve its overall gross barter terms of trade (i.e., the ratio of import to export volumes), by an annual average of more than 3 percent, thereby enjoying a net inward transfer of real resources for both current production and final demand, without having to incur trade deficits.[15] The terms of trade gain was reflected in the sharply rising share of NMP accounted for by foreign trade in the second half of the 1970s (Appendix Table A.3).

b. Broad sectoral developments

Although the share of investment going to industry remained constant in the 1970-85 period at around 35 percent, the proportion allocated to the oil and gas industries combined rose from about 4.5 percent in 1971-75 to almost 8 percent in 1981-85. Investment growth was kept at relatively high levels in these sectors partly to develop new gas fields but also in an attempt to maintain oil output which, by the mid-1980s, had fallen below the level of 1980 (Appendix Tables C.2-C.3 and B.3).

Agriculture continued to claim about 20 percent of total investment, although its share fell slightly below this range in the first half of the 1980s despite the launching of the so-called Food Program in 1982-83.[16] The secular shift of labor from agriculture into industry—and, increasingly, into the so-called nonmaterial sphere—continued during 1970-85 (Appendix Table F.2), although at a much slower rate than in the earlier decades. By 1985, almost 20 percent of the working population was still listed as being principally employed in agriculture. About 20 percent of NMP was also still accounted for by agriculture in 1985, up from about 15 percent in 1980 (Appendix Table A.5). This increase was not the result, how-

14

ever, of relatively rapid growth in real terms; indeed, agricultural value added in comparable prices grew by only 1 percent annually on average in 1981-85, whereas NMP increased at an annual rate of 3.2 percent (Appendix Table A.4). The big boost in agricultural value added in current prices was due to the decision—connected with the Food Program—to raise significantly the level of agricultural procurement prices relative to the cost of agricultural inputs.

In the mid-1980s, the food and light industries combined accounted for only 21.5 percent of industrial value added (down slightly from 1980), testifying to the continued low priority placed on consumer goods.[17] Personal consumption expenditure accounted for about 60-65 percent of Soviet NMP (Appendix Table A.7) and total consumption for about 55 percent of GDP. This compares with an estimated average share of consumption in world GDP of 78 percent. It is widely believed that one counterpart to this was a high, and possibly rising, share of defense expenditure in total national income. This is difficult to substantiate, however, from official figures; neither the budgetary nor the national accounts statistics permit a comprehensive assessment of defense spending.[18]

Foreign trade was dominated by exports of energy products and raw materials and imports of processed goods and food products. Foreign trade turnover rose from about 15 percent of GDP in 1980 to around 18 percent in 1985, largely reflecting higher world market prices for Soviet energy exports. Buoyed by these higher oil and gas prices, the share of energy products rose from 47 percent in 1980 to 53 percent of total exports in 1985 (Appendix Table G.2). At the same time, the share of manufactured products declined as the market shares of Soviet manufactures fell in industrial countries, reflecting a general decline in competitiveness. The terms of trade gains made it possible to raise the volume of imports by one third between 1980 and 1985 without incurring a major trade imbalance. The CMEA countries continued to be the most important trading partners. Because the sharp rise in world market prices of oil and gas around the beginning of the decade affected CMEA trade only with a lag, the share of CMEA countries in total trade expanded from some 49 percent in 1980 to around 55 percent in 1985 while the share of developed countries declined from 32 percent to 26 percent (Appendix Table G.7).

c. Incomes and expenditure

According to official statistics, the average annual rate of growth of private consumption in real terms fell from 4.2 percent in 1976-80 to 2.9 percent in 1981-85,[19] and the share of personal consumption in domestic expenditure fell by about 3 percentage points during the latter period (Appendix Tables A.6-A.7). Stockbuilding—broadly defined—increased in relative importance by roughly the same extent.[20] Equally striking, over the 15-year period ending in 1985, was the almost 30 percent decline in the share of domestic expenditure devoted to net

15

fixed "productive" investment, reflecting the slowdown in growth (during the 1970s) and then actual decline in net fixed investment during 1981-85.

The central regulation of wages, which was intended to keep the growth of real wages in line with gains in labor productivity, performed well in the period 1970-85. The rate of growth of the average monthly real wage declined in line with the falling rate of growth of labor productivity, and even nominal wages consistently grew less rapidly than labor productivity (Appendix Table E.2). The share of primary incomes of the population[21] in NMP fell, as a result, by 3 percentage points between 1970 and 1985. Thus, although the rigidity of the price structure almost certainly generated severe imbalances between the supply and demand for particular goods, there appears to have been no significant buildup of aggregate excess demand pressures.

One trend which emerged clearly in the early 1980s, and which would have a significant influence on economic developments later in the decade, was the progressive shift in income from the state budget to the industrial and agricultural sectors. Between 1980 and 1985, the share of profits in NMP rose by over 6 percentage points, less than one third of which was accounted for by a fall in the share of value added going to households (Appendix Table D.1). The remainder was at the expense of the budget and other miscellaneous categories.[22] Enterprises gained, in particular, from a significant increase in wholesale prices in 1982; while state and collective farms benefitted a year later, as part of the Food Program, from increases in agricultural procurement prices. In both cases, prices at the retail level remained more or less unchanged, and the state budget consequently bore the cost of higher subsidies and lower turnover tax receipts. In total, indirect taxes net of price subsidies fell as a share of NMP by almost 8 percentage points between 1980 and 1985.[23] As profits rose, remittances from enterprises to the budget increased, but by less than 2 percent of NMP. Consequently, by 1985, the state budget was showing a deficit of more than 3 percent of NMP, while enterprises' stock of financial assets—still, at this point, firmly under the control of the branch ministries—had climbed to 27 percent of NMP, from 15½ percent five years earlier (Appendix Tables A.2 and K.5).

NOTES

1. An overview of economic developments and reform in the USSR is contained on pages 2-16 of *The Economy of the USSR: Summary and Recommendations.*

2. More precisely, the Russian Soviet Federated Socialist Republic (RSFSR).

3. On an NMP basis (see section 3.a for an explanation of NMP as opposed to GDP).

4. For further details on republican issues, see Appendix II-4.

5. Over the past quarter century, however, the authorities have attempted in various ways and with some success to step up agricultural production.

6. Though residence permits continued to be required for work in Moscow and some other major cities, the main factor inhibiting labor mobility in the post-Stalin period was (and still is) the difficulty of obtaining housing.

7. One unintended consequence of this, together with various limitations imposed by Western governments, was that it severely curtailed the scope for spontaneous transfers of technology from the rest of the world. Great efforts were made to compensate for the deficiencies in Soviet research and development by the selective imports of Western technology, but with limited success.

8. The authorities also encouraged the population to hold its money in the form of savings deposits rather than currency, so as to discourage its expenditure and to rein in illegal activity. A more favorable conversion ratio had been applied to savings deposits in the early postwar currency reform.

9. Hidden inflation refers to the practice of state enterprises of introducing supposedly new products or claiming to have increased their output of higher quality goods so as to justify price increases that would not otherwise be permitted by the authorities. This phenomenon and others are covered in some detail in Appendix II-2.

   To the extent that unrecorded parallel market transactions involving more than simple retrading might have grown more rapidly than measured output, part of the official overstatement of growth may have been offset.

10. It should be noted at the outset that the reliability of official Soviet statistics in general is often questioned on grounds of methodology, coverage, consistency, issues of interpretation, and the incentives for enterprises, under central planning, to exaggerate their performance.

11. NMP differs from GDP largely due to the exclusion from the former of depreciation and of the value added of services provided by the so-called "nonmaterial" sector that do not directly contribute to material production. In recent years, Soviet official statistics have begun to include calculations of GNP (actually, GDP, inasmuch as net factor incomes from abroad are not included) and retroactively to estimate GDP for earlier years. These GDP estimates are open to several methodological objections, however (see the statistical issues appendix) and for this reason, as well as the fact that most other time series in Soviet official statistics are closely linked to production in the so-called material sphere, this chapter and Chapters II.2 and II.3 discuss Soviet aggregate economic developments largely in terms of NMP.

12. The Soviet concept of "comparable" prices does not strictly correspond to the usual notion of constant prices. See Appendix II-2.

13. Much of the controversy stems from the fact that total factor productivity growth is not directly measurable and is the residual element in econometric estimations of Soviet production functions, about which there is little consensus on functional form. Uncertainties about the data for real growth in NMP and the capital stock are also an important problem.

14. Efforts to keep the system manageable by concentrating production in one or a few firms may ultimately have hampered the process, by magnifying the consequences of shortfalls in one industry or enterprise on others further along the chain of production.

15. Nonfactor service transfers are not included here. To the extent that both exports and imports are composed of raw materials and intermediate products, an improving gross barter terms of trade may be viewed, in a supply-constrained economy, as a factor that positively influences the rate of growth of output.

16. The Food Program consisted of a package of measures designed to improve the efficiency of food production through unified agro-industrial management, greater investment in food storage and processing, and financial incentives for higher output and retention of young workers in agriculture.

17. These figures of course understate the relative importance of consumer goods production in the Soviet economy, as much of agricultural output is sold on collective farm markets and many enterprises nominally in heavy industry also produce industrial consumer products.

18. See Appendix II-2 and Chapter III.1. Following a reclassification of state budget expenditures in 1989, official statistics indicated defense spending in that year of around 8 percent of GDP (Appendix Table J.2). Most of this amount had previously been spread across other categories of state expenditure. Many Western estimates, however, continue to put total defense expenditure substantially higher (in some cases, by as much as a factor of two) than the new official figures would suggest.

19. These estimates probably overstate real consumption growth, because actual inflation was most likely understated. A partially mitigating factor, however, would be the possibility of above-average growth of the informal economy, as noted earlier.

20. Unfortunately, stockbuilding or "the change in material circulating means and reserves" cannot be easily decomposed into its parts, which consist of stockbuilding—as conventionally understood—the change in unfinished construction and changes in "reserves" of the defense sector and those held by the government in connection with natural disaster relief programs.

21. Excluding social security contributions and other social welfare deductions out of enterprise profits, which are classified in the Soviet accounts within the category "surplus product" of economic units.

22. It is not possible, from the statistics, to identify the effect on the budget *per se*. In Appendix Table D.1, the "other" category includes some items which themselves affect the budget—for example, net price equalization taxes on foreign trade. The latter probably rose as a share of NMP in the early 1980s, reflecting continuing improvements in the terms of trade.

23. This fall was accentuated by the early effects, in the second half of 1985, of the anti-alcohol campaign, which reduced alcohol sales sharply (see Chapter II.2).

Chapter II.2

Economic Developments And Reform Since 1985

Numerous steps had been taken by the authorities in the early 1980s to raise productivity, including measures to strengthen labor discipline, tighten surveillance of output quality, improve enterprise rewards for plan fulfillment, give firms incentives for reducing the material and energy intensity of output, and redirect investment toward renovation. These partial reforms foundered, however, on a fundamental contradiction. If efficiency were to be encouraged, bonuses could no longer depend so heavily on the fulfillment of gross output targets. Yet, the coherence and effectiveness of the existing planning and administrative system depended on the ability to generate, at least approximately, a consistent set of inputs and outputs in gross terms. These reform measures were therefore not generally successful, and were seldom pursued beyond an initial experimental phase. Bolder initiatives awaited the arrival of a new leadership in 1985.

1. 1985-87 "CAMPAIGNS"

Soon after assuming the post of General Secretary in March 1985, Mr. Gorbachev began to promote a policy of economic "acceleration" (*uskorenie*) designed to revive economic growth and to tackle three main defects of the economy: inefficiency, poor quality, and lagging technological development. Although the problems to be addressed were mainly systemic in nature, the strategy generally followed the model of earlier partial reforms in that it attempted to improve the functioning of the existing system, rather than changing its fundamental characteristics. The chosen path to *uskorenie* was incorporated into the 12th Five-Year Plan (FYP), which was formulated in 1985 for the period 1986-90, and a series of laws and decrees issued between 1985 and 1987. This strategy had several elements.

First, a major retooling of Soviet industry was planned. During 1986-90, gross fixed investment was set to grow at an annual average rate of 4.9 percent, up from the 3.5 percent achieved during the previous FYP.[1] Within the total, the proportion of investment devoted to modernization and retooling, as opposed to capacity expansion, was to rise from about 38.5 percent in 1985 to 50.5 percent in 1990. The corresponding need for additional machinery was supposed to be met through an enormous increase in investment in the civilian machine-building sector over the FYP period, which was expected to increase its output by 43 percent. Retooling was assumed to require an approximate doubling of the annual retirement rate of machinery and equipment, to over 6 percent (and to almost 10 percent in the machine-building industry). The idea behind this "campaign" was that large-scale re-equipping of industry would quickly raise the average level of technology employed and therefore increase both the efficiency and the quality of production. Consequently, although it involved a higher investment share in output, it was presented as a strategy for "intensive" rather than extensive growth. Among the secondary objectives of the strategy was a shift away from the traditional reliance on imported manufactures paid for by exports of fuel and raw materials, which was viewed as being inappropriate for a modern industrial nation. The success of the strategy was also to be a key ingredient in providing the basis for the very ambitious targets for the growth of consumer goods output by the year 2000.

A second campaign emphasized the strengthening of quality control. In the past, Gosstandart had set technical requirements for products which were supposed to be enforced by enterprises' own quality-control departments. But these departments were under the direction of enterprise managers (except, significantly, in the defense industry). Consequently, when plan fulfillment was threatened or the product was in severe excess demand, managers could override their quality controllers and substandard output would be released. In May 1986, a decree (implemented in the autumn) created a new agency, Gospriemka, which would act as an independent enforcer of state standards in the production of machines and consumer goods. Its inspectors were to be highly paid, with bonuses related to the decline in the number of customer complaints, and were accountable only to Gospriemka (which in turn was subordinate to Gosstandart). The stated aim was to bring 95 percent of Soviet machines up to the "highest world standards" by 1991-93.

Third, a series of measures were taken with the intention of stimulating the "human factor." These included high-level personnel changes, both in the government and in the Party, and the policy of *glasnost'*, which was aimed partly at increasing the accountability of bureaucrats and enterprise managers by exposing them to open criticism. It was also recognized that work incentives were being significantly impaired by the gradual compression of wage differentials and the loss of a clear relationship between bonuses and performance. A decree issued in September 1986 therefore proposed the "increased perfection of the wage system," abolishing some of the more arbitrary bonuses equal to about 20 percent of the total wage; increasing base wages by 20 percent for blue-collar workers and 30 percent for specialists;[2] and giving greater freedom, indeed incentives, for managers to shed surplus labor and permit the existing wage fund to be shared amongst the remaining staff.

A fourth policy, with perhaps the greatest short-term (albeit largely unintended) impact, was the anti-alcohol campaign. The relevant measures, beginning in May 1985, included a cut in alcohol production and an increase in prices (by 50 percent between 1984 and 1987); a reduction in the number of shops, cafes and restaurants allowed to sell alcohol and a time restriction on their sales; an increase in the minimum drinking age; and fines for drunkenness.

Finally, believing that some forms of private enterprise were beginning to encroach on the efficiency of the state sector, the leadership instituted measures to "clarify" the role of private activity in the economy. On the one hand, the campaign against unearned incomes, instituted in the summer of 1986, was supposed to stamp out speculation,[3] embezzlement, bribery and the widespread practice of using state facilities for private purposes. On the other hand, the Law on Individual Labor Activity (effective May 1987) was designed to specify more clearly than before the rules under which legitimate private enterprise could operate, by requiring participants to obtain licenses and making it explicit that private activity was to be part-time only and would not be considered as a substitute for a proper job in the state sector.

2. DEVELOPMENTS IN 1986-87

During its first year, the program to retool Soviet enterprises appeared to be broadly on track. Gross investment in the machinery branch increased by 12.4 percent in 1986 (1985: 4.5 percent—Appendix Table C.2), and production in the machine-building sector rose by 7.1 percent (Appendix Table B.1), although at a rate essentially unchanged from 1985. There was a marked increase in the share of investment in production accounted for by project design as well as by the reconstruction and technical refitting of enterprises (Appendix Table C.4).[4]

By 1987, however, severe bottlenecks were emerging in machine-building. Gross investment in this branch grew by less than 1 percent, and its output growth slowed to 5.6 percent—somewhat below the average of 1981-85—and continued to fall in subsequent years. By the end of 1989, with only one year of the 12th Five-Year Plan period remaining, the cumulative increase in output from the machine-building industry was only half that originally planned for 1986-90.

This campaign appears to have run into a series of problems, the first being one of sequencing. Machines are themselves important inputs into the machine-building process, and capacity at the outset was insufficient both to raise capacity further in the machine-building industry and satisfy the burgeoning demand for machinery from other sectors at the same time. A related difficulty was that the surge in economy-wide investment in 1986 (Appendix Table C.1)—including a rise of almost 10 percent in housing investment—had put strains on the supply of

21

other resources needed for project implementation, notably manpower and materials from the construction sector. These strains may be reflected in the sharp reduction in stockbuilding in 1987 (Appendix Table C.7). Finally, the campaign had failed to ease the traditional trade-off between quality and output. This time, unusually, it appeared to be quality-control which dominated, initially at least. Gospriemka began in the autumn of 1986 to pursue its mandate with zeal. Some 15-18 percent of output examined was rejected on first inspection and rub 6 billion worth of output was reportedly rejected altogether in 1987. The impact was greatest in the machine-building sector, where 60 percent of production was subject to Gospriemka's scrutiny, compared with an average of 20 percent for industry as a whole. The resulting disruption was widely and publicly blamed for a stall in output in early 1987, and political pressure intensified as production targets were missed and wage bonuses fell. From about March 1987, quality controls were eased and, although their coverage was subsequently extended, Gospriemka's effective impact was significantly curtailed.

On its own terms, the anti-alcohol campaign also began well. By 1987, the volume of alcohol sales was less than half what it had been in 1980, and the numbers of alcohol-related crimes, diseases and accidents were reported to have fallen significantly in just two years. However, illegal brewing and distilling rapidly began to fill the gap left by cuts in official production. The prevalence of drunkenness in the work place, one of the prime targets of the campaign, appears to have diminished only briefly, if at all; in 1987, the number of reported cases more than doubled by comparison with the previous year. In 1984, alcohol had accounted for about 16 percent of retail sales; consequently, the cutbacks were a major factor in the slowdown of total retail trade, which rose in current prices by only 2.5 percent and 2.8 percent in 1986 and 1987, respectively, compared with average annual growth of 4 percent in 1980-84.[5] As noted earlier, the budget suffered significantly from the decline in turnover taxes on alcohol. Moreover, it appears that the hoped-for improvements in productivity failed to materialize— perhaps partly because the campaign reduced further the range of goods available in the stores, with adverse effects on work incentives, and partly because of its limited impact on overall alcohol consumption due to the induced growth in non-state distilling.

Despite the measures intended to clarify the role of private activity, private enterprise may have been more hindered than helped by the political environment during the early years of the Gorbachev administration. Local authorities proved generally uncooperative in issuing new licenses, which in any case were limited to five years' validity and therefore did not provide entrepreneurs with the degree of security they required. The framework for price-setting remained unclear in law, while in practice prices continued to be partly regulated. The lack of legal access to transport facilities, material inputs,[6] and suitable work premises (which local authorities were often unwilling or unable to provide) were all serious impediments to private sector activity. The campaign against unearned incomes had a negative impact on the collective farm markets, which were affected by the catch-all prohibition against speculation.

In sum, the effects of Gorbachev's early campaigns were, at best, mixed, and the strategy of "acceleration" faltered at a disappointingly early stage. Under the impetus of the machine-building program, value added in the industrial and construction sectors rose by 5½ percent and 12 percent, respectively, in 1986.[7] In the following year, however, as the program ran into capacity constraints, industrial growth slowed to about 4½ percent, and the rate of output growth in construction fell by more than half. The slowdown also spilled over into the transportation and distribution sectors (Appendix Table A.4). Agricultural performance appeared to improve markedly in 1986, with net output rising by over 7 percent, but this too turned out to be transitory, and was probably little more than a reflection of poor harvests in the preceding two years. In 1987, following a particularly severe winter, value added in agriculture fell by almost 1½ percent. Growth in aggregate NMP, having picked up slightly to 2.3 percent in 1986, fell back to only 1.6 percent in 1987 (Table II.2.1). Given hidden inflation, NMP may well have stagnated in 1986-87.

Despite the continued decline in the growth rate of value added in this period, growth in the average nominal wage accelerated slightly—reaching 3.7 percent in 1987—perhaps reflecting the changes in wage regulations noted earlier. Real private consumption, while increasing more rapidly than NMP in these years, still rose on average by only 2.3 percent, less than the average annual rate of growth achieved in 1981-85. As a result, the measured household saving rate rose from 6.3 percent in 1985 to 7.6 percent in 1987 (Table II.2.2), and household broad money increased at an average annual rate of just less than 10 percent (Table II.2.5).

The problems of economic management were compounded by the drop in world oil prices. Although the effects were mitigated somewhat by a contemporaneous fall in prices of imported grain, and by the five-year moving average mechanism used in setting intra-CMEA trade prices, the terms of trade declined by a cumulative 12 percent during 1986-87, and by 16 percent vis-à-vis the non-socialist area (Appendix Tables G.4-G.5). In addition, exports of processed goods to the convertible area were adversely affected by the lack of adaptation of the Soviet system to an increasingly competitive world market. Furthermore, exports to developing countries (primarily arms and raw materials) could only be sustained through a further extension of sizable export credits averaging US$10.5 billion per annum during 1986-87 (Appendix Table I.1), many of which were not serviced on a timely basis because of these countries' own payments difficulties.

The authorities responded in several ways. First, exports to the convertible area, particularly of fuels and raw materials, were substantially boosted; overall, export volume to the nonsocialist area increased by 22 percent during 1986-87. Second, over the same period, the volume of imports from the nonsocialist area was slashed by 17 percent (Appendix Table G.5). As a result, the trade surplus vis-à-vis the nonsocialist area rose by rub 4 billion between 1985 and 1987. Third, gold exports were reportedly raised substantially, implying sales both from current production and official reserves.

The external adjustment was mirrored in the balance of payments on both a settlements (cash) basis and a transactions basis.[8] A comparison between the two presentations shows that the decline in exports and imports in convertible currencies between 1985 and 1987 was much sharper on a cash basis than on a transactions basis, which suggests that both exports and imports were increasingly supported by trade credits. The deficit on the services balance in convertible currencies declined slightly as increasing net interest payments (reflecting payments difficulties of debtor countries and the growing convertible debt) were more than compensated by rising net receipts on transport and insurance and on other services. The capital account with the convertible area, which had recorded a surplus of US$2.0 billion in 1985, swung into a deficit of US$4.4 billion in 1987, partly because the USSR encountered increasing difficulties in obtaining syndicated credits in the international capital market, amortization payments rose, and also because there was a sharp reduction in actual repayments of loans extended by the USSR to developing countries. While an overall balance of payments deficit in convertible currencies of about US$1.7 billion was recorded during 1986-87, this was not reflected in gross foreign exchange reserves as measured in U.S. dollar terms (Table II.2.7). This was partly related to valuation changes, as the U.S. dollar declined sharply against major European currencies,[9] and partly to the fact that gold reserves probably declined during this period.

The effects on the state budget of the oil price decline and the costs associated with the "campaigns" were contained much less effectively. The budget deficit rose from about 2½ percent of GDP in 1985 to over 6 percent in 1986 and almost 8½ percent in 1987 (Table II.2.3). In 1986, besides the loss in revenues from foreign trade—due to a narrowing of the gap between domestic and world prices for oil—and from the turnover tax in the wake of the anti-alcohol campaign,[10] there were increased investment expenditures connected with the machine-building program and higher outlays associated with the full-year costs of pension increases implemented in the previous year as well as with the Chernobyl accident. Meanwhile, higher wholesale prices (with unchanged retail prices) increased subsidies and further reduced turnover tax receipts; the latter decline, however, was almost fully offset by increased profit transfers from enterprises to the budget.

The position changed somewhat in 1987, when aggregate budgetary expenditure was kept largely stable as a proportion of GDP, and the increase in the budget deficit, by over 2 percent of GDP, was due partly to a fall in enterprise profit remittances.[11] In an attempt to improve incentives facing enterprises, the authorities had sought to replace a large part of the requisition by the budget of

24

residual profits with fixed-rate taxes—albeit with differing implicit rates across branches. In practice, this led to a reduction in the share of profits remitted to the budget from nearly 60 percent in 1986 to around 56 percent in 1987 (Appendix Table D.6). The decline in revenues from profits was to become a serious problem for the state budget in subsequent years, even though the revenue loss would increasingly be compensated for by cuts in investment expenditures. Some of the reduction in enterprise transfers to the budget seems to have been replaced, however, by a significant increase in financial flows among enterprises through extrabudgetary centralized funds under the control of branch ministries.

In the monetary sector, the 1986-87 period marked the beginning of a series of attempts to compensate for the increased borrowing requirement of the Government by curtailing credit to enterprises. In 1986, bank credit to the state rose by almost 20 percent, while growth in enterprise credit was close to zero;[12] in the following year, credit to enterprises was reduced by 4.8 percent and lending to the state rose by 42.7 percent (Appendix Table K.2). Despite the squeeze on their borrowing, enterprises' bank deposits rose by 37 percent in 1987 alone (Appendix Table K.6), reflecting an increase in pre-tax profits and the fall in the effective profit tax rate (Appendix Table D.5). The increase in enterprise deposits, in combination with the rise in household savings, led to an acceleration of the growth rate of broad money from 8½ percent in 1986 to more than 14½ percent in 1987. With administrative control over enterprise deposits still more or less intact, however, the impact of the monetary expansion was for a time largely suppressed.[13]

3. THE 1987-89 REFORMS AND THEIR EFFECTS

Together with the industrial modernization and discipline campaigns, the Government subsequently introduced a third scheme of "radical reform," which was explicitly endorsed at the 27th Party Congress in February 1986. Reform and industrial modernization were intended to be complementary, but they were bound to conflict initially if the reform were truly radical, as it would involve at least short-run disruption of traditional links between suppliers and customers and modernization based on an evolving restructured base rather than the traditional industrial structure. The reform measures announced over the next 18 months aimed, however, for a hybrid "market socialism," with increased economic autonomy for enterprises and individuals, but still within a framework of predominantly state ownership. Key prices and investment decisions would continue to be controlled by the state, with factor markets narrowly circumscribed. In parallel to the diminishing role of central planning and greater enterprise autonomy, the conduct of fiscal and monetary policy was to become, at least in principle, increasingly independent of the plan.[14]

a. Reforms in planning, management, and distribution[15]

The cornerstone of the reforms was intended to be the Law on State Enterprises, promulgated on July 1, 1987 in time to be reflected in the 1988 Plan. Abolishing the traditional mandatory output targets, it allowed enterprises to contract directly with their suppliers and customers, and gave them greater freedom in decisions concerning investment and the deployment of profits.[16] Central planners and branch ministries would concentrate on formulating long-term investment objectives and putting out procurement contracts ("state orders") for direct government needs.[17] Enterprises were now given centrally-determined profit norms and remained subject to rules governing the setting of prices, but would otherwise be free to produce and trade as they wished. Their profits would be taxed at rates which would be reasonably stable and homogeneous. The residual would be available for allocation across various funds, from which investment would be financed and bonuses and other nonwage remuneration paid.[18] In addition, workers were given an expanded role in the selection of enterprise managers.

In practice, however, state orders accounted for over 90 percent of all industrial production in 1988, and the degree of enterprise autonomy in respect to inputs and outputs was less than had been envisaged. This was partly a result of planners and branch ministries wanting to ensure supplies of low-profit or loss-making items. But it also reflected pressure from enterprises themselves who, in an economy prone to chronic shortages and distribution failures, wanted the assurance of a guaranteed source of inputs to meet their own state orders.

State orders were, however, less tightly specified than the previous production targets. Thus, enterprises, when producing under these new contracts, were able to switch the composition of their deliveries toward higher-priced products. This may have contributed to the very rapid increase in total enterprise pre-tax profits in 1988 (up 16 percent from the previous year (Table II.2.2)), as the gross operating surplus of enterprises (i.e., profits before payment of turnover taxes and receipt of subsidies) increased by 2 percentage points of GDP (Appendix Table D.6).[19] Having generated larger profits, however, enterprises were not in fact subject to a markedly more stable or less differentiated profit tax system than before. *Ex post* tax rates continued to vary from zero to 90 percent, and ministries continued to confiscate profits arbitrarily in order to cross-subsidize loss-making enterprises. Nevertheless, total profit remittances to the budget actually fell in nominal terms in 1988, and after-tax profits in relation to GDP rose by over 4 percentage points. In the face of low or negative real interest rates,[20] and to guard against possible confiscation of funds by branch ministries or the budget, enterprises used much of their increased liquidity to accumulate excess inventories and hoard investment goods. One approach was to launch new investment projects, in the expectation but with no guarantee of being able to procure the additional resources necessary to ensure completion. Following two years in which changes in total "material circulating means and reserves" (i.e., stockbuilding broadly defined) made little or possibly even a negative contribution to NMP growth, the build-up in these resources unambiguously made a significant contribution to NMP in 1988 (Appendix Tables A.6 and C.7).[21] At the same time, the change in unfinished construction almost tripled as a proportion of gross fixed investment (to 9.8 percent) and of GDP—to 2.2 percent (Appendix Table C.5).[22]

The pervasiveness of state orders began to diminish in 1989, leaving an increased proportion of output to be traded on inter-enterprise wholesale markets. This was in the spirit of the provisions of the Law on State Enterprises but under the circumstances it proved to be highly disruptive. The first problem was that a comprehensive network of market contacts between enterprises did not exist. While it should have begun to develop as soon as the new law came into operation, the domination of state orders in 1988 had almost certainly stunted its growth. A significant number of enterprises had so-called "stable links" with their main suppliers and customers, but these would not have provided enterprises with much flexibility in the event of shifts or disruptions in demand and supply conditions of the kind that prevailed in 1989.[23]

The lack of well-functioning markets interacted with the continued growth of enterprise liquidity (Appendix Table K.7) to induce an apparent further increase in 1989 in stockbuilding—although at a slower rate than in 1988—and in unfinished construction.[24] As the role of the state wholesale distributor (Gossnab) declined, uncertainty regarding the availability of inputs and possibly rising inflationary expectations probably encouraged enterprises to accumulate excess inventories. This behavior was, of course, mutually-reinforcing, since hoarding could itself aggravate or even generate shortages, in turn creating the disruption in supply which enterprises had feared. It was also associated with an increasing prevalence of inter-enterprise barter and of a growing tendency toward enterprise self-reliance, whereby firms took on ancillary functions—such as producing their own machine-tools, or consumer goods for their workers—which they might normally have contracted out.

The distribution system for agricultural produce was also adversely affected by the weakening of central control. Farmers were increasingly reluctant to sell their output to the state procurement agencies at what they regarded as inadequate prices and given the growing shortages of various consumer goods available to them. Despite a 16 million ton rise in grain production in 1989, the share going to the state's All-Union Fund was the lowest in 30 years, and a full 30 percent short of the plan. While it had been deliberate policy to reduce reliance on the All-Union Fund, the aim was to spur local production, not simply redirect output onto local markets. The result was an increasingly uneven distribution of food between the cities—which relied heavily on state food stores—and the countryside, as well as across regions.

27

b. Wage reforms[25]

The Law on State Enterprises also substantively affected the growth of wages. Previously, firms were narrowly constrained in making individual wage and bonus payments, and the annual growth in the wage fund was governed by a so-called growth normative, which limited its rate of increase to a fraction (typically in the range of 30 percent) of the rate of growth of output. Under the principle of "full self-financing" advocated by the Law, enterprises could not only more flexibly adjust their production to increase profits, but were now permitted to retain a higher share of internally generated funds (i.e., including depreciation),[26] and to allocate these more freely among wages and the various "funds" to which after-tax profits had traditionally been allocated.[27] This expanded control over internally-generated funds was accompanied by a relaxation of various restrictions on the payment of premia and bonuses.

These changes, coupled with the increased prevalence of worker-elected managers now permitted under the Law, led wages to soar in 1988, with payments from the wage and material incentive funds rising by nearly 7.5 percent, "other remuneration" increasing by over 13 percent (Appendix Table D.3), and the average monthly wage in the material sector rising by close to 9 percent (Appendix Table E.2). In 1989, the growth of wages and other payments from state enterprises accelerated, with wages increasing by 8 percent (the average wage in the material sphere increased by almost 10 percent) and "other remuneration" rising by close to 14 percent.

Faced with the upsurge in wages, the authorities tried various expedients to restrain wage growth, all unsuccessful. In 1989, they attempted to enforce a "normative" guideline that would hold the growth of the wage fund to the growth rate of productivity. In the first three quarters of 1989, wages grew so much faster than productivity that enterprises would have had to institute wage cuts in order to comply with the norm for the year as a whole. The authorities therefore overrode the guideline and instituted in the last quarter of 1989 a highly progressive tax on "excessive" wage increases irrespective of productivity growth. Wage fund increases in excess of 3 percent but less than 5 percent were taxed at a 100 percent marginal rate, increases of 5 percent to 7 percent were taxed at a 200 percent marginal rate, and further increases were taxed at a 300 percent marginal rate. The authorities exempted various high priority branches of production from this tax, and with time the exemptions became so pervasive as to render the scheme ineffective. Indeed, despite an apparent further acceleration of wage growth, tax collections on excess wages actually declined in the first quarter of 1990 from the fourth quarter of 1989. A new scheme was introduced in February 1990, which exempted or partially exempted various branches of production from regulation and redefined thresholds for excess wage taxation in terms of output growth. The successive mechanisms for indirectly controlling wages, and their general ineffec-

28

tiveness, were reminiscent of similar approaches taken in Poland in the 1970s and 1980s.

c. Price reform[28]

Effective January 1, 1988, enterprises were permitted to negotiate "contract" (*dogovornye*) prices for so-called new goods. These prices were still subject to limits, however, and the limits varied across branches and over time. In heavy industry, contract prices applied for two years, after which the price was converted into an official list price compiled according to the standard pricing formulas developed by the State Committee on Prices (Goskomtsen). According to these rules, contract prices could not be higher than the base price of the closest comparable item plus 70 percent of the so-called marginal value of the new good, as documented by the supplier. Contract prices covered about 15 percent of machine-building output in 1989, but in heavy industry outside of machine-building, innovation was less frequent and contract prices were rare.

In light industry, contract prices were permitted on around 15 percent of goods on the grounds of improved quality. From January 1, 1989, these prices were limited to a maximum of 30 percent above list prices but, as opposed to heavy industry, were not subject to a time limit. A further 25 percent of light industry products were allowed a surcharge of up to 30 percent for two years for supposedly attaining world quality standards.

Outside these sectors, all but a few prices continued to be set by the authorities either at the central, republic or local level. The extent of price liberalization was therefore considerably less than had been pursued in, say, Hungary from 1968 or Poland beginning in 1982. The overall impact of the introduction of contract pricing on the wholesale price index cannot be evaluated, since the latter has been compiled only since 1988 after a 10-year hiatus. In 1989, however, the rise in the index was a seemingly modest 1.7 percent.

d. Private/cooperative activities

The authorities began to take a decidedly more liberal approach toward private activity in 1988. The Draft Law on Cooperatives, which appeared in March 1988, placed cooperative ownership—defined sufficiently broadly to include both large collective farms and three-person family cooperatives—on a legal par with state ownership. Cooperatives were allowed to engage in a broad range of activities, to lease property, to subcontract to other cooperatives or individuals, to hire outside labor, and to raise capital through issue of shares. Cooperative protection was further strengthened in the final version of the Law promulgated in May 1988 for implementation effective July 1, 1988. The revisions permitted additional activities, including recycling of waste materials, fishing, road construction, and sport and fitness services. They also simplified the procedures for registration,

29

strengthened legal protections against the withholding or withdrawal of registration, and affirmed the rights of cooperatives to refuse state orders. Nevertheless, some administrative barriers to registration remained (in particular, some local authorities refused to register cooperatives lacking an independent business address, which they knew was difficult to obtain given the shortage of office space and the restrictions on resale and subletting of apartments). Moreover, cooperatives had difficulty in gaining access to scarce supplies.

The initial supply increment from cooperatives was small and competition limited. However, the same price controls that made supplies scarce also provided substantial opportunities for quick profit for those cooperatives able to establish good connections. Public opinion began to associate cooperatives with high prices, speculative profits, and corruption, although quite often cooperatives were themselves reportedly the victims of corruption. The authorities' response, encouraged by state enterprises that were threatened by cooperative competition, was to tighten restrictions. In December 1988, the Council of Ministers forbade cooperative engagement in some activities, while for other activities (in direct violation of the Law on Cooperatives) it allowed cooperatives to engage only under contract with state enterprises and organizations "for which these activities are basic." In October 1989, the Supreme Soviet passed a resolution allowing local Soviets to set maximum prices for cooperative products and forbidding cooperatives from buying state goods for resale or selling imports for more than state stores charged for comparable goods. While attempts to impose surtaxes on cooperative incomes have been rebuffed, special charges are frequently levied on cooperative purchases of inputs.

By the spring of 1990, the official attitude toward cooperatives had become more relaxed, and open discussion of outright private enterprise became generally acceptable. Cooperatives were given the right to charge either state or negotiated prices for their output. Those that chose to charge negotiated prices, however, were required to pay three to five times the official prices for raw materials, according to list prices posted by Goskomtsen, with compliance monitored by inspectors of Goskomtsen and the Ministry of Finance. Fines equal to twice illegally-earned profits could be imposed. State enterprises were barred from supplying raw materials to nonregistered cooperatives or private parties.

According to data supplied by the Union of Cooperatives, the turnover of cooperatives increased from only rub 33 million in 1987 to rub 40 billion in 1989 and rub 32 billion in the first half of 1990 alone. By October 1990, there were some 215,000 cooperatives employing 5.2 million people, or more than 3.5 percent of total employment.[29] Wages earned by cooperative employees in 1989 were officially estimated as accounting for almost 3½ percent of total money incomes received from the socialized sector,[30] up from only about ½ percent in 1988 (Appendix Table D.4).[31]

e. Reforms in the banking system[32]

The authorities began in 1988 to restructure the Soviet banking system. The intention was to create a two-tier system, in which commercial banking functions would be performed by several state-owned banks, specialized by sector, with Gosbank retaining the role of a conventional central bank. It was envisaged that the new banks, though they would be expected to continue to accommodate enterprise demand for credit under the annual plan, would be free to extend additional loans on their own initiative, on the basis of assessment of risk, profitability and creditworthiness. There would be some degree of competition between the banks, subject only to centrally-imposed ceilings on total credit advanced by each bank. In the event, however, the system of specialized banks did little to advance the cause of decentralization and competition. The branch ministries dominated the banks' lending decisions, and the strict sectoral demarcation effectively precluded competition for loans.

Towards the end of 1988, a more radical liberalization began, as the newly legalized cooperatives and some (now more autonomous) enterprises found they had only restricted access to the state-owned banks. The cooperatives and those enterprises with surplus liquidity were permitted to establish their own ("commercial") banks. These were initially almost entirely unregulated, and substantially beyond the influence even of the central bank. They were free to attract deposits from households and extend credit to enterprises in any sector of the economy, and were not subject to the credit controls under which the specialized banks operated. In some respects, they formalized a system of inter-enterprise credit, easing the problem of unevenly distributed liquidity within the enterprise sector. Subsequently, a 5 percent reserve requirement was introduced,[33] along with a range of prudential ratios. Later still, as the state-owned Savings Bank began to lose household deposits—which are a primary indirect source of financing of the budget—a ceiling, equal to the guaranteed rate paid by the Savings Bank, was placed on the deposit rates of these commercial banks. This substantially curtailed their operations in the market for household deposits. Although they increased rapidly in number to more than 400 by September 1990, the commercial banks still accounted for only about 5 percent of all outstanding credit.

In macroeconomic terms, the most significant monetary reform in 1988 was the lifting of administrative control over enterprise deposits. With the extension of self-financing under the Law on State Enterprises, deposits which had previously been strictly earmarked, and often owned "jointly" with a branch ministry, became fungible and at the sole disposal of the enterprise. As a result, the "moneyness" of these deposits (and consequently their potential effect on aggregate demand) was increased dramatically.

31

f. External reforms[34]

Although external sector reforms had been initiated in 1986 with the tentative decentralization of trading rights and the reorganization of government bodies overseeing foreign economic relations, the effects of these measures on foreign trade flows and domestic economic activity remained minimal. Trade continued to be conducted mainly through foreign trade organizations (FTOs). More extensive reform was put off until April 1, 1989 when all state enterprises, joint ventures, production cooperatives and other entities judged by the Ministry of Foreign Economic Relations (MVES) to be competent to trade internationally were given the right to do so.[35] By the second half of 1990, some 20,000 firms were registered to participate directly in foreign trade (although the actual number of participants probably was closer to one third of this total), and their combined share of total transactions had risen significantly at the expense of the traditional FTOs. This dismantling of the state foreign trade monopoly and the licensing of imports under the principle of self-financing were to aggravate balance of payments difficulties in 1989-90 (see section 4.d. and 5.c).

Until 1987, the exchange rate served mainly as an accounting unit, with trade taxes and subsidies making up the difference between foreign and domestic prices. The introduction of differentiated foreign exchange coefficients (DVKs)[36] for most exports and imports from the start of 1987 was intended to give the exchange rate more of an economic function by making enterprises sensitive to changes in foreign currency prices. Trade flows were little affected, however, as most continued to be determined on the basis of plan targets. The dispersion and number of DVKs were subsequently reduced to cover mainly exports and imports of machinery.[37]

Of generally greater importance was the introduction in 1987 and subsequent enhancement of foreign exchange retention quotas, which represented the first breach of the state foreign exchange monopoly. Depending on the degree of processing of their output, enterprises were allowed to retain a portion of their foreign exchange earnings. The conditions under which these retained balances could be used were successively relaxed. Of some significance were the permission to use part of the retained amounts for imports of consumer goods for the benefit of workers, and the introduction of foreign exchange auctions in late 1989 at which excess holdings of foreign exchange could be sold at market exchange rates.[38] The foreign exchange retention scheme failed to promote rapid export expansion, however, due to quantitative restrictions on exports, the largely unchanged price system, and continued central allocation of most material inputs.

Attempts to attract foreign capital through joint-venture legislation failed to elicit a significant response. The initial legislation was passed in 1987 and liberalized in December 1988 to permit majority foreign ownership and enhanced tax benefits.[39] However, the number of joint ventures that actually commenced operation remained small and foreign exchange inflows limited. The reasons for this disappointing response seem to lie in the unstable legal framework, the great uncertainties about economic conditions in the USSR and the continued difficulties encountered by the private sector in securing inputs in the economy.

4. OTHER POLICIES AND DEVELOPMENTS IN 1988-89

a. Financial policies

Government finances continued to worsen in 1988, as revenues fell by a further 2 percent of GDP (Table II.2.3). A renewed deterioration in the terms of trade, and the associated restraint on imports, reduced budget receipts from foreign trade by over 11 percent. This was roughly offset, however, by the beginning of a recovery in turnover taxes, as the anti-alcohol campaign was gradually abandoned and official alcohol production resumed. The dominant factor reducing revenues was the enterprise reform. Self-financing led to a further reduction in transfers of profits to the state budget, equivalent to 1¾ percent of GDP between 1987 and 1988. The counterpart was supposed to be significantly less financing of enterprise investment directly from the budget. But, given the inertia inherent in the planning system and the legacy of investment decisions made in previous years, the anticipated savings did not materialize. In fact, state investment expenditure increased by 6½ percent in 1988, with capital transfers to enterprises and collective farms rising by 8 percent. While the budget's intervention in the use of enterprise earnings declined, financial flows through the so-called centralized funds showed a marked increase of about 70 percent—measured in terms of either inflows or outflows.[40]

In addition to the continued rise in capital spending, significant expenditure pressures came from increases in agricultural procurement prices, averaging 13 percent in 1988 (Appendix Table E.1), and hikes in coal prices at the wholesale level. As a result, consumer subsidies rose sharply and subsidy payments from all sources, including extrabudgetary agricultural price support (financed directly by Gosbank), reached 15 percent of GDP by 1988, one third of which consisted of subsidies on meat and dairy products.[41] Additional demands came from social security transfers, reflecting a 25 percent rise in the minimum pension, and payments to the victims of the Armenian earthquake. Notwithstanding these expenditure increases, it would appear that aggregate budget outlays fell in relation to GDP in part due to a substantial effort to rationalize public sector employment,[42] but a major reclassification of expenditures—notably, a shift of some expenditures from enterprises to defense[43]—means that no firm conclusions can be drawn regarding changes in budgetary outlays in 1988. Given the fall in revenues, the state budget deficit peaked at 9¼ percent of GDP, or 11 percent of GDP including extrabudgetary price support.

The year 1989 marked a turning point for budgetary policy, as the authorities sought actively to contain the deficit. Faced with the emergence of inflationary

33

and external pressures, they revised the deficit target down sharply from the initial limit—equivalent to 11½ percent of GDP—approved by the Supreme Soviet. In the event, the state budget deficit remained unchanged in nominal terms from that of the previous year, and fell to 8½ percent of GDP (9½ percent including extrabudgetary price support). This improvement was achieved entirely through expenditure cuts.

On the expenditure side, a further adjustment of agricultural procurement prices raised domestic subsidy payments from the state budget by the equivalent of half a percent of GDP, and the utilization of contingency reserves was relatively large in the aftermath of the Armenian earthquake. At the same time, however, there was a sharp cutback in budget-supported financing of capital formation—for the first time in recent history—amounting to 1½ percent of GDP. The picture is clouded by a further reclassification of defense outlays—which explains the bulk of the measured jump in military expenditures—but capital transfers to enterprises do appear to have declined in line with the policy of increased enterprise self-financing. The apparent increase in cross-subsidization through centralized funds was, however, inconsistent with that policy. Revenue continued to decline, by nearly one percentage point, to 41 percent of GDP, reflecting, in particular, the drop in enterprise income tax revenue. Part of this fall, however, was offset by increased revenue from income taxes on individuals and social insurance contributions.

As the budget deficit rose, enterprise credit was tightened further in an attempt to prevent serious monetary overruns. Credit to the nongovernment sector (mainly enterprises) as a share of total bank credit fell to around 50 percent by the end of 1989, from 82 percent in 1985. While the squeeze on enterprises was insufficient to offset the acceleration in government borrowing, and the growth rate of total credit more than doubled relative to the 1986-87 period (Appendix Table K.2), there were some corrective effects from the point of view of the banking system. The granting of bank credit to cover losses was reduced and the amount of overdue debt declined from rub 17 billion in 1985 to rub 4 billion in 1989. An exception was the agricultural sector, where the volume of bad loans continued to increase rapidly, leading to a substantial debt write-off (amounting to more than rub 70 billion) in the course of 1990.[44]

b. Organizational and structural problems

(1) Problems with industrial restructuring[45]

With the machine-building campaign having run out of steam and mounting pressures for increased output and quality of consumer goods, the leadership decided in 1988 to begin large-scale conversion of defense-related manufacturing facilities to the production of consumer products. The defense industries had always produced a significant proportion of the total output of consumer durables.[46]

But now it was envisaged that some plants would be completely retooled, and it was hoped that, with better equipment and the defense sector's traditionally higher technical standards, the quality as well as the quantity of consumer goods could be raised.

The growth rate of production of consumer goods—excluding alcoholic beverages—did accelerate somewhat in 1989 (to 5.9 percent), but this was still not much higher than in 1986-88 (average growth rate: 5.0 percent).[47] The conversion process apparently proved more difficult and costly than had been anticipated. The planners were accused of failing to allocate the resources necessary for retooling, and of making no allowance for the lags involved in switching production. It also seemed that some of the enterprise managers involved were less than enthusiastic, arguing that it would have been better to step up military exports to pay for imported consumer goods, so making use of the USSR's existing comparative advantage.

(2) Bottlenecks in transportation[48]

Almost a half of all freight in the USSR is distributed by rail (Table V.3.5). As with infrastructure in general, investment in expansion and renovation of the railroads had traditionally been accorded lower priority than the accumulation of "productive" plant and machinery. In the latter half of the 1980s, the share of total gross fixed investment allocated to the railroad system, having been on a rising trend, declined slightly (Appendix Table C.3). The rail network was perennially stretched to its capacity limits, and functioned relatively efficiently only because freight shipments and the deployment of rolling stock were tightly controlled and coordinated from the center. In 1989, this system was pushed seriously off-balance by the growing decentralization of distribution, increasing shortages of vital spare parts and fuel, and by the lack of labor and warehouse space at city terminals and ports, which frequently resulted in long delays in the unloading of freight. Added to this, a blockade imposed by Azerbaidzhan, during a territorial dispute over the Nagorno-Karabakh region, left a significant number of freight cars stranded in Armenia. The disruption caused by trains arriving late, or not at all, spread quickly from region to region. Bottlenecks intensified in the second half of 1989, as normal harvest-time demands were supplemented by a surge in imports of consumer goods. For the year as a whole, almost half of the nation's railroads failed to meet freight shipment targets.

(3) Problems in the energy sector[49]

As world market prices for oil fell in the mid-1980s, and oil output declined, the authorities attempted to sustain export revenues by rushing new wells into production. The share of total gross fixed investment directed to the oil and gas branches rose from about 8 percent in the 1981-85 period to 10.5 percent by 1989 (Appendix Table C.3). In 1986-89, gross investment in the oil and gas branches

35

increased at average rates, in comparable prices, of around 8 percent and almost 19 percent, respectively, while investment in the coal industry grew by an average of almost 7 percent (Appendix Table C.2). The energy sector as a whole accounted for over 15 percent of gross fixed investment by 1989.

The new oil wells, however, were sited in smaller and more remote fields that were less productive, and extraction techniques were often inefficient. Average unit extraction costs reportedly increased by over 60 percent between 1985 and 1989. By the end of the decade, reflecting the shift of priorities toward the production of consumer goods, the rate of investment growth in petroleum was cut back sharply; in 1988-89, it averaged only one-third the rate of 1986-87. The budget for repairs and maintenance was also apparently cut along with that for new capacity, so that stoppages and breakdowns of oil rigs proliferated. Ethnic unrest in Azerbaidzhan, the site of much of the Soviet oil-servicing industry, cut the supplies of valves and pipes to the Siberian fields. And the pipeline system, which had been in poor condition for some time and was largely neglected in the rush to raise extraction rates, continued to deteriorate. Reflecting these developments, oil output fell by 2.7 percent in 1989 (Appendix Table B.3).

In the coal industry, as production from underground mines in the European USSR fell, increasing reliance was placed on Siberian open-pit mining. This coal was relatively cheap to extract but, being difficult to burn, was frequently rejected by consumers. Relatively mild winters in the USSR in the last three years also tended to weaken demand. Coal output fell for the first time in 1989—by 4 percent (including the effects of major strikes in July)—and was down a further 5 percent for the first three quarters of 1990.

The growth in output of natural gas has also suffered in recent years from a maturing of the more accessible sources: all proven European reserves are now in production, while output from fields in Kazakhstan and Central Asia has already peaked. The main cause, however, of the sharp slowdown in 1989 (to 3.3 percent growth, from almost 6 percent in both 1987 and 1988) appears to be the increasing distribution problems. The Soviet gas pipeline system is enormous (215,000 kilometers in total) and, despite some increase in investment, it has not been possible to devote adequate resources to its upkeep. The pipeline leakage rate is high, and the need for reconstruction is said to be twice the actual rate. Added to this, in June 1989, a devastating explosion destroyed part of the Bashkiri pipeline, a major carrier of natural gas liquids (including 80 percent of all Soviet LPG, used by households for cooking and heating).

The energy sector also appears to be one of the main casualties from a rising wave of popular concern over the USSR's serious environmental problems. Responding to public pressure, the authorities (mostly at a local level) began in 1989 to force the closure of the worst-offending facilities, and to postpone or cancel the construction of others. The nuclear electricity industry suffered a particular backlash from the Chernobyl disaster. Plans for the construction or expansion of a number of nuclear plants were shelved, and the commissioning of others delayed. Local pressure has also postponed the development of natural gas fields on the Yamal peninsula in north-western Siberia. Elsewhere in industry, the most affected sectors were pulp and paper plants (forced to shut down or change their product mix) and some chemical and pharmaceutical industries.

The effects of fuel and raw material shortages, transport and distribution breakdowns, strikes, environmental shutdowns and ethnic disturbances were aggravated by the high concentration of production in Soviet industry.[50] Those industries which relied to a significant extent on imported inputs from the convertible currency area also began to suffer from the shortage of foreign exchange. This affected particularly industries producing intermediate and capital goods, as priority was given to reallocating the dwindling hard currency to industries producing consumer goods or machinery for their production.

c. Frictions in interrepublican trade[51]

As the power of the central authorities declined, the regional distribution of reserves, specialization in production and the structure of interrepublican trade began to have increasingly important implications for the Soviet economy.

Roughly 60 percent of NMP, including in industry, is reportedly generated in the RSFSR alone, with another 20 percent originating in Belorussia and the Ukraine. Only about half of agricultural value added is produced in the RSFSR, however, while 23 percent originates in Belorussia and the Ukraine and another 16 percent in the four Central Asian republics and Kazakhstan (Appendix II-4, Table 13). The Baltic republics emphasize the production of meat, milk and light consumer goods. Russia, the Ukraine and Kazakhstan are the major fuel and metals producers. Moldavia and the Caucasus specialize in fruit and vegetable production. The Ukraine is a major grain producer, while cotton comes from Central Asia, particularly Uzbekistan. Machine-building is concentrated in the European regions of the USSR and the Caucasus.

In terms of the proportion of NMP exported to other republics, the Baltic and Caucasian republics, Moldavia, and Belorussia exported the highest proportions of their value added (in most cases, over 60 percent in 1988) while the Central Asian republics (40-50 percent), the Ukraine (39 percent), Kazakhstan (31 percent) and the RSFSR (18 percent) followed. The RSFSR, by contrast, exported abroad the highest share of its NMP (measured in domestic prices)—almost 9 percent—while the Central Asian and southern republics exported abroad less than 5 percent of their NMP. The higher RSFSR share was due largely to the concentration of energy exports in that republic (Appendix II-4, Table 26).

If trade is valued in domestic prices, the RSFSR, Belorussia, the Ukraine and some of the southern republics have tended in recent years to run trade surpluses with the rest of the union, while every republic has incurred deficits in its trade with the outside world. At the same time, only the RSFSR has been running more than negligible surpluses with the outside world in valuta rubles, i.e., at border prices. Official Soviet re-estimations of interrepublican trade at valuta prices[52] suggest an enormous RSFSR surplus with the other republics (presumably, largely due to its net exports of energy)—equal to more than twice its valuta surplus with the rest of the world in 1987—while virtually all the other republics would be in deficit (Appendix II-4, Table 28).[53]

As shortages of food, consumer goods, and fuels spread in 1989, many of the individual republics—which under glasnost' were asserting increasing autonomy in any event—became more wary of exporting to other regions without greater assurance that their own supply needs would be met in turn. Increasingly, the notion of an all-union, integrated market—albeit the result of central planning rather than market forces—was being challenged. Barter transactions grew in importance, and the attitude of the republics became increasingly autarkic.

d. Economic outturn: growing internal and external imbalances

The sharp rise in the recorded growth of aggregate NMP in 1988—to 4.4 percent—is somewhat puzzling. In industry and agriculture, gross output rose by only 3.9 percent and 1.7 percent, respectively (Appendix Tables B.1 and B.4). But official statistics indicate growth in *net* output of 6.1 percent and 2.5 percent for the two sectors (Appendix Table A.4). Where the implied improvement in efficiency was concentrated, and what could have caused it, is not immediately apparent. Moreover, renewed deterioration in the overall terms of trade and the associated fall in value added generated in foreign trade are estimated to have contributed more than half a percentage point decline in NMP (Appendix Tables G.5, A.3, and A.6).[54] From the domestic expenditure side, the rapid growth in NMP is also difficult to explain. Aggregate consumption grew by 4.2 percent—or less than the rate of growth of NMP—while accumulation reportedly rose by over 5½ percent in real terms. Yet, net fixed investment declined by 7.4 percent, implying that the increase in real stockbuilding and other "material circulating means" must have been equal to some 2.5 percent of 1987 NMP (Appendix Table A.6). As noted earlier (section 3.a), there are reasons to believe that stockbuilding (including increases in unfinished construction) was significant in 1988, but official statistics would appear to imply that the deflator for stockbuilding was essentially unchanged in 1988 (Appendix Tables A.6 and C.7).

The comparatively modest growth rate for NMP in 1989 (2.5 percent) is more plausible, although it too may be exaggerated to the extent that accelerated hidden inflation was induced by the growing scope for negotiated "contract" prices discussed earlier. The recorded slowdown in growth affected virtually all major sectors, except distribution and foreign trade (Appendix Table A.4). Domestic expenditure was more buoyant than output in 1989, and the trade balance made an estimated negative contribution to NMP growth of about 0.7 percentage points.

Within domestic expenditure, the new priority attached to consumption was reflected in a fall in net fixed investment of 6.7 percent and a rise in real consumption of around 5 percent in 1989. Household incomes, however, were up by 13 percent in nominal terms, as growth in both wages and pensions accelerated. Consequently, the measured household saving rate rose by a further 2.8 percentage points in 1989, to a level almost twice that prevailing in 1985 (Table II.2.2).

Higher saving pushed the growth rate of households' financial assets from an average 9.3 percent in 1986-87 to 11.3 percent in 1988 and 14.6 percent in 1989 (Appendix Table K.6). Given that the real yield on households' deposits—if deflated by the underlying inflation rate—was negative in 1989, and with few alternative assets available to households, much of the additional saving is thought to have been involuntary. At the same time, there was a marked shortening in the maturity structure of household assets. The stock of demand deposits and, especially, currency grew more rapidly than the less liquid components (savings deposits, bonds, and insurance policies), reversing the trend of the previous two decades. The relatively rapid build-up in the most liquid assets may have been a symptom of increasing uncertainty—regarding the availability of goods, for example—or of rising fears of possible administrative measures (such as a temporary freeze) against bank deposits. But it is estimated that, by the end of 1989, the stock of currency and bank deposits in the hands of households exceeded their desired level by approximately rub 130 billion (around 30 percent of households' financial assets). Liquidity was also rising strongly during the 1988-89 period in the enterprise sector, where excess money holdings were estimated at close to rub 50 billion in 1989.[55] The inflationary risks this posed were heightened by the freeing of enterprise money from the control of branch ministries. By 1989, the growth rates of M1 and M2 had been in the range of 14-15 percent for three years running, compared to annual average growth of 6-8 percent in the 1981-85 period.

The external current account deteriorated progressively during 1988-89. A renewed drop of world market oil prices, a surge in grain import prices, and the lagged impact on export prices vis-à-vis CMEA countries of previous declines in world market oil and gas prices resulted in a further sharp decline in the terms of trade in 1988. Another factor behind the deterioration in the trade balance was a sharp increase in the volume of imports, particularly from the convertible currency area (Appendix Table H.8). This reflected in part some release of pent-up excess demand, following the decentralization of trade and financing, as well as imports to provide disaster relief after the Armenian earthquake in late 1988. Despite further growth in oil exports, which reached an all-time peak in 1988, and continuing expansion of natural gas exports (Table V.6.6), the trade balance with the convertible currency area deteriorated by more than US$8 billion (on a transactions basis) between 1987 and 1989. Meanwhile, the trade balance with socialist countries also deteriorated by nearly rub 5 billion (Appendix Table H.4), largely due to the lagged deterioration in the terms of trade (Appendix Table G.5).

The worsening in the trade balance was accompanied by growing deficits in the services balance, particularly in convertible currencies, as receipts on transport and insurance dwindled and net interest payments rose sharply. As a result, the current account balance in convertible currencies (on a transactions basis and excluding gold exports) swung from a surplus of almost US$7 billion in 1987 to a deficit of US$4 billion in 1989. Over the same period, the current account with socialist trade partners deteriorated by rub 5 billion to reach a deficit of rub 3 billion in 1989.

The current account deficits in convertible currencies were financed through continued borrowing in the international capital markets, including syndicated credits and bond placements abroad. However, as the possibilities for medium- and long-term financial loans were limited, the USSR stepped up its short-term borrowing in the form of deposits and credit lines with foreign banks. The stock of short-term debt doubled from US$9 billion at end-1987 to almost US$18 billion by end-1989 (Table II.2.7). No significant change took place in the stock of foreign exchange reserves, which appear to have amounted to five months of convertible currency imports by end-1989.

5. ECONOMIC POLICIES AND LIKELY OUTTURN IN 1990

The functioning of the economy continued to deteriorate in 1990, and at an accelerating rate. It became clear that the piecemeal reforms of the previous years had failed to stabilize the economy, let alone produce higher rates of growth. The combination of substantial monetary, fiscal and external imbalances with a disintegrating system of internal trade and distribution brought shortages in some cases to a crisis point. The authorities were faced with severe day-to-day problems of economic management and had, at the same time, to respond to growing pressures to formulate new and more radical reform plans.

a. Financial policies[56]

The authorities intensified their efforts in 1990 to bring monetary growth under control. Attention was focused primarily on fiscal measures—in particular, on recouping some of the drop in revenues (relative to GDP) which had occurred during the late 1980s. But there was also an unsuccessful attempt to move away from automatic money-financing of the deficit, by promoting debt sales outside the banking system.

The 1990 budget sought a cut in the deficit of more than half a percentage point, to below 8 percent of GDP; the adjusted budget deficit was projected to decline by 1¼ percentage points (Table II.2.3). On the expenditure side, investment was to be cut by nearly 3 percentage points of GDP, and defense by half a point. Subsidies were planned to increase by around 1 percent of GDP, and there was to be a 2 percentage point across-the-board increase in social outlays. Social security payments, in particular, were to rise by more than 16 percent in nominal terms. These increased payments, however, were less than half the projected increase in social insurance contributions, which were expected to rise by 35 percent compared with 1989, reflecting an increase in the average effective contribution rates—from around 9 percent to 12 percent—together with sharp increases in wages.

Total revenue was planned to recover by 1¾ percent of GDP. Besides the higher social security contributions, an increase of 1½ percent of GDP was projected for revenue from enterprise taxes and the turnover tax. Foreign trade tax receipts, however, were expected to decline, given the disarray in the oil and gas industry and the foreign exchange constraint on consumer imports.

Preliminary results for the first half of 1990 showed a deficit of rub 19 billion as against a target of rub 33 billion (Table II.2.4). Revenues were slightly above target, with individual income tax collections particularly buoyant as wages continued to rise, and turnover tax receipts marginally exceeding the planned level. However, the slump in production, in combination with a further decline in the effective rate of profit taxation, led to a decline in receipts from enterprises, which fell by 6 percent compared to the budget estimate. Total expenditures were 5 percent below the planned level, mainly because of investment cuts, while in defense and administration spending was precisely as planned.

It seems likely that these favorable outcomes masked upward pressures on the deficit in the second half of the year. The most vulnerable of the budget estimates were those for subsidies, the government wage bill, and revenue from enterprise taxation. Subsidies may have risen particularly as a result of procurement price increases for grain announced in May, and higher government purchase prices for meat effective in October, neither of which were followed by a comparable adjustment in retail prices. Also uncertain was the outlook regarding revenue from foreign transactions,[57] despite a possible windfall from the rise in the world price of oil in the last quarter.[58]

In August, the authorities issued a decree cutting expenditures by around rub 4 billion for the remainder of 1990. This decree, which was supposed to correct for possible slippages, annulled unspent appropriations remaining after the first semester; authorized the Ministry of Finance to prepare a list of nonessential expenditures to be cut in the rest of the year; disallowed funding of construction (except for special projects, particularly housing) not yet begun; and cut foreign grants by rub 0.6 billion. However, its budgetary effect was more than offset by a rub 7 billion spending package which provides rub 4.2 billion to cover the cost of higher prices for cereals, rub 1.5 billion to finance supplementary pensions for World War II veterans, and rub 1.2 billion for the Chernobyl cleanup.

As late as November, revised official projections suggested that the budget deficit may have remained on track for the year as a whole. There could, however, be a significant shift in its composition between the union and the republics. The union budget was expected to have a deficit of rub 67 billion instead of rub 49 billion as planned, while the consolidated republic budgets were expected to show a rub 8 billion surplus rather than the planned rub 11 billion deficit.[59] Shortfalls in tax revenues totaling more than rub 10 billion, mostly from enterprise tax revenue and to a lesser extent from oil exports, were expected to affect primarily the union budget, whereas a considerable portion of the rub 7 billion in revenue windfall from the turnover tax and from income taxes on individuals and cooperatives was to accrue to the republics—which presently retain a substantial share of this revenue. Similarly, on the expenditure side, the republics appeared to be shouldering a smaller portion of the overruns, especially as regards subsidies and possible budgetary assistance of enterprises, than the union.

The authorities had initially hoped to finance the deficit increasingly through the issuance of government bonds to the nonbank public. Bonds were to be placed on a voluntary basis with state enterprises, cooperatives and individuals, and warrants were to be sold to individuals, giving the right to purchase certain consumer durables at a fixed price on a specified maturity date. Most of these issues were unsuccessful. A rub 19 billion tranche of 10-year bonds remained unsold, and had to be taken up by Gosbank.[60] An issue of 5 percent fixed-coupon bonds to be sold to households was a total failure—even after the interest yield was doubled to 10 percent and the maturity halved to 8 years—and sales of the traditional "lottery bonds" were extremely slow. Only the warrants for consumer goods met with a reasonably positive response, although the total amount involved (rub 3 billion) was modest.

In sum, the growth in bank credit to the government is thought to have slowed in 1990 to around 16-17 percent, compared with over 30 percent in 1989—more on account of the reduction in the deficit than of changes in the sources of financing. At the same time, however, credit to enterprises—perhaps reflecting the expected 2 percent decline in pre-tax profits, and a growing unevenness in the distribution of liquidity across enterprises—began to rise again in 1990, and was estimated to be 4 percent higher than at the end of 1989 after four years of continuous decline.[61] As a result, total credit growth—which was originally planned to fall from a rate of 11 percent in 1989 to around 7½ percent in 1990—was expected to have slowed only marginally (Table II.2.5).

b. Economic developments

The energy sector continued to be hit by distribution problems,[62] strikes, interregional conflicts, shortages of spare parts, and a cutback in drilling activity. In the first nine months of 1990, oil and coal output both fell by 5 percent (compared with January-September 1989), while growth in gas production slowed further to 3 percent. In July, the authorities announced that oil exports would be curtailed in order to supply domestic needs, and in August the USSR became a net importer of gasoline for the first time in post-war history. The official estimate of the likely decline in oil output during 1990 as a whole was around 5 percent, implying a level well short of the authorities' original target. As a result, oil exports may have declined by as much as 19 percent in volume terms.

While in 1989 a shortage of foreign exchange had already begun to constrain some producers who relied on imported inputs, by the fall of 1990 this was being cited as one of the main causes of industry's problems. The automobile industry was short of cold-rolled steel sheets, the tire industry of critical additives, the furniture industry of imported dyes and lacquers, and the food processing industry of vital packaging materials.

The primary cause of the foreign currency shortage was the fall in energy exports, but the consequences may have been aggravated by a serious misallocation of the available hard currency. Prior contracts had led to continued high imports of grain being imported despite the record harvest. And enterprises had large quantities of imported machinery sitting idle, as the resources needed to complete the planned investment projects were unobtainable. Enterprises had to be asked to export part of their huge stocks of capital equipment and intermediate products in order to reallocate funds to more productive uses.

The grain harvest was officially estimated at around 220 million metric tons in 1990, up almost 12 percent over 1989. The increase in yields was ascribed mostly to very good weather, which is plausible since other factors were almost entirely adverse. Shortages of fuel, batteries and spare parts had, by July, reportedly put 120,000 combine harvesters and 40,000 tractors out of action. In addition, the usual exodus of students and factory workers to the countryside, upon which farms rely for harvest labor, was significantly smaller than in previous years—the instructions of the central government being in many cases simply ignored. Consequently, one in five of the combines that could be used had no driver.

Although the harvest appeared to be good despite these handicaps, serious distribution problems led to substantial losses of grain (around 30 million tons, on official estimates), and generated severe shortages of supply to the state bakeries during the summer. Among the causes of high losses were a lack of trains and functioning trucks, and a shortage of storage facilities (some of which were full of imported grain).[63] Meanwhile, possibly to an even greater extent than in 1989, farmers were withholding grain from the state partly to feed their livestock, given shortages of other animal feedstuffs,[64] and partly in anticipation of being able to sell on the private markets.[65] Aside from grain, the output of most agricultural products in 1990 was expected to be at, or slightly below, the levels of 1989. Aggregate gross output in agriculture was thought to have remained unchanged.

The authorities expected aggregate NMP to decline in 1990 by around 4 percent, in comparable prices; GDP was to fall by somewhat less, possibly around 2 percent, because of continued growth in the service sector. On the expenditure side, total consumption was expected to rise by 3 percent in real terms, and total fixed investment and stockbuilding were both expected to drop by around 20 percent.

The fall in gross industrial output in the first nine months was put at 0.9 percent, and was expected to exceed 1 percent by year-end. Profits in industry were officially estimated to fall by even more than the approximate 2 percent decline foreseen for enterprises as a whole. Production was hit by serious industrial unrest, leading to an estimated loss of 10 million workdays in the six months to July from strikes and absenteeism. Many of the strikes were related to ethnic and regional conflicts, affecting Armenia and Azerbaidzhan in particular (where industrial production fell 7½ percent and 13 percent, respectively, in the first half). The output of the defense sector fell, higher production of consumer goods failing to offset the fall in military output. Plants continued to be shut down for environmental reasons—in the cement industry, for example—although the authorities attempted to reverse some earlier closures where it was apparent that the impact on supply had been catastrophic (e.g., in the production of raw materials for medicines). With the transport and energy sectors continuing to deteriorate, shortages of fuel and other inputs intensified.

Output levels in the construction and transport sectors were also expected to decline in 1990. The former suffered primarily from a shortage of inputs; production of wood, cement, window-glass, asbestos, concrete-piping and other vital materials were all reported to have fallen in the first half of the year. The total volume of freight carried in the first nine months declined by close to 5 percent, with fuel shortages causing particular problems for road haulage (down 6 percent).

Total employment was estimated to have fallen by 0.8 percent in the first nine months of 1990. If the trend were to continue for the year as a whole, as the authorities expected, employment would have declined for the first time in the post-war history of the USSR. The shift in employment from state to cooperative sectors continued in 1990. During the first nine months, average employment in the state sector dropped by 1.5 percent (1.8 million workers), while the number working in nonagricultural cooperatives rose by 1.2 million, or 46 percent. There are no official statistics for unemployment; but since the labor force remained essentially unchanged in 1990, unemployment is likely to have risen, albeit remaining very low by the standards of most market economies. The official estimate was about 2 million unemployed on average in 1990, about 1.4 percent of the labor force.[66] At the same time, the continued existence of (localized) labor shortages was suggested by reported vacancies of around 3 million.

Household incomes were officially projected to rise by more than 14½ percent in 1990, after an increase of 13 percent in 1989. The growth in money expenditures was expected to reach 13.7 percent, sustained partly by additional imports of consumer goods and partly by increased production from the military conversion program. With overall consumption on a national accounts basis officially estimated to increase in 1990 by around 3 percent, however, the much

44

higher projected increase in nominal consumers' expenditure suggested that the official inflation estimate—at just under 5 percent—might have substantially underestimated the actual rate of open inflation in 1990.

The growing dissatisfaction of consumers, despite official statistics that indicate an increase in real consumption spending, suggests that the official estimates may be overly optimistic. Even if consumption spending had grown, however, the availability of goods was extremely uneven in 1990, with individual items appearing in abundance and then rapidly disappearing altogether. This was often, initially, a supply problem which, because of the uncertainty that the shortages generated, led to panic-buying, hoarding and further shortage. In fact, the large increase in retail sales in the first six months of 1990 is thought to have been partly due to a major episode of panic-buying in May, following an abortive proposal by the Government for large price increases on a range of consumer goods and services (including a tripling of bread and a doubling of meat and milk prices). Intermittent supply required people to stand even longer in queues for whatever product was available on the day, so reducing productivity (queuing often had to be done during work hours) as well as welfare. The worsening shortages also led to an increasing proportion of goods being distributed directly at the workplace, through "invitation only" sales, and on private markets—and therefore to a partial collapse of the traditional system of open sale through state outlets. Moreover, the growth in aggregate consumption may have encompassed forced switches from some products in short supply to others in relative abundance, the resulting "basket" yielding a less-than-normal level of utility. One reason given for the shortages of bread in late summer, for example, was that consumers were substituting bread for meat and other, more desirable but less available, foodstuffs. Indeed, by the summer, almost every major city had outright rationing of some products.

The continued rise in consumers' expenditure in 1990, however, did begin to reduce the rate of growth in households' financial assets—to an estimated 13.8 percent, from 14.6 percent in 1989 (Appendix Table K.6). At the same time, the growth rate of enterprise broad money rose from 14½ percent in 1989 to an estimated 20 percent in 1990 (Appendix Table K.7), partly reflecting enterprises' increased access to bank credit, and, possibly, a significant cutback in stockbuilding to the extent that this was reflected in a rundown of stocks of consumer goods. There was, however, some maturity lengthening, with time deposits growing substantially faster than holdings of M1. Broad money growth in 1990 was expected to be slightly above the 14.8 percent outturn for 1989 which, at a time when the economy was contracting in real terms, suggested that if anything overall monetary policy was being loosened rather than tightened. Indeed, it is estimated that the monetary overhang increased further in 1990, to rub 170 billion for households and rub 85 billion for enterprises (representing 32 percent and 43 percent of sectoral M2 holdings, respectively).[67]

Retail price inflation, as noted, was officially expected to move up close to 5 percent in 1990, compared with 2 percent in 1989. This reflected the growing prevalence of contract pricing and substantial price rises on the collective farm markets (24 percent in the first nine months of 1990). Measured inflation, however, has become an increasingly misleading indicator of excess demand (official estimates of repressed inflation reached almost 7 percent in 1990)[68] and of cost-of-living increases—particularly in the rural areas, where collective farm market prices have a much higher weight than is implied by the retail price index.[69]

c. External developments

There was a further sharp deterioration in the external accounts in 1990. The decline in exports of oil and oil products, in the wake of a further reduction in domestic oil output, is estimated at 19 percent in volume terms (and 31 percent vis-à-vis CMEA countries). At the same time, imports continued to rise, reflecting both planned state imports, which were not cut in parallel with the decline in exports, and direct enterprise imports of consumer durables and food products, as growing domestic demand coincided with disruptions in domestic supplies. In the first half of 1990, the trade deficit against developed countries was US$6 billion (transactions basis), while trade with the socialist countries was in deficit by rub 5 billion.[70] Reflecting seasonal factors and the sharp rise of oil prices from August 1990, however, it was expected that the overall trade deficit might be limited to rub 10 billion for the year as a whole, of which over rub 3 billion (US$6 billion) would be with the convertible area, rub 6 billion with the CMEA countries and the remainder with other countries with which the USSR has bilateral payments agreements (Table II.2.6).[71]

Increasing debt service payments in convertible currencies also strained the external situation. Debt service (excluding net repayments on short-term debt) which had remained almost stable at US$8-9 billion during 1986-89, rose to US$13 billion (33 percent of exports of goods and services in convertible currencies) in 1990, as both principal repayments and interest payments increased (Table II.2.7).[72] These obligations were, according to Soviet officials, serviced on a timely basis. Furthermore, as arrears began to emerge on suppliers' credits in late 1989 and continued growing during 1990, the USSR's credit rating plummeted. Consequently, it became increasingly difficult to renew short-term credit lines and deposits, and the stock of such debt fell substantially (by a projected US$13 billion in 1990 as a whole). In addition, access to syndicated credits and bond issues dried up. Borrowing became possible only with the guarantee of creditor country governments. Such guarantees for financial borrowing were issued by the German Government in the second half of 1990, and other governments made commitments for future loans. In addition, the USSR borrowed US$1 billion against future exports of diamonds[73] and reportedly made extensive use of gold swaps to boost official foreign exchange reserves. Nevertheless, official reserves declined by a projected US$9 billion during the year to US$5 billion by the end of 1990, and arrears accumulated during the year reached an estimated US$5 billion.[74]

In relation to CMEA countries, the USSR accumulated liabilities vis-à-vis all Eastern European countries, except Romania, with particularly large liabilities against the former GDR, Poland, the Czech and Slovak Federal Republic, and Hungary (see Appendix II-3). Total gross external debt, although smaller than for most Eastern European CMEA countries in relation to export earnings, has increased rapidly in recent years and, given the deficits in the current account, the maturities have shortened.[75] External debt contracted or guaranteed by the Vneshekonombank was US$52 billion in mid-1990, including 20 percent at short term.[76] In trade with developing countries, sizable claims were accumulated—more than US$130 billion by end-1989, including about US$29 billion in convertible currencies—though it is questionable how much of this debt will be repaid, at least for several years.

Although no exact information is available from Soviet sources on the share of debt which was extended or guaranteed by foreign governments, it is believed that virtually all of long-term bank loans, but only a small part of other debt, was extended or guaranteed by governments or official export agencies abroad. Based on this information, it appeared that about 33 percent of debt service obligations in 1990 were either official or officially-guaranteed, while 47 percent represented nonguaranteed debt service to banks and the remaining 20 percent nonguaranteed debt to foreign suppliers.

NOTES

1. *Narkhoz 1985* (1986), pp. 61-62.
2. The bonus and wage measures were to be phased in between 1987 and 1990.
3. The definition of speculation was never made clear but in practice it meant any activity which generated earnings deemed by the authorities to be excessive, including, typically, simple arbitrage transactions.
4. Indeed, one goal of the retooling strategy that may have been essentially fulfilled is the shift in the *composition* of investment toward reconstruction and refitting. In 1989, this type of investment accounted for 49.6 percent of the total, compared to the planned share of 50.5 percent mentioned earlier (Appendix Table C.4).
5. Imputed from *Torgovlia SSSR* (1989), pp. 127-28 and *Narkhoz 1984* (1985), p. 483.
6. Private firms were outside the Gossnab (state) distribution network.
7. The growth figure for industry is reported exclusive of turnover taxes so as to exclude the significant effect that the decline in output of highly-taxed alcohol had on overall growth.
8. The balance of payments on a *settlements basis,* as compiled by the Soviet authorities (Appendix Tables H.1, H.3, H.5 and H.7), records only cash transactions, i.e., trade data exclude trade on a barter basis, and trade on a credit basis is recorded only when settlement takes place. Imports financed from gold exports are also excluded. Similarly, the extension or receipt of trade credits is not recorded in the capital account. The balance of payments on a *transac-*

47

tions basis (Appendix Tables H.2, H.4, H.6 and H.8) has been estimated which, in principle, records all trade transactions, including gold, in the year when they take place, as well as trade credits.

9. According to the Soviet authorities, at the end of 1987, 60 percent of bank deposits abroad were denominated in U.S. dollars and the remainder primarily in European currencies and the ECU. The U.S. dollar declined by 32 percent against the ECU between end-1985 and end-1987.

10. Taxes on alcohol are thought to have financed over 12 percent of total state expenditure in the 1981-84 period. By 1987, this share was down to around 8 percent.

11. These remittances fell by a little less than 1 percent of GDP. A sharp drop in unidentified nontax revenue accounts for the remainder of the increase in the deficit.

12. In October 1986, in order to free banks from the burden of monitoring the progress of construction work and in recognition of the fact that a large share of delayed construction projects would never be completed, bank loans of about rub 70 billion to the construction sector were removed from the banks' balance sheets, together with the corresponding contracting enterprises' escrow accounts. (These had represented advance payments by the banks on account of construction projects in progress.) At the same time, it was decided that payment for new construction works would be made directly to the building firms. The 1986 growth rate of bank loans reported in the text has been adjusted for the amount of this operation, which did not imply an actual decrease in credit extended to firms.

13. As will be seen in Chapter II.3, this control was substantially weakened by the Law on State Enterprises, which became effective on January 1, 1988.

14. The shift in primary responsibility over the budgetary process from Gosplan to the Ministry of Finance did not, however, materialize until very recently. From July 1987 onward, Gosplan no longer issued directives, but instead provided "estimates" and "suggestions" to budgetary institutions. Yet, until 1989, spending ministries continued to be rewarded upon fulfillment of these suggestions. In July 1989, Gosplan was assigned an advisory role in the budgetary process. See Chapter III.1.

15. See also Chapters IV.2 and V.2.

16. The abolition of mandatory obligatory targets had in principle taken place in Hungary as early as 1968 and to some extent in Poland in 1982, but in practice, as long as the planning and ministerial apparatus remained fundamentally unreformed, a great number of enterprise output targets continued to be heavily influenced by the central authorities in these countries.

17. This system of state orders was similar in many respects to that used in Poland during 1983-89, although by the end of that period state orders in that country were estimated to have accounted for less than 5 percent of gross output.

18. Being an allocation of profits, these funds are distinct from the "wage fund," which is deducted from revenues in the calculation of profit.

19. The figures quoted here for growth in profits are derived from the aggregated financial accounts of enterprises. These, however, involve large unexplained differences between total sources and uses of enterprise funds and cannot easily be related to national accounts concepts. Any discussion of changes in profits is therefore subject to wide margins of error.

20. The positive real rates of interest in this period suggested by Table II.2.5 must be interpreted in light of the probable understatement of the open inflation rate—and almost certainly of underlying inflationary pressures—by the official deflator.

21. As suggested by the estimates for the contribution of stockbuilding to NMP growth reported in Appendix Table A.6, however, the quantification of "stockbuilding" (broadly defined) may be subject to wide margins of error.

22. Ironically, the hoarding of investment materials and the long gestation periods for construction projects were two of the phenomena which enterprise self-financing under the Law on State Enterprises was supposed to discourage.

23. These "stable links" were to remain in force until 1993. A stable link was defined as a supplier-customer relationship that had been in effect for at least two years prior to the coming into effect of the Law on State Enterprises. It could not be broken without the consent of the customer.

24. The increase in unfinished construction projects may also have been related to the diversion of construction resources to Armenia, following the earthquake there in December 1988.

    The pattern of stockbuilding is somewhat different in the derived financial accounts of enterprises (Appendix Table D.5), which show a fairly moderate increase in stocks in 1988 (about 1 percent of GDP) but an enormous increase in 1989 (about 4.5 percent of GDP).

25. See Chapter IV.6 for a detailed discussion of this issue.

26. The shares of internally generated funds that had to be paid to the branch ministries and the budget were reduced.

27. The main funds are the fund for development of production, science and technology, the fund for social-cultural measures and housing, and the material incentive fund (from which various premia and bonuses are paid). Under the Law on State Enterprises, enterprises were also allowed to amalgamate the material incentive and wage funds into a single labor payment fund, with corresponding adjustments in tax obligations.

28. See Chapter IV.1 for further details.

29. Goskomstat reported average cooperative employment of only 3.8 million for the first nine months of 1990.

30. Cooperatives have been classified as part of the socialized sector by the Ministry of Finance for purposes of compiling the statement on money incomes and expenditures of the population (vis-à-vis the socialized sector).

31. The very rapid growth of this type of private activity compares favorably in magnitude with the experiences of Hungary after 1968 and Poland after 1981.

32. See Chapter IV.5 for further details.

33. This was raised to 10 percent in August 1990.

34. See also Appendix III.4 and Chapter IV.3 for details.

35. Exceptions were retained for certain strategic products (mostly fuels and raw materials).

36. DVKs are coefficients that are multiplied by the official (or valuta) exchange rate to yield the value of domestic rubles to be paid by importers or received by exporters. For further discussion, see Chapters III.2 and III.4.

37. The DVKs were withdrawn with the introduction of the commercial exchange rate on November 1, 1990.

38. The amounts offered in these auctions have remained small. Rates in these auctions have varied, during the first ten months of 1990, between rub 10 and rub 24 per U.S. dollar, compared to an average official exchange rate of rub 0.58 per U.S. dollar.

39. For details, see Chapter IV.4.

40. Even after enactment of the Law on State Enterprises, firms were required to make certain allocations of after-tax profits to their respective branch ministries, which redistributed these funds among enterprises by means of so-called centralized funds that mirrored the types of enterprise "funds" discussed in section 3.b.

41. See the discussion of consumer price subsidies in Chapter III.1. Subsidy rates, calculated in reference to retail price, stood at 233 percent for meat, 247 percent for butter and 171 percent for milk in 1988.

42. As part of this effort, the number of all-union ministries was reduced from 64 to 55 in March 1988. Between 1986 and 1988, the number of workers in state administration (at all levels of government) fell by 523,000, or more than 25 percent.

43. See Chapter III.1.

44. The significance of this write-off will depend on the extent to which it sets a precedent, relieving the recently-imposed pressure on banks to assess the creditworthiness of their borrowers. In itself, it simply involved a shift of nonperforming loans from the state-owned agricultural bank to Gosbank, leaving the state's total assets and liabilities effectively unchanged.

45. For details, see Chapter V.8.

46. In the early 1980s, for example, all television and radio receivers and cameras, around 30 percent of bicycles and vacuum cleaners, and 10 percent of passenger cars had come from industries that mainly produced for the military.

47. *SSSR v tsifrakh 1989* (1990), p. 7. It is unclear whether these data are in current or comparable prices.

48. Problems in the transport sector are discussed in detail in Chapter V.3.

49. See Chapter V.6 for further details.

50. The output of diesel locomotives, for example, fell in 1989 because of a shortfall in deliveries by the only manufacturer of vital electrical components; and the blockade of Armenia left a tractor factory near Moscow without tires—there was no other source in the USSR. One consequence of the highly concentrated industrial structure, together with the sheer size of the country, was that production tended to be relatively transport-intensive. The effects of failures in the transportation system on the overall functioning of the economy were therefore particularly severe.

51. For further detail on republican issues, see Appendix II-4.

52. It is unclear whether valuta prices in this case were meant to reflect world market prices, rather than some average of these and intra-CMEA trading prices.

53. The interpretation of these re-estimations of interrepublican trade is quite controversial, with some republics noting that such quantification overlooks other costs of their association with the union. In any event, a strong national element has been added to the already sensitive issues of property rights, while conversely, disputes over property rights have tended to exacerbate ethnic and interrepublican tensions. Uncertainty over the future political and economic relations within and among the republics has complicated the issue of reform as well as economic relations with the outside world.

54. A possible explanation of the puzzle would be that with the extension and formalization of "contract" pricing in 1988, the rate of hidden inflation may have increased significantly. The official retail price deflator actually registered a lower rate of inflation in 1988 than in 1987 (Appendix Table E.1).

55. See Chapter III.3 for a comprehensive discussion of the "monetary overhang" and a description of the methodology underlying these estimates.

56. See Chapter III.1 for further details on the fiscal system.

57. For instance, a failure to pass through the November 1 depreciation into higher domestic prices of imports could result in an unanticipated import tax shortfall.

58. The projected increase in bank credit to the government for agriculture, which should be seen as a quasi-fiscal operation of Gosbank, should also be mentioned.

59. After allowing for the proceeds of rub 20 billion—which did not materialize, as discussed below—from fixed coupon bonds and consumer durable warrants.

60. Gosbank also had to redeem rub 5.4 billion of government bonds issued in 1957.

61. The figure of 4 percent refers to the growth rate adjusted for the increase in credit extended to the construction sector as a counterpart of "escrow deposits" created by the contracting enterprises. This increase is due to the revival of the system by which building firms are not paid directly by the contracting entities but receive the funds required for the construction through the banking system as "loans" (see section 2).

62. Despite the obvious problems with the pipeline system, the 1990 budget allocated only rub 1 billion to the oil and gas construction ministry for work on pipelines, compared to rub 3.3 billion in 1989 and rub 5.1 billion in 1988.

63. It is not clear why this grain was not being used to supply the state bakeries.

64. Production of hay silage and other roughage crops (60 percent of all animal feed) had fallen in 1989.

65. In the Baltic republics, farmers were able to get prices as much as 5 times higher than the state would pay.

66. See Chapter IV.6 for a more detailed discussion of the issue of unemployment in the USSR.

67. See Chapter III.3.

68. Repressed inflation is defined by Goskomstat as the rate at which prices would have had to rise to maintain the ratio of retail trade turnover to the stock of household money unchanged for the year as a whole. It should be emphasized that this does not measure the rise in prices that would occur in any one year if administrative controls were suddenly lifted. The latter would depend on the *stock* of excess money outstanding, not the *flow* addition to the overhang for the year in question. Nor does the methodology allow for changes in the velocity of the demand for money.

69. Measurement of the living standards of the rural population is complicated by the likelihood that income in the form of home-grown food is underrecorded. In terms of a cost-of-living index, however, prices on the collective farm market would still be the relevant base, since these represent the opportunity cost to households of consuming their own food production.

70. Trade data for the first half of 1990 were not available on a country-by-country basis to permit calculation of the trade balance in convertible and nonconvertible currencies.

71. Soviet trade statistics for the period 1984-89 reveal a pronounced seasonality of exports and imports, which imply a considerable improvement in the second half trade performance relative to the first half. In all years, exports peaked in the fourth quarter and slumped in the first quarter of the following year, because enterprises stepped up their efforts to comply with export targets, including those under international agreements. By contrast, the seasonal peak of imports is in the second quarter. Two factors are likely to account for this phenomenon.

As domestic grain stocks are being depleted, deliveries of imported grain pick up in the second quarter. And, in the absence of interest rate penalties, enterprises rush to use the full annual allocation under the import plan early in the year.

72. These debt service figures relate to debt contracted or guaranteed by the Vneshekonombank (VEB). There is no official data on debt which is not guaranteed by the VEB. However, all such borrowing required licensing from the VEB. By October 1990, total licenses issued amounted to rub 1.7 billion (about US$3.6 billion). The actual use of the licenses, however, was not known.

73. Exports of diamonds are not specified in the published trade statistics. But according to the Soviet authorities, exports of diamonds, other precious stones and jewelry amounted to 905 million valuta rubles (US$1.6 billion) during the first nine months of 1990—15 percent lower than in the corresponding period of the previous year.

74. Arrears identified by the VEB amounted to US$5 billion in October 1990. In addition, there may have been other arrears outstanding.

75. At end-1989, external debt in convertible currencies amounted to 139 percent of exports of goods and services in the USSR, against 227 percent in Bulgaria, 104 percent in the Czech and Slovak Federal Republic, 319 percent in Hungary, 486 percent in Poland, and 2 percent in Romania.

76. It could be expected that the debt figures reported by the Soviet authorities would be slightly higher than those reported by the BIS, because they would be more comprehensive. This is indeed the case for end-1989. However, for the preceding years, the international banking statistics reported somewhat higher claims on the USSR than reported by the authorities. One possible explanation is that the BIS statistics include claims on the two CMEA institutions located in Moscow (the IBEC and IIB) which should be excluded from Soviet debt.

Table II.2.1. USSR: Output and Expenditure, 1976-90

(Annual average growth in percent, comparable prices)

	1976-80	1981-85	1986-89	1986	1987	1988	1989	1990 (official estimates)
NMP produced [1]	4.3	3.2	2.7	2.3	1.6	4.4	2.5	-4.0
by sector of origin:								
Industry	5.0	2.9	3.3	0.6	3.6	6.1	3.1	...
(excluding turnover taxes)	(5.1)	(3.9)	(4.2)	(5.5)	(4.6)	(6.3)	(0.4)	(...)
Agriculture	-0.2	1.0	2.4	7.1	-1.4	2.5	1.7	—
Construction	3.1	3.2	6.6	12.1	5.5	7.6	1.6	...
Transportation & communications	3.8	2.9	0.8	4.2	0.3	5.8	-6.5	...
NMP utilized	3.8	2.9	2.6	1.6	0.7	4.6	3.4	-2.6
Consumption	4.4	3.2	4.1	3.5	3.5	4.2	5.1	3.0
of which:								
private	(4.2)	(2.9)	(3.4)	(1.9)	(2.7)	(3.9)	(5.3)	(...)
public	(5.9)	(4.9)	(5.4)	(4.0)	(7.7)	(5.9)	(4.0)	(...)
Accumulation	2.3	2.8	0.6	3.0	-4.2	5.6	-1.6	-20.3
of which:								
net fixed investment	(2.6)	(-1.7)	(-1.1)	(4.9)	(5.7)	(-7.4)	(-6.7)	(...)
stockbuilding [2]	(...)	(...)	(...)	(0.1)	(-1.9)	(2.5)	(0.6)	(...)
Foreign trade balance [3]	...	...	...	2.0	0.6	-0.6	-0.7	-1.4

Source: Tables A.4 and A.6 of Appendix II-1.

1. As noted in the text, and as discussed in Appendix II-1, many unofficial Soviet and non-Soviet sources suggest that throughout this period official NMP growth rates have been overstated.
2. Implied contribution to NMP growth. For 1986-89, estimates were calculated using official growth rates for accumulation and net fixed investment and the previous year's weight of net fixed investment—in current prices—in accumulation. For 1986 and 1988-89 these estimates differ substantially from those derived from official current price data on stockbuilding.
3. Contribution to NMP growth; merchandise trade only, excluding exports of gold.

Table II.2.2. USSR: Incomes and Prices, 1986-90

(Annual growth in percent)

	1986	1987	1988	1989	1990 (official estimates)
Household money incomes	3.6	3.9	9.2	13.1	14.5
Household expenditures [1]	2.8	3.1	7.2	9.5	13.7
Saving rate (percent of disposable income)	6.9	7.6	9.2	12.0	...
Average monthly wage	2.9	3.7	8.3	9.4	...
Retail price index	2.0	1.3	0.6	2.0	4.8
Enterprise profits:					
pre-tax [2]	15.4	3.8	16.3	11.5	-1.8
post-tax [3]	27.2	11.8	45.5	23.2	...

Source: Derived from tables in Appendix II-1.

1. On goods and services only.
2. Profits before payments to the budget, as in Table D.5, Appendix II-1.
3. Defined in Table D.5, Appendix II-1.

Table II.2.3. USSR: Fiscal Developments, 1985-90

	1985	1986	1987	1988	Estimate 1989	Plan 1990
			(In billions of rubles)			
State budget revenue	367.7	366.0	360.1	365.1	384.9	410.1
Tax revenue and transfers [1]	337.1	335.6	342.9	340.0	361.6	387.8
Income taxes and transfers	148.4	159.7	158.8	154.3	157.3	168.0
of which:						
From state enterprises	115.9	125.9	123.4	115.6	111.4	120.4
Social security contributions	25.4	26.5	28.1	30.1	33.1	44.8
Turnover tax	97.7	91.5	94.4	101.0	111.1	121.9
Foreign activity	65.6	57.9	61.6	54.6	59.0	51.8
Other	—	—	—	—	1.1	1.3
Nontax revenue	30.6	30.4	17.2	25.1	23.3	22.3
State budget expenditure	386.0	415.6	429.3	445.9	465.1	485.6
Economy	217.2	234.1	234.0	203.1	200.1	188.2
of which:						
Investment	63.8	66.4	71.8	76.3	68.0	42.2
Subsidies [2]	69.2	75.2	76.8	88.1	99.7	112.7
Defense [3]	19.1	19.1	20.2	57.3	75.2	71.0
Social and cultural	111.9	119.3	127.6	134.3	139.3	160.5
Foreign activity	2.2	4.9	11.9	15.6	15.4	14.9
Interest payments [4]	...	...	...	4.5	5.3	6.3
Other	35.6	38.2	35.6	31.2	29.8	44.7
Overall balance	-18.3	-49.6	-69.2	-80.8	-80.2	-75.5
Extrabudgetary agricultural price support	...[5]	—	3.6	15.4	9.3	4.4
Adjusted balance	-18.3	-49.6	-72.8	-96.2	-89.5	-79.9
Financing (net)	18.3	49.6	72.8	96.2	89.5	79.9
Foreign	-7.4	-8.6	-7.1	-4.9	-4.6	-4.2
Domestic	35.8	66.4	85.3	95.3	97.1	79.4
Banks	29.4	63.0	79.8	87.5	89.2	60.0
Nonbanks	6.4	3.4	5.5	7.8	7.9	19.4
Overfinancing [6]	-10.1	-8.2	-9.0	-9.6	-12.3	...

Table II.2.3 (Concluded).   USSR: Fiscal Developments, 1985-90

	1985	1986	1987	1988	Estimate 1989	Plan 1990
			(In percent of GDP)			
State budget revenue	47.3	45.8	43.6	41.7	41.0	42.8
State enterprises	14.9	15.8	15.0	13.2	11.9	12.6
Turnover tax	12.6	11.5	11.4	11.5	11.8	12.7
Foreign activity	8.4	7.2	7.5	6.2	6.3	5.4
State budget expenditure	49.7	52.0	52.0	51.0	49.5	50.6
Investment in economy	8.2	8.3	8.7	8.7	7.2	4.4
Subsidies [2]	8.9	9.4	9.3	10.1	10.6	11.8
Defense [3]	2.5	2.4	2.4	6.5	8.0	7.4
Overall balance	-2.4	-6.2	-8.4	-9.2	-8.5	-7.9
Adjusted balance	-2.4	-6.2	-8.8	-11.0	-9.5	-8.3
Memorandum items:						
State budget total investment	9.3	9.4	9.9	10.0	8.4	...
Extrabudgetary centralized funds						
Inflows	0.3	...	3.3	5.2	5.5	...
Outflows	0.3	...	3.0	4.9	5.5	...
Government domestic liabilities	19.7	21.6	29.1	39.2	46.7	61.1

Sources: Ministry of Finance; Goskomstat; and estimates.

1. Includes also revenue derived from sources other than fixed-rate taxes.
2. Subsidy payments include the subsidies proper, expenditure on price differentials, and expenditure for increases in procurement prices.
3. Prior to 1988 only a fraction of actual defense outlays is shown; 1989 is the first year for which global defense data are available. Therefore, the institutional breakdown of budget expenditure is not fully comparable before or after 1988.
4. On domestic liabilities only.
5. Actual amount is unknown and assumed to be zero.
6. Excess of credit plan allocation over required financing.

Table II.2.4. USSR: State Budgetary Operations, 1989-90

(In billions of rubles)

	1989				1990			
	First half		Full year		First half		Full year	
	Plan	Outturn	Plan	Outturn	Plan	Outturn	Plan	Estimate
Total revenue	182.1	188.8	372.7	384.9	208.6	210.8	410.1	423.2
Tax revenue and transfers [1]	171.7	177.7	346.3	361.6	196.3	196.8	387.8	390.8
Income taxes and transfers	77.9	80.3	156.7	157.3	84.4	83.5	168.0	169.9
Individual income taxes	18.2	20.5	36.3	41.7	21.7	23.6	43.5	46.5
Profit taxes and transfers	59.7	59.8	120.4	115.6	62.7	59.9	124.5	123.4
Enterprises	58.1	57.8	117.7	111.4	60.7	57.0	120.4	117.5
Cooperatives and social organizations	1.6	2.0	2.7	4.2	2.0	2.9	4.1	5.9
Social security contributions	15.8	15.9	31.4	33.1	22.1	20.9	44.8	44.7
Turnover tax	52.0	54.4	104.8	111.1	58.8	60.2	121.9	122.5
Foreign activity	26.0	27.1	52.0	59.0	30.4	31.3	51.8	52.2[2]
Other tax revenue	...	...	1.4	1.1	0.6	1.0	1.3	1.5
Nontax revenue	10.4	11.1	26.4	23.3	12.3	14.0	22.3	32.4
Total expenditure	236.5	217.6	480.8	465.1	241.8	229.7	485.6	497.6
Economy [3]	105.1	91.2	203.2	200.1	97.3	88.9	188.2	196.0
Defense	30.1	29.9	78.5	75.2	35.0	34.9	71.0	70.8
Justice and internal security	3.4	3.4	8.5	8.2	5.0	4.9	9.6	10.2
Administration	1.6	1.5	2.5	2.9	2.2	2.2	2.9	4.5
Science	3.8	3.1	7.5	10.1	5.4	5.1	11.0	11.4
Social and cultural	73.4	70.8	143.8	139.3	81.1	77.6	160.5	163.8
Foreign activity	7.6	5.7	18.5	15.4	7.1	6.1	14.9	19.4[2]
Other [4]	11.6	12.0	18.3	13.9	8.7	10.0	27.3	21.5
Overall balance	-54.4	-28.9	-108.1	-80.2	-33.2	-18.9	-75.5	74.4
(In percent of GDP)	(...)	(...)	(-11.5)	(-8.5)	(...)	(...)	(-7.9)	(-7.8)

Source: Ministry of Finance.
1. Includes also revenue derived from sources other than fixed-rate taxes.
2. Foreign financing is estimated as a residual, given the estimated deficit.
3. Includes production-related investment and subsidies.
4. Totals may differ slightly from those in annual tables, as it was not possible to carry out all adjustments for financing elements in debt service.

Table II.2.5. USSR: Monetary and Credit Developments, 1981-90

(Period averages, in percent)

	1981-85	1986-87	1988-89	1990 (estimated)
	(Annual growth rates)			
Total bank credit [1]	8.7	5.2	11.2	10.5
Credit to the government [1]	8.6	30.4	39.4	16.6
Credit to the economy [1]	8.7	-2.3	-4.7	4.3
Of which: short term	10.3	-2.6	-7.4	5.9
Money (M2)	7.5	11.5	14.4	15.3
Of which: households	7.2	9.6	13.1	13.5
	(Interest rates)			
				1990 (Jan.-Sept.)
Nominal				
Demand deposits	2.0	2.0	2.0	2.0
Time deposits	3.0	3.0	3.0	4.0
Average on bank loans	2.4	2.3	2.5	2.8
Real [2]				
Demand deposits	0.9	0.3	0.7	-1.6
Time deposits	2.0	1.3	1.7	0.3
Average bank loans	1.4	0.6	1.2	-0.9

Source: Data provided by the Soviet authorities; projections for 1990.

1. Adjusted for changes in accounting procedures and for debt write-offs (see Table K.1 in Appendix II-1).

2. Nominal interest rates deflated by the official retail price index. The latter is widely considered to understate the actual rate of open inflation in retail sales by the socialized sector which, in turn, at least in recent years, is considered to have understated the underlying rate of inflation.

Table II.2.6. USSR: Balance of Payments on a Transactions Basis, 1985-90

	1985	1986	1987	1988	1989	1990 Projection
I. Balance of Payments in Nonconvertible Currencies (In billions of rubles)						
Current account (excluding gold)	1.6	3.0	1.7	-1.5	-4.0	-7.3
Trade balance	2.2	3.2	2.2	-0.8	-3.3	-6.7
Exports	(49.6)	(49.4)	(48.3)	(46.8)	(46.5)	(41.6)
Imports	(-47.4)	(-46.2)	(-46.1)	(-47.6)	(-49.8)	(-48.3)
Services balance	-0.2	-0.2	-0.6	-0.8	-0.7	-0.6
Transfers	-0.4	0.1	0.1	0.1	0.1	—
Capital account	-2.6	-2.4	-1.9	0.9	-0.2	7.3
Overall balance	-1.0	0.5	-0.3	-0.6	-4.2	—
II. Balance of Payments in Convertible Currencies (In billions of rubles)						
Current account (excluding gold)	-0.5	1.3	4.2	0.9	-2.4	-6.2
Trade balance	1.1	2.5	5.2	2.9	-0.1	-3.3
Exports	(23.1)	(18.9)	(19.9)	(20.3)	(22.2)	(21.4)
Imports	(-22.0)	(-16.3)	(-4.6)	(-17.4)	(-22.3)	(-24.7)
Services balance	-1.5	-1.3	-1.1	-2.0	-2.4	-2.9
Transfers	—	—	—	0.1	0.1	—
Gold exports	1.5	2.8	2.2	2.3	2.3	2.1
Capital account	-2.3	-3.6	-7.9	-3.7	-2.2	-4.2
Overall balance	-1.3	0.4	-1.5	-0.4	-2.4	-8.3
(In billions of U.S. dollars) [1]						
Current account (excluding gold)	-0.5	1.8	6.6	1.6	3.9	-10.7
Trade balance	1.3	3.6	8.2	4.8	-0.1	-5.7
Exports	(27.5)	(26.8)	(31.3)	(33.4)	(35.2)	(36.9)
Imports	(-26.3)	(-23.2)	(-23.1)	(-28.7)	(-35.4)	(-42.6)
Services balance	-1.8	-1.8	-1.7	-3.3	-3.8	-5.0
Transfers	—	—	—	0.1	0.1	—
Gold exports	1.8	4.0	3.5	3.8	3.7	3.6
Capital account	-2.8	-5.2	-12.4	-6.1	-3.5	-7.2
Overall balance	-1.5	0.6	-2.3	-0.7	-3.7	-14.3
Memorandum items:						
Crude oil price [2] (U.S. dollars per barrel)	27.3	14.5	18.3	15.0	18.2	23.7
Current account in convertible currencies as percent of GDP	—	0.2	0.5	0.1	-0.3	-0.6

Sources: Ministry of Finance, Vneshekonombank, Goskomstat, and estimates.
1. Converted at the average official exchange rate for each year.
2. U.K. Brent.

Table II.2.7. USSR: External Liabilities and Assets,
and Debt Service Obligations in Convertible Currencies, 1985-90

	1985	1986	1987	1988	1989	1990 Projection
	(In billions of U.S. dollars)					
External debt	28.9	31.4	39.2	43.0	54.0	52.2[1]
Of which:						
Medium- and long-term	22.0	24.0	30.6	31.8	36.3	42.2[1]
Short-term	6.9	7.4	8.6	11.2	17.7	10.0[1]
Foreign exchange reserves [2]	12.9	14.7	14.1	15.3	14.7	5.1
Net debt [3]	16.0	16.7	25.1	27.7	39.3	47.1
Other external assets [4]	...	18.5	22.9	25.2	28.6	...
External debt service	...	7.8	8.8	8.2	9.4	13.3
Of which:						
Medium and long term	...	7.3	8.2	7.3	7.8	12.1
Principal	...	5.6	6.2	5.3	5.6	8.7
Interest	...	1.7	2.0	2.0	2.2	3.4
Short-term	...	0.5	0.6	0.9	1.6	1.2
Interest	...	0.5	0.6	0.9	1.6	1.2
Memorandum item:						
	(In percent of exports of goods and services)					
External debt	101.8	111.1	117.3	120.5	139.4	129.1
External debt service	...	27.7	26.5	23.1	24.2	33.0

Sources: Data provided by the Soviet authorities; Bank for International Settlements (BIS); and projections.
1. June 1990.
2. BIS data, except end-1990 which is a projection.
3. External debt minus foreign exchange reserves.
4. Claims in convertible currencies on developing countries. In addition, the USSR has claims in nonconvertible currencies.

Chapter II.3

The New Reform Effort

1. THE REFORM DEBATE

The deterioration of Soviet economic performance during the late 1980s, continuing at an accelerating rate into 1990, pointed clearly to the inadequacies of the approach to reforms followed since 1985. In particular, it illustrated the risks of weakening the traditional command mechanisms regulating economic activity without at the same time making rapid progress towards the creation of markets and market-based control instruments and the elimination of price distortions. The worsening economic conditions, against a more difficult political backdrop, created the climate for, in President Gorbachev's own words, an "irrevocable choice" to move to a market economy.

While the goal was set, the path to it nevertheless remained far from clear. The second half of 1990 witnessed a sharp and wide-ranging debate on the means, timing and sequencing of the transition to a market economy, a debate which became intertwined with more political issues, notably the sharing of power between the union and the republics. No fewer than four alternative programs of transition were presented to the USSR Supreme Soviet[1] in the months before the "Guidelines for Stabilization of the Economy and Transition to a Market System" were unveiled by Mr. Gorbachev in mid-October.

At the risk of some oversimplification, the main issues can be highlighted through a brief, and somewhat stylized, comparison of two programs: the one presented in September 1990[2] by the Government (hereafter referred to as the Abalkin program),[3] and that prepared by the group set up under a Gorbachev-Yeltsin agreement in August, led by Academician Shatalin (the Shatalin program).

The two programs differed mainly on the following issues: (a) the roles of the union and the republics in economic policy making; (b) the pace of privatization and price decontrol; (c) the mechanisms of social protection; and (d) the strategy to reduce the budget deficit. Broadly speaking, the model of intergovernmental relations underlying the Abalkin program can be characterized as federal, and that of the Shatalin program as confederal. Accordingly, republics would have exercised much greater control over price policies, privatization and the distribution of deficit goods under the Shatalin approach than under the Abalkin program. In addition, the Shatalin program advocated that the taxing authority should be vested primarily in the republics, which would agree on a formula for sharing revenue with the union, to finance the latter's activities.

The Shatalin program set specific (rather ambitious) targets for the scale and pace of privatization of government property, including several large-scale industrial enterprises, while the Abalkin program envisaged both a more gradual approach to privatization, and the maintenance, even over the longer term, of direct state control over at least one third of the productive structure.

The programs differed also in the approach to price reform. The Abalkin program advocated the maintenance of union-level administrative controls over the bulk of prices in the first year of the transition, and a gradual liberalization, or decentralization of control to the republican and local levels, thereafter. Administered prices of subsidized commodities would be raised sharply at the beginning of the program, in order to drastically reduce consumer subsidies. The program envisaged that households would be compensated for these price increases and that wages and pensions would be indexed to subsequent price changes. The Shatalin program advocated instead faster price liberalization (prices of 70-80 percent of goods would be freed by end-1991), coupled with very tight financial policies, and extensive sales of government assets to absorb the excess liquidity in the economy. Prices of a narrow range of basic goods would remain frozen, however, through 1991; wages would be indexed to a "minimum consumer basket" in which these frozen prices would weigh heavily. This would help prevent triggering an inflationary spiral.

Although both programs emphasized the need to cut the budget deficit (Shatalin advocating its outright elimination at the union level), in neither instance did the measures proposed appear adequate to the task, especially in view of upward pressures on the deficit in 1991, stemming from already enacted tax and pension reform legislation (see section 2.b(1)).

2. THE PRESIDENTIAL REFORM PROGRAM

Following a period of intense debate on the two programs and unsuccessful attempts to work out a compromise, President Gorbachev, on the strength of emergency powers conferred on him in late September by the Supreme Soviet, took steps to arrest the threatening breakdown of economic relations by issuing a decree ordering enterprises to honor existing contracts and maintain established supply links through the end of 1991. At the same time, the President attempted to secure a minimum political consensus on a reform program by presenting the "Guidelines"—approved by the Supreme Soviet on October 19, 1990—a framework which left considerable scope to individual republics to determine the content and pace of reforms in their respective regions. In what follows, an overview is presented of the presidential program, the policies announced in the late autumn of 1990, and the outlook for 1991. Section 3 presents a summary assessment of the proposed policies and reforms.

a. Broad strategy and sequencing

Although the presidential guidelines, in contrast to the Shatalin program, do not specify a timetable for the various phases of the transition process, they outline a broad sequence. Emphasis is placed in the first stage of the program on: (a) stabilizing the financial situation, through steps aimed at reducing the budget deficit, absorbing excess liquidity in the economy and moderating monetary growth, reforming the banking system, tightening financial constraints on enterprises, and improving the external accounts; (b) preventing disruptions of production and established economic links, and improving the supply of consumer goods in the market; and (c) beginning systemic and structural reforms, notably the recognition of private property rights, sales of government property and land reform.

A second stage of the transition process would see a gradual liberalization of prices (still maintaining surveillance over those freed), accompanied by the maintenance of tight financial policies, the setting up of a social safety net and further progress in privatization and demonopolization.

Further structural reforms, including of the labor compensation system, the tax system, and the housing market, would follow. In the final stage, financial policies would be gradually eased, and foreign trade and payments progressively liberalized, as external constraints became less binding.

b. Macroeconomic policies

(1) Budgetary policies

The Soviet authorities made significant efforts in 1989 and 1990 to reverse the steady deterioration of the public sector finances which took place from the mid-1980s (see Chapter II.2). The presidential guidelines called for further progress in this respect, targeting that the state budget deficit should be contained to rub 25-30 billion, or 2½-3 percent of GDP,[4] in 1991, a level expected to require no resort to financing by the Gosbank. However, the draft budget for 1991, submitted to the Supreme Soviet in December 1990, foresaw a deficit (rub 59 billion) virtually double the target in the presidential guidelines. This budget clearly illustrated the difficulty of securing a substantial and lasting improvement in the public finances without fundamental reforms, not only in the fiscal but also in other systemic areas, in particular price and social policies.

63

The draft budget also highlighted the difficulty of conducting fiscal policies appropriate from a macroeconomic standpoint until clear rules for the apportionment of revenue raising powers and expenditure responsibilities between the union and the republics have been defined and accepted. Indeed, since agreement could not be reached between the authorities of the union and of some republics on the proposed budgets of the latter, the budget submitted to, and recently approved by, the Supreme Soviet refers only to the union. Preliminary projections for the consolidated state budget, based on current information on the republican budgets, are therefore subject to considerable uncertainty.

Given continuing uncertainty about the future course of price policies, in particular regarding retail prices (see section c.(6)), the draft 1991 budget was based on the assumption that the retail prices of subsidized commodities would remain unchanged. At the same time it was assumed that a number of retail prices of commodities subject to the turnover tax would be decontrolled, with a view to preventing a loss of tax revenue following expected adjustments in wholesale prices. Accordingly, total price subsidies paid from the union and republican budgets were projected to nearly double in nominal terms, and revenue from the turnover tax to decline markedly in relation to GDP. In the union budget approved by the Supreme Soviet, no revenue is, in fact projected for the turnover tax, on the assumption that it will be fully retained by the republics.

A further element of pressure on the 1991 budget will be represented by wide-ranging improvements in social benefits, including more liberal provision of various welfare payments and a comprehensive reform of pensions.[5] These improvements are expected to lead to an overall 45 percent increase in social benefits, even before allowance for their indexation to prices and for any cost entailed by a proposed new unemployment compensation scheme. Other substantial increases in spending (35 percent or more) are projected for R & D, environmental programs, health, education, and defense. The more than 35 percent increase in defense expenditures was considered by the authorities to be consistent with the previously announced target of a decline in real terms, since the deflator for defense expenditures was projected to rise by around 50 percent.

The growth of tax revenues in 1991 is likely to be adversely affected by the scheduled reduction in taxation of enterprise profits and by the replacement of much of the price equalization taxes from foreign trade with border taxes; in the union budget, receipts from profit taxes are projected to fall by nearly one third.

With a view to offsetting the adverse impact of some of these factors on the deficit, the authorities have taken a number of measures, some of which, however, will involve no lasting improvement in the public finances. Specifically, the measures include:

(1) a trebling (from 12 percent to 37 percent) of the present rate of the payroll tax on employers and the introduction of a payroll tax of 1 percent on employees;

64

(2) the introduction of a 5 percent broad-based sales tax;

(3) rental payments by enterprises engaged in the exploitation of nonrenewable natural resources, such as oil and gas—this levy was expected to yield rub 16.5 billion additional revenue in 1991;

(4) a (one-time) tax on the notional capital gains recorded by enterprises on their "excess" inventories due to the planned increases in wholesale prices—expected to yield rub 9 billion;

(5) a 20 percent levy on funds set aside by enterprises for depreciation (rub 13 billion);

(6) the shifting to extrabudgetary funds of large items of expenditures: pensions (rub 125 billion); capital expenditures (which amounted to rub 42 billion in 1990); transfers to less developed regions of the country (rub 10 billion); and support to restructuring programs for public enterprises. These funds are to be financed by receipts from privatization of state properties, in addition to some of the revenues referred to in (1) and (5) above.[6]

(2) Monetary and financial policies

The presidential guidelines call for measures to address both the "stock problem" of excess liquidity of households and enterprises, and the "flow problem" of effectively moderating the future growth of the monetary and credit aggregates. To absorb enterprise liquidity, the authorities proposed in late 1990 a partial freeze of their deposits, which would eventually be converted into shares and distributed to workers. As regards household excess liquidity, several types of measures were envisaged to absorb it, including the sale of physical assets (such as dwellings and land plots, military equipment with civilian uses, and small businesses in the retail and services sectors) and financial assets with attractive returns, such as the warrants for consumer goods mentioned in Chapter II.2. In January 1991, however, the authorities took more drastic steps to absorb household liquidity, by limiting monthly withdrawals from bank deposits and by confiscating the bulk of higher denomination banknotes, estimated to account for a significant share of currency in circulation.[7] Whether these measures will lead to a lasting reduction in excess demand, will depend, of course, on the stance of monetary and fiscal policies in the coming months.

The presidential guidelines call for a rise in interest rates to increase the attractiveness of bank deposits. Indeed, a first increase in these rates (up to 9 percent) was announced by Gosbank, effective November 1, 1990. There are suggestions in the guidelines that households might be compensated for losses of purchasing power of their deposits entailed by large increases in retail prices, through a revaluation of these deposits. Given the size of the latter (currently equivalent to about 35 percent of GDP), such a move would entail heavy costs either for the budget, the banks, or for borrowers from the banks to the extent that the cost of the revaluation was reflected in lending rates.

The presidential guidelines also refer to steps aimed at containing monetary growth in the near and longer term. No specific targets, however, have been announced to date for the growth of money and credit in 1991. These steps would include the elimination—except on a temporary basis under exceptional circumstances—of financing of budget deficits by Gosbank,[8] and a more active use of indirect means of monetary control, including reserve requirements, refinancing policies and the establishment of at least non-negative levels of real interest rates.

Following a long debate, the Supreme Soviet approved in December 1990 a new central bank law which establishes a Union Reserve System consisting of the USSR Gosbank and republican central banks.[9] The governing body of this system is envisaged to be a Central Council, consisting of 12 members: the President and the Vice President of Gosbank, appointed for six years by the Supreme Soviet, and 10 other members appointed by the President of the USSR on a rotation basis from the presidents of the republican central banks or other leaders of the republics. The Central Council will be responsible to the Supreme Soviet, and define and conduct monetary and credit policies for the whole union within the framework of guidelines approved each year by the Supreme Soviet. These guidelines will include limits on credit that can be extended by Gosbank and the republican central banks to finance the union and republics' budgets, respectively. The Council will also define uniform union-wide rules (including prudential standards) for licensing and supervision of new banks, with a view to promoting competition within the banking system without loosening prudential control. The licensing of all union banks is to be the responsibility of the USSR Gosbank, while republican central banks would be empowered to license banks operating within the territory of the respective republics.

The new law envisages continued reliance on administrative mechanisms of monetary control, including credit ceilings and the regulation of bank interest rates and commissions, although reaffirming the reserve system's powers to utilize mechanisms of indirect control, such as bank refinancing, reserve requirements, and purchases and sales of government securities.

(3) External policies[10]

While the presidential guidelines mention the objective of establishing ruble convertibility towards the end of the transition to a market economy, they do not spell out the steps for achieving it. They make passing references to the abolition of the DVK system, the establishment of a free exchange market and higher retention quotas. Several of these steps, however, have been subsequently enacted through presidential decrees. One of these decrees introduced a new commercial exchange rate, effective from November 1, 1990 and initially set at US$1 = rub 1.66[11] —compared with the level of the official rate of around US$1 = rub 0.55.

The new rate was chosen to ensure that, for 90 percent of exports, prices converted into domestic currency would at least equal present domestic wholesale prices. The commercial rate is to be applied to the bulk of current account transactions, in particular export proceeds subject to surrender, imports covered by the foreign exchange allocation plan and service of the foreign debt, and to inflows of financial loans. A special rate (equivalent to ten times the official rate) will remain in effect for tourist and other noncommercial current transactions.

The authorities also intend to create a free exchange market (possibly by expanding the scope of the existing auction market) in which exporters with surplus retained foreign exchange and importers without adequate foreign exchange allocations will be allowed to participate through the intermediation of banks and brokers. The existing provisions for foreign exchange retention have been modified by another presidential decree establishing a joint union-republic foreign exchange fund, to be fed with surrendered foreign earnings. This decree stipulates that 40 percent of all foreign exchange proceeds must be surrendered by exporters to the fund, for the service of the external debt of the union in 1991. New, generally higher, retention ratios would apply to the remaining 60 percent.[12] Foreign exchange to be surrendered after application of the retention ratios is to be allocated between the joint union-republican and local foreign exchange funds in a ratio of 9:1. It is unclear at the present time whether the republics will agree to the sharing of foreign exchange in the proportions envisaged in the presidential decree. There are also no clear indications at present regarding the extent to which the authorities envisage intervening in the free market, and which institutions (e.g., the union and republican central banks or Vneshekonombank) would be carrying out such interventions.

c. Systemic and structural reforms[13]

(1) The role of central planning

The emphasis placed on stabilizing supply conditions in the first phase of the guidelines is reflected in a presidential decree requiring the maintenance of stable supply links through 1991, and the expectation that state orders will continue to play a major role, at least for one year.[14] Gosplan has prepared directives for the sectoral ministries in the areas reserved to the union,[15] as well as in other areas of crucial importance in the short run, such as the agro-industrial complex and the part of foreign trade to be carried out under intergovernmental agreements.

For the remaining areas, Gosplan undertook more of an advisory and forecasting role for 1991 than in previous years. It remains unclear to what extent central planning at the union level will be replaced by central planning at the republican level.

(2) Ownership relations

Although the presidential guidelines call for legislation to establish private property rights and to promote privatization of state property, they do not specify the form and timing of these actions. In agriculture, the guidelines advocate the co-existence of different forms of land ownership. The extent of, and timetable for, sale or distribution of land is, however, to be decided by each republic. Therefore, it is difficult to foresee to what extent, or how soon, private ownership might replace the traditional, and largely inefficient, state and collective farms.[16] The guidelines also envisage extensive privatization of housing, but leave the definition of policies in this area to a future presidential decree, to be issued in the near future. Privatization is expected to proceed rapidly in the retail and services sector, and for small businesses in the industrial sector. For the larger industrial concerns, which account for a major share of industrial output, the guidelines envisage their transformation into joint stock companies and the eventual distribution or sale of their shares to private investors (with preference to be given to the workers in the firm). While no specific time horizon is indicated, the document suggests that the privatization process is likely to be stretched over a long period, in view of the large book value of state property.

(3) Market structure

The guidelines emphasize the need to promote competition, especially in areas such as agricultural procurement and processing. They call for the creation of anti-monopoly committees at various governmental levels, but do not specify their functions, powers, or timetables for action. Proposed antimonopoly policies center on the taxation of "excess profits" of firms deemed to be in a monopolistic position. By contrast, they make no mention of the potential roles for the dismantling of large industrial concerns and the elimination of product "profile restrictions," or for import liberalization in promoting competition.

(4) Enterprise management

While the guidelines envisage the tightening of budget constraints on—and financial accountability of—state enterprises, they remain silent on such important issues as: the criteria for selecting managers of enterprises which would remain under state ownership or control and for assessing their performance; the prospective role of workers' organizations in enterprise management; and the degree of autonomy that managers would be afforded in, *inter alia*, investment and employment decisions. For the near term, at least, the emphasis placed on maintaining existing economic links and on controls over prices and wages (see below) would appear to imply that enterprises' autonomy will remain substantially constrained.

(5) Industrial restructuring and military conversion program

The presidential guidelines call for a major redirection of resources and investment towards industries producing consumer goods. It envisages that certain current investment projects in non-priority sectors may be reconverted if possible, or halted altogether, and unfinished construction sold off to the extent feasible. The restructuring effort is to be fostered through the tightening of budget constraints on enterprises, increases in interest rates on investment loans and the closing of nonviable firms (which the guidelines estimate to number several hundred). The program envisages the creation of special "stabilization funds" to provide temporary support during the restructuring period to loss-making firms deemed economically viable. It says little, however, about the criteria for distribution of these funds or the duration of the proposed support.

Although the presidential program does not provide details on military conversion plans, the authorities have indicated that the production of civilian goods by defense industries is targeted to increase by 30 percent over the period 1989-91. Accordingly, the share of civilian goods in the output of defense industries would rise by about 10 percentage points, to over 50 percent, from 1988 to 1991. The military conversion process is expected to be guided primarily by state orders, rather than by market instruments.

(6) Price reform[17]

In the price policy area, the presidential guidelines follow more closely the approach envisaged in the Abalkin program than in the Shatalin plan. Liberalization is to proceed cautiously at both the wholesale and the retail levels, while an attempt is to be made to correct administratively the largest distortions in relative prices. As regards wholesale prices, the authorities envisage two categories. One group (consisting of energy products, raw materials, and strategic intermediate goods) is to remain controlled, with prices set on the basis of a new list established by the central and regional price authorities.[18] For other products, prices are to be set contractually between enterprises. However, it is also expected that these prices would be set on the basis either of guidelines prepared by the State Committee on Prices (Goskomtsen) or of cost developments plus a standardized markup. Preliminary indications suggest that administered wholesale prices would be increased at the beginning of 1991 on average by 50-60 percent, with some increases (e.g., for petroleum) ranging up to 130 percent. Agricultural procurement prices not already increased in 1990 were expected to rise on average by about 30 percent at the beginning of 1991.

As regards retail prices, 5-15 percent of these prices (mainly for "luxury goods") were expected to be liberalized before the end of 1990. The debate on further reforms in this area in 1991 continued, with union authorities advocating modest further liberalization but an administrative pass-through to the retail level of most increases in wholesale and procurement prices. Others, in particular in

69

some republics, supported rapid decontrol of most prices, with the exception of a few staple commodities which could be subject to rationing.

(7) Labor market, wages and social policies[19]

The presidential guidelines recognize that the necessary restructuring of industry is likely to entail losses of jobs in many state enterprises, which are currently substantially overmanned. They give no estimate, however, of either the scale of these losses or the scope for creation of new jobs in the emerging private sector activities. Estimates by government agencies of the foreseeable increase in unemployment range widely, from under 1 million to 4-6 million. The presidential program calls for measures—such as the creation of a state employment service—to facilitate retraining and the dissemination of information on available vacancies, for the provision by local authorities of public work opportunities to temporarily unemployed workers, and for the early introduction of an unemployment compensation scheme. While some details of this scheme—including notably the sources of its financing—were still under debate, the draft law provided for benefits broadly equivalent to 50 percent of the tariff wages of eligible displaced workers for a period of up to six months. Given the uncertainty about the prospective size and composition of unemployment, estimates of the respective costs of training, public works and unemployment compensation programs are also subject to wide variance.

The prospective role and instruments of incomes policy are not clearly set out in the presidential program. In order to promote greater productivity of labor, the guidelines call for freedom for enterprise managers to determine the form and level of individual workers' compensation, subject only, during the transition period, to the minimum wage regulations for the relevant skill level. Minimum wage scales will be set nationwide, but it is envisaged that individual republics could set higher minimum wages for workers in their respective territories. The guidelines are unclear about the prospective role for government intervention in collective bargaining, in particular whether guidance would continue to be provided to enterprises on the growth of their overall wage bill, or of the average wage per worker, and what, if any, would be the penalties for "excessive" wage increases. The presidential document makes no reference to the "consumption fund" tax, which according to legislation passed in June 1990, is to replace the so-called Abalkin tax on wage increases in excess of government guidelines. It is anticipated, however, that this tax would be in effect at least until 1992.

The likely marked acceleration of retail prices in 1991 will pose difficult choices in economic and social policy, in particular as regards the degree of protection to be provided to various groups. Although the presidential guidelines do not fully clarify intentions in this area, they appear to envisage different degrees of compensation for different income groups. Accordingly, pensions and family allowances would be fully indexed, while the degree of indexation of wages would range up to 70 percent, declining for higher wage brackets—a feature which would tend *ceteris paribus* to compress differentials. Apparently, the index to be used for these adjustments would not be the overall price index but an index of prices for a "minimum consumer basket," which would be calculated at the republican level (to allow for regional differences in living standards and consumption patterns) and would give heavy weight to the prices of subsidized commodities subject to rationing.

(8) *Liberalization of foreign trade and investment* [20]

The presidential program envisages further progress in eliminating the state monopoly on foreign trade, except for energy products, gold, diamonds, and a few high-technology goods. This will make the development of exports less predictable than they have been in a system dominated by state trade, e.g., with the CMEA countries.

The guidelines, though not specific, suggest that the authorities envisage relatively slow progress in trade liberalization, given in particular the balance of payments prospects (see section d). State orders for basic export goods will be maintained through 1992, and export quotas are likely to be maintained for some time. A new tariff has been prepared but it will continue to be supplemented by selective import and export taxes, in some instances with quite high rates.

Liberalization is likely to proceed much faster with respect to foreign investment. A recent presidential decree allows for the first time full foreign ownership. A draft foreign investment law is under preparation which, *inter alia*, is intended to protect foreign investors against future adverse changes in Soviet legislation, and would liberalize rules for the transfer abroad of profit and capital.

d. The macroeconomic outlook for 1991

The macroeconomic outlook for 1991 is clouded by greater than usual uncertainty regarding not only the external environment (in particular, the price of oil and the evolution of CMEA trade and financing) but also the domestic political and social context, as well as important aspects of economic and financial policies. The assumptions are made here that increased barriers would not arise to inter-republican trade and that a single currency would be maintained; also that arrangements for sharing of revenue and expenditure responsibilities and for financing budget deficits would eventually be agreed and be conducive to adequate budgetary discipline by sub-national governments.

As regards economic policies, it is assumed, on a general level, that the pace of systemic reforms would be relatively slow, but that efforts would be made to tighten financial policies and moderate wage pressures. Specifically, it is assumed that:

71

(a) a considerable share of production would continue to be governed by state orders, and existing trade links would also be largely maintained, as called for by the presidential decree of September 1990.

(b) administered wholesale prices would be increased as planned, and contractual prices would rise broadly in line with centrally established guidelines;

(c) retail prices would be adjusted upwards sufficiently to prevent a major loss of turnover tax revenue and to restrict the growth of subsidies;

(d) the growth of nominal wages would be moderated by allowing only partial indexation and by tightening enterprise liquidity. In these conditions, real wages might record a modest decline. However, overall money incomes of the population would rise in real terms, reflecting the projected improvements in pensions and other social benefits. It is further assumed that these benefits would be fully indexed to prices, in accordance with the presidential guidelines. This indexation, and the implementation of the proposed unemployment compensation scheme, would boost social expenditures well above budgeted levels. At the same time, however, the measures taken to confiscate part of household currency holdings and limit deposit withdrawals might reduce somewhat the pressure of existing household liquidity on the market for consumer goods;

(e) tax revenue would fall somewhat short, in relation to GDP, of the projection contained in the draft budget; thus the consolidated deficit of the state would exceed by a nonnegligible margin the preliminary projection of rub 59 billion;

(f) the tax measures and the partial freeze of enterprise deposits would absorb most excess liquidity in this sector. In addition, tight control would be kept on bank credit to enterprises, and interest rates would be raised significantly, albeit remaining negative in real terms. In reflection of this tightening of credit policy and of the steps taken to drain household liquidity, the overall ratio of money to GDP could, for the first time in years, decline significantly.

(g) the commercial exchange rate would be kept at its current level.

On balance, these policies would probably result in a net transfer of resources from enterprises to households. Accordingly, investment would continue to fall at a rapid rate, and some decumulation of inventories could be anticipated—unless supply uncertainties were exacerbated by political developments. On the other hand, private consumption might continue to rise, but its growth would be curbed by the tightening of liquidity. Although the intent of the presidential program is to restore order in the production and distribution systems, this could be expected to take some time. Meanwhile, shortages and disruptions in internal trade could increase. On the whole, net material product could fall by around 5 percent, with GDP declining by less. The behavior of retail prices would continue to be largely determined by administrative intervention, but there is likely to be a considerable acceleration of inflation in 1991.[21]

These relatively unfavorable prospects for the short-run, which—given the foreseeable slow pace of restructuring and lack of a major supply response—are unlikely to be significantly improved upon in subsequent years, raise serious concerns about the sustainability of the authorities' overall reform strategy.

A plausible range of possible outcomes for the balance of payments in 1991 could be provided by two alternative scenarios (Table 5, Appendix II-3). In an optimistic one, oil prices would average US$26 per barrel and oil exports would decline by 17 percent. In a more pessimistic scenario, oil prices would decline to US$20 per barrel, and oil exports would fall by 25 percent. In both scenarios it is projected that the introduction of a depreciated commercial exchange rate, coupled with the abolition of the differentiated foreign exchange coefficients, would not strengthen competitiveness enough to prevent a fall in manufactured exports, particularly to the CMEA area. Imports would be constrained by foreign exchange availability, but would also be affected by the projected decline in investment. Accordingly, in both scenarios import volumes are assumed to fall by 7 percent on average, a decline which would still allow modest growth in imports of food and consumer durables. Under these assumptions, the current account deficit vis-à-vis the traditional convertible currency area (excluding gold exports) could range between US$10 billion and US$14½ billion. In addition, the Soviet authorities would face in 1991 large amortizations of medium- and long-term debt (amounting to about US$12 billion). Given already secured financing, amounting in all to US$17 billion, and assuming no further decline in foreign interbank deposits, the financing gap in convertible currencies would range between US$5½ billion and US$10 billion. Part of this gap, however, could be filled by the prospective current account surplus vis-à-vis the CMEA area (estimated at between US$10 billion and US$6½ billion under the two alternative scenarios), depending on the financing available to these countries, and on the disposition of the accumulated debts in transferable rubles of the USSR, which is now under discussion.

3. AN ASSESSMENT OF PROPOSED POLICIES AND REFORMS

a. The role of the republics in the implementation of reforms

The presidential guidelines envisage considerable freedom for the republics to choose the specific modalities and timing of reforms, in particular regarding the privatization process, land reform, price liberalization and/or adjustments— and consequently the evolution of commodity taxation and consumer subsidies— and the design of social safety nets. In addition, the republics would have

73

responsibility for the provision of a substantial share of public goods and services, and for designing and administering an important portion of the tax system. In these circumstances, given the wide differences in demographic composition, political conditions, economic structure and living standards among the republics, and even within some of them, the pace of reform would probably tend to vary significantly across the country. Moreover, important differences would tend to emerge in the level and composition of taxation and public expenditures, including on consumer subsidies and social benefits.

The crucial question is the extent to which these divergent developments would be consistent with the maintenance of a unified economic space (i.e., the avoidance of a proliferation of new barriers to interrepublican trade and to labor and capital mobility across republican borders, and indeed the elimination of existing obstacles), as well as with a single currency within the union. This question requires first and foremost a political answer, which could be provided by a new union treaty, if it were to include a constitutional (and enforceable) commitment by the republics to refrain from the introduction of barriers to interrepublican trade and labor mobility. The effective maintenance of free flows of goods and factors of production would prevent the emergence of excessive differentials in their prices, and would also promote a degree of harmonization of taxation across the republics. Since, however, taxing capacities are likely to differ significantly (reflecting, in particular, different resource bases, levels of economic development and demographic structures), appropriate mechanisms for intergovernmental transfers would need to be devised and agreed among the union and the republics, to ensure adequate minimum levels of public services and social benefits, while preserving firm budgetary discipline at all levels of government.[22]

Such discipline would be essential to maintain unity of the currency. A single currency clearly requires central management of the monetary and credit aggregates. The new central bank law attempts to provide an institutional framework for a unified conduct of monetary policy, but leaves open a number of operational issues which could affect importantly the consistency of credit policies at the republican and local levels. Moreover, it remains unclear to what extent the accountability of the new Union Reserve System to a political authority (the Supreme Soviet) and the role envisaged for the latter in the definition of monetary and credit policies—including limits on central bank financing of the union and republics' budgets—will be conducive to adequate monetary and financial discipline. In this respect, it would be preferable to ban altogether financing of the budget deficits of the union and subnational governments by the respective central banks and to rely on rules,[23] rather than discretion, in the setting of annual limits on borrowing by the various levels of government from commercial banks.

The proposed creation of a joint union-republic foreign exchange fund, which would be a separate body fully independent of Gosbank, raises concerns not only about an orderly servicing of the external debt of the country, but also as regards the unified management of the foreign exchange reserves and the commercial exchange rate. It also leaves open important operational issues regarding, in particular, procedures for decision making within the ruling council of this fund.[24] In principle, given the close interrelation of monetary and exchange rate policies—which should be defined and implemented in a consistent and mutually reinforcing manner—it would seem appropriate to entrust the management of the foreign exchange fund to the Central Council of the newly created Union Reserve System, in which both union and republican authorities are represented.[25]

The joint union-republic foreign exchange fund is also to service the external debt outstanding of the union as well as debt incurred in the future for all-union projects. Foreign debt incurred by individual republics (possibly against collateral of their foreign exchange earning assets) will be serviced by them. The resulting foreseeable loss of central control over external indebtedness is a cause for concern. It would also seem important that, with the further planned decentralization of foreign trade activities, an effective mechanism be put in place as soon as possible to monitor and control external financing obtained by enterprises engaged in foreign trade.

b. Some observations on the authorities' reform strategy

(1) Systemic reforms

This brief review of the presidential guidelines, and of the policies announced so far for 1991, suggests that the pace of transition to a market economy envisaged by the Soviet authorities is a gradual one, and that emphasis will be placed in the near future on stabilizing economic conditions, beginning to correct some major relative price distortions and financial imbalances, and striving to shelter socially (and politically) sensitive segments of the population from the impact of the adjustment. It would seem likely that:

(a) production carried out under state orders will continue to account for a large share (albeit varying by sectors) of enterprise output. This will not promote enterprise autonomy nor a reallocation of resources toward more productive uses; it may also hinder sustained progress in the reconversion of military industries to the production of civilian goods;

(b) similarly, the injunction to companies to maintain stable supply links, albeit understandable as a short-run response to disintegrating economic structures, will not foster the necessary shifts in internal trade flows, nor promote managerial initiative in seeking out more profitable business opportunities. The extent to which the injunction can be effectively enforced remains, in any event, unclear;

(c) the envisaged reliance on ceilings on profit margins, and on a heavy taxation of "excess profits," as antimonopoly devices, in lieu of steps to promote internal and external competition, will not provide incentives

75

to enterprises to increase productivity and contain costs, and will tend to perpetuate existing monopoly positions;

(d) the proposed maintenance of extensive controls on wholesale prices will not foster managerial autonomy and responsibility in the state enterprises, which, given the foreseeable slow pace of privatization, will continue to account for the preponderant share of output, especially in industry. A substantial degree of freedom from government intervention in the pricing of inputs and outputs would be a necessary, though not sufficient, condition for the imposition of an effective budget constraint on state enterprises;

(e) a slow pace of decontrol of retail prices would hinder not only budgetary discipline but also the rapid elimination of shortages of consumer goods and queuing.

(2) Fiscal policy

The 1991 budget highlights some of the most difficult tradeoffs facing economic policy makers in the USSR today. In particular, it shows the difficulty of securing a fundamental improvement in the public sector finances without reducing price subsidies, moderating the growth of social benefits and carrying out a major reform of indirect taxation. In the absence of progress on all these fronts, it is not surprising that: (a) the forecast deficit of the draft state budget for 1991 was virtually double the level targeted in the presidential guidelines; (b) the deficit may only be contained to this (higher) level through measures which are partly of a temporary and somewhat "cosmetic" nature; and (c) there are serious risks that the actual deficit may significantly exceed the forecast level.

A more sustainable improvement in the budgetary position for 1991 could be achieved through a comprehensive alternative package of measures. Specifically:

(a) existing turnover taxes should be quickly replaced with fixed rate ad valorem taxes, implying a full pass-through to the retail level of any increase in wholesale prices of taxed commodities. In the process, it would be most desirable to improve the turnover tax further by streamlining its rate structure and broadening its base, *inter alia* to include imports, and to complement it with excise duties on, for example, alcohol, petroleum products, tobacco and luxury goods. In addition to yielding additional revenue in the short run, these reforms would lay the foundation for the introduction of a value-added tax within two or three years;

(b) price subsidies, which were projected to nearly double in 1991, should instead be significantly reduced from their 1990 level, for example by allowing prices to rise and limiting the quantity of subsidized commodities;

(c) the proposed levy on enterprise depreciation charges could be replaced with a uniform mandatory dividend payout (a percentage of after-tax profits) for state enterprises, which would be in line with a policy of placing state and private enterprises on a more equal footing;

(d) existing tax preferences and exemptions should be further reduced;

(e) sharper cutbacks should be made in lower priority expenditures, including subsidies to loss-making enterprises, defense outlays (which, even at the probably understated level of about 7 percent of GDP, absorb a higher share of resources than in most countries), and expenditures on personnel and administration; and

(f) adequate financing should be secured for the proposed new unemployment compensation scheme.

In a longer term perspective, wide-ranging further reforms in the tax system, tax administration, the structure of expenditures, and budgeting and expenditure control procedures will be needed to complement and support the overall reform process in the economy.[26]

(3) Monetary policy

The authorities have recently announced measures to absorb or tie up existing excess liquidity in the economy. As regards enterprise liquidity, the proposed conversion of a part of enterprise deposits into shares to be distributed to workers by boosting household wealth might add to excess demand for consumption goods in the short run. It would also tend to give an excessive weight to workers' ownership, thereby hindering the efficient management of enterprises. The steps taken to confiscate or freeze household liquidity may have some dampening effect on inflationary pressures in the short run, but they also threaten to further undermine confidence in the currency and popular support for the reform effort. It would be preferable to concentrate instead on sales of government property and financial assets, as proposed in the presidential guidelines. Since these sales might not materialize in the short term at a scale sufficient to absorb a substantial part of the "monetary overhang,"[27] it might be useful to supplement them with offers to the public of relatively short-term (2-3 years) bonds with indexed principal to be used at maturity (or even earlier, at the option of the holder) to buy public assets (including shares of enterprises to be privatized) or as downpayment for the purchase of housing.

In addition to asset sales, a more appropriate level of interest rates could play an important role in promoting the voluntary holding of financial assets (as well as a more efficient allocation of credit). The initial steps taken recently by the authorities in this direction are to be welcomed. It is clear, however, that the current level of interest rates remains well below the foreseeable rate of inflation in 1991. It would be important that, as prices are liberalized, interest rates be moved rapidly to a level that provides the prospect of a positive real return on financial assets, and that they be adjusted flexibly thereafter. Although a full liberalization of interest rates should probably await the development of a competitive banking system, steps could begin to be taken in that direction, for example, by limiting direct intervention by the monetary authorities on deposits and lending rates to the setting of a floor and a ceiling, respectively. Adequate flexibility in the conduct of interest rate policy would be essential to support the planned gradual shift towards indirect instruments of monetary control. In the near term, however, the authorities will probably need to continue to rely on quantitative limits to the growth of bank credit. The implementation of effective controls in the context of a more decentralized and competitive banking system will require significant and timely adaptations in the operations of the central bank.

(4) Incomes policy[28]

In a context of reduced direct government intermediation in the wage determination process, as envisaged in the presidential guidelines, an effective tightening of monetary policy would be an important indirect instrument in promoting wage moderation. In the near term, however—as financial discipline on enterprises is progressively tightened and trade unions develop a role more in line with western models—it seems desirable that the authorities continue to provide close guidance to the collective bargaining process, supported by nondiscriminatory and firmly enforced taxation of wage increases in excess of the guidelines. The proposed indexation of wages may well be necessary to secure social acceptability of a rapid price reform. It must be recognized, however, that it introduces an element of rigidity in the wage determination process which is undesirable from a purely economic perspective. To moderate its inflationary potential, it is essential that the degree of indexation be kept relatively low. As the experiences of several other countries show, it would be preferable to replace indexation to past price increases with a mechanism linking wages to a (realistic and credible) target for inflation.

(5) External policies

The recent introduction of a commercial exchange rate, substantially depreciated in comparison to the official exchange rate, and the elimination of the differentiated foreign exchange coefficients, represent steps in the direction of a more realistic and less discriminatory exchange rate policy. The present narrowness of the auction market implies, however, that the gap between rates prevailing in this market and the commercial rate is likely to remain large for the foreseeable future, fostering "leakages" between the two markets. More importantly, if the auction market remains thin, the authorities will continue to lack adequate guidance from market forces as to the appropriate level of the exchange rate. It would therefore appear important to move quickly towards unification of the rates in the two markets by reducing progressively the share of export proceeds to be surrendered at the commercial exchange rate,[29] by requiring exporters to promptly sell in the free foreign exchange market retained export earnings which are not used for imports, and by increasing rapidly the share of imports channeled through this market. It would also be important quickly to establish adequate arbitrage facilities between regional foreign exchange markets, to avoid the emergence of multiple exchange rates in these markets.

A more difficult question—and one that would best be answered in the light of the overall policy stance and conditions of the economy at the time of unification of the exchange rate—is whether the rate should then be allowed to float, at least for some time, or whether an attempt should be made to stabilize it at a particular level, presumably somewhat undervalued at the start. The latter alternative would have the advantage of providing a nominal policy "anchor" and would tend, therefore, to moderate inflationary expectations, provided that it was supported with appropriately tight financial policies and adequate foreign exchange reserves (or lines of credit). By contrast, floating would provide greater flexibility in the management of other policies and, at least in the short run, better safeguard the balance of payments, albeit probably at the cost of higher inflation.[30]

The proposed liberalization of foreign investment is generally to be welcomed. However, the extent to which it will ultimately benefit the Soviet economy will depend on the speed with which distortions between domestic and world prices are eliminated. So long as those distortions remain, free access to inward direct investment could leave the USSR worse off than before, as foreign investors capture and repatriate the implicit economic rents. Ideally, therefore, price and trade liberalization should proceed at least as quickly as the liberalization of foreign investment.

NOTES

1. Following the reforms of the government structure at the special conference of the Communist Party of the Soviet Union in mid-1988, the supreme organ of power in the USSR is the 2,250 member Congress of People's Deputies (CPD) which was first elected by popular vote in March 1989. The CPD meets at least twice a year, and elects, from its ranks, the 542 member bicameral Supreme Soviet, which functions as the USSR's full time working legislature. The Supreme Soviet passes laws, ratifies international treaties, and approves economic plans and the union budget. It must also ratify all appointments (including that of the Prime Minister) to the Council of Ministers, the body in charge of the vast Soviet bureaucracy as of late 1990. Symmetrically, each republic has its own Supreme Soviet and Council of Ministers (only the Russian Republic has a congress of people's deputies as well). There are also local soviets at the regional, city and district levels.

In March 1990, a new post, Executive President of the USSR, was created by the CPD. The President has the right to declare a state of emergency (subject to a two-thirds approval of the Supreme Soviet), and to nominate the Prime Minister. He can veto legislation proposed by the Supreme Soviet (although this can be overridden by a two-thirds vote of the Supreme Soviet), and can issue binding decrees that do not require the Supreme Soviet's approval. The President is advised by a Presidential Council (which he appoints) the role of which appears to include many functions previously undertaken by the Politburo of the Communist Party. The President is also assisted in policy making by the Federation Council, on which sit representatives of the republic governments. The executive powers of the Council were to be substantially strengthened in late 1990.

2. The September program of the Government had been preceded by previous versions more or less publicly debated since the latter part of 1989.

3. The name refers to the then Deputy Prime Minister for economic reforms, Academician Abalkin.

4. It is not clear whether the target was actually intended to be set as an absolute amount or in relation to GDP, in which case its nominal equivalent could exceed significantly the rub 25-30 billion range.

5. For a description and analysis of these reforms, see Chapter III.1.

6. Specifically, 11 percentage points of the combined payroll tax of 37 percent were designated as revenue for the "stabilization" (restructuring) funds.

7. The confiscation of higher denomination banknotes reportedly only led to a fairly negligible decline in currency in circulation within the USSR, however, as holders of most of these banknotes were permitted to exchange them for lower denomination bills.

8. It is envisaged, however, that the deficits could be financed through recourse to the Savings Bank, which is to remain under state control, although such borrowing would take place at market rates.

9. Chapter III.2 provides a more detailed analysis of the law.

10. For further details, see Chapters III.4 and IV.3.

11. The commercial rate will be pegged to the same basket of six currencies as the official rate (which remains in effect for ruble-denominated claims of the USSR on developing countries). Thus, the commercial rate will fluctuate weekly vis-à-vis the U.S. dollar, reflecting changes in the rate of the latter vis-à-vis the other currencies in the basket.

12. See Table III.4.12.

13. These areas are covered in greater detail in Part IV and Chapter V.8.

14. The draft plan for 1991 provided that over 95 percent of petroleum, 70-90 percent of various petroleum products, and some two-thirds of coal would be delivered under state orders. The role of state orders in most other areas, however, was expected to be considerably lower.

15. The guidelines propose that responsibility for the following areas of economic activity be delegated by the republics to the union: basic research and technological development; national defense; the fuel and energy systems; major transportation systems; and the union emergency response system. The union's jurisdiction over some of these areas (e.g., energy) is still contested by certain republics and autonomous regions.

16. The program stresses, however, the need for interrepublican agreements to secure the free flow of agricultural commodities among republics, and calls for the retention of the All-Union

Fund—to be now managed jointly by the union and the republics—with pre-established contributions of each republic, to ensure minimum supplies of basic food products and agricultural raw materials.

17. The subject of price reform is covered in more detail in Chapter IV.1.

18. For 1991 many of these prices will in fact be set by Presidential decree, under the emergency powers granted by the Supreme Soviet.

19. These issues are covered in detail in Chapter IV.6.

20. These issues are covered in detail in Chapter IV.3.

21. Prior to the January measures taken to reduce liquidity, it was considered that the rate of recorded retail inflation could well exceed 40 percent. At this time, it is difficult to assess the impact of these measures on the rate of either underlying or open inflation in 1991, due to the uncertainties regarding, respectively, the stance of monetary and fiscal policies, and the policy with respect to administered price increases.

22. For a fuller discussion of intergovernmental fiscal relations see Chapter III.1.

23. For example, it could be stipulated that bank financing for each budget could not exceed a certain proportion of its revenues.

24. These are to be defined in implementing guidelines to be issued by the Council of Ministers of the USSR.

25. For a further discussion of these issues see Chapter III.2.

26. These reforms are discussed in some detail in Chapter III.1.

27. See Chapter III.3 for an econometric analysis of the "monetary overhang" in the household and enterprise sectors.

28. See Chapter IV.6 for a more detailed discussion.

29. The large gain that would thus accrue, for example, to exporters of oil and other natural resources could be subjected to a high export tax, shared between the union and the republics.

30. For a further discussion of considerations affecting the choice of exchange rate policy, see Chapter III.2.

Appendix II-1

Statistical Tables on Macroeconomic Activity

This appendix contains statistical tables regarding the following areas of macroeconomic activity: (A) aggregate output and expenditure; (B) sectoral output; (C) fixed investment and stockbuilding; (D) incomes and sources and uses of funds; (E) prices, wages, and labor productivity; (F) the labor force and employment; (G) foreign trade; (H) the balance of payments; (I) external claims and debt; (J) the fiscal accounts; and (K) money and credit. These tables serve as background mainly for Part II, but also to some extent for other chapters of this study.

Table A.1. USSR: Sources of Economic Growth, 1961-90

(Average annual growth rate, in percent)

| | Net Material Product [1] | Employment [2] | | Gross Fixed Capital Stock [4] | | Gross Barter Terms of Trade[5] |
		Total	Material Sphere [3]	Total	Productive Capital Stock	
1961-65	6.5	...	0.4 [6]	8.5	9.6	-3.0
1966-70	7.8	...	1.0 [6]	7.5	8.1	-3.0
1971-75	5.6	...	1.1 [6]	7.9	8.7	5.2
1976-80	4.3	1.4	1.0	6.8	7.4	0.6
1981-85	3.2	0.7	0.5	6.0	6.4	4.0
1986-89	2.7	0.4	-0.1	4.8	4.7	-2.4
1986	2.3	0.6	0.1	5.3	5.2	-14.5
1987	1.6	0.4	—	4.9	4.8	-4.9
1988	4.4	0.1	-0.4	4.7	4.4	-1.0
1989	2.5	0.5	-0.1	4.4	4.2	6.9
1990 (first nine months)	-2.5 [7]	-0.8 [8]	...	...	...	...

1. In comparable prices; sources are *Narodnoe khoziaistvo SSSR za 70 let* (1987), p. 51 for 1961-70, and Goskomstat for 1971-89.
2. Source is Goskomstat.
3. Includes some employment in the transport and communications sector that is not included in the material sphere.
4. "Basic funds," including changes in livestock, without taking into account wear and tear, valued in 1973 comparable prices according to published Soviet statistics. Sources are *Narodnoe khoziaistvo SSSR za 70 let* (1987), p. 51 through 1985; *Narkhoz 1988* (1989), p. 259 for 1986-89; and *Osnovnye pokazateli* (1990), p. 49, for 1989.
5. Table G.4.
6. Derived from *Narodnoe khoziaistvo SSSR za 70 let* (1987), p. 51.
7. Source is *Sotsial'no — ekonomischeskoe razvitie* (1990).
8. Goskomstat estimate.

Table A.2. USSR: Net Material Product and
National Income Utilized, 1970-89

(In billions of rubles, current prices)

	NMP [1] (1)	Adjusted Valuta Trade Balance [2] (2)	Losses [3] (3)	National Income Utilized [1] (1)-(2)-(3) (4)
1970	289.9	2.2	2.2	285.5
1975	363.3	-3.0	3.3	363.0
1980	462.2	3.7	4.4	454.1
1981	486.7	3.2	5.6	477.9
1982	523.9	5.1	5.9	512.9
1983	548.3	5.5	6.4	536.4
1984	570.5	6.4	5.1	559.0
1985	578.5	3.1	6.7	568.7
1986	587.4	3.3	8.1	576.0
1987	599.6	4.9	8.9	585.8
1988	630.8	1.4	10.3	619.1
1989	673.7	-2.3	10.0	666.0

1. Source is Goskomstat.
2. Equal to $B_t'\alpha_x$ when $B_t'>0$ and $B_t'\alpha_m$, when $B_t'<0$, where α_x and α_m refer respectively to the implicit internal exchange rate for exports and imports, respectively, and B_t' denotes the valuta trade balance. Source is Goskomstat. See Appendix II-2 for further details.
3. Residual.

Table A.3. USSR: Value Added in Foreign Trade, 1970-1989

(In current prices)

	Adjusted Valuta Trade Balance [1] (1)	Trade Balance in Domestic Prices [2] (2)	Value Added in Foreign Trade [3] (1)-(2)	Valued Added in Foreign Trade as Percent of NMP
1970	2.2	-8.6	10.8	3.7
1975	-3.0	-22.1	19.1	5.3
1980	3.7	-40.7	44.4	9.6
1981	3.2	-47.7	50.9	10.5
1982	5.1	-49.6	54.7	10.4
1983	5.5	-52.0	57.5	10.5
1984	6.4	-52.9	59.3	10.4
1985	3.1	-60.6	63.7	11.0
1986	3.3	-55.4	58.7	10.0
1987	4.9	-50.4	55.3	9.2
1988	1.4	-50.4	51.8	8.2
1989	-2.3	-59.5	57.2	8.5

1. Column (2) of Table A.2.
2. Source is Goskomstat.
3. Equal to $(B_t'\alpha_x-B_t)$ when $B_t'>0$ and $(B_t'\alpha_m-B_t)$, when $B_t'<0$, where α_x and α_m refer respectively to the implicit internal exchange rate for exports and imports, respectively, and B_t' and B_t denote the valuta trade balance and the trade balance evaluated in domestic prices, respectively. See Appendix II-2 for further details.

Table A.4. USSR: Growth in NMP by Sector of Origin, 1971-89

(In percent)

	Real Rates of Growth (In Comparable Prices)						Share of of 1989 total output (in current prices)
	1981-85	1986-89	1986	1987	1988	1989	
Total	3.2	2.7	2.3	1.6	4.4	2.5	100.0
Industry	2.9	3.3	0.6	3.6	6.1	3.1	41.9
(excluding turnover taxes)	(3.9)	(4.2)	(5.5)	(4.6)	(6.3)	(0.4)	(40.4)
Agriculture	1.0	2.4	7.1	-1.4	2.5	1.7	23.4
Construction	3.2	6.6	12.1	5.5	7.6	1.6	12.8
Transport and communication	2.9	0.8	4.2	0.3	5.8	-6.5	5.6
Transport	2.8	0.4	4.1	-0.1	5.7	-7.4	5.3
Communication	5.8	7.6	6.2	8.3	8.0	8.0	0.3
Trade, procurement, and supply	2.4	3.3	1.2	-0.5	4.6	8.2	6.5
Trade	2.5	3.4	0.2	-2.6	7.7	8.6	5.0
Agricultural procurement	0.7	7.8	4.9	6.2	6.7	13.5	0.6
Material-technical supply	3.2	0.4	3.7	5.4	-9.5	2.9	0.9
Data processing	3.6	22.0	3.0	15.9	13.5	63.7	0.2
Forestry	1.9	3.8	0.7	0.9	2.1	12.0	0.1
Other branches	0.1	7.6	0.3	5.2	22.8	3.5	0.9
Receipts from foreign trade	9.5	-4.2	-8.8	-4.7	-6.6	3.8	8.5

Source: Goskomstat.

Table A.5. USSR: Distribution of NMP by Sector,[1] 1970-89

(In percent of NMP; in current prices)

	1970	1975	1980	1985	1989
Industry	51.2	52.6	51.5	45.5	41.9
Agriculture	21.8	16.9	14.9	19.5	23.4
Construction	10.3	11.4	10.3	10.8	12.8
Transport and communications	5.6	6.3	5.8	6.1	5.6
Trade, procurement and supply	6.2	6.5	7.0	6.3	6.5
Others	1.2	1.0	0.9	0.8	1.3
Foreign trade	3.7	5.3	9.6	11.0	8.5
	100.0	100.0	100.0	100.0	100.0

1. Including turnover taxes; source is *Osnovnye pokazateli* (1990), p. 22, and Goskomstat for all years except 1989, in which only the latter source is used.

Table A.6.   USSR: Growth in NMP by Expenditure Category, 1971-89 [1]

(Percentage change in comparable prices)

	1976-80	1981-85	1986-89	1986	1987	1988	1989
Domestic expenditure	3.8	2.9	2.6	1.6	0.7	4.6	3.4
Consumption	4.4	3.2	4.1	3.5	3.5	4.2	5.1
Private	(4.2)	(2.9)	(3.4)	(1.9)	(2.7)	(3.9)	(5.3)
Public	(5.9)	(4.9)	(5.4)	(4.0)	(7.7)	(5.9)	(4.0)
Accumulation	2.3	2.8	0.6	3.0	-4.2	5.6	-1.6
Net fixed investment	(2.6)	(-1.7)	(-1.1)	(4.9)	(5.7)	(-7.4)	(-6.7)
Stockbuilding and other (est. 1) [2]	(0.2)	(0.9)	(0.3)	(0.1)	(-1.9)	(2.5)	(0.6)
(est. 2) [3]	(...)	(...)	(...)	(-0.8)	(-1.6)	(1.7)	(-0.5)
Change in merchandise trade balance [4]	...	...	...	2.0	0.6	-0.6	-0.7

1. Source for most items is Goskomstat.
2. Contribution to growth rate of NMP, in percentage points. Estimate calculated using official growth rates for accumulation and net fixed investment and the previous year's weight of net fixed investment—in current prices—in accumulation.
3. Contribution to growth rate of NMP, in percentage points. Estimate based on *Osnovnye pokazateli* (1990), pp. 19, 20 and 113 using the implicit NMP price deflator.
4. Contribution to growth rate of NMP, in percentage points. Estimate based on *Osnovnye pokazateli* (1990), p. 19 and *Vneshnie ekonomicheskie sviazi* (1990), p. 6., and use of trade volume indices from various issues of *Vneshniaia torgovlia* and from *Vneshnie ekonomicheskie sviazi* (1990), p. 18. The special conversion coefficient, discussed in Appendix II-2, is not applied.

Table A.7.   USSR: Components of Domestic Expenditure
(National Income Utilized)

(Percent share; in current prices)

	Consumption Fund		Accumulation Fund		
	Personal	Other	Net fixed productive investment [1]	Net fixed unproductive investment	Change in "material circulating means" and reserves
1970	62.3	8.2	11.3	6.6	11.6
1975	63.7	9.7	11.2	6.0	9.4
1980	65.6	10.5	10.0	5.3	8.6
1981	65.9	10.5	8.7	5.1	9.8
1982	63.4	10.4	9.1	4.5	12.6
1983	62.7	10.6	8.5	5.3	13.0
1984	62.3	10.6	8.7	5.8	12.8
1985	62.8	10.8	8.1	6.0	12.3
1986	63.1	11.1	8.7	6.4	10.7
1987	63.8	11.6	9.2	6.9	8.5
1988	63.5	11.7	7.4	7.1	10.3
1989	65.1	11.8	5.9	6.4	10.8

Source: Osnovnye pokazateli (1990), pp. 112, 114-115; 1989 figures are subject to revision.
1. "Accumulation of basic funds." Includes changes in livestock herds.

Table A.8.   USSR: Material Intensity of Gross Output, 1970-88 [1]

	Including Depreciation	Excluding Depreciation
	(1970 = 100)	
1975	105.5	103.4
1980	104.0	100.2
1985	106.0	100.6
1988	106.7	100.0
1989	105.0[2]	...
	(Previous year = 100)	
1986	100.7	100.2
1987	100.7	100.1
1988	99.4	99.1

1. Index of ratio of material costs per unit of gross output, measured in current prices. Source: *Osnovnye pokazateli* (1990), pp. 74-75.
2. Source is Goskomstat (provisional).

Table B.1.   USSR: Growth in Gross Value of Industrial Output, 1971-89
(Percentage change, in comparable prices)

	1981-85	1986-89	1986	1987	1988	1989	1989 Output Shares as Percent of the Total
Total	3.6	3.4	4.4	3.8	3.9	1.7	100.0
of which:							
Electricity	3.7	2.7	3.1	4.8	1.9	1.1	3.5
Fuel industry	1.2	1.4	3.7	1.9	1.7	-1.5	6.8
Ferrous metals	2.0	2.3	4.4	2.0	3.0	—	5.7
Nonferrous metals	2.1	2.5	3.5	2.2	3.2	0.9	3.8
Chemicals	5.0	4.0	6.0	4.5	4.6	0.9	6.8
Machinery	6.2	5.1	7.1	5.6	5.3	2.5	28.1
Forest and paper products	3.5	3.3	5.1	2.5	4.4	1.4	4.6
Construction materials	2.9	3.9	5.3	3.5	4.5	2.1	3.8
Light industry	1.5	2.3	1.7	1.3	3.6	2.5	13.8
Food products	2.7	3.4	1.8	4.3	3.4	4.2	15.2

Source: Goskomstat.

Table B.2.   USSR: Industrial Value Added by Main Branch, 1980-89

(Share in percent, in current prices) [1]

	1980	1985	1989
Electrical energy	3.8	4.5	3.8
Fuels	7.8	9.1	8.1
Metallurgy	8.4	9.5	9.2
Machinebuilding and metalworking	39.1	37.8	39.0
Chemicals and petrochemicals	8.1	6.6	7.1
Forestry, woodworking and paper	5.6	6.4	6.6
Construction materials	4.2	4.7	4.9
Light industry	11.5	11.1	11.9
Food industry	11.6	10.4	9.4
	100.0	100.0	100.0

Source: Goskomstat.
1. Excluding turnover taxes.

Table B.3.   USSR: Production of Major Energy Products, 1960-89

	1960	1970	1980	1985	1986	1987	1988	1989	(First nine months) 1990
Crude petroleum [1] (millions of tons)	148	353	603	595	615	624	624	607	433
Natural gas (billions of cubic meters)	45	198	435	643	686	727	770	796	528
Coal (millions of tons)	510	624	716	726	751	760	772	740	602
Electricity (billions of kilowatts)	292	741	1,294	1,544	1,599	1,665	1,705	1,722	...

Sources: 1960 and 1970: *Narodnoe khoziaistvo SSSR za 70 let* (1987), pp. 162-63; 1980-89: *Narkhoz 1989* (1990), pp. 375 and 377; 1990 (first nine months): *Sotsial'no ekonomicheskoe razvitie* (1990), p. 21.
1. Including gas condensate.

Table B.4. USSR: Growth in Agricultural Production, 1981-89

	Annual Percentage Rates of Growth, in Constant Prices							Share of 1989 Gross Value of Output [1]
	1981-85	1986-89	1985	1986	1987	1988	1989	
Gross value of agricultural output (in comparable prices)	2.1	1.9	0.1	5.3	-0.6	1.7	1.3	
Output (in physical volume):								
Grain [2]	0.3	2.4	11.8	8.3	-0.1	-7.0	9.2	10.8
Meat [3]	2.5	4.1	0.6	5.3	5.0	4.2	2.0	31.1
Milk	1.6	2.4	0.7	3.7	1.6	2.9	1.6	19.1
Eggs	-0.1	0.8	-2.7	—	-0.9	1.4	2.8	3.6
Potatoes	1.7	-0.3	-14.6	19.5	-13.0	-17.4	15.2	6.1
Vegetables	0.6	0.5	-10.8	5.7	-1.7	0.3	-2.0	3.8
Fruit – including grapes	2.3	-2.7	-10.8	10.9	-21.3	4.2	-1.3	2.8
Sugar beets	0.3	4.3	-3.5	-3.8	14.4	-3.0	10.7	2.2
Cotton lint	0.6	-1.1	7.1	-4.4	-5.9	9.8	-3.1	3.2
Wool	0.2	1.8	-4.0	5.0	-1.6	3.6	0.3	1.8
Other	...	...	...	...	...	...	...	15.5

Source: SSSR v tsifrakh (1989), p. 223, Goskomstat, and U.S. Department of Agriculture (for cotton lint).
1. Gross value of output shares are calculated from data in 1983 comparable prices.
2. Grain output statistics here are not traditional "bunker weight" figures, but reportedly exclude dirt, moisture, and other foreign matter.
3. Meat's share of gross value of agricultural output for 1989 includes the output value of cattle and poultry raising.

Table C.1. USSR: Growth of Net and Gross Fixed Investment, 1971-89
(Average annual growth rate in comparable prices; in percent)

	Gross Fixed Investment [1]		Net Fixed Investment [2]
	Total	Material sphere	
1971-75	6.8	8.1	5.2 [3]
1976-80	3.3	3.5	2.6
1981-85	3.5	3.1	-1.7
1986-89	6.2	5.6	-1.1
1986	8.4	7.4	4.9
1987	5.6	4.2	5.7
1988	6.2	6.2	-7.4
1989	4.7	4.7	-6.7

1. Refers to investment in the total economy; source is Goskomstat.
2. Source is Goskomstat.
3. Average for 1973-75 only.

Table C.2. USSR: Growth of Fixed Investment by Sector and Branch, 1971-1989

(Average annual growth rate in comparable prices; in percent)

	1971-75	1976-80	1981-85	1986-89	1985	1986	1987	1988	1989
Total	6.8	3.3	3.5	6.2	3.0	8.4	5.6	6.2	4.7
Industry	6.5	3.4	4.2	7.0	4.4	8.4	5.7	5.9	7.8
Electricity	3.6	3.9	5.1	0.7	12.4	0.1	2.1	3.0	-0.3
Coal	2.4	3.9	3.6	6.9	2.4	6.8	10.7	10.8	-0.2
Oil	8.7	12.2	8.8	8.2	11.3	10.6	14.4	3.5	4.5
Gas	11.6	2.9	12.5	18.8	15.8	14.4	8.7	10.0	45.6
Metallurgy	5.6	2.2	—	3.2	-7.0	14.7	9.8	-11.6	2.0
Chemicals	9.5	-0.2	-0.2	-0.9	8.5	0.6	3.3	0.7	-1.4
Machinery	9.4	4.0	4.0	5.0	4.5	12.4	0.9	9.2	-1.8
Forest and paper products	4.4	-0.2	1.6	6.6	5.6	10.9	-1.4	3.7	13.9
Construction materials	1.6	-0.2	1.8	9.9	7.8	-2.8	21.6	12.3	10.0
Light industry	5.0	2.6	2.0	7.7	-5.0	4.3	-11.5	17.9	23.6
Food products	4.9	1.8	1.9	12.0	-1.4	5.3	3.5	21.2	19.2
Other	5.1	-1.6	4.5	12.4	8.0	4.9	9.1	7.1	29.9
Agriculture	10.3	2.7	1.1	5.1	1.3	6.5	2.4	6.3	5.2
Transport	10.0	4.9	3.8	-1.5	-2.3	3.5	4.4	4.6	-16.6
Rail	5.6	5.8	1.5	3.2	-0.1	5.6	6.5	1.4	0.4
Other	11.8	4.5	4.6	-3.1	-3.0	2.8	3.8	5.7	-21.8
Communication	6.0	3.4	5.0	10.8	6.8	15.3	11.0	6.6	10.7
Construction	7.7	4.5	0.4	14.9	5.0	11.6	1.8	19.0	28.8
Trade and related supply	3.4	6.3	4.3	-0.5	6.7	11.3	-9.6	-0.4	-2.2
Data processing	—	—	—	—	—	—	—	-34.1	73.6
Forestry	2.3	3.2	6.1	-16.0	4.6	-5.6	-8.1	6.9	95.3
Semi-processed goods	8.9	-6.1	-2.5	-1.2	-12.5	14.3	-16.6	-1.2	1.2
Housing	4.0	1.9	5.9	7.6	2.9	9.9	8.7	6.2	5.8
Utilities and other [1]	3.9	3.3	3.1	8.0	5.5	11.5	10.6	6.3	3.7

Source: Goskomstat.

1. Includes municipal services, public health, education, science, culture and art.

Table C.3. USSR: Gross Fixed Investment by Sector and Branch, 1971-89

(Percent of total, in comparable prices)

	1971-75 [1]	1976-80 [2]	1981-85	1986-89	1986	1987	1988	1989
Total	100.0	100.0	100.0	100.0	100.0	100.0	100.0	100.0
Industry	35.2	35.2	35.6	36.8	36.5	36.5	36.4	37.5
Electricity	3.6	3.4	3.4	3.2	3.4	3.3	3.2	3.0
Coal	1.7	1.6	1.6	1.7	1.6	1.7	1.7	1.7
Oil	3.2	4.2	6.0	6.9	6.6	7.1	6.9	6.9
Gas	1.4	1.5	1.9	2.8	2.4	2.5	2.6	3.6
Metallurgy	4.2	4.0	3.6	3.2	3.5	3.6	3.0	2.9
Chemicals	3.2	3.1	2.7	2.1	2.3	2.1	2.0	1.9
Machinery	8.0	8.5	8.7	8.9	9.2	8.8	9.0	8.5
Forest and paper products	1.6	1.4	1.2	1.2	1.2	1.1	1.1	1.2
Construction materials	1.9	1.5	1.3	1.4	1.2	1.3	1.4	1.5
Light industry	1.4	1.3	1.3	1.1	1.2	1.0	1.1	1.3
Food products	2.6	2.4	2.2	2.3	2.1	2.0	2.3	2.6
Other	2.5	2.1	1.9	2.1	1.9	2.0	2.0	2.4
Agriculture	19.0	20.0	18.5	16.9	17.2	16.7	16.7	16.8
Transport	9.7	10.7	11.5	10.0	10.8	10.6	10.5	8.3
Rail	2.7	2.8	2.9	2.6	2.7	2.7	2.6	2.4
Other	7.0	7.9	8.6	7.4	8.1	8.0	7.9	5.9
Communication	0.9	0.9	0.9	1.0	1.0	1.0	1.0	1.1
Construction	3.7	3.8	3.6	3.9	3.5	3.4	3.8	4.6
Trade and related supply	2.0	2.1	2.3	2.0	2.4	2.0	1.9	1.8
Data processing	—	—	—	—	—	0.1	—	0.1
Forestry	0.1	0.1	0.1	0.1	0.1	0.1	0.1	0.2
Semi-processed goods	0.5	0.4	0.3	0.2	0.3	0.2	0.2	0.2
Housing	15.8	14.4	15.1	16.3	15.9	16.3	16.3	16.5
Utilities and other [3]	13.0	12.3	12.0	12.8	12.4	13.0	13.0	12.9

Source: Goskomstat.
1. Based on the average of 1970 and 1975 values.
2. Based on the average of 1975 and 1980 values.
3. Includes municipal services, public health, education, science, culture and art.

Table C.4. USSR: Composition of State Capital Investment in Production, by Type of Project, 1980-89

(Share in percent)

	1980	1985	1986	1987	1988	1989
Reconstruction and technical refitting of active enterprises	33.0	38.7	43.0	43.7	45.7	49.6
Expansion of active enterprises	29.0	23.6	20.3	19.2	17.9	16.7
New construction	38.0	36.5	35.1	35.3	34.1	30.6
Individual projects of active enterprises	—	1.2	1.6	1.8	2.3	3.1
	100.0	100.0	100.0	100.0	100.0	100.0

Source: Goskomstat.

92

Table C.5. USSR: Change in Unfinished Construction in Relation to
Gross Fixed Investment by State Enterprises and Organizations
and in Relation to GDP, 1986-89 [1]

	As Percent of Gross Fixed Investment	As Percent of GDP
1986	6.5	1.4
1987	3.5	0.8
1988	9.8	2.2
1989	11.3	2.4

1. Unfinished construction for a given year is measured in the current prices of the different years in which its components were expended. Gross capital investment is in comparable prices, whereas GDP is in current prices. Source is Goskomstat.

Table C.6. USSR: Change in Unfinished Construction in Relation to Gross Fixed
Investment of the National Economy, by Sector and by Branch, 1987-89

(In percent)

	1987	1988	1989
Total	3.1	8.7	9.9
Industry	4.6	15.4	14.5
Of which:			
Electricity	9.9	21.6	29.3
Coal	-5.4	17.5	9.5
Oil and gas	6.1	7.9	11.0
Ferrous metals	...	...	...
Chemicals and petrochemicals	2.0	6.4	10.4
Machinery	1.0	15.7	10.1
Forest and paper products	6.5	1.7	20.2
Building materials	43.1	15.3	19.6
Light industry	2.7	6.8	16.1
Food industry	7.7	15.4	16.1
Agriculture	-5.1	4.1	3.7
Transportation and communications	-1.8	5.4	-1.9
Construction	14.7	9.7	16.5
Other	6.3	4.4	10.3

Source: Calculated from data provided by Goskomstat. The aggregate figures in this table differ slightly from those in Table C.5 because the change in unfinished construction is related to a larger gross fixed investment magnitude (i.e., investment of the "national economy," rather than simply of "state enterprises and organizations").

93

Table C.7. USSR: Change in Material Circulating
Means and Reserves in Relation to NMP, 1970-89

(Percent share; in current prices)

	Change in Material Circulating Means and Reserves [1]		Of which	
	As percent of NMP	Contribution to NMP growth [2]	Change in material circulating means [3]	Change in reserves and other expenditures [3]
1970	11.4	...	...	...
1975	9.4	...	...	...
1980	8.5	...	...	...
1985	12.1	-0.2	5.4	6.7
1986	10.5	-1.5	3.7	6.8
1987	8.3	-2.0	1.4	6.9
1988	10.1	2.4	4.5	5.6
1989	10.7	1.3	5.8	4.9

1. Represents essentially changes in stocks, but also includes the change in unfinished construction; sources are *Osnovnye pokazateli* (1990), pp. 19 and 113 prior to 1985, and Goskomstat for 1985-89.
2. In percentage points of NMP growth; in current prices. Source is identical to that in footnote 1.
3. Derived from *Osnovnye pokazateli* (1990), p. 19 (revised) and Goskomstat.

Table D.1. USSR: Distribution of Value Added in the Material Sphere, 1980 and 1985-89

(In percent of NMP, at current prices)

	1980	1985	1986	1987	1988	1989	Change in Share		
							1980-85	1985-89	1980-89
Workers and employees									
Wages	...	31.9	32.6	33.3	33.1	32.2	...	0.3	...
Premia [1]	...	2.6	2.7	2.6	2.8	2.7	...	0.1	...
Subtotal	36.5	34.5	35.3	35.9	35.9	34.9	-2.0	0.4	-1.6
Incomes of collective farm workers	4.4	4.4	4.6	4.5	4.2	4.1	—	-0.3	-0.3
Incomes of co-operative workers	—	—	—	—	—	2.0	...	2.0	2.0
"Subsidiary" incomes	7.8	8.0	8.1	8.0	8.1	8.4	0.2	0.4	0.6
Current primary incomes of the population	48.7	46.9	48.0	48.4	48.2	49.4	-1.8	2.5	0.7
Enterprise profits, net of premia	20.0	24.2	27.1	28.5	31.3	30.0	4.2	5.8	10.0
Profits (and social security and other contributions) of collective farms	0.4	2.5	2.7	3.1	3.6	3.8	2.1	1.3	3.4
Profits (before profit taxes)	20.4	26.7	29.8	31.6	34.9	33.8	6.3	7.1	13.4
Social security contributions of enterprises	2.2	3.3	3.3	3.3	3.3	3.2	1.1	-0.1	1.0
Indirect taxes (net)	14.8	6.9	4.4	4.1	1.8	1.5	-7.9	-5.4	-13.3
Other [2]	13.8	16.2	14.4	12.6	11.7	12.1	2.4	-4.1	-1.7
Budget and other	30.8	26.4	22.1	20.0	16.8	16.8	-4.4	-9.6	-14.0
Total [3]	100.0	100.0	100.0	100.0	100.0	100.0	—	—	—

Source: Derived from *Osnovnye pokazateli* (1990), pp. 12-13, with revisions noted by Goskomstat.
1. Paid out of after-tax profits.
2. Includes net price equalization taxes on foreign trade and other unspecified items, including, in 1989, the profits of cooperatives.
3. May not add to 100 percent due to rounding.

Table D.2. USSR: Money Incomes and Expenditures of the Population, 1985-89

(In billions of rubles, at current prices)

	1985	1986	1987	1988	1989
(+) Income	420.1	435.3	452.1	493.6	558.0
Wages and salaries	312.8	322.8	334.3	361.8	406.8
Wages	279.3	288.4	299.5	321.5	347.1
Other remuneration from enterprises	9.6	9.8	9.8	11.1	12.7
Income of collective members	23.9	24.6	25.0	26.2	28.2
Wages in co-ops	—	—	—	3.0	18.9
Receipts from sales of agricultural products	17.3	16.7	16.8	19.2	23.5
Pensions and allowances	57.6	62.3	64.7	69.1	74.7
Stipends	2.6	2.6	2.7	2.8	2.8
Receipts from financial system	15.7	15.4	16.8	19.6	20.6
Other income	14.1	15.5	16.7	21.1	29.7
(-) Taxes and duties	31.2	32.2	33.6	36.8	42.8
(=) Disposable income	388.9	403.1	418.6	456.7	515.2
(-) Total expenditure	364.5	375.1	386.6	414.8	453.4
Expenditure on goods and services	347.3	356.9	367.8	394.4	431.7
Purchases of goods	311.2	318.6	327.1	349.3	383.5
Purchases of services	36.2	38.3	40.7	45.1	48.2
Other expenditure	17.1	18.2	18.7	20.4	21.6
(=) Saving	24.4	28.0	32.0	41.9	61.8
Accumulation of savings deposits	20.1	23.9	26.1	32.7	45.2
Cash accumulation	4.3	4.1	5.9	9.2	16.6

Source: Goskomstat.

Table D.3. USSR: Growth of Money Incomes and Expenditures of the Population, 1986-90 [1]

(Annual percentage rate of growth, at current prices)

	1986	1987	1988	1989	(Jan.-Oct.) 1990
(+) Income	3.6	3.9	9.2	13.1	14.5
Wages and salaries	3.2	3.6	8.2	12.4	...
Wages	3.2	3.8	7.4	8.0	...
Other remuneration from enterprises	1.9	0.2	13.2	13.8	...
Income of collective members	3.1	1.5	4.8	7.6	...
Wages in co-ops	—	—	...	530.4	...
Receipts from sales of agricultural products	-3.7	0.9	14.1	22.1	...
Pensions and allowances	8.1	4.0	6.7	8.1	...
Stipends	—	3.9	4.5	1.3	...
Receipts from financial system	-1.6	9.2	16.3	5.0	...
Other income	10.0	7.9	25.9	41.1	...
(-) Taxes and duties	3.0	4.4	9.7	16.3	...
(=) Disposable income	3.7	3.8	9.1	12.8	...
(-) Total expenditure (excluding taxes)	2.9	3.1	7.3	9.3	...
Expenditure on goods and services	2.8	3.1	7.2	9.5	14.4
Purchases of goods	2.4	2.7	6.8	9.8	...
Purchases of services	5.8	6.5	10.6	7.0	...
Other expenditure	6.2	2.8	9.1	5.9	...
(=) Saving	14.6	14.3	30.9	47.6	...
Accumulation of savings deposits	19.1	9.1	25.1	38.5	...
Cash accumulation	-6.3	44.9	57.0	79.7	...

1. Derived from Table D.2 for 1986-89; for January-October 1990 the source is *Sotsial'no-ekonomicheskoe razvitie* (1990), p. 5.

Table D.4. USSR: Shares of Income, Expenditure and Saving in Total Income of the Population, 1985-89 [1]

(In percent, at current prices)

	1985	1986	1987	1988	1989
Income	100.0	100.0	100.0	100.0	100.0
Wages	66.5	66.3	66.2	65.1	62.2
Other remuneration from enterprises	2.3	2.3	2.2	2.3	2.3
Income of collective members	5.7	5.7	5.5	5.3	5.0
Wages in co-ops	—	—	—	0.6	3.4
Receipts from sales of agricultural products	4.1	3.8	3.7	3.9	4.2
Pensions and allowances	13.7	14.3	14.3	14.0	13.4
Stipends	0.6	0.6	0.6	0.6	0.5
Receipts from financial system	3.7	3.5	3.7	4.0	3.7
Other income	3.4	3.6	3.7	4.3	5.3
Expenditure including taxes	100.0	100.0	100.0	100.0	100.0
Purchases of goods	78.6	78.2	77.9	77.3	77.3
Purchases of services	9.1	9.4	9.7	10.0	9.7
Taxes and duties	7.9	7.9	8.0	8.2	8.6
Other	4.3	4.5	4.5	4.5	4.4
Private Saving Rate Definitions (in percent)					
Saving/Total Income [2]	5.8	6.4	7.1	8.5	11.1
Saving/Disposable Income	6.3	6.9	7.6	9.2	12.0
Saving/GDP	3.1	3.5	3.9	4.8	6.7

1. Derived from Table D.2.
2. Saving defined as the change in savings deposits plus change in currency.

Table D.5. USSR: Sources and Uses of Funds of State Enterprises and Organizations [1], 1985-89

(In billions of rubles, at current prices)

	1985	1986	1987	1988	1989
Sources					
Gross operating surplus	215.4	231.8	241.2	273.0	301.5
(-) Turnover tax [2]	97.7	91.5	94.4	101.0	111.1
(+) Net price subsidies [3]	69.2	75.3	76.9	88.1	99.7
Profit before payments to the budget [4]	186.9[13]	215.6	223.7	260.1	290.1
Payments to budget out of profits [5]	118.4	128.5	126.3	118.4	115.5
After-tax profits (derived)	68.5	87.1	97.4	141.7	174.6
(+) Depreciation [6]	103.1	110.0	118.1	125.6	134.5
Internally generated funds (derived)	171.6	197.1	215.5	267.3	309.1
memo: allocation to enterprise funds [7]	(41.4)	(77.4)	(126.4)	(264.2)	(334.2)
(+) Transfers from budget for investment [8]	57.6	60.8	65.2	70.4	61.9
Internal funds plus transfers (derived)	229.2	257.9	280.7	337.7	371.0
Net borrowing from banks [9]	20.8	-3.7	-44.3	-57.0	-32.1
Borrowing from banks	(26.9)	(0.9)	(-21.2)	(-30.2)	(-15.1)
Accumulation of deposits and money (M2)	(6.1)	(4.6)	(23.1)	(26.8)	(17.0)
Total	250.0	254.8	236.4	280.7	338.9
Uses					
Fixed capital investment [10]	140.5	167.1	173.4	193.8	201.2
Change in stocks [11]	21.0	6.0	-1.0	9.4	41.9
Expenditure from funds [12]	28.8	59.8	70.9	151.3	219.0
Total	190.2	232.9	243.2	354.5	462.1
Residual and missing items					
(excess of sources over uses)	59.8	21.9	-6.8	-73.8	-123.2
memo: payments to budget net of transfers	60.8	67.7	61.1	48.0	53.6
also net of taxes and subsidies	89.3	83.9	78.6	60.9	65.0

1. Including collective farms and cooperatives.
2. *Narkhoz 1988* (1989), p. 624, and Ministry of Finance.
3. From Ministry of Finance; includes expenditure on economy for price differentials, price subsidies, and compensation for increases in procurement prices.
4. *Finansy SSSR 1987-88* (1989), p. 110 for 1987-88. Source for other years is Goskomstat.
5. Ministry of Finance.
6. Excludes collective farms; sources are for 1985, 1987 and 1988: *Narkhoz 1988* (1989), p. 622; 1986: *Narkhoz 1987* (1988), p. 585; 1989: *Narkhoz 1989* (1990).
7. *Finansy SSSR 1987-88* (1989), p. 164 for 1987-88; source for other years is Goskomstat.
8. Ministry of Finance.
9. Gosbank; 1986 borrowing excludes change in loans and deposits due to canceling of rub 70 billion of escrow accounts. Deposits include construction accounts of firms.
10. *Kapital'noe stroitelstvo SSSR* (1988), pp. 214-215 for 1985-86 and *Finansy SSSR 1987-88* (1989), p. 193 for 1987-88, and *Finansy SSSR 1989* (1990), p. 218 for 1989; *less* investment of budgetary institutions, from the Ministry of Finance.
11. Goskomstat.
12. *Finansy SSSR 1987-88* (1989), p. 164 and *Finansy SSSR 1989* (1990), p. 88 "expenditure from funds" less *Finansy SSSR 1987-88* (1989), p. 193 and *Finansy SSSR 1989* (1990), p. 111 financing of "investment from the production fund" (to avoid double-counting of investment expenditure). An alternative would be to subtract "own financing of investment" reported in the same sources.
13. Includes estimate of profits of collective farms.

Table D.6 USSR: Sources and Uses of Funds of State Enterprises
and Organizations as a Share of GDP,[1] 1985-89

(In percent of GDP, at current prices)

	1985	1986	1987	1988	1989
Sources					
Gross operating surplus (derived)	27.7	29.0	29.2	31.2	32.1
(-) Turnover tax	12.6	11.5	11.4	11.5	11.8
(+) Net price subsidies	8.9	9.4	9.3	10.1	10.6
Profit before payments to the budget	24.1	27.0	27.1	29.7	30.9
(-) Payments to budget out of profits	15.2	16.1	15.3	13.5	12.3
After-tax profits (derived)	8.8	10.9	11.8	16.2	18.6
(+) Depreciation	13.3	13.8	14.3	14.4	14.3
Internally generated funds (derived)	22.1	24.7	26.1	30.5	32.9
memo: allocation to enterprise funds	(5.3)	(9.7)	(15.3)	(30.2)	(35.6)
(+) Transfers from budget for investment	7.4	7.6	7.9	8.0	6.6
Internal funds plus transfers (derived)	29.5	32.3	34.0	38.6	39.5
Net borrowing from banks	2.7	-0.5	-5.4	-6.6	-3.4
Borrowing from banks	(3.5)	(0.1)	(-2.6)	(-3.5)	(-1.6)
Accumulation of deposits and money (M2)	(0.8)	(0.6)	(2.8)	(3.1)	(1.8)
Total	32.2	31.8	28.7	32.1	36.1
Uses					
Fixed capital investment	18.1	20.9	21.0	22.1	21.4
Change in stocks	2.7	0.8	-0.1	1.1	4.5
Expenditure from funds	3.7	7.5	8.6	17.3	23.3
Total	24.5	29.2	29.5	40.5	49.2
Residual and missing items ..,...................	7.7	2.7	-0.8	-8.4	-13.1
memo: payments to budget net of transfers	7.8	8.5	7.4	5.5	5.7
also net of taxes and subsidies	11.5	10.5	9.5	7.0	6.9
memo: GDP, in billions of rubles	777	799	825	875	940

1. Derived from Table D.5 and Table 1 of Appendix II-2.

Table E.1. USSR: Price Developments, 1971-89

	(Annual Average Percentage Change)								Jan.-Sept. 1990
	1971-75	1976-80	1981-85	1986-89	1986	1987	1988	1989	
Retail prices[1]	-0.1	0.7	1.1	1.5	2.0	1.3	0.6	2.0	3.7
Food	0.3	0.5	1.7	2.8	5.2	4.9	0.5	0.8	2.5
Alcoholic beverages	(0.4)	(0.7)	(4.7)	(9.1)	(23.4)	(14.7)	(—)	(—)	(...)
Nonfood products	-0.3	0.8	0.5	0.3	-1.5	-0.8	—	3.5	...
Collective farm market prices	4.8	6.4	2.0	2.7	-3.6	2.6	2.6	9.5	24
Agricultural procurement prices[2]	...	...	...	5.6	0.8	3.0	13.0	6.0	...
Wholesale industrial prices[2]	...	...	...	...	...	...	...	1.7	...

Sources: Goskomstat and *Torgovlia SSSR* (1989), pp. 75, 314; *Narkhoz 1989* (1990) p. 138; for the first nine months of 1990: *Sotsial'no-ekonomicheskoe razvitie* (1990), pp. 5-6.
1. In state and cooperative trade.
2. The index of agricultural procurement prices is not available before 1984, and the index of wholesale industrial prices is not available before 1989.

Table E.2. USSR: Growth in the Average Monthly Wage and Labor Productivity, 1966-1989

	Average Annual Rate of Growth, in Percent				Primary Incomes of Population Received in Material Sphere as Percent of NMP[4]	
			Average Monthly Wage[2]			
				Material sphere		
	Labor productivity[1]	Total economy	Nominal	Real[3]		
1966–70	6.8	...	...	...	1970:	50.1
1971–75	4.5	3.6	3.9	4.0	1975:	50.6
1976–80	3.3	3.0	2.9	2.2	1980:	48.7
1981–85	2.7	2.4	2.8	1.7	1985:	46.9
1986–89	2.7	6.0	6.3	4.7	1989:	50.9
1986	3.8	2.9	3.1	1.1		
1987	2.4	3.7	3.5	2.2		
1988	2.3	8.3	8.9	8.3		
1989	2.3	9.4	9.9	7.7		
1990 (First nine months)	...	8.4[5]	...			

Source: Narkhoz 1988 (1989), p. 62 for 1966-75; *SSSR v tsifrakh* (1989), p. 53 for 1976-89. Sources for individual years are *Trud v SSSR* (1988), p. 233 from 1986; Narkhoz 1988 (1989), p. 11 and the foregoing for 1987 and 1988; and *SSSR v tsifrakh* (1989), p. 13 for 1989.
1. Refers to labor productivity in activities whose value added is included in NMP.
2. *Source:* Goskomstat.
3. Using Table E.1.
4. *Source: Osnovnye pokazateli* (1990), p. 12.
5. *Source: Sotsial'no-ekonomicheskoe razvitie* (1990), p. 5; may not be strictly comparable with earlier figures.

Table F.1. USSR: Growth of Population of
Working Age and Employment, 1980-88

	Absolute Increase		Average Annual Rate of Growth	
	Population of working age [1]	Employment in socialized sector [2]	Population of working age [1]	Employment in socialized sector [2]
	(in thousands of persons)		*(in percent)*	
RSFSR	900	396	0.1	0.1
Central Asia, Kazakhstan, and Azerbaidzhan ..	4,628	2,358	2.3	1.6
Other republics	596	468	0.2	0.2
USSR	6,124	3,222	0.5	0.3

1. Period covered is 1979-87; source is *Naselenie SSSR 1987* (1988), pp. 48-94.
2. Includes the categories "workers and employees" and "collective farm workers," which have typically accounted for more than
   95 percent of total employment. Source is *Sotsial'noe razvitie SSSR* (1990), p. 49.

Table F.2. USSR: Distribution of Employment by Sector, 1975-89
(In percent)

	1975	1980	1985	1989
Industry	29.1	29.4	29.3	28.6
Agriculture and forestry	22.2	20.3	19.5	18.5
Construction	9.1	8.9	8.8	10.8
Transport and communications	8.8	9.1	9.2	7.5
Trade, etc.	7.8	7.9	8.0	7.5
Other material sphere [1]	1.2	1.4	1.5	1.8
Nonmaterial sphere [1]	21.8	23.1	23.8	25.3
	100.0	100.0	100.0	100.0

Source: Goskomstat.
1. These figures may differ from other official figures due to the inclusion here, for simplicity, of all employment in transport and
   communications as employment in the material sphere.

101

Table G.1 USSR: Structure of Foreign Trade, 1980-90 [1]

	1980	1985	1986	1987	1988	1989	First Half 1989	First Half 1990
	(Shares in percent, in current prices)							
Total exports, f.o.b.	100.0	100.0	100.0	100.0	100.0	100.0	100.0	100.0
Machinery & equipment								
including transport	15.8	13.9	15.0	15.5	16.2	16.4	14.5	19.5
Fuels & electricity	46.9	52.7	47.3	46.5	42.1	39.9	53.3	52.0
Ores, concentrate								
metals & fabrications	8.8	7.5	8.4	8.5	9.5	10.5		
Chemicals, fertilizers & rubber	3.3	3.5	3.4	4.0	4.0	4.0	4.4	4.1
Wood, cellulose, paper products	4.1	3.0	3.4	3.3	3.5	3.5	...	...
Textile, fibers & other								
semifinished goods	1.9	1.3	1.4	1.5	1.6	1.6	...	...
Food raw materials & products	1.9	1.5	1.6	1.6	1.7	1.6	1.6	2.0
Manufactured consumer goods	2.5	2.0	2.4	2.6	2.8	2.6	2.9	3.8
Other	14.8	14.2	17.0	17.1	18.6	19.9	...	...
Total imports, f.o.b.	100.0	100.0	100.0	100.0	100.0	100.0	100.0	100.0
Machinery & equipment								
including transport	33.9	37.1	40.7	41.4	40.9	38.5	36.2	41.1
Fuels & electricity	3.0	5.3	4.6	3.9	4.4	3.0	10.4	8.9
Ores, concentrates,								
metals & fabrications	10.8	8.3	8.3	8.1	8.0	7.3		
Chemicals, fertilizers, & rubber	5.3	5.0	5.1	5.3	5.0	5.1	5.2	4.4
Wood, cellulose, paper products	2.0	1.3	1.3	1.2	1.2	1.2	...	...
Textile fibers & other								
semifinished goods	2.2	1.7	1.3	1.5	1.6	1.6	...	...
Food raw material products	24.2	21.1	17.1	16.1	15.8	16.6	20.6	20.4
Manufactured consumer goods	12.1	12.6	13.4	13.0	12.8	14.4	12.7	15.8
Other	6.2	7.6	8.2	9.5	10.3	12.3	...	...
	(In billions of rubles)							
Memorandum items:								
Total exports	49.6	72.7	68.3	68.1	67.1	68.7	33.4	30.4
Total imports	44.7	62.4	52.6	60.7	65.0	72.1	36.0	38.0

Sources: Ministry of Foreign Economic Relations; and Goskomstat.
1. Tables G.1-G.8 exclude gold and are based on data in valuta rubles, i.e., foreign currency values multiplied by the official exchange rate. The resulting ruble values are not directly comparable to statistics in domestic prices.

Table G.2. USSR: Composition of Exports, 1980-89

(In percent at current prices)

	1980	1985	1986	1987	1988	1989
Total exports, f.o.b. [1]	100.0	100.0	100.0	100.0	100.0	100.0
Machinery, equipment, and						
transportation items	15.8	13.6	15.0	15.5	16.2	16.4
Machine tools and presses	0.5	0.3	0.4	0.5	0.5	0.5
Energy and electrical equipment ...	2.1	2.2	2.1	2.2	2.4	2.7
Mining, drilling, and						
metallurgy equipment	2.1	1.6	1.6	1.7	1.5	1.5
Lifting, conveying, and						
road equipment	2.4	0.2	0.6	0.7	0.6	0.7
Tractors and agricultural						
equipment	0.7	0.4	0.6	0.6	0.9	0.7
Vehicles (including ships						
and planes) and parts	4.7	4.3	4.7	4.9	5.2	5.2
Other	3.3	4.6	5.0	4.9	5.1	5.1
Fuels and energy	46.8	52.7	47.3	46.5	42.1	39.9
of which:						
Oil and oil products	36.4	38.9	32.9	33.5	29.4	27.1
Natural gas	7.4	10.6	10.8	9.4	8.8	8.9
Metal ores, pig iron, alloys	2.0	1.7	2.1	2.2	2.1	2.2
Rolled products and pipe	3.1	2.6	2.9	2.8	2.8	3.0
Chemicals and fertilizer	2.5	3.1	2.7	2.6	3.1	3.2
Logs and lumber	2.8	1.9	2.1	1.9	2.3	2.2
Pulp, paper, and cardboard	0.8	0.8	1.0	1.0	1.0	1.0
Cotton and fibers	1.8	1.1	1.2	1.3	1.3	1.3
Furs and pelts	0.2	0.2	0.2	0.2	0.2	0.1
Agricultural and fishing products	0.8	0.7	0.8	0.8	0.9	0.8
Consumer appliances	0.8	0.5	0.6	0.6	0.6	0.5
Other [2]	22.6	21.1	24.1	24.6	27.4	29.4

Sources: Ministry of Foreign Economic Relations (MVES) and Goskomstat.
1. Excludes gold.
2. Other exports includes unallocated exports by new export firms.

Table G.3. USSR: Composition of Imports, 1980-89
(In percent at current prices)

	1980	1985	1986	1987	1988	1989
Total imports, f.o.b.	100.0	100.0	100.0	100.0	100.0	100.0
Machinery, equipment, and						
transportation items	33.9	37.2	40.7	41.1	40.9	38.5
Machine tools and presses	1.8	2.2	2.4	2.6	2.6	2.1
Energy and electrical equipment,						
wire, and cable	2.7	2.7	2.9	3.0	2.8	2.4
Mining, lifting and						
conveying equipment	2.1	2.8	3.0	3.1	3.0	2.7
Industrial machinery						
and equipment	5.2	4.2	4.0	3.9	3.9	4.6
Agricultural machinery						
and equipment	1.7	1.9	2.0	2.0	1.8	1.4
Railroad equipment	1.3	1.7	2.0	2.0	1.8	1.4
Vehicles (including						
ships) and parts	5.5	7.3	7.3	6.5	6.5	5.6
Other	13.6	14.4	17.1	17.8	18.3	17.8
Rolled products and pipe	5.8	5.3	5.4	5.1	5.2	4.2
Chemicals, paints, and dyes	3.6	3.1	3.1	3.3	3.4	3.8
Pulp and paper	1.0	0.6	0.6	0.6	0.7	0.7
Wool, cotton thread	1.0	0.8	0.7	0.9	1.0	0.9
Grain (including rice)	7.5	7.1	3.3	2.8	3.8	4.5
Coffee, tea, cocoa	1.1	1.1	1.0	0.9	0.7	1.0
Sugar	4.9	5.6	5.2	5.0	4.2	3.9
Tobacco and cigarettes	1.1	1.0	1.0	0.9	0.8	0.7
Meat	2.0	1.2	1.4	1.4	1.1	1.0
Fruits and vegetables	2.1	1.6	2.0	1.8	1.8	1.4
Textiles, clothing, and shoes	6.9	7.2	7.5	6.8	6.5	7.2
Furniture	0.9	0.8	0.9	0.9	0.9	0.8
Medicines	1.2	1.7	2.0	2.1	2.0	2.6
Domestic and cultural goods	0.8	0.7	0.8	0.8	0.8	0.7
Other	26.2	25.0	24.4	25.6	26.2	28.1

Sources: Ministry of Foreign Economic Relations (MVES) and Goskomstat.

104

Table G.4. USSR: Gross and Net Barter Terms of Trade, 1960-89

(Average annual growth rate, in percent)

	Net Barter Terms of Trade [1] (nbtt) (1)	Gross Barter Terms of Trade [2] (gbtt) (2)	Ratio of nbtt to gbtt [3]	Cumulative Trade Balance (In billions of valuta rubles)
1961-65 [4]	-1.9	-3.0	1.1	0.9
1966-70 [4]	-1.9	-3.0	1.1	5.2
1971-75 [5]	1.4	5.2	-3.7	0.1
1976-80 [5]	5.0	0.6	4.4	13.1
1981-85 [6]	2.9	4.0	-1.0	31.9
1986-89 [7]	-4.7	-2.4	-2.3	12.0
1986 [6]	-11.5	-14.5	4.7	5.7
1987 [6]	-1.0	-4.9	3.2	7.5
1988 [6]	-9.7	-1.0	-9.1	2.1
1989 [7]	-1.0	6.9	-7.5	-3.3

Sources: Derived from *Vneshniaia torgovlia* (1987 and 1988), Table VII; and *Vneshnie ekonomicheskie sviazi* (1990), Tables I, VII and VIII.
1. Defined as the ratio of the valuta export price index to the valuta import price index, for total foreign trade.
2. Defined as the ratio of the import volume index to the export volume index, for total foreign trade.
3. An increase (decrease) in this ratio means that the normalized trade balance (i.e., the trade balance divided by the base period value of exports) is rising (falling) and the net inward transfer of real resources is smaller (larger) than would be possible given a fixed financing constraint.
4. 1960 base year weights.
5. 1970 base year weights.
6. 1980 base year weights.
7. 1985 base year weights.

Table G.5. USSR: Foreign Trade Developments by Main Trading Regions, 1985-89
(Percentage change)

	Exports		Imports		Terms of Trade
	Values	Volumes	Values	Volumes	
Nonsocialist countries [1]					
1986	-19.5	15.5	-23.0	-14.3	-22.4
1987	5.5	6.0	-10.3	-2.8	7.8
1988	1.2	6.3	16.4	8.6	-11.2
1989	9.4	-1.0	26.8	18.5	3.3
1986-89 (Annual average) ..	-1.5	6.5	0.5	1.8	-6.4
CMEA countries					
1986	4.9	3.9	-0.2	0.7	1.9
1987	-3.5	0.9	2.8	1.5	-5.6
1988	-4.0	—	2.5	—	-6.3
1989	-2.8	1.9	1.9	2.0	-4.5
1986-89 (Annual average) ..	-1.4	1.7	1.7	1.0	-3.7

Sources: Vneshniaia torgovlia (various issues) and *Vneshnie ekonomicheskie sviazi* (various issues).
1. Nonsocialist countries comprise all countries except the nine CMEA partner countries, Albania, the People's Republic of China, the Lao People's Democratic Republic, the Democratic People's Republic of Korea, and Yugoslavia.

Table G.6. USSR: Export and Import Values,
Volumes and Unit Values, 1981-89[1]
(1980 = 100)

	1981	1982	1983	1984	1985	1986	1987	1988	1989
Exports									
In current prices	115	127	137	150	147	138	138	135	139
In 1980 prices	101	107	111	115	110	121	125	131	131
Unit values	114	119	123	130	133	114	110	103	106
Imports									
In current prices	118	127	134	147	156	141	136	146	162
In 1980 prices	108	117	123	128	134	126	124	129	141
Unit values	110	108	109	115	116	112	110	113	115

Sources: Ministry of Foreign Economic Relations (MVES) and Goskomstat. Implicit net barter terms of trade figures may differ from those in Table G.4 due to differences in some base year weights and rounding.
1. 1975 base year weights for 1980-84 and 1980 base year weights for 1985-89.

Table G.7. USSR: Direction of Trade, 1980-90

(In billions of rubles)

	1980	1984	1985	1986	1987	1988	1989	First Half 1990
I. Exports	49.6	74.4	72.5	68.3	68.1	67.1	68.7	30.4
Socialist Countries	26.9	42.1	44.3	45.6	44.2	42.9	42.2	18.2
CMEA	24.3	38.2	40.1	42.2	40.7	39.0	38.0	16.4
Cuba	2.3	3.8	3.8	3.8	3.7	3.7	3.8	...
Czechoslovakia	3.6	6.6	6.8	6.9	6.8	6.4	6.3	...
GDR	4.9	7.5	7.7	7.9	7.6	7.2	6.7	...
Poland	4.4	6.1	6.5	6.8	6.5	6.3	5.8	...
Other	2.6	3.9	4.2	3.5	3.5	3.8	4.3	1.8
China	0.2	0.5	0.8	0.9	0.7	1.0	1.3	...
Yugoslavia	2.1	3.1	2.7	1.7	1.9	1.7	1.9	...
Non-Socialist Countries	22.7	32.3	28.2	22.7	23.9	24.2	26.5	12.2
Developed Countries	15.9	21.3	18.6	13.1	14.2	14.7	16.4	7.9
Finland	2.0	2.4	2.3	1.6	1.7	1.5	1.8	...
France	2.2	2.4	2.1	1.5	1.5	1.6	1.3	...
German (Fed. Rep.)	2.9	4.2	4.0	2.7	2.3	2.4	2.5	...
Italy	2.1	3.2	2.5	1.6	1.8	1.7	1.9	...
United Kingdom	...	0.9	1.4	1.2	1.3	1.6	1.8	2.2
United States	0.2	0.3	0.3	0.3	0.3	0.3	0.5	...
Less Developed Countries	6.9	10.9	9.6	9.6	9.8	9.6	10.1	4.3
India	0.9	1.5	1.6	1.0	1.1	1.1	1.1	...
Iraq	0.5	0.3	0.3	0.3	0.3	0.3	0.2	...
II. Imports	44.5	65.4	69.1	62.6	60.7	65.0	72.1	38.0
Socialist Countries	23.6	8.3	42.2	41.8	42.1	43.4	44.7	22.8
CMEA	21.4	34.6	37.6	37.8	38.9	39.8	40.6	20.7
Cuba	2.0	3.5	4.1	3.8	3.8	3.8	3.9	...
Czechoslovakia	3.5	6.0	6.6	6.6	6.9	6.8	6.6	...
GDR	4.3	7.4	7.6	7.1	7.1	7.0	7.2	...
Poland	3.6	5.3	5.5	6.1	6.3	7.1	7.4	...
Other	2.2	3.6	4.6	4.0	3.3	3.5	4.1	2.1
China	0.1	0.5	0.5	0.8	0.9	0.8	0.8	1.1
Yugoslavia	1.8	2.8	3.3	2.7	2.1	2.1	2.4	...
Non-Socialist Countries	20.8	27.1	26.9	20.7	18.6	21.7	27.5	15.2
Developed Countries	15.7	19.6	19.3	15.9	13.9	16.3	20.5	11.4
Finland	1.9	2.3	2.7	2.4	2.0	2.2	2.1	...
France	1.5	1.8	1.6	1.1	1.1	1.2	1.2	...
Germany (Fed. Rep.)	2.9	3.3	3.1	2.9	2.6	3.2	4.1	...
Italy	0.9	1.3	1.3	1.5	1.7	1.3	1.6	...
United Kingdom	1.0	0.8	0.7	0.5	0.5	0.6	1.0	...
United States	1.4	2.8	2.4	1.1	0.9	1.8	2.9	...
Less Developed Countries	5.1	7.5	7.6	4.9	4.7	5.3	7.0	3.8
India	0.9	1.3	1.5	1.2	1.1	1.1	1.8	...
Iraq	0.3	0.7	0.6	0.3	0.8	1.0	1.0	...

Sources: Ministry of Foreign Economic Relations (MVES) and Goskomstat.

107

Table G.8. USSR: Seasonal Variation of Aggregate Trade Flows, 1984-89

	Q1	Q2	Q3	Q4
		I. (In billions of rubles)		
Exports				
1984	17.1	18.7	18.5	19.9
1985	15.6	18.6	18.3	20.0
1986	16.2	16.9	16.2	19.0
1987	15.1	16.9	16.9	19.1
1988	15.8	17.2	16.1	18.1
1989	15.9	17.2	15.9	19.6
Imports				
1984	15.9	17.2	15.0	17.2
1985	16.9	19.4	15.7	17.2
1986	16.1	17.0	14.1	15.4
1987	14.1	17.2	13.9	15.5
1988	15.8	17.6	14.6	17.1
1989	17.3	18.5	16.5	19.8
		II. (In percent of average quarterly levels)		
Exports				
1984	23.0	25.1	24.9	26.7
1985	21.5	25.7	25.2	27.6
1986	23.7	24.7	23.7	27.8
1987	22.2	24.8	24.8	28.0
1988	23.5	25.6	24.0	27.0
1989	23.1	25.0	23.1	28.5
Imports				
1984	24.3	26.3	23.0	26.3
1985	24.5	28.0	22.7	24.9
1986	25.7	27.1	22.5	24.6
1987	23.2	28.3	22.9	25.5
1988	24.3	27.1	22.5	26.3
1989	24.0	25.7	22.9	27.5
		III. Average (1984-89)		
Exports				
average per quarter	22.8	25.2	24.3	27.6
Imports				
average per quarter	24.3	27.1	22.8	25.9

Sources: Ministry of Foreign Economic Relations (MVES) and Ministry of Finance.

Table H.1. USSR: Balance of Payments in Convertible Currencies
on a Settlements Basis, 1970-89

(In millions of rubles)

	1970	1980	1985	1986	1987	1988	1989
Current Account	114	1,482	-2,920	1,169	1,328	-1,025	-4,455
Trade balance	-70	1,881	-1,392	2,421	2,364	919	-2,109
Exports	1,942	15,959	19,694	16,834	12,349	12,667	13,171
Imports	-2,012	-14,078	-21,086	-14,413	-9,985	-11,748	-15,280
Services balance	184	-398	-1,541	-1,285	-1,064	-2,009	-2,420
Transport and insurance ...	202	499	-212	165	232	-222	-264
Travel	20	44	95	93	121	125	127
Interest	-32	-617	-553	-966	-1,169	-1,245	-1,838
Other	-6	-324	-871	-577	-248	-667	-445
Transfers	—	-1	13	33	28	65	74
Capital Account	73	1,065	1,647	-721	-2,792	587	2,096
Medium-term and long-term capital	73	1,065	547	-1,121	-2,192	-1,013	-1,604
Foreign direct investment .	-12	-22	-26	-148	-124	305	-165
Loans received (net)	...	...	-1,223	-1,424	-2,464	-1,647	-1,548
Disbursement	...	...	2,396	2,377	1,403	1,538	1,992
Amortization	...	...	-3,619	-3,801	-3,867	-3,185	-3,540
Medium term	...	...	-744	-571	-499	-300	-735
Long term	...	-1,274	-1,760	-1,969	-2,001	-1,722	-1,689
Commercial credit ...	-89	-518	-1,115	-1,261	-1,367	-1,163	-1,116
Amortization received ..	124	1,192	1,935	621	545	500	319
Other	-39	-105	-139	-170	-149	-171	-210
Short-term capital net	...	...	1,100	400	-600	1,600	3,700
Overall Balance	187	2,547	-1,273	448	-1,464	-438	-2,359

Sources: Ministry of Finance, Vneshekonombank, and estimates.

109

Table H.2. USSR: Balance of Payments in Convertible Currencies
on a Transactions Basis, 1985-89

(In millions of rubles)

	1985	1986	1987	1988	1989
Current account (excl. gold)	-450	1,266	4,181	943	-2,438
Current account (incl. gold)	1,057	4,080	6,398	3,253	-128
Trade balance	1,078	2,518	5,217	2,887	-92
Exports	23,052	18,860	19,856	20,320	22,208
Imports	-21,974	-16,342	-14,639	-17,433	-22,300
Services balance	-1,541	-1,285	-1,064	-2,009	-2,420
Transport and insurance	-212	165	232	-222	-264
Travel	95	93	121	125	127
Interest, net	-553	-966	-1,169	-1,245	-1,838
(interest gross)	(...)	(-1,654)	(-1,680)	(-1,726)	(-2,316)
Other	-871	-577	-248	-667	-445
Transfers	13	33	28	65	74
Gold exports [1]	1,507	2,814	2,217	2,310	2,310
Capital account	-2,330	-3,632	-7,862	-3,691	-2,231
Medium- and long-term	547	-1,121	-2,192	-1,013	-1,604
Foreign direct investment	-26	-148	-124	305	-165
Loans received (net)	-1,223	-1,424	-2,464	-1,647	-1,548
Disbursement	2,396	2,377	1,403	1,538	1,992
Amortization paid	-3,619	-3,801	-3,867	-3,185	-3,540
Medium term	-744	-571	-499	-300	-735
Long term	-1,760	-1,969	-2,001	-1,722	-1,689
Commercial credit	-1,115	-1,261	-1,367	1,163	-1,116
Amortization received	1,935	621	545	500	319
Other	-139	-170	-149	-171	-210
Short-term financial credits	1,100	400	-600	1,600	3,700
Trade credits	-3,977	-2,911	-5,070	-4,278	-4,327
Overall balance	-1,273	448	-1,464	-438	-2,359

Sources: Goskomstat, Ministry of Finance, Vneshekonombank, and estimates.
1. Estimates.

110

Table H.3. USSR: Balance of Payments in Nonconvertible Currencies
with Socialist Countries on a Settlements Basis, 1970-89 [1]

(In millions of rubles)

	1970	1980	1985	1986	1987	1988	1989
Current Account	-64	1,223	470	3,613	216	-732	-3,447
Trade balance	10	1,762	823	3,634	664	-152	-2,810
Exports	6,773	24,669	41,360	43,642	42,140	40,987	38,810
Imports	-6,763	-22,907	-40,537	-40,008	-41,476	-41,139	-41,620
Services balance	-74	-31	1	-103	-595	-650	-698
Transport and insurance . . .	116	333	483	534	567	393	434
Travel	-4	-2	-25	-226	-42	-301	-439
Interest	—	—	—	104	131	83	35
Other	-186	-362	-457	-515	-1,251	-825	-728
Transfers	—	-508	-354	82	147	70	61
Capital Account	657	-442	-1,681	-2,779	-1,481	-645	6
Medium and long-term capital	654	-331	-1,333	-2,341	-1,175	-323	394
of which:							
Amortization paid	-62	-122	-264	-245	-229	-101	-206
Amortization received . .	773	596	1,770	1,162	1,617	1,905	2,594
Government credit extended [2]	-57	-805	-2,839	-3,258	-2,563	-2,127	-1,994
Foreign direct investment . . .	-2	-121	-376	-364	-345	-379	-478
Other	5	10	28	-74	39	57	90
Total (Net)	593	781	-1,211	834	-1,265	-1,377	-3,441

Sources: Ministry of Finance, Vneshekonombank, and staff estimates.
1. Socialist countries comprise CMEA countries, Albania, the People's Republic of China, the Lao People's Democratic Republic, the Democratic People's Republic of Korea, and Yugoslavia.
2. Government refinancing of CMEA trade credits.

111

Table H.4. USSR: Balance of Payments in Nonconvertible Currencies
with Socialist Countries on a Transactions Basis, 1980-89 [1]

(In millions of rubles)

	1980	1985	1986	1987	1988	1989
Current account	2,659	1,931	4,016	1,956	-770	-2,988
Trade balance	3,198	2,284	4,037	2,404	-190	-2,351
Exports	26,984	44,068	45,410	44,197	42,867	41,765
Imports	-23,786	-41,784	-41,373	-41,793	-43,057	-44,116
Services balance	-31	1	-103	-595	-650	-698
Transport & insurance	333	483	534	567	393	434
Travel	-2	-25	-226	-42	-301	-439
Interest	—	—	104	131	83	35
Other	-362	-457	-515	-1,251	-825	-728
Transfers	-508	-354	82	147	70	61
Capital account	-1,878	-3,142	-3,182	-3,221	-607	-453
Medium-term and long-term capital	-452	-1,709	-2,705	-1,520	-702	-84
Foreign direct investment	-121	-376	-364	-345	-379	-478
Amortization paid	-122	-264	-245	-229	-101	-206
Amortization received	596	1,770	1,162	1,617	1,905	2,594
Government credit extended [2]	-805	-2,839	-3,258	-2,563	-2,127	-1,994
Other	10	28	-74	39	57	90
Trade credits	-1,436	-1,461	-403	-1,740	38	-459
Total (net)	781	-1,211	834	-1,265	-1,377	-3,441

Sources: Ministry of Finance, Goskomstat, and estimates.
1. Socialist countries comprise CMEA countries, Albania, the People's Republic of China, the Lao People's Democratic Republic,
the Democratic People's Republic of Korea, and Yugoslavia.
2. Government refinancing of CMEA trade credits.

Table H.5. USSR: Balance of Payments in Nonconvertible Currencies
with Nonsocialist Countries on a Settlements Basis, 1970-89 [1]

(In millions of rubles)

	1970	1980	1985	1986	1987	1988	1989
Current Account	-282	-806	-540	-1,143	-201	-660	-1,524
Trade balance	-301	-472	-342	-952	-112	-522	-1,488
Exports	734	3,488	4,379	3,189	3,437	3,269	3,388
Imports	-1,035	-3,960	-4,721	-4,141	-3,549	-3,791	-4,876
Services balance	19	-331	-189	-134	-38	-148	-48
Transport and insurance	21	-76	-32	-3	-7	-35	-15
Travel	1	9	9	9	5	—	-18
Interest	—	—	16	23	-9	20	18
Other	-3	-264	-182	-163	-27	-133	-33
Transfers	—	-3	-9	-57	-51	10	12
Capital account	378	634	748	834	1,203	1,477	726
Medium-term and long-term capital . . . . of which:	390	645	807	905	1,371	809	912
Amortization paid	—	-2	-63	-86	-87	-88	-132
Amortization received . .	390	647	870	991	1,458	897	1,044
Foreign direct investment . . .	-11	-11	-58	-70	-167	669	-185
Other	-1	—	-1	-1	-1	-1	-1
Total (net)	96	-172	208	-309	1,002	817	-798

Sources: Ministry of Finance, Vneshekonombank, and estimates.
1. See Table H.3 for a listing of socialist countries.

Table H.6. USSR: Balance of Payments in Nonconvertible Currencies
with Nonsocialist Countries on a Transactions Basis, 1980-89 [1]

(In millions of rubles)

	1980	1985	1986	1987	1988	1989
Current account	-762	-325	-1,047	-309	-760	-987
Trade balance	-428	-127	-856	-220	-622	-951
Exports	3,811	5,544	4,015	4,089	3,928	4,769
Imports	-3,383	-5,671	-4,871	-4,309	-4,550	-5,720
Services balance	-331	-189	-134	-38	-148	-48
Transport and insurance	-76	-32	-3	-7	-35	-15
Travel	9	9	9	5	—	-18
Interest	—	16	23	-9	20	18
Other	-264	-182	-163	-27	-133	-33
Transfers	-3	-9	-57	-51	10	12
Capital account	590	533	738	1,311	1,577	189
Medium-term and long-term capital	645	807	905	1,371	809	912
of which:						
Amortization paid	-2	-63	-86	-87	-88	-132
Amortization received	647	870	991	1,458	897	1,044
Foreign direct investment	-11	-58	-70	-167	669	-185
Other	—	-1	-1	-1	-1	-1
Trade credits	-44	-215	-96	108	100	-537
Total (net)	-172	208	-309	1,002	817	-798

Sources: Ministry of Finance, Vneshekonombank, and estimates.
1. See Table H.3 for a listing of socialist countries.

114

Table H.7. USSR: Balance of Payments in Convertible Currencies on a
Settlements Basis, in U.S. Dollars, 1985-90 [1]

(In millions of U.S. dollars)

	1985	1986	1987	1988	1989	First Half 1990
Current account	-3,489	1,662	2,097	-1,687	-7,068	-1,969
Trade balance	-1,663	3,441	3,732	1,513	-3,346	434
Exports	23,529	23,929	19,496	20,851	20,896	10,728
Imports	-25,192	-20,488	-15,764	-19,338	-24,242	-10,293
Services balance	-1,841	-1,827	-1,680	-3,307	-3,839	-2,403
Transport and Insurance	-253	235	366	-365	-419	-154
Travel	114	132	191	206	201	141
Interest	-661	-1,373	-1,846	-2,049	-2,916	-2,401
Other	-1,041	-820	-392	-1,098	-706	12
Transfers	16	47	44	107	117	—
Capital account	1,968	-1,025	-4,408	966	3,325	-9,780
Medium-term and long-term capital	654	-1,593	-3,461	-1,667	-2,545	-2,322
Foreign direct investment	-31	-210	-196	502	-262	—
Loans received	-1,461	-2,024	-3,890	-2,711	-2,456	-2,461
Disbursement	2,863	3,379	2,215	2,532	3,160	815
Amortization paid	-4,324	-5,403	-6,105	-5,243	-5,616	-3,276
Medium-term	-889	-812	-788	-494	-1,166	-1,163
Long-term	-2,103	-2,799	-3,159	-2,835	-2,680	-1,558
Commercial credit	-1,332	-1,792	-2,158	-1,914	-1,771	-555
Amortization received	2,312	883	860	823	506	355
Other	166	-242	-235	-281	-333	-215
Short-term capital (net)	1,314	569	-947	2,634	5,870	-7,458
Overall balance	-1,521	637	-2,311	-721	-3,743	-11,749

Sources: Ministry of Finance, Vneshekonombank, and estimates.
1. Excluding gold exports.

115

Table H.8. USSR: Balance of Payments in Convertible Currencies
on a Transactions Basis, in U.S. Dollars, 1985-89

(In millions of U.S. dollars)

	1985	1986	1987	1988	1989
Current account (excl. gold)	-538	1,800	6,601	1,552	-3,868
Current account (incl. gold)	1,263	5,800	10,101	5,355	-203
Trade balance	1,288	3,579	8,237	4,752	-146
Exports	27,541	26,809	31,348	33,449	35,234
Imports	-26,253	-23,230	-23,112	-28,696	-35,380
Services balance	-1,841	-1,827	-1,680	-3,307	-3,839
Transport and insurance	-253	235	366	-365	-419
Travel	114	132	191	206	201
Interest, net	-661	-1,373	-1,846	-2,049	-2,916
(interest, gross)	(...)	(-2,351)	(-2,652)	(-2,841)	(-3,674)
Other	-1,041	-820	-392	-1,098	-706
Transfers	16	47	44	107	117
Gold exports [1]	1,800	4,000	3,500	3,802	3,665
Capital account	-2,784	-5,163	-12,412	-6,076	-3,540
Medium- and long-term	654	-1,593	-3,461	-1,667	-2,545
Foreign direct investment	-31	-210	-196	502	-262
Loans received (net)	-1,461	-2,024	-3,890	-2,711	-2,456
Disbursement	2,863	3,379	2,215	2,532	3,160
Amortization paid	-4,324	-5,403	-6,105	-5,243	-5,616
Medium term [2]	-889	-812	-788	-494	-1,166
Long term	-2,103	-2,799	-3,159	-2,835	-2,680
Commercial credit	-1,332	-1,792	-2,158	-1,914	-1,771
Amortization received	2,312	883	860	823	506
Other	-166	-242	-235	-281	-333
Short-term financial credits	1,314	569	-947	2,634	5,870
Trade credits	-4,751	-4,138	-8,004	-7,042	-6,865
Overall balance	-1,521	637	-2,311	-721	-3,743

Sources: Ministry of Finance, Vneshekonombank, and estimates.
1. Estimates.
2. Financial credits.

116

Table I.1. USSR: External Claims of the USSR, 1985-90

(In billions of U.S. dollars; end of year) [1]

	1985	1986	1987	1988	1989	Arrears as of June 30 1990 [2]
Total	75.5	95.7	121.4	127.5	138.2	10.0
In convertible currencies	...	18.5	22.9	25.2	28.6	7.2
In nonconvertible currencies	...	77.2	98.5	102.3	109.6	2.8
Of which:						
Socialist countries [3]	40.7	52.0	65.7	67.3	70.8	1.4
In convertible currencies	...	0.1	0.1	0.1	0.1	0.1
In nonconvertible currencies	...	52.0	65.6	67.2	70.7	1.3
Developing countries	34.8	43.7	55.7	60.2	67.4	8.8
In convertible currencies	...	18.4	22.8	25.1	28.5	7.3
In nonconvertible currencies	...	25.2	32.9	35.2	38.9	1.5

Source: Ministry of Finance.

1. Converted from rubles to U.S. dollars at the official exchange rate at the end of each period.
2. Arrears of foreign countries on debt obligations to the USSR. Includes unpaid interest.
3. Socialist countries comprise the CMEA member countries, Albania, the People's Republic of China, the Lao People's Democratic Republic, the Democratic People's Republic of Korea, and Yugoslavia.

117

Table I.2. USSR: External Assets by Debtor Countries
at end-October 1989 [1]

(In millions of U.S. dollars)

	Total	Of which: Written off [2]	Of which: Rescheduled
Total	133,119	866	27,664
Of which:			
Socialist countries	67,581	768	15,242
Of which:			
Albania	128	31	—
Bulgaria	689	—	—
People's Democratic Republic of China	10	—	—
Democratic People's Republic of Korea	3,552	—	664
Cuba	23,997	—	3,753
German Democratic Republic	175	—	—
Hungary	990	—	—
Lao, P.D.R.	1,206	—	79
Mongolia	14,281	91	3,230
Poland	7,874	—	5,021
Viet Nam	14,082	646	2,495
Yugoslavia	597	—	—
Developing countries	64,538	98	12,422
Of which:			
Algeria	3,892	—	890
Angola	3,069	—	1,221
Afghanistan	4,609	—	992
Cameroon	1,520	—	453
Egypt	2,721	—	13
Ethiopia	4,531	82	1,359
India	14,163	—	—
Iraq	5,588	—	2,250
Libya	2,520	—	573
Nicaragua	1,332	—	752
Syria	10,359	3	1,578
Yemen Arab Republic	1,519	—	453
Yemen, P.D.R.	2,919	1	924
Others	5,796	12	964

Source: Ministry of Finance.
1. Converted from rubles to U.S. dollars at the official exchange rate on October 31, 1989.
2. Including future interest payments.

Table I.3. USSR: External Debt and Foreign Exchange Reserves
in Convertible Currencies, 1985-90

	1985	1986	1987	1988	1989	June 1990
	(In billions of U.S. dollars, end of period)					
Long-term credits	16.7	18.1	20.9	18.1	19.9	22.7
Bank loans	(9.9)	(11.2)	(12.1)	(10.9)	(13.3)	(14.4)
Commercial credits	(6.2)	(6.2)	(7.9)	(6.4)	(5.8)	(7.5)
Official loans	(0.6)	(0.7)	(0.9)	(0.8)	(0.8)	(0.8)
Short- and medium-term financial credits .	12.2	13.3	18.3	24.9	34.2	29.5
Bonds	(—)	(—)	(—)	(0.3)	(1.4)	(1.7)
Medium-term loans	(5.3)	(5.9)	(9.7)	(13.4)	(15.1)	(17.8)
Short-term loans	(6.9)	(7.4)	(8.6)	(11.2)	(17.7)	(10.0)
Total debt	28.9	31.4	39.2	43.0	54.0	52.2
Foreign exchange reserves [1]	12.9	14.7	14.1	15.3	14.7	8.5
	(In percent)					
External debt, in percent of						
GDP [2]	3.1	2.8	3.0	3.0	3.7	...
Exports of goods and services [3]	102	111	117	121	139	128
Memorandum item:						
	(In billions of U.S. dollars, end of period)					
Total bank loans, by data source:						
USSR authorities	22.1	24.5	30.4	35.8	47.5	43.9
International banking statistics	22.8	29.1	33.3	36.9	44.8	41.2

Sources: Ministry of Finance, Vneshekonombank, Bank for International Settlements, and estimates.
1. BIS data.
2. GDP is converted from rubles to U.S. dollars at the official exchange rate. If a more market-related exchange rate were used, the debt-GDP ratio would be higher.
3. In convertible currencies.

Table I.4. USSR: External Bonds Outstanding, 1988-90 [1]

End of Period	1988	1989	June 30, 1990
Currency of issue (In millions of units):	*(In millions of U.S. dollars)* [2]		
1988 issues			
Swiss francs 100	66.5	64.7	70.5
Deutsche mark 500	280.9	294.5	299.1
1989 issues			
Italian lire 75,000		59.0	61.2
Deutsche mark 1,250		736.2	747.8
Netherlands guilder 250		130.5	132.9
Austrian schillings 1,000		84.6	85.1
1990 issues			
Deutsche mark 500	347.4	1,369.5	1,695.7

Sources: Vneshekonombank and estimates.
1. No bonds were outstanding prior to 1988.
2. Valued at end-of-period exchange rates.

Table I.5. USSR: External Debt Service Obligations in Convertible Currencies, 1986-91 [1]
(In billions of U.S. dollars)

	1986	1987	1988	1989	1990 Estimates	1991 Projections
Long-term bank credits	3.6	3.9	3.6	3.5	4.5	5.3
Principal	(2.8)	(3.1)	(2.8)	(2.7)	(2.4)	(4.3)
Interest	(0.7)	(0.8)	(0.8)	(1.0)	(1.0)	(1.0)
Commercial credits	2.4	2.8	2.6	2.4	3.8	6.4
Principal	(1.9)	(2.3)	(2.1)	(1.8)	(3.1)	(5.7)
Interest	(0.5)	(0.6)	(0.7)	(0.8)	(1.7)	(0.7)
Medium-term financial credits	0.7	1.4	1.2	1.9	4.0	3.6
Principal	(0.7)	(0.8)	(0.5)	(1.1)	(2.2)	(1.7)
Interest	(0.6)	(0.6)	(0.7)	(0.8)	(1.7)	(1.9)
Interest on short-term deposits	0.6	0.6	0.8	1.6	1.2	0.5
Total	7.8	8.8	8.2	9.4	13.4	16.9
Principal	(5.5)	(6.2)	(5.4)	(5.7)	(8.8)	(11.7)
Interest	(2.4)	(2.7)	(2.8)	(3.7)	(4.6)	(5.2)
In percent of exports of goods and services (in convertible currencies)	27.7	26.5	23.1	24.2	33.0	...

Sources: Derived from data provided by Vneshekonombank.
1. The projections for 1991 include obligations on external debt projected to be disbursed in 1991. External debt service obligations relate only to debt contracted or guaranteed by Vneshekonombank.

Table J.1. USSR: State Budget Revenue, 1976-90 [1]

(In billions of rubles)

	Average 1976-80	1981	1982	1983	1984	1985	1986	1987	1988	Estimate 1989	Plan 1990
Total revenue	266.0	320.6	353.0	357.9	376.7	367.7	366.0	360.1	365.1	384.9	410.1
(in percent of GDP)	(...)	(48.7)	(50.9)	(49.2)	(49.6)	(47.3)	(45.8)	(43.6)	(41.7)	(41.0)	(42.8)
Tax revenue	199.2	235.2	253.8	262.4	274.2	337.1	335.6	342.9	340.0	361.6	387.8
Income taxes and transfers [2]	103.9	119.8	130.9	136.4	147.0	148.4	159.7	158.8	154.3	157.3	168.0
Individual income taxes	22.0	25.5	26.6	27.6	28.8	30.0	31.2	32.5	35.9	41.7	43.5
Income tax	20.5	23.9	25.0	26.0	27.1	28.3	29.5	30.9	33.9	37.5	40.2
Agriculture tax	0.3	0.3	0.3	0.3	0.2	0.2	0.2	0.2	0.2	0.2	0.2
Bachelor/small family tax	1.2	1.3	1.4	1.4	1.4	1.5	1.5	1.4	1.4	1.5	1.5
Patent/other income taxes									0.4	2.5	1.6
Profit taxes and transfers	81.9	94.3	104.3	108.8	118.2	118.4	128.5	126.3	118.4	114.6	124.5
State enterprises [3]	80.3	92.4	102.4	106.6	115.6	115.9	125.9	123.4	115.6	111.4	120.4
Profit/income deductions, etc.	13.5	18.8	19.7	22.1	25.3	30.2	43.4	66.7	61.0	66.0	78.8
Fixed payments	1.3	0.3	5.2	5.4	5.5	0.5	3.2	2.2	0.6	0.6	—
Residual profit payments	39.1	45.3	46.3	45.9	49.2	47.1	38.5	12.8	9.5	4.8	3.0
Wage tax [4]									4.9	6.2	
On fixed/working capital	26.4	28.0	31.2	33.3	35.5	38.1	40.8	41.7	39.5	33.8	38.6
Cooperatives and other	1.6	1.9	1.9	2.2	2.6	2.5	2.6	2.9	2.8	4.2	4.1
Collective farms	0.7	0.8	0.8	1.0	1.4	1.2	1.2	1.3	1.3	1.6	1.4
Cooperatives, etc.	0.9	1.1	1.1	1.2	1.3	1.3	1.4	1.6	1.6	2.6	2.7
Social insurance contributions	12.9	15.0	22.3	23.1	24.5	25.4	26.5	28.1	30.1	33.1	44.8
Turnover tax	82.3	100.4	100.6	102.9	102.7	97.7	91.5	94.4	101.0	111.1	121.9
Alcohol	...	...	...	...	...	30.1	27.2	29.1	33.4	40.4	39.0
Other	...	...	...	...	...	67.6	64.3	65.3	67.6	70.7	82.9
Revenue from foreign activity	...	...	...	...	...	65.6	57.9	61.6	54.6	59.0	51.8
Exports	...	...	...	...	...	33.8	26.3	29.4	24.0	23.8	16.0
of which: oil and gas	...	...	...	...	...					14.0	11.5
Imports	...	...	...	...	...	31.2	31.0	31.5	29.9	34.3	33.3
Other	...	...	...	...	...	0.6	0.6	0.7	0.7	0.9	2.4
of which: foreign exchange revenue	...	...	...	...	...	—	—	—	—	—	1.0
Tax on motor vehicles	...	...	...	...	...					1.1	1.3
Nontax revenue [5]	66.8	85.5	99.2	95.5	92.5	30.6	30.4	17.2	25.1	23.3	22.3
Geological fees	—	—	—	—	—	3.7	3.9	4.0	4.1	4.1	4.2
Movies	—	—	—	—	—	1.3	1.3	1.4	1.6	1.6	1.5
Forestry	0.5	0.5	0.8	0.8	0.8	0.8	0.8	0.9	0.8	0.8	0.8
Water	—	—	—	—	—	0.5	0.5	0.5	0.5	0.5	0.5
Lotteries	0.9	0.7	1.3	1.3	1.3	0.3	0.3	0.3	0.3	0.4	0.3
Other	65.4	84.2	97.0	93.4	90.4	24.0	23.6	10.1	17.8	15.9	15.0

Source: Ministry of Finance; and estimates.

1. Data since 1985 are not comparable to those of previous years.
2. Includes also revenue from sources other than fixed-rate taxes.
3. Enterprise contributions include geological fees in 1981-84.
4. Labor resource tax in 1988 and the excess wage fund tax in 1989-90.
5. Nontax revenue includes revenues from foreign activity and unidentified financing through 1984.

Table J.2. USSR: State Budget Expenditure, 1976-90 [1]

(In billions of rubles)

	Average 1976-80	1981	1982	1983	1984	1985	1986	1987	1988	Estimate 1989	Plan 1990
Total expenditure	260.1	309.8	343.1	354.3	371.2	386.0	415.6	429.3	445.9	465.1	485.6
(in percent of GDP)	(…)	(47.1)	(49.4)	(48.7)	(48.8)	(49.7)	(52.0)	(52.0)	(51.0)	(49.5)	(50.6)
Economy	140.4	169.8	197.3	201.8	211.7	217.2	234.1	234.0	203.1	200.1	188.2
Investment	…	…	…	…	…	63.8	66.4	71.8	76.3	68.0	42.2
Subsidies	…	…	…	…	…	3.4	2.2	1.9	1.9	1.8	16.8
Operational expenditures	…	…	…	…	…	13.2	13.6	13.0	12.7	8.0	11.8
Price differentials	…	…	…	…	…	65.8	73.0	74.9	64.3	66.3	95.9
Increases in procurement prices	…	…	…	…	…	…	…	…	21.9	31.6	…
Other	…	…	…	…	…	71.0	78.9	72.4	26.0	24.4	21.5
Defense	17.2	17.1	17.1	17.1	17.1	19.1	19.1	20.2	57.3	75.2	71.0
Procurement	…	…	…	…	…	…	…	…	…	32.6	31.0
R & D (including space)	…	…	…	…	…	…	…	…	…	15.3	13.2
Wages and salaries	17.2	17.1	17.1	17.1	17.1	19.1	19.1	20.2	20.2	20.2	19.3
Pensions	…	…	…	…	…	…	…	…	…	2.3	2.4
Military construction	…	…	…	…	…	…	…	…	…	4.6	3.7
Other	…	…	…	…	…	…	…	…	…	0.2	1.3
Justice and internal security	…	…	…	…	…	5.7	6.0	6.2	6.6	8.2	9.6
Administration	2.3	2.6	2.8	2.9	2.9	3.0	3.0	2.9	3.0	2.9	2.9
Science	9.0	10.9	11.7	12.7	13.2	13.7	14.4	12.4	16.9	10.1	11.0
Social and cultural activities	80.2	92.8	97.8	102.1	106.4	111.9	119.3	127.6	134.3	139.3	160.5
Education	27.9	30.8	32.2	32.4	34.0	35.9	38.1	42.3	42.7	44.5	49.6
Health and physical cultural	13.4	15.2	16.0	16.5	17.2	17.6	18.0	19.5	21.9	24.6	27.6
Budget of national social insurance	14.1	16.9	18.0	20.8	22.3	22.8	23.6	24.0	25.5	25.3	4.9
Grant to central collective farm insurance	3.0	3.9	3.9	3.9	2.8	3.1	4.0	3.8	4.1	4.0	6.6
Mothers	0.3	0.3	0.5	0.5	0.6	0.6	0.6	0.7	…	0.7	0.8
Social security	21.5	25.7	27.3	28.0	29.6	31.9	35.0	37.3	40.1	40.2	71.0
On account of national social insurance	17.3	20.5	21.9	22.6	24.1	25.8	28.7	30.8	…	35.8	41.2
Other	4.2	5.1	5.4	5.4	5.5	6.1	6.3	6.5	…	4.4	29.8
Lottery	…	…	…	…	…	0.2	0.2	0.2	0.2	0.2	0.2
Foreign economic activity	…	…	…	…	…	2.2	4.9	11.9	15.6	15.4	14.9
Trade subsidies	…	…	…	…	…	0.9	1.5	8.1	9.7	9.6	7.4
Exports	…	…	…	…	…	…	0.5	5.9	6.7	6.9	6.8
Imports	…	…	…	…	…	…	1.0	2.2	3.0	2.7	0.6
Subsidies to industry	…	…	…	…	…	…	2.0	2.1	2.2	2.1	2.3
Unilateral aid	…	…	…	…	…	1.3	1.1	1.7	2.1	1.5	2.0
Interest payments	…	…	…	…	…	…	…	…	0.8	1.3	1.9
Other	…	…	…	…	…	…	0.4	…	0.8	0.9	1.3
Other expenditures	11.1	16.7	16.4	17.8	19.9	13.0	14.6	13.9	9.1	13.7	27.3
Internal interest payments	…	…	…	…	…	…	…	…	4.5	5.3	6.3
Gosbank	…	…	…	…	…	…	…	…	4.5	5.3	6.3
Price diff. on agricultural products	…	…	…	…	…	…	…	…	…	…	0.4
From reserve funds	…	…	…	…	…	…	…	…	0.4	4.5	4.1
USSR Council of Ministers	…	…	…	…	…	…	…	…	0.4	1.8	1.0
Republic Council of Ministers	…	…	…	…	…	…	…	…	…	2.2	2.6
USSR Ministry of Finance	…	…	…	…	…	…	…	…	…	0.5	0.5
Other	11.1	16.7	16.4	17.8	19.9	13.0	14.6	13.9	4.2	3.9	16.9

Source: Ministry of Finance and estimates.

1. Data since 1985 are not comparable to those for previous years.

Table J.3. USSR: State Budget Financing, 1976-90[1]

(In billions of rubles)

	Average 1976-80	1981	1982	1983	1984	1985	1986	1987	1988	Estimate 1989	Plan 1990
Overall balance	5.9	10.8	9.9	3.6	5.6	-18.3	-49.6	-69.2	-80.8	-80.2	-75.5
(In percent of GDP)	(...)	(1.6)	(1.4)	(0.5)	(0.7)	(-2.4)	(-6.2)	(-8.4)	(-9.2)	(-8.5)	(-7.9)
Financing	-5.9	-10.8	-9.9	-3.6	-5.6	18.3	49.6	69.2	80.8	80.2	75.5
Foreign financing (net)	...	...	...	...	...	-7.4	-8.6	-7.1	-4.9	-4.6	-4.0
Drawings	...	...	...	...	...	5.5	6.5	7.7	8.0	8.2	7.9
Amortization	...	...	...	...	...	-12.9	-15.1	-14.8	-12.9	-12.8	-12.0
Domestic financing (net)	...	...	...	...	...	35.8	66.4	85.3	95.3	97.1	79.4
Banking system	...	...	...	...	...	29.4	63.0	79.8	87.5	89.2	60.0
Gosbank loan of 1982	...	...	...	...	...	10.5	19.0	19.0	21.0	19.8	—
State-wide loan fund	...	...	...	...	...	6.0	28.9	35.5	66.5	62.4	—
Other[2]	...	...	...	...	...	12.9	15.1	25.3	—	5.8	60.0
Nonbank public	...	...	...	...	...	6.4	3.4	5.5	7.8	7.9	19.4
Liquidation of 1957 loan	...	...	...	...	...	—	-1.0	-1.0	—	-1.4	-1.6
Loan of 1982 (3 percent interest rate)[3]	—	—	...	...	...	0.9	1.4	0.6	1.3	1.7	1.0
Social security receipts of 1982 loan	—	—	...	...	...	1.5	—	2.6	2.6	2.6	—
Eight-year loan (10 percent interest rate)	—	—	—	—	—	—	—	—	—	—	10.0
Consumer durable bonds	—	—	—	—	—	—	—	—	—	—	10.0
Residuals from republic budgets	—	—	—	—	—	4.0	3.0	3.3	3.9	5.0	—
Over-financing (-)[4]	-5.9	-10.8	-9.9	-3.6	-5.6	-10.1	-8.2	-9.0	-9.6	-12.3	—
Memorandum items:											
Union balance	...	...	...	...	...	...	...	...	-90.0	-92.0	-64.6
Republics' balance	...	...	...	...	...	...	...	...	7.6	8.5	-10.9
Social security balance	...	...	...	...	...	...	...	...	1.8	2.8	—

Sources: Ministry of Finance and estimates.
1. Data since 1985 are not comparable to those for preceding years.
2. Ministry of Finance documents identify "other financing" as "state loan for the development of the national economy, distributed among the firms, organizations and banks."
3. Includes lottery payments in 1985-88.
4. Excess of credit plan allocation over required financing.

123

Table J.4. USSR: Centralized Funds of State Enterprises, 1985-89

(In billions of rubles)

	1985			1986			1987			1988			1989		
	Inflow	Outflow	Year-end balance	Inflow	Outflow	Year-end balance	Inflow	Outflow	Year-end balance	Inflow	Outflow	Year-end balance	Inflow	Outflow	Year-end balance
Total	2.7	2.7	1.8	...	...	...	27.1	24.9	9.4	45.9	43.0	9.9	52.0	51.9	11.3
Distribution by fund:															
Material incentive fund	1.3	1.3	0.9	...	...	...	1.7	1.4	1.4	1.5	1.3	1.1	1.6	1.6	1.6
Social, cultural and housing construction fund	0.5	0.5	0.4	...	...	...	1.5	1.4	0.8	1.7	1.6	0.7	1.6	1.5	0.9
Production development fund	0.7	0.7	0.2	...	...	...	13.8	13.2	1.2	28.3	27.4	2.9	48.9	48.9	8.8
Other funds	0.3	0.2	0.2	...	...	...	10.2	8.9	6.0[1]	14.4	12.7	5.2	—	—	—
Distribution by activity:															
Industry	1.6	1.6	1.0	...	...	...	14.1	13.4	2.2	20.7	20.2	2.9	25.3	25.2	4.1
Agriculture	0.3	0.4	0.2	...	...	...	5.3	5.3	2.7	9.6	8.5	3.9	8.8	8.7	3.6
Transport	0.1	0.2	0.1	...	...	...	1.8	1.6	0.3	6.5	6.1	0.7	5.4	5.5	0.6
Communications	—	—	—	...	...	...	0.0	0.0	0.0	0.8	0.7	0.2	0.7	0.7	0.1
State procurement	0.1	0.1	0.0	...	...	...	0.0	0.0	0.0	0.2	0.1	—	0.7	0.6	0.1
Supply and marketing	—	—	—	...	...	...	—	—	—	—	—	—	0.5	0.5	-0.1
Trade	0.1	0.1	0.1	...	...	...	2.5	1.2	2.0	3.3	3.0	1.0	3.1	3.1	0.9
Personal services	0.3	0.2	0.1	...	...	...	0.6	0.6	0.1	0.6	0.7	0.2	0.6	0.6	0.1
Municipal services enterprises	0.1	0.1	—	...	...	...	0.1	0.1	0.0	0.1	0.1	0.1	0.1	0.1	0.1
Scientific organizations	—	—	—	...	...	...	—	—	—	—	—	—	0.4	0.4	0.1
Construction and assembly organizations	0.1	0.1	0.2	...	...	...	2.5	2.4	1.7	3.2	3.0	0.8	5.0	5.0	1.2

Source: Goskomstat.

1. Fund for production and social development (trade); agro-industrial reserve fund.

Table J.5. USSR: Domestic Government Debt Outstanding, 1975-90

(In billions of rubles, at end of year)

	1975	1980	1984	1985	1986	1987	1988	Estimate 1989	Plan 1990
I. Bank credit	29.2	70.7	96.2	106.7	125.7	180.2	267.7	349.9	349.9
Credit against deposits of the public [1]	29.2	70.7	96.2	106.7	125.7	144.7	165.7	185.5	185.5
Free reserves of state loan fund	—	—	—	—	—	35.5	102.0	164.4	164.4
II. Nonbank debt	33.2	33.1	32.1	34.9	35.6	39.6	44.7	48.8	191.0
From insurance funds [1]	5.0	7.7	10.1	11.9	12.3	15.3	18.4	21.6	22.2
Debt on account of loans accumulated before 1957	23.8	18.4	13.4	12.0	10.6	9.6	9.6	8.4	—
1982 loan [1]	4.4	7.0	8.6	11.0	12.7	14.7	16.7	18.8	20.5
Loan from cooperatives, enterprises, etc.	—	—	—	—	—	—	—	—	60.0
Treasury obligations to public [2]	—	—	—	—	—	—	—	—	10.0
Consumer durable bonds	—	—	—	—	—	—	—	—	10.0
Debt write-off on agricultural banks/enterprises in 1990	—	—	—	—	—	—	—	—	68.3
III. Official domestic debt (I+II)	62.4	103.8	128.3	141.6	161.3	219.8	312.4	398.7	540.9
IV. Agricultural Price Support Fund	...	...	...	11.3	11.3	20.5	30.3	39.6	45.0
V. Domestic debt, adjusted (III+IV)	...	...	...	152.9	172.6	240.3	342.7	438.3	585.9

Sources: Ministry of Finance and Gosbank.

1. At 3 percent interest rate.
2. At 10 percent interest rate and 10-year maturity period.

Table K.1. USSR: Total Domestic Credit, 1980-90

(In billions of rubles, end of period)

	1980	1985	1986	1987	1988	1989	1990 June	1990 Dec. Proj.
Bank credit to firms	342.5	519.4	450.2	427.8	398.8	383.7	385.8	367.4
Short-term	261.4	426.5	356.6	333.5	302.3	287.1	293.4	294.0
Long-term	81.1	92.9	93.6	94.3	96.5	96.6	92.4	73.4
Bank credit to households [1]	0.7	2.0	2.4	3.1	5.8	7.4	8.9	10.6
Total bank credit to economy	343.2	521.4	452.6	430.9	404.6	391.1	394.7	378.0
of which: long term	81.1	94.9	96.0	97.4	102.3	104.0	101.3	84.0
(adjusted) [2]	343.2	521.4	452.6	430.9	404.6	391.1	410.0	408.0
Bank credit to government	78.2	118.0	140.6	200.7	298.0	390.1	427.9	524.9
Ordinary credit	70.7	106.7	125.7	180.2	267.7	350.5	385.8	474.9
Agricultural credit	7.5	11.3	14.9	20.5	30.3	39.6	42.1	50.0
(adjusted) [3]	78.2	118.0	140.6	200.7	298.0	390.1	392.6	454.9
Total bank credit	421.4	639.4	593.2	631.6	702.6	781.2	822.6	902.9
(adjusted) [4]	421.4	639.4	593.2	631.6	702.6	781.2	802.6	862.9
Government bonds	7.0	11.0	12.7	14.4	16.1	18.1	21.2	23.5
Total domestic credit	428.4	650.4	605.9	646.0	718.7	799.3	843.8	926.4
(adjusted) [4]	428.4	650.4	605.9	646.0	718.7	799.3	823.8	886.4

Sources: Data provided by the Soviet authorities; and estimates.

1. Households are granted only long-term credit.
2. Credit to the economy has been adjusted by adding rub 70 billion in 1990 (35.3 billion in June 1990) on account of loans to the agricultural sector taken up by the Government; rub 20 billion and rub 40 billion for new construction on credit (matched by deposits in escrow accounts) have been subtracted respectively in June and in December 1990.
3. Credit to the Government in 1990 has been adjusted for the acquisition of bad loans written-off by the enterprise sector (see footnote 2).
4. Total bank credit has been adjusted by subtracting rub 20 billion and rub 40 billion for new construction credit respectively in June and in December 1990 (see footnote 2).

Table K.2. USSR: Growth in Domestic Credit, 1971-90

(Annual growth rates in percent)

	1971-80	1981-85	1986	1987	1988	1989	1990 June	1990 Proj.
Bank credit to firms	10.5	8.7	-13.3	-5.0	-6.8	-3.8	-2.6	-4.2
Short-term	9.6	10.3	-16.4	-6.5	-9.4	-5.0	-2.2	2.4
Long-term	14.4	2.8	0.8	0.7	2.3	0.1	-4.0	-24.0
Bank credit to households	1.5	23.4	20.0	29.2	87.1	27.6	53.4	43.2
Total bank credit to economy	10.5	8.7	-13.2	-4.8	-6.1	-3.3	-1.8	-3.3
Of which: long-term	14.2	3.2	1.2	1.5	5.0	1.7	-0.7	-19.2
(adjusted) [1]	10.5	8.7	0.2	-4.8	-6.1	-3.3	2.0	4.3
(adjusted and in real terms) [1]	10.6	7.2	1.0	-5.3	-6.8	-7.2	...	...
Bank credit to government [2]	...	8.6	19.2	42.7	48.5	30.9	26.7	34.5
(adjusted) [3]	...	8.6	19.2	42.7	48.5	30.9	16.3	16.6
Total bank credit	...	8.7	-7.2	6.5	11.2	11.2	11.2	15.6
(adjusted) [4]	...	8.7	4.0	6.5	11.2	11.2	8.5	10.5
Government bonds [5]	...	9.5	15.5	13.4	11.8	12.4	23.4	29.8
Total domestic credit	...	8.7	-6.8	6.6	11.3	11.2	11.5	15.9
(adjusted)	...	8.7	4.2	6.6	11.3	11.2	8.8	10.9
Memorandum items:								
Net material product (nominal)	4.8	4.6	1.5	2.1	5.2	6.8	...	...
Net material product (real)	4.9	3.2	2.3	1.6	4.4	2.5	...	...
NMP deflator (implicit)	-0.1	1.4	-0.8	0.5	0.8	4.2	...	...

Sources: Data provided by the Soviet authorities; and estimates.
1. The growth rate of credit to the economy in 1986 has been adjusted for rub 71.6 billion of canceled construction credit. Credit to the economy in 1990 has been adjusted by adding rub 70 billion (35.3 billion in June 1990) on account of loans to the agricultural sector taken up by the Government. Rub 20 billion and rub 40 billion for new construction credit (matched by deposits in escrow accounts) have been substracted respectively in June and in December 1990. The NMP deflator was used to compute the growth rate in real terms.
2. Including agricultural credit.
3. The growth rate of credit to the Government in 1990 has been adjusted for the acquisition of bad loans written-off by the enterprise sector (see footnote 1).
4. The growth rate of total credit in 1986 has been adjusted for rub 71.6 billion of cancelled construction credit. The same growth rate in 1990 has been adjusted by subtracting rub 23 billion for new construction credit (see footnote 1).
5. Including bonds to be paid back in consumer durables.

127

Table K.3. USSR: Growth in Short-Term Credit to Enterprises, 1981-90

	Percentage Growth Rates							Composition in Percent
	1981-85	1986-89	1986	1987	1988	1989	June 1990	1989
By sector:								
Industry	8.0	-8.8	3.5	-13.1	-13.8	-10.8	-3.9	25.3
Agriculture	7.4	-2.1	2.7	3.0	-6.2	-7.5	-29.9	26.3
Transports and communication	12.1	-18.8	2.2	-12.8	-43.9	-13.0	59.1	0.7
Construction	19.0	-33.1	-60.9	-31.8	-32.6	-16.9	47.6	7.7
Trade	8.9	-6.0	-11.7	-8.9	0.4	-3.3	21.9	23.8
Wholesale trade	7.3	1.0	6.3	0.8	-0.8	-2.1	2.6	8.0
Procurement of farm products	4.1	-1.1	3.6	8.7	-8.0	-7.8	21.7	3.7
Other	13.3	45.6	3.6	-3.4	57.1	186.4	260.0	4.4
Total	10.3	-9.4	-16.4	-6.1	-9.7	-5.0	-0.3	100.0
(excluding construction)	8.0	-4.3	-0.7	-5.8	-6.6	-3.9	-4.7	92.3

Source: Data provided by the Soviet authorities.

Table K.4. USSR: Republican Distribution
of Bank Deposits and Loans, 1970-89
(Percentage composition)

	1970	1980	1987	1988	1989
	(Bank Deposits)				
RSFSR	60.3	57.2	56.9	57.0	...
Ukraine	19.6	22.0	22.2	22.2	...
Belorussia	3.2	4.0	4.4	4.5	...
Estonia	0.9	0.7	0.7	0.7	...
Latvia	1.3	1.1	1.1	1.1	...
Lithuania	1.5	2.0	2.1	2.1	...
Moldavia	0.6	1.0	1.1	1.1	...
Georgia	2.6	2.2	2.1	2.1	...
Armenia	1.3	1.3	1.2	1.1	...
Azerbaidzhan	1.1	1.0	1.0	0.9	...
Kazakhstan	3.9	3.8	3.6	3.6	...
Turkmenistan	0.4	0.4	0.4	0.4	...
Uzbekistan	2.1	2.2	2.1	2.1	...
Tadzhikistan	0.6	0.5	0.5	0.5	...
Kirgizia	0.6	0.6	0.6	0.6	...
Total	100.0	100.0	100.0	100.0	100.0
of which:					
rural	26.8	27.0	25.2	24.5	...
urban	73.1	73.0	74.8	75.5	...
	(Bank Loans)				
RSFSR	56.9	59.0	59.6	55.1	54.8
Ukraine	16.8	15.2	13.6	12.9	12.4
Belorussia	2.8	3.2	3.6	3.0	2.8
Estonia	0.5	0.4	0.3	0.3	0.4
Latvia	1.0	1.0	0.8	0.8	0.8
Lithuania	1.2	1.2	1.1	1.1	1.2
Moldavia	1.2	1.3	1.2	1.2	1.0
Georgia	1.6	1.5	2.4	2.3	2.2
Armenia	0.9	0.8	1.0	1.1	1.1
Azerbaidzhan	1.3	1.2	2.0	1.8	1.8
Kazakhstan	5.4	5.6	6.5	6.8	7.1
Turkmenistan	0.8	0.6	0.8	0.8	0.8
Uzbekistan	3.9	3.6	4.4	4.3	4.2
Tadzhikistan	0.8	0.7	0.7	0.7	0.7
Kirgizia	0.9	0.7	0.9	1.0	1.0
Unspecified	3.9	4.0	1.7	6.8	7.8
Total	100.0	100.0	100.0	100.0	100.0

Source: Data provided by the Soviet authorities.

Table K.5. USSR: Financial Assets, 1980-90
(In billions of rubles, end of period)

	1980	1985	1986	1987	1988	June 1989	1989	June 1990	Proj. 1990
Narrow money (M1)	198.4	276.1	297.0	343.6	396.4	416.2	453.1	464.8	514.0
Currency	52.6	70.5	74.8	80.6	91.6	100.8	109.5	119.5	133.0
of which: firms	1.7	1.6	1.8	1.7	3.3	2.8	4.5	3.8	6.1
Demand deposits	145.8	205.6	222.2	263.0	304.8	315.4	343.6	345.3	381.0
Households	102.4	134.7	146.5	159.2	176.2	187.3	201.6	211.6	221.0
Enterprises	43.4	70.9	75.7	103.8	128.6	127.8	142.0	133.7	160.0
Broad money (M2)	262.6	377.0	409.0	469.2	535.4	561.3	614.8	643.1	708.8
M1 plus:									
Time deposits	62.6	95.3	104.7	116.6	128.3	133.4	149.0	164.5	179.8
Households	52.2	83.7	93.5	104.5	116.1	123.4	130.5	137.0	147.8
Enterprises [1]	10.4	11.6	11.2	12.1	12.2	10.0	18.5	27.5	32.0
Lottery bonds	1.6	5.6	7.3	9.0	10.7	11.7	12.7	13.8	15.0
Total financial assets	300.1	475.8	438.0	500.0	575.1	600.7	656.6	711.3	797.2
M2 plus:									
Other bank deposits	18.7	74.0	2.8	3.2	10.8	10.1	12.2	36.4	55.2
Households									
Long-term deposits	1.9	2.4	2.8	3.2	5.5	5.6	8.4	8.8	11.4
Enterprises									
Construction funds	16.8	71.6	—	—	5.3	4.5	3.8	27.6	43.8
Bonds (1957 ser.)	5.4	5.4	5.4	5.4	5.4	5.4	5.4	5.4	—
Bonds (1990 ser.)	—	—	—	—	—	—	—	2.0	8.5
Insurance policies	13.4	19.4	20.8	22.2	23.5	23.9	24.2	24.4	24.7
Households' assets									
M1	153.3	203.6	219.5	238.1	264.5	285.3	306.6	327.3	347.9
M2	207.1	292.9	320.3	351.6	391.3	420.4	449.8	478.1	510.7
Total financial assets	227.8	320.1	349.3	382.4	425.7	455.3	487.8	518.7	555.3
of which:									
savings deposits	156.5	220.8	242.8	266.9	297.8	316.3	340.5	357.4	380.2

Sources: Data provided by Gosbank; and estimates.
1. Including incentive funds of enterprises; technically, these are not time deposits since they could be used for specific purposes without previous notice.

Table K.6.   USSR: Growth in Financial Assets, 1981-90

(Growth rates in percentage)

	1981-85	1986	1987	1988	1989	June 1990	Proj. 1990
Narrow money (M1)	6.8	7.6	15.7	15.4	14.3	11.7	13.4
Currency	6.0	6.1	7.8	13.6	19.5	18.6	21.5
Demand deposits	7.1	8.1	18.4	15.9	12.7	9.5	10.9
Households	5.6	8.8	8.7	10.7	14.4	13.0	9.6
Enterprises	10.3	6.8	37.1	23.9	10.4	4.6	12.6
Broad money (M2)	7.5	8.5	14.7	14.1	14.8	14.6	15.3
of which:							
time deposits							
of households	9.9	11.7	11.8	11.1	12.4	11.0	13.3
Households' assets							
M1	5.8	7.8	8.5	11.1	15.9	14.7	13.5
M2	7.2	9.4	9.8	11.3	15.0	13.7	13.5
Total financial assets	7.0	9.1	9.5	11.3	14.6	13.9	13.8
of which:							
savings deposits	7.1	10.0	9.9	11.6	14.3	13.0	11.7

Sources: Data provided by Gosbank; and estimates.

Table K.7.   USSR: Financial Assets of Enterprises,[1] 1980-90

	1980	1985	1986	1987	1988	1989	1990[2]
			Stock at the end of the period				
			(in billions of rubles)				
Narrow money (M1)	45.1	72.5	77.5	105.5	131.9	146.5	166.1
Currency	1.7	1.1	1.8	1.7	3.3	4.5	6.1
Demand deposits	43.4	70.9	75.7	103.8	128.6	142.0	160.0
Broad money (M2)	55.5	84.1	88.7	117.6	144.1	165.0	198.1
M1 plus:							
Incentive funds	10.4	11.6	11.2	12.1	12.2	11.2	16.0
Time deposits	—	—	—	—	—	7.3	16.0
Construction funds	16.8	71.6	—	—	5.3	3.8	43.8
Total financial assets	72.3	155.7	88.7	117.6	149.4	168.8	241.9
Memorandum item:							
Funds in transfer							
between enterprises	20.3	30.9	42.9	43.1	47.0	68.0	...

		1980-85	1986	1987	1988	1989	1990
			Selected growth rates				
M1	...	10.0	6.9	36.1	25.0	11.1	13.4
M2	...	8.9	5.5	32.6	22.5	14.5	20.0

Source: Data provided by the Soviet authorities; and estimates.
1. Including nonprofit organizations.
2. Projections.

131

Table K.8. USSR: Monetary Survey, 1988-90

	1988	1989 June	1989 Dec.	1990 June	1990 Dec.[1]
Monetary assets					
Money (M1)	396.4	416.2	453.1	464.8	514.0
Currency in circulation	91.6	100.8	109.5	119.5	133.0
Demand deposits	304.8	315.4	343.6	345.3	381.0
Households	176.2	187.3	201.6	211.6	221.0
Enterprises	128.6	127.8	142.0	133.7	160.0
Time deposits	128.3	133.4	149.0	164.5	179.8
Households	116.1	123.4	130.5	137.0	147.8
Enterprises	12.2	10.0	18.5	27.5	32.0
Other bank deposits	10.8	10.1	12.2	36.4	55.2
Households' long-term deposits	5.5	5.6	8.4	8.8	11.4
Enterprises' construction funds	5.3	4.5	3.8	27.6	43.8
Total monetary assets	535.5	559.7	614.3	665.7	749.0
Liabilities					
Total domestic bank credit	702.6	740.1	781.2	822.6	902.9
Credit to government	298.0	338.0	390.1	427.9	524.9
Ordinary credit	267.7	304.0	350.5	385.8	474.9
Agricultural credit	30.3	34.0	39.6	42.1	50.0
Credit to the economy	404.6	402.1	391.1	394.7	378.0
Short term (only firms)	302.3	300.1	287.1	293.4	294.0
Long term	102.3	102.0	104.0	101.3	84.0
Enterprises	96.5	...	96.6	92.4	73.4
Households	5.8	...	7.4	8.9	10.6
Other items (incl. nfa)	-167.1	-180.4	-166.9	-156.9	-153.9
Interenterprise settlement (MFO)[2]	-47.0	-57.0	-68.0	-80.0	...
Interbank settlement	-38.8	-29.7	-14.7	-7.9	...
Settlements through					
Ministry of Communication	20.5	-0.2	-0.6	-0.1	...
Budgetary transit accounts	-62.9	-66.0	-59.4	-59.4	...
Other debtors/creditors (+ net credit)	6.6	10.3	-6.2	14.1	...
Others	-45.5	-37.8	-18.0	-23.6	...
of which: estimated net foreign assets	-35.0	-37.1	-41.5	-43.5	...

Sources: Data provided by the Gosbank; and estimates.
1. Figures for December 1990 include the write off of agricultural debt (rub 70 billion) and the repayment by Gosbank of rub 5.46 billion on account of outstanding bonds issued in 1957.
2. The figures for June 1989 and 1990 are estimates.

Statistical Issues

1. INTRODUCTION

As a country's economy evolves, it typically finds that it must adapt its statistical system to meet changing circumstances. Nowhere is this phenomenon more apparent than in the USSR. Reform initiatives in the 1980s have underscored problems with the existing statistical system, and created a demand for new indicators and methods of gathering data. These initiatives have prompted major changes in Soviet statistical work that can be expected to continue as the USSR undergoes further reform. The purpose of this appendix is to provide an overview of the Soviet statistical system, evaluate the reliability of selected indicators it produces, and suggest areas in which changes might prove fruitful. It should be noted at the outset that its objective is not to dwell on the problems with Soviet statistics. The existence of some degree of error is normal in statistical work, and Soviet statisticians were fully prepared to discuss these problems. It is also true, however, that an understanding of the systematic biases of Soviet statistics is essential to the analysis of current economic developments.

As regards the future, it is clear that changes to both the accounting systems used in enterprises and in government statistics would help accelerate the transition to a market economy. Efficient decentralization of decision-making will take place only if managers and investors have a full and fair view of an enterprise's financial performance. Achieving this will require the implementation of uniform accounting standards, training in these new concepts, auditing of accounts to ensure that the standards are being met, and the dissemination of audited accounts for use by shareholders, creditors, and supervisory authorities. Just as improved accounting systems are a prerequisite for efficient microeconomic decision-making, so are improved macroeconomic statistics necessary for improved policy formation. Converting the balance of payments from a settlements basis—which excludes transactions related barter trade, gold exports and trade credits—to a transactions basis would provide a more comprehensive picture of the USSR's external position. Adapting the national accounts to the SNA framework and revis-

133

ing the methodology used to calculate implicit price deflators for these accounts would permit a more accurate measurement of real growth. Introducing comprehensive measures of unemployment and modifying the methods used to calculate retail and wholesale price indices would provide a clearer picture of the social impact of policy changes. Soviet authorities have already sought outside advice in some of these areas; further technical assistance could play an important role in promoting the transition to a market economy.

2. OVERVIEW OF THE SOVIET STATISTICAL SYSTEM

a. Organization of the statistical system

Although the Soviet statistical system is relatively centralized, there are no fewer than five organizations involved in statistical work. The chief coordinator is the State Committee on Statistics (Goskomstat USSR), but as shown in Chart 1, it shares the responsibility for statistical collection with several other agencies. Banking, monetary, and budgetary statistics are compiled by the Ministry of Finance, although the source of most financial and balance of payments statistics is Gosbank. Statistics on crime, corruption, alcoholism, and other social problems are the domain of the Ministry of Internal Security. Until 1989, foreign trade statistics were the exclusive responsibility of the Ministry for Foreign Economic Relations (MVES). Although many of these data are now compiled directly by Goskomstat, this ministry continues to gather a number of important external sector statistics, as does Vneshekonombank. Finally, the Ministry of Defense maintains all statistics on military production and other defense- related activities.[1]

The sources of data for statistics on the domestic economy, external sector, fiscal accounts, and money and credit are summarized in Chart 2. Given that it requires specialized expertise to compile many of these series, it is not surprising that a few institutions are the sole providers of certain statistics. The degree to which access to a given organization's statistics is restricted, however, is surprising. For example, Goskomstat has a legitimate interest in acquiring data on net factor income from abroad to compile GNP statistics for the USSR, but has yet to obtain these data from the other agencies. As a result, its GNP statistics exclude net factor income from abroad and therefore are actually GDP figures, though no statistical compendia mention this. Similarly, one cannot go to a single ministry for a composite picture of external settlements, although this would seem to be of interest to a variety of Soviet organizations in carrying out their official activities.

Goskomstat, the central coordinator of statistical work in the USSR, has evolved a highly structured internal organization to compile the data for which it is responsible. As shown in Chart 3, the national office is organized into 14 sectoral departments and divisions, with five affiliated organizations that cut across sectoral lines. Administrative regions at the union republic level and below each have their own Goskomstats, which serve as the link between the national headquarters and reporting units within each enterprise and collective farm. The organization of these regional statistical offices parallels that of the national office, although they are subordinate not only to Goskomstat USSR but to regional administrative authorities as well.

Glavlit, the state censorship office, is not formally part of the national statistical network, but has nonetheless played an important role. By forbidding publication of articles containing statistics not authorized by the central statistical authorities, it traditionally controlled the dissemination of information on the Soviet economy. Glavit's degree of control, however, has been reduced. For example, since 1987 Soviet scholars have been able to publish growth rates that differ from official statistics. Legislation has been introduced that would restrict the scope of state censorship.[2]

b. The role of statistical agencies

Soviet statistical agencies provide indicators of macroeconomic performance, as do their western counterparts. They are also expected, however, to serve as a mechanism for monitoring plan fulfillment by individual enterprises. This latter role has given rise to several notable characteristics of the Soviet statistical system, which include the following:

(1) Complete enumeration preferred to sample surveys

The success of enterprises in meeting plan targets cannot be assessed unless data are gathered for all relevant establishments. The practice of compiling statistics based on comprehensive reports filled out by each firm is at considerable variance with western methods of data collection, which are based primarily on sample surveys.

(2) Large statistical workforce

Monitoring individual enterprise performance is labor intensive. For example, to process the forms it receives, Goskomstat currently employs 27,000 persons—down from 41,000 employed as recently as 1987. By contrast, approximately 13,000 full-time employees are involved in federal statistical work in the United States (where sample surveys predominate).[3] The relatively high employment figures reflect not only the practice of gathering data via complete enumeration, but also the poor quality of much of the available data processing equipment. This frequently necessitates hand tabulation of many indicators.

135

(3) Emphasis on data processing over data analysis

Given finite resources and the plethora of reports submitted by individual enterprises, the attentions of Goskomstat and other Soviet statistical organizations have traditionally been focused on data processing rather than data analysis. Statistics thus tend to be gathered in a manner that facilitates easy compilation, though not necessarily easy interpretation or use.

(4) Incentives to distort

Because bonuses have generally been paid upon proof of plan fulfillment, enterprises have had a strong incentive to exaggerate their performance. Goskomstat maintains a large force of investigators to audit reports, but falsification is still widespread.[4] Soviet analysts estimate that exaggerated reporting inflated output by three percent on average during the late 1980s, but was as high as 25 percent for some raw material sectors.[5] It is not possible to judge whether the incidence of inflated reporting has risen over time. To the extent that reforms have substituted state orders and autonomous direct contracts among enterprises for planning norms, there are now fewer output targets and thereby fewer incentives to falsify production levels.

c. Reform and the statistical system

The *glasnost'* and *perestroika* campaigns had a delayed impact on the Soviet statistical system.[6] The campaign for change began in earnest in 1987, following the publication of an unprecedented series of challenges by Soviet scholars regarding the accuracy of official statistics.[7] Soviet authorities responded to these criticisms in 1987 by mandating a restructuring of the country's statistical system.[8] In the following months, the former Central Statistical Administration (TsSU) was renamed Goskomstat, and elevated to state committee status. Indicators that had been omitted from existing yearbooks for decades were restored, the Information and Publishing Center was created, and many new, sector- specific statistical handbooks were published. Concerted efforts were made to increase Soviet participation in international statistical conferences, and a new director for Goskomstat was appointed in 1989 to oversee the continuation of reform initiatives.

While these measures represent a substantial change from past practices, many problems remain. Goskomstat still monitors fulfillment of plan targets, and the systemic problems that role engenders (noted above) continue to be in evidence. The statistical agency's work force has been reduced by a third at a time when increasing demands are being made of its services. Finally, there is still widespread uncertainty regarding various methodological approaches and the quality of many macroeconomic indicators. The following sections review selected statistical issues regarding the domestic economy, the external sector, the fiscal accounts, and the banking system.

3. DOMESTIC ECONOMY

a. National accounts

Most of the criticism of Soviet economic statistics has been directed at its national accounts. The problem most frequently noted is that real growth rates for these accounts are upwardly biased by the failure to account fully for inflation. But there are also problems of coverage, undocumented changes in methodology, and distortions imposed by the economic system, all of which complicate comparisons of Soviet national accounts statistics with those from other countries as well. Each of these issues is discussed below.

(1) Problems of coverage

Traditional Soviet national accounts are prepared in accordance with the System of Balances of the National Economy (MPS). This means that unlike the national accounts of most countries (which are prepared according to the U.N. System of National Accounts (SNA)), Soviet accounts exclude depreciation and the output of most so-called nonmaterial services.[9] Levels of output implied by traditional Soviet indicators, such as national income produced (hereafter referred to as net material product, or NMP), therefore understate the true level of economic activity.

An additional consequence of adopting the MPS accounting framework is that final expenditure statistics cannot be easily used to check the accuracy of NMP calculated on a sector of origin basis. National income utilized—the final expenditure equivalent of NMP—is simply the sum of consumption and accumulation. It is thus a measure of domestic absorption rather than total final expenditure, and differs from NMP whenever the combined net exports and loss figure it excludes is not zero.[10] Although Goskomstat has all the elements needed to conduct a consistency check between NMP and national income utilized (see Table A.2 of Appendix II-1), it is unclear whether or not such checks are regularly used by Goskomstat to assess the reliability of the national accounts. But it is clear that no explicit allowance is made for statistical discrepancy, meaning in effect that all errors and inadvertent omissions are buried within national income utilized or "losses". Finally, the net export figure is defined differently than under the SNA system. Rather than simply valuing net exports at border prices, which would be the standard SNA practice, Goskomstat multiplies the valuta trade balance by an average export conversion factor if the trade balance is positive, and by an import conversion factor if it is negative.[11] This practice introduces a bias in the calculation of one or more of the components of the national income accounting identity whenever the valuta trade balance is nonzero and the conversion factor is different from unity. The degree of bias, given the differences between domestic and valuta prices, may not be negligible.[12]

137

Goskomstat has moved in recent years to address these coverage problems by also compiling national accounts estimates on an SNA basis.[13] As shown in Table 1, gross national product (GNP) statistics produced on this basis to date have been built up from NMP data using translation keys, although corresponding GNP estimates have been developed from the expenditure side that are fully consistent with these figures.[14] While broader in scope than traditional NMP statistics, these GNP estimates are not without problems. On the one hand, Goskomstat has been unable to obtain statistics on net factor income from abroad. This means that their GNP estimates are effectively gross domestic product (GDP) figures, and would generally be different if net overseas income were taken into account. On the other hand, the difference between NMP and GDP—40 percent in 1989— is much larger than for Eastern European economies,[15] suggesting that GDP estimates may be overstated.

The largest part of this difference is depreciation, which in the Soviet case includes both capital renovation and capital repair. The latter is generally regarded as an intermediate expense in western countries, and excluded from the GDP accounts. Soviet statisticians justify its inclusion by noting that depreciation rates for renovation are so low that capital repair must be used by enterprises to prolong the life of not fully depreciated equipment. There is some appeal to this argument: Soviet GDP statistics imply an aggregate depreciation rate of only six percent (including the capital repair adjustment), which is quite low by international standards.[16] Even after including capital repair, this low depreciation rate might lead one to conclude that depreciation is underestimated in the national accounts. Offsetting this, however, is the immense capital stock base to which the relatively low depreciation rates are applied. This base may owe its impressive size at least in part to valuation problems, which could in turn impart some upward bias to depreciation.[17] In addition, it is difficult to justify the inclusion of all capital repair as true depreciation, for only a portion is devoted to extending the life of the existing capital stock. It is possible that the upward bias imposed by valuation problems and inclusion of capital repair is roughly compensated by the downward bias introduced through the use of relatively low depreciation rates. This would yield reported depreciation figures that are close to their true values, though further study would be necessary to draw firm conclusions.

Finally, it is important to note that neither the NMP nor GDP statistics compiled by Goskomstat take into account levels of activity in the "second," or shadow economy. Estimates of gross output in the shadow economy vary considerably, with Goskomstat estimating a figure of rub 70 billion, and the Chairman of the Soviet KGB maintaining that it is closer to rub 150 billion.[18] Even if only half of these estimates represent undocumented value-added, they would imply that official GDP statistics are understated by 4 to 8 percent. While figures such as these are quite rough, they are consistent with other estimates of the output of the shadow economy, and highlight continuing problems of coverage in Soviet national accounts [19]—a problem also noted in the national accounts of western countries.[20]

(2) *Methodological uncertainties*

Methodological changes to Soviet national accounts are not always well documented. At worst, this can allow unflattering economic results to be concealed. A recent example of this was the revelation that the statistical authorities had originally excluded declining alcohol sales from the national accounts for 1985 and 1986 to boost artificially rates of aggregate growth.[21] At best, incomplete documentation still has the potential to mislead users of data, even if that is not the intention. For example, one methodological problem not publicly documented concerns the valuation of inventories in calculating stockbuilding. Soviet statisticians apparently make no adjustments for inflation in inventories when calculating changes in stocks. During periods of low inflation this has little effect on national income utilized, but as prices increase, the consequent rise in inventory values imparts an upward bias to national income accounts.[22] This problem could seriously distort measurement of economic activity in the USSR if controls on prices were lifted as part of economic reforms.

There are also problems in defining stockbuilding. For example, besides net fixed investment ("accumulation of basic funds"), the accumulation component of national income utilized includes (1) accumulation of "material circulating means" and (2) accumulation of "reserves and other expenditures" (Table C.7, Appendix II-1). According to Goskomstat, the change in unfinished construction is included in the first category—under the "change in material circulating means" in the construction sector— although in many countries it is customary to include changes in certain types of unfinished construction (structures, highways, and rail lines) in net fixed investment.[23] The second category includes changes in inventories in the defense sector and in those held by the government in connection with disaster relief programs. In Chapter II.2, the two categories together are taken to be equal to "stockbuilding," as conventionally defined.

It should be noted, finally, that there remains uncertainty regarding the scope of coverage of the defense sector in the Soviet national accounts. Available budget figures on defense procurement[24] are broadly consistent with the accumulation of "reserves and other expenditures" component of national income expended, which would seem to make sense because, as noted, the latter apparently consists primarily of changes in defense sector inventories. This consistency could be misleading, however, for some western analysts have suggested that the budget figures may not include all defense expenditures.[25] On the production side of the national accounts, Goskomstat has indicated that NMP includes the earnings of defense workers previously omitted from the employment rolls (see section 3.d). Some wage data suggest that these defense workers may be included in the non-productive sphere, meaning that their earnings would be included in GDP, but not necessarily in NMP. Further information is necessary to draw firmer conclusions on the extent of defense sector coverage in the USSR's national accounts.

(3) Distortions imposed by the economic system

The fact that the USSR is a planned economy has traditionally made interpretation of its national accounts problematic. Foremost of the difficulties imposed by the economic system are problems of valuation. As resources have traditionally been allocated by plan rather than market, most prices in the USSR are set administratively. This means that national accounts are valued at prices that do not necessarily reflect consumer preferences, and increases in NMP or GDP may thus not indicate an improvement in consumer welfare. In addition, the sectoral composition of value-added is distorted by the presence of large turnover taxes and subsidies.[26] Finally, comparisons of output per capita with other countries are complicated by vast differences in relative prices, as well as the absence of a market-clearing exchange rate to convert Soviet national accounts into dollars.

These problems of valuation have been the driving force behind western estimates of Soviet GNP, most notably the "adjusted factor cost approach."[27] They are, however, not the only distortions introduced by the economic system. For instance, as already noted, considerable rewards have accrued to enterprises reporting fulfillment of their economic plans, providing an incentive for these firms to exaggerate their output.

(4) Biased rates of growth

Few indicators have been singled out for greater criticism than the official real growth rates for NMP. Soviet critics maintain that official growth rates are overstated because of inadequate accounting for inflation.[28] Soviet growth rates are calculated in "comparable prices," which until 1989 were simply official list prices.[29] Since list price increases associated with the introduction of new or improved products were not regarded as inflationary (even if there was no actual improvement in product quality), price deflators implicit in "comparable price" rates of growth for NMP tended to underestimate actual inflation, and therefore overstated official growth rates.[30]

How large is this bias? Official NMP growth rates for 1966-85 averaged 5.3 percent, compared to much lower alternative estimates by Soviet analysts ranging from 2.2 to 2.9 percent.[31] Researchers at the USSR Institute of World Economy and International Relations have recently estimated that real growth in NMP between 1913 and 1987 was approximately one-third the official rate.[32] Soviet scholars have gone as far as to use CIA estimates of real growth in Soviet GNP to suggest that official growth rates are twice as high as actual growth.[33] In an even more unusual turn, Goskomstat has used CIA estimates of real growth to call into question the reliability of even lower growth rates set forth by Soviet critics.[34]

140

While these alternative estimates of real growth should be regarded with caution, the message they send is unmistakable. Official growth rates are upwardly biased because inflation has not been accounted for fully. The only point of contention is the magnitude by which growth has been overestimated. Goskomstat has sought to address these problems by introducing an improved method for calculating real growth rates in 1990 (for 1989 data). This involves the calculation of actual NMP deflators, which are reportedly developed according to international standards on the basis of changes in prices of a representative sample of commodities. Conceptually, this is a departure from earlier practices, where real rates of growth were derived by first literally calculating output in comparable prices— a complicated procedure that led to the problems outlined above. To the extent that better efforts are now made to account for inflation, this is a welcome change.

b. Price indices

Official price indices that are used simply to monitor price developments in the economy have also come under fire.[35] Problems with Soviet price indices are threefold. First, there are problems of availability. While a retail price index has been compiled for decades, an agricultural procurement price index has been calculated only since 1984, compilation of a wholesale price index was resumed only in 1988 after a 10 year hiatus, and a price index for services did not exist until 1990. Significantly, the USSR still has no true consumer price index (with weights drawn from household budget surveys rather than retail trade statistics), although income-indexing called for in some reform plans would require such an index.[36]

Second, there are problems of measurement. Prior to 1989, the retail price index was not particularly good in picking up so-called hidden inflation, that is, inflation associated with the introduction of new models or quality improvements. If a product in the sample was upgraded or a new model introduced, standard practice was simply to ignore price increases that were accompanied by the supposed increase in product quality. It is widely believed, however, that in many cases these price increases could not be fully justified by quality changes. The official price index thus failed to account for a fairly pervasive form of inflation in the USSR. Goskomstat introduced changes in 1989 aimed at capturing this so-called hidden inflation.[37] The improved price index for that year shows a rate of inflation of 2.0 percent—a full 1.5 percentage points higher than would have resulted from simply assuming all so-called quality improvements were non-inflationary.

Finally, there are problems of sample design, and more generally of measuring so-called repressed inflation. For its retail price index, Goskomstat attempts to gather prices for a remarkably large sample of 3,000 commodities. Not every commodity is in stock when the survey is conducted, however, meaning that the effective sample used for the retail price index is smaller than stated, and changing every month.[38] Goskomstat's apparent solution to this problem is to use official list prices when shortages preclude obtaining prices in the field. The problem with this approach is that shortages indicate excess demand, strongly suggesting that the true transaction prices of these goods in parallel markets are above the state list prices. Of course, to the extent that the retail price index also includes cooperative prices, some of the effective price increases manifested by shortages in state-run stores are captured, but directly addressing this problem is not an easy task. The U.S. Bureau of Labor Statistics has been working with Poland to devise methodologies for imputing prices of scarce goods in the context of measuring inflation—research that is obviously relevant to the USSR as well.

Goskomstat has recently attempted to quantify the extent of repressed inflation in the state retail sector, and estimates that in 1989 it amounted to approximately 5.5 percent.[39] Although the methodology used to arrive at this estimate is quite rough, it would suggest that the true rate of inflation for the USSR in 1989 was in the neighborhood of 7.5 percent (the official rate of 2.0 percent, together with repressed inflation of 5.5 percent). It should be kept in mind, however, that little research has been conducted in the USSR on direct measurement of inflation in parallel markets, providing no real benchmark against which Goskomstat's estimates of repressed inflation can be assessed.

c. Investment and the capital stock

Statistics on investment and the capital stock are among the most difficult to compile. Issues such as the valuation, useable life, depreciation, and retirement of fixed assets are unavoidably complex. Soviet investment and capital stock statistics also have their own peculiarities.[40] One problem is that both sets of data are expressed in "comparable prices," although this point is rarely made clear for capital stock data.[41] More important is the fact that both investment and capital stock data from 1983 to the present are calculated in 1983 prices, though data for earlier periods use different price bases. This complicates the interpretation of capital-output ratios for the country over time (output is typically expressed in current prices, but capital stock is in comparable prices of different years), and can introduce problems in the estimation of aggregate production functions. Goskomstat has made appropriate adjustments for the base year changes in available gross investment statistics, although there is some uncertainty whether capital stock data have been similarly revised for earlier periods.[42]

Also troubling are potential problems of valuation in connection with the capital stock statistics. As noted earlier (see section 3.a.(1)) the aggregate capital output ratio for the USSR is quite high by international standards, at approximately 3.2:1. Even if one allows for inefficiency in capital use, it is probable that part of the reason this ratio is so high is because capital is overvalued. Goskomstat assesses capital stock data at original purchase prices (or more specifically, at 1983 purchase prices for recent capital stock data), but not at replacement values.

If there were a long-term tendency for prices of industrial goods (such as capital equipment) to fall relative to other prices in the Soviet economy,[43] depreciation calculated on an asset base valued at original purchase prices could be higher than if replacement values were used. This in turn would tend to inflate the GDP estimates that are shown in Table 1.[44] While some research by western economists suggests that prices of machinery in the USSR have actually risen at a faster rate than shown by official price indices,[45] capital stocks could still be overvalued if the rate of increase was less than for prices in the economy overall.[46]

The apparent contradiction between the rapid growth of gross investment in the late 1980s and the decline in net investment in the national accounts in 1988-89 (see Tables A.6 and C.1, Appendix II-1) is largely attributable to fundamental definitional differences between the two concepts, and the growth of depreciation.[47]

d. Employment and living standards

The availability of standard labor indicators has traditionally been a problem in the USSR. Although comprehensive labor balance tables are regularly compiled, comprehensive sectoral employment figures are typically provided only in percentage terms in statistical publications. Goskomstat does not compile labor force statistics as they are understood in the West (i.e., the employed population, plus those who are unemployed but who desire work), and thus has no official measures of unemployment that are comparable to western statistics. It instead prepares estimates of total "labor resources," which divide the working age population into those who work, and those who for various reasons do not (housewives, students, prisoners, the handicapped, and individuals who are involuntarily unemployed). Experimental unemployment rates that have been computed to date are generally the ratio of a subset of nonworkers to total labor resources, despite the fact that not all of these individuals desire work or are even capable of it.[48] The crux of the problem is that official accounting of unemployment cannot formally proceed until the government adopts the Law on Unemployment, which provides a definition of the status of unemployed individuals. Pending approval of this law, Goskomstat expects to begin compiling official unemployment statistics in 1991. Accelerating work on these statistics is particularly important in the context of the economic reform initiatives now under discussion, for most reform programs assume that unemployment will rise at least temporarily as inefficient firms are closed.

Although concern has been expressed by western scholars over possible discontinuities in Soviet employment statistics posed by the sudden appearance in the statistics of approximately 4 million workers involved in defense-related activities in 1989,[49] aggregate and sectoral employment trends noted in the tables in Appendix II-1 include these workers throughout. While these employment figures are consistent with sectoral employment data published in percentage terms in

Soviet statistical handbooks, they are higher than average annual employment totals shown elsewhere in these publications.

Soviet authorities have expressed increasing interest in data on standards of living. Goskomstat has acted to meet the growing demand for this type of data by increasing the sample size in its family budget surveys by 45 percent, thereby increasing the representativeness of household income and expenditure statistics.[50] The record of reporting on other aspects of living standards is less commendable. For example, grain output per capita is an important measure of the USSR's ability to meet its food needs, yet until 1989 grain output statistics were reported in "bunker weight," which includes dirt and other foreign matter that clearly cannot be consumed.[51] Similarly, official statistics on meat consumption are inflated by the inclusion of substandard cuts, lard and bones.[52] Statistics on the sales of passenger cars were also artificially boosted in the early 1970s by the undocumented inclusion of used cars.[53] While a careful reader of Soviet statistics on living standards may be able to allow for these peculiarities, they may well prove misleading to others.

e. Enterprise finances

Although the statistical authorities compile a wide variety of financial statistics, they have yet to assemble a unified set of tables on sources and uses of funds for state enterprises. Data on sources and uses of funds cited in Chapter II.2 are therefore estimates that have been developed on the basis of several different available statistical series. Unfortunately, considerable uncertainty exists regarding the definitions and coverage of some of the statistics on which these estimates are based. As a result, there are large, unexplained discrepancies between the sources and uses of funds (see Table D.5, Appendix II-1). For example, preliminary estimates for 1989 suggest that state enterprises used rub 123 billion (or 13 percent of GDP) more than they had at their disposal to spend.[54] It is also difficult to reconcile the large increases in profits in the financial accounts in 1989 (Table D.5, Appendix II-1) with a virtual leveling-off of profits as reported in the distribution of NMP in the national accounts (Table D.1, Appendix II-1).

4. EXTERNAL SECTOR

a. Foreign trade

Foreign trade statistics, as compiled by the Ministry for Foreign Economic Relations (MVES), differ from general international practice in six respects in terms of their coverage.

(1) All deliveries are on a commercial basis, i.e., grants (foreign aid given and received), parcel post, and traveler's baggage remain excluded.

(2) Both exports and imports are on an f.o.b. basis.[55]

(3) Re-exports and imports also include merchandise which is resold without entering Soviet territory; e.g., Iraqi oil sold to India.

(4) Exports recorded in connection with turnkey projects implemented abroad or imports recorded for those carried out domestically include all services (labor, feasibility studies, etc.) in addition to exported/imported machinery, equipment, and raw materials.

(5) Only value added in the USSR is included in the case of goods imported for transformation in the USSR and subsequently re-exported to the country of origin, e.g., import of wool from Viet Nam for the production of carpets sold to Viet Nam. In such cases, no imports are recorded and the corresponding exports are reduced by the value of the imported inputs.

(6) Exports of gold are excluded. However, unlike the foreign exchange settlements balance (see section b), which deletes all counterpart entries, the trade balance records all merchandise imports financed through gold sales.

Starting with 1991, the methodology for compiling foreign trade statistics is to be brought in line with the U.N. methodology, except for turnkey projects, the services content of which was estimated by the authorities at rub 1.3 billion for exports and rub 0.7 billion for imports in recent years. The c.i.f. adjustment on imports would add about rub 3 billion a year while grant-financed exports and imports may amount to about rub 0.5 billion and rub 0.1 billion a year, respectively.[56]

The value of diamond exports is not shown separately in published data but it is included in section 9 of the unified customs nomenclature. Exports and imports of production cooperatives and joint ventures are included, as are those under barter arrangements.

b. The foreign exchange settlements balance

The Soviet authorities do not yet compile a balance of payments on a transactions basis.[57] In the past, there were separate foreign exchange plans for the 15 foreign trade organizations (FTOs) controlled by the Ministry of Foreign Trade (now, the MVES). Their aggregation represented the annual foreign exchange allocation plan. In addition, there was an ex post presentation of the execution of this plan. As payments began to exceed receipts and foreign indebtedness began to rise, a foreign exchange settlements balance was developed in the Ministry of Finance that incorporated certain elements of debt servicing. Gosbank is currently developing a methodology to compile a balance of payments on a transactions basis, which is scheduled to be implemented in 1991. Several of the presentational problems (e.g., with respect to the recording of interest and amortization payments) were corrected in collaboration with the Soviet authorities for purposes of preparing Tables H.1-H.8 of Appendix II-1, as highlighted below.

The settlements balance, for which the responsibility for preparation has recently been shifted from the Ministry of Finance to Gosbank, relies primarily on data supplied by the Vneshekonombank (VEB). Reflecting the different means of settlement employed in Soviet foreign transactions, three separate settlement balances are prepared: (1) in convertible currencies; (2) in transferable rubles and currencies of other socialist countries; and (3) in clearing currencies under bilateral agreements with Finland and various developing countries. All three balances follow the same classification scheme but the convertible currency balance has some methodological complications that arise from borrowing operations to bolster reserve holdings.[58]

The bulk of transactions included in the settlements balance in convertible currencies are those with countries with which transactions normally are settled in convertible currency. Also included are convertible currency settlements with CMEA member countries and such payments whenever required by the provisions of bilateral clearing agreements with other countries (recently, only in the case of Finland). The settlements balance excludes transactions between residents and nonresidents in rubles but it includes, as explained in section (3), some transactions between residents.[59]

(1) Trade account

(a) While MVES data discussed in section a are based on transactions records, the trade data of the settlements balance reflect only cash settlements (see, however, (c)). As a result, there is no possibility to break them down by commodity groups or countries of origin and destination.

(b) These payments data are converted from valuta rubles — which reflect the official exchange rates in effect when each payment is made/received—to U.S. dollars by applying the average annual rub/US$ rate.

(c) Export receipts include amounts retained by exporters. The VEB invests the amounts retained in deposits abroad and the Soviet convention is to assume that imports are made the moment the investment takes place. Therefore, the settlements balance erroneously records imports instead of an increase in reserves, which results in a smaller trade surplus (or larger trade deficit) in the year retention quotas are introduced or in any subsequent year when the outstanding foreign exchange rights or deposits increase.

146

(d) Exports and imports with financing terms show up only with their downpayments in the year the trade transaction takes place, while the amortization of such credits is shown as trade transactions in future years.

(e) Soviet donations of goods (or services)—or receipts of such transfers—do not show up at all in the settlements balance.

(2) Services account

(a) Transportation reflects on a gross basis the settlements between Soviet and foreign companies (airlines, railroads, trucking, river and ocean shipping).

(b) Tourism receipts are based on the receipts of tour operators (Intourist). There is a small amount of tourism expenditure abroad.

(c) Interest receipts appear to be understated in each year, as stock data published by the BIS would suggest a minimum of US$1-1.3 billion (see, however, section (3)). Trade credits extended should yield additional interest receipts.

(3) Balance on nontrade transactions

This balance includes maintenance of representative offices (including embassies) abroad and in the USSR, contributions to international organizations, outlays for official travel, and bank operations. The first category encompasses only current payments and receipts—the acquisition of real estate having been included in the category "balance on credit and capital placements abroad" (see section 4.b.(4))—and might be reclassified as "other services" along with outlays for official travel. Contributions to international organizations ought to be included in the capital account. Bank operations are the receipts and expenditures of the VEB's own foreign exchange budget. (The debt service on government credits channeled through the VEB is included in the flows noted under section 4.b.(4)). The VEB's own transactions include, among receipts: interest earned on assets held abroad, embassy operations, and the purchase of foreign exchange from the public (foreign tourists). Included in interest receipts are interest on the placement of foreign exchange retained by exporting enterprises and interest on the placement of excess of borrowing over use of loans by the government. On the expenditure side, the VEB's budget includes the sale of foreign exchange to the public; noncommercial transfers; diplomatic expenses; interest and capital amortization on long-term project loans, and on medium-term financial credits (i.e., balance of payments support); and on interest on deposits. The latter includes interest on foreign currency deposits by enterprises, usually at LIBOR-1 1/2 percent; since this transaction represents a transaction among residents, it ought to be excluded from the balance of payments.

The recording of interest and capital amortization has changed over time. Until 1988, the full amount of short-term credits outstanding and all medium-term financial loans obtained in a given year were considered to be amortized in full in the succeeding year. As the original disbursements of financial loans were not recorded, any ex post correction of the assumed amortization of medium-term financial loans through an offsetting credit item (i.e., a fictitious disbursement) also could not be shown. In 1989, only the repayment of short-term credits and interest on new medium-term borrowing were included in the settlements balance. From 1990, in yet another change, only amortization of long-term loans and interest on all maturities (short-, medium-, and long-term loans) have been included.[60] As a result, the balance on nontrade transactions still excludes financial loan disbursements. It also excludes the amortization of financial loans and the net changes in short-term credits. In the balance of payments presented in Appendix II-1, Tables H.1-H.2 and H.7-H.8, however, net changes in the stock of short-term credit and the recording of amortization payments according to actual repayments have been incorporated.

(4) Balance on credits and capital placements abroad

This category encompasses amortization of government, commercial and bank credits and the purchase and sale of property. The USSR extends only government and commercial credits, but it receives all three aforementioned categories of credit. While disbursements (even those of a cash nature) are not shown in the settlements balance, the debt service is. In principle, only debt service received or paid in cash is included in the settlements balance. However, until 1987—i.e., while the Ministry of Foreign Trade had full control over the operations of FTOs—debt service on a Soviet credit (e.g., for arms exports) that was to be repaid in kind (e.g., with oil) would appear as both "imports" and "amortization" in the settlements balance as and when these oil shipments in fulfillment of the repayment-in-kind obligation were made. Internally, Soyuznefteexport (the oil-trading FTO) would be debited, and the arms exporter would be credited, with "accounting foreign exchange" (*razchotnie rubli*) in recognition of the execution of the foreign exchange allocation plan. Now, these transactions remain outside the settlements balance and only the corresponding internal transaction in accounting foreign exchange is carried out.

(5) Overall balance

The overall balance in the Soviet statistics, as pointed out above, is distorted by the omission of all cash disbursements, by the full amortization (without rollover) of all short-term debt outstanding at the end of the preceding year and, in the years before 1989, by the inclusion of the full amount of medium-term borrowing as amortization in each following year. The settlements balance presented in this study has been adjusted for these flows with the assistance of the Soviet authorities, using, as noted in section (1)(b), average annual official exchange rates between the ruble and the U.S. dollar.

c. External assets and liabilities

External assets and liabilities, as presented in Soviet statistics, include future interest payments on fixed rate loans. Only in the case of variable rate loans (essentially, medium-term financial loans from foreign banks) are the indebtedness data identical with principal outstanding. Data presented in Tables II.7 and Appendix II-1, Table I.3) have been adjusted to show only principal amounts. External liabilities refer only to debt contracted or guaranteed by the VEB; no statistical information is available on external debt contracted without its guarantee.

It should also be noted that a distinction is made between assets denominated in convertible and nonconvertible currencies, as is common for many socialist countries. Most of the assets in nonconvertible currencies are denominated in transferable rubles. Although these assets do represent a measure of liquidity (for financing inter-CMEA trade), it is doubtful that they perform any meaningful reserve function in a larger sense. For this reason, assets in nonconvertible currencies should generally be excluded from total reserves.

International reserve holdings of gold and foreign exchange continue to be treated as state secrets. The absence of such data makes a reconciliation of monetary and balance of payments accounts impossible. As to foreign exchange holdings, the data prepared by the Bank for International Settlements (BIS) have been acknowledged by Soviet officials to track very closely the USSR's foreign exchange holdings, and have been used in this report. However, in interpreting the BIS data, it should be borne in mind that they exclude foreign exchange held with banks outside the BIS reporting area—thought to be rather small—and that they include foreign exchange holdings of the two multinational CMEA banks headquartered in Moscow.

5. FISCAL ACCOUNTS

The fiscal accounts of the USSR are not presented in a form easily reconcilable with the Government Finance Statistics (GFS) format.[61] Divergences occur in several dimensions, which are noted below. It should be stressed, however, that the problems outlined below are problems of degree that occur to some extent in almost every other country. There is always scope for reform, refinement and reclassification of government statistics. Since statistics form the basis for appropriate policy making, they must change as the structure of the economy and its available policy instruments change. In the USSR, the pace of change is sufficiently rapid that the reform of fiscal statistics has become urgent.

a. The definition of government

The state budget of the USSR is probably the most comprehensive budget in the world, consolidating as it does more than 52,000 different governments according to a common framework. Hence, a frequent complaint when compiling GFS statistics—lack of adequate data on levels of government below the central administration—does not apply. Such richness of information is an important aid to fiscal policy analysis and implementation in any economic regime, and it would be important to maintain the continuity and consistency of budgetary statistics in the event of far-reaching reform of the fiscal system.

At the same time, however, the coverage of government in the state budget of the USSR is deficient, by GFS criteria. Many activities that affect the financial position or behavior of enterprises and individuals through the use of taxes and subsidies rather than indirect market mechanisms would be deemed "governmental" by GFS, yet are not included in the state budget. For instance, the cross-subsidization of enterprises effected by their branch ministries represents two activities carried out on governmental authority—a tax on the profitable enterprise and a transfer to the loss-maker—which do not appear in the budget record of taxes and expenditures. The state budget therefore does not describe the full extent of governmental intermediation of resources in the Soviet economy, and consequently gives policy-makers only a partial idea of the scope for fiscal policy management.

As economic reforms take place, some of these extra-budgetary functions are expected to disappear (such as the independent taxing and spending powers of branch ministries), and some are expected to be transferred to the state budget (for instance, the social welfare support offered by enterprises and trade unions). For a full understanding of the role of government in the economy in the meantime, the budget should be expanded to include all remaining extra-budgetary operations. In analyzing the budget deficit during the transition to a more market-oriented economy, however, care needs to be taken to distinguish between "new" revenues and expenditures, and those that always existed but have only now been made explicit in the budget.[62]

b. The distinction between ordinary revenues and expenditures, and financing

The Soviet concept of financing government differs in several respects from that of GFS. In the Soviet presentation of the budget, foreign borrowing and repayments of loans made by the USSR abroad, are included as revenue, as are receipts from the sale of bonds and drawings from reserve funds of subordinate levels of government. All external debt service is considered expenditure. If an imbalance between revenues and expenditures remains, it is financed by the banking system.[63]

150

In the GFS presentation of the budget, foreign borrowing and repayments, bond sales and retirements, and use of reserve funds are all recognized as financing items, and to the extent that the sum of such operations is positive, the budget deficit will be larger under this presentation. The exact composition of the Soviet position for foreign financing is still somewhat clouded. Despite the inclusion of interest payments on balance of payments support above the line, it is likely that the foreign outflows which would normally be classified as negative financing items incorporate some interest payments as well as lending and amortization (on official loans, banking and commercial credits, construction credits, credits by foreign trading organizations, and the operations of Vneshekonombank).[64] Likewise, foreign financing inflows include some interest income, along with repayments received, new official loans and commercial bank credits.

In sum, the state budget includes borrowed funds (except from the banking system) as income and the repayment of these funds as expenditure. GFS, on the other hand, draws a line between fiscal policy actions and the financial consequences (the creation or extinction of liabilities for government) of these actions. There are four main issues to be addressed in reconciling the government financing statistics of the USSR.

(1) Interest versus principal

GFS distinguishes between the interest and principal components of debt service, with regard to both debt and lending. It does so on the grounds that interest represents the purchase of a desired service—the loan of funds—while the loan or collection of principal represents the creation or extinction of a claim or liability, affecting net asset positions, and offsetting past or future operations. Hence, according to GFS, interest, unlike borrowing and amortization, is included above the line, as a determinant of the deficit. The Soviet presentation includes interest and principal together (for most but not all of debt service), and thus a strict GFS deficit cannot be derived.[65]

(2) Government lending

GFS makes a distinction between government lending for policy purposes, and lending undertaken to manage the government's liquidity. Policy lending is considered an expenditure rather than negative financing although it does create a financial asset for government, because it is considered as simply an alternative way of implementing desired government actions—such as investment in preferred sectors. Although some government lending is included in the state budget, it is not possible at this time to separate policy loans from management of the government's liquidity position. Therefore, all such lending is included here below the line (Table J.3, Appendix II-1). In a market economy, the equivalent lack of information would probably have resulted in the classification of all such lending above the line, because government lending is relatively unusual and

151

therefore its motives are usually not market-based. In the USSR, however, where the financial structure has not been diversified, government entities are likely to have played an important role in intermediation. In particular, it is not clearly understood to what extent the foreign trade financing activities of Vneshekonombank are included in the budget. To the extent that a portion of loans now undertaken by the government does not reflect financial intermediation, their inclusion below the line may lead to an understatement of the GFS deficit.

(3) Arrears

Though the GFS deficit is presented on a cash basis, it is frequently considered useful for policy purposes to make a supplementary calculation of expenditures made but not paid for, and add these to total expenditures, thus raising the recorded deficit. The financing item that offsets the increase in the deficit is a forced loan to government by those sectors of the economy or the rest of the world that provided the goods, services, or funds to government, and expected to be paid but were not. In other words, since the buildup in arrears on expenditure creates a liability for government, they should be considered as extraordinary financing. The deficit should reflect the actual resources preempted by government and not just the payment for them, particularly if arrears become significant.

Although the USSR has contracted significant external arrears, no adjustment has been made to the state budget in the main report to take them into account, since it is not clear exactly how large are the arrears which should be included in the state budget. In the future, however, the budget presentation should be seen as a useful tool for highlighting the impact of arrears on the economy and for reminding policy-makers that deficit reduction through arrears is artificial and temporary.

(4) Reserve funds

The state budget counts as revenue the residuals of republican budgets from past years.[66] According to the GFS presentation, this represents a double-counting, because income can only be earned once. If earnings are recorded as revenue in the year they are earned, and then, having helped to generate a surplus, are deposited with the banking system — thereby improving government's net credit position—their eventual withdrawal from the banking system to finance new expenditures must be seen as an increase in net credit to government. The proper treatment of reserve funds is also important given the concern for the intertemporal consistency of statistics in different economic sectors, discussed in section d. The state budget's treatment of reserve funds could give a misleading economic signal about the expansionary or contractionary effect the current year's deficit will have on the economy.

It should be noted, finally, that the nature of the planning mechanism creates the possibility that the deficit may be overfinanced. This is because, prior to 1990, the Budget Plan was worked out in conjunction with the Plan for output and the Credit Plan, before the start of each fiscal year. The Credit Plan incorporated as an important element the required financing for the planned budget deficit, and the financing allocation was made to a government account at the central bank at the beginning of the year. Because the Budget Plan had been coordinated with the Plan for output, deviations of budgetary operations from Plan tended to be small (by Western standards) and thus financing allocations were rarely amended in the course of a fiscal year. If the budget outturn was better than expected, unused financing would remain in the government's account at the end of the year. Should this financing system continue unchanged, such overfinancing should be offset against net credit to government when the year is closed.

c. The classification of revenue and expenditures[67]

For a given budgetary coverage, GFS has certain basic rules for a classification of revenues and expenditures that facilitates economic analysis and policy management of the budget. On the revenue side, a distinction is made between: (1) the government's income from its power to tax (tax revenue), which is a specific characteristic of government; and (2) its income from the sale of goods or services, such as fees for the use of land or mineral resources (nontax revenue), which is comparable to the income of private entities in that it does not depend on coercive power. Within tax revenue, taxes collected on a common base, such as profits, or labor income, are grouped together so that the impact on the budget of changes in the economy, such as production downturns or wage increases, can immediately be calculated. In the USSR, the recent and impending tax reforms have vastly improved government's ability to monitor and control taxes with transparent bases. Prior to the enterprise tax reform, revenue was collected from the productive sector on a multitude of bases (the various funds, etc.) which were not easy to distinguish, and whose behavior was not easy to predict.

Outstanding issues of revenue classification include the economic separation of the different "revenues from foreign activity" (though grouping them together because they generate foreign exchange has its own logic), and a breakdown of the miscellaneous category "levies and non-tax revenue." This appears to include a melange of small taxes, fees, assets sales, and possibly some financing and debt repayment. Apart from the economic diversity of the items lumped together there, the category is too large (6 percent of state budget revenue in 1990) to remain as a single item.

On the expenditure side, the current outlays of government should be clearly separated from its capital formation. Though much government capital formation is infrastructural, with only an indirect (or social) rate of return, the conceptual reason for the separation is that capital expenditure should eventually pay for itself, either through profits or through the growth it induces in the economy, whereas current outlays are the operating expenses of running government, and cannot be recouped. Typically, too, the investment budget of government is managed differently than the current budget, with attention to its intertemporal aspects, its effect on sectoral growth, its recurrent cost implications, its accompanying debt service, and sometimes its foreign exchange implications.

The state budget of the USSR provides no easy way of grouping current and investment expenditures—though it is possible to calculate a seemingly global investment figure. Capital expenditures now included in "expenditure on the economy," "military construction," and "socio-cultural outlays," and probably in other expenditure categories as well, should at least be identified in each category, so that a coherent capital budget can be constructed.[68]

Within expenditures, finer economic distinctions are also found to be analytically useful. An important distinction is between government transfers and direct expenditures, because transfers represent mainly a redistribution of purchasing power from one part of the non-government economy to another rather than true operating expenditures. In the state budget, current transfers can be isolated from other current expenditures (and, usually, their recipients identified), but there is no indication of which investment expenditures are made directly by budgetary institutions and which by enterprises with transferred budgetary funds.

Other economic variables to be identified in the budget include the government's wage bill (and, more broadly, its total personnel costs), its non-wage operating expenses (supplies and maintenance), and its debt service (payment of both foreign and domestic principal and interest). Knowledge of its overall wage bill is an important management tool of any entity, and in countries where the government is large, control of the public sector wage bill can be one of the main instruments of labor market policy. In the state budget, wages are presently subsumed within expenditures in broad functional categories. Interest payments on debt measure the cost of past deficits to the present government, and their relative size provides an indicator of the sustainability of the government's fiscal policies. There can be no effective portfolio management by government (and in particular, no debt restructuring or rescheduling) without a full interest schedule. As discussed in section b.(1), however, interest payments are only partially identified in the state budget.

d. Consistency of budgetary accounts with the accounts of the rest of the economy

For accuracy in economic management, it is important that the same data collected by different sources be consistent. For instance, the government should be able to see in its Gosbank revenue account the exact amount of income recorded by the Ministry of Finance as having been collected. Government foreign

154

borrowing should be identifiable both in the balance of payments and in the budget.

A minimum condition for such consistency is that statistics should be recorded over the same period. In particular, while Gosbank closes its books on January 1, the state budget includes a so-called complementary period after the fiscal year, during which extra revenues are recorded and payments made to cover unpaid bills and deficits. At the end of the budget exercise, the government's financial position may look very different from that recorded by Gosbank at the end of the year. GFS recommends the reconciliation of accounts by a subtraction of transactions that take place during the complementary period, and their addition to transactions of the following budgetary exercise. This ensures that all operations taking place in any calendar year are grouped together, as they are in the banking system and in the balance of payments.

It is not possible at present to make an adjustment for complementary period transactions in the state budget. However, discrepancies between banking sector statistics and Ministry of Finance data appear to be very small, at least since 1987. This suggests that complementary period transactions may not vary substantially from year to year. Further work needs to be done, however, to determine whether this is a permanent feature of Soviet budget statistics.

6. FINANCIAL INSTITUTIONS

This section concentrates on statistical methodology as it affects the collection and consolidation of financial statistics. Financial accounts on which this discussion is based include those related to enterprises and households, as well as government accounts held with the banking system, and data related to the financing of the budget through the banking system. There is, however, a substantial gap regarding information on similar aspects of foreign financing, which is handled through Vneshekonombank. Apart from financial institutions, there are a few additional sources of domestic credit (mainly government bond issues). There may also be substantial interenterprise credit on an informal basis (which was illegal prior to 1989), however, and an accumulation of domestic arrears which are not reflected in the accounts of financial institutions.

a. Institutional organization and statistical reporting

Data collection for financial institutions is carried out by Gosbank. It does not publish any of the data it collects on financial institutions, but both the Ministry of Finance and Goskomstat compile statistical compendia on the financial sector based on Gosbank data. The most important of these volumes in recent years is the financial statistics yearbook (*Finansy SSSR*), which includes selected data on deposits and credit to the economy. It does not include, however, the complete aggregate balance sheet of the banking system or the credit plan.

155

Gosbank has a reporting system in place which collects balance sheet information for all banks within the first two weeks of each month.[69] This statistical information reflects the administrative needs of implementing and controlling the credit plan, which remains the main instrument of monetary policy. For this purpose, the Gosbank relies on a system of data collection which is outside the balance sheet framework. In this system, deposits and credits specified in the credit plan are reported in a manner which differs from the definitions used in the balance sheets.

The reform of the banking system in 1987-88 resulted in the split-up of Gosbank into a central bank and five specialized banks which are organized along sectoral lines. It also allowed the creation of cooperative and joint stock commercial banks. The restructuring of Gosbank, the reconstitution of its functions as a central bank, and the allocation of its commercial banking operations to the specialized banks have posed special problems for the preparation of monetary aggregates. In addition, there are major problems arising from the monetary authority functions of Vneshekonombank, which manages a large part of international liquidity as well as the foreign debt.

b. The accounting system of banks

The system of accounting used in banking in the USSR is changing in response to the banking reform measures that have been implemented. However, reporting continues to be geared towards implementing the credit plan. As a result, the classification of accounts according to financial instruments as defined in the credit plan continues to take precedence over a sectoral classification, and there are a number of accounts in which the ownership is indeterminate.

Prior to financial reform in 1987, this classification of deposits dominated the reporting of holdings by the enterprise sector, whose financial assets were divided among a large number of funds with dedicated uses. Some of the accounts are essentially trust deposits, as in the case of the "escrow account for construction expenditure", which is offset directly by a corresponding credit to the building industry. For financial analysis, it may be useful to exclude these paired accounts from domestic credit and the overall money supply. It should be noted, that the degree of *de facto* liquidity of enterprise deposits and even of household deposits has been quite constrained by Western standards.

An aggregate statement of assets and liabilities of the banking system is compiled by the authorities. Classification in this statement reflects the most recent format for reporting. These data, combined with separate information on government net debt to the banking system, could be used to derive a monetary survey. These particular data were not, however, used to derive the monetary survey discussed in Chapters II.2 and III.2, because they are incomplete. The study relies instead on current data on credit to the enterprise sector and to households, as well as data on deposits by enterprises and households that are not collected within a balance sheet framework, all based on sources other than balance sheets. The major disadvantage of this methodology is that there is no assurance that the financial aggregates in the monetary survey are internally consistent.

c. Data gaps and methodological uncertainties

In the framework of the aggregate balance sheet of banks, the claims on and liabilities to nonresidents are included in "other net assets." As a result, this category was derived as a residual by Gosbank. This is unsatisfactory, because the banking system holds foreign exchange positions vis-à-vis resident enterprises resulting from the financing of exports and imports.

As noted, the data in the aggregate statement of assets and liabilities of the USSR banking system are incomplete. The following items are missing, or are currently being netted out in "other assets":[70]

(1) Total assets of the banking system are smaller than total liabilities because data on certain claims of the banking system have not been provided.

(2) Government internal debt held with the banking system has not been provided in a balance sheet format. The following detail would be required for financial analysis:

Claims on the union government,
  claims on republics, claims on other
  levels of government . . . . Loans, bonds, other
                                      instuments

Liabilities to union government,
  liabilities to republics, liabilities to
  other levels of government . . . . Current accounts (outside
                                        budgetary operations),
                                        transit accounts (after
                                        closing of fiscal year),
                                        other instruments

---

(3) The claims on government are also affected by credit to the foreign exchange stabilization fund, the price stabilization fund, and other "centralized funds" net of deposits of these institutions with the banking system. All of these are missing from the authorities' balance sheets.

157

Also, the offset in claims on government for the currency issue needs to be specified.

(4) It needs to be clarified to what extent the claims on and liabilities to the Ministries of Transport, Post and Telecommunications are part of credit to enterprises, credit to government, or part of the domestic clearing system.

(5) The residual estimates of "net foreign assets" may include banks' foreign currency claims on and liabilities to resident entities.[71] It would be useful to obtain a detailed breakdown of this net position into the following components:

Foreign assets
  Gold
  Foreign exchange (convertible)
  Other claims in convertible currencies
    of which in arrears
  CMEA transferable ruble claims
  Other nonconvertible assets

Foreign currency claims on residents
  Government:
    Union
    Republics
  Enterprises
  Other

Foreign liabilities
  Short-term liabilities to banks (convertible)
  Short-term liabilities to non-banks (convertible)
  Other liabilities in convertible currencies
  CMEA transferable ruble liabilities
  Other nonconvertible liabilities

Foreign currency liabilities to residents
  Government
  Enterprises
  Other

(6) The claims on and liabilities to government resulting from the foreign exchange operations of Vneshekonombank need to be identified, and the management of government foreign debt by this institution should be excluded from the monetary accounts.

(7) In order to fully construct a time series for money, it would be necessary to analyze in greater detail the liquidity of different types of deposits by the enterprise sector. This is especially relevant for periods prior to

158

financial reforms, when many of these deposits were not readily available for making payments. In addition, it would be desirable to obtain data on the deposits of non-profit institutions with the banking system, as well as deposits of enterprises, and savings deposits. Savings deposits which are reported outside the balance sheet context apparently include deposits by banks, nonprofit institutions, and households, as well as centralized funds and clearing balances. There are also deposits by enterprises and nonprofit institutions which are not included in the broad definition of money, because they may be fungible among enterprises and may not be available to the specific institution that has made the deposit. These restricted accounts need to be studied in detail and the likely effects of financial reform on these deposits need to be scrutinized.

(8) The classification of certain long-term deposits and the domestic credit created from such deposits poses a particular problem. These include investment and other long-term funds, which are partly but not fully offset by capital investments on the assets side of the banks' balance sheets. It is not clear whether the latter should be included in domestic credit, or be netted against the corresponding deposits. It is also not clear whether these deposits should be included in a broad definition of money, or be reported separately as lending funds with an indeterminate ownership.

(9) Interbank balances, which reflect the process of settlement among banks as well as interbank lending, have a profound effect on the development of the other financial aggregates. It is necessary to review these accounts in greater detail and link their developments more closely with the payments system. However, even a closer scrutiny of these accounts would not provide sufficient information about the development of enterprise credit and domestic arrears accumulating outside the banking system. It would be desirable if the credit provided by Gosbank could be reported separately from the clearing balances.

(10) The arrears on credit to enterprises have at times been transferred to the government. This raises the question of how to classify current arrears reported on short-term and long-term loans.

(11) In addition to short-term and long-term credit (provided under the credit plan), banks in recent years have been able to provide additional credit and what is reported as "temporary help" in the parlance of bank balance sheets. It needs to be clarified how such credit is reported in the credit control series of the Gosbank, as long as the monetary survey is not fully based on balance sheet information.

159

NOTES

1. See Treml (1990b), pp. 6-7.

2. Under the proposed legislation, state censorship would be restricted only to published materials that have a bearing on national security.

3. These figures exclude temporary census workers. It should be noted that some analysts believe a greater investment in additional manpower and other resources would benefit U.S. statistical work.

4. Statistical agencies revealed 28,000 cases of falsified accounts in 1986 alone, and spot checks in 1987 exposed inflated reporting by 10 to 30 percent of all enterprises in certain regions. See Korolev (1987), pp. 3-16.

5. Shmelev and Popov (1989) p. 44.

6. For a more extensive discussion, see Treml (1988).

7. These critiques include articles by Selyunin and Khanin (1987), Khanin (1989), Ivanova (1989), Faltsman (1989), and Aganbegyan (1989). Further details on challenges to the Soviet statistical system may be found in Central Intelligence Agency (1988), Treml (1990a), Ericson (1990), and Kostinsky and Belkindas (1990).

8. This came in the form of a Council of Ministers decree, "Measures for the Radical Reform of the Statistical System in the Country." For a detailed discussion of this and subsequent statistical reform measures, see Heleniak and Motivans (1990).

9. Nonmaterial services include personal transport, banking and insurance, medical care, education, scientific research, housing, and government services. Services that facilitate material production—such as construction, freight transport, communications, and trade—are by contrast included in the national accounts.

10. The formal accounting identity would be: NMP = National income utilized + net exports in "adjusted" valuta prices + losses + statistical discrepancy, except that, as discussed in the text, the statistical authorities do not report an explicit "statistical discrepancy." The adjustment made to net exports in valuta prices is discussed below.

11. Holzman (1974). The valuta trade balance is simply exports minus imports expressed in valuta ruble prices, which are foreign currency prices multiplied by the official exchange rate. As noted by Holzman (1974), Chap. 13 and Wolf (1985), valuta ruble prices are rarely equal to domestic prices, which are set independently to insulate the domestic economy from international price movements. The Soviet statistical authorities attempt to take this factor into account in the national accounts. Specifically, the "adjusted valuta trade balance" is calculated:

$$B_T' = (V_x' - V_m')\alpha,$$

where B_T' is the adjusted valuta balance, V_x' is exports in valuta rubles (exports at foreign currency prices multiplied by the official exchange rate), V_m' is imports in valuta rubles (imports at foreign currency prices multiplied by the official exchange rate), and α is a general conversion factor which varies according to whether the valuta trade balance is positive or negative. If the valuta trade balance is positive $(V_x' - V_m' > o)$, then $\alpha = \alpha_x$, which is a weighted average of domestic prices to valuta prices for exports. If the valuta trade balance is negative $(V_x' - V_m' < 0)$, then $\alpha = \alpha_m$, which is a weighted average of domestic prices to valuta prices for

160

imports. The bias introduced by this "adjustment"—vis-à-vis the trade balance that would be incorporated in the national accounts on the basis of SNA methodology—is equal to $(V_x' - V_m')(\alpha - 1)$. For further details, see Wolf (1987).

12. For example, if the SNA methodology is employed to value the trade balance in the national accounts, the contribution of the change in the nominal trade balance to nominal NMP growth in 1988 would be about -0.9 percentage points. If the "adjusted" valuta trade balance is used instead (see Table A.2, Appendix II-1), the contribution would be calculated as -0.6 percentage points.

13. Goskomstat officials have indicated that they intend to convert their entire national accounting system to an SNA basis within the next few years. For further information on GNP accounting methods and future plans, see Ryabushkin (1989), Kostinsky and Belkindas (1990), and State Committee of the USSR on Statistics (1990).

14. Translation keys are lists of data that must be added and subtracted from NMP to arrive at GDP. They are frequently used by countries that have not fully completed the conversion from the MPS accounting system to the SNA approach. It is important to note that the translation key approach focuses on developing GDP from the production side. GDP estimates by final expenditure consistent with these production-based estimates are also available, but it is evident that while they are also generated with the aid of translation keys—applied to national income utilized—these estimates are not derived independently of the aggregate figure for GDP on the production side.

15. For most Eastern European countries, the estimated difference between NMP and GDP is in the range of 20 to 30 percent. This is consistent with research by the U.N. Statistical Office, which estimated that the GDP/NMP ratio for Hungary in 1976 was 1.19, and that the GDP/NMP ratio for Yugoslavia in 1970 was 1.29. Similar ratios of GDP to NMP were calculated by the U.N. for selected developing economies, and slightly higher ratios were shown for developed countries. For further details, see United Nations (1981).

16. 1988 depreciation of rub 166 billion divided by the capital stock of rub 2.8 trillion yields an aggregate depreciation rate of 6 percent.

17. One way of illustrating this is to observe that if the Soviet capital stock figures are correct, they imply an aggregate capital output ratio of 3.2:1 in 1988. This ratio is quite high by international standards, suggesting that Soviet capital is either overvalued, phenomenally inefficient, or possibly both.

18. These estimates were respectively obtained from conversations with Goskomstat officials, and from Kryuchkov (1990), p. 1. Goskomstat maintains that the KGB estimates improperly include payments for idle time, unproductive expenditures, material and labor expenses in connection with "above-norm" unfinished construction, and unsubstantiated losses. It is interesting to note that according to Yuryev (1990), p. 12, losses from short-changing, stealing, and falsified enterprise accounts actually documented by Soviet inspectors in 1989 totaled rub 468 million. This figure may appear small compared to an NMP of rub 674 billion for 1989, but it represents only that fraction of illegal activity outside the statistical system that was actually detected. Such activities undoubtedly affect national accounts to a greater degree than Yuryev's figure suggests.

19. See Grossman (1987), Bakatin (1990), p. 2, and Treml (1990b), pp. 11-12.

20. Numerous studies have been carried out in the U.S. by economists who have attempted to document the magnitude of shadow economy activities, and several years ago Italy revised its GDP to reflect activities outside the scope of the nation's statistical system.

21. See Treml (1990b), p. 16, and Volkov and Samokhvalov (1989). As noted in Kirichenko (1990), p. 22, the national accounts have since been corrected.

22. For example, output levels for Yugoslavia were substantially overstated by inflation in inventories until valuation corrections were recently made by the statistical authorities.

23. Galkin (1989), pp. 651-652, notes that there have been changes in payment practices for unfinished construction in the USSR, though this is apparently not the cause of sharp increases in stockbuilding in the construction sector in recent years. This can be confirmed by comparing data on changes in stocks of unfinished construction with construction stockbuilding figures in the national accounts. There is a broad consistency between these two sets of data, suggesting that Goskomstat's accounting practices have indeed not changed over time.

24. See Chapter III.1.

25. A discussion of defense expenditures in the state budget may be found in Treml (1990b), pp. 17-20. Wiles (1987) and Steinberg (1987) have suggested that coverage problems result in defense activities being understated in national income utilized.

26. This also makes valuation of capital stock and stockbuilding extremely difficult. See section 3.c for further details.

27. This approach was pioneered by Bergson (1961). Also see Becker (1969), and Central Intelligence Agency (1982).

28. See, for example, Selyunin and Khanin (1987), Khanin (1988), and Aganbegyan (1988).

29. Comparable prices are often mistakenly referred to as constant prices by western economists, but the sets of prices differ both by sector and era. For example, 1982 list prices are the comparable prices currently used to calculate real rates of growth for industry, but 1955 prices were used from 1956 to 1957, 1952 prices were used for 1951 to 1955, and 1926/27 prices were used for years prior to 1950. For agriculture, the current comparable price base is 1983, though real growth rates prior to 1986 are calculated in 1973 prices. The current comparable price base used in construction is 1984, although real growth rates for earlier years are calculated in 1969 and 1974 prices. NMP output indices in comparable prices are calculated on a sector of origin basis via double-deflation (recalculating gross output and inputs in comparable prices by sector of origin, deriving NMP as a residual, and calculating indices of real growth from these NMP estimates). National income utilized in comparable prices is calculated by revaluing components of final expenditure in comparable prices, then calculating rates of growth from these new series.

30. See the discussion of so-called hidden inflation in section 3.b. Treml (1990b), p. 11, notes that Soviet criticism of official real growth rates is virtually identical to complaints made long ago by Western analysts.

31. See Selyunin and Khanin (1987) and Aganbegyan (1988), respectively.

32. Kostinsky and Belkindas (1990).

33. See Yasin (1989), pp. 773-781, and Zoteyev (1989), pp. 789-800.

34. See Korolev (1989), p. 2.

35. See Bogomolov (1989), pp. 2-4, and Deryabin (1989), p. 43.

36. Research by Guryev and Zaitseva (1990) suggests that Goskomstat is working on a "cost of living index," which appears to bear close resemblance to traditional consumer price indices in the West.

37. See Guryev and Zaitseva (1989), pp. 7-18, and Belyayevskiy (1989), pp. 19-27.

38. Presentation by Dr. Janet Norwood, Director of the U.S. Bureau of Labor Statistics, on statistical reform in the Soviet Union, September 13, 1990, Washington, D.C.

39. See Guryev and Zaitseva (1990), pp. 20-29. This estimate of repressed inflation is based on the assumption that *ceteris paribus*, free prices would rise at a rate that ensures identical rates of growth of the stock of savings and total trade turnover. When savings grow faster than trade turnover, there is said to be evidence of forced saving, and therefore of repressed inflation. It should be pointed out, however, that there is by no means a universally accepted methodology for attempting to measure repressed inflation. See Chapter III.3.

40. See Falt'sman (1989) and Khanin (1989a).

41. As noted in section 3.a.(4), comparable prices are essentially constant prices, though the base year for prices varies both by sector and over time.

42. Compare with footnote 4 to Table A.1, Appendix II-1.

43. See Gerschenkron (1947).

44. See section 3.a.(1).

45. Treml (1990a).

46. Some economists have argued, however, that the relative price of capital equipment has actually been rising in recent years. See Kontorovich (1989) and Rumer (*Soviet Studies*, 1989).

47. According to Goskomstat, gross investment in 1989 was equal to net investment in the national accounts (rub 89.8 billion), plus depreciation (111.6 billion), increases in unfinished construction (rub 22.8 billion), the remaining value of liquidated capital (rub 5.1 billion), and investment write-offs for incomplete construction (rub 5.5 billion); less the increase in livestock and herds (rub 3.2 billion) and Article 12 funds of the state budget (rub 5.3 billion). The total, rub 226.3 billion, differs slightly from the aggregate figure reported elsewhere by Goskomstat for capital investment of rub 228.5 billion, presumably reflecting minor adjustments. The foregoing depreciation figure here apparently excludes capital repair, which is included in depreciation in the GDP accounts (Table 1). Net fixed investment ("accumulation of basic funds") in the national accounts is equal to the sum of (i) fixed assets actually put into operation (i.e., excluding the change in unfinished construction), and (ii) completed capital repairs; less (iii) depreciation (including for capital repair); and (iv) fixed assets removed from operation.

48. To date, these unemployment estimates have been estimated for several central Asian republics. For further details, see Heleniak (1990b), pp. 2-3, and Peterson (1989), p. 5.

49. These include non-military personnel involved in defense- related activities in the Communist Party, the Communist Youth League, the Ministry of Defense itself, and other government agencies. For further details, see Heleniak (1990b).

50. See Korolev (1987).

51. See Treml (1990b), p. 5. It should be noted that grain output data in Table B.4 of Appendix II-1, however, are new figures, in which dirt, moisture, and other foreign matter have been netted out.

52. See Chernichenko (1990), p. 1.

53. See Treml (1990b), p. 5.

54. Moreover, note that this residual had shifted from an excess of sources over uses of some 8 percent of GDP, in 1985, to a shortfall of around 13 percent of GDP by 1989 (Table D.6, Appendix II-1).

55. Soviet export and import statistics distinguish between socialist and nonsocialist trade. Socialist trade includes transactions with CMEA member countries, Albania, Yugoslavia, Lao, P.D.R., Democratic People's Republic of Korea, and the People's Republic of China.

56. It should be noted that with the introduction of the revised System of National Accounts (SNA), exports as well as imports will be shown on an f.o.b. basis.

57. The balance of payments tables on a transactions basis included in Appendix II-1 are estimates. They differ from balance of payments estimates on a settlements basis in that the merchandise trade account includes barter and gold transactions, with accommodating adjustments made to the capital account.

58. Convertible and nonconvertible currency transactions are dealt with separately on the grounds that the valuation of trade flows in nonconvertible trade is not comparable with convertible currency trade values due to significant price distortions. Moreover, foreign assets in nonconvertible currencies cannot be equated with international reserves.

59. For the special meaning of residents and nonresidents in the present Soviet context, see Chapter III.4.

60. Instead of repayment of short-term debt, a new indicator of short-term indebtedness is included as a memorandum item.

61. The *Manual on Government Finance Statistics* (GFS), IMF (1986), is the point of reference for compilation of government statistics in the International Monetary Fund's framework.

62. Data on the enterprise sector are not currently collected and presented in such a way that the relations of firms with the government can be separated from their business operations. Hence, the budgetary tables in Chapter II.2 and Appendix II-1 do not add extrabudgetary functions to the state budget, except in one, easily identifiable instance: the fund for agricultural price support administered by Gosbank.

63. Under the existing system, financing by the banking system has taken place in two steps. First, the equivalent of any buildup of savings deposits in savings banks may be drawn down via a transfer of funds to the state budget from Gosbank; because this is comparable to using the private sector surplus to finance the public sector deficit, it is considered non-inflationary financing. If increases in savings deposits are inadequate to cover the fiscal deficit, Gosbank resorts to monetary financing — "free credit."

64. It should be noted, too, that with better information about the composition of these external flows, some or all of official lending might be included above the line as expenditure, given that it may act as a policy instrument of government.

65. In tables II.2.3, and J.3 of Appendix II-1, therefore, all debt service other than identifiable interest on balance of payments support was considered as financing.

66. In the GFS classification, the stock of those residuals is referred to as reserve funds. The state budget also includes expenditures on account of the "reserve funds" of the Council of Ministers and the Ministry of Finance. These appear to be the equivalent of ordinary budget expenditures.

67. See also Chapter III.1.

68. On a broader scale, all "state investment expenditure" should be in the budget, and the distinction between budget expenditure and expenditure from so-called centralized funds of the branch ministries should be abolished.

69. The banks report to the regional computer centers of Gosbank according to a system of administrative accounts. This system is basically unchanged from the system in effect during the monobank era.

70. Since these other assets are net of the currency issue of Gosbank, it is difficult to identify the link between currency issue and credit to government in the balance sheet of Gosbank.

71. For more detail on the statistical issues related to the external accounts see section 4 of this appendix.

Table 1. USSR: Derivation of Official Gross Domestic Product Statistics, 1985-1989

(Billion rubles, in current prices)

		1985	1986	1987	1988	1989 [1]
Net Material Product Produced		579	587	600	631	674
Plus:	Wages and salaries of organizations in the nonproductive sphere (including income from private activities, less income of domestic servants)	99	103	108	121	143
Plus:	Social insurance allocations in the nonproductive sphere	6	7	8	8	10
Less:	Funds for business travel in the material production sectors	7	7	6	6	6
Plus:	Profits less subsidies in the nonproductive sphere	6	6	4	4	4
Less:	Nonmaterial services performed by material production sectors, and expenditures by these sectors on social-cultural services and entertainment.	40	39	40	42	51
Plus:	Depreciation in both spheres	139	148	157	166	174
Less:	Losses of material stocks	5	6	6	7	8
Gross Domestic Product		777	799	825	875	940

Source: Goskomstat.
1. Provisional.

Chart 1. **USSR: INSTITUTIONAL RESPONSIBILITIES IN STATISTICS**

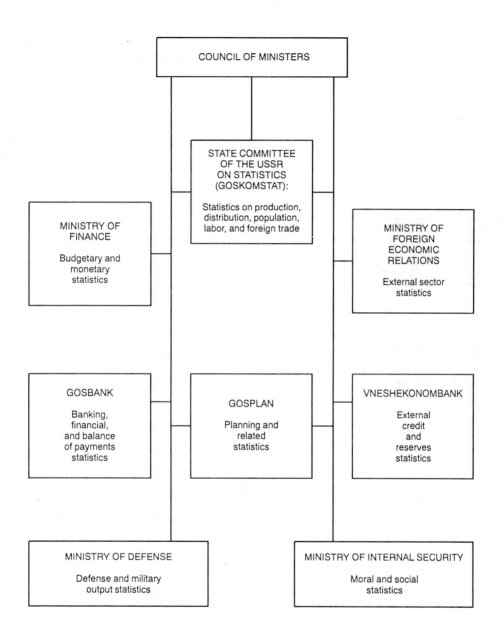

Chart 2. **USSR: SOURCES OF DATA BY SECTOR**

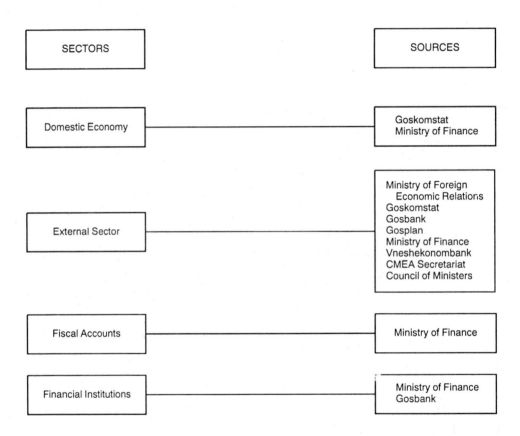

SECTORS

SOURCES

Domestic Economy — Goskomstat
Ministry of Finance

External Sector — Ministry of Foreign
  Economic Relations
Goskomstat
Gosbank
Gosplan
Ministry of Finance
Vneshekonombank
CMEA Secretariat
Council of Ministers

Fiscal Accounts — Ministry of Finance

Financial Institutions — Ministry of Finance
Gosbank

Chart 3. **USSR: ORGANIZATION OF GOSKOMSTAT**

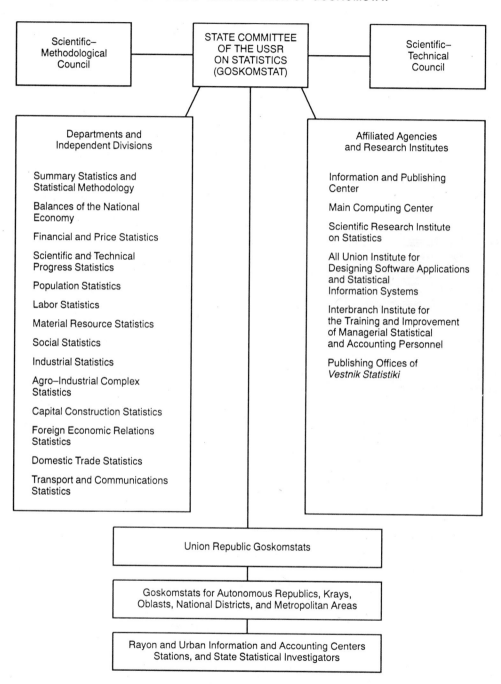

Scientific–Methodological Council	STATE COMMITTEE OF THE USSR ON STATISTICS (GOSKOMSTAT)	Scientific–Technical Council

Departments and Independent Divisions

Summary Statistics and Statistical Methodology

Balances of the National Economy

Financial and Price Statistics

Scientific and Technical Progress Statistics

Population Statistics

Labor Statistics

Material Resource Statistics

Social Statistics

Industrial Statistics

Agro–Industrial Complex Statistics

Capital Construction Statistics

Foreign Economic Relations Statistics

Domestic Trade Statistics

Transport and Communications Statistics

Affiliated Agencies and Research Institutes

Information and Publishing Center

Main Computing Center

Scientific Research Institute on Statistics

All Union Institute for Designing Software Applications and Statistical Information Systems

Interbranch Institute for the Training and Improvement of Managerial Statistical and Accounting Personnel

Publishing Offices of *Vestnik Statistiki*

Union Republic Goskomstats

Goskomstats for Autonomous Republics, Krays, Oblasts, National Districts, and Metropolitan Areas

Rayon and Urban Information and Accounting Centers Stations, and State Statistical Investigators

Appendix II-3

Changes in Trade and Payments with CMEA Countries[1]

1. INTRODUCTION

CMEA transactions have played the dominant role in the external economic relations of the USSR over the past 40 years. The long regional isolation of the CMEA countries has led to interdependence and—to some extent—specialization of their economies. The structure of trade (i.e., Soviet net exports of energy products and raw materials and net imports of manufactures, mainly machinery products) and relative prices (i.e., low energy and raw material prices relative to machinery product prices, in comparison to relative world market prices) have meant implicit Soviet subsidization of trade with its CMEA partners in recent years. Disruptions in the traditional trade links occurred during 1990. More fundamental changes in CMEA arrangements are expected in 1991 when trade is to take place, in principle, at world market prices to be settled in convertible currencies. A transition to world market prices could be expected to result in a major improvement in the terms of trade of the USSR. Trade developments will also be affected by several other factors, including production and distribution problems, further decentralization in trade in the USSR and in several of its CMEA partner countries, and German unification. This appendix seeks to quantify the balance of payments consequences of these changes, following a brief description of the most recent developments in trade. It does not cover the institutional features of the currently existing CMEA trade and payments system, which are described in Chapters III.4 and IV.3.

2. RECENT DEVELOPMENTS IN CMEA TRADE

CMEA trade accounted for well over one half of total trade of the USSR during 1985-90 (Table 1).[2] The major trading partners were—in descending order of importance—the German Democratic Republic (GDR), Bulgaria, the Czech and Slovak Federal Republic, and Poland. While the USSR recorded a trade

171

surplus with the CMEA area from 1980 to 1987, since 1988 growing deficits have emerged. The deficit in 1990 was expected to reach rub 5.7 billion (rub 6.6 billion against the six European CMEA members), corresponding to nearly one fifth of total exports to these countries. The deterioration in the trade balance with the CMEA area has followed the same trend as the trade balance vis-à-vis the convertible area. The major factors have been the decline in oil prices in the world market since 1986, which had a delayed impact in CMEA trade because of the practice of using five-year moving averages of world market prices; the decline in Soviet oil production and exports since 1989; and the continued strong demand for imports because of rising domestic demand and increasing shortfalls in domestic supplies.

During 1988-90, the USSR recorded cumulative deficits with all Eastern European countries, except Romania, with particularly large deficits vis-à-vis Poland and the GDR. Outside Eastern Europe, the USSR also incurred a small deficit against Cuba, but maintained surpluses in its trade with Mongolia and Viet Nam. Moreover, in addition to the aggregate merchandise trade deficit, the USSR also had a small overall deficit on the services balance, partly relating to the stationing of troops in other CMEA countries and payments for pipeline and other transportation services.

On the export side, energy products were the most important category in this period, accounting for about 40 percent of total Soviet exports to the CMEA area (Table 2). By contrast to Soviet exports to industrial countries, oil exports to CMEA countries were composed primarily of crude oil, since the CMEA countries had sufficient refining capacity and also limited demand for heavy fuel oil products (which tend to make up the bulk of Soviet exports of refined products to industrial countries (Table 3)). The largest oil recipients were the GDR, followed by the Czech and Slovak Federal Republic, Poland and Bulgaria (the export figure for Bulgaria includes reexport of crude oil originating in the Middle East). Other raw materials and other basic inputs, including metals and chemicals, accounted for more than 10 percent and exports of machinery and equipment accounted for another 21 percent of total exports. While a certain proportion of exports of energy and raw materials could relatively easily be diverted to other markets (given pipeline, transmission line and port constraints), the quality of Soviet machinery and equipment is such that it would be difficult for the USSR to sell these products in other markets without substantial reductions in prices. A relatively large proportion of exports, 19 percent in 1989, remained unclassified; presumably it included military equipment and direct exports by enterprises with newly acquired trading rights.[3]

On the import side, machinery and transportation equipment comprised the largest category, accounting for nearly half of total trade with CMEA countries in 1989 (Table 4). The majority of these products were tailored to Soviet specifications and came exclusively from Eastern European countries. They encompassed a wide variety of products, but the most important were buses and trucks (from Hungary and the Czech and Slovak Federal Republic), mining equipment (from Romania and Poland), ships (from the GDR and Poland), agricultural machinery (from Bulgaria and Hungary), railroad equipment, including locomotives (from the Czech and Slovak Federal Republic and the GDR), and heavy lifting equipment (from Bulgaria and Poland). The second most important category of imports was industrial consumer goods, with their share in trade being rather similar among the Eastern European countries. Finally, imports of food and food products accounted for about 10 percent of imports from all CMEA countries and 4 percent from the five Eastern European countries (excluding the GDR) in 1989. The largest food imports came from Cuba (sugar and citrus fruit), followed by Hungary (meat and meat products, seeds, and canned vegetables) and Bulgaria (wine, processed fruit products, and canned meat and vegetables).

In 1990, CMEA trade was already undergoing radical changes in response to the transition of the Eastern European member countries to market economies. The partial decentralization in the USSR, and particularly in some Eastern European countries, began disrupting trade because it was no longer fully covered by annual trade protocols and state orders; meanwhile, direct enterprise trade, outside the traditional foreign trade organizations, gained in importance. Furthermore, in the USSR the question of the legal right to trade in natural resources also began hampering trade. In addition to these systemic changes, the USSR did not fulfill its contracts for oil deliveries as a result of a drop in domestic production and the diversion of shipments to convertible currency markets. The CMEA countries bore the brunt of the decline in exports (an estimated decline of 31 percent in exports of oil and oil products as against an overall decrease of 21 percent). The diversion of Soviet exports from the CMEA countries to the convertible currency area was a deliberate attempt to stem the growing shortage of convertible foreign exchange in the USSR. The CMEA countries responded by not meeting some of their planned deliveries to the USSR, particularly of food products, in an attempt to arrest the export to the USSR of so-called hard goods (i.e., goods that could be sold outside CMEA for convertible currency without a price discount). By contrast, the USSR experienced no shortages in supplies of machinery and equipment from these countries, as domestic investment activity in the USSR was contracting sharply and Eastern European partners were keen on keeping up their sales of those products that were tailored to the Soviet market and could not easily be sold elsewhere.[4] After the establishment of the monetary union with the Federal Republic of Germany on July 1, 1990, exporters in the GDR were not allowed to conclude new contracts for settlement in transferable rubles except for spare parts, foodstuffs and compensation deals. On October 3, 1990, at the time of German reunification, even these exceptions were abolished. Soviet exports of military equipment and machinery suffered from cancellations of orders in the GDR, while oil exports to the GDR fell because of domestic production difficulties.[5]

The trade deficits with some of the Eastern European countries resulted in an accumulation of current Soviet liabilities at the IBEC (i.e., those resulting from trade in goods and services). By end-1990 the largest liabilities were expected to have accumulated vis-à-vis the previous GDR (some TR 4.5 billion) and Poland (about TR 4 billion). In addition, current liabilities against Bulgaria, the Czech and Slovak Federal Republic and Hungary were expected to amount to TR 0.5 billion, TR 0.7 billion, and TR 1.2 billion, respectively. By contrast, a small current IBEC surplus of the USSR of TR 0.3 billion was expected to have accumulated vis-à-vis Romania. In addition to the current IBEC balances, the USSR had other claims on and liabilities to CMEA countries, including project loans; total claims amounted to TR 39 billion at end-October 1989 (no later information is available), of which four fifths were claims on non-European members, but the exact magnitude of liabilities has not been revealed.

3. CHANGES IN 1991

From 1991, the CMEA trade and payments system will be fundamentally changed. Six major factors will influence trade developments. First, as mentioned above, trade will generally take place at world market prices. Second, in principle, trade will be settled in convertible currencies. Third, trade might be influenced by the use of some proportion of outstanding IBEC balances for settlement. Fourth, trade will be affected by the further decentralization of trading activities and restructuring in the USSR and its Eastern European CMEA partners. Fifth, it will be influenced by the extent to which the USSR and its CMEA partners can provide export financing for investment goods. Finally, trade with the former GDR will be affected by the unification of Germany.

a. World market prices

World market prices were to be applied in CMEA trade as from January 1, 1991. While it is relatively straightforward to calculate the impact of this change for commodities such as oil, gas and other relatively homogenous commodities for which there exist clearly documented world market prices,[6] it is a matter of debate as to what constitute world market prices for goods such as machinery and equipment that are tailored to specific markets in the CMEA countries and not currently sold elsewhere. As most manufactured products traded within the CMEA have been overpriced vis-à-vis the prices they could command in world markets,[7] their prices will need to be lowered substantially in order for them to continue to be sold within the CMEA area, once convertible currency settlement is required. Care should be taken when making such estimates, however, not to double count in the sense of also assuming a large decline in mutual trade volumes in manufactures due to their overpricing vis-à-vis the world market.

Such calculations are complicated by the fact that the cross rates between the transferable ruble and the U.S. dollar are markedly different among CMEA countries. For example, in October 1990 the cross rates for one U.S. dollar were about TR 0.6 in the USSR, TR 1.7 in the Czech and Slovak Federal Republic, TR 2.4 in Hungary and TR 4.5 in Poland. This means that the transition to U.S.dollar pricing may lead to different perceptions as to its resulting gain for the exporting country (e.g., the USSR) and its loss for the importing country (e.g., in the Czech and Slovak Federal Republic). For example, unchanged raw material prices according to the official IBEC rate imply only a small increase in export prices for the USSR, but nearly a trebling of raw material import prices for the Czech and Slovak Federal Republic measured by the cross rate prevailing there.

b. Settlement in convertible currencies

Settlement of trade will also, in principle, take place in convertible currencies. However, the modalities of settlement are still under negotiation between the USSR and its CMEA partner countries. Based on the early indications in trade discussions, e.g., with the Czech and Slovak Federal Republic, it seems that a combination of barter trade (based on indicative lists of goods), payments in convertible currencies, and clearing accounts might be used in the transition phase. The lack of banking facilities for trade finance in the USSR and in some of its partner countries is one reason for establishing clearing arrangements.[8] It was envisaged, however, that the transferable ruble would no longer be used for denomination of trade or accounts in transactions in which the USSR is a partner.

c. Outstanding IBEC balances

The use of current IBEC balances and the settlement of other financial obligations are currently under discussion. It is likely that part of the IBEC claims of other CMEA countries on the USSR will be used as payments for imports in 1991. However, the amounts have not yet been agreed between the partners. An additional issue to be settled is the rate of conversion of the transferable ruble balances into convertible currencies. By end-December 1990, the USSR had reached agreement only with Hungary (US$0.92 per transferable ruble) and the Czech and Slovak Federal Republic (US$1 per transferable ruble), but the conversion rate is likely to differ among individual countries. Agreement with all of the CMEA countries and Germany on the conversion rate and the possible use of the IBEC balances is not expected to be completed before mid-1991.

d. Decentralization of trade

The decentralization of trade will have unpredictable effects on the pattern of trade. While trade among CMEA countries in the past was governed by annual trade protocols, it will now be conducted through a combination of state orders, agreements with individual Soviet republics or so-called autonomous republics, and direct enterprise deals. Soviet officials have indicated that trade conducted through state orders in 1991 was expected to amount to about half of the total value of Soviet trade with CMEA countries in 1990. State orders were likely to comprise a higher than average proportion of trade with Cuba, Mongolia, Romania, and Viet Nam. On the export side, a relatively large part of trade in oil and oil products, gas, cotton, and other raw materials was to take place through state orders, but state orders in these commodities were also expected to be supplemented by direct enterprise exports.

On the import side, state orders were to comprise the basic needs (such as food and medical supplies), spare parts and components, and some finished capital goods (e.g., locomotives, vessels and aircraft). Beyond state orders, it remains an open question whether enterprises will choose to continue with their previous trading partners or whether they will switch to other countries for imports and exports. It is likely that some shift will take place towards the non-CMEA area if enterprises are given freedom to choose their trading partners.

e. Export credits

The extension of export credits for large pieces of machinery and equipment (e.g., locomotives or ships) in intra-CMEA trade was unusual in the past. The outlook for such trade after the transition to convertible currency settlement depends partly on whether financing terms that are customary in the rest of the world can be provided to importers of goods from CMEA countries. For the USSR, export financing for machinery and equipment could possibly be provided by the Vneshekonombank (although the present regulations prevent it) or, with its guarantee, by foreign banks. Also, the exporting firms could supply such financing, provided that they had enough liquidity and could obtain forward cover against changes in the commercial exchange rate.

f. Trade with the former GDR

Finally, the unification of Germany will affect trade with the previous GDR, which will no longer be a member of the CMEA system. The trade of goods considered particularly important for the USSR is likely to continue under state orders in the USSR and to be encompassed by a trade agreement between the two countries. A framework agreement between Germany and the USSR was signed in November 1990, but it contained no specifics as to the goods to be traded or their value. Soviet exports, particularly of machinery and chemical products, are likely to drop substantially, although exports in general are likely to benefit from exemption from customs duties, quota restrictions and quality norms of the European Communities for a transitory period. At the same time exports from the

176

territory of the former GDR will no longer be entitled to subsidies, but from January 1, 1991, export insurance coverage through the German export insurance agency (Hermes) for sales by firms in the former GDR to the USSR will be enhanced.[9] It is expected that repayment of the outstanding IBEC balances due the GDR will be postponed for five years.

g. Balance of payments assumptions for 1991

For the balance of payments projections for 1991 two scenarios have been considered (Table 5). In the base scenario, it has been assumed that exports, excluding energy and raw materials, and imports will decline on average by 20 percent in volume terms vis-à-vis CMEA countries against an overall decline of 15 percent and 7 percent, respectively. Moreover, oil exports are projected to decline by 21 percent to CMEA countries (overall by 16 percent), and the oil price to average US$26 per barrel. These projections assume a decline in real GDP by 5 percent and oil production by 6 percent and maintenance of the commercial exchange rate at the level of the end of 1990. In the alternative scenario, lower oil export volumes (a decline of 27 percent to CMEA countries and 25 percent in overall oil exports) and a lower oil price (US$20 per barrel) have been assumed. The Soviet authorities have indicated that the structural changes in trade will be surrounded by great uncertainty. But they have stressed that the decline in trade volume would probably be limited in the short run because of the traditional dependence of production on inputs according to certain technological specifications, and familiarity with existing trading partners. By contrast, the authorities of other CMEA countries have tended to be more pessimistic on the prospects for maintaining trade with the USSR, pointing also to the uncertainties regarding the organization and division of responsibilities for trade between the union and republican levels.

For prices, the working assumption is based partially on information from the Soviet authorities and the Eastern European CMEA partners. Prices of imports and exports, other than those of energy and raw materials, are projected to decline on average by 50 percent in U.S. dollar terms measured at the IBEC exchange rate prevailing at end-1990. For energy products, it is assumed that intra-CMEA prices will equal those in the world market, and for raw materials the prices are assumed to be unchanged from 1990 at the prevailing IBEC rate. Altogether, the above assumptions—with unchanged world market prices between 1990 and 1991—would imply a terms of trade improvement for the USSR of about 50 percent vis-à-vis CMEA countries, which is equivalent to a one third decline in the terms of trade of the CMEA countries in trade with the USSR.[10]

In sum, trade between the USSR and its CMEA partners will be subject to considerable uncertainties next year. Based on the above working assumptions under the base scenario and the alternative scenario, the USSR might record a trade surplus vis-à-vis the eight other CMEA countries (excluding the GDR) of

US$11 billion or US$8 billion respectively, of which US$9 billion or US$6 billion would be with the five Eastern European members. Under the same scenarios, the current account surplus might be US$10 billion and US$7 billion, respectively, with the eight CMEA countries. This would represent a substantial improvement relative to the trade deficit of rub 5-6 billion and current account deficit of rub 6-7 billion estimated for 1990 with all CMEA countries.[11] As noted earlier, however, it is unlikely that all this trade will actually be settled in convertible currencies in 1991; consequently the current account surplus in convertible currencies of the USSR with the CMEA region is expected to be smaller than these figures might suggest.

NOTES

1. CMEA members in 1990 were Bulgaria, the Czech and Slovak Federal Republic, Cuba, the (former) GDR, Hungary, Mongolia, Poland, Romania, the USSR, and Viet Nam.

2. It should be noted, however, that such shares reflect the average degree of distortion—vis-à-vis world market prices—of intra-CMEA foreign trade prices.

3. It is likely that many of these exports had previously been channeled through foreign trade organizations, which had reported them under the appropriate classification.

4. In fact, on October 15, 1990, the USSR introduced license requirements for imports above planned targets for goods from the Czech and Slovak Federal Republic and Hungary.

5. Existing export commitments of the GDR to the USSR were subsidized by the German government through the Treuhandanstalt and a special export support fund.

6. Differences in transportation costs, including in the form of sunk costs for pipelines, leave some room for negotiation of prices of homogeneous goods.

7. Overpriced in the sense that if their TR prices are converted into U.S. dollars at the IBEC exchange rate, they would be substantially higher than the U.S. dollar prices of comparable quality items sold on world markets.

8. In the USSR, trade financing by banks was not permitted in 1990. Only enterprises were allowed to extend trade credits.

9. Preferential export credit insurance conditions would exempt the USSR from the usual 15-20 percent downpayment. Credits would run 10 years instead of 8 1/2 years and first repayments would be due after three years instead of six months. The preferential conditions would remain in effect through 1991.

10. Kenen (1990) estimates the terms of trade effects of the transition to world market prices on the basis of data disaggregated by SITC and CMEA commodity groups. Using national cross rates between the transferable ruble and the U.S. dollar, the author arrives at a deterioration of the terms of trade of the five European CMEA countries ranging from 24 to 37 percent based on 1989 trade flows.

11. The conversion of the 1990 ruble balances into U.S. dollars for comparative purposes with 1991 should probably be avoided due to the aforementioned distortions in relative prices in intra-CMEA trade.

Table 1.   USSR: Trade with CMEA Countries, 1985-90

	1985	1986	1987	1988	1989	1990 Proj.	1990 Share in Total	
							Exports	Imports
	(In millions of rubles)						*(In percent)*	
Bulgaria								
Exports	6,435	6,752	6,276	6,094	6,122	5,977	18.0	
Imports	-6,040	-6,191	-6,552	-6,873	-7,301	-6,573		16.9
Trade balance	395	561	-276	-779	-1,179	-596		
Cuba								
Exports	3,849	3,802	3,731	3,727	3,760	3,693	11.1	
Imports	-4,140	-3,800	-3,827	-3,837	-3,867	-4,061		10.4
Trade balance	-291	2	-96	-110	-107	-368		
Czechoslovakia								
Exports	6,813	6,947	6,777	6,385	6,254	5,380	16.2	
Imports	-6,587	-6,556	-6,907	-6,817	-6,607	-5,840		15.0
Trade balance	226	391	-130	-432	-353	-460		
GDR								
Exports	7,652	7,884	7,636	7,193	6,662	5,230	15.7	
Imports	-7,553	-7,128	-7,093	-7,024	-7,177	-8,526		21.9
Trade balance	99	756	543	169	-515	-3,296		
Hungary								
Exports	4,560	4,678	4,600	4,484	4,186	3,827	11.5	
Imports	-4,850	-4,873	-5,080	-4,943	-4,815	-4,071		10.4
Trade balance	-290	-195	-480	-459	-629	-244		
Mongolia								
Exports	1,114	1,138	1,140	1,131	1,005	1,083	3.3	
Imports	-387	-410	-401	-406	-397	-398		1.0
Trade balance	727	728	739	725	608	685		
Poland								
Exports	6,517	6,814	6,542	6,298	5,770	4,125	12.4	
Imports	-5,525	-6,127	-6,329	-7,109	-7,410	-7,227		18.5
Trade balance	992	687	213	-811	-1,640	-3,102		
Romania								
Exports	1,949	2,823	2,539	2,344	2,681	2,729	8.2	
Imports	-2,277	-2,415	-2,347	-2,431	-2,489	-1,648		4.2
Trade balance	-328	408	192	-87	192	1,081		
Viet Nam								
Exports	1,165	1,318	1,455	1,394	1,371	1,230	3.7	
Imports	-281	-294	-319	-389	-520	-616		1.6
Trade balance	884	1,024	1,136	1,005	851	614		
Total CMEA-9								
Exports	40,054	42,156	40,696	39,050	37,811	33,274	100.0	
Imports	-37,640	-37,794	-38,855	-39,819	-40,583	-38,960		100.0
Total balance	2,414	4,362	1,841	-779	-2,772	-5,686		
Total CMEA-5 [1]								
Exports	26,274	28,014	26,734	25,605	25,013	22,038		
Imports	-25,279	-26,162	-27,215	-28,173	-28,622	-25,359		
Trade balance	995	1,852	-481	-2,568	-3,609	-3,321		
Memorandum item:								
CMEA trade in percent of total trade:	*(In percent)*							
Exports	55.3	61.8	59.7	58.1	55.3	52.9		
Imports	54.4	60.4	64.1	61.2	56.3	53.4		

Source: Vneshniaia torgovlia and *Vneshnie ekonomicheskie sviazi,* various issues; and projections.
1. Bulgaria, Czechoslovakia, Hungary, Poland, and Romania.

Table 2. USSR: Soviet Exports to CMEA Countries by Commodities, 1989

(In percent of total)

	Bulgaria	Cuba	Czechoslovakia	GDR	Hungary	Mongolia	Poland	Romania	Viet Nam	CMEA-9	CMEA-5[1]
Machinery, equipment and transportation	29.4	31.6	14.0	17.6	14.6	55.6	15.7	17.2	29.1	21.1	18.6
Fuel and electric power	38.4	26.1	51.5	42.6	36.7	13.9	45.4	48.1	28.2	41.3	44.1
Ores and concentrates metals, metal products	3.9	6.1	5.6	13.0	6.5	2.6	7.7	11.8	9.6	7.6	6.5
Chemical products, fertilizers, rubber	1.2	3.8	3.3	1.4	6.9	2.0	2.4	2.1	5.5	2.9	3.0
Lumber and pulp and paper articles/goods	1.4	3.7	0.9	3.8	5.7	0.5	2.3	1.8	0.3	2.5	2.2
Textile raw materials and semi-finished products	1.1	1.8	1.6	1.6	1.8	0.7	2.3	2.2	5.6	1.8	1.7
Food and raw materials for food	0.1	7.8	0.5	0.2	0.5	3.7	1.0	0.4	0.2	1.2	0.5
Industrial consumer goods	2.1	4.5	2.0	0.6	3.1	8.4	4.3	1.2	2.5	2.6	2.6
Total exports categorized	77.5	85.6	79.5	84.3	75.9	87.4	81.0	84.7	81.0	81.1	79.3
Overall exports	100.0	100.0	100.0	100.0	100.0	100.0	100.0	100.0	100.0	100.0	100.0

Sources: Ministry of Foreign Economic Relations and Goskomstat.
1. CMEA-5 comprises Bulgaria, Czechoslovakia, Hungary, Poland, and Romania.

Table 3. USSR: Exports of Crude Oil and Oil Products, 1987-1990

	1987	1988	1989	Proj. 1990	1987	1988	1989	Proj. 1990
	(In millions of metric tons)				*(Percentage change)*			
Crude oil								
Total exports	136.6	144.2	127.3	100.0	5.5	5.6	-11.7	-21.5
of which:								
CMEA-9	78.2	75.9	74.9	50.7	-1.4	-3.0	-1.3	-32.3
of which:								
CMEA-5	54.5	52.4	51.4	34.3	-3.1	-3.9	-1.9	-33.2
Bulgaria	11.6	11.5	11.5	6.4	-0.9	-0.8	-0.1	-44.2
Czechoslovakia	17.0	16.4	16.6	13.0	0.5	-3.3	1.1	-21.7
Hungary	7.5	6.9	6.3	4.5	0.5	-7.4	-8.7	-28.8
Poland	13.8	13.5	13.0	8.0	0.1	-1.5	-3.7	-38.6
Romania	4.7	4.2	3.9	2.4	-27.2	-14.4	-1.9	-39.1
Cuba	4.0	3.8	3.5	2.2	3.5	-4.5	-7.3	-37.5
GDR	19.8	19.7	20.0	14.2	2.3	-0.5	1.5	-29.0
Oil products								
Total exports	59.2	61.0	57.4	50.0	4.1	3.1	-5.8	-12.9
of which:								
CMEA-9	11.0	10.1	9.8	10.7	-2.7	-8.9	-3.0	-18.1
of which:								
CMEA-5	5.5	5.2	5.0	3.9	0.4	-4.6	-3.6	-21.5
Bulgaria	1.4	1.2	1.2	0.9	-4.3	-13.9	-0.8	-20.5
Czechoslovakia	0.4	0.4	0.3	0.2	0.5	3.8	-33.2	-21.6
Hungary	1.4	1.4	1.5	1.3	0.2	0.3	2.6	-11.0
Poland	2.3	2.2	2.1	1.5	3.5	-3.6	-4.2	-29.4
Romania	—	—	—	—	—	—	—	—
Cuba	2.7	2.1	1.9	1.6	-14.2	-23.1	-9.0	-16.7
GDR	0.2	0.1	0.1	0.1	43.0	-22.2	4.2	-17.7
Mongolia	0.8	0.9	0.8	0.7	6.0	2.9	-2.3	-11.2
Viet Nam	1.8	1.8	1.9	1.6	2.2	-4.3	5.4	-13.3

Source: Ministry of Foreign Economic Relations; Goskomstat, and projections.

181

Table 4. USSR: Soviet Imports from CMEA Countries by Commodities, 1989

(In percent of total)

	Bulgaria	Cuba	Czechoslovakia	GDR	Hungary	Mongolia	Poland	Romania	Viet Nam	CMEA-9	CMEA-5 [1]
Machinery, equipment and transportation	53.2	0.4	56.5	62.2	48.0	—	48.4	48.9	—	47.3	51.5
Fuel and electric power	—	—	—	—	—	—	8.5	—	—	1.6	2.2
Ores and concentrates metals, metal products	0.3	5.4	9.9	0.4	0.5	49.6	3.9	6.4	—	3.9	4.0
Chemical products, fertilizers, rubber	1.4	—	3.2	4.9	2.3	1.5	1.3	4.9	4.8	2.5	2.3
Lumber and pulp and paper articles/goods	—	—	—	0.6	1.0	1.5	—	1.2	2.7	0.4	0.3
Textile raw materials and semi-finished products	1.3	—	—	—	0.2	5.0	0.4	0.7	11.2	0.6	0.5
Food and raw materials for food	5.5	68.7	0.1	—	12.9	15.1	0.3	3.1	15.0	9.7	3.9
Industrial consumer goods	16.5	0.3	16.5	17.3	14.5	15.4	14.6	9.7	54.6	14.6	15.1
Total exports categorized	78.3	74.8	86.2	85.4	79.4	88.2	77.4	75.0	88.3	80.5	79.8
Overall imports	100.0	100.0	100.0	100.0	100.0	100.0	100.0	100.0	100.0	100.0	100.0

Sources: Ministry of Foreign Economic Relations and Goskomstat.
1. CMEA-5 comprises Bulgaria, Czechoslovakia, Hungary, Poland, and Romania.

Table 5. USSR: Balance of Payments Scenarios for 1991 [1]

(In billions of U.S. dollars)

	Total	Of which: Convertible currency area	Of which: CMEA area
		Base scenario [2]	
Trade balance	5.4	-4.1	11.1
Services balance	-7.2	-6.0	-1.2
Current account balance (excl. gold)	-1.8	-10.1	9.9
Current account balance (incl. gold)	1.7	-6.5	9.9
Capital account, net	...	-11.0	...
Overall balance	...	-17.5	...
Arrears	-5.0	-5.0	—
Financing requirement [4]	...	22.5	...
Of which: Identified financing	...	16.9	...
		Alternative scenario [3]	
Trade balance	-3.6	-8.7	7.8
Services balance	-7.2	-6.0	-1.2
Current account balance (excl. gold)	-10.9	-14.7	6.6
Current account balance (incl. gold)	-7.3	-11.1	6.6
Capital account, net	...	-11.0	...
Overall balance	...	-22.1	...
Arrears	-5.0	-5.0	—
Financing requirement [4]	...	27.1	...
Of which: Identified financing	...	16.9	...

Source: Projections.

1. The balance of payments is broken down by the traditional convertible currency area, CMEA area (excl. the former German Democratic Republic) and countries with which the USSR had bilateral payments agreements in 1990 (which is not shown separately), although a large part of trade with the latter two areas will also be conducted in convertible currencies in 1991.
2. The base scenario assumes a 17 percent volume decline in the exports of crude oil and oil products to all countries (27 percent to CMEA countries) compared with 1990 and an oil price of US$26 per barrel.
3. The low export scenario assumes a 25 percent volume decline in the exports of crude oil and oil products compared with 1990 and an oil price of US$20 per barrel.
4. Official foreign exchange reserves and gold reserves have in this presentation been projected to remain unchanged.

183

Appendix II-4

Republican Aspects of Soviet Economic Reform

1. INTRODUCTION

This appendix provides a brief survey of interrepublican relations in the USSR and many of the issues they raise for economic reform.[1] Section 2 provides background information on the ethnic composition of the USSR, its territorial governmental organization; the spatial distribution of natural resources, production and human capital; and republican trade, income and consumption patterns. Recent political developments involving interrepublican and union-republican relations are also summarized. Several policy issues relating to economic reforms in the context of interrepublican and union-republican relations are discussed in Section 3, including the question of sovereignty, ownership relations, goods and labor mobility, and social transfers.

The survey shows that the social and economic differences between republics are substantial and that in some respects they appear to be widening. These differences infuse a strong nationalist element into debates over economic reform.

2. THE DIMENSIONS OF REGIONAL DIVERSITY

a. Ethnic geography

The USSR is one of the most ethnically diverse states in the world, embracing over 90 indigenous nationalities among its 290 million people. According to the 1989 census, 22 of the nationalities number more than one million and another 32 number between one hundred thousand and one million. The predominant national group is Russian, comprising 145 million people in 1989 or 51 percent of the total Soviet population (Table 1). Russians are concentrated in the European interior and southwestern Siberia, but a century of spontaneous and planned migration has spread Russians throughout the settled regions of the USSR. The Ukrainians and Belorussians, speaking Slavic languages closely related to Russian, make up 15 percent (44 million) and 4 percent (10 million) respectively of

185

the total population. Ukrainians and Belorussians are concentrated southwest and west respectively of the main Russian centers. For the most part, the three Slavic peoples share Orthodox Christian traditions, though in the western Ukrainian areas the Uniate movement is strong.[2] Poles, Bulgarians, and other Slavs live mainly along the western borders and account for another 1.5 million people.

The largest non-Slavic contingent is formed by Turkic Muslim peoples, sub-divided into Uzbeks (17 million people in 1989, or 6 percent of the Soviet total), Kazakhs (8 million), Azeris and Tatars (7 million each), Turkmen and Kirgiz (3 million each), and other smaller nationalities. Closely related by culture and by generations of intermarriage are the Tadzhiks (4 million), a people of mostly Iranian stock.

Most of the Muslim peoples, who together comprise over 50 million people, are concentrated in Central Asia and neighboring areas. The main exception is the Tatars: a major Tatar concentration can be found in the Russian Republic (RSFSR) interior near the big bend of the Volga river, but the remainder of the population is fairly dispersed, partly reflecting the Soviet authorities' decision during World War II to expel a large Tatar community from the Crimea.

About half of the remaining people are non-Slavic Christians living along the western or southwestern Soviet borders. The historically Orthodox Armenians (4½ million people in 1989) and Georgians (4 million) are concentrated in the south-central and west-central Caucasus respectively. Most Moldavians (3½ million), who ethnically might be considered Romanians, inhabit an area next to Romania that used to be called Bessarabia. Lithuanians (3 million), Latvians (1½ million), and Estonians (1 million), live mainly along the Baltic Sea, with the Lithuanians bordering Poland in the southwest and the Estonians, whose language is similar to Finnish, residing in the northeast across the straits from Finland.

German and Jewish communities flourished for centuries in what is now the USSR, but both groups have suffered population losses as the result of war and emigration. The 1989 census reported 2 million Germans and 1.4 million Jews; the latter tend to reside in the larger European cities, whereas almost one-half of the Germans live in Kazakhstan, to whence many Soviet Germans were deported during World War II.

The remaining dozen or so million people comprise an extraordinarily diverse ethnic mix, with most nationalities unique to the USSR. Many of them are interspersed in the mountains and valleys of the Caucasus and the bordering areas to the north, where they have lived for centuries on the periphery of competing empires. A score of other peoples live in sparsely-settled central and eastern Siberia and the Arctic. While small on an all-union scale, in certain areas these peoples form significant minorities or even majorities.

Demographic trends (including changes in ethnic identification by adults) are sharply differentiated by nationality. Jews, Poles, and Mordvinians, 3 of the 25

186

largest nationalities, have experienced population declines since 1959 of 10 percent or more. Among the Baltic peoples, the numbers of Estonians and Latvians have barely changed since 1959 (up 4 percent), but the mostly-Catholic Lithuanians have become about one third more numerous. The Russians, Ukrainians, and Belorussians as a group increased in numbers by one quarter from 1959 to 1989. Substantially faster population growth since 1959 has been registered among Moldavians, Georgians, and Armenians, with increases of one half to two thirds, while the largest Muslim peoples have more than doubled in number.

Population growth rates are generally declining, but since the slowdown has been more gradual among the Muslim than the non-Muslim peoples, the ethnic differentials are widening. Muslim peoples currently account for about one third of all Soviet army recruits. Among the Tadzhiks, population growth has actually accelerated in recent years and now ranks among the highest in the world, with a doubling time of less than twenty years.

Russian is the most common means of interethnic communication. Instruction in Russian is mandatory in schools, and a good working knowledge is indispensable for advancement in most central Soviet institutions, including the army. However, 53 million Soviet citizens, or almost one fifth of the total, reported to the 1989 census neither native nor second-language fluency in Russian (Table 2).[3] Knowledge of Russian is weakest among the Central Asian peoples, with barely a quarter claiming Russian language fluency, and in rural Central Asia the proportion is even smaller.

Conversely, 89 percent of the non-Slavic peoples are native speakers of their national language, and among the four main Central Asian peoples the proportion is 98 percent, while barely 1 percent of Slavs report fluency in non-Slavic tongues. Of course, most of the Slavs live in overwhelmingly Slavic-speaking regions, where other languages are of little practical use, but even in non-Slavic regions the share of Slavs speaking the indigenous languages tends to be small. It ranges from over a third in Lithuania and Armenia, where Russian national communities are small and intermarriage with Russians frequent, to less than 5 percent in Central Asia. It follows that disputes over formal and informal language requirements for jobs have an enormous bearing on various ethnic groups' employment and career advancement opportunities.

b. Territorial organization

In recognition of national differences, the USSR is divided administratively into 15 republics, each of which is associated with one of the larger Soviet nationalities. There are three Slavic republics (the RSFSR, Belorussia, and the Ukraine), three Baltic republics (Estonia, Latvia, and Lithuania), Moldavia, three Caucasian republics (Georgia, Armenia, and Azerbaidzhan), four Central Asian

187

republics (Uzbekistan, Turkmenistan, Tadzhikistan, and Kirgizia), and Kazakhstan, which lies between the RSFSR and Central Asia and shares some characteristics of each. In a few cases republics contain non contiguous regions.

The republics differ widely in area and population (Table 3). Largest by far is the RSFSR, which embraces both the major ethnic Russian concentrations and vast but sparsely settled territories in Siberia, the Arctic, and the Far East. The RSFSR accounts for three quarters of total Soviet area and half of total population. An independent RSFSR would be the world's largest country in area and the fifth most populous. Kazakhstan, the second largest republic in area (12 percent of the total), is nearly as large as Argentina. The second most populous republic is the Ukraine with 51 million people (18 percent of the total), followed by Uzbekistan with 20 million people and Kazakhstan with 17 million. The area of the smallest republic, Armenia, about matches that of Belgium, while the least populous republic is Estonia, with 1.6 million inhabitants.

Every nationality having a titular republic is concentrated in it, but all republics except Armenia also have minorities exceeding 15 percent of the total population, and Kazakhstan has a nontitular majority (Table 4). Large minorities result primarily from the migration over the last few decades of Russians and other Slavs. Indigenous majorities have been shrinking in all of the northern and western republics, especially in Latvia and Estonia (Table 5).[4] However, in recent years each southern republic has been growing significantly more ethnically homogeneous, reflecting both high titular nationality growth rates and the emigration of Russians and other non-titular peoples. Indeed, from 1979 to 1989 the number of Russians fell absolutely in every southern republic except Kirgizia, where it rose by 0.5 percent. Increased ethnic violence and fears of violence over the last few years are significantly accelerating this "unmixing" of nations, particular with respect to the Armenian and Azeri peoples.

Of course, no amount of border redrawing and migration could squeeze 90-plus Soviet nationalities into 15 internally homogeneous republics. To facilitate the formation of ethnically less heterogeneous administrative units, the RSFSR and a few other republics contain some so-called autonomous republics. There are 16 autonomous republics in the RSFSR, 2 in Georgia, and 1 each in Uzbekistan and Tadzhikistan. Like the republics, the autonomous republics vary significantly in area and population (Table 6). The smallest in area, the Adzhar autonomous republic of Georgia, is roughly the size of Luxembourg, while the largest, Yakutsk in eastern Siberia (part of the RSFSR), is larger than Western Europe but has barely a million people. In population, the autonomous republics range from 300 thousand to almost 4 million.

The autonomous republics tend to be much more closely bound to their host republics than the republics with each other. Only in 8 of the autonomous republics, all of them in the RSFSR, does a single titular nationality comprise more than 40 percent of the population, and only in 3 does it comprise more than

188

55 percent of the population (Table 7). Of the 20 autonomous republics, 7 lie in the interior of the RSFSR, while another 6 have external borders solely with other Soviet republics or with an inland sea. Only Tuva, north of Mongolia, has both a titular ethnic majority and a non-Soviet border.

On a lower administrative level than autonomous republics are 8 autonomous *oblasts* and 10 autonomous *okrugs*, most of which are in the RSFSR (Table 8). Only 4 have ethnic majorities different from the host republic, and only one, the Nagorno-Karabakh autonomous *oblast* in Azerbaidzhan, has a non-host majority numbering over a hundred thousand. According to the 1989 census, there were 145 thousand Armenians in Nagorno-Karabakh, less than 500 of whom were fluent in Azeri, while of the 41 thousand Azeris less than 1,000 professed fluency in Armenian.[5]

c. Natural resources

As in area and population, the republics vary enormously in natural resource wealth. Outside of some sheltered lowlands in or near the Caucasus, and parts of the Ukraine, few Soviet regions are naturally ideal for agriculture. Most of the country lies too far north to receive sufficient solar radiation, and too far inland to receive much ocean-generated rain. Rivers through most of Siberia tend to flow northward, which causes extensive flooding during spring thaws. Most of central and eastern Siberia is characterized as well by extremely cold winters, permafrost, hilly or mountainous terrain, and great distance from major population centers. Unblocked by mountains, the marine influence of the Atlantic makes winters in the northwestern quarter of the country much warmer than at equivalent latitudes in the northeast or in Canada; nevertheless, growing seasons are short and soils often waterlogged. In the south, where growing seasons are longer, precipitation is generally inadequate; most of Central Asia is desert. Offsetting these disadvantages are the abundance of land, the extensive drainage and irrigation network put in place in the Soviet period, and, in some areas, extremely rich topsoils. The famed *chernozem* or black-earth belt, a few hundred kilometers wide, extends for four thousand kilometers from the western Ukraine and northern Moldavia to the Urals and across southwestern Siberia to the Altai mountains.

Central Asia faces a growing challenge in meeting its water needs. Diversion for irrigation purposes of rivers feeding the Aral Sea is causing the latter to dry up, with serious health and ecological consequences. Other local water supplies in Central Asia have mostly been tapped, and the planned redirection of Siberian rivers southward was suspended in 1986 due to mounting concern over its environmental impact. Extensive conservation would appear to require large-scale restructuring of Central Asian agriculture, and is rendered especially difficult by high rates of rural population growth. A water challenge of a different sort is faced by the RSFSR and the Ukraine: how to stop the pollution of the Sea of Azov.

189

Forests cover over half of the USSR, with the overwhelming share located in the Far East, Siberia, Urals, and Northwest regions of the RSFSR, which accounts for 92 percent of Soviet commercial wood production. Forestry is being converted to a sustained yield basis, and in recent years more area seems to have been forested than deforested. Outside the commercial timber areas, trees are planted extensively to form shelterbelts, to combat air pollution and erosion, and to provide beauty and recreation.

Fuel and mineral reserves, in which the USSR is extremely rich, are predominantly concentrated in the RSFSR and in the heavily Russian-settled areas of the eastern Ukraine (especially the Donets basin) and northern Kazakhstan (Tables 9-12). The Baltic republics are poorly endowed with fuels and minerals. Supplies are more plentiful in the southern republics, but except for natural gas in Turkmenistan and Uzbekistan and some non-ferrous metals, the contribution to the Soviet total is modest.

Over time the fuel and mineral balance is tilting even more towards the eastern Ukraine, the RSFSR, and northern Kazakhstan, and to Siberia in particular. This reflects, on the one hand, the exhaustion (except for coal and iron ore) of European and Caucasian reserves; on the other hand, the enormous finds in Siberia and growing investment there in extraction and transport. Tyumen *oblast* in Western Siberia—as large as the U.K., France, Germany, and Italy together, but with only 3 million people—accounts for about two-thirds of all Soviet oil production, with a world market value at US$26/barrel of approximately US$75 billion. Tyumen *oblast* also accounts for two-thirds of Soviet natural gas production and holds about 30 percent of confirmed world gas reserves. Elsewhere in Siberia are massive coal reserves, but due to high extraction and transportation costs only the Kuznetsk basin in south-central Siberia is currently a major producer.[6]

d. Production and investment

Over 60 percent of NMP is generated in the RSFSR alone, with another 20 percent originating in Belorussia and the Ukraine. On a per capita basis, the RSFSR, Belorussia, and the Baltic republics are considerably more productive and the Central Asian republics considerably less productive than the rest. Industrial value added per capita in the RSFSR, Estonia, Latvia, and Belorussia is three to four times that in Central Asia. In agriculture, the RSFSR and the Ukraine together account for 68 percent of total value added, about equal to their share of the population. The leading agricultural producers on a per capita basis are Lithuania and Belorussia, followed by Latvia, Moldavia, and Estonia; while mountainous Armenia comes in last. Despite their agricultural focus, Uzbekistan and Tadzhikistan trail all other republics except Armenia in agricultural value-added per capita (Tables 13-14).

190

From 1970 to 1985, productivity gaps relative to the Baltic republics and the RSFSR narrowed considerably for the Caucasian republics and Belorussia, but widened for Central Asia. During 1986-89, NMP per capita tended to grow most rapidly in the Baltic republics, the Ukraine and Belorussia and most slowly in the southern republics and Central Asia (Table 15). Overall, the ratio of the RSFSR/Baltic NMP per capita to Central Asian NMP per capita has grown by about a third since 1970. Reflecting their high birth rates, however, Uzbekistan and Tadzhikistan have matched or exceeded the all-union pace in aggregate NMP growth.

One should be careful not to read too much into the republican value added figures, as they are easily distorted by domestic pricing decisions and changes in the allocation of turnover taxes.[7] However, the general productivity differentials seem to be confirmed by more disaggregated commodity breakdowns. The share of a Central Asian republic in Soviet industrial output rarely exceeds its population share and usually is considerably less, while the RSFSR and the Ukraine typically have more than proportionate shares, especially in heavy industry. Belorussia is an important producer (over 10 percent of the Soviet total, or roughly three times its population share) of electric motors, dairy equipment, fertilizer, synthetic fibers, and an assortment of consumer durables. The Baltic republics and to a lesser extent Moldavia are major producers, on a per capita basis, in light industry, food-processing, building materials, paper (except Moldavia), and some machines and consumer durables. The Caucasian republics and Kazakhstan, with light industry, some machine building, and (in the case of Kazakhstan) bulk heavy industry and building materials are industrially intermediate between Central Asia and the European republics (Table 16).

In agriculture, Moldavia and the Ukraine are relatively high per capita producers of most products other than cotton, citrus fruits, and wool, and the Baltic republics are important producers of meat, milk, eggs, and potatoes. Besides eggs and grain, agricultural output per capita tends to be below average in the RSFSR. Both Armenian and Georgian agriculture focus on fruits and vegetables, but climate and soil give an undisputed advantage to the latter; Georgia is the only significant domestic citrus producer. Azerbaidzhan exceeds its population share in cotton, grapes, other fruits and berries, and vegetables. Kazakhstan raises primarily grain and livestock, while Kirgizia is a major Soviet wool producer. The remaining Central Asian republics specialize in cotton-growing although they do raise fruits and vegetables on the side (Table 17). On a per capita basis, these republics are falling further behind in agricultural production. Apart from cotton, both state and collective farms in Azerbaidzhan, Turkmenistan, Uzbekistan, and Tadzhikistan tend to be high-cost producers, while the western republics tend to be relatively low-cost areas of production.

Fixed assets employed in the material sphere of production are concentrated in absolute terms in the RSFSR, the Ukraine, and Kazakhstan, which together account for 83 percent of the total. Fixed assets per capita are highest in the Baltic republics and the RSFSR, and lowest in Central Asia (except Turkmenistan), the Caucasus, and Moldavia. Once again, on a per capita basis the gaps have been widening since 1970, with a marked acceleration after 1985. In just 4 years, republican fixed assets per capita grew 17 percent more rapidly in Lithuania than in Uzbekistan (Table 18).

e. Labor and human capital

With the exception of Moldavia and Armenia, the labor force is distinctly more oriented to agriculture in the southern republics than in the North and the West. In 1987 (the most recent year for which data are available), agricultural and forestry employment ranged from 34-42 percent of total employment in Central Asia, to 13-20 percent of total employment in the Baltic and Slavic republics. Meanwhile, industry and construction absorbed 39-42 percent of employment in Armenia and the Baltic and Slavic republics, versus 21-31 percent elsewhere (Table 19).

Labor force organization also varies considerably across republics. In 1988, 80 percent of the labor force in the RSFSR was employed in state enterprises, 5 percent worked on collective farms, and only 2 percent were (officially) mainly employed privately, including in cooperatives. In contrast, only 52 to 55 percent of the labor force in Turkmenistan, Uzbekistan, and Tadzhikistan worked in state enterprises, with 11 to 19 percent working on collective farms and 11 to 14 percent engaged primarily in private activity (Table 20).

Labor force participation rates are relatively low in the southern republics. This reflects in part the greater share of students and draftees in the population and in part cultural pressures on women in southern republics to stay home and raise large families. The proportion of women among workers and employees is 16 percentage points less in Tadzhikistan than in Estonia and Latvia, a difference only modestly offset by the higher share of Tadzhik women among collective farmers (Table 21). The lower officially-recorded labor force participation rates may also reflect a greater propensity of people in the southern republics to engage in black market activities.[8]   Indeed, north-south differentials in non-reported economic activity might significantly mitigate the interrepublican income differentials reported below, although at the same time they might heighten the interrepublican social differentials.

The 1988 employment figures miss the recent explosion in cooperative membership. The most recent republican-level breakdown available shows that over the last part of 1988 and in 1989 an additional 1.5 percent of the labor force shifted its primary employment affiliation to the cooperatives. Latvia and Armenia stand out as centers of cooperative activity. Cooperative membership is relatively more common in the northern and western republics than in Central Asia (Table 22).

The regional distribution of skilled industrial workers and engineers, not surprisingly, generally corresponds with that of industry. Central Asia is at the bottom in terms of concentration of specialists and scientists while the RSFSR is near the top (Table 23). The main discrepancy in regional supply and demand concerns the high concentration of scientists and specialists in Armenia and Georgia relative to the level of industrial development, a discrepancy which is partly resolved through migration.

Of nationalities with a titular republic, Georgians, Armenians, and Estonians are the most likely to have advanced scientific degrees, while the Central Asian peoples and the Moldavians lag behind. However, of all the nationalities, Jews are by far the most likely to have advanced degrees, and hence their exodus from the USSR might be expected to have a disproportionately severe economic impact (Table 24).

In recent years, the republican authorities have typically tried not so much to attract skilled labor from without—which would often involve a dilution of titular republican majorities—as to cultivate it from within. In most of the European republics, the main concerns are low birth rates and an ageing population. In the predominantly Muslim areas, by contrast, the principal concern is high birth rates, especially in rural areas offering poor-quality education and limited on-the-job training. In general, the titular nationality in a republic is more likely than average to engage in agriculture and less likely to engage in industry. The two exceptions are Armenia, which until recently had a sizeable rural Azeri minority, and the RSFSR, which is home to a number of smaller nationalities (Table 25). As noted earlier, regional and ethnic differentials in human capital tend to be particularly pronounced between Muslim and non-Muslim women (Table 21). Deficient education and employment opportunities discourage restraints on child-bearing, while the need to care for large families in turn discourages outside employment and tends to reduce the educational investment per child.

f. Trade

The Soviet economy embraces a substantial interregional division of labor, arising in part from varying comparative advantages and a common economic union. The division of labor is reinforced by two factors more peculiar to the Soviet economic system. The first is the organization of economic ministries along branch lines, which often favors interrepublican trade within a ministry over intra-republican trade across ministries. The second is the emphasis on economies of scale, which sometimes leaves only 1 or 2 enterprises supplying the entire union.

In domestic prices, interrepublican trade (excluding "nonproductive" services") in the USSR amounted to 21 percent of GDP in 1988, about four times the size of exports abroad. For comparison, in the European Community both trade in goods and services among members and trade with the rest of the world are about 14 percent of GDP.[9] The Soviet economy is therefore relatively more integrated internally than the EC but relatively less open to foreign markets. The ratio of interrepublican exports to republican NMP[10] is least in the RSFSR (18 percent in 1988), Kazakhstan (31 percent), and the Ukraine (39 percent). Belorussia is the most oriented to interrepublican trade, with an interrepublican export to NMP ratio of almost 70 percent, while the ratio exceeds 60 percent in the Baltic republics, Moldavia, and Armenia. As for exports abroad relative to NMP, the RSFSR has the highest share (almost 9 percent in 1988) while Kirgizia and Armenia have the lowest (barely 1 percent) (Table 26).

In domestic prices, Azerbaidzhan and Belorussia tend to run total trade surpluses (respectively 10 and 8 percent of NMP in 1988) while the other republics run deficits ranging in 1988 from slightly under 3 percent of NMP in the Ukraine to 27 percent in Kazakhstan. All of the republics run deficits in trade with the outside world in domestic prices, although these deficits are relatively small for Uzbekistan, Tadzhikistan and Turkmenistan (1 to 4 percent of NMP). In interrepublican trade, the RSFSR tends to be roughly in balance while Belorussia and Azerbaidzhan run substantial trade surpluses as a percent of NMP (15 percent and 19 percent, respectively, in 1988).

These figures are significantly distorted by the uneven allocation of turnover taxes and consumer subsidies across republics, however, and by purchases and sales of goods by visitors from other republics. When turnover taxes are allocated in proportion to labor expenditures incurred in production, subsidies for consumer goods are charged to the consuming republic, and transactions by visitors are assigned to the republic of permanent residence, official Soviet sources report that total trade balances deteriorate for the RSFSR, Armenia, and Georgia, remain unchanged for the Ukraine, and improve for all other republics. The biggest improvement is registered by Moldavia, which moves from a deficit of 13 percent of NMP to a surplus of 10 percent (Table 27).

However, the preceding adjustments do not address the artificially low domestic price of fuels (of which the RSFSR is a large net exporter), relative to food and consumer goods (of which it is a net importer). When trade is revalued at world market prices, both the foreign and interrepublican trade balances of the RSFSR improve drastically. According to official Soviet reestimations, other republics run smaller foreign deficits at world market prices or, in the case of Uzbekistan and Tadzhikistan, modest surpluses; however, for most republics the improvements are outweighed by the enormous deterioration relative to the RSFSR. Apart from the RSFSR, only Azerbaidzhan would have had a net surplus at world market prices in interrepublican trade in 1987, and most republics accrue substantial deficits (Table 28).[11]

Over time, economic restructuring might significantly reduce the net transfers or even reverse their direction. For example, the consumption of fuels and materials from the RSFSR in importing republics might drop significantly in response to higher prices and greater market orientation. The Baltic states, which were economically similar to Finland prior to World War II, might in the future emulate its development pattern, while Central Asia conceivably could become a major exporter of fruits and vegetables. In the short run, however, a shift to world market prices uncompensated by budgetary shifts would yield a tremendous windfall for the RSFSR, or for Siberia to the extent it received fiscal autonomy.

Over the last two years, interregional deliveries appear to have significantly declined. The adverse economic impact is magnified by the high degree of monopoly in Soviet industry and the limited flexibility of the transportation network, which cause bottlenecks at one stage of production to be transmitted to the next. Some of this reduction can be ascribed to political conflict; such as the blockade of Armenia by Azerbaidzhan in the winter of 1988-89 and the central authorities' blockade of Lithuania in the spring and summer of 1990. In general, however, the contraction in trade reflects the difficulty, under conditions of worsening shortages, of securing an exchange of comparable values without resort to barter.

g. Income, savings, and consumption

Labor earnings tend to be highest in Siberia and the Far North, where wage premia are set high to attract and retain workers, and in the Baltic republics, where labor productivity is high. They are lowest in the southern republics. In 1989, average monthly salaries for workers and employees in the socialized sector were 12 percent higher than the national average in Estonia and 8 percent higher in the RSFSR but some 22 percent and 26 percent lower in Tadzhikistan and Azerbaidzhan, respectively. The implied ethnic differentials are even steeper, since a disproportionate share of the better-paid jobs in Central Asia is held by Europeans. For collective farmers, average monthly pay in 1989 exceeded the union norm by 28 to 58 percent in the Baltic republics (with Estonia again the leader) but fell short of the union norm by 17-18 percent in Uzbekistan and Tadzhikistan. Moreover, judging from the trends of the 1980s, the gaps appear to be widening over time (Table 31).

The regional differentials are compensated to some extent by more fertile private agricultural plots and lower collective farm market prices in the southern republics. However, workers there tend to have more dependents (Table 32), and relatively fewer goods are available at low state prices. According to official sources, per capita income in 1988 in Tadzhikistan was less than half that in the RSFSR and only 41 percent of the Estonian level, with the gaps growing about 1 percentage point per year since 1975 (Table 33). Especially stark are the republican differences in the size of savings deposits per capita, with the Lithuanian level five times the levels of Uzbekistan and Tadzhikistan as a whole and tens times the levels if rural areas only are compared (Table 34). However, a large part of this differential probably reflects a greater propensity in southern republics to hold savings in the form of cash.[12]

Poverty levels are also higher in Central Asia, particularly in rural areas. In 1989, only 2 percent of the population in the Baltic republics, and 3 to 6 percent of people in the mainly Slavic republics, lived in households with per capita incomes of less than rub 75 per month, compared with 33 to 51 percent in the predominantly Muslim republics.[13] Two thirds of the population in Estonia lived in households with per capita incomes of over 150 rubles per month, contrasted with 8 percent in Tadzhikistan (Table IV.6.14).

Differences in income, family size, and culture are reflected in different consumption patterns. Sales of alcoholic beverages in 1989 amounted to 5.3-6.8 liters of pure alcohol per person in the RSFSR and the Baltic republics but only 1.3-3.4 liters per capita in the predominantly Muslim republics, with the Slavic population probably accounting for a large proportion of purchases. Meat consumption is barely one third as high in Uzbekistan as in Lithuania (Table IV.6.15), but bread consumption is 50 percent greater. There are less than half as many automobiles per person in Central Asia as in the Baltic republics, and concentration of other durable goods is also less. However, because families are so much larger in Central Asia than in the Baltic republics, durable good possession per family is roughly comparable.

Health indicators also differ markedly by republic. Infant mortality rates range from 32-55 in the Central Asian republics compared to 11-15 in the Baltic republics. Alcoholism is from 12-17 times as prevalent in the RSFSR as in the Caucasus, and abortions are 1.8-4.8 times more frequent relative to the number of women in child-bearing years (Table 35). Central Asia fares worst in housing conditions, with rural Central Asians having on average less than one half the dwelling space of rural Baltic residents (Table 36).

h. Political developments

Relations between the union government and the republics have deteriorated markedly over the last five years. Paradoxically, the prime catalyst was the decision of the union's leadership, under *glasnost'*, to permit more open expression of grievances. Since many non-Russians perceive their regions as having been forcibly seized and colonized, serious nationalist grievances were not hard to find, and even complaints that were essentially non-nationalist in character easily took on a nationalist tinge. As elections became freer, republican nationalist parties grew in strength, and Communist Party branches in the republics were themselves forced to respond more to nationalist interests.

The growing assertiveness of republican governments has triggered a number of concessions from the center, which, in conjunction with the weakening of the Communist Party and the breakdown of central planning, have encouraged more assertiveness. All republican governments have officially proclaimed their sovereignty, which at the minimum is interpreted to deny the supremacy of union over republican laws and to assert control over most natural resources within their borders. Most of the republics are organizing bilateral barter trade with other republics and with foreign trade partners, and some have set up border controls. Several republics are preparing to introduce their own currency and some have already restricted the use of the ruble on their territory.[14]

In March 1990, the newly-elected Lithuanian government announced its secession from the USSR. Although this declaration was later suspended under pressure, Lithuania continues to affirm its intent to eventually secede from the union, as do the other two Baltic republics and Georgia.

Declarations of sovereignty extend to the sub-republican level. Attempts by the Armenian majority in Nagorno-Karabakh to secede from Azerbaidzhan and join Armenia brought the two neighboring republics to the verge of war in 1988-89. More recently, attempts by the Southern Osetian autonomous *oblast* in Georgia to join with the neighboring Northern Osetian autonomous republic in the RSFSR have prompted the Georgian parliament to revoke Southern Osetian autonomy. Many minority national communities, including Russians living outside the RSFSR, are clamoring for territorial recognition, while several autonomous republics in the Russian Republic seek full republic status. Even where ethnic control is not at issue, the desire to control local resources sometimes precipitates assertions of independence.

There remain powerful centripetal forces opposed to dissolution of the union. The most important are the still-powerful central institutions—the army, the Communist Party, and the KGB. Preservation of the union also appeals to many Russians and other minorities living outside the RSFSR, who fear that independence would come at their expense. Indeed, at present most republics contemplating secession are themselves facing internal secessionist movements. Feelings of ethnic affinity among Slavs tend to temper separatist tendencies in the Ukraine and Belorussia, while the relatively conservative republican governments in Central Asia are concerned to retain transfers from the union budget.

As the indispensable core of the USSR, the RSFSR is a special case. In recent months, the RSFSR has declared in favor of accelerated economic reform and looser, more confederal relations among republics. Its leadership has also endorsed greater decentralization to local and regional authorities within the federation and more sovereignty (albeit vaguely defined) for minority nationalities.

A new union treaty is currently under discussion, which seeks to reconcile republican sovereignty with strong central authority; a draft was published in November 1990. The governments of the Baltic republics and Georgia have said they will not sign it, and in any case its impact on actual relations will depend on the President's exercise of his emergency powers and/or on judicial enforcement

197

mechanisms yet to be created. The existing Constitution grants extensive formal rights to the republics, but in practice these were largely ignored in the past.

3. POLICY ISSUES

a. Sovereignty

The precise meaning of sovereignty is subject to debate, but generally it is taken to mean a state's decisive control over its territory and its internal social and economic order. With Soviet society in upheaval, the question of sovereignty is crucial to economic reform. In particular, sovereignty bears immediately on the ownership and disposal of state property, and most Soviet property is owned by the state.

The draft union treaty affirms the republics' rights to "independently determine their governmental system, administrative-territorial divisions, and system of organs of power and management". The republics for their part would guarantee basic human rights to their own citizens and citizens of other union republics, cooperate with other republics and pledge noninterference in their internal affairs, foreswear the stationing of foreign troops on their territory, and delegate certain political and economic powers to the union government. Those political powers would include internal enforcement of the Constitution, defense and national security, and foreign policy.

The union's economic powers would include the implementation of unified monetary, credit, and financial policies based on a common currency, the formulation and implementation of the union budget, the safekeeping of gold and diamond reserves, and the right to levy union-level taxes. In conjunction with the republics, the union government would also manage the fuel and energy system, the transportation and communication networks, defense production, space research, meteorology, geodesy, and cartography; formulate social, environmental, and scientific policy; and work out proportional republican deductions for all-union programs.

According to the draft treaty, union and republic laws would each be supreme in areas of their sole jurisdiction. Where jurisdiction is joint, union law would prevail unless an affected republic objected. Each side could protest the other's actions, with disagreements resolved through "agreed procedures" or through a union Constitutional Court. The union's legislative body, the Supreme Soviet, would have two chambers. One chamber, the union Council, would be elected by the entire population based on election districts with an equal number of inhabitants. The second, a Council of Nationalities, would consist of representatives from republics, from nationally autonomous regions within republics, and from other nationality-based organizations.

The President, who would have supreme executive power, would be elected by a majority of votes in the union as a whole and in the majority of republics. The President would be assisted at a policy-formulation level by a Federation Council consisting of the Vice President (elected in the same manner as the President) and the presidents of the republics. Government administration would be directed by a Cabinet consisting of presidentially-appointed union ministers (subject to approval of the Supreme Soviet) and chief republican administrators. The Cabinet would be supervised by the President and be legally responsible to the Supreme Soviet. Some administrative questions would be decided by collegia of union and republic ministers.

The draft treaty does not provide much more detail. It does not specify how and with what degree of independence the Constitutional Court would operate, how disagreements among the two parliamentary chambers and the President would be handled, how often elections would be held or how runoffs or recalls would be organized. The requirement that the President receive both an absolute electoral majority and the support of a majority of republics could in theory leave the office vacant.

In essence, it appears that the draft union treaty envisages a strong centrally-led federation with a strong Presidency. The Federation Council might have mainly an advisory role, as most of its members would hold full-time jobs outside Moscow. The treaty does not mention procedures for voluntary secession, although it does appear to allow for expulsion of republics not living up to the agreement. It also does not allow for the rearrangement of borders or the formation of new republics without the consent of affected parties.

b. Ownership

As suggested in the presidential guidelines of October 1990, the draft union treaty would cede to the individual republics the ownership of the natural resources lying within their borders. In principle, this means that, say, citizens of republics other than the RSFSR would have no direct claim on Siberian oil and natural gas.[15] However, the guidelines also suggest that the union government should administer the "common fuel and energy system" of the country, including major pipeline transport, which might give it *de facto* a strong ownership claim. The draft union treaty modifies exclusive administration by the union to joint union-republic administration, but adds that "the regulation through republican legislation of property relations pertaining to land, its underground resources, and other natural resources must not impede the implementation of the union's powers". Again, an individual republic's ownership of natural resources would seem to be substantially though imprecisely qualified. Similar issues appear in internal republic relations as well, especially between the RSFSR and its internally autonomous republics, *oblasts,* and *okrugs.*

The draft union treaty is even less clear on the disposition of state enterprises. It declares that the republics own "state property other than that portion required for implementation of [union] powers". Since in 1988 the share of state industry under direct republic or local control was 7 percent,[16] even a broad interpretation of union requirements would appear to imply a substantial property transfer to the republics. However, it should be borne in mind that even now there is a large intermediate category of state property administered by republic-level branch ministries (31 percent of industry in 1988).[17] The actual disposition of such property will depend on whether such ministries are to report primarily to republican governments or to union-level superiors. Over the last few years control has been shifting to the republic governments, but future recentralization cannot be ruled out.

According to the presidential guidelines, the union and to some extent the republics will temporarily be allowed to impose mandatory state requisition orders, which would in effect override ownership rights. It is possible that the authorities intend to impose state orders only on enterprises within their immediate jurisdiction. Even with the best of intentions, however, there are bound to be disagreements over jurisdiction, not just for state orders but also for other activities. There is as yet no established judicial mechanism for resolving disputes among the republics or between the republics and union. As for property claims in one republic by individual or corporate citizens of another, little recognition has been given even to their possible emergence.[18] Ironically, foreign investment has much better protection than interrepublican investment.

Indeed, ownership rights are even difficult to clarify at a local level. Privatization of housing in Moscow, for example, has recently been mired in disputes over rights of disposal, not only between the Moscow city government and higher authorities, but also between the city government and neighborhood councils. In the past, vertical disputes between lower and higher authorities were typically resolved in the latter's favor, while horizontal disputes were often mediated by the Communist Party. There is an established state arbitration system, but substantial work is required to transform it into a strong independent judiciary.[19]

c. Mobility of goods and labor

The existing interregional division of labor, while extensive, rests on a central administrative fiat that has become increasingly difficult to sustain. It follows that a common all-union market, which has figured so prominently in reform discussions, might to a considerable extent have to be recreated. One way an all-union market is being recreated is through direct trade agreements between republics. These agreements typically amount to government-managed barter, however, which should not be confused with free trade.

The legal foundation of a common market is a blanket prohibition of constraints on interrepublican trade, often referred to as an "interstate commerce clause". The closest the presidential guidelines come to such a clause is a statement that trade in "an agreed list of goods" not be constrained. Even with an interstate commerce clause, however, interregional trade is bound to be stunted as long as shortages at official prices are widespread. The latter make producers reluctant to sell for money, so that exchange tends to degenerate into barter. The greater information needs of barter (since demand and supply for real commodities must be matched on each side of the transaction) make it cumbersome and encourage government intervention. Moreover, with price controls many goods are bound to be in shortage, and republics frequently try to prevent the export of locally deficit goods. Allowing more prices to be set by local and republican governments, as the presidential guidelines propose, increases the opportunities and incentives for interregional arbitrage and hence is bound to provoke either protectionism or abandonment of controls. Intergovernmental negotiations are no panacea either, as evidenced by the history of the CMEA. Indeed, negotiations have already in some cases limited the development of spontaneous trade, as republic and local governments strive to improve their bargaining positions.

As for interregional labor mobility, the main constraints are housing shortages and the *propiski*, or permits, required for residence in large cities. The presidential guidelines call for a housing market but decline to elaborate, saying that this is a matter for subsequent union and republican decrees. The *propiski* are not mentioned at all. Given the sensitivity of housing and nationalist issues, large in-migration of nationalities other than the locally dominant one could create serious problems.

d. Pacing of reform

The presidential guidelines propose for the republics substantial autonomy to determine their own forms and pacing of economic reform. However, under conditions of generalized shortages, it would be difficult for an individual republic to pursue radical reform very far on its own within the confines of a common economic and monetary union. Internal decontrol of prices would tend to draw in more supplies from other republics, but their authorities might respond with direct export controls, just as the recent hike in procurement prices for meat in the RSFSR prompted the Ukraine to restrict meat exports. If the ruble were maintained as a common currency, and barring immediate price decontrol throughout the union, attempts by a republic to implement radical reform on its own could lead to increased trade and capital restrictions between republics and/or abandonment of its reform effort.

201

NOTES

1. Issues of fiscal federalism and interrepublican monetary relations are discussed respectively in Chapters III.1 and III.2; the regional dimensions of issues of social protection are covered in Chapter IV.6.

2. Uniates are Catholics following many of the Orthodox rites. The Ukrainian Uniate Church was amalgamated into the Russian Orthodox Church in 1946, but has recently been relegalized.

3. Fluency in third or subsequent languages is not reported. Given that 62 million non-Russians claim fluency in only one language and less than 19 million non-Russians are native Russian speakers, it would appear that at least 43 million Soviet citizens claim not to be fluent in Russian.

4. Migration rates of ethnic Slavs to non-Slavic republics are thought to have been particularly high in the 1950s, but statistical data are not available.

5. Goskomstat notes that, due to the Armenian earthquake and civil strife, these figures, such as those for Azerbaidzhan and Armenia more generally, may be imprecise.

6. For more information on natural resource distribution in the Soviet Union, see Lydolph (1990).

7. The limitations of republican-level national accounts are examined more closely in Belkindas and Sagers (1990) and Belkindas and Brown (1990).

8. For survey evidence on this subject, see Grossman (1989).

9. Commission of the European Communities (1990).

10. GDP estimates are not available on a republican basis. For the union as a whole, NMP in 1988 equalled 72 percent of officially reported GDP.

11. Breakdowns of republican external trade at world market prices into foreign and interrepublican components are available only for 1987. Judging from its aggregate figures, the main features of trade in 1988 would appear to be the same.
   As with the trade balances in domestic prices, these reestimations in world market prices should be treated cautiously. It is not clear how world prices for commodity aggregates are chosen—in particular, what if any corrections are made for quality, and to what extent intra-CMEA foreign trade prices, which in general are distorted from those on world markets, are used in these calculations. Given that the RSFSR is a large net importer from abroad of machinery and a large net exporter of machinery to other republics (Tables 29-30), it is difficult to explain how revaluation at foreign prices would improve its aggregate machinery and equipment balance by 13 billion rubles, or 3 percent of republican NMP (see *Narkhoz 1989* (1990), p. 640; republican NMP are from *Osnovnye pokazateli*, p. 34).

12. See Grossman (1989).

13. Soviet researchers often consider the poverty threshold to be a household per capita income of rub 75 a month. Of course, because of economies of scale in household formation, the poverty threshold may differ by size of family, and the cost of living also varies by regions. In general, comparisons based on household per capita income tend to exaggerate the relative incidence of poverty in Central Asia. For further discussion see Chapter IV.6.

14. A recent example is the introduction of the *khavronets*—a coupon issued for use with rubles—in the Ukraine.

15. For comparison, in the United States natural resources in the public domain typically belong to the federal government rather than to the states. In Canada, however, subsurface mineral

202

rights are typically vested in the provincial governments. See Chapter III.1 for further discussion.

16. *Narkhoz 1988* (1989), p. 332.

17. *ibid.* According to *Narkhoz 1989* (1990), p. 331, the share of industry under republic, local, or union-republic ministry jurisdiction rose by 1 percentage point in 1989, but no disaggregation is provided. Such industry, which is primarily light and food industry, accounted in 1989 for 36 percent of total industrial employment but only 19 percent of industrial fixed capital.

18. The Shatalin reform program did call for the formation of transrepublican stock companies.

19. Issues of legal reform are discussed extensively in Chapter IV.7.

Table 1. USSR: Nationality Composition of the Population, 1959-89

	Population in 1989		Percent of total	Percentage Change			
	(1,000)	Rank		1959-89	1959-70	1970-79	1979-89
USSR	285,743		100.0	36.8	15.8	8.4	9.0
Russian	145,155	1	50.8	27.2	13.1	6.5	5.6
Ukrainian	44,186	2	15.5	18.6	9.4	3.9	4.3
Uzbek	16,698	3	5.8	177.6	52.9	35.5	34.1
Belorussian	10,036	4	3.5	26.8	14.4	4.5	6.1
Kazakh	8,136	5	2.8	124.6	46.3	23.7	24.1
Azeri	6,770	6	2.4	130.3	49.0	25.1	23.6
Tatar	6,649	7	2.3	33.8	19.4	6.5	5.2
Armenian	4,623	8	1.6	65.9	27.7	16.6	11.4
Tadzhik	4,215	9	1.5	201.8	52.9	35.7	45.5
Georgian	3,981	10	1.4	47.9	20.6	10.0	11.5
Moldavian	3,352	11	1.2	51.4	21.9	10.0	12.9
Lithuanian	3,067	12	1.1	31.9	14.6	7.0	7.6
Turkmen	2,729	13	1.0	172.5	52.3	33.0	34.6
Kirgiz	2,529	14	0.9	161.1	49.9	31.3	32.7
German	2,039	15	0.7	25.9	14.0	4.9	5.3
Chuvash	1,842	16	0.6	25.3	15.3	3.4	5.2
Latvian	1,459	17	0.5	4.2	2.2	0.6	1.4
Bashkir	1,449	18	0.5	46.5	25.3	10.6	5.7
Jewish	1,378	19	0.5	-39.2	-5.2	-15.8	-23.9
Mordvinian	1,154	20	0.4	-10.2	-1.7	-5.6	-3.2
Polish	1,126	21	0.4	-18.4	-15.4	-1.4	-2.1
Estonian	1,027	22	0.4	3.8	1.9	1.2	0.7
Chechen	957	23	0.3	128.5	46.3	23.4	26.6
Udmurt	747	24	0.3	19.5	12.7	1.3	4.6
Mari	671	25	0.2	33.1	18.7	3.9	7.9
All other	9,766		3.4	35.3	-1.6	11.7	23.1

Source: Census data for 1959, 1970, and 1979 from *Naselenie SSSR 1987* (1988), pp. 98-99. Census data for 1989 from *Vestnik Statistiki*, No. 10, 1990, p. 69. Figures for 1979 and 1989 include permanent residents only.

Table 2. USSR: Linguistic Affiliation by Republic, 1989

	Percent of Total Fluent in		Percent of Russians Fluent in		Percent of Titular Nationals Fluent in		Percent of Others Fluent in	
	Russian	Republican tongue	Russian	Republican tongue	Russian	Republican tongue	Russian	Republican tongue
USSR	81.4	...	99.9	...	...	...	62.3	...
RSFSR	97.8	97.8	100.0	100.0	100.0	100.0	88.0	88.0
Ukraine	78.4	78.0	99.6	34.3	71.7	94.7	81.9	29.5
Belorussia	82.7	77.7	99.5	26.7	80.2	89.7	80.5	48.2
Estonia	58.9	67.4	99.7	15.0	34.6	99.6	89.9	19.5
Latvia	81.6	62.4	99.8	22.3	68.3	98.7	86.8	24.7
Lithuania	47.3	85.3	98.9	37.5	37.6	99.8	73.2	22.0
Moldavia	68.5	67.0	99.7	11.8	57.6	97.1	81.7	12.7
Georgia	41.2	77.2	99.4	23.7	32.0	99.8	52.7	24.0
Armenia	44.3	95.4	99.5	33.6	44.6	99.8	23.3	34.1
Azerbaidzhan	38.4	86.5	99.9	14.4	32.1	99.6	53.3	28.4
Kazakhstan	83.1	40.2	100.0	0.9	64.2	98.8	88.2	2.7
Turkmenistan	38.6	74.7	99.9	2.5	28.3	99.4	47.2	15.7
Uzbekistan	33.4	75.4	99.9	4.6	22.7	99.0	43.5	21.5
Tadzhikistan	36.4	66.6	99.9	3.5	30.5	99.4	32.3	14.7
Kirgizia	56.7	53.6	100.0	1.2	37.3	99.6	60.2	4.6

Source: Natsionalnyi sostav naseleniia SSSR (1990). Figures include permanent residents only.

Table 3. USSR: Territory and Population of Republics, as of January 1, 1990

	Territory		Population		Percent Growth Rate [1]	Density per sq. km.	Percent Urban
	Thousand sq. km.	Percent of USSR	In thousands	Percent of USSR			
USSR [2]	22,403	100.0	288,624	100.0	0.66	12.9	66
Slavic							
RSFSR	17,075	76.2	148,041	51.3	0.43	8.7	74
Ukraine	604	2.7	51,839	18.0	0.26	5.9	67
Belorussia	208	0.9	10,259	3.6	0.58	49.4	66
Baltic/Moldavia							
Estonia	45	0.2	1,583	0.5	0.89	35.1	72
Latvia	65	0.3	2,687	0.9	0.26	41.7	71
Lithuania	65	0.3	3,723	1.3	0.64	57.1	68
Moldavia	34	0.2	4,362	1.5	0.55	129.4	47
Caucasus							
Georgia	70	0.3	5,456	1.9	0.24	78.3	56
Armenia	30	0.1	3,293	1.1	0.15	110.5	68
Azerbaidzhan ...	87	0.4	7,131	2.5	1.32	82.3	54
Kazakhstan							
Kazakhstan	2,717	12.1	16,691	5.8	0.94	6.1	57
Central Asia							
Turkmenistan ...	488	2.2	3,622	1.3	2.49	7.4	45
Uzbekistan	447	2.0	20,322	7.0	2.09	45.4	41
Tadzhikistan	143	0.6	5,248	1.8	2.72	36.7	32
Kirgizia	199	0.9	4,367	1.5	1.79	22.0	38
Composition by regions							
Slavic	17,886	79.8	210,139	72.8	0.40	11.7	73
Baltic/Moldavia ...	209	0.9	12,355	4.3	0.60	59.3	62
Caucasus	186	0.8	15,880	5.5	0.70	85.3	56
Kazakhstan	2,717	12.1	16,691	5.8	0.94	6.1	57
Central Asia	1,277	5.7	33,559	11.6	2.20	26.3	40

Source: Narkhoz 1989 (1990), pp. 17, 19-24.

1. Percentage growth in population 1989-90.

2. USSR territory includes 127,300 square kilometers for the White Sea and the Sea of Azov, not included in the area of individual republics.

206

Table 4. USSR: Percentage Nationality Composition by Republic, 1989

		Nationality																		
	Total	Russ.	Ukrain.	Belor.	Eston.	Latvi.	Lithua.	Moldav.	Georg.	Armen.	Azerb.	Kazakh.	Turkmen.	Uzbek.	Tadzh.	Kirg.	Tatar	Jew	German	Other
USSR	100	50.8	15.5	3.5	0.4	0.5	1.1	1.2	1.4	1.6	2.4	2.8	1.0	5.8	1.5	0.9	2.4	0.5	0.7	6.1
RSFSR	100	81.5	3.0	0.8	—	—	—	0.1	0.1	0.4	0.2	0.4	—	0.1	—	—	3.8	0.4	0.6	8.5
Ukraine	100	22.1	72.7	0.9	—	—	—	0.6	—	0.1	0.1	—	—	—	—	—	0.3	0.9	0.1	2.1
Belorussia	100	13.2	2.9	77.9	—	—	0.1	—	—	—	—	—	—	—	—	—	0.1	1.1	—	4.4
Estonia	100	30.3	3.1	1.8	61.5	0.2	0.2	0.2	0.1	0.1	0.1	—	—	—	—	—	0.3	0.3	0.2	1.8
Latvia	100	34.0	3.5	4.5	0.1	52.0	1.3	0.1	0.1	0.1	0.1	—	—	—	—	—	0.2	0.9	0.1	3.0
Lithuania	100	9.4	1.2	1.7	—	0.1	79.6	—	—	—	—	—	—	—	—	—	0.1	0.3	0.1	7.2
Moldavia	100	13.0	13.8	0.5	—	—	—	64.5	—	0.1	0.1	—	—	—	—	—	0.1	1.5	0.2	6.2
Georgia	100	6.3	1.0	0.2	—	—	—	0.1	70.1	8.1	5.7	—	—	—	—	—	0.1	0.5	—	7.8
Armenia	100	1.6	0.3	—	—	—	—	—	—	93.3	2.6	—	—	—	—	—	—	—	—	2.1
Azerbaidzhan	100	5.6	0.5	0.1	—	—	—	—	0.2	5.6	82.7	—	—	—	—	—	0.4	0.4	—	4.4
Kazakhstan	100	37.8	5.4	1.1	—	—	0.1	0.2	0.1	0.1	0.5	39.7	—	2.0	0.2	0.1	2.0	0.1	5.8	4.7
Turkmenistan	100	9.5	1.0	0.3	—	—	—	0.1	—	0.9	0.9	2.5	72.0	9.0	0.1	—	1.1	0.1	0.1	2.3
Uzbekistan	100	8.3	0.8	0.1	—	—	—	—	—	0.3	0.2	4.1	0.6	71.4	4.7	0.9	3.3	0.5	0.2	4.5
Tadzhikistan	100	7.6	0.8	0.1	—	—	—	—	—	0.1	0.1	0.2	0.4	23.5	62.3	1.3	1.6	0.3	0.6	1.0
Kirgizia	100	21.5	2.5	0.2	—	—	—	—	—	0.1	0.4	0.9	—	12.9	0.8	52.4	1.7	0.1	2.4	3.9

Source: 1989 census data in *Natsional'nyi sostav naseleniia SSSR* (1990). Some missing data for Jews, Tatars, and Germans (including subgroups of Jews and Tatars) taken from *Vestnik Statistiki*, No. 10, 1990, pp. 69-79, and also from the preliminary report *Natsional'nyi sostav naseleniia SSSR, Chast' II*, (1989). Figures from the latter do not always match revised estimates but the discrepancies appear to be small, with a total residual of less than one thousand.

Table 5. USSR: Changes in Nationality Composition by Republic, 1939-89

	Titular Nationality Change in percent			Russian Nationality Change in percent	
	1939-59	1959-79	1979-89	1959-79	1979-89
USSR	...	...	...	-2.2	-1.6
RSFSR	0.4	-0.7	-1.1	-0.7	-1.1
Ukraine	3.3	-3.1	-1.0	4.3	0.9
Belorussia	4.0	-1.6	-1.6	3.7	1.3
Estonia	-17.2	-9.9	-3.2	7.8	2.4
Latvia	-15.4	-8.3	-1.7	6.2	1.2
Lithuania	5.6	0.7	-0.4	0.4	0.5
Moldavia	-1.2	-1.4	0.5	2.7	0.1
Georgia	2.9	4.4	1.4	-1.8	-1.1
Armenia	5.2	1.7	3.6	-0.9	-0.7
Azerbaidzhan	9.1	10.7	4.5	-5.7	-2.3
Kazakhstan	-7.9	6.0	3.7	-1.9	-3.0
Turkmenistan	1.7	7.6	3.5	10.9	-3.1
Uzbekistan	-2.5	6.7	2.5	-2.7	-2.5
Tadzhikistan	-6.4	5.8	3.4	8.5	-2.8
Kirgizia	-11.2	7.5	4.4	13.1	-4.4

Source: Data for 1979 from *Naselenie SSSR 1987* (1988), pp. 101-106. Data for 1959 and 1989 from *Natsionalnyi sostav naseleniia SSSR*, 1990, pp. 5-15. Data for 1939 from *Trud v SSSR* (1988), p. 19. Errors of 0.1 percent may occur due to rounding.

Table 6. USSR: Territory and Population of Autonomous Republics, as of January 1, 1990

	Territory		Population		Density per sq. km.	Density urban
	1,000 sq. km.	Percent of USSR	In thousands	Percent of USSR		
USSR	22,403	100	288,624	100	12.9	66
In RSFSR:						
Bashkir	144	0.6	3,964	1.4	27.6	64
Buryat	351	1.6	1,049	0.4	3.0	62
Dagestan	50	0.2	1,823	0.6	36.2	44
Kabardino-Balkir ...	13	0.1	768	0.3	61.4	61
Kalmyk	76	0.3	325	0.1	4.3	46
Karelia	172	0.8	796	0.3	4.6	82
Komi	416	1.9	1,265	0.4	3.0	76
Mari	23	0.1	754	0.3	32.5	62
Mordvinian	26	0.1	964	0.3	36.8	57
North Osetian	8	—	638	0.2	79.8	69
Tatar	68	0.3	3,658	1.3	53.8	74
Tuva	171	0.8	314	0.1	1.8	47
Udmurt	42	0.2	1,619	0.6	38.5	70
Chechen-Ingush	19	0.1	1,290	0.4	66.8	41
Chuvash	18	0.1	1,340	0.5	73.2	59
Yakut	3,103	13.9	1,099	0.4	0.4	67
In Uzbekistan:						
Kara Kalpak	165	0.7	1,245	0.4	7.6	48
In Georgia:						
Abkhaz	9	—	538	0.2	62.6	48
Adzhar	3	—	382	0.1	127.3	48
In Azerbaidzhan:						
Nakhichevan	6	—	300	0.1	54.5	54

Source: Narkhoz 1989 (1990), pp. 19-24.

209

Table 7. USSR: Nationality Composition of Autonomous Republics, 1989
(In percent of total)

Autonomous Republic	Largest Titular Nationality	Host Republican Nationality	Other Nationalities
In RSFSR:			
Bashkir	21.9	39.3	38.3[1]
Buryat	24.0	69.9	6.0
Dagestan	27.5	9.2	63.3[2]
Kabardino/Balkar	48.2	31.9	19.8[3]
Kalmyk	45.3	37.7	17.0
Karelia	10.0	73.6	16.4
Komi	23.3	57.7	19.0
Mari	43.2	47.5	9.3
Mordvinian	32.5	60.8	6.6
North Osetian	52.9	29.9	17.2
Tatar	48.5	43.3	8.3
Tuva	64.3	32.0	3.7
Udmurt	30.9	58.9	10.2
Chechen-Ingush	57.8	23.1	19.1[4]
Chuvash	67.7	26.7	5.6
Yakut	33.4	50.3	16.3
In Uzbekistan:			
Karakalpak	32.1	32.8	35.2
In Georgia:			
Abkhaz	17.3	46.2	36.5
Adzhar	...[5]	82.8	17.2
In Azerbaidzhan:			
Nakhichevan	...[5]	95.9	4.1

Source: Natsionalnyi sostav naseleniia SSSR (1990).
1. Largest non-Russian nationality is Tatar, with 28.4 percent of total.
2. Total for all Daghestani nationalities is 80.1 percent.
3. Largest nationality is Kabardinian; Balkars are 9.4 percent.
4. Largest nationality is Chechen; Ingush are 12.9 percent.
5. No separate titular nationality.

Table 8. USSR: Territory, Population, and National Composition of Autonomous Oblasts and Autonomous Okrugs, 1989

	Area 1,000 sq. km.[1]	Population 1,000 [1]	Population Density per sq. km.[1]	Percent Urban [1]	Percent Largest Titular Nationality [2]
USSR	22,403	288,624	12.9	66	...
Autonomous oblasts					
In RSFSR:					
Gorno-Altai	93	194	2.1	27	31.0
Adyge	8	436	57.3	52	22.1
Khakass	62	573	9.3	73	11.1
Karachai-Cherkess	14	422	29.9	49	31.2
Jewish	36	218	6.1	66	4.2
In Georgia:					
South Osetian	4	99	25.4	51	66.2
In Azerbaidzhan:					
Nagorno-Karabakh	4	192	43.7	52	76.9
In Tadzhikistan:					
Gorno-Badakhshan	64	164	2.6	13	...[3]
Autonomous okrugs					
In RSFSR:					
Taimyr (Dolgo-Nenets)	862	55	—	67	8.9
Evenki	768	25	—	30	14.0
Nenets	177	55	0.3	62	11.9
Ust-Orda Buryat	22	137	6.1	19	36.3
Koryak	302	39	0.1	38	16.5
Chukchi	738	156	0.2	73	7.3
Komi-Permyatsk	33	160	4.9	30	60.2
Khanti-Mansi	523	1,301	2.5	91	0.9
Yamalo-Nenets	750	495	0.7	78	4.2
Aga-Buryat	19	77	4.1	33	54.9

Source: Narkhoz 1989 (1990), pp. 19-24, and *Natsionalnyi sostav naseleniia SSSR* (1990).
1. As of beginning of 1990.
2. From 1989 census.
3. No titular nationality.

Table 9. USSR: Soviet Oil Production (Including Natural Gas Liquids) by Republic, 1970-89

	1970	1975	1980	1985	1989	1970	1975	1980	1985	1989
	(In million metric tons) [1]					*(As percentage of total)*				
USSR	353	491	603	595	607	100	100	100	100	100
RSFSR, of which:	285	411	547	542	552	81	84	91	91	91
Siberia	31	151	316	371	409	9	31	52	62	67
Ukraine	14	13	8	6	5	4	3	1	1	1
Belorussia	4	8	3	2	2	1	2	—	—	—
Georgia	—	—	3	1	—	—	—	1	—	—
Azerbaidzhan	20	17	15	13	13	6	4	2	2	2
Kazakhstan	13	24	19	23	25	4	5	3	4	4
Turkmenistan	15	16	8	6	6	4	3	1	1	1
Uzbekistan	2	1	1	2	3	1	—	—	—	—
All Other	—	—	1	1	—	—	—	—	—	—

Sources: Promyshlennost' SSSR (1990), p. 136; *Promyshlennost' SSSR* (1988), p. 142; and Sagers (1990), p. 281.
1. 1 million metric tons/year = 20 thousand barrels/day.

Table 10. USSR: Natural Gas Production by Republic, 1970-89

	1970	1975	1980	1985	1989	1970	1975	1980	1985	1989
	(In billion cubic meters)					*(As percentage of total)*				
USSR	198	289	435	643	796	100	100	100	100	100
RSFSR, of which:	83	115	254	462	616	42	40	58	72	77
Siberia	11	40	162	383	542	5	14	37	60	68
Ukraine	61	69	57	43	31	31	24	13	7	4
Azerbaidzhan	6	10	14	14	11	3	3	3	2	1
Kazakhstan	2	5	4	6	7	1	2	1	1	1
Turkmenistan	13	52	71	83	41	7	18	16	13	5
Uzbekistan	32	37	35	35	90	16	13	8	5	11
All other	1	1	1	1	1	—	—	—	—	—

Sources: Promyshlennost' SSSR (1990), p. 139; *Promyshlennost' SSSR* (1988), p. 147; and Sagers (1990), p. 290.

Table 11. USSR: Coal Production by Republic, 1970-89

	1970	1975	1980	1985	1989	1970	1975	1980	1985	1989
	(In millions of metric tons)					*(As percentage of total)*				
USSR	624	701	716	726	740	100	100	100	100	100
RSFSR, of which:	345	381	391	395	410	55	54	55	54	55
Siberia	200	243	264	279	...	32	35	37	38	...
Ukraine	207	216	197	189	180	33	31	28	26	24
Kazakhstan	62	92	115	131	138	10	13	16	18	19
Uzbekistan	4	5	6	5	6	1	1	1	1	1
Kirgizia	4	4	4	4	4	1	1	1	1	1
All other	3	3	3	2	2	1	—	—	—	—

Sources: Narkhoz, various issues, and Sagers (1990), p. 298.

Table 12. USSR: Iron-Ore Production by Republic, 1970-89

	1970	1975	1980	1985	1989	1970	1975	1980	1985	1989
	(In million tons of usable ore)					*(As percentage of total)*				
USSR	197	235	245	248	241	100	100	100	100	100
RSFSR, of which:	67	89	92	104	107	34	38	38	42	44
Siberia	13	16	17	17	...	7	7	7	7	...
Ukraine	111	123	125	120	110	56	52	51	48	46
Azerbaidzhan	1	1	1	1	1	1	1	—	—	—
Kazakhstan	18	22	26	23	24	9	9	11	9	10
All other	—	—	1	—	—	—	—	—	—	—

Sources: Promyshlennost' SSSR (1990), p. 147; *Promyshlennost' SSSR* (1988), p. 155; and Sagers (1990), p. 391.

Table 13. USSR: Net Output by Sector by Republic, 1988

(As percent of total value added in sector)

	Total	Industry	Agriculture	Construction	Transport/ Commu- nication	Other
USSR	100.0	100.0	100.0	100.0	100.0	100.0
RSFSR	61.1	63.7	50.3	62.5	65.6	66.9
Ukraine	16.2	17.2	17.9	13.5	13.8	14.5
Belorussia	4.2	4.2	5.1	3.4	2.9	3.8
Estonia	0.6	0.7	0.7	0.6	0.7	0.6
Latvia	1.1	1.1	1.3	0.8	1.4	1.0
Lithuania	1.4	1.1	2.0	1.5	1.1	1.4
Moldavia	1.2	1.1	1.9	0.9	0.8	1.2
Georgia	1.6	1.5	2.1	1.6	1.0	1.4
Armenia	0.9	1.2	0.7	0.8	0.6	0.7
Azerbaidzhan	1.7	1.7	2.3	1.8	0.9	1.2
Kazakhstan	4.3	2.5	6.4	6.0	6.7	3.5
Turkmenistan	0.8	0.5	1.3	1.2	0.8	0.4
Uzbekistan	3.3	2.4	5.5	3.8	2.7	2.4
Tadzhikistan	0.8	0.6	1.3	0.9	0.5	0.6
Kirgizia	0.8	0.6	1.4	0.8	0.5	0.5

Source: Osnovnye pokazateli (1990), pp. 34-39.

Table 14. USSR: Per Capita Net Output by Sector by Republic, 1988

(USSR = 100)

	Total	Industry	Agriculture	Construction	Transport/ Commu- nication	Other
USSR	100	100	100	100	100	100
RSFSR	119	124	98	122	128	130
Ukraine	90	95	99	75	77	80
Belorussia	117	117	144	96	82	107
Estonia	117	121	124	101	125	107
Latvia	119	123	134	85	146	103
Lithuania	110	89	152	118	87	108
Moldavia	81	70	126	56	50	77
Georgia	86	79	113	86	54	76
Armenia	80	102	65	67	54	61
Azerbaidzhan	70	69	94	74	37	50
Kazakhstan	74	44	111	104	117	61
Turkmenistan	61	37	104	97	62	33
Uzbekistan	47	35	79	55	39	34
Tadzhikistan	43	31	70	50	27	34
Kirgizia	53	42	91	54	32	33

Sources: Osnovnye pokazateli (1990), pp. 34-39. Population at beginning of 1989 from *Narkhoz 1989* (1990), p. 17.

Table 15. USSR: NMP Growth Rates by Republic, 1971-89

(Average annual growth rates in percent)

	Total		Per Capita	
	1971-85	1986-89	1971-85	1986-89
USSR	4.4	2.7	3.5	1.7
RSFSR	4.4	2.5	3.7	1.8
Ukraine	3.8	3.0	3.3	2.6
Belorussia	6.2	3.8	5.5	3.1
Estonia	4.2	3.2	3.4	2.5
Latvia	4.2	3.9	3.6	3.3
Lithuania	4.1	6.0	3.2	5.1
Moldavia	4.1	3.6	3.1	2.2
Georgia	5.9	-0.1	5.2	-1.2
Armenia	6.9	1.9	4.9	2.0
Azerbaidzhan	6.4	0.7	4.6	-0.8
Kazakhstan	3.1	1.9	1.8	0.9
Turkmenistan	3.1	4.9	0.4	2.2
Uzbekistan	5.1	2.9	2.2	0.3
Tadzhikistan	4.4	3.2	1.4	0.0
Kirgizia	4.2	4.9	2.1	2.9

Sources: Growth rates 1971-85 from *Osnovnye pokazateli* (1990), pp. 29-30, 33. Growth rates for 1986-89 from *Narkhoz 1989* (1990), p. 13.

215

Table 16. USSR: Republican Share of Output for Major Industrial Products, 1989

(In percent)

Product	RSFSR	Ukrain.	Belor.	Eston.	Latvi.	Lithua.	Moldav.	Georg.	Armen.	Azerb.	Kazakh.	Turkmen.	Uzbek.	Tadzh.	Kirg.
Electric power	62.5	17.2	2.2	1.0	0.3	1.7	1.0	0.9	0.7	1.4	5.2	0.8	3.3	0.9	0.9
Cast iron	54.0	40.8	—	—	0.4	—	—	0.6	—	—	4.6	—	—	—	—
Steel	57.9	34.2	0.7	—	0.7	—	0.4	0.9	—	0.5	4.3	—	0.7	—	—
Rolled ferrous metal	57.1	34.5	0.6	—	—	—	0.4	1.0	—	0.6	4.3	—	0.8	—	—
Steel pipe	60.7	33.5	0.4	—	—	—	—	2.5	—	2.8	0.1	—	—	—	—
A.C. electric motors	22.6	35.8	13.5	2.3	—	4.6	1.9	2.5	7.7	3.9	—	—	1.8	3.8	3.4
Metal-cutting machines	46.6	22.6	10.4	—	—	6.6	—	1.4	5.5	0.6	1.6	—	—	—	0.9
Forging & stamping machines	66.0	25.3	1.8	—	0.1	—	—	—	1.1	—	2.8	—	2.1	—	—
Oil equipment	81.6	16.8	—	0.6	—	—	—	—	—	—	—	1.0	—	—	0.8
Chemical equipment & spare parts	63.1	28.5	1.1	0.4	—	0.1	0.7	0.1	—	0.3	—	—	3.9	0.3	—
Agricultural machinery	57.1	27.9	1.7	0.4	0.2	0.2	1.2	0.1	—	0.4	1.8	0.1	4.1	0.3	—
Equipment for livestock-raising & fodder production	31.6	28.8	23.0	4.5	4.2	2.6	0.4	0.1	0.2	—	6.2	—	—	—	—
Excavators	62.3	29.2	0.4	—	—	—	—	—	—	0.2	5.7	—	0.6	—	2.4
Electric hoists	50.7	22.6	0.9	—	—	—	—	—	—	1.9	1.4	—	2.2	—	—
Soda ash	73.7	26.3	—	—	—	—	—	—	—	—	0.6	—	25.2	—	—
Caustic soda	73.0	14.8	—	—	—	—	—	—	1.5	6.9	2.0	—	—	1.8	—
Mineral fertilizer (100 percent concentration)	51.1	15.0	18.3	0.6	0.5	1.8	—	0.5	—	0.8	5.0	0.5	5.6	0.3	—
Synthetic fibers	46.9	12.3	28.9	—	3.3	0.9	—	2.4	0.7	—	1.3	—	3.3	—	—
Tires	69.2	16.3	7.2	0.6	0.8	0.9	—	0.5	1.9	1.9	3.5	0.1	0.6	0.2	—
Lumber	82.0	8.2	3.3	1.5	2.2	1.9	0.3	0.4	0.1	0.2	2.0	—	0.4	—	0.2
Paper	84.6	5.6	3.2	0.8	0.5	2.4	—	1.1	0.2	0.7	—	—	4.4	0.8	—
Cement	60.2	16.7	1.6	0.8	1.0	1.3	1.6	0.4	1.2	0.9	6.2	0.8	4.8	1.0	1.0
Sheet rock	55.7	16.2	4.9	—	—	—	1.8	3.1	0.8	—	7.7	0.8	6.6	0.5	1.9
Roofing materials	56.8	15.3	7.1	—	—	2.4	—	—	—	—	6.6	1.6	—	—	—

Table 16 (Concluded). USSR: Republican Share of Output for Major Industrial Products, 1989

(In percent)

Product	RSFSR	Ukrain.	Belor.	Eston.	Latvi.	Lithua.	Moldav.	Georg.	Armen.	Azerb.	Kazakh.	Turkmen.	Uzbek.	Tadzh.	Kirg.
Bricks	53.8	22.6	5.0	0.6	1.0	2.4	0.5	0.6	—	0.3	5.4	1.1	4.7	0.7	1.3
Window glass	61.9	20.9	5.5	0.8	1.6	1.7	1.9	—	—	2.2	1.9	2.2	5.8	—	3.2
Cotton cloth	71.9	7.0	1.7	2.3	0.7	1.2	—	0.6	0.3	1.5	4.7	0.3	0.1	1.6	1.3
Woolen cloth	65.3	10.3	6.7	1.1	2.2	3.1	2.1	1.3	0.9	2.0	3.5	0.4	6.7	0.3	1.6
Silk cloth	50.4	14.1	10.0	0.5	1.3	2.4	2.0	2.2	0.9	1.4	3.9	0.4	5.4	3.5	0.6
Hosiery	40.2	20.3	8.3	0.8	3.7	5.0	3.5	1.5	2.3	2.0	6.4	0.9	5.7	2.1	1.6
Knitted garments	39.2	18.3	8.0	1.2	2.2	3.2	2.8	2.9	4.7	2.2	4.3	0.6	—	0.8	1.1
Shoes (except rubber & felt)	45.7	23.4	5.4	0.9	1.2	1.4	1.2	2.0	2.2	2.1	0.6	—	5.3	1.3	1.4
Radios	65.0	6.7	10.3	—	17.4	6.2	1.9	0.7	—	—	—	—	—	—	—
Televisions, all	44.9	35.9	11.1	—	—	4.6	—	1.0	—	—	—	—	—	—	—
Televisions, color	37.4	37.7	17.4	—	—	3.3	—	—	1.7	—	—	—	—	—	—
Tape recorders	51.9	31.7	2.0	—	1.7	—	2.2	—	—	—	2.8	—	—	—	2.7
Refrigerators & freezers	55.6	13.6	11.1	—	3.2	5.5	5.4	—	—	—	—	—	3.0	2.6	—
Vacuum cleaners	78.6	17.8	—	—	—	3.6	—	—	—	—	—	—	—	—	—
Electric irons	53.2	29.6	0.1	—	8.2	—	—	—	—	—	3.1	2.7	—	3.7	3.1
Washing machines	67.2	9.7	0.3	—	4.2	—	7.5	—	—	—	4.0	1.8	—	—	9.1
Bicycles, adult's	61.5	14.9	15.2	—	—	—	—	—	—	—	0.9	—	—	—	—
Bicycles, children's	60.2	19.9	5.8	—	4.0	2.6	—	—	—	—	7.5	—	—	—	—
Motorcycles & mopeds	68.4	—	—	—	—	—	—	—	—	—	—	—	—	—	—
Furniture	56.3	18.7	5.7	2.2	2.1	2.3	1.9	1.3	1.0	1.1	3.4	0.2	2.7	0.5	0.6
Sugar	31.6	52.6	2.7	—	1.9	1.8	3.3	0.2	—	—	2.8	—	—	—	3.1
Meat products	50.1	21.3	6.8	1.4	1.9	3.4	1.9	0.8	0.5	0.7	7.3	0.3	2.1	0.5	1.0
Fish & other sea products	74.0	10.1	0.2	3.6	4.9	3.7	0.1	1.3	0.1	0.5	0.8	0.5	0.2	—	—
Lard	47.3	25.4	9.1	1.8	2.7	4.5	1.7	0.1	—	0.3	4.8	0.2	0.9	0.4	0.8
Vegetable oil	34.7	33.2	0.8	—	0.4	—	3.6	0.3	0.2	1.5	2.8	3.3	15.8	2.9	0.5
Canned goods	39.1	23.3	3.8	1.7	2.4	2.0	8.3	3.4	1.9	3.5	2.1	0.4	5.5	1.8	0.8
Memorandum: Share of population	51.3	18.0	3.6	0.5	0.9	1.3	1.5	1.9	1.1	2.5	5.8	1.3	7.0	1.8	1.5

Source: Narkhoz 1989 (1990), pp. 17, 338-339.

Table 17. USSR: Republican Share of Output of Major Agricultural Products, 1986-89 (Average)

(In percent)

	RSFSR	Ukrain.	Belor.	Eston.	Latvi.	Lithua.	Moldav.	Georg.	Armen.	Azerb.	Kazakh.	Turkmen.	Uzbek.	Tadzh.	Kirg.	Residual
Grain	52.9	24.3	3.5	0.4	0.8	1.6	1.3	0.3	0.1	0.6	12.0	0.2	0.9	0.2	0.9	—
Cotton (incl. seeds)	—	—	—	—	—	—	—	—	—	8.0	3.8	15.3	61.1	11.0	0.9	—
Sugar beets	37.6	54.2	1.8	—	0.4	—	2.9	0.1	0.1	1.1	1.7	—	—	—	—	—
Sunflower seeds	49.4	44.4	—	—	—	—	4.1	0.1	—	—	1.8	—	—	—	—	0.1
Flax	37.3	30.2	26.7	0.3	1.4	4.1	—	—	—	—	—	—	—	—	—	—
Potatoes	49.8	24.5	14.8	1.2	1.7	2.5	0.5	0.5	0.3	0.2	2.8	—	0.4	0.3	0.4	—
Vegetables	39.0	26.2	3.0	0.5	0.7	1.2	4.5	2.1	1.9	3.0	4.3	1.3	8.9	1.8	1.8	—
Grapes	12.2	13.0	—	—	—	—	19.2	10.7	3.2	23.0	1.9	2.6	10.5	3.0	0.7	4.2
Citrus fruits	—	—	—	—	—	—	—	95.8	—	—	—	—	—	—	—	—
Other fruits/berries	27.7	26.5	5.2	0.5	0.8	1.7	11.3	6.9	2.0	4.5	2.6	0.5	6.3	2.2	1.3	—
Meat	49.8	22.4	5.9	1.2	1.8	2.8	1.8	0.9	0.6	1.0	7.5	0.5	2.2	0.6	1.1	—
Milk	51.1	22.7	6.9	1.2	1.9	3.0	1.4	0.7	0.5	1.0	5.0	0.4	2.6	0.5	1.0	—
Eggs	57.5	20.9	4.2	0.7	1.1	1.5	1.4	1.1	0.7	1.3	5.0	0.4	2.7	0.7	0.8	—
Wool	47.7	6.3	0.3	—	0.1	—	0.6	1.4	0.8	2.4	22.8	3.4	5.2	1.1	7.9	—
Memorandum: Share of population	51.3	18.0	3.6	0.5	0.9	1.3	1.5	1.9	1.1	2.5	5.8	1.3	7.0	1.8	1.5	

Source: Narkhoz 1989 (1990), pp. 436-452, 467-470.

Table 18. USSR: Fixed Assets in the Material Sphere of Production by Republic [1]

(Including livestock)

| | Fixed Assets at end of 1989 | | Average Annual Growth Rates in Percent | | | |
| | As percent of USSR total | Per capita as percent of USSR average | Total | | Per Capita | |
			1971-85	1986-89	1971-85	1986-89
USSR	100.0	100	7.5	4.7	6.6	3.8
RSFSR	61.8	120	7.7	5.0	7.0	4.3
Ukraine	15.2	85	6.6	3.5	6.1	3.0
Belorussia	3.4	96	8.6	5.3	7.9	4.7
Estonia	0.7	126	6.3	4.5	5.6	3.8
Latvia	1.1	114	6.6	4.3	6.0	3.7
Lithuania	1.4	111	7.2	6.1	6.4	5.3
Moldavia	1.1	70	8.2	4.1	7.3	2.9
Georgia	1.4	73	6.6	4.0	5.9	3.0
Armenia	0.8	70	8.0	4.7	6.1	5.2
Azerbaidzhan	1.5	62	6.9	4.0	5.2	2.4
Kazakhstan	5.9	102	7.3	5.1	6.0	4.0
Turkmenistan	1.0	76	9.2	4.5	6.6	1.9
Uzbekistan	3.3	47	8.9	3.7	6.1	1.3
Tadzhikistan	0.7	38	7.8	5.2	4.8	2.2
Kirgizia	0.7	49	7.5	3.7	5.5	1.8

Sources: Narkhoz 1989 (1990), pp. 278; *Narkhoz 1988* (1989), p. 262; *Osnovnye pokazateli* (1990), pp. 57, 59. Population figures from *Narkhoz 1989* (1990), p. 17, and *Naselenie SSSR* 1987 (1988), pp. 8-15.
1. In comparable prices, without adjustment for wear and tear.

Table 19. USSR: Sectoral Distribution of Employment by Republic, 1987

	Industry/ Construction	Agriculture/ Forestry	Transport/ Communication	Trade/ Catering	Health/ Science/ Education/ Art	Other
USSR	38	19	9	8	18	8
RSFSR	42	14	9	8	19	8
Ukraine	40	20	7	8	17	8
Belorussia	40	22	7	8	16	7
Estonia	42	13	9	9	18	9
Latvia	40	15	9	9	17	10
Lithuania	41	18	8	8	17	8
Moldavia	28	35	7	7	17	6
Georgia	29	27	9	7	20	8
Armenia	39	19	7	6	21	8
Azerbaidzhan	26	34	8	7	18	7
Kazakhstan	31	23	11	8	19	8
Turkmenistan	21	41	8	6	17	7
Uzbekistan	24	38	7	6	19	6
Tadzhikistan	21	42	7	6	17	7
Kirgizia	27	34	7	7	18	7

Source: Trud v SSSR (1988), pp. 16-17.

Table 20. USSR: Labor Force by Employment Status by Republic, 1988

(In percent of total for republic)

	Total Labor Resources	Employed Total	Employed in State enterprises	Employed in Collective farms	Employed in Private activity	Students	Other [1]
USSR	100	85	75	7	3	7	8
RSFSR	100	86	80	5	2	7	7
Ukraine	100	86	72	12	2	7	7
Belorussia	100	87	74	11	1	7	6
Estonia	100	85	76	8	2	7	8
Latvia	100	87	76	9	2	7	7
Lithuania	100	86	73	10	2	8	7
Moldavia	100	87	67	13	7	7	6
Georgia	100	88	74	8	6	7	5
Armenia	100	81	70	3	8	8	12
Azerbaidzhan	100	70	56	8	6	8	22
Kazakhstan	100	81	75	3	3	8	11
Turkmenistan	100	82	52	19	11	9	9
Uzbekistan	100	76	55	11	11	10	14
Tadzhikistan	100	77	53	11	14	10	13
Kirgizia	100	80	62	9	9	10	11

Source: Statisticheskie materialy (1989), p. 30.
1. Includes housewives, soldiers, religious functionaries, and the unemployed.

Table 21. USSR: Gender Composition of Labor Force by Republic, 1989

(Percent of females in category)

	Workers/ employees	Collective farmers	Specialists with higher education	Specialists without higher education
USSR	51	44	55	65
RSFSR	52	39	57	67
Ukraine	52	45	55	66
Belorussia	53	43	56	67
Estonia	55	47	57	63
Latvia	55	41	60	66
Lithuania	53	46	55	64
Moldavia	53	46	56	67
Georgia	47	49	52	62
Armenia	48	47	50	60
Azerbaidzhan	43	53	44	48
Kazakhstan	49	36	56	66
Turkmenistan	42	55	43	55
Uzbekistan	43	54	47	55
Tadzhikistan	39	52	38	47
Kirgizia	49	43	56	62

Source: Narkhoz 1989 (1990), pp. 56-59.

Table 22. USSR: Employment in Cooperatives by Republic, 1988-90

	Primary Employment in Cooperatives as Percent of Labor Force		Including Part-Time Employment January 1, 1990
	Average 1988	January 1, 1990	
USSR	0.4	2.0	3.1
RSFSR	0.4	2.2	3.3
Ukraine	0.4	1.7	2.8
Belorussia	0.3	1.2	2.1
Estonia	0.7	2.1	4.7
Latvia	0.5	4.6	8.8
Lithuania	0.5	1.9	3.8
Moldavia	0.6	2.4	3.7
Georgia	0.6	3.2	4.6
Armenia	2.1	4.4	7.4
Azerbaidzhan	0.3	1.2	1.7
Kazakhstan	0.5	1.9	2.6
Turkmenistan	0.1	1.4	1.9
Uzbekistan	0.5	1.9	2.7
Tadzhikistan	0.3	1.4	1.8
Kirgizia	0.5	1.4	1.9

Sources: Narkhoz 1989 (1990), pp. 19-24, 52, 269; and *Statisticheskie materialy* (1989), p. 30.

Table 23. USSR: Training Levels by Republic, January 1989
(Per 10,000 inhabitants)[1]

	Specialists		Scientists [2]	
	All	With higher education	All	Doctors/ candidates
USSR	1272	553	53	19
RSFSR	1396	589	70	24
Ukraine	1319	569	42	16
Belorussia	1408	627	43	15
Estonia	1451	643	45	22
Latvia	1335	607	52	21
Lithuania	1443	623	42	19
Moldavia	1091	476	24	12
Georgia	1091	643	53	24
Armenia	1175	654	66	25
Azerbaidzhan	864	455	32	16
Kazakhstan	1112	464	25	10
Turkmenistan	781	363	16	8
Uzbekistan	817	386	20	9
Tadzhikistan	668	343	18	7
Kirgizia	889	417	24	9

Source: Nauchno-tekhnicheskii progress v SSSR (1990), pp. 23-24; *Narkhoz 1989* (1990), pp. 17, 58.
1. Includes relatively small numbers of social scientists and humanities scholars.
2. A Soviet rank of "candidate" roughly corresponds to a North American Ph.D, while a Soviet doctorate is typically awarded only to senior scholars.

Table 24. USSR: Number of Scientific Workers by Nationality, End-1987
(Per 10,000 nationals in 1989)

	Total	Doctor/ Candidate
USSR	53	19
Titular republican nationalities		
Russian	71	22
Ukrainian	39	14
Belorussian	38	13
Estonian	61	31
Latvian	51	23
Lithuanian	44	21
Moldavian	16	8
Georgian	67	32
Armenian	70	28
Azeri	29	15
Kazakh	23	10
Turkmen	13	7
Uzbek	14	7
Tadzhik	12	6
Kirgiz	18	8
Ten largest other nationalities		
Tatar	32	11
German	...	...
Chuvash	19	7
Bashkir	22	9
Jewish	424	216
Mordvinian	17	6
Polish	...	...
Chechen	5	3
Udmurt	15	4
Mari	8	3
All other	29	14

Sources: Nauchno-tekhnicheskii progress v SSSR (1990), pp. 21, 25-27. Population from Narkhoz 1989 (1990), p. 17.

Table 25. USSR: National Composition of Workers and Employees[1] by Republic, 1989
(In percent)

			Share of Non-Titular Nationalities		
	Total Economy	Agriculture	Industry	Transport/ Communication	Construction	Trade/ Catering
RSFSR	18	25	17	15	22	16
Ukraine	30	21	32	29	31	27
Belorussia	22	11	23	22	24	19
Estonia	41	16	57	53	39	38
Latvia	52	31	62	62	54	51
Lithuania	24	16	29	33	19	21
Moldavia	41	21	52	46	48	45
Georgia	28	23	39	32	30	30
Armenia	7	15	7	4	5	6
Azerbaidzhan	22	10	31	26	27	22
Kazakhstan	67	48	79	72	79	71
Turkmenistan	41	19	47	52	46	35
Uzbekistan	39	24	47	45	50	34
Tadzhikistan	46	37	52	43	52	39
Kirgizia	59	31	75	65	74	66

Source: Trud v SSSR (1988), pp. 22-23.
1. Not including collective farmers and private producers.

Table 26. USSR: Republican Trade[1] in Relation to Value Added, 1988

(In domestic prices)

	Exports			Trade Balance		
	Inter-republican	Abroad	Total	Inter-republican	Abroad	Total
	(As percent of GDP)[2]					
USSR	21.1	5.4	26.5	—	-5.8	-5.8
	(As percent of NMP)					
USSR	29.3	7.5	36.8	—	-8.0	-8.0
RSFSR	18.0	8.6	26.6	0.1	-8.7	-8.6
Ukraine	39.1	6.7	45.8	3.5	-6.4	-2.9
Belorussia	69.6	6.5	76.1	15.5	-7.5	7.9
Estonia	66.5	7.4	73.9	-8.2	-10.2	-18.4
Latvia	64.1	5.7	69.8	-1.7	-8.2	-9.9
Lithuania	60.9	5.9	66.9	-9.1	-8.1	-17.2
Moldavia	62.1	3.4	65.5	-2.4	-10.8	-13.2
Georgia	53.7	3.9	57.6	2.8	-8.6	-5.8
Armenia	63.7	1.4	65.1	-5.8	-13.4	-19.2
Azerbaidzhan	58.7	3.7	62.3	19.2	-9.1	10.2
Kazakhstan	30.9	3.0	33.8	-19.9	-7.1	-27.0
Turkmenistan	50.7	4.2	54.9	-2.0	-3.9	-6.0
Uzbekistan	43.2	7.4	50.5	-8.0	-0.8	-8.9
Tadzhikistan	41.8	6.9	48.7	-20.8	-2.8	-23.7
Kirgizia	50.2	1.2	51.4	-8.7	-14.3	-23.1

Sources: Osnovnye pokazateli (1990), pp. 4, 34-39, 43, 44; *Narkhoz 1989* (1990), p. 634.
1. Trade figures exclude "non-productive" services.
2. GDP figures are not available on a republican basis.

Table 27. USSR: Adjustments to Trade Balances of the Republics, 1988[1]

	Unadjusted Balance (1)	Turnover Tax (2)	Consumer Subsidies (3)	Trade by Visitors (4)	Adjusted Balance (5)= {(1)+(2)+ (3)+(4)}	World Prices (6)	Balance Adjusted for Foreign prices (7)= {(1)+(6)}
			(In billions of rubles)				
USSR	-50.4	—	—	—	-50.4	52.3	1.9
RSFSR	-33.3	-3.4	-5.1	0.1	-41.7	64.1	30.8
Ukraine	-2.9	-1.2	1.6	-0.4	-2.9	—	-2.9
Belorussia	2.1	-1.1	1.7	0.6	3.3	-4.2	-2.1
Estonia	-0.7	-0.1	0.2	0.3	-0.3	-0.6	-1.3
Latvia	-0.7	-0.2	0.4	0.5	—	-0.6	-1.3
Lithuania	-1.5	-0.4	0.8	0.5	-0.6	-2.2	-3.7
Moldavia	-1.0	0.9	0.3	0.6	0.8	-1.6	-2.6
Georgia	-0.6	0.6	-0.3	-0.7	-1.0	-1.3	-1.9
Armenia	-1.1	0.2	-0.3	-0.2	-1.4	-0.3	-1.4
Azerbaidzhan	1.1	1.8	-0.4	-0.4	2.1	-1.6	-0.5
Kazakhstan	-7.3	0.2	1.0	-0.5	-6.6	0.7	-6.6
Turkmenistan	-0.3	0.5	0.1	-0.2	0.1	0.3	—
Uzbekistan	-1.8	1.5	—	-0.4	-0.8	-0.7	-2.5
Tadzhikistan	-1.1	0.4	-0.1	0.2	-0.6	-0.1	-1.1
Kirgizia	-1.1	0.3	0.1	—	0.7	-0.1	-1.0
			(As percent of NMP)				
USSR	-8.0	—	—	—	-8.0	8.3	0.3
RSFSR	-8.6	-0.9	-1.3	—	-10.8	16.6	8.0
Ukraine	-2.9	-1.2	1.6	-0.4	-2.9	—	-2.8
Belorussia	7.9	-4.2	6.5	2.3	12.5	-16.0	-8.0
Estonia	-18.4	-2.5	4.9	7.4	-8.6	-14.8	-33.2
Latvia	-9.9	-2.8	5.7	7.1	0.1	-8.5	-18.4
Lithuania	-17.2	-4.5	9.0	5.6	-7.1	-24.3	-41.5
Moldavia	-13.2	11.7	3.9	7.8	10.1	-20.2	-33.4
Georgia	-5.8	5.9	-2.9	-6.8	-9.7	-12.8	-18.6
Armenia	-19.2	3.5	-5.2	-3.5	-24.4	-4.8	-24.0
Azerbaidzhan	10.2	16.5	-3.7	-3.7	19.3	-14.7	-4.5
Kazakhstan	-27.0	0.7	3.7	-1.9	-24.4	2.6	-24.4
Turkmenistan	-6.0	10.6	2.1	-4.2	2.4	6.3	0.3
Uzbekistan	-8.9	7.2	0.0	-1.9	-3.6	-3.2	-12.1
Tadzhikistan	-23.7	8.4	-2.1	4.2	-13.2	1.3	-22.4
Kirgizia	-23.1	6.0	2.0	0.1	-15.0	2.2	-20.9

Source: Vestnik statistiki, Nos. 3 and 4, 1990.
  Explanation of columns:
  (1) Net trade balance in existing domestic prices.
  (2) Change in trade balance if turnover tax were reallocated in proportion to labor expenditures incurred in production.
  (3) Change in trade balance if consumer subsidies were charged to consuming republic.
  (4) Change in trade balance if adjusted for sales and purchases by visitors to republic.
  (6) Change in trade balance if revalued at world market prices.
1. Combined trade balance with other republics and in foreign trade.

Table 28. USSR: Interrepublican and Foreign Trade Balances by Republic, 1987

(In billions of rubles)

	At Domestic Prices [1]			At World Market Prices [2]		
	Inter-republican	Abroad	Total	Inter-republican	Abroad	Total
USSR	—	-50.4	-50.4	—	7.7	7.7
RSFSR	3.6	-32.4	-28.8	28.5	12.8	41.3
Ukraine	1.6	-7.7	-6.2	-3.9	-1.5	-5.4
Belorussia	3.1	-2.0	1.2	-2.2	-0.2	-2.5
Estonia	-0.2	-0.4	-0.7	-1.1	-0.2	-1.4
Latvia	-0.3	-0.6	-0.9	-1.4	-0.3	-1.7
Lithuania	-0.4	-0.7	-1.1	-3.3	-0.2	-3.5
Moldavia	0.6	-0.9	-0.3	-1.5	-0.4	-1.9
Georgia	0.6	-0.9	-0.3	-1.5	-0.2	-1.8
Armenia	0.6	-0.7	-0.1	-0.3	-0.3	-0.5
Azerbaidzhan	2.0	-0.8	1.2	0.2	-0.3	—
Kazakhstan	-5.4	-2.1	-7.5	-6.6	-1.1	-7.7
Turkmenistan	-0.3	-0.2	-0.5	—	-0.1	-0.1
Uzbekistan	-3.9	-0.1	-4.0	-4.5	0.1	-4.4
Tadzhikistan	-1.1	-0.1	-1.2	-1.4	0.1	-1.3
Kirgizia	-0.5	-0.7	-1.2	-1.0	-0.4	-1.4

1. *Osnovnye pokazateli* (1990), p. 41.
2. *Ekonomika i zhizn'*, No. 10, 1990.

Table 29. USSR: Interrepublican Trade Balances by Sector by Republic, 1988

(In millions of domestic rubles)

	Residual [1]	RSFSR	Ukrain.	Belor.	Eston.	Latvi.	Lithua.	Moldav.	Georg.	Armen.	Azerb.	Kazakh.	Turkmen.	Uzbek.	Tadzh.	Kirg.
Total	—	260	3,624	4,050	-332	-118	-808	-186	290	-335	2,099	-5,349	-97	-1,667	-997	-435
Industry	-882	3,833	1,966	4,079	-299	-274	-837	-388	246	-243	1912	-6,691	-211	-2,517	-983	-476
Electric power	-104	-36	2	-110	101	-59	73	-2	-51	22	7	-145	50	-11	7	48
Oil and gas	-1,347	5,868	-3,574	-644	-256	-483	-741	-514	-375	-437	544	-455	650	-349	-279	-303
Coal & other fuel	81	255	-41	-60	11	-3	-23	-136	-12	-17	-7	159	-7	-23	-7	-10
Ferrous metals	-1,087	-996	3,757	-1,131	-133	-297	-340	-259	-148	-252	-192	-148	-104	-541	-124	-179
Non-ferrous metals	12	1,459	-983	-337	-80	-123	-172	-157	-60	-29	2	241	-4	104	110	41
Chemicals	-748	2,064	-895	275	-139	4	-408	-392	-194	53	133	-496	-50	-163	-226	-314
Machine-building	1,842	6,266	2,632	2,958	-462	-300	-404	-679	-623	-106	-153	-3,870	-881	-1,949	-576	-10
Wood and paper	304	3,381	-1,167	72	47	-6	26	-118	-164	-98	-134	-747	-103	-483	-100	-103
Building materials	161	401	385	-8	-10	-15	-18	-37	-99	-26	-58	-142	-33	-105	-24	-52
Light industry	1,335	-5,168	-2,299	2,351	292	296	615	347	381	621	871	-138	721	1,786	479	180
Food-processing	-1,494	-10,537	4,318	658	343	677	620	1,557	1,621	-10	912	-745	-339	-649	-178	258
Other industry	163	877	-171	55	-14	34	-66	3	-29	36	-15	-205	-113	-133	-65	-33
Agriculture	181	-3,617	1,432	52	-28	-14	29	219	63	-95	182	1,356	109	469	-22	43
Other material sphere	702	45	226	-81	-6	170	—	-18	-20	3	5	-14	5	381	7	-2

Source: Vestnik Statistiki, No. 3, 1990.

1. Residual calculated as sum of republican balances.

Table 30. Foreign Trade Balances by Sector by Republic, 1988

(In millions of domestic rubles)

	USSR	RSFSR	Ukrain.	Belor.	Eston.	Latvi.	Lithua.	Moldav.	Georg.	Armen.	Azerb.	Kazakh.	Turkmen.	Uzbek.	Tadzh.	Kirg.
Total	-50,431	-33,588	-6551	-1,977	-416	-578	-722	-837	-882	-775	-990	-1,906	-187	-174	-136	-714
Industry	-41,812	-28,054	-5549	-1,382	-281	-463	-520	-724	-754	-671	-800	-1,706	-177	9	-78	-663
Electric power	742	101	525	21	-10	—	—	94	11	—	—	—	—	—	—	—
Oil & gas	9,746	8,664	357	338	2	—	178	—	62	—	142	13	—	-10	—	—
Coal & other fuel	925	424	573	-12	-7	-24	-35	-1	—	—	—	6	—	—	—	—
Ferrous metals	308	-1,005	1407	-49	-13	2	-22	1	34	-5	-89	99	-8	-23	-12	-8
Non-ferrous metals	552	344	-120	-50	—	—	-5	-22	2	—	13	292	—	-10	92	16
Chemicals	-3,787	-2,649	-538	-79	-61	-53	-59	-98	-31	-50	-72	-51	-7	4	-23	-20
Machine-building	-18,724	-14,981	-1996	-375	-114	25	-220	-154	-62	-54	-147	-548	-21	-41	-6	-31
Wood & paper	845	1,712	-395	-55	16	14	5	-38	-27	-31	-42	-166	-26	-87	-21	-15
Building materials	-634	-410	-63	-19	-6	1	-2	-13	-22	-20	-14	-27	-4	-25	-7	-4
Light industry	-19,047	-12,422	-3417	-759	-110	-245	-247	-406	-326	-237	-324	-890	11	584	-1	-258
Food-processing	-12,199	-7,418	-1768	-402	24	-175	-108	-86	-387	-267	-260	-414	-119	-379	-97	-343
Other industry	-539	-415	-114	59	-1	-9	-5	-1	-8	-7	-7	-20	-3	-6	-2	-1
Agriculture	-8,382	-5,291	-1023	-546	-124	-136	-202	-114	-132	-102	-196	-201	-20	-185	-59	-52
Other material sphere	-236	-243	22	-48	-11	21	—	1	4	-2	6	1	10	2	—	—

Source: Vestnik Statistiki, No. 3, 1990.

229

Table 31. USSR: Average Monthly Salaries by Republic, 1989

	Workers and Employees			Collective Farmers		
	In 1989 relative to USSR average	Annual growth rate in percent		In 1989 relative to USSR average	Annual growth rate in percent	
		1981-85	1986-89		1981-85	1986-89
USSR	100	2.4	6.0	100	5.3	7.0
RSFSR	108	2.5	6.4	110	6.0	7.5
Ukraine	91	2.3	5.8	92	5.5	8.0
Belorussia	95	3.0	7.0	105	8.7	8.1
Estonia	112	2.7	5.9	158	5.7	3.9
Latvia	104	2.7	6.3	132	7.0	5.6
Lithuania	102	2.7	6.5	128	6.5	8.8
Moldavia	83	2.7	6.2	98	7.0	8.4
Georgia	82	2.9	4.2	85	5.7	3.9
Armenia	91	2.0	5.1	102	5.1	3.7
Azerbaidzhan	74	1.8	2.4	91	4.7	-3.2
Kazakhstan	97	2.2	5.8	105	3.6	6.0
Turkmenistan	92	1.6	3.7	102	1.2	5.9
Uzbekistan	81	1.1	4.2	82	—	6.1
Tadzhikistan	78	1.6	4.5	83	1.6	4.3
Kirgizia	82	1.9	5.0	99	6.4	5.5

Source: Narkhoz 1989 (1990), pp. 78-79.

Table 32. USSR: Dependency Ratios[1] by Republic, 1989
(In percent)

	Child	Old Age	Both
USSR	49.0	30.7	79.7
RSFSR	43.0	32.5	75.5
Ukraine	41.2	37.9	79.1
Belorussia	43.7	34.9	78.6
Estonia	42.1	35.9	78.0
Latvia	40.2	36.7	76.9
Lithuania	42.4	33.3	75.6
Moldavia	53.6	27.8	81.4
Georgia	46.8	30.9	77.7
Armenia	57.0	20.8	77.8
Azerbaidzhan	62.6	18.0	80.6
Kazakhstan	61.1	20.1	81.2
Turkmenistan	85.9	15.2	101.1
Uzbekistan	87.5	16.3	103.8
Tadzhikistan	95.3	16.0	111.2
Kirgizia	78.4	20.2	98.6

Source: Census data from Goskomstat.

1. Dependency ratio is calculated as the population in specified age group divided by the working-age population, where the latter is defined as men aged 16-59 plus women aged 16-54. To the extent that people outside these age groups work, the calculated dependency ratio is an overestimate of the true value.

Table 33.   USSR: Income Per Capita by Republic, 1975-88

(As percent of the USSR average)

	1975	1980	1985	1988
USSR	100	100	100	100
RSFSR	109	110	109	110
Ukraine	92	91	96	96
Belorussia	96	98	102	102
Estonia	128	131	128	133
Latvia	123	123	121	123
Lithuania	114	110	108	114
Moldavia	79	81	82	84
Georgia	83	88	99	108
Armenia	76	80	82	86
Azerbaidzhan	63	64	68	71
Kazakhstan	92	93	91	93
Turkmenistan	77	73	71	71
Uzbekistan	66	67	64	62
Tadzhikistan	61	58	55	54
Kirgizia	73	70	70	72

Source: Sotsial'noe razvitie SSSR (1990), p. 119.

Table 34.   USSR: Savings Deposits Per Capita by Republic, End-1989

(As percent of USSR overall average)

	Savings Deposits (overall)	Of which:	
		Urban	Rural
USSR	100	115	70
RSFSR	111	115	98
Ukraine	123	134	99
Belorussia	127	135	111
Estonia	126	144	81
Latvia	114	126	87
Lithuania	158	188	94
Moldavia	77	109	49
Georgia	108	166	35
Armenia	131	160	73
Azerbaidzhan	36	58	10
Kazakhstan	63	75	47
Turkmenistan	35	63	13
Uzbekistan	30	63	8
Tadzhikistan	27	67	9
Kirgizia	39	74	18

Source: Finansy SSSR 1989 (1990), p. 13.

Table 35. USSR: Social Indicators by Republic, 1989

	Average Family Size (number)	Crude Birth Rate (per 1,000)	Crude Death Rate (per 1,000)	Natural Growth Rate (per 1,000)	Infant Mortality Rate (per 1,000)	Life Expectancy at Birth (Years)	Diagnosed Alcoholism (per 1,000)	Doctors (per 10,000)	Hospital Beds (per 10,000)	Abortions (1988) (per 1,000 women aged 15-49)	Sports Establishments (1987) (per 1,000)
USSR	3.5	17.6	10.0	7.6	22.7	69.5	14.9	44.4	133	82	102
RSFSR	3.2	14.6	10.7	3.9	17.8	69.6	19.1	47.3	139	105	110
Ukraine	3.2	13.3	11.6	1.7	13.0	70.9	15.2	43.9	135	62	102
Belorussia	3.2	15.0	10.1	4.9	11.8	71.8	13.2	40.6	135	54	146
Estonia	3.1	15.4	11.7	3.7	14.7	70.6	8.5	48.3	122	77	80
Latvia	3.1	14.5	12.1	2.4	11.1	70.4	16.5	50.0	147	77	94
Lithuania	3.2	15.1	10.3	4.8	10.7	71.8	12.9	45.7	126	38	95
Moldavia	3.4	18.9	9.2	9.7	20.4	69.0	14.9	40.1	127	88	99
Georgia	4.1	16.7	8.6	8.1	19.6	72.1	1.6	58.5	110	57	95
Armenia	4.7	21.6	6.0	15.6	20.4	72.0	1.1	42.7	90	30	66
Azerbaidzhan	4.8	26.4	6.4	20.0	26.2	70.6	1.5	39.0	100	22	71
Kazakhstan	4.0	23.0	7.6	15.4	25.9	68.7	12.0	40.9	136	72	116
Turkmenistan	5.6	35.0	7.7	27.3	54.7	65.2	4.2	35.5	111	43	49
Uzbekistan	5.5	33.3	6.3	27.0	37.7	69.2	4.4	35.8	123	51	66
Tadzhikistan	6.1	38.7	6.5	32.2	43.2	69.4	3.4	28.5	105	39	47
Kirgizia	4.7	30.4	7.2	23.2	32.2	68.5	6.8	36.6	119	68	62

Sources: Narkhoz 1989, (1990), pp. 37, 38, 41, 43, 225, 230, 234; and Sotsial'noe razvitie SSSR (1990), p. 272, 282.

232

Table 36. USSR: Urban and Rural Housing Conditions by Republic, 1989
(Relative to all USSR = 100)

	Overall	Urban	Rural
USSR	100	97	106
RSFSR	102	97	114
Ukraine	111	103	129
Belorussia	111	96	140
Estonia	136	125	164
Latvia	124	111	155
Lithuania	121	106	152
Moldavia	111	89	131
Georgia	116	103	134
Armenia	92	85	107
Azerbaidzhan	74	77	70
Kazakhstan	89	91	85
Turkmenistan	65	71	66
Uzbekistan	75	77	73
Tadzhikistan	58	74	51
Kirgizia	75	76	74

Source: Derived from *Narkhoz 1989* (1990), p. 170, on the basis of square meters of total usable space per person.

233

Part III

Macroeconomic Policies
and Reform

Chapter III.1

Structural Fiscal Issues

1. INTRODUCTION

The evolution of the public finances in the USSR has been dominated for decades by allocative and distributional concerns, with little weight attached to macroeconomic stability considerations. In the traditional system, the state budget and the centralized funds of branch ministries effected a massive reallocation of resources among state enterprises, in accordance with the dictates of the national economic plan. At the same time, the elaborate system of product-specific turnover taxes and subsidies resulted in a large and growing redistribution of resources among households. The planned environment—involving guaranteed job security, wage, price and external trade controls—virtually obviated the use of fiscal instruments for macroeconomic stabilization. Close adherence to the plan in the preparation and execution of the budget, and strict controls of the government authorities over the finances of enterprises—often through discretionary ad hoc measures—helped ensure broad balance in the public sector finances until the mid-1980's.

In the second half of the decade, the relaxation of the planning process and increased autonomy of state enterprises, in combination with adverse external shocks and growing macroeconomic disequilibria, led to a progressive deterioration of the public finances. While profit remittances by enterprises to the budget and receipts from the turnover tax—the major sources of revenue—declined in relation to GDP, social spending and price subsidies rose rapidly, the defense burden remained high, and the authorities found it difficult to cut back investment significantly. As a result, the fiscal imbalance widened rapidly, peaking in 1988 with an adjusted deficit equivalent to some 11 percent of GDP (Table II.2.3).

More recently, significant efforts have been made to reduce the budget deficit and its contribution to liquidity creation (Chapter II.2). At the same time, a beginning has been made toward structural reform in various areas of the public finances, to adapt them progressively to a more market-oriented economy. In the revenue area, these reforms have centered on the taxation of enterprises and individual incomes. Although these initial reforms involve some progress in the direction of neutrality and transparency of income taxation, they will need to be followed by additional steps to broaden their base and eliminate remaining distortions and preferences. They will also need to be complemented by an early and wide-ranging reform of the taxation of goods and services, to ensure adequate elasticity of revenue with respect to income and output in the years ahead. A substantial strengthening of tax administration will be essential to ensure that legislative reforms of the tax system are implemented effectively, and that capabilities to collect and enforce taxes are adapted to the requirements of a more market-oriented economy.

Economic reform will require a substantial restructuring of governmental spending over the next few years. On the one hand, the imposition of a hard budget constraint on enterprises will require the elimination of budgetary and extrabudgetary support to loss-making enterprises, although it may be necessary to provide temporary aid to enterprises and banks undergoing well defined and closely monitored restructuring programs. Price reform should entail a major cutback of budgetary subsidies, which in 1989 amounted to over 13 percent of GDP (Table III.1.9). The social acceptability of these reforms will, however, require the early implementation of an effective safety net, involving unemployment compensation and other targeted income support schemes. The authorities have already introduced an ambitious program of reforms of pensions and other welfare benefits. While adequate funding appears to have been secured for these schemes in the short run, illustrative scenarios point to significant risks to their financial viability over the medium term, in the absence of steps to tighten eligibility requirements and/or to raise contribution rates (Appendix III.1-3).

An active monetary policy, involving flexible interest rates, will inevitably increase substantially the burden of servicing the domestic public debt in the years ahead. These foreseeable pressures on public spending, plus large needs for investment in a deteriorated public infrastructure, will require a determined effort to cut back other more discretionary spending, if the overall deficit is to be adequately reduced. In particular, it will be important to carry out fully the proposed reductions in defense expenditures, which remain significantly higher in relation to GDP than in most large industrial countries.

The restructuring of expenditures should be accompanied by wide ranging reforms of the budgetary process, in order to improve coordination between various levels of government, introduce effectively macroeconomic analysis in the budget preparation, strengthen expenditure control and introduce modern cash management procedures. It would also be important, for purposes of transparency and financial discipline, to minimize the use of extrabudgetary funds.

A precondition for effective reforms of the public finances is an early definition of respective responsibilities and powers in taxation and expenditure for different levels of government, as well as of the scope of budgetary transfers among

238

these levels. Also essential to the maintenance of a unified economic space—involving a single currency and consequently a unified monetary policy—is the acceptance by all levels of government of strict and effective limits, and preferably a ban, on monetary financing of budget deficits. Admittedly, however, intergovernmental fiscal relations, particularly in a large country encompassing a multitude of ethnic and cultural differences, cannot be decided on efficiency considerations alone. Indeed, a conclusive and durable settlement of this issue must be based on a broad consensus, taking fully into account trade-offs between regional or local socio-political preferences and economic efficiency.

2. INTERGOVERNMENTAL FISCAL RELATIONS

a. Past relations

The general government of the USSR encompasses the union and 15 union republics, which in turn include 20 autonomous republics and more than 52,000 local governments (*oblasts, okrugs, krays, rayons,* cities) headed by soviets of people's deputies. The autonomous republics, concentrated mainly in the Russian Republic, are established along minority nationality lines.[1] The administrative status of cities depends on size, as well as political and economic importance.[2]

The state budget is a consolidation of the union budget, including the social security accounts, and the state budgets of the union republics. Likewise, the state budget of each level of government is a consolidation of its own budget and the budgets of all lower levels of government under its jurisdiction (Chart 1). Traditionally, despite the formal federal structure of public administration, the formulation and execution of fiscal policy has been highly centralized to ensure full conformity with the plan.

In essence, the minimum level of revenue and maximum expenditure (by category and program, respectively) were determined at each level of government for the budgets of the immediately lower level under its jurisdiction, with the global amounts being set for the state budget by the union authorities. Deficits at any level could be covered with transfers from the budget of the next higher level government, as in principle there was no recourse to transfers between budgets at the same level or from a lower level. Some of the transfers from the union to the republican governments consisted of loans subject to repayment by the republics. Also, republic or local budget surpluses could be transferred to higher levels or carried over to the following year, upon approval by the central authorities. The high degree of centralization is evident from the almost complete control that the union authorities have exercised over the imposition of taxes (or requisition of enterprise profits) at various levels of government. Similarly, spending directives were issued by the union authorities—specifically by Gosplan—and then delegated consecutively to each level of government.

As regards the mechanics of intergovernmental relations, each year governments at every level were allocated a certain proportion of tax or nontax revenue in a given category collected within their territory. The allocations were more or less linked to the expenditure directives for that year. In 1990, the allocations were clustered in the 70-100 percent range for turnover tax revenue, were raised from around 50 percent to 100 percent for personal income tax revenue in half of the republics, and were kept at 20 percent or less for union-subordinated enterprise profit tax revenue, except in the Baltic republics where allocations exceeded 50 percent (Table III.1.1). Revenues from most other tax and nontax sources (especially local charges, profits of regionally-subordinated enterprises and cooperatives, and the agricultural tax) were allocated fully to republic or local budgets. Although financing normally was obtained only to cover deficits at the union level, 50 percent of the proceeds from the sale of "lottery loans" accrued to the union republics.[3] In addition, the republics received from the union budget transfers for meat and milk subsidy payments, while Central Asian republics also received regional grants—totaling up to almost one third of total budgetary revenue in the case of Turkmenistan (Tables III.1.1 and III.1.2).

In the aggregate, in 1989, the state budgets of the union republics (i.e., republic plus local budgets) obtained the bulk of the revenue from the turnover tax (86 percent), and from income taxation of individuals (61 percent) and cooperatives (93 percent), while the union budget received all foreign trade revenue, including external financing, and the major share of revenue from state enterprise profits (61 percent). Revenue from social security contributions—assisted with general revenue—was channeled to beneficiaries through both the union and the union republic budgets (Table III.1.3).

On the expenditure side, the picture that emerges is one of a division of fiscal responsibilities, broadly along functional lines, under tight centralized control: union republics and the local soviets being responsible for social expenditures, and the union government for defense, foreign economic relations and support of state enterprises. The principal items financed solely from the union budget were defense, justice, internal security, subsidies to the external sector, and most budgetary investment in the economy (61 percent). By contrast, given their first-hand contact with the community, local governments were primarily responsible for outlays on health (86 percent) and education (66 percent), while union republics disbursed most price subsidies (78 percent) and the majority of social security benefits (Table III.1.3).

To this effect, roughly in line with the balance between economic endowment and social needs, union republics have been permitted to retain a certain proportion of revenue allocations. This is best illustrated by the full turnover tax retention in Central Asian republics—with the lowest per capita income—supplemented with grants from the union budget, with allocation subject to yearly variations depending largely on changing needs.

b. Recent developments

Fueled by ethnic, cultural, and political differences, pressures have been building in recent years toward substantial regional fiscal decentralization. These pressures led to outright declaration of sovereignty by union republics, and in several instances, by autonomous republics and local governments. To contain this centrifugal trend, in April 1990 a law was enacted on the basic principles that would govern relations between the union and the republics.[4]

The law confirms union jurisdiction in the following areas involving fiscal policy: determination and administration of the Soviet tax system, including tax rates and bases, as well as other mandatory payments to the union budget; determination of customs duties; and preparation, approval and execution of the union budget, including expenditures on subsidies to the republics. In addition, the union would retain responsibilities for many areas that have fiscal implications.[5]

The law entrusts the union republics and autonomous republics with the fiscal responsibilities within their territory, subject to compliance with USSR legislation, relating to determination of republic taxes and other mandatory payments (including for natural resources) levied on their territory and entered in their budgets, and the preparation, approval, and execution of the republic budgets by the legislature of each republic.[6]

In conjunction with the republics, the union authorities are authorized to form regional development funds, as well as reserve, innovation, environmental protection and other union-level funds, to finance economic and social programs. Furthermore, the law calls for the preservation of a common union-wide market, above all by prohibiting the erection of barriers or discrimination against inter-republican commodity and financial flows. However, it allows republics to tax and to control the price of goods and services within their territory and to provide incentives or subsidies for the production or sale of specific commodities, from their own budgetary resources. Republics are also empowered, within their territory, to set rules regarding investment or acquisition of property and disposal of profits.

This enabling legislation was, in many respects, reaffirmed by the presidential guidelines issued in October 1990. Once again, the union was entrusted with the tasks of, among others: drawing up long-term forecasts; developing and implementing a uniform customs legislation; managing and financing common functions (defense, energy, transport, etc.); and servicing foreign and domestic government debt. To meet the corresponding expenditure responsibilities, the union budget would be financed from union taxes and from other revenue sources under direct union control. Meanwhile, the republics would be expected to promote the development of their territories, conduct economic policy, determine their systems of republic and local tax and nontax payments, and regulate prices, income and social protection within their boundaries.

If there is a difference between the law of April 1990 and the presidential guidelines, it is that the guidelines seem to stress rule by consensus among the republics, focusing on organizational rather than substantive aspects. This approach is evidenced,[7] for example, by the proposal that union tax rates and taxable objects be determined by agreement with the republics. More broadly, the guidelines envisage creation of an Interrepublic Economic Committee—composed of plenipotentiary representatives of the republics, under the Federation Council[8] to coordinate measures introduced by all republics. Coordinated and prompt implementation of financial measures is called for, including curtailment of the state budget deficit, to a target of 2½ to 3 percent of GDP for 1991.

In addition, a number of regulatory agencies and extrabudgetary funds (including a State Property Fund, a Regional Development Investment Fund, an Employment Promotion Fund, and an unspecified number of stabilization funds) is to be established at the union and republic levels to carry out new functions emerging from the increased market orientation (for instance, privatization, infrastructure investment, and enterprise restructuring). From an efficiency viewpoint, it is difficult to justify the creation of these funds with distinct policy goals, to be financed through earmarked taxes; moreover, such extrabudgetary funds are bound to weaken budgetary control. Yet, one possible explanation for establishing some of them is to counteract, in part, what may be viewed as a process of excessive regional decentralization.

On the whole, although they represent a step toward a genuine federal structure, neither the enabling legislation nor the presidential guidelines offer a detailed solution for the reform of intergovernmental fiscal relations. Presumably, the extent and limits of union authority in fiscal matters, as well as intergovernmental relations, would be decided through a constitutionally binding union treaty. There are, however, a few initiatives that are likely to shape these relations at least in the near term. For 1991, the union and republic budgets have been prepared on separate tracks—following to an extent the familiar functional division—with considerable ad hoc coordination among different levels of government. Revenue sharing remains one of the most contentious issues, and some republic and local governments are reportedly embarking on their own tax reform programs. In general, however, as the republics retain an increased portion of revenue, some of them will make negotiated upward transfers to the union budget. Should these transfers prove to be insufficient, it will be necessary to reopen negotiations.

The past formula for the central allocation of revenue shares to the republics no longer appears politically tenable. In fact, in 1990, several republics and local governments already retained a higher share of turnover and income tax revenue than allocated. According to the tax reform enacted at the union level, from 1991 onward revenue from the new 45 percent enterprise income tax is to be divided between the union and republic budgets, with 22 percentage points accruing to the former and 23 percentage points to the latter. Foreign trade tax revenue has

242

been assigned to the union and revenue from property taxes and local levies to the republics and local governments. In addition, agreement appears to have been reached to the effect that the republics will receive all turnover tax revenue but that the union will receive the entire proceeds from a newly-introduced 5 percent sales tax.

c. Options and constraints

If the USSR is to move to a federal fiscal system, a number of issues would need to be dealt with in the context of a union treaty or some other agreement between the union and the republics. These issues include the assignment of budget revenue and expenditure flows as well as the stock of government assets and liabilities. Furthermore, clear rules must be set on intergovernmental transfers and on permissible financial operations, i.e., lending and borrowing. It is important to recognize that the alternatives under consideration would be limited if consensus is reached to maintain an open and integrated economic space and to preserve a central role for fiscal policy as an instrument of macroeconomic stabilization within that space.

More generally, whereas there are many potentially useful lessons to be derived from international experience in fiscal federalism, ultimately each country must find its own unique approach that is most suitable for satisfying not only efficiency criteria, but national, cultural, or linguistic aspirations as well. A common lesson from various country experiences is that the most durable federal fiscal systems are those characterized by objective, transparent, and accepted rules for allocating revenue and expenditures among government levels, for determining intergovernmental transfers, and for limiting financial activities at lower levels of government.

(1) Division of government assets and liabilities

As regards public nonfinancial assets, there seems to be broad agreement—whatever the nature of the union—on explicitly assigning the ownership of real property: housing to local governments; nonrenewable resources to union republics and autonomous republics; state enterprises, including unfinished construction and inventories, to the corresponding government of subordination, except that many union-subordinated enterprises are being claimed by republic or local governments; while pipelines and transport facilities could probably remain under union jurisdiction. In any event, most of these assets—except for public utilities—are likely to be partially or wholly offered or transferred to private owners as privatization proceeds, with any proceeds accruing to the budget of the selling government.

More controversial is the status of financial assets, especially official foreign exchange and gold reserves, to which some republics apparently want to establish a direct ownership claim. By contrast, joint responsibility for the servicing of outstanding public debt, including external obligations, has been widely accepted among the republics—although without agreement as to the basis for determining each republic's share in these obligations. Joint debt service and unified monetary control imply the need for joint ownership of external reserves under central bank management.

(2) Assignment of budget revenues and expenditures

On expenditure responsibilities, most republics—except those that favor secession—recognize the union's role in assuming certain common functions, such as defense, energy, space activities, and foreign economic relations—albeit without prejudice to direct foreign contacts by republic governments—while decisions concerning all other programs would be left to republic and local levels of government. On the revenue side, however, controversy reigns. Most republics want to dispose freely of the bulk of revenue from taxes and from property (including asset sales), leaving locally-raised revenue to local governments.[9] The final outcome will probably lie somewhere between, on the one hand, the present revenue allocations as a minimum—including perhaps the split of the enterprise income tax—and, on the other, full accrual of revenue to the republic and local budgets.

Besides the determination of revenue shares among various government levels, agreement is necessary on the definition of tax bases and on tax rates and on the latitude for variation that may prevail among jurisdictions. The new enterprise income tax already allows for variations in the republic revenue shares for incentive purposes through a reduced tax rate and a narrower base.

In this respect, it is worth recalling that arrangements for tax assignment in other countries with a federal system can be classified under three approaches: tax sharing (with revenues from a single tax being divided among various levels of government, as in Germany), tax overlapping (under which different levels of government compete in the same tax field, allowing for some variation in the determination of tax bases, exemptions and tax rates, as in Canada and the United States), and tax separation (where each level of government raises revenue from separate tax categories, as in Switzerland and Yugoslavia).

In Germany, most of the major taxes and the largest component of the local business tax are shared between two or three levels of government. The rates and bases of the shared taxes are uniform, with the respective shares of the Federal Government, the Länder and the municipalities being fixed in the constitution at 43-43-14 percentage points for the personal income tax and 50-50-0 percentage points for the corporation income tax. These shares are applied to income taxes collected at the Land level, corrected by a measure of the "true effective tax capacity" of a Land before sharing the revenue with the Bund, and before equalizing the tax capacity across Länder. The VAT shares, distributed among Länder according to population and fiscal capacity, are frequently changed by the Federal Government. The main exclusively federal taxes are customs duties and excises. Although there are some distortions arising from the way taxes are collected, the German system has proved quite effective in providing stability and transparency to government finances.

Canada has tried many forms of tax sharing and tax overlapping arrangements in the past. When the provinces gained more legislative autonomy in the 1970s, they became free under the tax overlapping approach to set their own rates as long as they conformed to the federal base; later, a tax supplement method was introduced whereby provincial taxes were calculated as an additional percentage to the federal rates. Tax collection arrangements between the federal and provincial authorities are extensive, although some provinces collect their own personal or corporation income taxes. The system allows decentralized fiscal macroeconomic policy; provinces can, for example, reduce their sales tax rates in order to stimulate consumer spending. Also relevant for the Soviet case is the role of natural resource taxes. In Canada, the central government is given authority to raise revenue from export taxes on oil, but because the ownership of natural resources is held by the provinces through their retention of subsurface mineral rights when surface rights are sold, the provinces also derive revenue from resource rents. This gives a much higher revenue raising capacity to resource-rich provinces, and the existing fiscal equalization program has been inadequate to keep fiscal disparities within an acceptable range.

In Yugoslavia, a notable example of tax separation, the only tax whose proceeds are shared between republics and the federal government is the general sales tax, which also happens to be the single most important revenue source, accounting for nearly one half of total budget revenues. However, unlike in Germany, there are no predetermined shares for this tax and the republics exercise considerable autonomy over its disposition. All other taxes are effectively controlled by one or the other level of government, so the degree of tax separation is nearly complete.

In the USSR, if consensus on revenue assignment in the framework of a Union Treaty were not attainable, at a minimum interrepublic differences in effective tax rates on income or goods and services, or differences in subsidy rates, would be constrained by the desired preservation of a common economic space, especially since the transition to a market economy would entail integration of currently segmented commodity and factor markets. Otherwise, with the economy becoming increasingly market-oriented, active arbitrage by consumers, producers and investors would develop across republic boundaries, in response to tax rate or subsidy differentials.[10] The erosion of tax revenue ensuing either from such tax avoidance or evasion practices, or from the tax competition, mainly on the part of economically less developed jurisdictions which experience the most acute revenue need and seek to attract investment inflows (by offering tax holidays, reduced tax rates, etc.), could only be prevented through elaborate administrative arrangements among republics.[11]

(3) Intergovernmental transfers

Apart from tax and expenditure assignment, an essential aspect of federal structures involves intergovernmental transfers to satisfy vertical and/or horizontal redistribution criteria. Whereas vertical redistribution is usually directed at compensating for imbalances at a given level of government (due to a mismatch between revenue and expenditure at that level), horizontal redistribution is aimed specifically at reducing inequities among regions. In practice, the two criteria are not really separable. It can be argued that, under the existing system, the USSR has actually been applying both criteria through union transfers to the republics in connection with meat and milk subsidies and through republic-specific grants.

Interestingly, however, neither the enabling legislation nor the presidential guidelines focus on the scope for compensatory intergovernmental transfers, presumably leaving this matter to negotiation between the union and the republics, while perhaps (by omission) attempting to preserve downward transfers from higher to lower levels of government.[12]

In theory, the direction, mechanics, and criteria governing intergovernmental transfers may have no bearing on the global budgetary outcome, and specifically on the state budget balance. In practice, however, fiscal discipline can be affected adversely by the nature of such transfers. The experience of other federal fiscal structures indicates that revenue sharing rules must be accompanied by transparent ex ante rules on compensatory transfers among different levels of government. Moreover, although in principle the direction of the transfers is immaterial, upward transfer schemes are particularly vulnerable to negotiation, and are likely to have a destabilizing effect on government finances, unless they are buttressed by an objective and solid enforcement mechanism. In addition, lack of a centralized revenue raising power is likely to deprive the federal government of an important tool for macroeconomic stabilization.

There are several examples that serve to illustrate these views. In Spain, for instance, upward yearly transfers from the Basque Country to the central government have been subject to protracted negotiations that, despite their relatively small size, have contributed to uncertainty in the budgetary outcome. Perhaps even more instructive is the experience of Yugoslavia, where republics regularly transferred to the federation an amount almost equal to two fifths of federal budget revenues and shared with the federation the general sales tax revenue in about the same proportion. The amounts of these upward transfers were subject to annual negotiation, and until recently there was no effective enforcement of a republic's payment once the agreement on the distribution of tax burden was reached. As a result, the federation often had to resort to borrowing, with negative consequences for macroeconomic stability. Since 1989, upward transfers have declined in rela-

246

tive importance due to the introduction of a special defense tax at the federal level and a rule whereby payment to the federation of sales tax shares became automatic. With these changes, the revenue assignment seems more stable, although republics often still exercise their discretionary control of fiscal revenue as a powerful bargaining tool. On a far smaller relative scale, the system of upward and downward transfers within the European Community—viewed as having a federal fiscal structure—is among the most stable. All EC member countries are required to transfer a small percentage of their VAT base to the Community budget, from which, in turn, structural funds are disbursed to economically backward regions on the basis of objective formula of need.

A critical aspect of a federal system is the extent to which lower level governments are able to finance their deficits at home or abroad. In most countries, such financing is ordinarily subject to statutory limits; in others it is preempted by stop-gap budgetary transfers from the central government. Rarely can lower level governments resort directly to central bank or even commercial bank financing; in the USSR, the enabling law and the presidential guidelines are silent on this issue.[13] Nonetheless, financial discipline requires that lower level governments be barred from borrowing from the banking system.[14] As an extension of this argument, both the extent and terms of borrowing from the nonbank public should be freely dictated by the borrowing government's rating in financial markets, without guarantees from a higher level of government,[15] unless on an exceptional basis to secure external credits for sound infrastructure projects. There is considerable accumulated evidence that countries can face both substantial fiscal imbalances and external debt problems because of easy access to foreign borrowing by lower level governments (as well as state enterprises) under liberal central government guarantees.

3. THE REVENUE SYSTEM

a. Introduction

The USSR state budget relies on four major revenue sources. Since the tax consolidation of 1930,[16] state enterprise profits and the turnover tax have been the most important sources of expenditure financing, followed in importance by foreign trade taxes and taxes on households. State budget revenue as a percentage of GDP fell steadily from 47 percent in 1985 to 41 percent in 1989 (Table III.1.4). The decline in revenue is largely due to the reduction in transfers from state enterprises, and would have been larger were it not for the recovery over the period of the turnover tax on alcoholic beverages. As of 1989, revenue from state enterprises and turnover tax each accounted for less than one third of budget revenue, while foreign trade taxes provided about one eighth, and individual income taxes one tenth of revenue.

247

Transfers from state enterprises, which had several different components prior to the recent introduction of the enterprise income tax, consist of distribution to the budget of part of enterprise profits; in the past, substantial amounts of enterprise income were also earmarked for extrabudgetary centralized funds under the control of industrial branch ministries. Most of these transfers—just like reverse transfers from the budget and centralized funds—have been largely a matter of negotiation. As a rule, the turnover tax consists of commodity-specific wedges between administratively fixed retail and wholesale prices, minus notional wholesale and retail margins. In other words, it lacks explicit fixed rates and is not comparable to any conventional turnover tax found in a market-oriented economy. Similarly, taxes on foreign trade generally have arisen from the price equalization system which effectively taxes away the profits of enterprises arising from the difference between the foreign prices of traded goods converted into valuta rubles at the official exchange rate, and the fixed domestic wholesale prices.[17]

Around 90 percent of the revenue from the income tax on households is composed of a withholding tax on wage income.[18] The remainder is composed of schedular income taxes, levied mainly on self-employment income, taxes on personal property (land, buildings, and motor vehicles), and other receipts. The relatively small weight of taxes on households is confirmed by the fact that altogether they provide almost the same amount of receipts as the turnover tax on alcoholic beverages alone.

b. Taxes on business income

(1) Transfers from state enterprises

Transfers from state enterprises to the budget and to the extrabudgetary centralized funds have been regulated since 1987 under the system of enterprise self-accounting.[19] According to the system, which ultimately is to be fully replaced by the profit tax, profits of a state enterprise were apportioned to the centralized funds under the control of its branch ministry and to the state budget. The enterprise would pay to the centralized funds about one half the amount of recorded depreciation, in principle to finance investment within the same industrial branch, and an enterprise-specific amount, used by the branch ministry to cover its running expenses and to cross-subsidize loss-making enterprises.[20] The transfers to the state budget consisted of: (1) payments from profits, corresponding to the planned profit of the enterprise, after certain allocations (mostly for fixed investments and loan repayments); (2) fixed payments, levied as specific amounts or as a percentage of profits, on enterprises deemed to have made extraordinary profits from favorable natural resource or transport conditions; (3) a contribution (introduced in 1988) based on the use of labor resources, amounting each year to rub 200-300 per manual worker and rub 600 per white-collar

248

worker; (4) a contribution (introduced in 1965) on "basic production funds and normalized circulating capital," ranging from 2 percent to 8 percent of fixed assets and working capital, the rates increasing with the profitability of the firm; and (5) residual profit payments, representing the transfer to the budget of remaining actual profits after all other authorized profit allocations.[21] Enterprises made these payments monthly, sometimes even three times per month, depending on the annual cash plan, revised quarterly. Since 1988, state enterprises were no longer required to surrender depreciation allowances and were allowed to retain a larger share of earnings, while enjoying increased freedom in distributing profits among various funds.[22]

(2) The enterprise income tax

With the advent of foreign investment in 1987, in the form of joint ventures, the authorities realized the inadequacy of the existing profit transfers, geared to the state enterprise sector, for the taxation of the emerging private enterprises. Accordingly, a special tax treatment was created for joint ventures under which book profits would be liable to a 30 percent tax, and dividend remittances abroad were taxed at 20 percent.[23] A two year tax holiday was granted from the time the joint venture first netted a profit,[24] and the Ministry of Finance was empowered to grant partial or total exemption to specific taxpayers.[25] In order to promote foreign investment and reinvestment, generous rules were established for the determination of the tax base. Most accounting criteria—including depreciation methods and rates—were acceptable if established under the joint venture's statute. Also, a number of items, not fully deductible by state enterprises, could be deducted by joint ventures: R & D expenditure, interest and principal paid on bank loans, and capital expenditures (in addition to depreciation). Finally, the tax could be reduced further for retaining profits in a general reserve, up to the equivalent of 25 percent of equity, and for unlimited allocations to investment. Also, joint ventures, like state enterprises, could not deduct bonuses paid to employees.

The purpose of the new enterprise income tax law,[26] which entered fully into force in January 1991, was to establish a uniform tax environment for all state-, cooperative-, or privately-owned enterprises. In preparing for the transition to the generation of budget revenues on the basis of taxes rather than transfers, the Government attempted during 1988-90 to reduce the degree of discretion and to stabilize the contributions of state enterprises to the budget and funds at around 50 percent of the net profit. Under the new legislation, state enterprises are subject to a basic 45 percent statutory rate on profits, plus a progressive rate of up to 90 percent on "excess profits," payable to the budget.[27] The substitution of the 45 percent profit tax for the system of transfers is likely to cause *ceteris paribus* a significant loss of revenue, on the order of rub 30-40 billion in constant prices. A revenue neutral changeover would have required a 55 percent profit tax rate.

249

Although the initial draft law envisaged such a statutory rate, the USSR Supreme Soviet reduced the rate to 45 percent. According to official estimates, this measure implies a cut from 49 percent to 37 percent in the average effective tax rate. (Table III.1.5 summarizes the main features of the tax reform initiated in 1990 and extending through 1991.)

Besides replacing the system of profit transfers, the reform sought to put state enterprises on an equal competitive footing with the emerging private sector, including joint ventures (except those with significant foreign participation) and cooperatives, which had been subject to a relatively low tax on gross profits and had expanded rapidly since mid-1988. Although the new law has removed the preference enjoyed by joint ventures in deducting the amortization of bank loans, it allows for the first time the deduction of bonuses paid to employees and interest on long-term bank loans, in addition to standard depreciation. Also, joint ventures with foreign participation continue to be subject to the reduced 30 percent profit tax rate, while the withholding tax on dividend remittances was cut from 20 percent to 15 percent on July 1, 1990.[28]

The enterprise tax law represents a step in the direction of uniform and transparent treatment of profits. However, serious obstacles remain to revenue neutrality and to allocative efficiency. The tax base is either not yet well defined or determined in an arbitrary manner, incorporating conservative depreciation rates, notional deduction of wages and salaries calculated on the basis of industry-specific coefficients, and limitation on interest deductions; also, the criteria for assessment of "excess profits" have not been set. The law creates an excessive number of tax preferences (exemptions, credits, special regimes, and reduced rates differentiated according to the type of activity or legal form).[29] These preferences narrow the coverage of the tax, making it complex and difficult to administer, while at the same time reducing its effective rate and hence its revenue yield. Statutory tax rates of up to 90 percent on excess profits may not deter state enterprises from exploiting a monopoly position, but certainly provide a strong incentive for tax evasion. Furthermore, the tax liability is reduced by deductions of, or credits which are not permitted in most other countries.[30] Yet, except for joint ventures, rates for straight-line depreciation—the only method permitted—are lower than those common in other countries, and loss carryover is not allowed. The lack of uniform accounting standards contributes to the creation of uncertainty about the taxable base. In particular, the current tax structure lacks a definition of profit which could be consistently applied to both state enterprises and private businesses.

Finally, the present structure of the profit tax lacks any adjustment for inflation. Although the real value of revenue is reasonably protected by short collection lags,[31] the effective tax rate is influenced by the rate of inflation inasmuch as the determination of taxable income does not recognize gains and losses for inflation on an accrual basis. Distortions arise, for example, from depreciation based on historical costs, incomplete recognition of exchange gains and losses on liabilities or assets denominated in foreign currency, and presumptive taxation of gains from inventory revaluation. As a result, the real tax burden becomes volatile in an inflationary environment, placing an unintended tax liability on the enterprise.

(3) Scope for a compulsory dividend

Under a uniform enterprise income tax, state enterprises would enjoy a competitive advantage vis-à-vis privately-owned enterprises that are expected to pay some rate of return to their owners in addition to tax payments to the budget. Therefore, there is a strong case for imposing on state enterprises an obligatory dividend payout to the budget, so as to place them on a comparable footing with private enterprises. One approach would be to predetermine the dividend as a uniform proportion of the government's paid-in capital in all enterprises. However, in view of the practical problems of valuing the equity of Soviet state enterprises, and the arbitrariness of profits in a system full of price distortions, as well as the remarkable stability of corporate dividend-profit ratios in market economies, such an approach would appear to be less preferable than one which sets the dividend at a uniform predetermined percentage (say, 25 percent) of after-tax profit of state enterprises in all industrial branches.

(4) Tax on excess wage increases

The present tax on the growth of the wage fund is a regulatory device intended to constrain wage increases that exceed official guidelines. It represents the latest in a series of schemes since 1989 designed to indirectly control the growth of wages (see Chapter II.2). According to legislation of June 1990, effective January 1, 1991, a modified excess wage tax was to apply which would make increases in enterprise wage bills subject to taxation if the resulting share of labor remuneration in value added were not to decline by a specified margin, which would vary across sectors. The tax rate schedule is steeply progressive, with a maximum rate of 200 percent if the threshold for tax-free wage increases is exceeded by more than 3 percent.[32]

c. Taxes on personal income

The income tax consists of a set of schedules for various types of personal income. The present system, overhauled in April 1990, is characterized by progressive rates, reaching a top 60 percent marginal rate for most kinds of income. With regard to both wage and nonwage incomes, there are a large number of exemptions, credits and other kinds of benefits, the most significant being the personal exemptions. The executive committees of regional and local soviets of people's deputies may grant partial or complete exemption for a certain type of income or class of taxpayer, and even to a particular taxpayer. As a result, effective tax rates depend not so much on the level of income as on the kinds of activity through which the income is earned. Due to the overwhelming state control of economic activity, until recently the actual income tax base was very narrow, consisting of not much more than wage income, subject to withholding tax. Other individual income taxes include those on income of residents from self-employment, intellectual property, household business activity, peasant farm activity, and foreign sources,[33] and on domestic source income earned by foreign residents.

A recent change in the tax system, effective July 1990, increased the progressivity of the wage tax, set a maximum marginal rate of 60 percent for most kinds of income, and increased the already large number of brackets. Thus, in many respects, this reform was no more than an updating of the old tax system. New elements were introduced, however, in line with the emergence of new forms (e.g., profits of cooperatives) and levels of income, and with the objective of attracting foreign investment. Under the new system, the tax from family business income is collected under a separate schedule; the taxation of foreign residents is simplified; the treatment of royalty income is unified; and the tax on single individuals and childless persons is to be phased out.[34]

However, over the medium term, and until the development of other tax bases with more effective administrative mechanisms, the most important schedule, in terms of both coverage and revenue, will remain the withholding tax on wage income. Until June 1990, the withholding tax on wages was set at moderate average rates, with a top marginal rate of 13 percent applicable to wages over rub 100 per month, and an exemption limit of rub 70, equivalent to the minimum wage. Since July 1990, the first 100 rubles of wage income are exempt from the tax, but marginal rates of about 30 percent apply to wages between rub 100-150;[35] for earnings between rub 150-700 per month the marginal rate is a modest 13 percent; and it rises in the following six income brackets and reaches 60 percent for wages exceeding rub 3,000 per month (Chart 2).

Traditionally, wages have been strictly regulated, allowing for small differentials. In mid-1990, the average wage was about rub 260 per month. The emergence of highly differentiated wages in the private sector, however, prompted lawmakers to increase taxation on higher incomes, partly as a response to popular perceptions of the need for greater equity. The U-shaped marginal rate structure, already present in the earlier schedule, was preserved, perhaps on revenue grounds.

The taxation of personal income continues to be applied strictly on an individual basis. The new legislation retains the tax credit for wage earners having many dependents,[36] which may be claimed by both working spouses, without adjustment for global family income. As the value of the credit (set at 30 percent of the tax due) rises with income, it provides an increasingly larger relief to high income taxpayers.

The taxation of self-employment income incorporates a negligible basic exemption (up to rub 5 per month), but has low marginal rates from 1.5 percent to

13 percent on monthly income up to rub 700. For incomes exceeding rub 700, the rates are the same as for wages, but rise continuously over 14 income brackets, or twice as many as those for the tax on wages, running counter to tax simplicity.[37]

The authorities' avowed aim regarding personal taxation is to introduce within a few years a comprehensive personal income tax with the various rate schedules converging to a single rate structure, although some schedular elements may be preserved, especially in relation to capital income. Notwithstanding the progress this would represent in many respects, as compared with the current situation, the introduction of an annual declaration for wage earners who are currently subject to withholding would, at this stage, increase costs and administrative complexity without a significant increase in revenues.

d. Taxes on domestic sales of goods and services

Since the beginning of the 1930s, the turnover tax has been an integral part of the system of centrally fixed prices. It is levied at a single stage on the production of a few intermediate and most final goods (excluding domestic services and imports) and consists of the difference between retail and wholesale prices, minus a notional trade margin. More than four fifths of turnover tax revenue is generated from the sale of products for which the tax is simply the residual between administratively fixed retail and wholesale prices. For a minority of products—most petroleum derivatives, tobacco products, matches, and bread and other wheat products—the turnover tax is calculated at specific rates (i.e., a fixed amount per unit of the commodity). Finally, for a few goods produced under a local jurisdiction (e.g., agricultural inputs) or subject to local price regulations, the rates are ad valorem, ranging from 5 to 50 percent of the retail price net of a trade margin.[38]

Almost one half of the revenue from the turnover tax is raised in the food and beverages industry (Table III.1.6), with the bulk provided by alcoholic beverages, mainly vodka. Estimates for 1989 indicate that on the average the turnover tax amounted to 27.5 percent of gross retail commodity sales; for alcoholic beverages, the tax revenue was equivalent to 82.4 percent of recorded sales.

Besides an unknown number of implicit rates (probably in the thousands), the turnover tax contains a large number of tax preferences. Some incentives are provided to encourage compliance. For instance, enterprises are allowed to retain 30 percent of the increase in turnover tax payments above the previous year's level. Other preferences are granted for social purposes; for example, 30 percent of the increase in turnover tax can also be retained to provide social benefits to employees. The turnover tax has been dispensed with altogether for certain enterprises that keep wholesale markups below 20 percent.

Under the reform of June 1990, joint ventures and other private businesses were made liable to an ad valorem turnover tax, beginning July 1990.[39] The base of the tax is defined as the retail price minus wholesale and retail margins, with rates ranging from 15 percent on unlisted goods to 90 percent on liquor. While the number of these rates (eight) is still too large, the definition of the base and the use of different rates for the same goods—depending on whether they are produced by joint ventures or by state enterprises—are likely to introduce serious distortions.

The authorities envisage the adoption over the medium term—at the earliest in 1993—of a general tax on the sales of goods and services, preferably of the value-added type. Initial steps towards that objective should be taken in the near future by transforming the present turnover tax into a fixed rate ad valorem tax, drastically simplifying its rate structure and broadening its base. Specifically, at the very outset, the turnover tax rate should be recalculated as a percentage of the price at the wholesale or production/import stage—without discounts for trade margins or other notional allowances. This initial recalculation into an explicit ad valorem rate need not be accompanied by any price adjustment, but would ensure in the transition period a certain degree of elasticity of the tax with respect to any price changes. Subsequently, the desirable progressive reduction in the number of rates (eventually to one or two only) would require a realignment of relative prices. Thereafter, the maintenance of the resulting fixed ad valorem tax rates would, of course, require that retail prices be adjusted to reflect changes in wholesale prices, as a precondition for the eventual transformation of the turnover tax into a general sales tax. The coverage of the tax should be progressively extended to encompass all domestic production and imports, while exempting exports. The shift from the present turnover tax toward a general sales tax should be accompanied by the introduction of excise duties—at relatively high rates—on selected "nonmerit" or luxury goods, such as cigarettes, distilled spirits, automobiles and a few other high price items.

e. Taxes on international trade

Traditionally, so-called valuta prices (foreign currency prices converted at the official exchange rate) have differed—often significantly—from domestic wholesale prices for traded goods. The difference between the valuta and domestic values for traded goods was largely offset by so-called price equalization taxes paid by trading enterprises to the budget or subsidies received from the budget.[40] Part of the difference was also accounted for by customs duties and explicit import taxes levied on certain consumer goods. Import tax rates ranged up to over 2,000 percent. In recent years, the customs tariff has been based on the 1984 version of the CMEA Unified Classification System—a nomenclature consisting of only about 300 three-digit entries. In principle, duty rates are applied to the valuta value, with rates varying between zero and 70 percent, but with an average—on an unweighted basis—of only 3.5 percent. Raw materials were exempt from duty, while equipment was mostly exempt or subject to low rates. The higher rates were imposed on foodstuffs and consumer durables.

The authorities intend over time to adopt international trade practices, including the Harmonized System of the Customs Cooperation Council (CCC), and to join the GATT.[41] As a step towards replacing quantitative controls and administrative allocation of foreign exchange with explicit taxes, a new tax regime for some exports and imports was created effective from January 1, 1991. Ad valorem taxes now apply to the main energy and raw material exports at rates ranging between 5-50 percent of the ruble value, converted at the new commercial exchange rate.[42] The new import tax rate schedule covers about 200 items classified in 95 commodity groups under two separate columns depending on whether the goods are imported from the CMEA countries or from other origins;[43] the CMEA rates are lower, except for citrus fruits and sugar. Effective November 1, 1990, when the new commercial exchange rate was set at rub 1.66 per U.S. dollar (three times the former official rate), import tax rates were reduced correspondingly, and now range between 10-630 percent.

As groundwork for trade liberalization, a new classification, in line with the Brussels Tariff Nomenclature (BTN), is under preparation to replace the CMEA classification. The new customs tariff is envisaged to cover up to 10,000 items with rates averaging 7-10 percent, under MFN treatment, and ranging up to 100 percent on a few goods. Semifinished goods bear lower rates and consumption goods the highest.

f. Taxes on natural resources

Since the USSR is well endowed with natural resources, the value of their extraction and sale constitutes an important potential tax base, which has not been fully tapped. Until recently the extraction of natural resources was taxed with some degree of discretion in the form of rental payments from the extraction enterprises to the budget. Although usually set as a fixed rate per unit of output,[44] these payments were intended to capture profits which were derived from especially favorable natural, transportation, technical, and other economic conditions. The revenue system also included charges for water use and forest exploitation, which do not generate significant receipts.

The presidential guidelines contemplate an updating of the charges for water use and forestry and the taxation of land and natural resources, both to raise revenue and to encourage environmental protection. The budget envisages that in 1991 substantial additional revenue will be collected from rental payments on the use of natural resources.

255

g. Tax and customs administration

(1) Organization

To the extent that under central planning most revenues were transferred directly to the budget through debiting of enterprise accounts at Gosbank or its branches, tax administration weakened over time, culminating in the dismantling of the tax administration system in the 1960s. Since then, tax administration has been performed by the finance departments of the ministries of finance at various levels of government. The fact that these departments had a number of other responsibilities, mostly related to budget execution, and that tax officers were poorly rewarded, hindered the development of expertise in tax administration.

With the movement toward decentralization and market-oriented policies, the need arise for the establishment of specialized services to administer the existing taxes and those anticipated in connection with the process of economic reform. In January 1990, the USSR Council of Ministers created the State Tax Service (STS), which encompasses republic and local tax offices (Chart 3). To manage the system, the Main State Tax Inspectorate (MSTI) was installed on July 1, 1990 as a new department in the Ministry of Finance of the USSR, with jurisdiction over tax offices at all levels of government (Chart 4). The personnel of the STS, most of them former employees of finance ministries or departments at lower levels of governments, totaled 40,000 initially, and was supplemented by another 25,000 by the end of 1990. The authorities foresee the need to employ as many as 100,000 people when the STS is fully operative, possibly within one year.

The very short time spent on the organization of the STS may explain the impractical configuration given to the organizational structure. The various departments are not organized along functional lines (technical, collection, information processing, auditing, etc.), but according to the taxes they are assigned to administer, and this structure is replicated at all levels of the organization. This structure is conducive to duplication of work, poor coordination, and higher costs.

(2) Procedures[45]

The "taxes on the population" are well established in the USSR and their collection on a withholding basis is fairly efficient. However, Soviet tax agencies have yet to develop basic skills in tax administration for an environment of unregulated prices and private activity. Although in principle the current network of services reaches quite a wide universe of taxpayers, its approach relies on procedures built on the assumption that all operations take place within the public sector. For instance, in the case of workers holding two jobs, the tax adjustment is made by one of the employers, not by the taxpayer or the tax office. Such an arrangement places on the enterprises the costs and responsibility for an activity which, in market-oriented economies, would be regarded as onerous for taxpayers and withholding agents alike.

256

In fact, the STS is far from prepared to handle a large number of taxpayers independent from the Government. Problems of tax evasion and tax fraud, which currently are not serious, will over time oblige the tax authorities to develop adequate enforcement mechanisms and techniques of desk and field audits. The setting up of independent accounting and auditing companies, an idea under examination by the authorities, could certainly improve the quality of accounting, but would not substitute for in-house audit and investigative capacity.

Finally, the resource base of the tax administration is still fragile. Most of the recently recruited staff lack skills in tax matters, and the improvement of the situation will be hampered, at least in the immediate future, by the lack of resources for in-house training. On the positive side, the recent doubling of wages paid to tax officers should help to attract and retain qualified staff, thus modifying the perception that jobs in the tax area are not sufficiently remunerative. Inadequate physical installations of tax offices are a major obstacle to efficient operation; this problem will become more acute as important tax reforms take place, requiring extensive education of taxpayers and more intensive contacts with tax offices. Current procedures for tax administration are based on manual control and paperwork. There are plans for the introduction of personal computers; the few now available are outdated and do not play an important role in tax administration. Modernization of routines and procedures will require not only adequate equipment but also the design of a system of information, linking processing to reporting and control, as well as a sizable investment in training.

Since the effectiveness of any tax system is limited by the ability of the tax administration to implement it, insufficient preparation both of the administrative apparatus and the taxpayers is likely to represent a major weakness of the recent tax reform. The design of a specific and effective program to strengthen tax administration would, however, need to await the definition of respective responsibilities of the union and subnational levels of government in the collection of tax revenues.

(3) Customs

Although the foreign trade organizations are still conducting most functions of processing, clearance and tariff collection for most imports, the Customs Department will be responsible increasingly for the collection of customs duties and the import and export taxes. The Customs Department is four years old, and still being set up. Currently there are 104 customhouses, operating in four regions. Further expansion depends on the stabilization of the relations between the union government and the various republics, as a number of republics seem to be intent on creating their own customs, and some (Ukraine, Belorussia) have reportedly already done so. A single customs service for the country, under a single customs code, would be necessary if agreement is reached for the preservation of an all-union market.

The authorities intend to expand rapidly the current manpower strength of the all-union customs service (some 9,000 persons), to reach as many as 20,000-25,000 officers when the setup is complete. The authorities have actively sought foreign assistance, and the CCC and the EC Commission have provided seminars and technical assistance, contributing to the preparation of new tariff classification and law. The organization and procedures largely draw on CCC conventions and recommendations.

4. THE BUDGET PROCESS

a. Institutions

In the USSR, budget preparation, implementation, accounting, reporting, and audit involve a large number of institutions at various levels of government. The main participants in the budget process are: the ministries of finance at the union and republican levels, and finance departments at local levels; the councils of ministers of the union and each republic; the supreme soviets of the union and each republic; the local soviets of people's deputies; Gosplan; Goskomstat; Gosbank, including 200 regional offices and more than 6,000 branches; Promstroibank and Vneshekonombank.

Traditionally, as the principal fiscal agent of the government, the USSR Ministry of Finance has played a key role in the budget process. In general, it has been responsible for carrying out the national economic plan and the government's financial policies, as well as for supervising all financial operations of lower-level governments. After approval by the USSR Council of Ministers and enactment by the USSR Supreme Soviet of the budget, the Ministry of Finance monitors its implementation. The responsibilities of the republican ministries of finance, as well as their organizational structure, are very similar to those of the Ministry of Finance. At lower levels of government, these functions are assumed by finance departments, with a much simpler organizational structure.

Responsibility for accounting is exercised jointly by the ministries of finance or finance departments, at each level of government, and Goskomstat. The Ministry of Finance, through its Directorate for Accounting, is the authority in accounting practices and methods. Goskomstat has responsibility for preparing reports on the operations of budgetary institutions and state enterprises with regard to real variables (such as material stocks, employment, wages and salaries, and fixed assets).

Until 1987, Gosplan controlled virtually all major budgetary decisions; it was in charge of the preparation of the plan and in this capacity it was the essential link between the economic directives set by the USSR Council of Ministers and preparation of the state budget. Budgets of all levels of government were prepared following the directives of Gosplan, consistent with the targets and limits in the

258

plan. After July 1987, Gosplan's role in the budget process became less prominent. It began to issue estimates and suggestions instead of the earlier plan directives. Until July 1989, however, spending ministries continued to be rewarded according to the fulfillment of plan objectives. During this period, the Ministry of Finance has progressively displaced Gosplan in the formulation of the budget for enactment by the Supreme Soviet. For 1991, the Ministry has been responsible for the preparation of the draft union budget, while the ministries of finance of each republic assumed responsibility for preparing their respective draft budgets for legislative action at the republican level.

Gosbank, the government's banker, and in some important respects also its fiscal and accounting agent—sharing the role of fiscal agent with the Ministry of Finance—has primary responsibility for intermediating all financial transactions involving domestic current operations in the state budget. As part of these functions, Gosbank acts as the depository of budget revenue collected at all levels of government, and maintains the government accounts. Promstroibank performs the same functions for financial transactions relating to investment operations in the budget. Vneshekonombank is in charge of all foreign transactions recorded in the budget.

Budget expenditures are actually undertaken by two kinds of spending units: directly by budgetary institutions, and indirectly by state enterprises, to the extent that expenditures of the latter are supported by transfers from the budget. Budgetary institutions carry out spending functions in the administrative, defense, social, cultural, and scientific areas. Altogether, 90 percent or more of their activities is financed with general budget revenue, while the remainder—mainly in the health, educational, and other cultural areas—is financed from own resources. By contrast, state enterprises are increasingly expected to operate with economic and financial autonomy and to generate profits. Nevertheless, several state enterprises continue to receive significant support from the government, especially for investment outlays, but also for certain (social, educational, and cultural) expenditures for their employees.

b. Budget preparation

Until 1987, the USSR state budget was an integral part of the consolidated financial plan for the economy, which included also the financial plans of extrabudgetary funds and state enterprises. Prepared jointly by Gosplan and the Ministry of Finance in a highly aggregated form, it was used to establish the financial consistency of the economic plan. A first draft of the state budget was derived on the basis of indicators contained in the preliminary draft of the plan elaborated by Gosplan. Gosplan was also responsible for ensuring the conformity of the budget with the plan, and for submitting the resulting draft budget with recommendations to the Council of Ministers. As noted, the role of Gosplan in

259

budget preparation has been reduced while that of the ministries of finance has been progressively enhanced in recent years (Table III.1.7).

Until recently, due to the consolidated nature of the state budget, two budgets were prepared at each level of government (with the exception of the lowest one): the budget of the government at that level and the consolidated budget of all lower-level governments. Each budget was scrutinized and approved by administrative and legislative organs at different levels of government. For instance, the budget of a local government was examined not only by its local finance department, but also by the ministry of finance of its union republic. Similarly, each local budget needed approval by the local soviet of people's deputies and by the republic's supreme soviet. An important feature of the budget preparation process has been the incremental nature of the annual budget. Budget instructions sent by the USSR Ministry of Finance to various levels of government and subsequent negotiations required that estimates for the coming year be compared to those of the current year. Some of the features of budget preparation, particularly insofar as relations between the union and union republics are concerned, have begun to break down as republican ministries of finance have acquired considerable independence in formulating their own 1991 budgets.

The enhanced role of the Ministry of Finance and of the ministries of finance at lower levels of government in the budget preparation process has not been accompanied by desirable changes in complementary areas. In an increasingly market oriented setting, macroeconomic analysis for revenue and expenditure forecasting should be developed and applied on a routine basis by the Ministry of Finance, and within their respective territorial context, by the republican ministries of finance. In addition, a reorganization of the Ministry of Finance may be appropriate, especially involving a restructuring of the Main Budget Directorate along functional lines which would replace the division between the so-called productive and nonproductive sectors (Charts 5 and 6), and assign the responsibility to the Directorate for the preparation of both the current and investment budgets. But probably the most difficult, yet necessary, task ahead will be to install a mechanism for technical coordination of budget preparation among various levels of government—in particular between union and republican ministries of finance—within an agreed macroeconomic framework,[46] in place of the relatively weak ad hoc intergovernmental contacts that seem to prevail at present.

c. Budget implementation

Normally, the implementation of the state budget begins before its formal enactment by the USSR Supreme Soviet. Such a procedure reflects the necessity of transmitting information through five levels of government. In principle, the Ministry of Finance would complete preparation of the draft budget by the first week of October, so as to permit timely communication of the necessary information to all levels of government. After receiving this information, the ministries of finance of republics would break down their approved consolidated budgets into the republican and local budgets. A similar process would take place at lower levels of government. Thus, by the time the state budget was approved by the Supreme Soviet, detailed budgets at each level of government would be ready for implementation. It is unclear how this process has been evolving for the 1991 budgets, given the difficulties in reaching agreement between the union and the republics on their respective budgets. The following subsections describe procedures in effect through 1990.

(1) The budget schedule

At each level of government, the detailed budget is the basic input for preparing the budget schedule, namely, the operational version of the budget. The budget schedule shows not only the full detail of the budget classification, but also the quarterly apportionment of expenditures in the course of the fiscal year. It is, therefore, the principal instrument of budget execution and monitoring. The budget schedule is usually prepared in a very short period of time and is made available to spending ministries in February. At each government level, the budget schedule is subject to approval by the legislative organ of that level.

(2) Expenditure authorizations

Each spending unit, regardless of size, has an account with a Gosbank branch. At the beginning of each year, a line of credit is opened for the spending unit within the limits of the budget appropriation for that unit. In most cases, these credits can be regarded simply as expenditure authorizations. However, credit is in fact granted by each branch of Gosbank if at that branch, in any period, there are no revenue accounts or if deposits are insufficient for financing expenditures. For the state budget as a whole, Gosbank is in a net creditor position when revenues deposited therein are less than disbursements effected on account of the budget. To the extent that receipts in the revenue account may offset expenditures, budgetary credits or expenditure authorizations are not recorded as assets on the balance sheet of Gosbank, but in single-entry accounts. Only when there is genuine financing of budget expenditures will these operations be reflected in the monetary accounts. Before July 1990, the consolidation of budget operations in the Gosbank's accounts took place once a year. Since then, subject to technical feasibility, the authorities intend to undertake a monthly consolidation.

As the budget schedule contains quarterly apportionments, expenditure authorizations are granted for each quarter.[47] Expenditures are authorized by so-called credit administrators.[48] Each spending ministry has a chief credit administrator and subordinated credit administrators to whom he may delegate parts of his responsibilities, which may in part be delegated further to a lower level administrator. Following this mechanism, the Ministry of Finance authorizes spending only at the top level. The allocation of credits or expenditure authorizations to other budgetary institutions is accomplished through the above mechanism of delegation of expenditure administration.

(3) Payments

As each spending unit has its own bank account, the bulk of payments, other than for salaries and wages, is effected through bank transfers. One method consists of a payment request sent by the supplier of goods and services to his bank branch for collection; after confirmation of the transaction by the payer, the payer's branch makes the necessary payment. Another method involves a payment authorization, that is, a document prepared by the spending unit authorizing its bank branch to make a noncash transfer of funds to the payee's account. Although available for any kind of payment, it is mostly used for payments where, due to the nature of the transaction (e.g., payment for invoiced deliveries, prepayment for delivery of goods and services, debt amortization, payment of insurance premia), a payment request is not expected. Other less widely used methods of noncash payments are letters of credit and settlement checks. Cash payments are strictly limited to wages and salaries.

(4) Expenditure control

The Ministry of Finance monitors the realization of revenues and expenditures on a continuous basis, and if necessary, it restricts expenditure authorizations. Specifically, expenditure control is exercised through quarterly release of funds, credit or expenditure authorizations, and exceptional expenditure restriction measures. The quarterly release of funds ensures that they are made available according to an appropriate expenditure pattern and with due regard to the availability of funds. Credit or expenditure authorizations granted to each spending unit, through Gosbank, sets an automatic control under the limit of budget appropriations. Although control is effected through the services of the Gosbank network, any decision as to the timing or the level of authorized expenditure remains with the Ministry of Finance.

In case of a revenue shortfall, the Ministry of Finance has a limited number of options for restraining expenditures. Modification of the approved budget is not an often used option, since it requires a decision of the Council of Ministers. Another technique, which can be used at the discretion of the Ministry of Finance, involves freezing expenditure authorizations for selected ministries. This option has been used frequently because the budget classification permits identification of ministries that are lagging behind in revenue collection and thus can be easily selected for expenditure restriction. Although in the past such ministries were not always singled out for restriction, it is intended that from 1991 onward expenditure authorizations for these ministries be automatically restricted until revenue collections catch up with targets.

(5) Cash management

At present, spending units are not concerned with the management of financial resources mainly because short-term investment of cash resources is not rewarded by interest income, and the cost of borrowing is not borne by the spending units. Clearly, such behavior is incompatible with the increasing market orientation of the economy which would imply, *inter alia,* an active interest rate policy. Gosbank's responsibility for budget revenue and expenditure accounting—inherited from the period when Gosbank was effectively an integral part of the Ministry of Finance—continues to impede the development of a cash management capacity in the Ministry. Therefore, the fiscal and accounting functions of Gosbank, Promstroibank, and Vneshekonombank should be shifted to the Ministry of Finance.

d. Accounting and financial reporting

The authority of the Ministry of Finance over general accounting practices extends in principle to lower-level governments. However, detailed rules and regulations are developed at the republic level with due regard for local needs, and are subject to approval by the council of ministers of the republic. At the union and republican budget levels, each spending ministry has its own accounting service. Accounting for local budgetary institutions is provided by 66,000 local offices of the Central Accounting Service.

(1) Classification of accounts

The standard classification of double-entry accounts, introduced in the early 1960s, provides a comprehensive coverage of budgetary institutions and of types of operations—that is, operations financed with budgetary as well as nonbudgetary resources. Although accounts are usually aggregated at three levels (summary or first-order accounts, second-order accounts, and analytical or detailed accounts), it appears that for budgetary institutions no analytic or detailed accounts are provided. Small budgetary institutions having a limited volume of transactions tend to use single-entry accounts.

(2) Centralization of accounting data

Accounting data are centralized through the network of Gosbank's regional offices and branches. Information collected at the local level is first centralized at the oblast level, then at the republic level, before being sent to Gosbank's head office. Reporting is by telex or cable, as the system is not yet linked with a computer network. In order not to overload the information system, centralization is carried out at a high level of aggregation. For the union and republican budgets, the preparation of consolidated monthly budget balances, showing only total revenues and total expenditures, requires about eight to ten days. At the end of the year a provisional annual balance is prepared in five days. Revenue and expenditure operations which cannot be classified in such a short time period are accounted for in a transit account, and then classified in the final balance prepared before the end of January. Surplus funds at a given level of government are not necessarily transferred to a higher level. Subject to prior authorization by the Council of Ministers or the appropriate executive authority at the local level, they may be used for financing an eventual deficit during the following year.

(3) Reporting

Reporting is restricted to external reports, that is, excluding operational reports intended for internal use. External reports of primary budgetary units are divided into statistical and accounting reports. Statistical reports are primarily concerned with plan-fulfillment control. Accounting reports are used for the control of budget operations or enterprise financial flows.

Although reports are compiled quarterly, no report is prepared for the first quarter of the year because results for that quarter are considered unreliable. In some cases, cumulative data is incorporated into quarterly reports so that the report prepared at the end of December will become the annual report. A complete annual report, prepared at a later date, will also include statistical data obtained from extra accounting sources. Reports prepared at organizational levels lower than that of a republic follow simplified procedures. Accounting reports of primary units are submitted to the higher-level government, where they are consolidated and sent to the next higher-level organization for further consolidation. The USSR Ministry of Finance prepares a union-wide consolidated annual report and submits it to the Council of Ministers and the Supreme Soviet.

e. Control and audit

The control and audit functions are entrusted to the ministries of finance at the union and republican levels and to the appropriate financial authorities at the lower levels of government. At all levels of government, there are about 9,000 auditors who perform work in three different areas. First, they inspect and audit financial documents in ministries and other administrative units at their respective levels. Second, they audit the operation of the finance ministry or financial administration immediately below their own level, paying particular attention to budget implementation. Third, they audit the operations of Gosbank pertaining to budget execution. The extent to which these functions (especially the third one) will continue to be carried out in the future is unclear.

The frequency of audit varies according to the economic activity and the importance of financial operations carried out by a given entity. For instance, state enterprises are to be audited once a year and budgetary institutions once every two years. It appears, however, that the prescribed frequency is not observed at present because of the limited number of auditors, or because audits of agencies that do not meet their budgetary obligations are thorough and time-consuming.[49]

Controller-auditors are authorized to: inspect economic and monetary transactions, all supporting documents, including books of account, cash on hand and other assets; take inventories; seal cash on hand, warehouses, stores and archives; obtain all bank documents connected with financial operations of any enterprise or institution where the operations are conducted; obtain all bank documents of enterprises doing business with the enterprise under investigation; obtain from other enterprises and institutions documents concerning transactions between them and the enterprise or institution under investigation; and propose and/or adopt measures to eliminate shortcomings and to stop deliberate violation of financial discipline.

Audit reports prepared on the activities of specific state enterprises and budgetary institutions are submitted to the corresponding branch ministry and the Ministry of Finance. A general report pertaining to a given sector of the economy is submitted to the Council of Ministers. If there is evidence of willful wrongdoing, the report will be automatically submitted to the judiciary.

5. SELECTED EXPENDITURE ISSUES

The proportion of government expenditure to aggregate income or output does not fully reflect the overwhelming presence of the public sector in the Soviet economy. Indeed, state budget outlays amount to about one half of GDP, which is broadly comparable to the corresponding share in a number of European countries. More informative is the composition of outlays. Subsidies and social security transfers are the largest components, accounting respectively for one fourth and nearly one fifth of global budget expenditure in 1990. Recorded expenditures on defense, justice, and internal security represent about one sixth of the total. Outside the state budget, cross subsidies have been provided within the state enterprise sector through the centralized funds of the branch ministries; in 1989, gross flows through these funds were equivalent to nearly 5½ percent of GDP (Table J.4, Appendix II-1). Similarly, quasi-fiscal operations of official financial institutions, in the form of implicitly subsidized credit to government, appear to be substantial. Interest payments recorded in the state budget grossly understate the true cost of government borrowing.

This section focuses on three areas of special interest in the transition to a market economy, namely, expenditure on defense, producer and consumer subsidies, and social security.

265

a. Defense

(1) Definition and measurement

Defense expenditure in 1989, as recorded in the state budget, amounted to 8 percent of GDP, and was expected to fall to 7.4 percent of GDP in 1990.[50] Of this amount, two thirds consists of material procurement, R & D and construction, while one third represents personnel costs, including wages and pensions (Table III.1.8). While these data are not comparable to those of previous years,[51] questions arise as to the extent to which the magnitudes currently presented fully reflect Soviet defense expenditures. First, it can be argued that state budget coverage of defense is narrower than that of the U.N. classification of military expenditures. Elements of civilian R & D (in particular, on the space program) and of internal security spending may be in many respects indistinguishable from defense-related items. If all R & D and internal security were to be defined as defense outlays, defense spending in 1990 would amount to rub 92 billion (9.6 percent of GDP). While for budgetary analysis it is important that all defense be appropriately categorized, it should be noted that application of the U.N. classification has remained a grey area for many U.N. member countries.[52]

A second question concerns the possible substantial underpricing of defense goods and activities. Weapon procurement prices are apparently out of line with other durables because prices of raw materials, land use, and other inputs are set very low, or because defense industries are permitted to operate at low or negative profit margins.[53] Furthermore, military pay, while in some respects higher than in other sectors, is on average very low, reflecting the widespread use of conscripts. In addition, state enterprises engaged in civilian production may be providing part of their output (e.g., uniforms, shoes) free of charge, and thus cross-subsidizing the military. Correcting for these distortions, estimates of the defense burden of as high as rub 200 billion have been made; yet any estimate of this burden is subject to considerable controversy even among non-Soviet analysts.

From the standpoint of the financial impact of the budget, these arguments would appear to have limited relevance. For instance, it would be meaningless to include in the state budget the imputation of a market wage for conscripts, to the extent the government does not need to finance such imputed costs.[54] Thus, the presentation of defense expenditure in the state budget seems to be the correct basis for financial management purposes, and adjustments to the budget because of price distortions should take place only for explicit cross subsidies.[55]

Besides possible cross-subsidization throughout the enterprise sector in general, defense-related enterprises and their suppliers may be allowed to operate on low or negative profit margins, with subsidies from non-defense enterprises to cover these losses. However, neither these cross subsidies nor direct budget subsidies to defense-related enterprises can be identified in the state budget as presented.[56]

(2) *Policy prospects*

In his December 1988 U.N. speech, President Gorbachev announced cuts in defense spending to begin in January 1989. Military personnel were to be cut by 500,000, overall outlays to drop by 14.2 percent, and procurement to be reduced 19.5 percent. It has generally been understood that these cuts were to take place in real terms, by the end of 1991, on the base of 1988 spending.[57] However, it is not clear whether the 39 percent nominal increase in defense allocations contained in the draft budget for 1991 is in line with the targeted cuts.[58]

The envisaged conversion of military industry into civilian production, and repatriation of Soviet troops from Central and Eastern Europe, complicate any discussion of the defense budget for 1991 and beyond. Their combined impact on the 1991 fiscal deficit has been initially anticipated at around rub 9 billion. Production in the defense complex has always included output of civilian goods, a share estimated at around 50 percent in 1990. The target of the conversion program is to raise that share to 60 percent or above by the mid-1990s.[59] According to preliminary official views, nearly rub 8 billion (in end-1990 prices) would be allocated to the conversion program. Clearly, the cost of the conversion program will depend on the nature of the projects involved. Conversion has been targeted to ten priority areas: food, consumer goods, light industry, electronics, computers, medical equipment, communications, civil aircraft, shipbuilding, trade and catering. However, domestic pressures to avoid a shift from high- to low-tech industry appear to have retarded restructuring in some sectors.

Insufficient information is available on either the timing or cost of troop withdrawal. The German aid package, intended to finance some or all of the withdrawal, is to amount to rub 18 billion over the period 1990-94, with some rub 5 billion to be disbursed in 1991.[60] The net adverse impact on the budget deficit would be reduced insofar as rub 4 billion of the assistance comes in the form of a grant, covering troop withdrawal, transportation, housing and manpower retraining.

b. Subsidies

In an economy where practically all commodity and factor prices are administered, the economic concepts of subsidies and taxes can become so broad as almost to lose their meaning, insofar as administered prices, wages, interest rates, and the exchange rate all deviate from market-clearing values. Similarly, there are serious difficulties in measuring the resulting distortions, as there are no market benchmarks against which equilibrium prices or economic costs can be constructed. Explicit subsidies, measured by money transfers (or tax preferences) from government to enterprises or consumers, provide a poor approximation of total price support in the economy. And the measurement even of explicit subsidies is incomplete as it is limited to those financed from the state budget and

267

from certain extrabudgetary operations, excluding cross subsidies among enterprises through the centralized funds controlled by branch ministries, and subsidized transactions (partly through preferential interest rates) in the financial sector. However, as the economy moves toward the market, an increasingly clear subsidy accounting should emerge.

Budgetary subsidies in the 1990 plan amounted to around 13 percent of GDP (Table III.1.9). The changes in procurement prices in 1990 not foreseen in the plan suggested that the 1990 subsidy outturn would be higher still.[61] Four fifths of budgetary subsidies go to agriculture; nearly two thirds of agricultural subsidies are used to support basic food prices, with most of the remainder provided directly to farmers. Subsidies for milk and meat products alone account for almost two fifths of budgetary subsidies. However, food subsidy rates by commodity are very dispersed. The average subsidy rate (measured in reference to retail price) is estimated at around 65 percent; as of 1988, meat was subsidized by at least 230 percent, butter 240 percent, and milk 170 percent,[62] and since then subsidy rates have risen.

By contrast, subsidies to heavy industry (for which typically the price structure is more consistent with costs than for goods where social considerations are dominant), amount to some 7 percent of budgetary subsidies, and four fifths of these are to the coal industry, for which the subsidy has risen markedly over the last two years. Other domestic subsidies for services, mainly housing and culture, have remained relatively small.[63] Around 8 percent of budgetary subsidies support foreign trade and industries, such as tourism, that use foreign exchange intensively. These subsidies, which are largely related to exports, were expected to fall in connection with the November 1990 devaluation.

Gross budget figures mask some small implicit subsidies (that for children's clothes being the most significant), financed by tax offsets or outside the budget. Extrabudgetary agricultural price support administered by Gosbank, which supplements the budgetary allocation for essential commodities, totaled rub 9.3 billion in 1989 but was estimated to drop to rub 4.4 in 1990. The authorities planned to raise agricultural procurement prices on average by about 32 percent from the beginning of 1991 (for grain and meat already in the second half of 1990), and industrial wholesale prices by 50-60 percent. Unless a comparable retail price increase takes place, budget subsidies—as price differentials widen and profit margins remain unchanged—are estimated to rise by 50 percent in 1991.[64]

While the containment of subsidies is recognized as a key component of any reform effort, subsidy growth has become so rapid as to create a short-term dilemma for policymakers. If subsidies are removed, retail prices will have to move upwards significantly, with a disproportionate adjustment falling on basic foods whose subsidy rates are high. If they are maintained, however, the fiscal deficit is likely to require inflationary financing. In principle, the presidential guidelines envisage a gradual dismantling of subsidies, along with at least partial income compensation to the population. Indeed, the phaseout of price subsidies, as well as industrial restructuring, can be discussed only in the context of social security reform.

c. Social security

Social security reform is in many ways at the center of the economic and social policy agenda. Besides addressing the need to restore some of the loss in real benefits that resulted from accelerating rates of inflation, the reform is crucial to a successful transition to a market economy. Changes are needed, for instance, to avoid a future systematic decline in real (and relative) benefits as wages and prices rise, to enhance the mobility of labor, and to increase the tax-benefit linkage that would confer transparency on the social security system. Of paramount importance is the need to implement an unemployment compensation scheme designed as a catalyst to a more efficient allocation of resources in the economy. The often overly tight dependency on specific occupations for eligibility for various social insurance allowances also should to be reconsidered in the move toward a market economy.

Accordingly, 1990 witnessed adoption of a broad reform of public pensions, modification of existing allowances and the introduction of some new ones, and a major restructuring of the financing of social security. According to the draft Employment Law approved by the Supreme Soviet in October 1990, an unemployment compensation scheme was to be introduced beginning in 1991. It was also anticipated that some form of compensation of low-income persons for the effect of the much-needed price adjustments would be adopted as an integral part of economic reform.

(1) The existing system[65]

Social security in the USSR is a pay-as-you-go scheme which provides old-age, disability and survivors' pensions to workers, self-employed and state farm workers, and sick pay, maternity benefits and family allowances. More than two thirds of expenditures is for pensions (72 percent in 1990), with sick pay representing the largest of the allowances (Table III.1.10).[66] The historically large contribution of general revenues to the financing of social security is also evident.[67] Social security contributions—all from employers—varied across enterprises from 4 percent to 14 percent of total wages, in part depending on the degree of hardship associated with the location and nature of the employment. In 1989, the average payroll tax rate for the system as a whole was 9 percent, and was expected to increase to 12 percent in 1990.

(2) Recent and prospective reforms

The pension reform enacted in May 1990 was aimed explicitly at increasing the share of national income allocated to pensioners, both by raising benefits and by expanding eligibility. Significantly, beginning in 1991, the government is to provide a basic social pension to retirees without any work history. This represents a notable departure from the traditional employment-benefit linkage which has characterized social security in the USSR.

The reform explicitly raises pension benefits on a permanent basis via an increase in the replacement rate (defined as the percentage of average past earnings replaced by the pension following retirement) from 50 percent to 55 percent; by working beyond the minimum required time, the rate can be raised to 75 percent. The reform appropriately enhances the actuarial basis of the pension by lengthening the effective period to 15 years from 10 years over which the 5 consecutive years with the highest earnings are averaged;[68] however, a longer period could be justified. The monthly benefit is to be equal at least to the minimum wage, and is subject to a maximum of five times the latter, resulting in a somewhat progressive benefit formula.

The statutory retirement age, 55 for women and 60 for men, low in comparison with those of most OECD countries, is left unchanged. This and other eligibility requirements warrant review in the near future in light of the eventual aging of the Soviet population (see Appendix III.1-3). However, two features of the new pension law will operate in opposite ways to influence incentives to retire and, therefore, the effective retirement age. While higher benefits provide an inducement to retire, removal of the ceiling on post-retirement earnings provides an incentive to remain in the labor force. It is, therefore, difficult to ascertain the net effect of these changes on the labor force activity of the elderly.

Perhaps the most significant provision introduced by the pension reform is the full indexation of benefits to changes in the cost of living, beginning in January 1992, aimed at both preserving the purchasing power of retirees and assuring greater stability of the overall replacement rate (or in the relative incomes of pensioners and workers). If the minimum wage relative to the average wage remains constant, then the earnings base will effectively also be indexed. Although the introduction of automatic indexation is crucial for limiting the decline in the real incomes of pensioners in the future, such a measure must be implemented in close concert with wage policies. In effect, indexation of pensions but not of wages might over time lead to increases in the average replacement rate beyond those explicitly sought in the reform. With perhaps the exception of very low-income pensioners, there is little justification for insulating fully the population of retirees from the real income changes needed to restore equilibrium to the Soviet economy.

Eligibility for full sick pay has been further broadened to all workers regardless of work affiliation or trade union membership. During 1990, a number of measures were adopted which aim to improve the size and scope of family allowances. First, a grant for each birth equal to three times the minimum wage (currently rub 70 per month) replaces the birth grant that has been provided heretofore, which ranged from rub 50 to rub 250 per child. Second, the previously available allowance for raising children to age one is to be extended to age one and a half, and is to be raised to 100 percent of the minimum wage for working mothers and 50 percent for nonworking mothers. Third, a monthly allowance equal to 50 percent of the minimum wage is to be paid for each child age one and a half to age six in families in which the family income is less than twice the minimum wage; and for each child of single mothers until the child reaches 16 years of age. Fourth, an allowance equal to the minimum wage is to be paid for each child of military personnel serving fixed tours of duty, as well as to foster children under age 16.[69]

A draft law instituting an unemployment insurance scheme has been approved on a first reading in the USSR Supreme Soviet. Under this law, unemployment compensation would be normally provided for up to 26 weeks, and up to 39 weeks for workers of pre-retirement age. During this time, the beneficiary will be required to search for a job commensurate with his or her experience and skill level. The program will provide tax exempt benefits equal to 50 percent of the wages (excluding bonus payments) earned by an unemployed worker at his last job, or the minimum wage, whichever is greater. In addition to unemployment compensation, the program would provide public works jobs as well, at not less than half the wage earned in the previous employment or the minimum wage.

An area of considerable uncertainty at the current stage of reform is the scope of income protection and the manner in which it would be administered, both in terms of new social assistance programs and for indexation of existing social security benefits. On the one hand, the presidential guidelines call for the establishment in 1991 of an index of a consumer basket, composed of selected essential goods and eventually to be broadened to include other goods, and adjustment of most social security benefits by changes in this index;[70] wage and salary increases would be limited to no more than 70 percent of the rise in the cost of the minimum consumer budget. At the same time, the guidelines envisage maintenance of relatively low fixed prices on essential goods during the transition. Moreover, the guidelines also explicitly reject the idea of extending direct material assistance and support to households, except in special cases.

Three important objectives should guide the design of an income protection scheme.[71] First, to maximize its cost effectiveness, the program should be targeted as much as possible to the households in need.[72] The whole population should not and cannot be compensated for price increases. Second, the removal of consumer subsidies should not be offset by the increased compensation of the needy. Thus, besides the welfare gains due to the removal of distortions, the scheme can be expected to yield net budgetary savings. A third objective must be to avoid using

271

schemes that would perpetuate or compound the existing distortions, except during brief emergency situations.

A major additional goal of social security reform has been to move its financing to an extrabudgetary basis, establishing a greater degree of transparency in the tax-transfer nature of the program. Two off-budget funds have been established: the Pension Fund, for all pension, maternity and child-rearing support payments, and the Social Security Fund, for temporary disability benefits, prenatal assistance, childbirth payments, and death benefits. Under the reform law, union republics are responsible for benefits to single mothers and the children in poor families, as well as the operation of homes for the elderly and the administration of local social security offices. The employer's and employee's pay-as-you-go contribution rates have been set initially at 26 percent and 1 percent of wages, respectively, beginning January 1, 1991. Thus, the restructuring of social security financing creates a closer linkage between benefits and contributions because of the elimination of the dependence on general revenue and the introduction of the employee's contribution. However, the phase-in of higher pension benefits over the period to 1995 will inevitably require an increase in the employer's contribution rate to 37 percent; the rate may have to be raised even higher when the effects of potentially higher unemployment than currently officially expected are taken into account.[73]

It is intended that unemployment compensation be financed through an additional 1 percent payroll tax on employers earmarked for the newly-established Employment Fund. However, the benefit provisions are likely to require a tax rate increase, or recourse to general government revenue. If, for instance, the current minimum wage of rub 70 per month were (hypothetically) paid to each unemployed worker for 26 weeks, benefits could be provided to about 10 million unemployed workers (or somewhat in excess of the official unemployment estimates for the first year of the transition, which range from 3 to 8 million) with a 1 percent payroll tax. As the average unemployment benefit is likely to exceed the minimum wage, however, the 1 percent tax rate could well be inadequate to cover the total cost of unemployment compensation.[74]

(3) Assessment and outlook

Social security reform should be viewed in the broader context of the overall reform of the economic system, with an eye on the longer run. In particular, the Soviet population is set to undergo a gradual ageing, as the old-age dependency rate increases over time during the first quarter of the next century. For instance, the percentage of the population age 65 and older could rise from 9.4 percent in 1990 to 16.9 percent in 2025, a rise broadly comparable to that anticipated in most OECD countries. The retirement policies put in place today therefore have implications for the budgetary pressures which future demographic conditions will create. Although the somewhat lower life expectancy in the USSR than in other developed countries can possibly justify correspondingly lower retirement ages, improved economic conditions that would follow the move to a free market would weaken this argument.

The greater risk, however, rests with the near and medium term. First, high rates of unemployment during the transition could noticeably reduce the contributory base for financing social security transfers. The induced higher payroll tax rates could in turn seriously harm the dynamism of the nascent private sector.[75] Second, while compensation to contain the hardship on the poor population should be an essential part of any transition program, protection of the large majority of the population from the adverse effects of inflation is not feasible economically.

NOTES

1. For further details on republican and national issues, see Appendix II-4.

2. For instance, the legal status of Leningrad and Moscow is comparable in many respects to that of a union republic.

3. The "lottery loans" (literally translated from Russian) appear to function as premium bonds.

4. Law on the Fundamentals of the Economic Relations of the USSR and the Union and Autonomous Republics, of April 10, 1990. Most principles affecting fiscal relations were further incorporated in the Decree on the Delimitation of Powers Between the USSR and the Subjects of the Federation, of April 26, 1990.

5. These areas include elaboration of forecasts—formally replacing the plan—of national social and economic developments; formulation and execution of union programs; implementation of general pricing policy; authority over the financial and credit system, including money in circulation; establishment of reserve, insurance, and other funds; determination of environmental protection and use of natural resources; management of transportation, communication, defense, space programs, energy and power systems, and union-owned property; coordination of the republics' activities regarding investment and depreciation policies, science, technology, employment, migration, education, health care and culture; extension of grants and loans to foreign governments, and contracting credits from abroad; and determination of the minimum wage, pensions and other social security benefits.

6. Other relevant republic responsibilities include: possession and disposal of natural resources in their own interest and in the interest of the USSR; regulation of economic activity and social development on their territory; participation in the formulation and implementation of union decisions on economic development; regulation of investment activity, and in particular, construction, on their territory; control of prices on the basis of union pricing policy; participation in the control over money in circulation and direction of the activities of republic-based banks; and decisions regarding social development, employment, income regulation (including minimum wage), pensions, and other social security benefits. In each of these areas, the republics' sphere of influence is narrowly circumscribed by the overriding USSR laws and regulations.

7. The emphasis on joint policymaking can be found also in the draft Union Treaty, elaborated by the central authorities in November 1990.

273

8. In turn, the members of the Federation Council are heads of the union republic governments, chaired by the President of the USSR. The executive powers of the Council have been substantially strengthened following the session of the USSR Supreme Soviet held on November 17, 1990.

9. The sharing of revenue and outlays between the republic and local jurisdictions depends in part on administrative considerations. International experience suggests that local (municipal, county, etc.) governments are in a relatively better position to collect taxes on real estate, as well as user fees, and have an advantage in investing in, and operating, local infrastructure projects, up to secondary school facilities, and in providing certain health care services and social assistance.

10. Reportedly, consumers and producers are already engaged in arbitrage of products subsidized at different rates (e.g., meat in certain Baltic republics).

11. International experience in federal tax structures reveals that in an open economic space it is necessary to introduce automatic border tax adjustments, coupled with administrative mechanisms, to offset existing differentials. For instance, in the European Community, a number of enforcement techniques have been considered (clearing houses, bonded warehouses) to affect the transfer of domestic indirect tax revenue collected on imports between trading partner countries. By contrast, in the United States, the lack of such a mechanism limits sales tax rate differentials across states. Analogously, in the area of company income taxation, to neutralize the effect of tax rate differentials on enterprises operating through affiliates, it is necessary to provide credits for taxes paid under other jurisdictions. Alternatively, as practiced in the United States, a multistate corporation's state tax base is determined by somewhat arbitrary apportionment rules (based on assets, sales, and/or work force). In Germany, the Länder choose to tax corporations at the location of the head office, automatically limiting tax rate differentials.

12. By contrast, the Shatalin reform plan envisaged upward transfers from the republics to finance union budget expenditures. Under this approach, transfers would be based on each republic's GDP or per capita GDP, and the republics could exercise considerable control over the union budget by determining the overall magnitude and timing of the transfers.

13. The Shatalin reform program essentially ruled out central bank financing of republic or local budget deficits.

14. By the same token, any drawdown of local government deposits with the banks should be consistent with any overall limits on *net* domestic bank credit to the consolidated budget and extrabudgetary funds.

15. New borrowing should be serviced by the debtor government, as against the present outstanding government liabilities or future debt contracted by the union, which are to be financed at the union level.

16. During the course of the New Economic Policy more than 60 kinds of taxes were introduced, including the personal income tax (1922). Most of these taxes disappeared in 1930, being replaced by the present turnover tax and system of payments of enterprise profits.

17. See Chapters III.4 and IV.3 for details.

18. Although the tax base consists of wage income, the tax is deemed to be an enterprise liability in the sense that individuals or households are, in practice, unaware of the tax.

19. The system (a form of financial autonomy) was adopted in 1987 by firms belonging to five ministries. In 1988 it was extended to an additional 20 ministries, and in 1989 to all enterprises.

20. The magnitude of the centralized fund operations in the period 1985-89 is shown in Appendix II-1, Table J.4.

21. Other authorized allocations included the enterprise's allocations to the fund for the development of production and science and technology; a reserve for interest payments on bank loans; deductions to the social consumption fund, to provide meals, medical care, and other benefits to workers; the material incentive fund, from which various premia and bonuses were paid; and allocations to the centralized production development fund.

22. Transfers to the budget are estimated to have declined from 50-60 percent of profits before the law was adopted to 35-42 percent, while payments to centralized funds were reduced from 30-40 percent of profits to less than 10 percent.

23. Decree of the USSR Council of Ministers of January 13, 1987, Section IV. See also Regulation of the USSR Ministry of Finance No. 124, of May 4, 1987.

24. Decree of the CPSU and the USSR Council of Ministers No. 1074, of September 17, 1987. The USSR Ministry of Finance set the corresponding regulation through Executive Order No. 226, of November 30, 1987.

25. Decree of the Presidium of the USSR Supreme Soviet of January 13, 1987.

26. Law on Taxes on Enterprises, Associations, and Organizations, of June 14, 1990. The law applied as of July 1, 1990 to joint ventures with a foreign equity participation exceeding 30 percent.

27. In late 1990, the elimination of centralized funds and most branch ministries by 1991 was envisaged. However, the draft state budget for 1991 included a tax on depreciation allowances and a one-time levy on the revaluation of inventories earmarked for newly created stabilization funds.

28. In principle, upon full repatriation of profits abroad, the Soviet tax burden would total 40.5 percent of profits.

29. See Appendix III.1-1.

30. For example, the deduction of repayment of loans used to finance centralized state investment, depreciation on the basis of the criteria set out in a firm's statute, a tax credit on the rental paid to state enterprises on goods made available in the process of restructuring, a tax credit on the interest on long-term bank debt of joint ventures, and a tax credit on the expenses made by joint ventures on account of scientific research and experimental design work.

31. The system of advance payments is described in Appendix III.1-1.

32. For details, see Appendix III.1-1. For a discussion of this tax scheme in the light of incomes policy considerations, see Chapter IV.6.

33. Income from abroad is taxed, but a foreign income tax credit is provided within the limits of Soviet law.

34. Starting in 1991, this tax will not be levied on married women; in the following year married men will be exempted, and in 1993 the tax (by then levied only on unmarried men) will be eliminated.

35. In this income interval, the average tax rate ranges from 0.3 percent to 9.8 percent.

36. From January 1, 1991 the tax credit can be claimed by employees having three or more economic dependents. Earlier it was necessary to have at least four dependents to qualify.

37. Here, as in all graduated rate schedules of the Soviet tax system, the tax (T) is computed using the formula $T = t(Y - L) + C$, where t is the marginal rate corresponding to the bracket, Y is taxable income, L is the lower limit of the income bracket, and C is a constant, capturing cumulative taxation in previous brackets. The adoption of a subtractive method—represented by the formula $T = t\,Y - C'$ where C' is also a constant—would simplify computation.

38. The determination of ad valorem rates has been made by using the formula

$$t = 1 - \frac{C\ (1+a)}{P\ (1-b)}$$

where C is planned cost, grossed up by a, a planned industry-specific markup or gross profit ranging from 0.15 to 0.23 but typically 0.20; and P is the retail price, discounted by b, a trade margin or retail markup on the order of 0.10. The rate thus determined is used for some period of time, usually for five years, before it is revised.

39. The regulations and rates were laid down by Decree No. 815 of the USSR Council of Ministers of August 13, 1990, and Letter No. 03-02-02 of the USSR Ministry of Finance, of August 22, 1990. Joint ventures were allowed to pay the tax retroactively without penalty or interest.

40. See Chapters III.4 and IV.3 for details.

41. At which the USSR already has the status of observer.

42. For details on the new commercial exchange rate, see Chapter III.4.

43. See USSR Council of Ministers decree No. 815 of August 13, 1990, applicable to joint ventures with at least 30 percent foreign participation retroactively since July 1, 1990. The new import tax structure, effective November 1, 1990, applies to all economic entities.

44. However, the fixed payments were sometimes based on the value of the output or as a percentage of the wholesale price or of the profit of the enterprise.

45. For more details, see Appendix III.1-2.

46. In order to make such a system operational, lower-level governments would need to be provided with qualified manpower for preparing and implementing their budgets without the involvement of ministries of higher-level government.

47. Although authorizations may be carried over from quarter to quarter, at the end of the year they are canceled.

48. To the extent that credits are expenditure authorizations, it would be more appropriate to view credit administrators as budget administrators.

49. In addition to these tasks, the Audit Department has the duty to conduct an audit where wrongdoing is suspected. The Economic Police, in charge of investigating economic crimes, is not allowed to present a case to the courts until the audit report is completed.

50. By comparison, U.S. budget defense outlays totaled 5.9 percent of GDP in 1989 and are estimated at 5.4 percent of GDP for 1990. For industrial countries as a whole, the figure was 4.4 percent in 1987, the last year for which comparable figures are available.

51. Prior to 1989, data on defense expenditure recorded in the state budget were incomplete and reflected only an amount equivalent to wages, salaries, and operational expenses. In May 1989, President Gorbachev announced a planned 1989 global defense expenditure figure of rub 77.3 billion, and stated that this followed two years in which defense outlays had been frozen. Reportedly, defense expenditure grew at around 1 or 2 percent a year in the 1960s and 1970s. In the mid-1980s, growth is said to have accelerated to around 3 percent per annum. It is likely that capacity had been building up since the early part of the decade, with the objective

of modernizing the existing stock of military assets. The Twelfth Five-Year Plan, starting in 1986, placed a strong priority on defense spending, which was to grow by 40 percent over the period of the plan, compared with a targeted 22 percent growth in national income. Around 1987, however, it appears that the build-up was reappraised.

52. In Japan, for example, military pensions are considered outside the defense budget. In the United States, internal security is classified as a civilian expenditure, while military R & D is defined as including spin-offs to civilian industry.

53. Attempts have been made to value weapons by using Soviet prices and Western production functions, but these have been recognized as questionable. Besides obvious differences in efficient techniques (not least because, given prices, relative scarcities in the USSR and the West are so different), account must be taken of possible economies of scale. It has been suggested that the USSR produces relatively few undifferentiated weapons, in long production runs. It is hence likely that per unit production costs in the USSR would turn out to be much lower than would be estimated by a Western manufacturer accustomed to producing a more specialized armament in lower quantities and with a shorter economic life.

54. In contrast, national income accounts do include imputations for unpriced services (including imputations for land use which might be considered analogous to rent imputations made on owner-occupied houses), but at domestic prices. Only a full economic accounting would attempt to apply shadow prices to correct all domestic price distortions. Nonetheless, in an economy where all prices are administered and there may not be equilibrium in the market for any single good, the question of which prices are "out of line" is a matter of degree and of judgment. From a narrow methodological point of view, it seems inconsistent to accept the Soviet social valuation of consumer goods in the construction of the national income accounts, but to reject the social valuation of military inputs and output.

55. Nevertheless, it remains a cause for concern that national income estimates of defense-related production are larger than financial data on defense expenditure.

56. Identifiable direct subsidies to loss-making enterprises (in all sectors) were at most rub 1.8 billion in 1989 and rub 16.8 billion in 1990 (i.e., the "subsidies" line in "state budget expenditure on the economy"). Losses could conceivably also have been covered under the rubric of "operational expenditures" (also part of expenditure on the economy). These amounted to rub 8 billion in 1989 and rub 11.8 billion in 1990 (Table III.1,8).

57. This assumes that, as President Gorbachev stated, defense expenditure in 1988 was the same as in 1989.

58. To make this assessment, it would be necessary to know the relevant price deflator and the extent to which the above growth rate includes conversion expenditures.

59. While this target does not presume that the size of the defense complex remains as large as at present, the conversion program does not plan to dismantle the defense complex; indeed, it is possible that civilian industries could be incorporated in it.

60. These figures are obtained using an exchange rate of rub 1.2 per DM, following the introduction of the commercial exchange rate in November 1990.

61. The plan does not include the cost of increasing procurement prices in May 1990, effective for the 1990 grain harvest. While supplementary costs of rub 9 billion for the state budget as a whole, and a possible further rub 5 billion for the RSFSR, have been projected, the seasonality involved makes these preliminary calculations subject to a wide margin of error.

62. The underlying data (in rubles) are as follows, with the subsidy being larger than the difference shown between producer and retail prices to the extent of the markups excluded from the producer price:

	Producer Price	Retail Price	Difference
Meat (kg)	6.0	1.8	4.2
Butter (kg)	11.8	3.4	8.4
Milk (liter)	0.65	0.24	0.41

63. Most of the economic subsidy to housing actually stems from the treatment of land as essentially free and probably also from the low costing of buildings and maintenance services. Two other possibly significant sources of housing subsidy are preferential credits for reconstruction and the provision of housing services by enterprises, neither of which appears in the budget.

64. For instance, the subsidy on grain could rise from its 1988 level of rub 64.8 per ton to rub 176 per ton.

65. Also see Chapter IV.6.

66. Other sources of assistance consist of goods and services (such as day care) provided through social consumption funds at the enterprise, and consumer subsidies.

67. Transfers from the budgets of union republics and receipts from the sale of sanitaria tickets to temporarily disabled workers have provided the remainder of revenue.

68. Until now, retirees have been free to choose between having the pension computed on the basis of earnings during the past 12 months prior to retirement and the 5 best consecutive years in the past 10.

69. An allowance of rub 12 per child per month that has until now been paid to low income unmarried mothers from the union budget will hereafter be paid by each separate union republic out of its own revenues.

70. The guidelines thus seem to bring forward the full indexation of pensions provided for in the pension reform.

71. For a more detailed discussion, see Chapter IV.6.

72. There currently exists some means testing insofar as allowances for raising children in poor families are provided, as described above.

73. The original proposal was for the employer's contribution rate to be set at 37 percent of wages, resulting in a surplus equivalent to 11 percentage points in the initial year. Instead, as part of the 1991 draft budget, a separate 11 percent payroll tax has been temporarily earmarked for the newly-created stabilization funds.

74. Moreover, these estimates do not take into account the costs of the employment service and of retraining programs (see Chapter IV.6).

75. Simulations presented in Appendix III.1-3 bring out clearly the potential impact of high unemployment rates on required pay-as-you-go contribution rates.

Table III.1.1. USSR: Breakdown of State Budget Revenue of Union Republics, by Republic, 1990 [1]

Union Republic	Total Revenue (Billions rubles)	Total Revenue (Percent of total)	Turnover Tax (Percent allocation) 1989	Turnover Tax (Percent allocation) 1990	Turnover Tax (Percent of total revenue)	Personal Income Tax (Percent allocation) 1989	Personal Income Tax (Percent allocation) 1990	Personal Income Tax (Percent of total revenue)	Enterprise Taxes [2] (Percent allocation) 1990 [3]	Enterprise Taxes [2] (Percent of total revenue)	Grants from Union (Percent of total revenue)	Other Sources (Percent of total revenue)
All republics [4]	248.7	100.0	74	82	37.5	51	57	8.2	14	6.6	3.5	44.2
RSFSR	137.5	55.3	71	84	37.7	50	50	9.2	12	7.6	—	45.5
Ukraine	39.5	15.9	61	68	31.3	50	50	7.8	12	5.8	—	55.1
Belorussia	11.8	4.7	86	71	47.5	50	50	5.5	20	5.9	—	41.1
Estonia	1.9	0.8	84	76	47.4	84	100	11.6	84	11.0	—	30.0
Latvia	3.2	1.3	58	57	43.8	58	100	7.5	58	15.6	—	33.1
Lithuania	4.3	1.7	78	94	41.9	78	50	10.0	78	9.3	—	38.8
Moldavia	3.4	1.4	69	87	44.1	50	50	5.6	20	4.1	—	46.2
Georgia	4.4	1.8	100	100	48.7	50	100	6.4	20	4.5	—	41.4
Armenia	3.5	1.4	100	77	57.1	50	50	5.1	20	5.1	2.9	29.8
Azerbaidzhan	4.4	1.8	81	75	47.7	50	50	4.8	20	4.5	—	43.0
Kazakhstan	15.2	6.1	100	100	30.3	50	100	7.2	20	3.3	25.0	34.2
Turkmenistan	2.3	0.9	100	100	34.8	50	100	5.2	20	2.2	30.9	26.9
Uzbekistan	11.6	4.7	100	100	34.5	50	100	5.2	20	3.4	26.7	30.2
Tadshikistan	2.7	1.1	100	100	40.7	50	100	4.8	20	2.6	15.2	36.7
Kirgizia	3.0	1.2	100	100	40.0	50	100	5.0	20	3.4	18.3	33.3

Sources: Ministry of Finance and estimates.

1. Consolidated budget of union republics and local soviets of people's deputies. Data refer to budget plan for 1990, unless otherwise noted. Allocation refers to the proportion of revenue to be retained by union republic from revenue collected within the republic in a given revenue category.
2. Revenue from profits of union-subordinated state enterprises from: allocation of profit tax, as shown; 100 percent allocation of tax on labor resources; and 100 percent of water charges.
3. Profit tax only.
4. Weighted average of republic amounts, except for first two columns which represent totals.

Table III.1.2.   USSR: Breakdown of State Budget Revenue, by Government Level, 1989

	State Budget of USSR	Union Budget	State Budgets of Union Republics (In billions of rubles)			Union Budget	State Budgets of Union Republics (Percent of state budget)		
			Total	Repub-lics¹	Local		Total	Repub-lics¹	Local
Total revenue [2]	393.9	208.6	185.3	103.5	81.8	53	47	26	21
Tax revenue	372.8	196.8	176.0	99.5	76.5	53	47	27	20
Income taxes and transfers	161.4	86.7	74.7	28.1	46.6	54	46	17	29
Profit taxes and transfers	119.7	70.4	49.3	23.5	25.8	59	41	20	22
State enterprises	115.5	70.1	45.4	23.5	21.9	61	39	20	19
Cooperatives	4.2	0.3	3.9	—	3.9	7	93	—	93
Personal income tax	41.7	16.3	25.4	4.6	20.8	39	61	11	50
Turnover tax	111.1	15.1	96.0	66.1	29.9	14	86	59	27
Social insurance contributions ...	33.1	27.8	5.3 [3]	5.3	—	84	16	16	—
Foreign activity [2]	67.2	67.2	—	—	—	100	—	—	—
Nontax revenue	21.1	11.8	9.3	4.0	5.3	56	44	19	25
Memorandum items:									
Financial revenue									
Lottery loan	2.6	1.1	1.5	0.7	0.8	42	58	27	31
Surplus from republics	6.3	—	6.3	2.6	3.7	—	100	41	59
Intergovernmental transfers		8.5	31.3						
Transfers from union		—	31.3						
Livestock and milk subsidy ...		—	13.4						
Republic-specific grants		—	5.9						
Other transfers [4]		—	12.0						
Transfers from republics [4]		8.5							

Sources: Ministry of Finance; and estimates.
1. Calculated as a residual from the data for state budgets of union republics and local budgets.
2. Net of intergovernmental transfers, but includes financing from abroad.
3. Calculated as a residual from state budget of USSR and union budget.
4. Largely lending from, or repayments to, the union.

Table III.1.3.   USSR: Breakdown of State Budget Expenditure, by Government Level, 1989

	State Budget of USSR	Union Budget	State Budgets of Union Republics			Union Budget	State Budgets of Union Republics		
			Total	Repub-lics	Local		Total	Repub-lics	Local
	(In billions of rubles)					*(Percent of state budget)*			
Total expenditure [1]	480.1	242.3	237.8	157.9	79.9	51	49	33	16
Economy	200.1	74.6	125.5	102.2	23.3	37	63	51	12
Investment	68.0	41.4	26.6	13.3	13.3	61	39	20	19
Operational expenditures	8.0	7.2	0.8	—	0.8	90	10	—	10
Price compensation	66.3	19.5	46.8	44.6	2.2	29	71	67	3
Procurement prices	31.6	—	31.6	31.6	—	—	100	100	—
Social and cultural activities	139.2	35.8	103.4	51.1	52.3	26	74	37	37
Education	44.4	4.2	40.2	10.7	29.4	10	90	24	66
Health	24.6	1.5	23.1	1.8	21.2	6	94	7	86
Social insurance	25.2	25.2	—	—	—	100	—	—	—
Social security pensions	35.8	—	35.8	35.8	—	—	100	100	—
Other benefits	9.2	4.9	4.3	2.6	1.7	53	46	28	18
Science	10.1	8.3	1.8	1.7	0.1	82	18	17	1
Defense	75.2	75.2	—	—	—	100	—	—	—
Justice and internal security	8.2	8.2	—	—	—	100	—	—	—
Other expenditures [2]	18.7	11.7	7.0	2.7	4.3	63	37	14	23
Foreign activity [1]	28.4	28.2	0.2	0.2	—	99	1	1	—
Memorandum item:									
Intergovernmental transfers		31.3	8.5						
Transfers to union [3]			8.5						
Transfers to republics		31.3	—						
Livestock and milk subsidy ...		13.4	—						
Republic-specific grants		5.9	—						
Other transfers [3]		12.0	—						

Source: Ministry of Finance; and estimates.
1. Net of intergovernmental transfers, but including financing flows to abroad.
2. Including administration.
3. Largely repayments by, and lending to, union republics.

281

Table III.1.4. USSR: State Budget Revenue, 1985-90

(In billions of rubles; percent of GDP in parentheses)

	1985	1986	1987	1988	Estimate 1989	Plan 1990
Total revenue	367.7	366.0	360.1	365.1	384.9	410.1
	(47.3)	(45.8)	(43.6)	(41.7)	(41.0)	(42.8)
Tax revenue	337.1	335.6	342.9	340.0	361.6	387.8
Income taxes and transfers [1]	148.4	159.7	158.8	154.3	157.3	168.0
Individual income taxes	30.0	31.2	32.5	35.9	41.7	43.5
Income tax	28.3	29.5	30.9	33.9	37.5	40.2
Agriculture tax	0.2	0.2	0.2	0.2	0.2	0.2
Tax on adults without children	1.5	1.5	1.4	1.4	1.5	1.5
Patents and other income taxes	—	—	—	0.4	2.5	1.6
Profit taxes and transfers	118.4	128.5	126.3	118.4	115.6	124.5
Enterprises	115.9	125.9	123.4	115.6	111.4	120.4
Profit transfers and deductions	30.2	43.4	66.7	61.0	66.0	78.8
Fixed payments	0.5	3.2	2.2	0.7	0.6	—
Residual profit payments	47.1	38.5	12.8	9.5	4.8	—
Wage taxes [2]	—	—	—	4.9	6.2	3.0
On fixed and working capital	38.1	40.8	41.7	39.5	33.8	38.6
Cooperatives and social organizations	2.5	2.6	2.9	2.8	4.2	4.1
Collective farms	1.2	1.2	1.3	1.3	1.6	1.4
Cooperatives, other	1.3	1.4	1.6	1.6	2.6	2.7
Social insurance contributions	25.4	26.5	28.1	30.1	33.1	44.8
Turnover tax	97.7	91.5	94.4	101.0	111.1	121.9
Alcohol	30.1	27.2	29.1	33.4	40.4	39.0
Other	67.6	64.3	65.3	67.6	70.7	82.9
Taxes on foreign trade	65.0	57.3	60.9	53.9	58.2	49.4
Exports	33.8	26.3	29.4	24.0	23.8	16.0
Of which: oil & gas	...	...	...	...	14.0	11.5
Imports	31.2	31.0	31.5	29.9	34.3	33.3
Revenue from other foreign activity	0.6	0.6	0.7	0.7	0.9	2.4
Of which: foreign exchange	—	—	—	...	...	1.0
Tax on owners of vehicles	—	—	—	—	1.1	1.3
Nontax revenue	30.6	30.4	17.2	25.1	23.3	22.3
Geological fees	3.7	3.9	4.0	4.1	4.1	4.2
Movies	1.3	1.3	1.4	1.6	1.6	1.5
Forestry	0.8	0.8	0.9	0.8	0.8	0.8
Water	0.5	0.5	0.5	0.5	0.5	0.5
Lotteries	0.3	0.3	0.3	0.3	0.4	0.3
Levies and other nontax revenues	24.0	23.6	10.1	17.8	15.9	15.0

Sources: Ministry of Finance; and estimates.
1. Includes revenue from sources other than fixed-rate taxes.
2. Refers to the labor resource tax in 1988 and to the excess wage tax in 1989-90.

Table III.1.5. USSR: Summary of the 1990-91 Tax Reform

Tax	Before Reform	After Reform
1. PROFIT TAX		
1.1 *On enterprises*	Enterprises would pay to the budget part of the planned profit, fixed payments for the use of labor and natural resources, payment on the value of fixed and working capital, and residual profit payments. The enterprise would also make payments to centralized funds managed by the corresponding branch ministry.	Uniform transfer to the budget, on the base of a 45 percent (normal rate) tax on profit. No payments to centralized funds.
	R & D and environment-protection expenses: not deductible.	30 percent deductible.
1.2 *On joint ventures*	Profit taxed at 30 percent.	Joint ventures with at least 30 percent foreign capital: profit taxed at 30 percent (10 percent in the Far East economic region);
		Other joint ventures: profit taxed at the same rate as enterprises.
	Two-year tax holiday.	Two-year tax holiday for joint ventures with at least 30 percent foreign capital.
	Uniform taxation.	Excess profits taxed at 80-90 percent.
	Dividend distribution: not taxed (there were no joint stock companies).	Dividend distribution: a tax of 15 percent is withheld at source.
	Remittances of profit abroad: taxed at 20 percent.	taxed at 15 percent.
	Repayment of principal of bank loans: deductible.	not deductible.
	Bonuses paid to employees, interest on long-term bank loans: not deductible.	deductible.
	R & D expenditure, environment-protection expenses, capital investment: deductible.	deductible.
1.3 *On cooperatives*	No tax on profit at Union level. A tax on gross income.	No tax on gross income.
		Profit taxed on the same basis as profit of enterprises.
1.4 *On the net income of public entertainment*	Not taxed in separate.	Taxed at 70 percent.
1.5 *On foreign companies with a permanent establishment*	Profit taxed at 40 percent.	Profit taxed at 30 percent.

Table III.1.5. (Continued)   USSR: Summary of the 1990-91 Tax Reform

Tax	Before Reform	After Reform

2. INDIVIDUAL INCOME TAX

2.1 *Wage income tax*

	First rub 70 per month exempt.	First rub 100 per month exempt.
	Marginal rate of 13 percent on monthly income over rub 100.	Marginal rate of 60 percent on monthly income over rub 3,000.
	Tax reduced by 30 percent if employee has four or more dependents.	Tax reduced by 30 percent if employee has three or more dependents.

2.2 *Tax on the income of the self-employed*

	Marginal rates ranging from 1.5 percent to 13 percent.	Marginal rates ranging from 1.5 percent to 60 percent.

2.3 *Tax on the income from intellectual property*

	Works intended for use inside the country: marginal rates ranging from 1.5 percent to 13 percent.	Marginal rates ranging from 1.5 percent to 60 percent.
	Works intended for use abroad: marginal rates ranging from 30 percent to 75 percent.	
	Heirs of authors taxed at rates ranging from 60 percent to 90 percent.	Heirs of authors taxed at rates ranging from 60 percent to 90 percent.

2.4 *Tax on other income of individual activity*

	Handicraft and artisanal activities: annual income over rub 840 taxed at rates up to 65 percent.	Annual income taxed at rates up to 60 percent.
	Professional and religious activities: annual income over rub 300 taxed at rates up to 69 percent.	
	Other activities:	
	annual income over rub 300 taxed at rates up to 81 percent.	

3. TAX ON EXCESS WAGE INCREASES

	Rates of 100, 200, and 300 percent.	Rates of 100, 125, 150, and 200 percent.

4. TURNOVER TAX

	In general calculated as the difference between administratively-fixed retail and wholesale prices, minus trading margins	In general expressed in ad valorem rates.
	Joint ventures exempt.	Joint ventures taxed at rates ranging from 15 percent to 90 percent.

284

Table III.1.5. (Concluded)   USSR: Summary of the 1990-91 Tax Reform

Tax	Before Reform	After Reform
5. TAXES ON FOREIGN TRADE		
5.1 Customs duties	A tariff on 300 items of import, averaging 3.5 percent.	A modern tariff on 10,000 items, with rates up to 100 percent and average below 10 percent.
5.2 Import and export tax	Tax computed as the difference between the fixed domestic price and the world price.	Rates up to 2,090 percent (to be reduced to 500 percent when the exchange rate is unified) on 200 items of import.
		Old system of price differentials to be used only for some government transactions.
	Joint ventures operations exempt.	Joint ventures operations taxed.

Source: Ministry of Finance.

Table III.1.6. USSR: Turnover Tax Revenue, 1989

	In Billions of Rubles	As Percent of Total	As Percent of Net Output [1]
Total	111.1	100.0	...
Heavy industry	36.5	32.9	...
Metallurgy	0.6	0.5	2.5
Petroleum products	12.0	10.8	60.9
Chemical and petrochemical	4.3	3.8	24.6
Chemical industry	2.0	1.8	...
Petrochemicals	2.3	2.1	...
Electric power	2.4	2.1	25.9
Machine building	6.6	6.0	7.0
Forestry industry	0.4	0.3	2.4
Building materials	1.3	1.2	11.3
Other [2]	9.0	8.1	...
Light industry	19.8	17.9	68.4
Textiles	9.3	8.4	...
Footwear	1.9	1.7	...
Knitwear	5.4	4.9	...
Other	3.2	2.9	...
Food and beverages industry	52.0	46.8	227.9
Fats and oils	1.6	1.4	...
Confectionary	1.7	1.6	...
Alcoholic beverages	41.9	37.7	...
Beer	1.8	1.6	...
Spirits	31.0	27.9	...
Wine	9.1	8.2	...
Tobacco products	1.8	1.6	...
Grain products	1.9	1.7	...
Other	3.1	2.8	...
Other industry	3.4	3.0	...
Refunds	(0.6)	(0.5)	...

Sources: Ministry of Finance; Goskomstat; and estimates.
1. In wholesale prices of enterprises, excluding turnover tax.
2. Includes Main Directorate for Diamonds and Gold.

Table III.1.7. USSR: Summary of Budget Preparation Process[1]

Principal Activities	Institutions	Timetable

I. *USSR State Budget*

1. *Union budget*

Principal Activities	Institutions	Timetable
a. The USSR Ministry of Finance prepares instructions, forms, and schedules for the forthcoming budget year. The Ministry also prepares a preliminary balance of revenues and expenditure using estimates provided by the Gosplan. The preliminary balance accompanied by comments and explanation and instructions is sent to the all-union ministries and to the ministries of finance of union republics.	Gosplan, USSR Ministry of Finance	March-April
b. Union branch ministries and spending agencies prepare budget estimates based on information received from lower level units but within the framework of the preliminary balance provided by the USSR Ministry of Finance.	Union republic ministries of finance; branch ministries; spending agencies	April-May
c. Preliminary draft of the consolidated state budgets of union republics are analyzed in the USSR Ministry of Finance.	USSR Ministry of Finance	May-July
d. Exchange of additional information between the USSR Ministry of Finance and the ministries of finance of union republics.	USSR Ministry of Finance; Union-republic ministries of finance	May-July
e. Budget negotiations between the USSR Ministry of Finance and the ministries of finance of union republics	USSR Ministry of Finance; Union-republic ministries of finance	May-July
f. Preparation of the draft of the consolidated state union budget and submission to the Council of Ministers	USSR Ministry of Finance; USSR Council of Ministers	September-October
g. Submission of the draft of the consolidated state union budget to the Economic Committees of the Supreme Soviet	USSR Council of Ministers; USSR Supreme Soviet	November
h. Review of the draft in the committees prior to submission to the plenary services of the two houses of the Supreme Soviet	Economic Committees of USSR Supreme Soviet	December
i. Adoption of the USSR state budget law.	USSR Supreme Soviet	December

287

Table III.1.7 (Concluded).   USSR: Summary of Budget Preparation Process [1]

Principal Activities	Institutions	Timetable
2. *State budgets of union republics*		
The stages in the preparation of union republican budgets are the same as the ones of the all-union budget. One important difference is that the first input for the preparation process comes from the USSR Ministry of Finance and not from Gosplan.	USSR Ministry of Finance; ministries of finance of union republics; department of finances of oblasts and krays; supreme soviets of union republics	March-December
II. *Local Budgets*		
The finance departments of oblasts, krays, rayons and cities (fourth-level governments) as well as the finance committees of small cities and rural settlements (fifth-level governments) prepare budget estimates based on information received from lower level units but within the framework of the preliminary balance provided by an upper level unit.	Ministries of finance of union-republics; departments of finance of oblasts and krays; finance offices of lower-level governments	March-May
Steps c, d, e, and f are the same as the steps of the union or the union republican budgets. Budget preparation as well as budget negotiations follow much simplified procedures.	Departments of finance of oblasts and krays; finance offices of lower-level governments	September-December
Steps g, h, and i are the same as for the union or the union republican budgets. Submission for review and adoption is effected by the relevant institutions or organizations.	Executive committees of lower-level governments	September-December

Source: Ministry of Finance.
1. With respect to 1990 budget.

288

Table III.1.8.   USSR: State Budget Expenditure, 1985-90
(In billions of rubles)

	1985	1986	1987	1988	Estimate 1989	Plan 1990
Total expenditure	386.0	415.6	429.3	445.9	465.1	485.6
(in percent of GDP)	(49.7)	(52.0)	(52.0)	(51.0)	(49.5)	(50.6)
Economy	217.2	234.1	234.0	203.1	200.1	188.2
Investment	63.8	66.4	71.8	76.3	68.0	42.2
Subsidies	3.4	2.2	1.9	1.9	1.8	16.8
Operational expenditures	13.2	13.6	13.0	12.7	8.0	11.8
Price differentials	65.8	73.0	74.9	64.3	66.3	95.9
Increases in procurement prices	—	—	—	21.9	31.6	—
Other	71.0	78.9	72.4	26.0	24.4	21.5
Defense	19.1	19.1	20.2	57.3	75.2	71.0
Procurement	...	...	...	...	32.6	31.0
R & D (including space)	...	...	...	...	15.3	13.2
Wages and salaries	19.1	19.1	20.2	20.2	20.2	19.3
Pensions	...	...	...	...	2.3	2.4
Military construction	...	...	...	...	4.6	3.7
Other	...	...	...	...	0.2	1.3
Justice and internal security	5.7	6.0	6.2	6.6	8.2	9.6
Administration	3.0	3.0	2.9	3.0	2.9	2.9
Science	13.7	14.4	12.4	16.9	10.1	11.0
Social and cultural activities	111.9	119.3	127.6	134.3	139.3	160.5
Education	35.9	38.1	42.3	42.7	44.5	49.6
Health and physical cultural	17.6	18.0	19.5	21.9	24.6	27.6
Budget of national social insurance ..	22.8	23.6	24.0	25.5	25.3	4.9
Grant to central collective						
farm insurance	3.1	4.0	3.8	4.1	4.0	6.6
Mothers	0.6	0.6	0.7	...	0.7	0.8
Social security	31.9	35.0	37.3	40.1	40.2	71.0
On account of national						
social insurance	25.8	28.7	30.8	...	35.8	41.2
Other	6.1	6.3	6.5	...	4.4	29.8
Lottery	0.2	0.2	0.2	0.2	0.2	0.2
Foreign economic activity	2.2	4.9	11.9	15.6	15.4	14.9
Trade subsidies	0.9	1.5	8.1	9.7	9.6	7.4
Exports	...	0.5	5.9	6.7	6.9	6.8
Imports	...	1.0	2.2	3.0	2.7	0.6
Subsidies to industry	...	2.0	2.1	2.2	2.1	2.3
Unilateral aid	1.3	1.1	1.7	2.1	1.5	2.0
Interest payments	...	...	...	0.8	1.3	1.9
Other [1]	...	0.4	...	0.8	0.9	1.3
Other expenditures	13.0	14.6	13.9	9.1	13.7	27.3
Internal interest payments	...	...	...	4.5	5.3	6.3
Gosbank	...	...	...	4.5	5.3	6.3
Price diff. on agricultural products .	—	—	—	—	—	0.4
Reserve funds	...	...	...	0.4	4.5	4.1
USSR Council of Ministers	...	...	...	0.4	1.8	1.0
Republic Council of Ministers	...	...	...	...	2.2	2.6
Ministry of Finance	...	...	...	...	0.5	0.5
Other	13.0	14.6	13.9	4.2	3.9	16.9

Source: Ministry of Finance; and estimates.
1. Including exchange rate-related expenditure.

289

Table III.1.9.   USSR: Subsidy Payments, 1988-90

	1988	1989	Plan 1990
	(In billions of rubles)		
Total subsidies	131.5	126.5	129.4
Budget subsidies to domestic producers and consumers	102.1	103.0	112.8
Agro-industrial complex	89.6	91.1	100.4
Food production	57.3	55.6	62.7
Livestock prices	26.8	22.7	28.2
Milk products	16.4	17.1	18.1
Grain and oilseed prices	6.0	6.8	6.8
Grain and bread products	0.2	0.3	0.3
Potatoes and vegetables	2.0	2.3	2.4
Conserved fruits and vegetables	1.3	1.4	1.5
Supplies to public cafeterias	0.1	...	...
Sugar	1.7	1.9	2.0
Potatoes for alcohol/starch products	0.2	0.3	0.3
Fish	2.6	2.8	3.1
Farmers	27.1	32.0	33.0
Low profit	1.8	...	...
Ordinary	25.3	32.0	33.0
Other agro-industrial subsidies	5.2	3.5	4.7
Animal fodder and seeds	0.1	0.1	0.1
Light industry (textiles)	3.2	3.4	4.6
Fish meal	0.1	...	...
Tractors and fertilizers	1.8	...	...
Other subsidies to consumers	5.9	4.4	3.9
Central Cooperative Union	—	0.1	0.1
Theaters	0.2	0.3	0.3
Cinemas	—	—	...
Housing and utilities (operational costs)	1.4	0.1	0.1
Housing (local soviets)	2.1	1.7	1.7
Municipal utilities of local soviets	1.0	0.9	0.4
Other public consumption goods	1.1	1.3	1.4
Subsidies to heavy industry	6.7	7.5	8.5
Thermal energy	1.3	1.0	1.1
Coal	5.4	6.4	7.3
Pharmaceuticals	...	0.1	0.1
Subsidies financed by tax offsets or outside the budget [1]	2.1	2.5	2.5
Construction of farmers' markets	0.2	0.2	0.2
Clothes for children	1.6	2.1	2.0
Ministry of non-ferrous metals	0.3	0.2	0.3
Agricultural support fund	15.4	9.3	4.4
Subsidies for foreign activity	11.9	11.7	9.7
Trade subsidies	9.7	9.6	7.4
Exports	6.7	6.9	6.8
Imports	3.0	2.7	0.6
Subsidies to foreign exchange using industries	2.2	2.1	2.3

Table III.1.9. (Concluded): USSR: Subsidy Payments, 1988-90

	1988	1989	Plan 1990
	(In percent of GDP)		
Total subsidies	15.0	13.5	13.5
To domestic producers and consumers	11.7	11.0	11.8
Agro-industrial complex	10.2	9.7	10.5
Of which:			
Food production	6.5	5.9	6.5
Other subsidies to consumers	0.7	0.5	0.4
Subsidies to heavy industry	0.8	0.8	0.9
Subsidies financed by tax offsets or outside the budget [1]	0.2	0.3	0.3
Agricultural price support fund	1.8	1.0	0.5
Subsidies for foreign activity	1.1	1.0	0.8
Trade subsidies	1.1	1.0	0.8
	(In billions of rubles)		
Memorandum item:			
Domestic subsidies [2]	119.6	114.8	119.7
State budget subsidies [3]	114.0	114.7	122.5

Source: Ministry of Finance; and Gosbank.

1. Farmers' markets are offset against income tax; children's clothes are offset against turnover tax; and presumably the subsidy to the Ministry of Non-Ferrous Metals is financed by enterprise payments. Excluding cross-subsidies provided through centralized funds.
2. Domestic subsidies to producers and consumers, plus subsidies financed by tax offsets or outside the budget, plus agricultural price support fund.
3. Domestic subsidies to producers and consumers plus subsidies for foreign activity.

Table III.1.10. USSR: Social Security Operations, 1985-90

(In billions of rubles; in percent of GDP in parentheses)

	1985	1986	1987	1988	Estimate 1989	Preliminary 1990
Receipts	61.1	65.9	69.2	73.6	76.4	91.9
	(7.9)	(8.2)	(8.4)	(8.4)	(8.1)	(9.5)
From the union budget	54.4	59.1	61.5	67.6	...	...
Social insurance contributions	25.4	26.5	28.1	30.1	33.1	44.7
General revenue	29.0	32.6	33.4	37.5	...	...
From budgets of union republics	4.0	4.2	4.3	4.5	...	...
Other revenue	2.7	2.6	3.4	1.5	2.6	2.7
Expenditure	61.1	65.9	69.2	73.6	76.4	91.9
	(7.9)	(8.2)	(8.4)	(8.4)	(8.1)	(9.5)
Old-age, disability and						
survivors' pensions	45.0	49.3	51.7	54.9	58.6	65.6
Allowances	14.4	14.6	15.2	16.4	17.8	24.0[1]
Of which:						
Sick pay	7.3	7.4	7.2	8.2	8.6	9.6
Maternity	2.0	2.2	2.3	2.4	2.3	3.0
Family allowances	3.6	3.7	3.7	3.8	3.5[2]	8.5
Other expenditure	1.7	2.0	2.3	2.3	—	2.3

Source: Ministry of Finance; and estimates.

1. Disaggregated data for some of the allowances (temporary disability, maternity and childbirth, and sanitaria visits) are not available for 1990 and the allocation shown in this column has been made using the shares of each of these in the previous year.
2. Separate data were not available for these benefits for collective farmworkers, and therefore the figure for this year should be considered with caution.

Chart 1. **USSR: STRUCTURE OF THE STATE BUDGET**

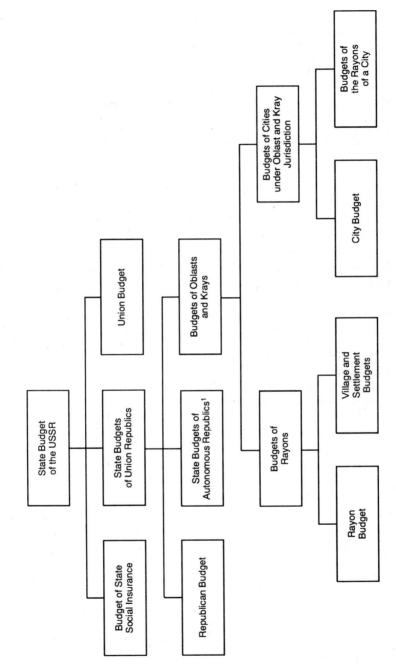

1. Constructed similarly to the state budgets of the union republics.

Chart 2. **USSR: AVERAGE AND MARGINAL TAX RATES BY WAGE INCOME LEVEL**[1]

(percent of taxable income)

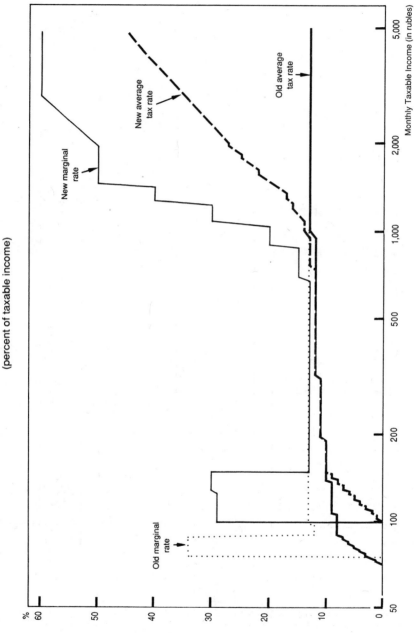

1. Old rates refer to those prior to July 1990, while the new rates have been effective thereafter.

294

Chart 3. USSR: STRUCTURE OF THE STATE TAX SERVICE

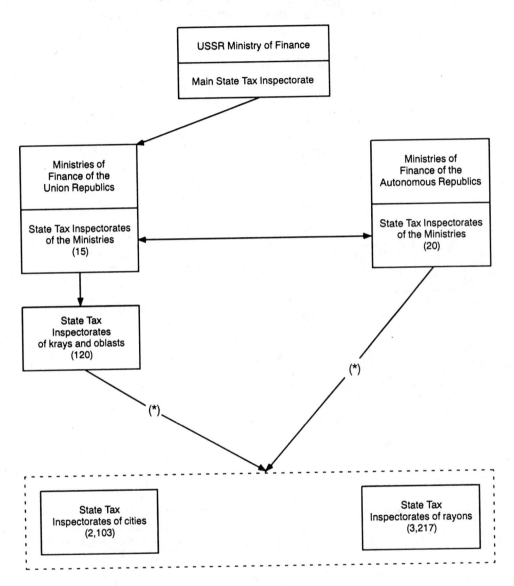

Total: 5,476 Inspectorates

(*) Whenever the city or rayon belongs to an autonomous republic, the corresponding tax inspectorate reports to the tax inspectorate of that republic's ministry of finance. Otherwise the tax inspectorate reports to the tax inspectorate of the kray or oblast to which it belongs.

Chart 4. USSR: STRUCTURE OF THE STATE TAX INSPECTORATE OF THE USSR MINISTRY OF FINANCE

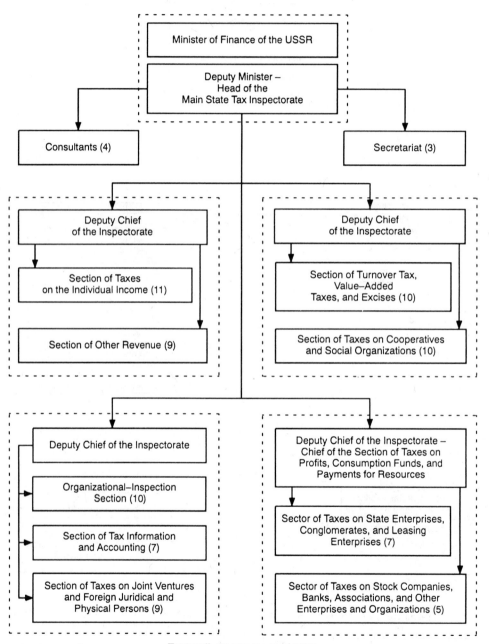

Total staff: 91 persons as of 1990

Chart 5. **USSR: ORGANIZATION OF THE USSR MINISTRY OF FINANCE**

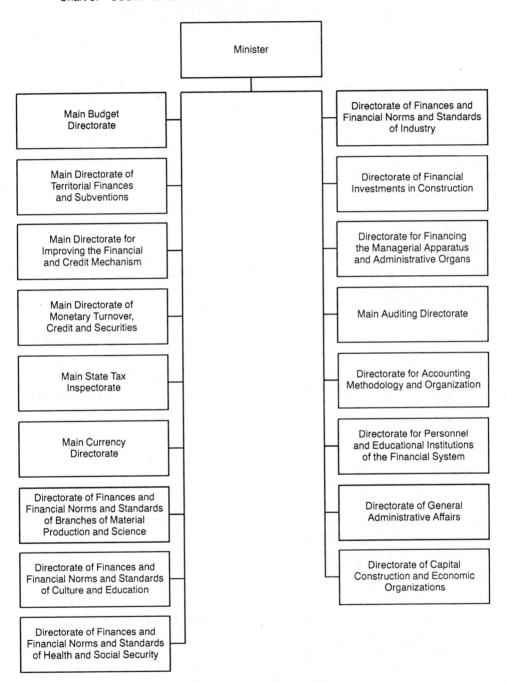

297

Chart 6. USSR: ORGANIZATION OF THE MAIN BUDGET DIRECTORATE

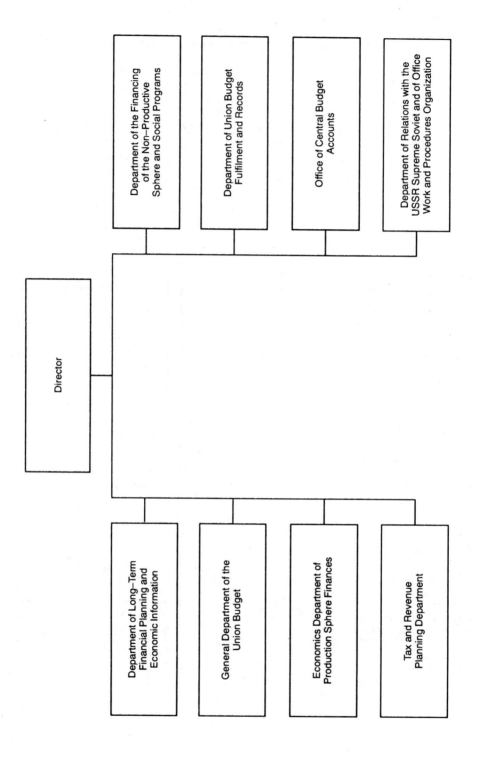

Director

Department of the Financing of the Non–Productive Sphere and Social Programs

Department of Union Budget Fulfilment and Records

Office of Central Budget Accounts

Department of Relations with the USSR Supreme Soviet and of Office Work and Procedures Organization

Department of Long–Term Financial Planning and Economic Information

General Department of the Union Budget

Economics Department of Production Sphere Finances

Tax and Revenue Planning Department

Appendix III.1-1

Summary of the Tax System[1]

I. TAXES ON NET INCOME AND PROFITS

1. PROFIT TAX

(Act of June 14, 1990, Ch.I)

(Effective January 1, 1991. Effective July 1, 1990, however, in relation to joint ventures with more than 30 percent foreign capital, and work centers for young people and youth centers of Konsomol.)

a. Nature of tax

A tax on the net income of *enterprises,* meaning private or public enterprises, associations, and organizations which are legal persons and have an independent balance sheet, including joint ventures, nongovernment foreign organizations, and non-budget government agencies deriving income from economic and other commercial activity. (Profit of foreign firms: see item 2 below.)

Deductible *costs and expenses* include labor, purchased goods, inputs, and services, social security and medical insurance payments, compulsory insurance, interest on short-term debt, depreciation and equipment repair, and expenditure related to natural resources and mining. Joint ventures may choose their own depreciation criteria.

Wage expenditure is adjusted upwards/downwards to conform to the standard set by the USSR Supreme Soviet. This rule does not apply to foreign investment (joint enterprises with foreign capital participation higher than 30 percent, international nongovernment organizations, and international associations engaging in economic activity).

Commercial and cooperative banks and joint ventures may deduct provisions to a *special reserve,* up to the point it reaches 25 percent of equity capital. On the liquidation of the joint venture, the tax applies to the unused portion of the reserve.

299

Main nondeductible items: sanctions pursuant to Soviet legislation and the following payments to labor: material help, participation in the annual results (except in agriculture), leave payments over and above the amounts mandated by law (including maternity, pension raises, and separation grants), and dividends paid to the working collective or its members.

Profit and other *income from abroad* are included in the tax base, but a credit is given for the tax paid to a foreign government.

A progressive surtax applies on profits exceeding the sectoral profitability levels defined by the USSR Supreme Soviet.

b. Exemptions and deductions

Exempt entities: Gosbank and apprentice enterprises and cooperatives. Special regime applies to state enterprises in the areas of transportation, civil aviation, and communications.

Entities exempt from the excess profit tax: banking and insurance organizations; and agricultural enterprises.

Exempt income: income from shares, bonds, and other securities, and income from shares in joint enterprises.

Tax incentives:

(1) Exemption:

(a) For two years, new enterprises (except those in the mining and extraction industry) set up in the Far East and Far North economic regions. In the second year of operations the exemption is 50 percent of the tax.

(b) For two years, new enterprises producing consumer goods (other than wine, vodka, tobacco and its products, perfume, and cosmetics) from local raw materials and waste, subject to input value content.

(c) For two years (three in the Far East region) from the time they become profitable, joint ventures engaged in material production (except mining and fishing) with at least 30 percent foreign capital. Joint ventures set up before January 1, 1991, are eligible regardless their sector of activity.

(d) Enterprises which develop their own material and technical base in rural areas, urban-type settlements, and regional centers.

(e) For two years, cooperatives for production and processing of agricultural products, construction and repair of buildings, and the production of building materials. Cooperatives engaged in other activities (except those in trade and purchasing, public catering, agency and entertainment, which have no tax incentives) will pay 25 percent of the tax in the first year and 50 percent in the second year. Restructuring restriction: the

300

exemption does not benefit cooperatives formed by the liquidation of enterprises, or their division; or cooperatives attached to enterprises, associations, and organizations working on equipment leased from the enterprises.

(f) For two years, small enterprises operating in specified sectors. Other small enterprises pay 25 percent of the tax in the first year and 50 percent in the second year. The restructuring restriction (see (e) above) applies.

(g) Collective farm markets, if their profit is used for specified purposes.

(h) Specified merit public organizations.

(i) Cooperatives of veterans of war and labor, if 70 percent or more of the workers are persons of pensionable age.

(j) Fishing enterprises, in relation to the profit from the sale of fish caught by the enterprise itself.

(2) Deductions:

(a) 30 percent of current expenditure on scientific research, experimental design, and absorption of new technologies.

(b) Repayment of credit used to finance centralized state capital investment, not covered by profit allocations to capital accumulation.

(c) 30 percent of expenditure connected with protection of nature.

(d) Approved expenditure on maintenance of facilities for housing, health, education, culture, and sports.

(e) Contributions to merit institutions, up to 1 percent of profit.

(f) Grants for construction of rural houses, up to 1 percent of profit.

(g) 30 percent of the profit of an enterprise operating in specified sectors, when more than half the personnel is old aged or disabled; or 20 percent of the profit, if they are between 30 and 50 percent of personnel.

(h) Losses incurred by joint ventures with at least 30 percent foreign capital, in the previous 5 years, provided the special reserve is insufficient.

(i) Expenditure on the construction, reconstruction, and renovation of basic resources, mastering new technologies, and training.

(j) The amount of profits used by joint ventures to develop production (expenditure on basic means of the formation of a reserve).

(k) Interest on the long-term bank debts of joint ventures, except overdue or deferred credits.

(l) Joint-venture expenditures on scientific research, experimental design and nature-conservation measures.

Additional relief may be provided by the USSR Council of Ministers, and the republics and local governments, within the limits of the respective tax shares.

c. Rates

Normal rate 45 percent. Applies to profits within the profitability limits set by the USSR Supreme Soviet. (Tax sharing: the 45 percent rate is split between the union budget (22 percent) and the republic and local budgets (23 percent). The limit of 23 percent encompasses also payments to local budgets for labor and natural resources, such that the enterprise's liability regarding those three levies is limited to 45 percent.)

Excess profits are taxed at the following rates:

(1) 80 percent on profits up to 10 percentage points above the limit;

(2) 90 percent on the remainder. (Tax sharing: the proceeds of the excess profit tax accrues half to the union budget and half to the republic and local budgets.)

Tax credits against the profit tax:

(1) Tax paid abroad, up to the level of domestic taxation on the same income.

(2) Rental paid to lessors by leasing enterprises.

(3) Amount of profit used by joint ventures for the development of production (expenditure on capital goods or reserve formation).

(4) Interest on long-term bank debt of joint ventures, except overdue or deferred debts.

(5) Expenses of joint ventures with scientific research and experimental design work and on measures to safeguard nature.

Special rates:

(1) 55 percent on banking and insurance organizations (half of the proceeds accrues to the union budget).

(2) 30 percent on joint ventures with at least 30 percent foreign capital.

(3) 10 percent on joint ventures set up in the Far East economic region with at least 30 percent foreign capital.

(4) 35 percent on consumer societies, unions and associations (proceeds accrue to local budgets).

(5) 35 percent on public and religious organizations and their enterprises (proceeds accrue to local budgets).

Differentiated rates up to 45 percent (as set by the Supreme Soviets of the republics) on non-agricultural production cooperatives and their unions and associations (proceeds accrue to the budget of the region or town of their place of registration).

Differentiated rates (as set by the Supreme Soviets of the republics) on: commercial purchasing, public catering, and agency and entertainment coopera-

302

tives (sharing of tax proceeds defined by the laws of the republics); agricultural enterprises, including state and collective farms; enterprises offering repairing services; and municipal services.

Differentiated rates up to 45 percent (as set by the local Councils of People's Deputies) on enterprises forming part of the local economy and relating to municipal property (proceeds accruing to local budgets).

Advance payments are due on the 15th and the 28th of each month, on the basis of the tax paid in the previous year. Small taxpayers may make a single payment each month, on the 20th. Every quarter the taxpayer estimates the cumulative actual tax liability. Cooperatives, public enterprises, and agricultural enterprises (including collective and state farms) determine the tax quarterly, taking account of the amounts calculated for the preceding quarters within the year. Joint ventures make quarterly advance payments on the 15th of March, June, September, and December; a final return is presented by March 15 of the following year.

2. TAX ON THE PROFIT OF FOREIGN LEGAL ENTITIES

(Act of June 14, 1990, Ch.II)

(Effective January 1, 1991)

a. Nature of tax

A tax on the profit of companies, associations, and any other type of foreign organization which carries out, through a permanent representation, economic activity in the territory of the USSR or its continental shelf or economic zone. (For the income of foreign participants in joint ventures, see item 3 below. For the passive income of foreign organizations, see item 4 below.) The profit is determined according to rules set by the USSR Council of Ministers. Whenever a direct determination is not feasible, the profit is estimated as 15 percent of the gross income or the expenses incurred. The profit is determined annually; a return is filed by April 15, and audited, at cost, by a Soviet auditing organization.

b. Exemptions and deductions

Tax incentives

Foreign firms are entitled to the same tax reliefs granted to joint ventures (see item 1 above) regarding philanthropic grants and expenditure to safeguard nature.

The tax on foreign firms may be forfeited or reduced on the basis of reciprocity, if the foreign tax authority confirms that a more favorable treatment is granted to Soviet firms with respect to the same or similar taxes.

c. Rates

The tax rate is 30 percent.

(*Tax sharing:* Half of the proceeds accrues to the union budget and half to the republican and local budgets.)

3. TAX ON CAPITAL INCOME

(Act of June 14, 1990, Ch.VII, Sec. 31)

(Effective January 1, 1991)

a. Nature of tax

A withholding tax:

(1) on the income received by enterprises, associations, and organizations (except foreign entities unconnected with activity in the USSR) from shares, bonds, and other securities, and the income received from joint enterprises by their Soviet participants; and

(2) on the transfer abroad of income of foreign participants in joint ventures.

The tax applies to income received in the territory of the USSR and its continental shelf and economic zone.

b. Exemptions and deductions

Exemption: interest from state bonds and other state securities.

Tax treaties may exempt, partially or totally, the income of foreign participants in joint ventures.

c. Rates

15 percent. In the case of transfer abroad, the tax is paid in the currency of transfer.

(*Tax sharing:* half of the proceeds accrues to the union budget and half to the republican and local budgets.)

4. TAX ON FREIGHT AND PASSIVE INCOME OF FOREIGN RESIDENTS

(Act of June 14, 1990, Ch.VII, Sec. 32)

(Effective January 1, 1991)

a. Nature of tax

A withholding tax on dividends, interest, copyright and license royalties, freight, rental payments, and other income from Soviet sources of foreign legal persons not connected with the USSR through a permanent representation.

b. Exemptions and deductions

Tax treaties may grant partial or total tax exemption.

c. Rates

Six percent on freight paid by foreign legal persons in connection with international transport; 20 percent in the remaining cases.

The tax is paid in the currency of transfer.

(*Tax sharing:* Half of the proceeds accrues to the union budget, and half to the republic in whose territory the enterprise or organization paying the tax is located.)

5. PERSONAL INCOME TAX

(Act of April 23, 1990)

(Effective July 1, 1990)

a. Nature of tax

A set of schedular taxes on income (items 5.1 through 5.7 below), representing the major component of the "taxes on the population" which also include the tax on adults without children (item 5.8 below), the agricultural and land taxes, and the taxes on owners of buildings and motor vehicles (see items VI.1-4 below).

For purposes of taxation, a permanent resident is a person who stays in the USSR for more than 183 days in a calendar year. Soviet citizens are taxed on worldwide income, and foreign residents on the income derived from Soviet sources. Foreign citizens and persons without citizenship ("foreign physical persons") with permanent residence in the USSR are taxed on the same basis as Soviet citizens.

Income received in foreign currency is converted at the official exchange rate.

b. Exemptions and deductions

Exempt persons: Heroes of the USSR, awardees of the Order of Glory, invalids of war and equivalent, participants in the Civil War, World War II, and other participants of military operations (even at headquarters), personnel of the organs of internal affairs who became invalid while carrying out official duties, invalids from childhood, people with blindness of the first and second group, Mother-Heroines, and citizens working in Leningrad from September 8, 1941 to January 27, 1944.

The executive committee of local Councils of People's Deputies at the *oblast,* municipal and regional level may grant partial or total exemption to individual taxpayers.

Exempt income: Social security benefits, state and voluntary pensions, alimony, scholarships, work retribution of students of vocational-technical schools, reward for donation of blood and breast milk, remuneration of workers of medical institutions for collecting blood, work income of members of cartels prospecting gold, compensation for injury and other health damage, compensation for loss of breadwinner, wages and other foreign currency income of Soviet citizens from work abroad for Soviet enterprises, institutions, and organizations, proceeds from the sale of property (except production for sale), income of private subsidiary farms, inheritance and gifts (except royalties received by successors), gains on state bonds, lottery winnings, interest and premia on deposits in state banks and on Treasury obligations, voluntary and compulsory insurance indemnization, rewards for rationalization suggestions, gifts up to rub 200 per year received from enterprises, institutions, and organizations, prizes received in international, all-union, and republican competitions, material assistance linked to natural disasters and other cases indicated by the USSR Council of Ministers, other material assistance up to rub 500 per year, reinvested dividends, income from work on collective farms, per diem and other allowances received by military personnel on active duty.

c. Rates

Tax reductions: The tax is reduced:

(1) by 50 percent, on all income received by invalids not exempt, and by parents and wives of military personnel who perished in or as a consequence of service;

(2) by 30 percent, on all income received by single mothers, widows, and widowers having two or more children under 16 and not receiving a pension for loss of a breadwinner;

(3) by 30 percent, on all income received by one of the parents who is raising and caring for an invalid from childhood.

306

Tax credit: The income tax paid abroad on taxable income is given credit, up to the amount of the Soviet tax liability.

5.1 WAGE INCOME TAX

(Act of April 23, 1990, Ch.II)

a. Nature of tax

A withholding tax on wages, salaries, and any other labor compensation, including dividends on the stocks of labor collectives, participation in profits (even by ex-employees), military allowances, and lawyers' compensation. The monthly payment is final, as there is no annual adjustment.

The taxable income of foreign physical persons includes bonuses paid in connection with residing in the USSR and compensation for expenditure such as children's school education, food, and leave trips for the family. It does not include, however, payments to social security and pension funds, or compensation for housing rent and maintenance of an automobile for official purposes.

b. Exemptions and deductions

Exemptions (in addition to those mentioned above):

(1) earnings of members of collective farms;

(2) income of work at the basic work place, not exceeding rub 100 per month;

(3) severance pay paid upon dismissal;

(4) legal compensation payments, except unused leave;

(5) payments in place of free housing and communal services.

The tax liability of foreign physical persons may be reduced or eliminated, on the basis of reciprocity, if the country of citizenship grants a more favorable tax treatment to Soviet citizens.

c. Rates

Monthly income (In rubles)	Tax (rubles + percentage on amount of income within the bracket)
0-100	Exempt
100-130	0.00 + 29
130-150	8.70 + 30

307

Monthly income (In rubles)	Tax (rubles + percentage on amount of income within the bracket)
150-700	.14.70 + 13
700-900	.86.20 + 15
900-1,100	116.20 + 20
1,100-1,300	156.20 + 30
1,300-1,500	216.20 + 40
1,500-3,000	296.20 + 50
over 3,000	1,046.20 + 60

Additional, together with bonuses over and above the base earnings for work in the far north and other areas with severe climatic conditions: tax rate 13 percent.

Tax reduction: The tax is reduced:

(1) by 50 percent, on wages, salaries, and allowances of military personnel who served in the contingent sent to the Republic of Afghanistan;

(2) effective January 1, 1991 by 30 percent, on the reward for working in the basic work place by a worker with three or more dependents.

5.2 TAX ON INCOME OF THE SELF-EMPLOYED

(Act of April 23, 1990, Ch.III)

a. Nature of tax

A withholding tax on the earnings from work on a nonrecurrent basis for enterprises, institutions, and organizations, including material assistance (bonuses, pensions, etc.) paid by those entities to people not working there. The monthly payment is final, as there is no annual adjustment.

b. Rates

Monthly income (In rubles)	Tax (rubles + percentage on amount of income within the bracket)
5-15	.0.00 + 1.5
15-20	.0.22 + 5.5
20-30	.0.50 + 6
30-40	1.10 + 7
40-50	1.80 + 8
50-70	.2.60 + 10

Monthly income (In rubles)	Tax (rubles + percentage on amount of income within the bracket)
70-100	4.60 + 12
100-700	8.20 + 13
700 & over	same as item 5.1 above

5.3 TAX ON INCOME FROM INTELLECTUAL PROPERTY

(Act of April 23, 1990, Ch.IV)

a. Nature of tax

A withholding tax on royalties and other compensation for the creation, publishing, performance, or other use of works of science, literature, and art, and also compensation for authors' inventions, discoveries, and industrial models. Legal successors and heirs are also liable. The tax is also levied on payments for translation, editing, and revising works of science, literature, and art, and on the sales of works of painting, sculpture, drawing, and other kinds of art and articles of decorative or applied art.

The tax is paid during the year, and with each payment the annual tax liability is recalculated.

b. Exemptions and deductions

Exemption: income not exceeding the exemption threshold for self-employed workers.

c. Rates

(1) Nonrecurrent payments:

Monthly income (In rubles)	Tax (rubles + percentage on amount of income within the bracket)
up to 180	0.00 + 1.5
180-240	2.70 + 5.5
240-360	6.00 + 6
360-480	13.20 + 7
480-600	21.60 + 8
600-840	32.20 + 10
840-1,200	55.20 + 12
1,200-8,400	98.40 + 13

Monthly income (In rubles)	Tax (rubles + percentage on amount of income within the bracket)
8,400-10,800	1,034.40 + 15
10,800-13,200	1,394.40 + 20
13,200-15,600	1,874.40 + 30
15,600-18,000	2,594.40 + 40
18,000-36,000	3,554.40 + 50
over 36,000	12,554.40 + 60

(2) Recurrent Payments to Heirs of Authors:

Annual income (rubles)	Tax (rub + percentage on amount of income within the bracket)
up to 500	0 + 60
500-1,000	300 + 65
1,000-3,000	625 + 70
3,000-6,000	2,025 + 75
6,000-10,000	4,275 + 80
10,000-15,000	7,475 + 85
over 15,000	11,725 + 90

Tax Reductions:

(1) by 50 percent, for heirs under 18, women over 55, and men over 60 years;

(2) effective January 1, 1991 by 30 percent, for authors having three or more dependents and no basic work place.

5.4 TAX ON INCOME OF HOUSEHOLD BUSINESS ACTIVITY

(Act of April 23, 1990, Ch.V)

a. Nature of tax

A tax on the net income of all types of individual business activity, including labor farms and private companies owned by foreign citizens and persons without citizenship ("foreign physical persons"). The base of the tax is the difference between gross income and documented expenditure associated with deriving the income. Expenditure includes material costs, amortization deductions, lease payments, wage payments to contract labor, payments to state social security, mandatory property insurance, interest payments for short-term bank credits (except on overdue and deferred loans), and repair of fixed production assets.

310

Advance payments are due quarterly, and an annual adjustment is made by March 15 on the basis of the return presented by January 15.

b. Exemptions and deductions

Exemptions: Income from individual labor activity, including from worker or peasant household businesses, not exceeding the exemption threshold for self-employed workers; men aged 60 or more, and women aged 55 or more, in relation to income from farming activity exempted from the agricultural tax.

Tax holiday: For two years since formation, the farm income of members of peasant household businesses.

c. Rates

Up to 3,000 (if average monthly income exceeds that of item 5.1 above for basic work place);

(1) If there is no basic work place: according to item 5.1 above;

(2) If there is a basic work place: according to item 5.2 above (adjusted for number of months)

Annual income (In rubles)	Tax (rubles + percentage on amount of income within the bracket)
3,000-4,000	332.40 + 20
4,000-5,000	532.40 + 30
5,000-6,000	832.40 + 50
over 6,000	1,332.40 + 60

Tax reduction: Effective January 1, 1991; the tax is reduced by 30 percent if the taxpayer has three of more dependents and does not have a basic work place.

5.5 TAX ON INCOME FROM PEASANT FARM ACTIVITY

(Act of April 23, 1990, Ch.VI)

a. Nature of tax

A tax on the net income derived from running a peasant farm, i.e., a farm engaged in raising, producing, or processing agricultural products. Net income is determined as in item 5.4 above. Joint partners are taxed separately following the income sharing they agree on.

Monthly advance payments are calculated as 10 percent of gross income, and the final tax liability is determined on the basis of a return presented by March 1.

311

The peasant farm is also liable to a withholding tax on wages paid to contract labor.

b. Rates

(1) if there is no basic work place: same rates as item 5.1 above;

(2) if there is a basic work place: same rates as item 5.2 above. In either case, adjusted for number of months.

5.6 TAX ON OTHER PERSONAL INCOME

(Act of April 23, 1990, Ch.VII)

a. Nature of tax

A tax on the net income not taxed under items 5.1 through 5.6 above. Net income is the difference between income received—in monetary form and in kind—and expenditures incurred in deriving the income. Expenditures include those mentioned in item 5.4 above and other expenditure specific to the type of activity.

Advance payments are due quarterly, and an annual adjustment is made by March 15 on the basis of the return presented by January 15 and other information gathered by the tax agencies. Enterprises, institutions, and organizations paying income to individuals must withhold tax in each payment, and adjust the tax liability in each subsequent payment.

b. Exemptions and deductions

Exemption: income not exceeding rub 300 per year.

c. Rates

Annual Taxable income (In rubles)	(rubles + percentage on amount of income within the bracket)
300-360	0.00 + 10
360-480	6.00 + 14
480-600	22.80 + 19
600-840	45.60 + 23.5

312

Annual Taxable income (In rubles)	(rubles + percentage on amount of income within the bracket)
840-1,200	102.00 + 29
1,200-1,800	206.40 + 33.5
1,800-2,400	407.40 + 40
2,400-3,000	647.40 + 46.5
3,000-5,000	926.40 + 52.5
over 5,000	1,976.00 + 60

5.7 TAX ON THE INCOME EARNED BY FOREIGN RESIDENTS

(Act of April 23, 1990, Ch.IX)

a. Nature of tax

A withholding tax on the non-labor income of nonresidents, derived from Soviet sources.

b. Exemptions and deductions

Tax treaties may grant partial or total exemption.

The tax may be waived or reduced, on account of reciprocity, if the country of residence grants a more favorable tax treatment to Soviet citizens.

c. Rates

20 percent.

5.8 TAX ON ADULTS WITHOUT CHILDREN

a. Nature of tax

A tax on the wage income of men from 20 to 50 years of age, and married women from 20 to 45 years of age, without children. (This tax is to be phased out from 1991 to 1993.)

b. Exemptions and deductions

Main exemptions: persons with monthly earnings of rub 100 or less, invalids of groups I and II, persons suffering from certain types of psychological ailments, and parents whose children have died, been killed, or are missing in action.

A one-year tax holiday applies following marriage.Maximum rate of tax: 6 percent of wages.

313

c. Rates

Maximum rate of tax: 6 percent.

II. SOCIAL SECURITY CONTRIBUTIONS

Effective January 1, 1991

a. Nature of tax

Compulsory contributions by enterprises and workers to the state social security system. Workers' contribution is withheld by the employers.

The contribution may vary according to a number of factors, such as the danger or difficulty of the work.

Neither the USSR Pension Fund nor the newly-created Social Security Fund are consolidated in the state budget.

b. Rates

Contributions:

(1) employers: 37 percent of total payroll; (only 26 percentage points will constitute a social security contribution in 1991)

(2) employees: 1 percent of paycheck.

III. TAXES ON DOMESTIC SALES OF GOODS AND SERVICES

1. TURNOVER TAX

(Act of June 14, 1990, Ch.III)

(Effective January 1, 1991, as a rule, but on July 1, 1990, for joint ventures.)

a. Nature of tax

A tax on the production of consumer goods by enterprises, associations, and organizations, including cooperatives and joint ventures. When both wholesale and retail prices are fixed, the tax is determined as the difference between the retail price, net of a trade discount allowance, and the wholesale price. In the absence of fixed wholesale prices, rates are established as percentages of the retail prices, taking into account average production expenditure for the area in question and a markup on the order of 20-25 percent on cost.

314

b. Exemptions and deductions

Exempt entities:

(1) For two years, new enterprises producing goods (other than vodka, wine and vodka products, beer, tobacco and its products, plastic goods, perfume and cosmetics) from local raw materials and waste.

(2) For two years (extendable by the union and autonomous republics within the limits of their tax share), folk-art enterprises in respect of the sale of the artistic goods they produce.

(3) Enterprises and societies for the blind, including production-training, if more than 50 percent of personnel has a limited capacity to work.

(4) Consumer cooperative enterprises for the sale of goods (except beer, spirits, and wines made from grapes and other fruits and berries) situated in mountainous and remote regions, up to 50 percent of the tax; and those situated in towns and cities under regional authority, urban-type settlements and rural areas, 25 percent of the tax.

(5) Agricultural enterprises, by the sale of products (other than plastic goods, dressed fur, fur and jewelry articles, and wine and vodka made with the use of spirits) made by them from local raw materials.

(6) Listed merit organizations, in respect of goods and products produced in accordance with the objects of their activity.

(7) Enterprises and economic organizations of creative unions, within the limits of the turnover tax amounts used by those unions for the activities under their rules.

(8) Cooperatives of war and labor veterans, with at least 70 percent of the workers being of pensionable age, producing goods from local raw materials and waste.

(9) Apprentice enterprises and cooperatives, in respect of the goods made by them.

The USSR Council of Ministers may establish additional relief from the turnover tax for individual payers.

Exempt goods (sample): meat, milk, newspapers, children's wear, eggs, medicine, coal, timber products, fruit and vegetables.

c. Rates

Rates are set by the USSR Council of Ministers.

Rates for joint ventures (in percent):

    Cotton & wool cloth, plastic products 20

Leather footwear for adults, other textiles, artificial leather, gold jewelry (without precious stones)	25
Wallpaper, refrigerators, computers, watches, VCRs, wine, cosmetics	30
Silk fabrics, beer	40
Carpets, artificial furs, cassettes, automobiles & parts, clothing made of synthetic fibers, silver jewelry	50
Jewelry with precious stones, fortified wines, champagne, cognacs	70
Liquor and vodka products	90
Other goods on which turnover tax is paid by Soviet enterprises	15

Tax retention:

(1) Enterprises producing consumer goods may retain up to 30 percent of the tax obtained from an increase in production by comparison with the preceding period, as defined by the USSR Council of Ministers.

(2) Enterprises may use up to 50 percent of the tax obtained from the sale of the additional goods to make for the insufficiency of the accumulation fund in paying a bank credit granted to increase production or improve quality and range of consumer goods produced.

Tax sharing: The tax proceeds accrue to the union budget, but the USSR Supreme Soviet Supreme and the Supreme Soviets of the union republics may assign shares to the union and autonomous republics.

2. TAX ON ENTERTAINMENT

(Act of June 14, 1990, Ch.VII, Sct.33)

(Effective July 1, 1990)

a. Nature of tax

A tax on the income of casinos, video salons (exhibition of videos), operation of gaming machines with money prizes, and from large-scale concerts and theatrical entertainments held in open spaces, stadiums, sport halls and other premises with seating for more than 2,000 persons.

316

Material expenses connected with obtaining the income is deductible in determination of taxable income.

b. Rates

70 percent.

Tax sharing: Half of the proceeds accrues to the union budget, half to republic and local budgets.

IV. TAXES ON INTERNATIONAL TRADE

1. CUSTOMS DUTIES

a. Nature of tax

A tariff based on the 1984 version of the CMEA nomenclature. The tariff is based on three digits (although the nomenclature has seven digits). There are only about 300 entries. The base of the tariff is the transaction value, which consists of the (valuta) ruble equivalent of the foreign currency price, converted at the official exchange rate. Payment may be made in rubles.

b. Exemptions and deductions

Exempt: raw materials and most capital goods. Goods imported from developing countries are generally exempt, in the framework of the GSP.

c. Rates

The tariff rates vary from zero to 70 percent, the unweighted average being 3.5 percent. For each entry there are two rates, the maximum—or basic—rate and a minimum rate applied to countries with MFN agreements with the USSR.

2. EXPORT AND IMPORT TAX

(Act of June 14, 1990, Ch.IV; Decree 815 of the USSR Council of Ministers, 1990)

(Effective July 1, 1990)

a. Nature of tax

A tax on enterprises, associations, and organizations subject to the profit tax (see item 1 above) which carry out foreign trade transactions. It is intended to capture the difference between international prices, converted into (valuta) rubles at the official rate, and internal prices for certain tradeable goods.

The rates are to be expressed:

(1) for private parties' transactions, at percentage rates of the foreign trade value of goods indicated in the customs declaration;

(2) for government transactions, as the difference between the foreign trade and internal price, after deduction of overheads.

b. Exemptions or deductions

Exemptions:

(1) Equipment, material, and other property imported for integralization of authorized capital (foreign direct investment).

(2) Temporary importation;

(3) Imports for sale for foreign currency.

Draw-back: The tax paid on imports is refundable with re-exportation within a year.

The USSR Ministry of Finance may change rates for individual commodities to adjust to new business conditions in the external and domestic markets.

c. Rates

Sample of rates:

	From CMEA Countries	From Other Countries
Personal computers	600	600
Automobiles	380	380
Vegetable fibers	130	130
Yarn	1,680	1,680
Coffee beans	300	480
Raw sugar	230	230
Oranges	430	330
Alcoholic beverages	200	610
Cigarettes	150	510
Jeans for adults	—	1,470
Umbrellas	470	2,030
Perfumes, cosmetics	—	210
Domestic appliances	460	460
Audio & video cassettes	500	2,090
Television sets	870	870
Unlisted consumer goods	160	160

The tax proceeds belong entirely to the union budget.

V. TAXES ON THE USE OF PRODUCTIVE RESOURCES

1. TAX ON PAY FUND FOR COLLECTIVE FARM WORKERS

(Act of June 14, 1990, Ch.V)

(Effective January 1, 1991)

a. Nature of taxes

A tax on the expenditure on labor over and above rub 100 per month per worker of collective farms, including fishing farms. The tax base includes additional pay, all kinds of bonuses and allowances, and payment in kind (goods valued at cost).

Payment dates and procedures to be set by the laws of the union and autonomous republics.

b. Rate

8 percent.

The tax proceeds belong entirely to the local budgets.

2. TAX ON EXCESS WAGE INCREASES

(Act of June 14, 1990, Ch.VI)

(Effective January 1, 1991)

a. Nature of tax

A tax on the excess of "funds used for consumption" (C) over the "nontaxable portion of funds used for consumption" (A), by enterprises, associations, organizations, foreign legal persons, international nongovernment organizations, international associations engaging in economic activity, and joint ventures with more than 30 percent of foreign capital. (C) includes all personnel expenditure (including labor pay, premia in cash or kind, material help, labor and social privileges, and other individual payments, but excluding royalties and rewards for discoveries) and dividend and interest income paid on shares of the working collective and individual investments by members of the collective. The non-state-financed income of the enterprises (V) is the total expenditure on pay for labor in the cost of the products sold plus the remaining profits, after adjustments are made to ensure comparability with that of the previous year. (A) equals the previous year's C times the ratio of the current year's V to the previous year's V, multiplied by k, where k (=0.98) is an adjustment coefficient allowing for V to increase relative to C. The USSR Council of Ministers may change k to take into account the specific features of production in individual sectors. An adjustment in the previous year's V may also be made to allow for the occurrence of surplus expenditure with payment of the corresponding tax. On the other hand, any margin of A over C may be included in the reserve fund and used by the enterprise for consumption in the subsequent periods without tax payment.

b. Deductions and exemptions

Exemptions:

(1) The increase in C in new enterprises, during the standard period of assimilation of designed technical and economic indices and the first year of operation.

(2) The increase in C in connection with the implementation of centralized measures for raising the standard of living, including the introduction of new conditions for labor and the eradication of the consequences of emergency situations.

(3) Payment for the work of disabled and handicapped persons, when they exceed 50 percent of the enterprise's personnel.

(4) Survival benefits for death, and financial compensation, above the statutory limits, to the victims of work accidents and professional diseases.

The USSR Council of Ministers may set additional tax reliefs.

c. Rates

Tax rates for 1991-92:

Percentage by which the nontaxable portion of the funds is exceeded	rubles per each ruble of the excess
Up to 1 percent	1.00
Over 1 percent, up to 2	1.25
Over 2 percent, up to 3	1.50
Over 3 percent	2.00

Tax sharing: Half of the tax proceeds accrues to the union budget, and half to the republic and the local budgets.

VI. TAXES ON PROPERTY

1. AGRICULTURAL TAX

a. Nature of tax

A tax on private holders of rural land, collected by the union budget and distributed to the local budgets where the tax was collected. These taxes are to be transferred, in 1991, to the republic level of government. This tax substitutes for other taxes, as the agricultural produce is not subject to any tax. Also, workers on collective farms are not liable to individual income tax; to the extent they also tend a small piece of land on their own, they pay this tax.

b. Exemptions and deductions

In the calculation of the tax, the area of the plot of land allotted to the farm is reduced by the area corresponding to buildings, gullies, and public roads.

Main exemptions include invalids, persons of advanced age, families of military servicemen, and agricultural specialists.

c. Rates

Annual rates per $\frac{1}{100}$ hectares vary from rub 0.20 to rub 2.20 from region to region, according to geographical and other factors. On average, the rate is rub 0.81 per $\frac{1}{100}$ hectares per year.

2. LAND TAX

a. Nature of tax

A tax on private holders of non-built-up urban plots, collected by local authorities for the benefit of local budgets.

b. Exemptions and deductions

Exemptions are numerous.

c. Rates

Annual rates per square meter range from 0.4 to 1.8 kopecks, and are distributed in six categories according to location.

3. TAX ON OWNERS OF BUILDINGS

a. Nature of tax

A local tax on the value of privately-owned urban buildings, including residential homes or part of them, outbuildings, garages, and *dachas*. Besides the tax, the owner has also to pay for compulsory state insurance for the building.

b. Exemptions and deductions

Exemptions are numerous.

c. Rate

1 percent.

4. TAX ON OWNERS OF MOTOR VEHICLES

a. Nature of tax

A tax paid by individuals and enterprises who own transport vehicles and other self-propelled machines and mechanisms, such as automobiles, motorcycles, motor boats, yachts, and motor-sledges. It is collected by the union budget in connection with the technical inspection or registration, and the proceeds are earmarked for projects of road conservation.

b. Rates

Rate per horsepower of the engine:

Light automobiles	rub 0.50
Motorcycles	rub 0.30
Cargo vehicles	rub 1.00
Cutters and yachts	rub 0.10-0.25

VII. OTHER TAXES

1. STATE DUTY

a. Nature of tax

A duty levied on delivery of various official documents and acts, including emigration permits, notarial services, and recognition of inheritance rights.

NOTES

1. Status as of July 1, 1990 unless otherwise indicated.

   The fiscal year runs from January 1 to December 31.

   Commercial contracts cannot stipulate the assumption of foreign firms' tax burden by the Soviet counterpart.

   Tax treaties, which have preference in application over internal tax laws, have been concluded with Austria, Bulgaria, Canada, Cyprus, the Czech and Slovak Federal Republic, Denmark, Finland, France, Germany (both the GDR and the FRG), Hungary, Italy, Japan, Malaysia, Netherlands, Norway, Poland, Romania, Spain, Sweden, Switzerland, the United Kingdom, and the United States.

Profile of Tax Administration as of December 1, 1990

I. TAX ADMINISTRATION

1. Organization

1.1 At national level

The State Tax Service (STS) is composed of the Main State Tax Inspectorate (MSTI—a department of the USSR Ministry of Finance set up in July 1990) and 5475 state tax directorates at all levels of government (union republics, autonomous republics, *krays*, *oblasts*, *rayons*, and cities). The STS is responsible for collection of all tax and nontax state revenue (except customs duties).

1.2 At central level

The MSTD is organized in six technical sections, each one administering a different tax or group of taxes, and two supporting sections (organizational-inspection and tax information and accounting). This structure is largely replicated at all levels of government.

2. Human Resources

2.1 Staff

The STS has a staff of 40,000 and is in the process of absorbing another 25,000; ultimately it will have 100,000 employees. Ninety one persons work for the MSTI. Eighty percent of the statutory strength consists of field officers, 13 percent of administrative and technical personnel, and 7 percent of heads and deputies of tax inspectorates.

2.2 Recruiting and training

Courses in finance and taxation are taught in a number of college programs, and specialization in taxation requires part-time work in a tax inspectorate beginning in the junior year, and one year of internship following

325

graduation. Those who have performed satisfactorily are hired. Staff are recruited mostly from graduates of vocational schools, which rank above schools (middle level) and institutes (higher education). Training centers are located in Moscow, Leningrad, Kiev, and other major cities. Knowledge of law and accounting is rare; typically the tax officer is an economist by formal training.

2.3 Pay

The nationwide average STS salary is rub 416 (after the 1990 increase from rub 190). Salaries vary according to the importance of the tax inspectorate. In a typical district tax inspectorate, the salaries are as follows: director, rub 460; director of department, rub 430; chief, rub 400; senior officer, rub 350; and tax officer, rub 320. In Moscow only, the salary is 30 percent higher. Seniority allowances (available only at the STS) range from 60 percent to employees with one year in the job to 150 percent to those with more than 15 years. An extra amount equal to a one month's salary is paid at the time of the annual leave.

3. Filing and payment

Profit tax: advance payments are due twice a month (once a month for small taxpayers, quarterly for joint ventures). The tax liability is reassessed quarterly. An annual return is filed by March 15. *Tax on excess wage increases*: is assessed and paid quarterly. *Wage income tax*: the withholding at source is final; no annual adjustment. Enterprises pay tax at the same time they pay wages (once a month). *Self-employed*: advance payments are due every quarter. The annual return is filed by January 15, with any tax supplement due immediately and any excess refunded by March 15. The taxpayer has the option of buying a patent (license to operate), which is valid for one year; the corresponding annual charge is related to the taxpayer's presumed income. *Tax on owners of buildings*: paid in two installments, by June 15 and August 15. *Tax on owners of vehicles*: paid at the time of annual inspection. *Tax payments* are made exclusively through the banking system, usually by transfer from the taxpayer's account to the budget.

4. Number of returns

Enterprises: there are about 46,000 state enterprises and 1,200 chartered joint ventures. *Self-employed*:

326

about one million, of which 350,000 present a return and pay tax, 350,000 are taxed under the system of patent, and 300,000 are tax exempt.

5. Collection

5.1 Amount

In 1989, rub 384.9 billion, or 41 percent of GDP, was collected.

5.2 Arrears

Figures not available. *Late payment*: an interest of 0.05 percent per day is applied (starting January 1, 1991, 0.2 percent per day). *Hardship*: to meet temporary financial hardship, payment may be deferred or made in installments (depending on tax officer's visit to taxpayer's place of business and examination of the bank account).

5.3 Delinquent accounts

Failure to file return (according to the law enacted on June 3, 1990): the chairman or chief accountant may be fined rub 100-200, and rub 200-300 for reincidence within one year. Recalcitrants may be reported to the procurator's office. (Until recently, when the taxpayer failed to file a return or pay the tax, the tax office would write him a reprimand letter, or, at most, would request the local council (soviet of people's deputies) to discuss the matter with the delinquent taxpayer. The council is, in principle, empowered to confiscate bank account balances.) *Failure to pay* (according to the new law): the tax office is empowered to impound and arrest funds from, and close, bank accounts of a delinquent taxpayer. At the office's request, the procurator's office may bring the taxpayer to trial. If a guilty verdict is reached, the court may determine the sale of the taxpayer's assets and close his/her business.

6. Audit

6.1 Internal

Returns are checked for arithmetic errors. Manual controls permit identification of taxpayers who fail to file a return. Joint ventures must have their financial statements audited (at cost, by a state auditing organization) before filing a return. The chief accountant of a state enterprise is independent from management

6.2 External

Tax officers in the taxpayer's premises check for tax payment. Once a year, each enterprise is checked regarding the withholding of the tax on wage income. In the past, emphasis has been placed on auditing 100 percent of enterprises. When a problem is found, the tax auditor fills out an inspection form (*akt*) demanding compliance within a specified period, usually three months. When this time expires, the officer follows up.

6.3 Administrative

The tax inspectorate staff check to see that tax offices are working properly, and organize training seminars.

7. Appeals system

An appeal may be filed within one year of tax payment, as follows: *first level*—the local tax office (which is required to resolve within one month); *second level*—the tax inspectorate immediately above (within one month of the first-level decision); *judicial level*—the tax inspectorate decision may be challenged through the courts. The filing of an appeal does not imply suspension of payment of the tax.

8. Registration

Prior registration with the tax inspectorate is required to open any business. There are no taxpayer identification numbers.

9. Material resources

9.1 Buildings

There is a great scarcity of office space, furniture, and other equipment. Only a few tax inspectorates are properly equipped. In some cases, one desk is shared by two officers.

9.2 Computers

The work done is done manually. A few microcomputers are available. In 1990, the STS was authorized to buy 1,000 microcomputers. The main computer center of the Ministry of Finance is expected to distribute the new equipment and to prepare tax programs.

10. Association

The USSR is not a member of any international tax administration association.

II. CUSTOMS ADMINISTRATION

1. Organization

Although the State Customs Administration is four years old, it is still being organized. It has 104 customs houses operating in four regions. The customs authority reports directly to the Council of Ministers (at least until the customs administration is set up).

2. Capacity

The customs administration is responsible for the collection of customs duties and the import/export tax. Presently, the foreign trade organizations still process their own imports and pay duties directly to the budget.

328

3. Personnel	The current staff of 9,000 will be increased gradually to 20,000-25,000.
4. Nomenclature	Until recently, the 1984 version of the CMEA nomenclature (seven digits) was used. A new classification has been prepared following the Brussels Nomenclature.
5. Tariff	The former tariff covered 300 entries based on three digits of the nomenclature. Annual collection has been about rub 200 million. A new tariff has been drafted to cover up to 10,000 items with rates typically below 10 percent, although rates up to 100 percent are levied on a few goods. Semifinished goods bear the lower rates, and consumption goods the highest. Developing countries benefit from preference in the framework of the GSP.
6. Association	The USSR has the status of observer at the GATT. The authorities' aim is to join the Customs Cooperation Council (CCC) and to become a full member of the GATT.

Appendix III.1-3

Social Security Reform and Budgetary Prospects

1. INTRODUCTION

Reform of the social security system is an important ingredient of the transition to a market-oriented economy. While the outlook for long-run growth will improve with increased reliance on market forces, the removal of the myriad of implicit and explicit tax-transfer schemes—which have pervasively distorted incentives in the Soviet economy—will impose substantial hardship on many groups of the population during the transition. To minimize this hardship and to assure political support for economic restructuring, it is necessary to design policies that cushion the less well-off from excessive burdens; any attempt at protecting all groups from the adverse consequences of reforms would be self-defeating. For instance, sizeable increases in inter-generational transfers, such as provided by the recent pension reform, at a time when the supply-side of the economy requires revitalization, could slow the transition to a market economy and make the social security reform wasteful and inadequate to assist those in need.

A major task for the authorities is to achieve an appropriate balance between improving social welfare, on the one hand, and transforming the economy so as to provide for providing sustained growth, on the other. This can be accomplished by reducing the policy-induced allocative distortions, including disincentives to work and to save, and by restoring soundness to the public finances. In sum, social security reform should be aimed at enhancing cost effectiveness, that is, maximizing benefits to those in need at the least budgetary and allocative cost.

This appendix examines some of the medium- and long-term budgetary implications of recently adopted or proposed social security and social assistance measures from a fiscal policy perspective.[1] Of particular interest are the implications for government outlays and/or revenues of alternative economic reform scenarios and benefit indexation. Despite the inevitable need to resort to a highly stylized methodology, the simulations serve to underscore the potential budgetary risks inherent in certain generalized schemes of social protection.

2. THE SOCIAL SECURITY SYSTEM

a. The pre-reform system

(1) Structure and finances

The social security system to date has been an employment-related benefit program which—along with job guarantees and an undifferentiated wage structure—was designed to promote simultaneously labor force participation and full employment. Although the scope of social security has evolved over the past seven decades, there has been little movement until very recently toward assigning to social insurance the "provider of last resort" role it serves in market-oriented economies, under the so-called Beveridge principle.[2]

Social security in the USSR is a pay-as-you-go scheme which provides old-age, disability, and survivors' pensions to workers, self-employed and state farm workers; sick pay and workman's compensation; maternity and childbirth payments; and a variety of family allowances. Until now, there has been no perceived need for unemployment insurance compensation since unemployment has not been officially recognized in the USSR for close to 60 years. Pensions have accounted for well over two-thirds of social security expenditure in recent years, with sick pay allowances making up for an additional 10-11 percent (Table III.1.10). In 1990 a considerable effort was made to increase the scope of family allowances.

The financing of social security since its inception has borne relatively little resemblance to that found in most market economies. In effect, basing their financing on the benefit principle—which helps assure that beneficiaries are cognizant of the cost of their social entitlements—a majority of countries relies on earmarked payroll taxes, usually assessed against both employers and workers. By contrast, social security in the USSR has been financed mainly, and in roughly equal proportions, by contributions from enterprises and general revenue of the union budget (Table III.1.10). The financing share of the union republics remained small and has declined in recent years.

This structure of financing has been deficient at least in two respects. First, it is based on a weak linkage between benefits and contributions because of reliance on general budget revenue and payroll tax contributions entirely from enterprises, without any contributions from workers. Second, the payroll tax has varied (between 4-14 percent) across sectors and enterprises, depending in part on the degree of hardship associated with the location and nature of the employment. The average payroll tax rate for the system as a whole was expected to increase from 9.1 percent in 1989 to 12.1 percent in 1990. Variation in tax rates further reduces the link between benefits and contributions and makes the insurance premia and rates of return variable across economic activities.

(2) Types of benefits

The existing public pension system was established in 1956 for workers, state farm workers and self-employed, and extended via a separate program in 1964 to collective farm workers. The system has provided earnings-related old-age, disability and survivors' pensions to approximately 44 million social security pensioners (out of a total of about 60 million) averaging approximately rub 89 per month in 1989, or about 40 percent of the average wage. Full old-age pensions are payable to men age 60 or older with 25 percent of work experience, and to women age 55 or older with 20 years of employment, with a lower age threshold for special circumstances or occupations. These statutory retirement ages are low in comparison with those in many industrial countries (Table 1), where the tendency has been toward raising the legal age, motivated by the rise in life expectancy and by concerns over the longer-term impact of aging populations on contribution rates.[3] Receipt of an old-age pension does not preclude continued work activity, although there have been limitations on the amount of wages that can be earned without a reduction in pension benefit. In 1989, approximately 9.5 million recipients were classified as working pensioners.

The pension benefit has been based on a 50 percent replacement rate of average gross income either during the last 12 months prior to retirement, or during any five-year period from the last ten years. A higher replacement rate has been applied to average incomes under rub 100 per month, rising to 100 percent at rub 70 per month. With an unindexed maximum set at rub 120 per month (rub 160 for miners), increasing nominal wages have led to a growing number of workers experiencing a fall in their effective replacement rate.

Disability pensions have been paid both for job-related loss of capacity to work and for invalidity induced by general illness, although the latter is subject to tenure requirements. Benefits have ranged from rub 30-120 monthly depending on the degree of disability and whether or not the disability is work related. The number of disabled pensioners has shown a remarkable stability since the middle of the 1970s, remaining essentially unchanged at 6.4 million. Survivors' pensions have traditionally been paid to female (age 55 or older or invalid) and male (age 60 and older or invalid) survivors of workers or retirees or to their dependent children, grandchildren, or parents, at slightly lower rates of replacement than in the case of old-age and disability pensions.

Sick pay (for temporary disability) has been available to all Soviet citizens insofar as medical care is concerned, with cash payments provided to students, employed persons, and state farm workers; a special system exists for collective farm workers. Membership in a trade union has been a prerequisite for receipt of full cash benefits. An additional related expenditure consists of the cost of visits to sanitaria and rest homes. By 1990, cash benefits and expenditure on sanitarium visits were estimated at rub 9.6 billion and rub 2.5 billion, respectively, totaling about 13 percent of total social security outlays. There is no minimum qualifying

333

period for receiving sick pay, which is available for a period of four months; thereafter, the beneficiary is considered to be permanently disabled and is entitled to a full or partial disability pension. An increasing proportion of the worker's income is replaced as the number of years of experience increases, from a 50 percent replacement rate for workers with less than a three-year work history to 100 percent for those with more than eight years of employment. Workers temporarily disabled by a work-related injury are also indemnified at a 100 percent replacement rate regardless of tenure. In all cases, if a worker has more than three dependent children, earnings are replaced at a 100 rate regardless of experience. For the average worker, these provisions resulted in a daily benefit of approximately rub 8 and rub 9, replacing 80 percent of the average wage in 1989 and 77 percent in 1990, respectively. Despite the generous sick pay provisions, the average number of sick days per worker in 1989 was 9.4, low by international standards.

Maternity benefits are available to all residents at a 100 percent replacement rate for a period of eight weeks before and eight weeks after confinement, although the average duration of paid maternity leave is much lower. Following maternity leave, a payment of rub 35-50 per month has also been made to the mother until the child reaches one year of age. Additional assistance is provided to low-income parents. In 1989 and 1990, the average duration of paid maternity leave was 58 and 53 days, respectively, with a 68 percent average replacement rate. Family benefits consist mainly of allowances to assist families to raise children. Grants were provided to families at the birth of each child: rub 50 for the first child, rub 100 for the second and third births, rising to rub 250 for the eleventh and subsequent births. In addition, an allowance of rub 4 per month was paid for a fourth child, rising to rub 15 for the eleventh and each additional child. Unmarried mothers, however, received rub 20 per month per child. Low-income assistance has been rather limited in the USSR; the only notable direct means-tested benefit has been an allowance of rub 12 per month until the child reaches age 8 for families with per capita monthly income under rub 50.

b. Recent and prospective reforms

(1) Pensions

The pension reform law enacted in May 1990 is broadly aimed at increasing the share of national income allocated to pensioners. It also aims to make the social security pension program substantially more universal than heretofore by bringing military pensions[4] into the scheme, folding in the pensions of collective farm workers, and providing a basic pension to retirees without any work history. The legislation introduces indexation to preserve the real and relative (to current wages) levels of pensions. Finally, the reform alters radically the structure of financing all social security benefits (Table 2).

All pension benefits—old-age, disability, survivors' and students' stipends—are scheduled to increase over the next several years by virtue of an explicit increase in the replacement rate. The monthly benefit, equal at least to the minimum wage, is to be based on a 55 percent replacement rate applied to the average of gross earnings in any five-year period during the last 15 years of work, up to a maximum of ten times the minimum wage. This ceiling, combined with the fact that a declining proportion of a pensioner's average earnings above four times the minimum wage are included in the earnings base, results in a progressive benefit formula; the effective replacement rate declines steadily from 55 percent to 38 percent as average earnings increase (Table 3). Another novel feature is that a pensioner's replacement rate can be increased by 1 percentage point for each year of work beyond the qualifying period, regardless of age, up to a maximum replacement rate of 75 percent. For example, for the male worker who begins work at age 20, the pension can be potentially based on a statutory rate of 70 percent (55 percent for the first 25 years, plus 15 percent for the years from age 45 to 60), and the effective replacement rate raised accordingly. Although the retirement age and qualifying periods of pensions are left unchanged, the net effect of the new pension law on the retirement decision cannot be ascertained *ex ante*. On the one hand, higher benefits provide an inducement to retire, but on the other, the removal of the ceiling on post-retirement earnings provides an incentive to remain in the labor force.

Perhaps the most significant provision introduced by the pension reform is the full indexation of benefits effective January 1992—brought forward to 1991 under a proposal in the presidential guidelines—aimed at both preserving the purchasing power of retirees and assuring greater stability of the overall replacement rate. In effect, the legislation calls for annual automatic adjustment of pension benefits for changes in the cost of living (without specifying the measure of these changes); the reform also establishes a minimum increase of 2 percent per year in pensions. Additionally, the reform provides for adjustments of the earnings base insofar as the minimum pension is equal to the minimum wage. Moreover, the reform introduces a minimum subsistence pension (or social pension) for women and men age 60 and 65, respectively, who have never been employed; persons disabled from childhood; disabled children under age 16; and children in the event of the wage earner's death. The benefit is generally 50 percent of the minimum wage, but can range from 30-100 percent of the minimum wage, with the higher amounts being paid to disabled pensioners. This represents a departure from the exclusively employment-related basis of pensions, making the government more of an insurer of last-resort than heretofore.

(2) Other benefits and allowances

Until now, relatively little change has been made to compensation for temporary disability, although a number of proposals are under consideration by the

335

authorities. One notable change is the extension of full sick pay to all workers regardless of trade union membership. During 1990, a number of measures was adopted to improve the size and scope of family allowances.[5] First, a one-time allowance equal to three times the minimum wage replaces the birth grants noted earlier, representing a significant increase in the average grant. Second, the previously available allowance for raising children to age one is to be extended to age one and a half, and is raised to 100 percent of the minimum wage for working mothers and 50 percent for nonworking mothers. Third, a means-tested monthly allowance (with family incomes less than twice the minimum wage) equal to 50 percent of the minimum age is to be paid to qualifying households for each child from age 1½ to age 6,[6] and for each child of single mothers until the child reaches 16 years of age. Fourth, allowances equal to the minimum wage are to be paid for each child of military personnel serving fixed tours of duty, as well as to foster children under age 16.

Under the only income support program targeted directly to the poor, responsibility for which was to be shifted to the union republics beginning January 1991, the eligibility for the rub 12 cash payment per child has been expanded from those under age 8 to those under age 12. The presidential guidelines call for policies which would protect the less well-off from the price increases that are likely to result from a removal of consumer subsidies. Considerable uncertainty remains, however, with respect to both the way in which compensation would be determined as well as to whom it would apply.[7]

A draft law has been approved on a first reading in the USSR Supreme Soviet for the introduction of an unemployment compensation scheme. Compensation would be provided for up to 26 weeks, and up to 39 weeks for pre-retirement workers.[8] During this time, the beneficiary will be required to search for a job commensurate with his or her experience and skill level. The program will provide tax exempt benefits equal to 50 percent of the last wage (excluding bonus payments) of the unemployed worker, or of the minimum wage, whichever is greater. In addition to unemployment compensation, the program would provide public works jobs as well, at not less than one half of the wage earned in the previous employment or at the minimum wage, whichever is greater.[9]

(3) Financing

Beginning in January 1991, social security operations were to be moved off budget. The transfer from general budget revenue was to be eliminated, and the system is hereafter to be financed fully from payroll taxes. The contribution rate of employers was to be set at 26 percent of the enterprise's wage bill. Significantly, the reform introduces a 1 percent tax on the wages of employees, a measure that can be expected to increase the linkage between benefits and contributions and to identify the beneficiary for administrative purposes. It is anticipated that the combined contribution rate will have to be adjusted over time—to the originally proposed 38 percent.[10] The contributions are earmarked for two funds: almost four fifths to the Pension Fund, out of which are to be paid all pensions, maternity and child-rearing support payments, with the remainder earmarked for the Social Security Fund, to finance temporary disability benefits, pre-natal and childbirth payments, and death benefits.

The unemployment compensation scheme is expected to be financed from a 1 percent payroll tax earmarked to the Employment Fund (the "State Fund for Occupational Orientation and Assistance to the Unemployed"). Three fourths of these tax receipts are to be retained by the union republic from which the funds originate, and the remaining one fourth are to be centralized at the union level. Other sources of revenue are to consist of allocations from the state budget, income earned from employment services, and voluntary contributions by enterprises and individuals. The Employment Fund would provide financing for labor creation programs (e.g., job training, employment in public works projects), in addition to unemployment compensation benefits.

3. MEDIUM- AND LONG-TERM OUTLOOK

Medium-term scenarios are presented below for the major components of social security, and long-run scenarios for old-age pensions. Neither set of simulations should be interpreted as projections, but should instead be seen as illustrative of the sensitivity of social security finances to variations, in key assumptions. For a given initial set of program parameters (e.g., the replacement rate and the degree of indexation), the most significant factors in the medium term are the rate of inflation, wage growth, labor force participation, unemployment, and the size of the beneficiary population. While these factors also influence the long-term outlook, demographic forces tend to play a dominant role in such a horizon.

a. Outlook for 1991 and beyond

A useful starting point in assessing the potential medium-term outlook for social security spending is the preliminary projection of outlays for 1991 by the Ministry of Finance (Table 4). This projection incorporates expected policy-related changes to beneficiary populations and benefit levels, as well as the new allowances scheduled for introduction this year. Significantly, the only important macroeconomic variable explicitly taken into account is a presumed nominal growth in aggregate wages of 12.3 percent, with no allowance for indexation, explicit compensation for price increases or unemployment compensation.

Overall, outlays are to rise substantially (42 percent), due mostly to increases in pensions, which account for the largest share of spending. Thus, even though pension benefit increases are phased-in over several years, there is nevertheless a sizable initial jump in benefits (34 percent). The other major item accounting for the large increase is the allowance for raising children from age 1½ to age 6, introduced in December 1990.

A projection of the (non-actuarial) balance of the Social Security and Pension Funds[11] for the period 1991-95 (Table 5) has been prepared by the Ministry of Finance simulating the effect of the 27 percent total contribution rate and the phase-in of changes in benefits. The simulation is based on an assumed average growth of wages between 4 and 5 percent per year—implicitly without retail price increases—for 1992-95 and a projection by Goskomtrud of underlying beneficiary populations. The projection suggests that financial balance cannot be maintained over the medium term if benefit levels, eligibility, and/or contribution rates are not adjusted. Payroll tax contributions appear to be insufficient to fully cover expenditure already in 1991; thus, the authorities may need to raise the combined contribution rate sooner and perhaps higher than the rate (38 percent) originally anticipated. Of particular concern is the possibility of an explosion of transfer payments as unemployment compensation and low-income support payments are introduced and if, as proposed in the presidential reform guidelines, indexation of pensions is brought forward from 1992 to 1991. When some of these considerations are taken into account, a vivid picture emerges of serious continuing pressure on the budget.

b. Medium-term scenarios

The official projection raises concern in view of the fact that the transition process is likely to entail temporary increases in unemployment and price rises which would feed through to both the revenue and expenditure sides of the social security accounts. First, unemployment, even if only frictional, would erode the contribution base, either generating a large deficit or necessitating a higher tax rate. Second, significant price increases, due to a reduction or removal of consumer subsidies, combined with indexation of pension and other benefits, would put significant upward pressure on outlays.[12]

Alternative scenarios through 1995 have been prepared using as a point of departure the official spending projection for 1991 (Table 4). A crude methodology has been adopted to generate a baseline scenario which closely approximates the official medium-term projection (Table 5) and which can accommodate various assumptions for the rates of inflation, unemployment and the degree of indexation (of wages and benefits), among others. The methodology, utilized to simulate the possible trajectory of aggregate spending in each category, can be summarized as follows:

Expenditure on benefits for single mothers and children in poor families (category 1 in Table 4) in 1991, $SMPC_{91}$, is estimated by multiplying the projected level by an assumed rate of inflation and an assumed degree of indexation (δ) for 1991. For subsequent years, $SMPC_t$ is obtained by adjusting the previous year's

338

value by the change in the size of the population age 0 to 15 ($POP_{t,0-15}$) (implicitly assuming that the beneficiary population remains a constant proportion of this age group), and the assumed rate of inflation π_t in year t:[13]

(1) $SMPC_t = SMPC_{t-1} (1 + \pi_t\delta) (POP_{0-15,t}/POP_{0-15,t-1})$.

For grants to institutions and other social security measures (category 2), G_t, a similar approach is employed, except that the value in each subsequent year is adjusted by the change in the size of the total population (POP_t), so that:

(2) $G_t = G_{t-1} (1 + \pi_t\delta) (POP_t/POP_{t-1})$.

Expenditure on pensions (category 3), P_t[14], is estimated by multiplying the number of pensioners in each period by the average pension in the same year, taking into account adjustments in the rate of inflation and the effects of any previous year's indexation.[15]

Expenditure on allowances for raising children up to age one and a half (categories 4 and 5) $FA1_t$, and allowances for raising children from 1½ to age 6, $FA2_t$, are simulated identically as $SMPC_t$, except for an adjustment for yearly change in the population under age 1½ ($POP_{0-1.5}$) and between age 1½ and age 6 ($POP_{1.5-6}$) respectively:

(3) $FA1_t = FA1_{t-1} (1 + \pi_t\delta) (POP_{0-1.5,t}/POP_{0-1.5,t-1})$, and

(4) $FA2_t = FA2_{t-1} (1 + \pi_t\delta) (POP_{1.5-6,t}/POP_{1.5-6,t-1})$.

Expenditure on each type of social security benefit (category 6) is simulated somewhat differently. Sick pay, SP_t, is estimated in each period by the product of a constant replacement rate of 80 percent,[16] the average wage (w_t), the average number of sick days per worker (9.3) in 1989-90 and the number of employed workers (E_t):

(5) $SP_t = 0.80 (9.3) w_tE_t$.

Similarly, maternity benefits, MB_t, are estimated by multiplying the average wage by the average 70 percent replacement and by the total number of days of maternity leave (DL_t), adjusted for the change in the female population of child-bearing age, roughly ages 15 to 45 ($FPOP_{15-45}$):

(6) $MB_t = 0.77 w_tDL_t(FPOP_{15-45,t}/FPOP_{15-45,t-1})$.

Outlays on sanitarium visits, S_t, are obtained by multiplying the average expenditure per worker in 1990 (S_{90}) by the number of workers in each subsequent year, adjusted by the rate of inflation and degree of indexation:

(7) $S_t = S_{90} (1 + \pi_t\delta)E_t$.

Population projections at five-year intervals to 2025, along with dependency rates (Table 6), have been used to simulate the number of employed workers in each year, by applying age- and sex-specific labor force participation rates (LFPR)[17] to the projected number of persons in the same age groups.[18] The resulting number is then multiplied by the assumed overall rate of unemployment (U_t) to obtain an estimate of the number of employed workers in each year:

(8) $E_t = LFPR_{j,k} \, POP_{j,k,t} \, (1-U_t)$,

where j = age group 16-29, 30-49, 50-54, 55-59, or 60 and over, and k = male, female.

The baseline medium-term scenario (Table 7) is simply the approximation of the official projection (Table 5) augmented to include those outlays which are financed by the union republics. This highly stylized scenario thus assumes no inflation (and, therefore, no indexation of benefits nor any low-income compensation beyond that provided by existing benefits), nor any additional unemployment.

In order to highlight the sensitivity of social security spending to alternative assumptions about inflation and unemployment, four different scenarios have been simulated, consistent with a "radical" and alternatively a "gradual" overall economic reform program,[19] and, for each of these, indexation or nonindexation of benefits beginning in 1991 is assumed—in all cases, pension benefits are fully indexed from 1992, as called for in the reform legislation.[20] In the radical reform, there is an immediate shock to the economic system, with inflation and unemployment rates reaching fairly high levels, especially in comparison with recent experience in the USSR. The counterpart to the increased burden of the transition is the more rapid adjustment to improved economic performance beyond the medium term. In the gradual reform, the initial policies have a lesser, although not insignificant, effect on prices and employment, but there is a slower improvement in economic performance.

The results obtained from these two alternative scenarios (Tables 8 and 9 and Chart 1) highlight the advantages of nonindexation from a financing perspective; the required tax rates[21] not only remain lower than otherwise, but begin to decline as early as 1992 under the radical reform. Immediate across-the-board benefit indexation significantly increases the initial and future required pay-as-you-go tax rates. Although the estimated required tax rate under radical reform is higher than under the gradual program until 1994, reflecting the much larger initial price adjustment in the former case, it is important to underscore the fact that the radical reform results in a more rapid restoration of higher real economic growth than under a gradual approach. This is reflected in lower rates of both unemployment and inflation by 1995. These simulations serve to highlight some of the pressure on the tax base of a large part of social spending. Left out of the analysis are the additional compensatory payments that are likely to be required, namely, for unemployment insurance and low-income protection.

c. Long-term scenarios

Given the latency of the growth of some benefits, pensions in particular, it is relevant to look to the distant future to determine the long-term financial sustainability of the social security system. As in many industrial countries, the Soviet

340

population is projected to experience a significant change in its age structure over the next 25-40 years as a result of declining fertility in recent decades (Table 6 and Chart 2).[22] The trends reflect not only the fact that the projected decline in the youth dependency rate is not expected to offset the rise in the elderly ratios, but that the earlier legal age of retirement in the USSR makes the ageing process more marked.

The importance of these demographic prospects for social security lies in the fact that in a pay-as-you-go (PAYG) system of financing pensions, the current period pensions of the retired population in each year are paid by the employed workers in the same period. Thus, as the number of retired persons per worker increases, a higher share of each worker's income must be transferred to retirees if the relative gross incomes of both retirees and workers are to remain fixed (as is often achieved either systematically via the pension formula, or on an ad hoc basis). The required PAYG contribution rates for public pensions in the USSR in each year to 2025 have been derived from the basic accounting identity that applies to a PAYG scheme, namely, that in each period t, total pension outlays must be financed by total contributions.[23] Defining the replacement rate, βt, as the ratio of the average pension in each period to the average gross wage, and the dependency ratio, D_t, as the ratio of the number of retired persons to the number of workers, the PAYG tax rate in each period is given by $\tau_t = \beta_t D_t$. The higher D_t, the higher must be τ_t; similarly, a rising or falling β_t will raise or lower τ_t.

A fundamental determinant of the PAYG tax rate is, thus, the average replacement rate. There is, of course, no necessity for the replacement rate to remain fixed, except insofar as it is ensured by the benefit formula.[24] However, authorities in most countries in recent years have typically endeavored to minimize major changes in the relative incomes of elderly and workers. Moreover, in the case of the USSR, the recent pension reform aims explicitly at increasing the pension replacement rate. For illustrative purposes, two alternative assumptions are made about the future path of the average replacement rate. In both cases, between 1991 and 1995, the replacement rate each year is determined by the baseline simulation reported above, which relies on official projections of the average pension. For the period beyond 1995, the replacement rate is assumed alternatively to remain constant from 1996 onward or to grow at a rate of a half of 0.5 percent per year to 2025.[25] In the latter case, the average replacement rate rises to 60 percent—the actual rate as of 1960. Projections of the dependency rate have been made by separately simulating the number of beneficiaries of old-age pensions and the size of the contributory base (i.e., the number of contributing workers). The number of beneficiaries in each period to 2025 is estimated by assuming that the number of recipients of old-age pensions, $B_{55/60}$,[26] grows in the first instance at the same rate as the size of the population of legal retirement age—women age 55 and older and men age 60 and older. On the assumption that the age and sex-specific labor force participation rates remain constant through time, and that the number of contributors, $C_{55/60}$, remains a constant proportion of the labor force, the

341

denominator of the dependency rate is obtained from projections of the population in each age group. The ratio of $B_{55/60}$ to $C_{55/60}$ provides an estimate of the dependency rate $D_{55/60}$ in each period.

In view of the projected population ageing, it is conceivable that the relatively low Soviet retirement ages will have to be reconsidered at some time in the future. Thus, it is useful to assess the extent to which increasing the legal pensionable age might reduce the future tax burden on workers. To quantify this, an alternative dependency ratio has been simulated assuming that the statutory retirement age for women and men is increased every two years by one-year increments over a ten-year period, beginning in the year 1995, so that by 2005 the legal ages for men and women would be 65 and 60, respectively. The ratio of the resulting number of pensioners to the contributor base yields the alternative dependency rate, $D_{60/65}$.

Four simulations of the required PAYG tax rate have been made. The first is based on the dependency rate $D_{55/60}$ and assumes, as noted, that the average replacement rate of old-age pensions rises to about 60 percent by 2025. The second simulation assumes the same pattern for the growth of the average replacement rate, but is based on a gradual increase of the retirement age (to be completed by 2005) and concomitantly of the dependency rate $D_{60/65}$. The third and fourth simulations are alternatively based on current and raised retirement ages, but in both cases the average replacement rate remains constant at 52 percent from 1996 onward.

In the case of retirement at ages 55 and 60 and a rising replacement rate, the estimated PAYG contribution rates rise quite considerably, reflecting the force of both demographic change and the replacement rate (Table 10 and Chart 3). The separate influence of population ageing in the USSR can be gauged from the constant replacement rate simulations. The very strong influence of the low retirement age on the per worker cost of future pensions is also evident; raising the pensionable age by five-year intervals reduces the increase in contribution rates by 6 percentage points. However, these simulations do not take into account unemployment, which can have an adverse effect on the contribution base.

Illustrative quantification of the potential implications of demographic conditions on payroll tax rates underscores their importance in the formulation of social security policy. At the same time, other factors should have opposite favorable effects. In particular, if labor productivity is significantly enhanced, the future burden per worker in the first instance will be lightened. However, if productivity gains, desirable in their own right, are passed through to pensions in order to maintain the relative incomes of workers and retirees, this will have little effect on the required tax rate. Thus, the large increase in the elderly dependency ratio that is projected over the next two to three decades in the USSR requires that eventually the authorities reassess the relative shares of national income of workers and retirees.

Although not captured by the present analysis, it is necessary to consider demographic differences among union republics; these differences partly explain current difficulties in establishing a centralized pension fund for the USSR (see Chapter IV.6). Moreover, besides variations in the present age structure (Table 11), differences in total fertility rates suggest that demographic diversity among the republics is likely to persist well into the next century.

NOTES

1. For further discussion, see Chapter IV.6.

2. See McAuley (1984).

3. Of course, effective retirement ages differ somewhat from statutory ones. As elsewhere, incentives to postpone retirement are present in the Soviet retirement system. For instance, the initial pension can be increased by 10 rubles per month for each additional year of work beyond the qualifying age. Conversely, penalties for early retirement have also been present, the pension being reduced proportionately if taken before reaching the legal age.

4. That is, for soldiers, as distinct from officers who are already covered by the scheme.

5. Decree of the USSR Supreme Soviet "On Urgent Measures to Improve the Status of Women, Protect Motherhood and Childhood, and Strengthen the Family,"and Decree No. 759 "On additional Measures for Social Protection of Families with Children in Connection with the Transition to a Regulated Market Economy" [no date].

6. The beneficiary population for this allowance is the same as for the allowance which previously was paid to mothers for raising children to age one.

7. See Chapter IV.6 for a discussion of alternative approaches.

8. It is not clear to what extent the proposed program would require prior employment for eligibility.

9. For a more elaborate discussion of this program, see Chapter IV.6.

10. The original rate was scaled back largely because it would have generated a surplus during the first two years of implementation. Instead, the 11 percentage point difference between the original and present rate is to be levied to finance the newly-created extrabudgetary stabilization funds.

11. A consolidated (union and union republic) balance for the two funds is not available because of a lack of revenue data for the union republics, which are excluded from the projection.

12. Although only pensions are to be explicitly adjusted for changes in the cost of living, all benefits tied to wages (e.g., sick pay and maternity leave benefits) will also change. At the same time, as wages grow so do receipts of social security contributions. In a broader budgetary context, however, it should be noted that the pressure on social security transfers would be compensated at least in part by the fall in state budget outlays on consumer subsidies.

13. Presumably, an interim effect of the transition to a market economy will be an increase in the size of the population below the poverty line. Thus, the assumption made here is unlikely to hold in reality, but insufficient information is available on which to project the number of poor population.

14. Based on data provided by the Ministry of Finance, the projected number (in millions) of pensioners (old-age, disabled, student, etc.) in each year to 1995 is: 60.8 for 1991; 61.9 for 1992; 63.0 for 1993; 64.1 for 1994; and 66.3 for 1995.

15. The estimates of average pension in each year to 1995 provided by the Ministry of Finance, as noted, do not take into account any possible future inflation, although they do incorporate the minimum 2 percent annual increase called for in the reform. In simulating aggregate pension spending, it has been necessary to adjust the average pension in subsequent years for inflation above 2 percent and for any indexation of benefits in previous years. In other words, if pensions are indexed fully only in 1991, but not in subsequent years, one would nevertheless expect the average pension in those subsequent years to be higher than otherwise.

16. The observed replacement rate of 77 percent in recent years is arbitrarily increased to 80 percent to take account of the extension of full cash benefits to nontrade union workers.

17. Labor force participation rates obtained from Oxenstierna (1990).

18. For simplicity, the labor force participation rates are assumed to remain constant over the simulation period.

19. See Chapter VI.1

20. Normally, indexation of benefits occurs with a lag of several months. The assumption made here, for simplicity, is that benefit adjustments are contemporaneous with inflation.

21. The required rate (to be distinguished from the statutory combined contribution rate, which remains 27 percent in each year for all scenarios) is equal to expenditures on all programs divided by the wage bill.

22. A decline in fertility rates today reduces the future size of the working age population relative to the number of elderly. This is often referred to as "ageing from the bottom," as opposed to "ageing from the top", which results from increases in the average duration of life (and unchanged fertility rates).

23. Halter and Hemming (1987), and Hagemann and Nicoletti (1989).

24. As a general rule, the more the initial pension depends on current period wages, and the greater the degree of post-retirement indexation of existing pensions, the more stable will be the average replacement rate.

25. It is not possible to project the level which the replacement rate might reach, as this depends on the income distribution of future retirees and the relative trends in wages over time, among other things.

26. Given projections through 1995, made available by the Ministry of Finance.

Table 1. USSR: Statutory Retirement Age in OECD Countries, 1989

	Standard Retirement Age		Early Retirement Age	
	Men	Women	Men	Women
Australia	65	60	—	—
Austria	65	60	60	55
Belgium	65	60	60	—
Canada	65	65	—	—
Denmark	67	67	60-66	60-66
Finland	65	65	60	60
France	60	60	—	—
Germany	63-65	60-65	—	—
Greece	58-65	55-57	...	...
Ireland	65	65	—	—
Iceland [1]	67	67	—	—
Italy	60	55	55	50
Japan	60	55	—	—
Luxembourg	65	65	60	55-60
Netherlands	65	65	—	—
New Zealand	60	60	—	—
Norway	67	67	—	—
Portugal	65	62	62	—
Spain	65	65	64	64
Sweden	65	65	60-64	60-64
Switzerland	65	62	—	—
Turkey [2]	65	60	... [3]	... [3]
United Kingdom	65	60	—	—
United States	65	65	62-64	62-64

Source: OECD Social Policy Data Bank.
1. Age 60 for seamen and fishermen having worked 25 years.
2. Age 50 for prematurely aged men; miners covered for 1,800 days.
3. Based on contribution.

Table 2. USSR: Summary of Pension Programs Before and After Reform

	Pre-Reform Scheme	Post-Reform Scheme
Coverage	Employed persons, disabled in public duties, and state farmworkers.	All persons, including those without a work history.
	Special provisions for certain subgroups.	Voluntary supplemental system retained.
	Special system for collective farmworkers, established in 1964.	
	Voluntary supplemental system for all workers.	
Source of funds	Insured person: none.	Insured person: 1 percent of wage.
	Employer: From 4-14.4 percent of payroll, variable across industries.	Employer: 26 percent of wage fund of enterprise. Government makes same contribution on behalf of its employees. Rate to vary by industry according to degree of difficulty of work and other conditions.
	Government: General revenues for excess of expenditure over employer contribution.	Possibility of use of funds from the state budget.
Qualifying conditions	*Old-age pension:* Age 60 (men) or 55 (women) and 25 (men) or 20 (women) years of work, with reduced work requirements for select groups (e.g., in far north regions). Lower age and shorter work history for certain groups.	*Old-age pension:* Generally unchanged from earlier law.
	Invalidity pension: Incapacity for any work (total invalidity) or usual (partial invalidity) injury. Tenure requirements of 2-20 years for men, 1-15 years for women, and 1-5 years (women) and 1-14 years (men) for dangerous work, according to age; reduced pension if fewer years.	*Invalidity pension:* Generally unchanged; provision for invalidity due to general illness as well, subject to minimum required years of work variable by age; up to 23 years–1 year of work; from age 23 to 26–2 years of work; from age 26 to 31–3 years of work; from age 31 to 34–5 years of work; from age 34 to 41–7 years of work; from age 41 to 46–9 years of work; from age 45 to 51–11 years of work; 51-56 years and older–14 years of work; 61 years and older–15 years of work.
	Survivor's pension: Insured has 20 (men) or 1-5 (women) years of work or 1-15 (women) years for dangerous work, according to age at death; reduced pension for shorter work history.	*Survivor's pension:* Nonworking members of the family of a deceased breadwinner, children, spouses and parents (whether or not they are dependent on the breadwinner), and the grandparents of the deceased when there are no others to provide support.

Table 2 (Continued).   USSR: Summary of Pension Programs Before and After Reform

	Pre-Reform Scheme	Post-Reform Scheme
Cash benefits	*Old-age pension:* 50 percent of average gross earnings in last 12 months (or best 5 consecutive years in last 10 years) if earnings above rub 100 per month; 55 percent if earnings rub 80-100 per month; 65 percent if earnings rub 60-80 per month; 75 percent if earnings rub 50-60 per month; 85 percent if earnings rub 35-50 per month; 100 percent if earnings under rub 35 per month. Higher rates for dangerous work. Supplemental of 20 percent of pensions for 10 years' work beyond qualifying 25 year period with uninterrupted employment in the same enterprise. For same longer work period but with only 15 years of service in the same enterprise, half the increment is received. Supplement of 10 percent of pension for one dependent; 15 percent for two or more. Supplement of rub 10 per month for each year pension is delayed after reaching age of entitlement (up to a maximum of rub 40). Minimum pension equal to rub 70 rubles, maximum equal to rub 120 (higher for select groups such as miners). No indexation, but adjustment of 10 year-old pension every two years. Reduced pension proportionate to number of years of work, with minimum equal to 25 percent of full pension. Pension also reduced when concurrent earnings exceed rub 150 per month.	*Old-age pension:* 55 percent replacement rate of average monthly earnings calculated from any consecutive five-year period in last 15 years of work before applying for pension, regardless of interruptions in work. If work history is shorter than 5 years, actual number of years is used. A decreasing share of average earnings in excess of four times the (indexed) minimum wage is included in pension determination; 100 percent of average earnings up to 4 times minimum wage; 85 percent of fifth multiple of minimum wage; 70 percent of sixth multiple of minimum wage; 55 percent of 7th multiple of minimum wage; 40 percent of 8th multiple of minimum wage; 25 percent of ninth multiple of minimum wage; and 15 percent of 10th multiple of minimum wage. Earnings in excess of 10 times the minimum wage are not included in base. Replacement rate is increased by 1 percent for each year of additional work beyond qualifying period, up to a maximum of 75 percent. Minimum pension is equal to the (indexed) minimum wage. Pensions are fully indexed for changes in wages and the cost of living, and are not subject to individual income tax. Minimum pension equal to (indexed) minimum wage. No limit on concurrent earnings from employment of pension. Introduction to a new *social pension*, payable to non-working citizens when they do not have a right to a labor pension. These are payable to totally disabled persons, to men age 65 or older and women age 60 or older, to disabled children under age 16 and to surviving children of an insured worker. Social pensions for disabled range from 50-100 percent of the minimum wage depending on the severity of invalidity or whether the beneficiary is a survivor of the injured worker.

347

Table 2 (Concluded). USSR: Summary of Pension Program Before and After Reform

Pre-Reform Scheme	Post-Reform Scheme
Disability pension:	*Disability pension:*
90 percent of old-age pension if totally disabled. 100 percent of old-age pension if minimum number of years for old-age pension is attained. Pension range: rub 7-120 per month. For partial invalidity, pension equal to 45 percent of earnings up to rub 40 per month, plus 10 percent of higher earnings. Minimum pension rub 26 per month; maximum rub 60.	For total disability, 55 percent replacement of earnings, equal to at least the (indexed) minimum wage or, if tenure requirement for old-age pension reached, old-age pension is assigned. For partial disability, 30 percent replacement of earnings, equal to at least half of the (indexed) minimum wage.
Supplement for dependents, additional years of continuous employment if constant nursing assistance needed, and for injury performing dangerous work.	*Survivor's pension:*
Survivor's pension:	Pensions are assigned to each survivor in the amount of 30 percent of the earnings of the deceased breadwinner, but no less than the social pension for the corresponding category of disabled (see below). For a child who has lost both parents, the pension is to be no less than twice the amount of the social pension.
One survivor, 45 percent of earnings up to rub 40 a month (full orphans, 65 percent) plus 10 percent of higher earnings. Pension range: rub 26-60 per month.	
Two survivors; 90 percent of old-age pension; minimum rub 50 per month; maximum rub 120 per month.	
Three survivors or more: 100 percent of old-age pension, in range of rub 75-120 per month.	
Pension increased 10-15 percent for 10 or 15 year period of continuous work.	

Source: Ministry of Finance.

Table 3. USSR: Hypothetical Pension Replacement Rates [1]

Average Earnings (In multiples of minimum wage)	Monthly Pension (In rubles)	Pension as a Ratio to Earnings
4	154	0.55
5	187	0.53
6	214	0.51
7	235	0.48
8	250	0.45
9	260	0.41
10	266	0.38

1. Assumes a minimum wage of rub 70 per month.

Table 4. USSR: Social Security Expenditure, 1990-91
(In billions of rubles)

Category	1990 Estimate	1991 Projection
1. Benefits for single mothers and poor families	2.1	2.2
For single mothers	0.8	0.8
For children in poor families	1.3	1.4
2. Grants to institutions and other social security measures	1.5	2.0
3. Pensions, including those to collective farmers	65.6	88.0
4. Benefits for raising children to age one and a half	5.6	5.6
5. Benefits for raising children from age 1.5 to 6	0.8	10.0
6. Sick pay, maternity, childbirth, burials and outlays for sanitaria	16.3	22.0
7. Benefits to single mothers and one time benefits for birth of a child	—	0.3
Total	91.9	130.1

Source: Ministry of Finance.

Table 5. USSR: Projection of Social Security Operations, 1991-95

(In billions of rubles)

	1991	1992	1993	1994	1995
Revenue					
Social security contributions[1]	120	126	133	139	147
Expenditure	125	143	155	168	178
Social Security Fund	22	24	26	28	30
Pension Fund	103	119	129	140	148
Pensions	88	103	112	122	128
Allowances	15	16	17	18	20
Balance	-5	-17	-22	-29	-31

Source: Ministry of Finance.
1. Assuming payroll-based rates of 26 percent on employers and 1 percent on employees.

Table 6. USSR: Population Projection, 1990-2025

(In millions of inhabitants)

Age Group	1990	1995	2000	2005	2010	2015	2020	2025
0–4	25.2	22.8	22.0	22.6	23.4	23.8	23.5	23.0
5–9	25.1	25.1	22.7	21.9	22.5	23.4	23.8	23.5
10–14	23.1	25.0	25.1	22.7	21.9	22.5	22.4	23.8
15–19	21.4	23.0	25.0	25.0	22.6	21.8	22.4	23.3
20–24	20.5	21.3	22.9	24.8	24.9	22.5	21.8	22.4
25–29	23.3	20.4	21.1	22.7	24.7	24.8	22.5	21.7
30–34	24.1	23.1	20.2	21.0	22.6	24.6	24.7	22.4
35–39	21.5	23.8	23.0	20.1	20.9	22.5	24.5	24.6
40–44	15.4	21.2	23.6	22.8	20.0	20.7	22.4	24.3
45–49	12.8	15.1	20.8	23.2	22.5	19.7	20.5	22.1
50–54	18.4	12.4	14.7	20.4	22.8	22.1	19.4	20.2
55–59	14.8	17.6	11.9	14.2	19.7	22.1	21.5	18.9
60–64	15.0	13.9	16.6	11.3	13.5	18.9	21.2	20.7
65–69	9.6	13.5	12.7	15.3	10.5	12.6	17.7	20.0
70–74	6.0	8.3	11.8	11.2	13.6	9.4	11.4	16.2
75 & over	11.5	10.8	12.6	17.2	19.8	23.2	22.3	23.0
Total	287.7	297.3	306.6	316.5	326.0	334.8	342.8	350.0
Memorandum items:								
Total fertility rate	2.186	2.106	2.097	2.091	2.084	2.078	2.072	2.065
Total dependency rate [1]	53.7	55.0	53.5	53.9	52.1	52.3	55.3	58.7
Old-age dependency rate [2]	14.5	17.0	18.5	21.2	20.5	20.6	23.3	26.8

Source: IBRD.
1. The total dependency rate is defined as the sum of the population aged 0-14 and 65 and over as a percentage of the population aged 15-64.
2. The old-age dependency rate is defined as the population aged 65 and older as a percentage of the population aged 15-64.

Table 7. USSR: Medium-Term Baseline Scenario for Social Security Operations, 1991-95

(In billions of rubles, unless otherwise noted)

	1991	1992	1993	1994	1995
Revenue	120	126	133	139	147
Pension Fund	103	109	114	120	126
Social Security Fund	17	18	19	19	21
Expenditure	125	140	150	160	167
Allowances	16	15	15	15	14
Pensions	88	103	112	122	128
Other [1]	21	22	23	23	24
Balance	-5	-14	-17	-21	-20
Required pay-as-you-go rate *(percent of payroll)*	24	30	30	31	31
Memorandum items (percent):					
Inflation rate	—	—	—	—	—
Unemployment rate	—	—	—	—	—
Wage growth	11	4	4	4	4

Source: Estimates.
1. Sick pay, maternity leave, rest home stays, burials.

Table 8. USSR: Medium-Term Radical Reform Scenarios
for Social Security Operations, 1990-95

(In billions of rubles, unless otherwise noted)

	1991	1992	1993	1994	1995
Without benefit indexation					
Revenue	136	158	190	228	280
Pension Fund	117	136	164	196	241
Social Security Fund	19	22	27	32	39
Expenditure	127	161	190	223	252
Allowances	16	15	15	15	14
Pensions	88	119	144	172	195
Other [1]	23	27	31	36	43
Balance	9	-3	—	5	28
Required pay-as-you-go rate *(percent of payroll)*	25	27	27	26	24
With benefit indexation					
Revenue	136	150	190	228	280
Pension Fund	117	136	164	196	241
Social Security Fund	19	22	27	32	39
Expenditure	193	247	292	344	388
Allowances	25	26	27	28	29
Pensions	143	193	233	279	316
Other [1]	25	27	32	37	43
Balance	-57	-88	-101	-116	-108
Required pay-as-you-go rate *(percent of payroll)*	38	42	41	40	37
Memorandum items (percent):					
Inflation rate	62	18	11	10	8
Unemployment rate	9	11	9	9	8
Wage growth	38	18	17	19	20

Source: Estimates.

1. Sick pay, maternity leave, rest home stays, burials.

352

Table 9. USSR: Medium-Term Gradual Reform Scenarios
for Social Security Operations, 1991-95

(In billions of rubles, unless otherwise noted)

	1991	1992	1993	1994	1995
Without benefit indexation					
Revenue	142	168	197	233	281
Pension Fund	122	145	169	201	242
Social Security Fund	20	24	28	33	39
Expenditure	128	166	205	254	300
Allowances	16	15	15	15	14
Pensions	88	123	158	201	241
Other [1]	24	28	32	38	44
Balance	15	2	-8	-21	-18
Required pay-as-you-go rate *(percent of payroll)*	24	27	28	29	29
With benefit indexation					
Revenue	142	168	197	233	281
Pension Fund	122	145	169	201	202
Social Security Fund	20	24	28	33	39
Expenditure	170	224	279	346	410
Allowances	22	23	24	26	27
Pensions	123	172	221	282	337
Other [1]	35	29	33	38	45
Balance	-20	-56	-82	-113	-128
Required pay-as-you-go rate *(percent of payroll)*	32	36	39	40	39
Memorandum items (percent):					
Inflation rate	40	22	10	17	14
Unemployment rate	4	7	9	10	10
Wage growth	39	20	19	19	19

Source: Estimates.
1. Sick pay, maternity leave, rest home stays, burials.

Table 10. USSR: Pay-As-You-Go Tax Rates for Old-Age Pensions
Under Alternative Long-Term Scenarios, 1990-2025 [1]

(In percent of payroll)

Year	Rising Replacement Rate		Constant Replacement Rate	
	Retirement at 55 & 60	Retirement at 60 & 65	Retirement at 55 & 60	Retirement at 60 & 65
1990	13.2	13.2	13.2	13.2
1995	19.7	19.7	19.7	19.7
2000	20.6	18.9	20.1	18.4
2005	20.8	17.6	19.8	16.8
2010	22.6	18.1	21.0	16.8
2015	25.7	20.0	23.3	18.1
2020	29.1	23.1	25.7	20.3
2025	31.5	26.1	27.1	22.5

Source: Estimates.
1. Each column refers to the average of ages shown for women and men, respectively.

Table 11. USSR: Selected Demographic Indicators,
by Union Republic, 1990

	Youth Dependency Rate	Old-Age Dependency Rate	Total Fertility Rate
USSR average	27.3	17.1	2.34
RSFSR	24.5	18.5	2.02
Ukraine	23.0	21.2	1.93
Belorussia	24.5	19.5	2.03
Estonia	23.7	20.2	2.22
Latvia	22.7	20.7	2.05
Lithuania	24.1	18.9	1.98
Moldavia	29.6	15.3	2.50
Georgia	32.6	15.8	2.14
Armenia	32.0	11.7	2.61
Azerbaidzhan	34.7	10.0	2.76
Kazakhstan	33.7	11.1	2.81
Turkmenistan	42.7	7.6	4.27
Uzbekistan	42.9	8.0	4.02
Tadzhikistan	45.1	7.6	5.08
Kirgizia	39.5	10.2	3.81

Source: Ministry of Finance.

354

Chart 1. **USSR : REQUIRED PAY-AS-YOU-GO TAX RATE UNDER ALTERNATIVE MEDIUM-TERM SCENARIOS, 1991-95**

(percent of payroll)

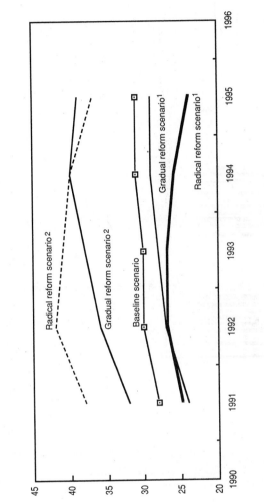

Source: Estimates.

1. Without benefit indexation.
2. With benefit indexation.

355

Chart 2. **USSR : PROJECTED DEPENDENCY RATES UNDER ALTERNATIVE RETIREMENT AGE PROVISIONS, 1990-2025**

(percent of labor-force-age population)

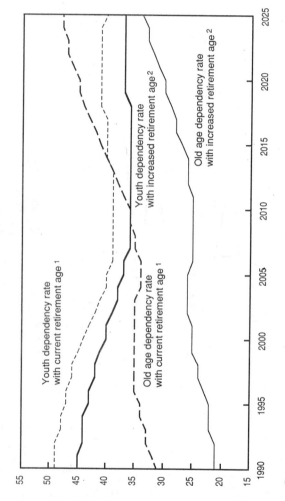

Source: International Bank for Reconstruction and Development.

1. The denominator is defined as the female population aged 16 to 54 and the male population aged 16 to 59. For the old age dependency ratio, the numerator is defined as the female population aged 55 and over and the male population aged 60 and over. For the youth dependency ratio, the numerator is defined as population aged 0 to 15.

2. The denominator is defined as the female population aged 16 to 59 and the male population aged 16 to 64. For the old age dependency ratio, the numerator is defined as the female population aged 60 and over and the male population aged 65 and over. For the youth dependency ratio, the numerator is defined as population aged 0 to 15.

Chart 3. **USSR : PAY-AS-YOU-GO TAX RATE FOR OLD-AGE PENSIONS UNDER ALTERNATIVE LONG-TERM SCENARIOS, 1990-2025**

(percent of payroll)

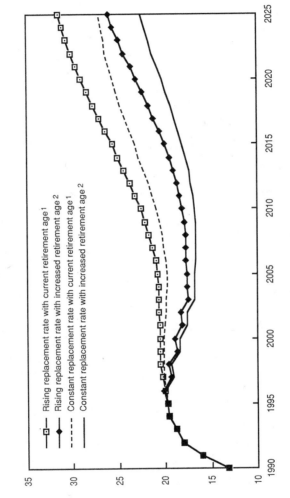

Source: Estimates.

1. Retirement age is set at 55 for females and 60 for males.
2. Retirement age is assumed to be 60 for females and 65 for males.

Chapter III.2

The Changing Roles of Monetary and Exchange Rate Policies

The introduction of economic reforms in the USSR has brought about some important changes in macroeconomic policy making. This chapter describes and analyzes the role and operation of monetary and exchange rate policies, and their implementation in the USSR before and after the reforms of 1987-88 (Sections 1 and 2). It also discusses the main points of the current proposals for further reforms in the financial sector (Section 3), with special emphasis on the issue of policy credibility for an economy in transition.

1. MONETARY POLICY BEFORE THE REFORMS

a. The role of monetary policy

The role and the instruments of monetary policy prior to the reforms of 1987-88 have to be considered in the context of the classical model of central planning that had prevailed in the USSR since the early 1930s. In that model, virtually all physical resources were allocated according to the central state plan, and the financial plan only mirrored the detailed quantitative plans for enterprise inputs and outputs. The subordination of financial planning to quantitative planning meant that real magnitudes would determine monetary aggregates, without in principle allowing for feedbacks. Planning started from the desired objective for production, which was apportioned between private consumption, public consumption, and investment. With the help of elaborate input-output models, the resulting main production objectives were translated into a detailed matrix of enterprise inputs and outputs. With prices being virtually fixed, and assuming a constant propensity to save out of disposable income, the desired (planned) stock of money in the economy could be derived. The role of monetary policy was to ensure that the liquidity injection into the economy took place in accordance with the plan.

To minimize any feedback that monetary variables might have on production and prices, the authorities pursued a policy of "dichotomized" money supply. In effect, credit to enterprises and their financial flows more generally were strictly separated from those of households in two respects. First, within the enterprise sector, and between that sector and the budget, all financial transactions were carried out in the form of transfers of bank deposits. Cash holdings by enterprises were virtually prohibited, and currency was drawn from enterprise deposits almost exclusively for payroll purposes. While households could hold savings accounts, only currency served as their means of payment. The interchangeability of currency and deposits within the household sector was not strictly limited, although the authorities always aimed at constraining cash holdings of households to the extent possible through regulating the supply of currency. Second, direct lending between the enterprise sector and households was prohibited; households were therefore not allowed to purchase enterprise securities and consumer credit was virtually nonexistent. These regulations effectively isolated the financial behavior and flows of firms and households, contributing to the reduced liquidity or "moneyness" of the currency (see below).[1]

The instruments of monetary policy were administrative in nature, and differed in the two financial circuits. Financial flows of enterprises were regulated through the Credit Plan, and those of households through the Cash Plan. The Credit Plan was the financial counterpart to the production plan. It was a "micro" plan in that it was built up from the disaggregated planned demand for credit by each enterprise. The planned demand for enterprise credit was aggregated at all territorial (local, regional, and union) levels, to determine the overall quarterly credit plan. Credit extended to enterprises was mainly short-term, aimed at supplying working capital, as virtually all investment was financed through budgetary transfers to enterprises (at the same time, the bulk of their profits had to be remitted to the budget). Indeed, until the mid-1960s, long-term credit to the economy was nonexistent, and increased only slowly thereafter. Enterprises faced a soft budget constraint which implied that shortfalls from planned profits would either be supported directly from the budget through increased net transfers or by bank credits. The difference between such credits and budgetary grants was rather blurred; and debt write-offs might occur following the accumulation of payments arrears.[2]

The complementary Cash Plan covered all the financial flows effected in currency. The particular importance that the authorities attached to the Cash Plan can be explained by the fact that only currency was regarded as a freely available source of purchasing power. As mentioned, enterprises were not allowed to hold significant amounts of cash, and their deposits were often held jointly with the branch ministries, with their use being earmarked. Savings deposits of households, which were encouraged by the authorities, tended to be stable and therefore were implicitly regarded as direct resources of the state budget (similar to government revenue), rather than a free claim by households on goods and services.

The Cash Plan specified both the factors that contributed to an injection of currency into circulation, and those that caused it to flow into the banking system—as reflected in the so-called balance of money incomes and expenditures of the population (see Table D.2 in Appendix II-1). Increases in currency in circulation arose most notably from wage and salary payments, social money benefits, state procurement of products grown on the private plots of collective farm members, and drawdowns of household deposits. Withdrawal of currency from circulation was mainly the result of household purchases of goods and services from state or cooperative outlets and increases in saving deposits, as well as of small purchases of government bonds.[3] Clearly, most of these factors were beyond the control of the banking system. Therefore, the implementation of monetary policy focused on closely monitoring the execution of the Cash Plan, and alerting the authorities when deviations occurred.[4]

The degree of moneyness of financial assets, and consequently the demand for money, differed substantially between the two separated financial circuits.[5] Households were, in theory, free to hold financial assets to the extent desired, although the range of these assets was rather limited (namely, to currency as well as demand and savings deposits).[6] Because the ownership of real assets was limited by law on ideological grounds, most household savings took the form of financial assets, almost exclusively in the form of money.

The high degree of moneyness of the available short-term financial assets of the household sector contrasted with the low degree of liquidity of the financial assets of enterprises, which had two main causes. First, as noted, the bank accounts of state enterprises were frequently jointly owned by the firms and their respective branch ministries.[7] Second, the use of enterprise own funds was strictly regulated, with funds being strictly earmarked and generally not fungible. Money holdings therefore did not play a decisive role in the decision-making of enterprises. The demand of enterprises for financial assets was largely determined by three major factors: (i) the requirements of the quantitative plan; (ii) uncertainties regarding the liquidity of available deposits; and (iii) the opportunity cost of holding money in terms of inventories (in the event of chronic shortages, inventories might substitute for money as a store of value). For these reasons, and due to the lack of attractive real rates of return on financial assets,[8] an enterprise may have sought to minimize its money (deposit) holdings. Over time, some of the rigidities were relaxed and, in line with the gradual decentralization of decision-making, enterprises gained greater freedom over the use of their accounts. However, the resulting higher degree of moneyness of enterprise accounts might not have increased the desired holding of financial assets insofar as growing liquidity was accompanied by greater shortages and possibly a heightened preference for stockbuilding.

b. Institutional features of the banking sector

Consistent with central planning and management, all central and commercial banking operations were centralized in Gosbank. A few state-owned specialized banks already existed prior to the reforms of 1987-88 (see Chapter IV.5), but they did not change the monolithic feature of the banking system because they were set up with well-defined tasks and were automatically assigned to specific enterprises; therefore, they did not compete with one another. Moreover, the banks worked under the direct control and supervision of Gosbank; one of them in fact as a Gosbank department (the Savings Bank).

The subordinated role of monetary and credit policy implied a generally passive role for Gosbank, reducing it to that of an administrative agency. Chief among its functions was to provide credit to enterprises necessary to carry out production and revenue plans. Moreover, since virtually all enterprise income and depreciation funds were transferred to the budget and branch ministries, enterprises were highly credit-dependent, giving Gosbank a considerable monitoring role over enterprise activity.[9] Gosbank also played an important role in the administrative control of the economy. It signalled deviations from plan targets or inconsistencies among plan objectives, and it suppressed these imbalances through the strict separation of the financial flows of enterprises from those of households and the supervision over the earmarked use of enterprise funds. In addition, the Gosbank network also provided the only settlement and clearing mechanism for the enterprise sector. Finally, like many central banks in market economies, Gosbank functioned as fiscal agency for the Government. Budgetary financing took different forms. All increases in households' savings deposits were made available automatically to meet planned budgetary financing needs. Moreover, indirect budget financing prevailed in the form of credit to enterprises to bridge the gap between planned and actual profits to be transferred to the budget.

c. Monetary policy before the reforms: an illustration

In a market economy, a monetary expansion that exceeds the growth of demand for money typically leads to some combination of an increase in prices and a deterioration in the balance of payments. However, in the Soviet system, where prices were controlled and foreign exchange operations restricted, excessive monetary expansion typically did not have such effects. Rather, it resulted in excess demand in the economy, which was manifested in shortages. In addressing the problem of excess demand, the authorities used administrative measures. A good example of this was the credit expansion during the first half of the 1980s. In the period 1981-1985, credit to the economy[10] grew by an average of 8.7 percent per annum, significantly exceeding the average annual rate of growth of production by around 3 percentage points.[11] As a counterpart, enterprise deposits also rose substantially. However, excess money supply could not manifest itself in an increase of the price level, or a spillover to the balance of payments, because of a set of administrative controls. First, excess enterprise liquidity in a particular sector was kept isolated in one product market due to the fact that deposits of enterprises were earmarked (in this case, mainly for construction purposes). Therefore, excess liquidity did not spill over to other product or factor markets. Second, in the given product market, shortages and overheating were subsequently addressed in a purely administrative manner: for example, at the end of 1986, the majority of money funds earmarked for construction were simply eliminated, and so were the corresponding credits to the construction sector.

This example highlights the reasons why the authorities did not pay particular attention to money creation in the enterprise sector. Any excess money creation was kept in isolation from other markets; and with prices in that particular market being controlled, and foreign trade operations restricted, excess liquidity was reflected in shortages which ultimately could be handled in an administrative manner. By contrast, the authorities paid close attention to money creation in the household sector, where such administrative measures were more difficult to apply. Therefore, the main source of possible excess liquidity in this sector was controlled through tight regulation of wages. Indeed, in this period, real wage increases were kept below increases in productivity (Table E.2 of Appendix II-1), and as a result, little, if any, excess liquidity emerged in the hands of the household sector.[12]

d. The role of the exchange rate[13]

Before 1987, the official exchange rate was merely used as an accounting unit and played no role in the allocation of resources. This was its traditional function in the central planning system in which foreign and domestic prices were separated through a system of variable taxes and subsidies, the so-called price equalization system. Under this mechanism, any change in the foreign currency price of imports or exports was offset by changes in taxes or subsidies and therefore had a budgetary effect but no impact on domestic prices, production or consumption.

2. MONETARY AND EXCHANGE RATE POLICY SINCE 1987-88

a. Restructuring of the banking system

In line with the general objectives of the reforms of 1987-88, i.e., to improve the efficiency of resource use and to grant more freedom of decision to economic agents, the banking system was restructured at the beginning of 1988. Given the increasing need to develop indirect levers for macroeconomic management, this restructuring was conceived as a first step in widening and strengthening the potential role for monetary policy.

Initially, the financial reforms had several objectives. First, it was intended to establish a two-tier banking system, in which all commercial bank functions would be detached from Gosbank. The new banks were to be established on the basis of full state ownership, and along sectoral lines. Assets and liabilities of the new banks were to be determined according to the deposits and indebtedness of enterprises that had been assigned to them. Second, they aimed at introducing a degree of competition among specialized banks by increasing their number. Third, increased independence was to be given to the specialized banks in credit allocation. While they were expected to continue to accommodate plan targets, they were also encouraged to extend credit within the established ceilings on the basis of risk assessment, profitability, and creditworthiness. Finally, new instruments of control were to be employed. With the dismantling of detailed quantitative planning, overall credit ceilings were to be introduced, replacing the disaggregated credit plan.

Two phases of the financial reforms can be distinguished in the process to date. During the first phase (mid-1987 to August 1988), five specialized banks were established to take over all the former commercial banking functions of Gosbank and to act as a treasurer for the Government.[14] Despite these institutional changes, however, the stated objectives remained largely unfulfilled in most respects during this first phase of reform. Most importantly, despite the transfer of virtually all commercial banking functions from Gosbank to the specialized banks, and the increase in their number, competition was not strengthened. This was due to the organization of banks along strict sectoral lines. Furthermore, credit allocation remained essentially administrative, with little emphasis on profitability and creditworthiness, owing to both the aforementioned weak competition among banks, and the dependence of the specialized banks on the branch ministries. Finally, the lack of consistency in the overall reform process reduced the effectiveness of credit policy. In particular, delays in price reforms severely impaired the task of providing loans on the basis of financial criteria.

The second phase of financial reforms began in mid-1988, when the Law on Cooperatives granted cooperatives the right to establish their own banks. This reflected general expectations that the large specialized banks would decline to service the infant cooperatives, placing them in an unfavorable position relative to the state-owned sector from the very start. Soon, state enterprises were also granted the right to establish their own financial institutions. In order to slow the growing shift of household deposits away from the Savings Bank and toward the emerging commercial banks, the authorities later introduced interest rate regulations that restrict the interest rates paid by commercial and cooperative banks (CCBs) on household deposits to the same levels as offered by the Savings Bank.[15] Especially in view of the implicit full government guarantee on savings deposits held at the Savings Bank, but not on those at CCBs, this measure effectively reduced competition in the financial sphere of the household sector[16].

b. The main consequences of the financial reforms

The reforms initiated in 1988 had an impact in four major areas:

(1) *Competition.* The reforms introduced an element of competition into the financial circuits of both enterprises and households, mainly as a result of the proliferation of CCBs. However, competition is still limited because of the sectoral organization of the big specialized banks, as well as the regulation that restricts interest rates that CCBs can offer on household deposits. Moreover, specialized banks still account for 95 percent of credit activity.

(2) *Liquidity of financial assets.* During the reforms, increased moneyness was established through several factors. Chief among these were the monetization of various enterprise accounts through the discontinuation of their joint ownership, as well as the increased fungibility of other enterprise funds. In addition, the artificial blocking of flows between the two financial circuits was reduced, as CCBs were allowed to compete for household deposits, and as households were allowed, at least in theory, to purchase shares of private cooperatives or of CCBs, or to establish such banks.

(3) *Financial intermediation.* The banking sector was given a more active role in resource allocation. State specialized banks could, within their credit ceilings, extend credit on a more commercial basis, rather than according to plan targets. Commercial and cooperative banks based their credit extension primarily on profitability and creditworthiness. In addition, if only on a small scale, commercial banks have also begun to act as financial intermediaries for the household sector.

(4) *Financial markets.* A first rudimentary step was taken toward establishing an interbank money market. State specialized banks were now allowed, at least in principle, to lend to and borrow from each other as well as CCBs. However, there was still no market for securities.

These positive elements have to be weighed, however, against the negative aspects that emerged on account of the incompleteness and the lack of proper sequencing of the reforms, as well as the reversal of certain measures. Competition remained extremely limited, and the monopoly position of the Savings Bank was effectively re-established. In addition, the annual economic plan still played an important, although not clearly defined, role in resource allocation. Moreover, the ability of the new credit policy to be based on more commercial criteria was severely hampered by the lack of proper progress in some areas of reform. In particular, price reforms have seriously lagged behind the decentralization of decision making, hampering the efficient use of indirect monetary instruments. Similarly, little progress has been made in introducing a hard budget constraint on both enterprises and banks, which again reduces the effectiveness of indirect instruments of monetary control, such as interest rates. Finally, the incompleteness of reforms has contributed to the emergence of increasing monetary disequilibrium in the second half of the 1980s.

c. The modified role of monetary policies and instruments

During the pre-reform period, credit to the economy occasionally exceeded targets due to the lack of corrective mechanisms to address deviations from the plan. In particular, credit to enterprises might have been higher-than-planned, owing in part to the automatic financing of the gap between planned and actual profits, and in part to the fact that key enterprises could easily bargain for higher credit. The absence of mechanisms to compensate by reducing the allocation of credit to other enterprises or, more generally, to react to negative supply shocks, would lead to money creation above the plan targets. With the shift toward less detailed quantitative planning, the consequence of monetary overruns had to be increasingly taken into account. Excess demand that emerged in a specific product or factor market following deviations from plan targets could now more easily spill over, in unforeseeable ways, to other markets. Moreover, the increasing financial requirements of the budget, in part also a product of the reform process, made necessary more active monetary and credit policies.

The role of monetary policy was modified in two important respects. First, it was given a greater responsibility in the attempt to maintain macroeconomic balance. Second, credit policy was assigned, albeit still more in theory than in practice, the task of ensuring a more efficient allocation of resources. To this end, within their credit ceilings, specialized banks were encouraged to extend credit on the basis of financial criteria. The modified role of monetary policy altered the characteristics of the Credit Plan. In contrast to the pre-reform period, the Credit Plan became a "macro" plan at a global level, in that it aimed—often unsuccessfully as in 1988-89—at equalizing public sector dissaving as well as enterprise credit needs with expected saving of the rest of the economy.[17]

The instruments of monetary control were also altered. Before the reforms, the quantitative administration of the Credit Plan was the main instrument of control. With the reforms, new direct instruments of control were introduced, which, however, differed, according to the type of bank. For the state-owned specialized banks, two instruments of control have been used:

(1) *Ceilings on credit extended by each bank* are determined, within the aggregate Credit Plan, through projected demand for credit by economic sectors. However, the banking regulations effectively permitted the possibility for indefinite credit extension. In particular, to the extent that banks raised more deposits than planned, they could exceed their credit ceiling. This could lead to a situation in which overall credit creation was uncontrolled, as banks raising more resources can extend more

credit, while those raising less could still fulfill their original (planned) credit ceilings.

(2) *Refinancing quotas of Gosbank* were determined in the light of the projected increase in each bank's resources (chiefly deposits), the targeted increase in the bank's total credit extension, and the maturity match between deposits and credit. Interest rates on refinancing have differed according to banks (i.e., sectors). Higher refinancing could be obtained at higher interest rates.

In contrast to the use of direct instruments for the specialized banks, monetary control over CCBs relied more on indirect instruments. Initially, there was virtually no control at all. Later, a reserve requirement of 5 percent was introduced, which was increased to 10 percent in August 1990.[18] Refinancing by Gosbank was also available, although in a very limited amount. Several prudential ratios were also introduced.[19]

d. Monetary developments since the reforms: the "overhang" problem[20]

The incompleteness and sequencing of the reforms were in large part responsible for the monetary disequilibrium that developed in the second half of the 1980s. The increased autonomy that was granted to the enterprise sector shifted resources from the budget towards the enterprises. In particular, enterprises were able to retain more of their own funds (profits and depreciation allowances), while the budget continued to finance much of their investment. This asymmetric decentralization process was accompanied by the increasing fungibility of enterprises' own funds; as a result, the effective moneyness of the resources of enterprises rose appreciably. To offset this impact, and to make room for the increased budgetary financing needs, the authorities adopted a more global monetary approach that required the tightening of credit policy toward enterprises in the second half of the 1980s. Despite an appreciable decline in credit to the enterprise sector, overall net domestic credit grew rapidly due to the rising budget deficits, which continued to be largely monetized. At the same time, rapid growth of internally generated resources of enterprises more than offset the effects of the credit crunch and led to an excess liquidity among enterprises. This enabled the management of increasingly autonomous enterprises repeatedly to raise wages at rates which outstripped the growth of real consumption possibilities and led to rising excess liquidity of the household sector as well.

More specifically, three periods can be distinguished (see Table III.2.1):

(1) *1986-87*. This period was characterized by the attempt of the authorities to offset the rapid acceleration in bank financing of the budget—at an average annual rate of 30.4 percent—by a reduction in credit to non-government at a rate of 2.3 percent.[21] However, already in this period the growth rate of monetary assets (M2) of both households and

enterprises accelerated (to 9.6 percent per annum, or about 8 percent in real terms for households; and to 18.3 percent in both nominal and real terms for enterprises).

(2) *1988-89.* With increasing bank financing of the budget, the squeeze on credit to the enterprise sector was inadequate to prevent a further acceleration in the rate of growth of the total money supply. Credit to the government rose by 39.4 percent per annum, while credit to nongovernment declined by only 4.7 percent; as a consequence, the growth rate of total bank credit accelerated to 11.2 percent per annum. Real money balances of households increased by over 10 percent per annum (13.1 percent in nominal terms); and their maturity shortened markedly. Enterprise liquidity rose at an even higher rate (18.4 percent per annum in nominal terms), while the liquidity of these funds also increased. As a result, a significant "monetary overhang" developed both in the household and enterprise sectors.[22]

(3) *1990.* While the growth rate of credit to government was cut by more than half, as the budget deficit fell, enterprise credit was permitted to increase for the first time since 1986. The growth of overall credit thus remained roughly unchanged, at more than 10 percent. While the growth rate in M2 of households remained broadly unchanged, the growth rate of enterprise money probably expanded, partly reflecting the increased access to bank credit and, possibly, a cutback in stockbuilding of consumer goods. As a result, the overall growth rate of money (M2) accelerated slightly.

e. Developments in exchange rate policy

With the beginning of decentralization of foreign trade in 1986, the authorities decided to give exchange rate policy a somewhat more active role. This policy was geared toward the convertible currency area, while exchange rate policy vis-à-vis CMEA countries remained passive. The main measures were the introduction of so-called differentiated foreign exchange coefficients (DVKs) and the foreign exchange retention scheme in 1987, and the introduction of foreign exchange auctions in 1989. All three initiatives, however, largely failed to achieve their objective of making the traded goods sector more responsive to changes in world market conditions, partly because of the restrictions attached to the measures, and also because of the way they were implemented. More fundamentally, their impact was constrained by the fact that the measures were not accompanied by supporting domestic policies, including price liberalization or substantial changes in the central allocation system.

In 1987, the system of price equalization was partially replaced by the DVK system.[23] These coefficients were set initially with a view to equating foreign and domestic prices for individual products (although some promotion of manufactured exports was also intended by setting particularly high DVKs). The coefficients not only differed by commodities, but also by countries of origin and destination. The advantage compared to the previous system was that—with fixed coefficients—changes in foreign currency prices for imports or exports would in principle be reflected in the profitability of the enterprises and thereby might make them more responsive to market conditions. However, the system was not implemented as intended. When enterprises faced pressures on their profits at the given exchange rate and DVKs, they frequently negotiated changes in the DVKs with the authorities. The DVKs were therefore often changed in an *ad hoc* manner, which meant increased budgetary support for the enterprises.

The foreign exchange retention scheme had limited coverage and was subject to various restrictions. Thus, until 1990, oil and other raw material exports were exempted from export retention, while retention rates varied from 0 to 100 percent for processed goods. On average, retained foreign exchange accounted for only 7-8 percent of total export earnings in convertible currencies. Moreover, retention rights were set by individual enterprise, which implied that different retention rights might apply for the same export goods produced by different enterprises. Until 1989, there were also several restrictions on the use of retained foreign exchange. It could only be spent in the year after it was received and only for imports of investment goods. These restrictions were relaxed in 1989, when also consumer goods for the benefit of workers (subject to certain limitations) could be imported in the same year as the foreign exchange was earned.

The foreign exchange auctions, which were established in November 1989, played a marginal role in exchange rate policy. During the first eleven auctions, only the equivalent of US$150 million was transacted. Therefore, the exchange rates established during the auctions, ranging from rub 9 to rub 24 per U.S. dollar, could not be considered as indicative of the market equilibrium exchange rate. Although foreign exchange retained by enterprises could be sold in the auctions, this was done only to a limited extent. This might be related to the fact that enterprises did not generally lack domestic financing but rather foreign exchange for imports, and they could not be certain that they would be in a position to purchase foreign exchange in the auctions at a later stage. Auction transactions were also initially restricted by confining participation in the foreign exchange auctions to only a few participants; subsequently, access by a broader group of enterprises and organizations was permitted, including joint ventures.

3. CURRENT REFORMS

Against this background, several proposals emerged with the aim of speeding up reforms of the financial and exchange systems.

a. The central banking law[24]

The central banking law that was finally approved in December 1990 focuses on the structure of the monetary system, including organizational aspects, and the role and independence of the monetary authority in shaping monetary, exchange rate, and prudential policies as well as managing international reserves. In addition, the questions of instruments of control, the types of commercial banks allowed to operate, their supervision, and competition in the banking system are determined in the new law and in the companion law on the banking system.

(1) *The structure of the monetary system.* The new law sets up a union reserve system, consisting of Gosbank and republican central banks. The system is based on a single currency. A board of governors, called the Central Council, will manage a unified monetary and credit policy and issue uniform prudential rules and regulations for the entire system. The republics will adopt their own banking legislation in accordance with the laws of the Union Reserve System. The Central Council will consist of twelve members: the President and the Vice President of Gosbank, to be appointed by the Soviet Supreme for six years, and ten other members appointed by the President of the USSR on a rotation basis from the presidents of the central banks or other leaders of the republics. The executive body of the Central Council will be the Monetary and Credit Council. As regards the role of the republican state banks, their activity would be subordinated to the Union Reserve System; and in terms of monetary and credit policies, their role would be limited to the implementation of policies as determined by the Central Council.

(2) *Independence of the central bank.*[25] There are three major aspects to the independence of a central bank: independence in terms of monetary and exchange rate policy, prudential policies and bank supervision, and its financial relations with government(s). The new law gives the central bank a central, active and independent role in the areas of monetary, exchange rate and prudential policies. In particular, it will determine the main guidelines and objectives of monetary and credit policy, which will be submitted to the Supreme Soviet for approval, contemporaneously with the annual union budget.

The law provides for coordination of monetary and exchange rate policies. However, at the same time, given that a joint union-republic foreign exchange fund[26] has been set up by an earlier presidential decree outside the domain of the union reserve system, it is unclear how monetary and exchange rate policies will be coordinated. A committee will be established to develop foreign exchange policy, including all-union responsibilities in this area, as well as to ensure external debt payment. Its operational features, however, including procedures for

370

decision-making and for the implementation of agreed policies, have yet to be defined.

As regards the third aspect of central bank independence, the new law allows for bank financing of the union and republic budgets to the extent approved by the Supreme Soviet. Gosbank and the central banks of the republics are authorized to purchase government securities within these established limits. Under exceptional circumstances, which are not specified by the law, the President of the USSR can authorize short-term credits in "limited" amounts in excess of the limits determined by the Supreme Soviet.

(3) *Monetary control instruments.* The law provides for the use of both direct and indirect instruments, of which refinancing quotas appear to be key. In addition, reserve requirements and interest rate policy—through changing the interest rate charged on credit by the central banks—will also be applied. Quantitative credit ceilings and interest rate regulations will be allowed, but only under "exceptional" circumstances, such as an excessive increase in money supply or in inflation. Such temporary measures can be introduced within the framework of the annual presentation of the monetary policy guidelines to the Supreme Soviet, or by the Central Council. As to their duration, a limit of six months is set only for such measures taken by the Central Council which, however, can be extended by the President of the USSR indefinitely.

(4) *Competition and interbank money markets.* Increased competition within the banking system is sought through the breaking up of the large state-owned specialized banks into independent joint stock companies and the establishment of new commercial banks. Most of the banks will be universal and free to choose their clientele on a competitive basis; and some specialized banks, yet to be set up, will be responsible for financing major union or republic projects. Foreign participation in bank ownership is allowed. Improved payment and settlement arrangements will remove existing limitations on the movement of monetary resources within the union. The registration and supervision of banks is to be the responsibility of the republican central banks.

The law on the banking system provides a special commercial bank status for the Savings Bank in two respects. First, Gosbank is to guarantee fully household deposits held at the Savings Bank, but not those with any other bank. Second, except for the Savings Bank, all commercial banks attracting household deposits must create a special reserve fund. The size of the fund is to be determined by the respective republican central banks. These regulations appear aimed at reducing competition for household deposits, so as to maintain the pre-emption of household savings for financing of the budget.

b. Other financial and exchange rate measures

Interest rates will continue to be administratively regulated but, as of November 1, 1990, the regulations were to be more uniform across banks. Interest rates on household deposits were increased to 5-9 percent, depending on maturities. Lending rates were also raised to a maximum of 15 percent.[27] The authorities have also discussed possibly indexing the savings deposits of households (principal and interest) to the price level. Such proposals have not, however, included indexation of the deposits of enterprises.

On November 1, 1990, a commercial exchange rate was introduced at a level that was two thirds depreciated in foreign currency terms compared with the official exchange rate. At the same time, the DVKs were eliminated. The commercial exchange rate will fluctuate in line with the exchange rates of the currencies in the basket to which it is pegged.[28] The commercial exchange rate would apply to most trade and capital transactions. In addition, a free exchange market will be established with supplies from foreign exchange retained by enterprises and official holdings. Banks and other brokers would be direct participants in the market. A special rate would remain in force for tourist transactions. But the commercial rate and the free market rate would be the key exchange rates vis-à-vis convertible currencies. It is unclear how the commercial rate will be managed in relation to the free market rate.

c. Effectiveness of the new reforms

A central question that arises at this point is how these monetary and exchange arrangements would operate as the reforms proceed, particularly in view of the existing monetary overhang, and how they would interact in maintaining monetary "flow" equilibrium. A substantial monetary overhang is often associated with shortages and typically with a large free foreign exchange rate premium (in this case, the difference between the free and the commercial exchange rates). A large premium involves some important costs. For example, if the free rate is more depreciated than the commercial rate, there is an incentive for arbitrage and circumvention of official regulations to exploit the differences in rates. Moreover, a large free market rate differential and surrender requirements introduce an anti-export bias, as exports are being implicitly taxed.[29]

Preliminary indications are that the authorities intend to stabilize the level of the commercial exchange rate in terms of a basket of currencies. Such a policy would be appropriate if the commercial exchange rate was tied to a basket of currencies close to a market clearing rate, and if the underlying rate of inflation was about the same as that of foreign trading partners and competitors. But that situation is not likely to prevail immediately following price liberalization. Therefore, either a flexible exchange rate system or initial overshooting of the depreciation, followed by fixing of the exchange rate, would appear to be appropriate.

372

A major problem for a fixed exchange rate in the present circumstances is that the fiscal deficit is not likely to be consistent with low inflation in the near future, and credit policies with respect to the rest of the economy, even if tightened, may not be expected to offset fully the expansionary fiscal stance. Therefore, in the course of a few months or a year, the gap between the exchange rates is likely to widen once again. Persistent inflation would call for a more flexible exchange rate.

As mentioned above, interest rates have been adjusted recently, and the Government has announced that in the future it will set interest rates at more realistic levels. This is, of course, a welcome development. Interest rate policy, however, cannot be relied upon to correct misalignments between the commercial exchange rate and the domestic price level, without changes in other fundamental factors, such as the fiscal deficit. Interest rates are effective for correcting a temporary widening of the gap between the free and the commercial exchange rates by enhancing the attractiveness of domestic financial assets vis-à-vis foreign assets, thereby lowering the free market premium. However, if the premium were driven by permanent forces, attempting to lower it by resorting to high interest rates could backfire for reasons similar to those discussed above.

A regime of multiple exchange rates is incapable, *per se,* of providing a long-run remedy to fundamental misalignments or inconsistencies among policy targets. The additional flexibility that is obtained by the existence of several exchange rates is rather limited because, as suggested above, substantial exchange rate differentials lead to distortions, arguing for a rapid convergence to a unified exchange rate system.

Exchange rate unification is consistent with both fixed and flexible exchange rates. Under fixed exchange rates, the ability of the monetary authorities to sustain the official exchange rate depends on the adequacy of international reserves and/or lines of credit from abroad (e.g., a stabilization fund). In contrast, the feasibility of a floating exchange rate regime depends much less on the country's reserves position. Therefore, a system of unified and floating exchange rates might be an attractive option for a country such as the USSR if it starts from a relatively low stock of international reserves and can obtain only modest amounts of international credit for stabilization purposes. A system of floating exchange rates, however, requires flexible domestic wages and prices and, given the latter, suitably tight financial policies if the exchange rate regime is not to reinforce existing inflationary pressures.

The current reforms of the financial system have been inspired by those of industrialized market economies. These systems have been designed in order to prevent political pressures from having a direct impact on the management of monetary and financial policies. In a more competitive environment, as envisioned by the new proposals, effective management of monetary policy is highly dependent on the credibility of policy announcements. The new proposals, however, fall short of ensuring policy credibility. Independence of the central bank, for example, may help to reduce outside pressures on the bank, but it does not completely eliminate the temptation to change policies in the future. Furthermore, central bank independence may easily become ineffective, since, as pointed out above, credit and monetary policy will have to be approved by the USSR Supreme Soviet simultaneously with the annual union budget.

Lack of credibility in a market environment is likely to be associated with high nominal and real market interest rates. This is so, because if the central bank is not credible, the public is likely to expect a future flare-up of inflation. In such a situation, the banking system would be forced to offer high nominal interest rates. Otherwise, depositors would prefer to hold their financial assets in the form of inventories or foreign exchange. To the extent that the central bank actually is able to persist with its intended anti-inflationary policy, the rate of inflation will tend to decline, thereby giving rise to rising real interest rates. High real interest rates, in turn, if maintained over a considerable period of time, may bring about serious disruption of the productive sector. Thus, it is very important under such a system that policy announcements become sufficiently credible within a reasonable period of time.

Credibility could be lost by faulty policy design, since the public will soon realize that policy will have to be subject to future adjustments. This points to the dangers of independent monetary and exchange rate policies, as suggested by the creation of the joint union-republic foreign exchange fund. In a well-functioning market system, monetary and exchange rate policies are intimately related. Attempts to manage them in independent ways are likely to result in exchange rate misalignments or sizable differentials between the commercial and free market exchange rates. As argued above, these phenomena bring about undesirable consequences, which eventually result in unforeseen accommodations of monetary policy to exchange rate policy, or vice versa, undermining policy credibility.

Credibility is likely to be more difficult to establish for a country such as the USSR than for the typical market economy. Soviet policy makers have not yet acquired much experience in a liberalized environment, and hence their competence and endurance are still largely unknown to the public. The presumption is that, not having had the chance to bloom under the old regime, expertise in market-oriented monetary policy may, indeed, be relatively scarce. This is an additional reason why monetary and financial policies need to be designed so as to avoid any unnecessary tension between the different policy targets. Ideally, one should aim for consistent monetary rules that operate most of the time with little human interference. Such a scheme may involve a form of exchange rate standard (e.g., anchoring to another currency), or pre-setting simple and transparent monetary rules (e.g., a pre-announced rate of increase in the money supply).

The above discussion suggests that the Soviet authorities would be well-advised to complement the new proposals with schemes that ensure a quick transition to a reasonably credible system. Policies and institutions are of the essence, but timing is too. Good policies that take long to be implemented may become ineffective because they may be overtaken by events, and hence lose their credibility. This highlights the importance of sending clear, early signals to the market about the authorities' intention to implement consistent and non-discretionary policies.

NOTES

1. "Moneyness" of short-term financial assets refers to the degree of their liquidity, which in turn reflects the degree of their unconditional conversion into goods, as well as the free flow of money between households and enterprises.
2. This occurred, for example, in 1986 and 1990.
3. Given the low level of direct and indirect taxation of the household sector, tax payments did not constitute a major source of cash withdrawal.
   In formalized terms, the cash plan can be described as follows:
   $$\Delta M(h) = WN + P(a)Q(a) + T + \Delta C(h) - P(c)Q(c) - \Delta S(h),$$
   where M(h) is currency in circulation, W is the average nominal wage rate, N is the level of employment; P(a) and P(c) are the average procurement price of agricultural products sold by the population and the price of consumer goods, respectively; Q(a) and Q(c) are the quantity of goods and services purchased from farmers by the state, and the purchase of goods and services by households from the state and cooperatives, respectively; T is the net cash transfer to the household sector, C is credit to households; S(h) is household savings deposits; and Δ denotes a change in a variable.
4. Monitoring of the execution of the Credit and Cash Plan was based on a number of indicators (e.g., the ratio of currency to retail trade).
5. For a detailed discussion of the demand for money of households and enterprises, see Chapter III.3.
6. Purchase of long-term financial assets in the form of government bonds was negligible (and occasionally compulsory). Moreover the degree of moneyness of savings deposits was occasionally reduced by the need to queue to make withdrawals.
7. Joint ownership of enterprise funds not only reduced the free availability of deposits, but sometimes resulted in the cancellation of certain deposits, if they were deemed excessive. An example is the cancellation of orderer's accounts in the context of the debt write-off operation of 1986.
8. Over the last three decades up to 1987/88, interest rates on enterprise deposits were fixed at 0.5 percent.
9. Another element of close monitoring was that, because enterprises were not allowed to hold currency in excess of a nominal amount, virtually all enterprise funds were held at Gosbank. Moreover, until recently, Gosbank was not only entitled to follow developments on enterprise accounts, but also to effect banking operations without the formal consent of an enterprise if envisaged in the plan (for example, profit transfers to the budget).
10. Almost exclusively credit to the enterprise sector, as credit to households was negligible.
11. See Tables III.2.1 and Table K.2 to Appendix II-1.
12. See also Chapter II.3.

13. For a detailed description of the exchange rate arrangements prior to the reforms, as well as to date, see Chapter III.4.

14. These reforms are described in greater detail in Chapter IV.5.

15. Some commercial banks have succeeded in finding ways to circumvent this regulation through offering, for example, special premia on deposits, or lottery drawings for deposits (i.e., the winners are rewarded with very high—25 percent—interest rates).

16. In addition, although prudential in nature, another measure limited the amount of deposits to the own capital of the commercial bank.

17. The concept of "expected" saving used in the Credit Plan does not necessarily coincide with the desired or voluntary saving of the population.

18. However, at the same time, commercial banks were allowed to meet the requirement through the purchase of government bonds.

19. Such as the ratio of own capital to total resources, a minimum capital requirement, and a stipulated ratio for the maximum exposure to one client.

20. For a detailed analysis of the monetary disequilibrium, see Chapter III.3.

21. Taking into consideration the impact of the already mentioned write-off of construction-related credit at the end of 1986. As credit to households was very small, this decline mainly reflected the fall in credit to enterprises.

22. For detailed data, see tables K.1-K.8 in Appendix II-1.

23. For a detailed description of this and other exchange system measures, see Chapter III.4.

24. The Law of the USSR on the USSR State Bank of December 11, 1990.

25. In the following, the proposed Union Reserve System will, for simplicity, be referred to as the central bank.

26. For a detailed description of the fund, see Chapter III.4.

27. Before this date specialized banks were not allowed to pay, on average, more than 2 to 4 percent on households deposits, depending on maturity; while for credit rates, they were given some leeway to vary rates according to the financial position of the borrower. Nevertheless, interest rates were highly regulated, as indicated by the fact that, except for the Agroprombank, bank lending rates were generally lower than the interest rate on refinancing by the Gosbank. In 1989 the average interest rate on credit and the rate on refinancing were the following, respectively. Promstroibank: 3.78 percent versus 4 percent; Agrobank: 1.77 percent versus 1.5 percent; Zhilsotsbank: 2.89 percent versus 4 percent. It has to be added, however, that some of these banks had government deposits, on which they did not pay any interest.
As regards commercial banks, they could freely determine their deposit and lending rates for all transactions until February 1990, when a regulation on interest rates was introduced, limiting interest rates that commercial banks can offer for household deposits to those offered by the Savings Bank. (Before the regulation, commercial banks offered a 6 percent interest rate on household deposits, which was 2.5 times more than the average rate in the Savings Bank.) Interest rates on credits extended varied between 5 and 60 percent, with an annual average of 9 percent.

28. For details see Chapter III.4.

29. See Chapter IV.3 for further discussions.

Table III.2.1. USSR: Main Monetary and Credit Aggregates

(Average annual growth rates)

	1981-85	1986-87	1988-89	1990
Total bank credit[1]	8.7	5.2	11.2	10.5
Government credit	8.6	30.4	39.4	16.6
Credit to the economy [1]	8.7	-2.3	-4.7	4.3
Money (M2)	7.5	11.6	14.4	15.3
Households	7.2	9.6	13.1	13.5
Enterprises	...	18.3	18.4	20.0

Source: Data provided by the Soviet authorities and projections for 1990.
1. After allowance for the debt write-offs at end-1986.

Chapter III.3

The Monetary Overhang: an Analytical and Empirical Study

1. INTRODUCTION

Official price indexes in the USSR have been remarkably stable over the last 30 years; between 1960 and 1980 the official retail price index remained almost unchanged and, even in the 1980s, official recorded inflation barely exceeded 1 percent per year. It is widely recognized, however, that inflationary pressures, particularly throughout the latter period, were substantially higher. On the one hand, official price indices almost certainly underestimated actual price increases, a phenomenon known in the Western literature as hidden inflation.[1] On the other hand, insofar as price controls prevented actual prices from reaching their equilibrium level, inflation remained artificially contained (repressed inflation). This constrained nominal consumption and led to involuntary savings. Since most of the involuntary wealth accumulation was in the form of liquid assets, it is described as a "monetary overhang." The monetary overhang, and the underlying repressed inflation that it represents, has potentially serious implications for the equilibrium of the Soviet economic system in the event of price liberalization. Section 2 presents some simple analytical considerations regarding the definition and implications of repressed inflation and the monetary overhang; section 3 provides quantitative measures of the overhang, while section 4 discusses possible ways to tackle the problem in the near future. Finally, section 5 draws the main conclusions.

2. CONCEPTS AND DEFINITIONS

In order to define the concept of repressed inflation, and the strictly related concept of a monetary overhang, consider initially a one good and one asset (money) economy. The good can be traded only on the official market by the Government (there is no black market). Real production in period t is equal to y_t; its market value is $p_t y_t = Y_t$. Repressed inflation can be defined as a situation in which, at price p_t, demand exceeds supply, so that the removal of price controls would lead to a price increase.[2] The excess of demand over supply implies some rationing;[3] if all demand is for consumption purposes (disregarding for the moment the existence of investment), the counterpart to a scarcity of goods is involuntary saving of households and therefore an involuntary increase in nominal wealth.[4] The wealth overhang can be defined as the difference between the nominal amount of wealth held by agents at the end of period t and the desired amount that would have been held in the absence of current and past rationing.

In the debate on repressed inflation in centrally planned economies (CPEs), it is usually assumed that all undesired accumulation of wealth is held as monetary balances; therefore, the terms monetary overhang and wealth overhang are often used synonymously. The two concepts, however, coincide only in a special case (which is only approximately met even in CPEs), i.e., when money is the only available store of wealth, or, equivalently, when, despite the existence of other stores of wealth, their supply and their price is fixed (so that additional resources can only be invested in money). In general, the concepts of wealth and monetary overhang differ; while "wealth overhang" refers to the stock of accumulated involuntary saving, monetary overhang is the difference between the amount of money held by agents and the amount that would have been held in the absence of current and past rationing (in the goods and financial markets). Clearly the existence of a monetary overhang can occur even in the absence of a wealth overhang; indeed, total consumption (and total wealth) could be in equilibrium, but, given the structure and regulation of financial and real asset markets, the *composition* of wealth might be biased towards money. Due to their different policy implications, both concepts are relevant and will be explored empirically. More precisely, in the empirical analysis of section 3, two questions will be addressed separately: first, to what extent has household consumption been rationed in the USSR and hence given rise to an involuntary accumulation of wealth. Second, to what extent is the composition of wealth of both households and enterprises biased towards financial and monetary assets.

In the presence of many goods, and of price controls, markets in which shortages and surpluses prevail can co-exist. How to define the concept of aggregate excess demand—from which that of the "overhang" is derived—under these conditions has been a subject of considerable controversy. On one side is the so-called "disequilibrium school."[5] According to this approach, the step from a one good economy to an economy with many goods is not a difficult one; if, at the current price vector, aggregate demand for goods and services (the sum of demands in all markets) is greater than aggregate supply (the sum of supplies in all markets), then the economy is in excess demand and, with sticky prices, it is subject to repressed inflation (i.e. the absolute price level is too low to clear the market). If, instead, aggregate demand and aggregate supply are in equilibrium, the contemporaneous existence of excess supply and excess demand in different markets requires an adjustment in relative prices, but does not imply the need to

380

adjust the price level. Certainly, in the presence of both shortages and surpluses, the measurement of excess demand may present some problems; however these problems can be tackled econometrically.[6]

On the other side is the so-called "shortage economy" school, which argues that the concept of aggregate disequilibrium, legitimate in market economies, becomes ill-defined in economies characterized by "chronic" shortages. Two specific points are raised: first, agents who are unable to buy the goods they desire almost always end up buying substitutes; very rarely do their savings rise involuntarily.[7] Second, the volume of voluntary savings may be directly affected by the existence of chronic shortages at the micro level;[8] the precautionary reserve of purchasing power (stored mainly in monetary assets) increases, artificially inflating the saving rate.[9]

The debate between these two points of view has been fruitful. From a theoretical standpoint, there seems to be no doubt that, in principle, the concept of aggregate disequilibrium can be extended from market economies to CPEs and that the distinction between distortion of the price level and distortion of relative prices is an important one. In this respect, the first point raised by the "shortage" school has to be interpreted properly. If forced substitution is widespread, consumers' utility is clearly affected, as their desired expenditure basket is distorted. Yet, it would be correct to say that there is no overhang; total expenditure may still, *ex post*, equal planned expenditure. The second point raised by the shortage school is, however, more important, as it implies that the desired accumulation of wealth (or, equivalently, the propensity to save) is not independent of current and expected market conditions and, more specifically, of the existence of shortages. Therefore, even if empirical evidence showed the absence of forced saving in a system in which shortages at the micro level are pervasive, it might still be possible that the (credible) announcement of a permanent change in regime regarding the supply of goods could increase desired consumption (with potentially inflationary effects on the price level).

One additional conceptual point could be mentioned. When both shortages and surpluses are present simultaneously, the size of forced saving may overstate the amount of macroeconomic disequilibrium. Consider the case of two markets— market A in which, at the current fixed prices, excess supply is present, and market B in which there is excess demand. Buyers would like to purchase 50 "rubles" worth of A and 50 "rubles" worth of B. But the equivalent of 70 rubles are offered of A and only 30 of B. Applying the min condition, transactions occur at 50 for A and at 30 for B. Aggregate expenditure is 80 and forced saving is 20. Yet, *ex ante*, aggregate demand and aggregate supply are equal (each sums to 100 "rubles"), implying no macroeconomic disequilibrium. This discrepancy disappears, however, when the involuntary accumulation of inventories (equal to 20 "rubles" of A in the previous example) is brought into the picture. This suggests that the existence of a macro-disequilibrium between demand and supply should, in principle, be measured taking into account not only the involuntary accumulation of wealth by buyers, but also the undesired accumulation of unsold products due to distortions in relative prices. It is for this reason that the ratio between monetary holdings of the population, which in some cases may be a good indicator of excess saving, and the stock of unsold consumer goods is sometimes used as an indicator of disequilibrium in CPEs.[10]

To take the analysis further, assume that, in addition to the official markets, parallel markets are also present. These may include legal and illegal (black) markets, in which suppliers can sell a portion of their total production at unregulated prices. In principle, parallel markets may eliminate macroeconomic rationing. If these markets are large enough (and in particular if they are accessible to everybody and can supply most goods), buyers will address to them all unused purchasing power left from shopping at state stores (less of course, desired saving). Prices on the parallel market will tend to be higher than those on the state market; and, in general, the two price levels will be respectively higher and lower than the single price level prevailing if controls were removed. In this case, relative prices would continue to be distorted but the average price level may be close to the unregulated equilibrium. Total expenditure may equal desired expenditure, involuntary accumulation of wealth may be zero, and the money market would be in equilibrium since the real amount of money (deflated by a weighted average of official and parallel market prices) would be equal to the desired demand.[11]

Several factors can, however, prevent the relevant level of prices from equilibrating the money market. Parallel markets may not be extensive enough: they may cover a limited spectrum of goods, may be geographically concentrated in some areas, and trade in these markets may be discouraged by legal sanctions. It has been shown that the existence of markets in which prices are free does not prevent the accumulation of excess saving if sales in these markets are an imperfect substitute for sales on the official market.[12]

Even if parallel markets are extensive, buyers may still be reluctant to purchase on these markets if they expect the price system to be liberalized (which would lead to a decline in parallel market prices). Thus, purchases on the parallel markets may be inadequate to prevent the buildup of a monetary overhang—albeit one that is "voluntarily held." Note that the same result is obtained when the availability of goods in the official market is expected to increase in the near future or when the probability of obtaining these goods in the official market increases with queuing.[13]

The extent to which the existence of parallel markets in the USSR has prevented a monetary overhang from emerging is ultimately an empirical question. Information on this subject is inadequate, but the size of the second economy may be fairly large and, as a consequence, official data on disposable income and expenditure are likely to underestimate their actual values.[14] Some information on price behavior in parallel markets is available, but, used in isolation, may provide misleading information on the degree of macroeconomic imbalance, for the reasons given earlier.

3. MEASUREMENT

a. The repressed consumption debate in the USSR

Few would argue that parallel market activity was extensive enough in the late 1980s to absorb all of the notional demand for consumption goods that could not be satisfied on official markets. It therefore seems reasonable to assume that households experienced some degree of involuntary saving in this period. There is less agreement, however, on the existence of involuntary saving before the most recent period, an issue which is important for establishing the current size of the monetary and wealth overhangs. The debate has been based on both theoretical and empirical arguments.[15]

Supporters of the thesis that repressed inflation and involuntary accumulation of wealth have always characterized the Soviet economy, as well as CPEs in general, stress the well known phenomena of shortages at the micro level and limits on the ability of households to respond to shortages of consumer goods by reducing labor supply.[16] The need for large voluntary savings in a society in which the state takes care of most of the basic "life cycle" requirements of the population has also been questioned.[17]

Three sets of indicators of repressed inflation have been proposed. First, there are indicators of shortages at the micro level,[18] ranging from the number of people in queues for officially allocated apartments, to measures of the time spent searching for goods, or the physical length of queues—unfortunately these indicators are based on data that are not readily available, and none appears to have been computed for the USSR.[19] A second set of indicators has been based on the ratio between prices in the collective farm (*kolkhoz*) markets and state prices for the same products, which shows a continuous increase throughout the last 30 years, albeit at a much faster rate at the end of the 1980s and in 1990 (Chart 1, upper panel). There are two problems, however, with this indicator. First, it has been suggested that this ratio should be weighted for the share of expenditure on the *kolkhoz* markets, with respect to total consumers' expenditure.[20] If this is done, the trend over the longer period disappears (Chart 1, lower panel), although a sharp increase in the most recent period remains. Second, as already mentioned, while the relative *kolkhoz* price may point to rising disequilibrium in state markets, it is not necessarily a good indicator of macroeconomic disequilibrium.

A third group of indicators, which has been applied frequently in the Soviet case, is based on ratios between financial (or monetary) holdings of the population and some "scale variable" (usually households' consumption or disposable income). These ratios exhibit spectacularly rising trends in recent years (Chart 2), strongly suggesting involuntary increases in saving. A clear upward trend is also apparent in the ratio between total wealth (defined as financial wealth plus houses and other real assets of the population) and the same scale variables.[21]

In spite of this evidence, the view that CPEs have been necessarily characterized by repressed inflation has been challenged by many authors. In addition to the claim discussed above that the indices of shortages at the micro level may only reflect microeconomic imbalances, but not an aggregate demand problem, it has been argued that: (a) there is some (albeit weak) evidence that labor supply is flexible in CPEs (and specifically in the USSR),[22] which might provide households with a way to reduce imbalances even in the presence of an initial disequilibrium; and (b) there are several reasons to have expected households' wealth to increase faster than consumption and income. An increase in the ratio of savings to income could have been connected to the general rise in the standard of living of the population (as saving is zero if income is at subsistence levels);[23] to a deterioration in the provision of public services and social security payments; and to increased expenditure on durables (given the absence of consumer credit, the purchase of durables requires previous accumulation of savings).[24] In addition, it has been observed that the initial level of wealth in the USSR was extremely low; total wealth represented only 70 percent of annual consumption in 1955, and financial wealth (for which a more precise measurement is possible) only 19 percent. By contrast, the wealth to consumption ratio in Western countries ranges from 400 to 600 percent and, for financial wealth, is close to 200 percent in many countries (Table III.3.1).[25] Even after 35 years of continuous increase, the comparable ratios in the USSR remained far below these levels. Given such a low starting point, it is not surprising that a steady rise in the wealth to income ratio should have occurred.[26] Finally, an increase in this ratio is also consistent with equilibrium consumption in the presence of a decelerating growth rate of real disposable income,[27] as was the case in the 1960s and, especially, the 1970s.

Critics of the repressed inflation hypothesis have argued that the ratio of saving to disposable income is a more revealing indicator of underlying behavior than the wealth-consumption ratio. The saving rate in the USSR does not appear particularly high, compared to Western countries (Table III.3.1). This may reflect the state's provision of "life cycle" services and cannot *per se* rule out the existence of rationing. However, the remarkable stability of the Soviet savings rate up to the late 1980s—with the exception of a step increase in the mid-1960s (Chart 3)—has been used to suggest that if rationing ever existed it remained relatively stable.[28]

All these arguments have been used to reject, *a priori*, the presence of involuntary saving in CPEs and several attempts have been made to reinforce the point empirically by estimating household consumption functions. Some studies have estimated consumption behavior under the hypothesis of equilibrium and have evaluated this hypothesis based on the performance of the estimated equation (in terms of fit and of the behavior of the residuals).[29] In all cases, households' disposable income (or its moving average) has been used as the main explanatory variable of consumption.[30] In some of these studies, indicators of possible disequilibrium (such as the ratio of *kolkhoz* to state prices or the rate of change in the CPI index) were introduced as explanatory variables, but did not produce satisfactory results.[31] These studies seem to indicate that consumption behavior in the USSR can be explained mainly in terms of disposable income with the exception of a structural break which occurred in the middle of the 1960s.[32] It is significant, however, that they focused on the period prior to 1980.

b. Econometric estimates of the consumption function

The preceding discussion suggests a strategy for the empirical analysis of consumption trends in the USSR and for the measurement of households' wealth overhang. As a working hypothesis, consumption behavior can be analyzed in terms of standard consumption theory. The life cycle approach, modelling consumption as a function of both human and nonhuman wealth, appears to be particularly appropriate as it takes into account explicitly the effect on consumption of (desired and undesired) accumulation of saving.

Under these assumptions, equations were estimated on a data set which excluded the second half of the 1980s, the period during which any existing overhang is likely to have increased substantially. The existence of possible forced saving over the estimation period (up to 1985) was taken into consideration by introducing, as an indicator of rationing, the ratio between *kolkhoz* and state prices. It was therefore implicitly assumed that the *kolkhoz* market is extended enough to provide a reliable indicator of excess demand, but is not sufficient (especially because of the limited number of products supplied) to eliminate excess demand at the macro level.[33] Any effects of shortages during the sample period, other than those captured by the rationing indicator, were assumed to remain approximately stable and therefore to leave unaffected the properties of the estimated equation.[34]

The equation was then used to project consumption in the second half of the 1980s, and forced saving could be measured as the difference between actual and projected saving *plus* the estimate of rationing derived from the inclusion in the equation of the rationing indicator *plus* a judgmental estimate of nonmeasurable "chronic" shortages.

The following model specification (in static form) was used as the base for the estimation:

(1) $LOGC = a_0 + a_1 log(W + H) + bX + a_2 IR$,

where C is households' consumption (including of consumer durables)[35]; W is non-human wealth[36] and H is human wealth[37]; X is a vector of variables influencing the steady state ratio between consumption and total wealth; IR is the index of rationing computed on the basis of *kolkhoz* prices; and a_0, a_1, and a_2 are parameters and b is a parameter vector. Note that $a_2 IR$ should approximate the percentage amount of rationing (possibly in excess of an unobservable fixed amount, included in the constant).

Vector X includes three variables: the real interest rate on deposits, computed as the nominal interest rate on bank deposits minus an estimate of actual (as opposed to official) inflation (see the statistical notes); the "dependency ratio", defined as the ratio of the nonworking population (children below 16 years of age and pensioners) to the remaining population; and the "benefit ratio," defined as total benefits extended by the social consumption fund to each nonworking member of the population, divided by the wage rate.[38] The expected sign is negative for the real interest rate and positive for the benefit ratio and the dependency ratio.

Equation (1) assumes that human and nonhuman wealth have the same effect on consumption; a less restrictive specification would be:

$$(2) \quad logC = a_0 + a'_1 \, log(W) + a'_1 \, log(1+\frac{H}{W}) + bX + a_2 \, IR,$$

which is equivalent to (1) if $a'_1 = a_1$. As a check of the model specification, the equations were estimated without imposing the equality constraint between the coefficient on $log(W)$ and the coefficient on $log(1+H/W)$. As to the dynamic specification, it is postulated that consumption adjusts slowly to changes in wealth; in particular, the following "quasi-error-correction mechanism" was adopted:

$$(3) \quad Dlog(C) = c_0 + c_1 \, log(\frac{W}{C})_{-1} + c_2 \, log(1+\frac{H}{W})_{-1} + cX + c_3 \, IR + c_4 \, Dlog(Y),$$

where Y is disposable income and D is the first difference operator.[39]

Tables III.3.2-III.3.4 report the OLS estimates of equation (3) (on annual data for the period 1965-85).[40] Three sets of results are presented. Table III.3.2 refers to equations in which nonhuman wealth is included in its broader definition (net financial assets plus houses and rural properties). On account of possible errors in the measurement of nonfinancial wealth, Table III.3.3 reports estimates for which only net financial wealth was used. Finally, Table III.3.4 reports results referring to a simpler specification based only on disposable income. Together with coefficient estimates, t statistics and the usual goodness of fit indicators, the tables show the results of a number of "diagnostic tests" on the normality of residuals, on the absence of autocorrelation and heteroskedasticity, and on the within-sample stability of the equation (see also Table III.3.5). The latter test is of particular relevance in this context because the measurement of the overhang as an "anomalous" increase in saving requires an equation that shows stability over the estimation period.[41]

The specification search process begins, for each of the three formulations, by estimating an equation containing all available regressors. Starting from Table III.3.2, the more general specification (equation A, which includes Holzman's indicator of rationing) shows a remarkably good fit, with an adjusted R^2 close to 0.9 (this is particularly high considering that the estimations are on percentage changes) and a standard error of around 0.8 percent. The normality and residual autocorrelation tests are easily passed, but one of the two heteroskedasticity tests shows unsatisfactory results. Traces of instability are also apparent; Harvey's Psi test, which is distributed as a Student's t, falls well beyond the 5 percent critical value. As to the coefficient estimates, the human and nonhuman wealth effects and the impact effect of disposable income have the correct sign; the sign of all other variables is opposite to the expected sign. Most t statistics, including the one on the variable containing human wealth, are low. In summary, while the overall performance of the equation appears to be adequate, there are signs of mispecification; or, possibly, the limited number of observations available does not allow the identification of all the expected effects according to economic theory.

In equation B, all variables that had the "wrong" sign and were not significant at the 5 percent level in equation A were removed. Specification B improves substantially over specification A. While there is some deterioration in the autocorrelation tests (which however remain much above their critical values), the heteroskedasticity and stability tests improve (the only exception being the variance ratio test). Note also that the t statistics on the coefficients on both human and nonhuman wealth increase well above the critical level. Finally, these coefficients, even if unrestricted, converge to a similar value (0.41), as predicted by the theory. The equality restriction is imposed in specification C and is easily accepted (see the last row of the table). Note that the equation's standard error is further lowered and that the variance ratio test improves. In summary, specification C seems to be entirely adequate in terms of goodness of fit, diagnostic tests and consistency of parameter values with what could be expected from economic theory. Actual and fitted values for this equation are shown in Chart 4.[42] Note that equation C implies that Soviet households maintain in the long run a broadly stable ratio between consumption and total (human and nonhuman) wealth; the fact that the coefficient on the change in disposable income is lower than unity implies that, in the short run, the saving ratio is correlated to the growth rate of disposable income, possibly because households try to offset partially the effect on consumption of changes in income that are perceived to be temporary.

In equation D the unweighted ratio between *kolkhoz* and state prices replaces Holzman's index as an indicator of rationing. Specification D has a slightly better fit, but shows signs of instability; and, while the rationing index and the benefit ratio have the expected sign, the interest rate level, the dependency ratio and the term including human wealth have the wrong signs. Some of these problems persist in the more parsimonious specification E (where the dependency ratio and the interest rate have been dropped).[43]

The specification using net financial wealth rather than total nonhuman wealth as a regressor (Table III.3.3) does not substantially alter the empirical results just described. The properties of the equation remain approximately unchanged and the specification search leads again to a parsimonious representation (equation C) in which, in the long run, the ratio between consumption and (human and nonhuman) wealth appears to be fairly stable. Note, however, that, contrary to equation D in Table III.3.2, the relative *kolkhoz* price has an extremely low coefficient and t statistic, suggesting that the correlation found before may have been spurious.

Finally, Table III.3.4 presents estimates of a more traditional specification in which only disposable income influences consumption expenditure. The performance of the equation remains satisfactory in terms of fit and diagnostic tests. Again, the relative *kolkhoz* price appears in specification C with a very low coefficient and t statistics.

In conclusion, the behavior of consumption between 1965 and 1985 can be adequately described by the evolution of total (human and nonhuman) wealth; the fact that a simpler specification in terms of disposable income (on which the computation of human wealth is based) closely approximates the results obtained by the more complete specification is probably a reflection of the fact that, in the USSR, households' wealth is predominantly "human".[44]

c. Estimates of households' accumulated excess savings

(1) The wealth overhang

The equations described above can be used to compute the size of the wealth overhang accumulated in the second half of the 1980s. A preliminary step is to show that the estimated consumption equations, very stable until 1985, present strong instability in the subsequent period. For this purpose, equation C in Tables III.3.2 and III.3.3 and equation B in Table III.3.4 were re-estimated over the 1965-90 period; the stability tests decisively rejected the hypothesis of structural stability.[45]

The calculation of the wealth overhang of households was then based on the difference between actual wealth accumulation and the amount of wealth that would have been accumulated in the absence of rationing on the basis of the estimated econometric equations. Table III.3.6 presents two sets of projections; the first is based on a simulation of equations C in Tables III.3.2 and III.3.3 and of equation B in Table III.3.4 for the period 1986-90; the second is based on a simulation of the same equations for the period 1983-90, as a check of the hypothesis that rationing (or rationing above a structural stable level) started in 1983.[46]

The first column of Table III.3.6 shows the estimates of the accumulated wealth overhang during the simulation period derived from the model simulations; they range from a minimum of around rub 95 billion to a maximum of rub 130 billion. As mentioned, these estimates do not include the "unobservable" chronic overhang which may have affected consumption even before 1986 (1983). Taking a figure of rub 59 billion (derived by the Soviet authorities from sample surveys of households' behavior) as the estimate of the "chronic" overhang at the end of 1985, and rub 48 billion for the end of 1982,[47] we obtain, in the last column of the table, estimates for the overhang in 1990 ranging between rub 159 billion and rub 183 billion with an average of rub 170 billion (around one third of households' financial wealth). Using the same procedure, we obtain an average estimate for the overhang at the end of 1989 equal to rub 128 billion. Thus, during 1990 the monetary overhang appears to have increased by around rub 42 billion (over 55 percent of households' saving in that year).[48]

Three observations must be made with reference to these figures. First, as mentioned in section 2, the measurement of consumption may be underestimated (and that of the overhang may be overestimated) by lack of adequate information on incomes generated on parallel markets.[49] In addition, the estimate of desired consumption, and hence that of the overhang, may be affected by lack of consideration of how expected future price increases may affect the desired intertemporal distribution of households' resources.[50]

Second, the amount of the overhang should be compared to the stock of unsold consumer goods. The latter appears to have declined sharply during the last twenty years; the estimated stock was rub 62 billion in 1970, rub 31 billion in 1985, and rub 15 billion at the end of 1989—a very modest proportion of the overhang, even at official prices. This finding suggests that, in the presence of price liberalization, the overhang would not lead simply to a change in relative prices (e.g., a decline in the price of the unsold inventories of consumer goods and an increase in the price of the goods for which shortages are observed) but would bring about an increase in the average price level.

Third, it must be recalled that the reported estimate of the overhang refers to the cumulative sum of involuntary saving incurred in past years. Under normal circumstances (i.e., assuming that behavior continues to conform to the estimated equations), Soviet households are unlikely to try to spend all the undesired accumulation of wealth in a single period (say one year). According to the life cycle hypothesis, they should allocate the expenditure of the undesired stock of wealth over time. Of course, a quantitative estimate of how rapidly the overhang would be released in the presence of price liberalization would be extremely difficult to make; it would depend on the type of consumption foregone in the past,[51] on price expectations and on the extent to which price liberalization was seen as temporary or permanent.

(2) The monetary overhang

Table III.3.7, describing the trends in the composition of households' wealth and savings, sheds some light on the question of what proportion of the estimated wealth overhang might have been accumulated in monetary assets. The table shows a steady increase in the financial component of total wealth, almost entirely matched by a decline in the share of housing. Although the latter may be influenced to some extent by miscalculations in the valuation of houses at current prices, the increased role played by financial wealth is confirmed by the data on the allocation of saving flows. Investment in real assets fell from around one-third of total saving during the late 1950s and early 1960s to less than 10 percent in subsequent years, mainly as a consequence of the decline in the share of private housing investment.[52]

Clearly, the composition of households' wealth is currently biased towards financial assets, which account for around 90 percent of both total wealth and saving.[53] In addition, financial wealth is almost entirely composed of monetary assets; throughout the period under consideration, M1 components (cash and demand deposits) represented around two thirds of total financial assets; and M2 components (including M1, time deposits and lottery bonds[54]) covered a share slightly above 90 percent.

The main conclusion that can be drawn from these data is that, given the limited share taken by the real component of saving in the last 20-25 years, almost all of the involuntary accumulation of saving is likely to have been in the form of financial, and specifically monetary, assets.

d. Estimates of the monetary overhang of enterprises

Enterprises' monetary holdings are likely to be determined basically by a transactions demand which, in theory, could be estimated. The approach used for households could then be applied, equating the overhang with the monetary accumulation that is not explained by the estimated equation. Two factors prevent the practical application of this procedure. First, the available information on enterprise money only extends back to 1980, which precludes econometric estimation techniques. Second, the reforms enacted in the second half of the 1980s significantly altered the nature of enterprise money, with potentially complex repercussions for the underlying demand function. On the one hand, the reforms increased the degree of control enterprises had over their resources; previously, their bank deposits had been held jointly with ministries and state organizations. The reform also raised the fungibility of different bank accounts, and therefore their liquidity.[55] On the other hand, the demand for money may have been increased by a tightening of enterprise credit, which accompanied the reforms and partially hardened the "soft" budget constraint of enterprises.[56] In addition, the increasing disruption in the distribution and trade system in the late 1980s may have increased enterprises' demand for liquidity, as they needed to be prepared to buy inputs as and when they became available. It is difficult to do other than assume that all these factors may have offset one another, although this is little more than a working hypothesis.

390

With this caveat, some indication of the involuntary accumulation of enterprise money can be obtained from both cross-sectional and time series empirical evidence. It is possible, in the first place, to compare the level of enterprise money in the USSR with that prevailing in Western European industrialized countries.[57] Enterprise holdings of M1 (cash and demand deposits) in relation to both NMP and GDP appears to be higher in the USSR than in the Federal Republic of Germany, France, Italy and the United Kingdom, although not dramatically higher (Table III.3.8). Corresponding ratios for M2 (M1 plus time deposits[58]) were lower than in the FRG, although higher than in the other countries. The ratio computed for total financial assets (which is also the M2 ratio in the USSR) fell close to the average in the five countries. Based on this evidence, it could be argued that Soviet enterprises are too liquid, given that the real yield of enterprise deposits in other countries exceeds that in the USSR.

Consider now the time series evidence, based on a plotting of the ratios of M1 and M2 to NMP (Chart 5). In 1987, both ratios started rising rapidly, doubling in four years. Notwithstanding some of the factors mentioned earlier, it is difficult to believe that this could have reflected equilibrium behavior. It may not necessarily reflect shortages of goods either, but may simply have been a short-run response to sharply increased profits during this period. In the long run, however, given the current level of interest rates, the high level of liquidity is likely to lead to increased expenditure.

How large is the excess accumulation of money by enterprises? One, admittedly rough, approximation could be derived by extrapolating the growth of liquidity that would have maintained the ratios of liquidity to NMP at their 1986 value. If this is done, the excess liquidity held in 1990 is rub 79 billion for M1 and rub 99 billion for M2. If, instead, we assume, as "normal" liquidity growth, the increase that would have kept the liquidity ratios close to the trend increase observed between 1980 and 1986, we obtain an estimate of the overhang equal to rub 65 billion for M1 (around 40 percent of the total) and to rub 85 billion for M2 (42 percent of the total). The corresponding figures for the end of 1989 are rub 48 billion for M1 and rub 53 billion for M2. Thus, the enterprise overhang is estimated to have increased in 1990 by rub 17 billion for M1 and by rub 32 billion for M2. Similar values are obtained by using ratios with respect to GDP instead of NMP.

4. A REVIEW OF POLICIES TO DEAL WITH THE LIQUIDITY OVERHANG

The apparent substantial (and rapidly rising) involuntary accumulation of monetary holdings for both households and firms suggests large and growing shortages. At the same time, it would be a cause for concern on the eve of a possible price liberalization, and dealing with it must be an integral part of any stabilization strategy. Certainly, all factors that could possibly determine a further increase in the overhang should be promptly removed: the expansion of monetary income has to be kept in line with the development of production, for both households and firms, which requires a tightening of fiscal, monetary, and possibly incomes policies. Even if this flow problem were solved, however, the stock of excess liquidity would remain. This section considers different possible ways to reduce that stock.

a. Price increases

One obvious way to eliminate the overhang is to liberalize prices and allow inflation to erode the excess purchasing power. Two problems have to be considered in this context: first, what is the type and magnitude of the price adjustment that would eliminate the overhang; and second, under what conditions could the adjustment be limited to a once-and-for-all increase in the price level, without triggering an inflationary spiral.

Let W and WF be the actual amounts of total and financial wealth, respectively, held by Soviet households in 1990, and W^d and WF^d the corresponding desired amounts. Under the assumptions that: (a) the desired amount of wealth in real terms and actual nominal wealth are constant[59]; and (b) the nominal value of the non-financial component of wealth (W-WF) (mainly houses) increases in line with prices, the price level which would have equated actual and desired wealth in real terms is obtained by solving for P in the equation:

$$(4) \quad \frac{WF}{P} + (W-WF) = W^d, \text{ or}$$

$$(5) \quad P\frac{WF}{(WF-OV)} = 1.453,$$

where OV is the overhang. This implies an increase in the price level of 45.3 percent with respect to 1990.[60]

Note that the price increase, at least in the short run, is not the only adjustment necessary for the elimination of the overhang. The overhang was created by an excess of income relative to the available supply of consumer goods; this disequilibrium fueled the increase in the stock of the overhang and has to be eliminated if the source of the overhang is to be eliminated permanently. This will probably imply a temporary drop in real households' disposable income with respect to its 1990 level.

A 45 percent price increase may be considered a reasonable cost to pay for price liberalization. Several factors, however, could push prices higher than this. First, some relative prices (e.g., energy prices) will have to increase much more than 45 percent. In the presence of downward price rigidity or of minimum price increases connected to wage indexation (a likely occurrence),[61] this may imply an average price increase above 45 percent. Second, a 45 percent price increase would be insufficient to absorb the enterprise overhang, which is estimated to equal 75 percent of this sector's desired money holdings;[62] moreover enterprise profits will probably rise as consumers' expenditure increases. Enterprises will therefore have an incentive to spend the undesired money accumulation, bidding up goods prices and, possibly, wages. Expectations would be likely to play a crucial role; in the current situation of political uncertainty, with fears of falling production, and a complete lack of experience in market mechanisms, initial price increases may easily be interpreted as signaling the beginning of an inflationary spiral. These expectations may be self-fulfilling as they could lead to increased hoarding of goods, highly negative expected yields on financial assets and, therefore, to a stronger increase in aggregate demand. Only through tight monetary and fiscal policies could this process be halted.

In conclusion, while in theory the absorption of the monetary overhang purely through price liberalization may involve moderate price increases, the practical difficulties in avoiding an inflationary spiral should not be underestimated. Consideration must be given to non-inflationary ways of eliminating the overhang.

b. Increased availability of goods

An increase in the supply of consumer goods has been one of the cornerstones of all recently proposed reform programs in the USSR. To the extent, however, that this involved shifting resources from the production of investment goods to consumer goods, it could reduce the overhang of households but at the risk of aggravating shortages in the investment goods market. Unable to increase capital investment (or facing higher prices for investment goods), firms might be induced to use their large liquidity holdings to bid for more labor, thus pushing up wages.[63] A solution might be to cut down the production of goods which do not supply the market (primarily military investment); or to increase overall productivity. In both cases, the supply responses would take time to materialize. A more rapid increase in the supply of consumer goods might be possible through stepped-up imports, but only if the external financing constraint would permit.

c. Monetary reform

The cancellation or write-down of outstanding monetary assets, i.e., monetary reform, has also been considered as a way to reduce the overhang. Here the problem is one of credibility. Some distinction can be made, however, between the deposits of households and enterprises.

For households, the distribution of bank deposits appears to be fairly concentrated in the USSR (and rather stable over time; see Chart 6): over 40 percent of bank deposits are accounted for by only 10 percent of bank accounts and over 60 percent by only 20 percent. At the end of 1988, around 35 percent of the entire stock of deposits consisted of accounts larger than rub 5,000 (3.5 times the value of per capita annual consumption in that year).[64] The distribution of bank deposits per capita (or household) is probably even more concentrated because of the widespread practice of breaking larger accounts into a number of smaller accounts, for fear of administrative measures against bank deposits.[65]

The high concentration of bank deposits implies, in principle, that a monetary reform that converted larger deposits at an unfavorable rate would affect a limited share of the population. Using end-1988 figures, for example, the conversion of deposits below rub 5,000 at par and of all deposits above rub 5,000 at, say, a 2:3 ratio (two new rubles for three old rubles) would have reduced the outstanding stock of deposits by around rub 60 billion and would have involved less than 20 percent of the stock of bank deposits. Assuming no change in bank distribution, the corresponding estimate for end-1990 would be around rub 80 billion.

There is, however, a political problem in implementing a reform of this kind; the last monetary reform in the USSR was implemented under Stalin (in 1947) and the practice of multiple accounts seems to indicate that the memory of that reform still lingers.[66] Instilling popular confidence in the inviolability of property rights is an important element in making a successful transition to a market economy. To begin such a transition with an arbitrary confiscation of assets (however illusory their purchasing power may have been) risks undermining the credibility of the entire strategy. This is not to say that some limited reform (possibly in the form of a temporary freeze), or some type of tax on wealth, should be entirely ruled out; but its contribution to the absorption of the households' overhang should, in most circumstances, be limited.

Administrative measures may possibly be politically more realistic with respect to enterprise deposits. Clearly, the advantage here would be that the "shareholder" is the state itself; the disadvantage is that a measure of confiscation (or conversion at very unfavorable rates) of enterprise liquidity would be against the free market spirit of the reforms and it may in particular discourage the profit motivation of enterprises. One risk is the possible disruptive effect on production of a sharp decline in the liquidity of firms; in order to reduce this risk, the targeted cut in liquidity should remain somewhat below the estimated monetary overhang.[67]

d. Sale of state property

The sale of state property represents, in theory, an effective way to reduce the monetary overhang. Since the composition of households' wealth in the USSR is severely biased towards monetary assets, it is likely that the potential demand for real forms of wealth is high. It is also likely that the increased availability of real stores of wealth could increase the desired amount of wealth (or, in other words, the propensity to save), thus bringing about not only a decline in the liquidity of the overhang, but also a decline in its absolute size.

Housing is obviously the first candidate for privatization. The pent-up demand of Soviet households for houses is well known.[68] Given the rather concentrated distribution of bank deposits, however, only a small proportion of households would have enough resources to purchase a house at nonsubsidized prices (or even to make a downpayment). Of course, credit could be extended to sustain the purchase of houses; in this case the initial amount of the overhang would not be immediately affected, but the gross saving rate in future periods might increase, as households had to face the repayment of the debt.[69]

The amount of resources that could be raised by the sale of houses, and land, will crucially depend on two factors. First, the Government must be able to offer a credible guarantee of property rights, which would require the introduction of legislation specifying in detail the procedures for the registration of property and for its transfer. Second, rents must be substantially raised (see Chapter V.9). On account of all these factors, any estimate of the amount of money that the Government could raise by selling property is extremely uncertain. The value of the stock of houses owned by the Government is officially put at about rub 800-900 billion at the end of 1989. The privatization of even a small proportion of this stock could offset a substantial share of the overhang.

As for the sale of enterprise shares on assets, again the authorities must develop a system of credible property rights guarantees.

e. Increase in interest rates and financial innovation

Until 1990, the yield on bank deposits in the USSR had remained fixed in nominal terms for more then 25 years. In real terms, it followed a slightly declining trend, becoming generally negative at the end of the 1980s, thus exacerbating the overhang. Despite increases toward the end of 1990, real interest rates remained negative. Raising the return on bank deposits and in general improving the conditions offered on financial assets is an effective way, under normal conditions, to increase saving rates and the demand for financial assets.

However, increasing deposit rates would require that loan rates on bank assets be raised accordingly. While this increase would certainly be beneficial in reducing the enterprise overhang, it could have a negative impact on the fiscal deficit as it would increase the cost of servicing the public debt. In addition, a rise in interest rates generally has (opposing) income and substitution effects on current saving rates. Given the relatively low total financial assets to income ratio (the income effect increases with this ratio), the substitution effect is likely to prevail and saving would therefore probably increase, though this has yet to be confirmed empirically in the case of the USSR. At the same time, efforts should be taken to develop a sufficiently wide market for bonds; in this context the issue of medium-term indexed bonds may represent the only way to support a bond market.[70]

5. CONCLUSIONS

During the second half of the 1980s, continued price controls, coupled with an increasingly inadequate supply of goods relative to nominal household and enterprise incomes, stimulated the accumulation of a substantial amount of unspent purchasing power held in the form of monetary assets. It is estimated that in 1990 this "monetary overhang" reached rub 170 billion for households and rub 85 billion for enterprises. These amounts represent fairly substantial shares of the monetary holdings of the two sectors (33 percent for households and 43 percent for enterprises). These estimates should be interpreted with some caution since they are based on several assumptions, the most important of which is that agents' underlying behavior has remained broadly stable over time. Should, for example, price expectations or lack of confidence in government policies destabilize established patterns of saving and expenditure, the amount of undesired money could easily and rapidly change.

While the stock of the overhang is significant, its high growth rate is particularly alarming. The total overhang is estimated to have increased in 1990 by over rub 75 billion (or by 41 percent). Clearly, a lasting solution to the problem requires the implementation of fiscal, monetary and incomes policies capable of checking the current income streams fueling the overhang. However, in the context of any stabilization effort, appropriate policies will also have to be implemented in order to reduce the current excess stock of money. Even in the absence of new liquidity injections, and without other measures to reduce the monetary surplus, the price increase required to remove the overhang could be fairly substantial (40-50 percent). The real risk is, however, that the first round of price increases would start an inflationary spiral. This, of course, is more likely in the presence of indexation mechanisms (of both labor incomes and interest rates), which may be difficult to avoid. In summary, relying on price increases to eliminate the overhang may involve a lengthy and potentially disruptive adjustment process. Other, noninflationary, ways to deal with the problem should also be considered.

Four such types of solution have been discussed. The sale of government assets is one option. While the overhang is large compared to the wealth of the population, it is small with respect to the value of state property, so that the sale of even a small part of the latter could easily absorb the overhang. The difficulties are in rapidly creating the legal and economic conditions that make the purchase of state properties attractive. Increased goods supply is another obvious solution and should be implemented through a cut in the production of goods which are not demanded by the market (mainly military hardware). Massive conversion in the composition of production has occurred in many economies in a relatively short time, but the same process may take longer in the USSR, given the current state of disarray in the economy. It is also possible that, given realistic exchange rates, a large portion of the overhang might be absorbed by a relatively modest expenditure of foreign exchange (if used to import goods in strong demand). Monetary reform is a third possibility; the highly concentrated distribution of bank deposits would imply that a relatively large share of households' excess money could be absorbed by penalizing a relatively small proportion of the population. However, this approach has the drawback that it would tend to work against the attempt to establish credibility and the population's confidence in the inviolability of property rights. More feasible could be the adoption of measures to reduce administratively, or to freeze, the excessive liquidity of state enterprises, possibly in the context of their conversion into joint-stock companies. Finally, an increase in the demand for financial assets, preferably less liquid than bank deposits, could be facilitated by an increase in interest rates and by the introduction of new financial instruments (such as indexed bonds).

All these instruments present advantages and drawbacks, and do not necessarily affect all population groups equally. In these circumstances, it would seem unrealistic to rely solely on any one instrument. Rather, recourse to a broad spectrum of measures is likely to prove the most effective strategy.

STATISTICAL NOTES

1. *Financial assets and saving*: all data on financial assets between 1964 and 1989 have been provided by the Gosbank; data on bank deposits for the previous period can be found in Hutchings (1983), who collected them from Soviet official publications; data on currency and other financial assets of households have been estimated by imposing a constant ratio with respect to bank deposits (at the 1964 level). This may underestimate the actual amount of cash before 1964 if the declining trend in the ratio between cash and deposits observable after 1964 had started before that date. In the absence of capital gains on financial assets, net financial saving has been equated to the change in the nominal stock of financial assets net of the change in households' credit, also available from the above sources.

2. *Households' disposable income*: data on disposable income for the 1980s have been provided by Goskomstat; the behavior of the series is similar for that period to the one published in CIA (1989), which has been used to extend the series back to 1965; information on the previous period has been derived from Pickersgill (1983).

3. *Real households' investment*: this is made of two components: houses and other real investment (both considered net of amortization). As to the first component, Goskomstat provided data from 1970 to 1989; data for the previous period have been derived from Smith (1973). The second component (including mainly livestock and other property of the rural population) has also been provided by Goskomstat from 1970 to

1989; for the previous period this series, for which the magnitudes are rather small, has been kept constant with respect to financial saving.

4. *Households' wealth*: total wealth has been derived as the sum of three components: net financial wealth, houses and the stock of other real wealth. For financial wealth see Note 1. The value of houses owned by the population, net of depreciation and at current (official) prices, has been provided by Goskomstat from 1965 to 1989. The housing investment series has been used to derive the stock of houses for the previous period. The value of the third component has also been provided by Goskomstat but only for 1970-1989 and not at current prices, but as a cumulative sum of previous investments. For the pre-1970 period the corresponding investment series has also been used to derive the stock of this wealth component. A "discrepancy", or "capital gain" series has also been derived by subtracting total (real and financial) investment from the change in wealth. Given the procedure followed above, this residual series represented entirely net capital gains on houses and was fairly small.

5. *Households' saving and consumption*: households' saving was derived as the sum of the three saving components (net financial saving, investment in houses, investment in other real assets). Consumption was derived residually as the difference between disposable income and net saving.

6. *Other series:* the inflation series was derived from CIA(1989) and from Pickersgill (1983); data on population are derived from *Narkhoz*, various issues; most recent estimates of the composition of the population by age have been published by Kingkade (1987a); data from Howard (1976) have been used for the previous period. Nominal interest rates have been provided by the Gosbank; real interest rates have been derived by using the above mentioned inflation series. Data on monthly wages and the expenditure of the social consumption fund are published regularly in *The USSR in Figures*. Data on the ratio between *kolkhoz* prices and official prices for the same products have been collected in Nove (1986); data published in the *Narkhoz 1988* (1989) and in Alexeev, Gaddy and Leitzel (1990) have been used for the most recent period. Data on the stock of unsold consumer goods have been provided by the Ministry of Finance.

All data for 1990 have been estimated, based on preliminary information.

NOTES

1. Hidden inflation can occur for several reasons: "Official price lists may lag behind actual prices... Quality may deteriorate at constant prices. State goods may be sold at prices higher than state prices by dishonest retailers...unrecorded open inflation can arise from quantity

weights in official price indices understating the relative weights of goods whose market prices (whether or not equal to the official price) rise relatively faster." Nuti (1989), p. 110.

2. Barro and Grossman (1974), p. 87; and Portes (1989). Nuti (1989) points out that, strictly speaking, the term "repressed inflation" should not be used in a situation in which the equilibrium price is simply *higher* than the actual price, but in a situation in which the difference between the equilibrium and actual price level *rises*. This point, while correct, seems to be purely semantic and the more common definition is adhered to here.

3. Following the literature on disequilibrium markets, "rationing" should be interpreted here purely as a situation where demand exceeds supply at current prices and does not imply a specific allocation mechanism (such as allocation through coupons).

4. There will also be an increase in real wealth at current prices, but not at the price level prevailing when equilibrium is restored.

5. This is epitomized by the work of Portes and Winter (1980), which has extended to CPEs the concept of macroeconomic disequilibrium proposed for market economies by Barro and Grossman (1974).

6. Burkett (1988). The main problem is the difficulty of applying at the macroeconomic level the "min condition" on which the econometric analysis of markets in disequilibrium is based. The "min condition" implies that, in the presence of disequilibrium, the observed quantity is the minimum of demand and supply. While this is an acceptable (although not necessarily correct) assumption in specific markets, at the macro level, in the presence of both shortages and surpluses, the observed quantity is always *lower* than the sum of all demands and of all supplies, if at the micro level the min condition prevails.

7. In this case "it is not clear what should be called aggregate excess demand on the macro level. Should it be only money which cannot be spent at all? But this is found only with a generally very intense shortage....Or should we interpret the notion widely and include all money that has not been spent according to initial demand? It seems that the term aggregate excess demand is not an operational category in an economy with chronic shortages." (*Kornai* (1982), p. 477). Also see *Kornai* (1980).

8. "In a shortage economy an alert buyer purchases not when he wants to consume a good but when the good is available" (*Kornai* (1982), p. 457).

9. Note that this component of saving can only be considered as "voluntary" given the state of chronic shortage affecting the economy. Should the state of the economy change, e.g., due to imminent price liberalization, the component of wealth previously accumulated for this motive would immediately become part of the overhang. Note also that this component should not increase over time, in relation to total consumption, unless shortages become more extensive or more severe.

10. Note, however, that to net out excess involuntary saving with the involuntary accumulation of stocks would require evaluating the latter at the correct (and lower) relative price, and not at the official price at which the goods remained unsold.

11. According to Nuti (1989), this is indeed the most common case in CPEs. In this respect, he argues that "By and large excess money holdings in the economy as a whole (i.e., with reference to the two-tier market) can be deemed to be small regardless of reliance on econometric evidence, except for the presence of lags and other minor factors which might slow down the adjustment of money balances to the actual two-tier price level. However, the small size or even absence of excess money holdings (and therefore of repressed inflation) is consistent with large-scale imbalance in the state sector, since consumers who—given the two-tier market—voluntarily hold liquid assets, do not refrain voluntarily from converting most or all

of them into goods in state shops where they *are* quantity-rationed." (p. 142) On this point see also Grossman (1977).

12. See Gardner and Strauss (1981).

13. As long as rationing is not implemented through coupons, but through queuing (so that the probability of being able to buy the desired amount of goods at the official prices is, for each individual, different from zero) it is possible that buyers prefer to delay purchases, increase queuing, and keep higher than desired money balances, rather than buying at the higher parallel market prices.

14. The most important legal parallel markets in the USSR have been the *kolkhoz* markets and the private market for housing services (mainly housing construction). Grossman (1977) estimates that in the middle of the 1970s "the contribution of private value added to household consumption must have been at least 15 percent, and, in regard to household food consumption, perhaps around 25 percent". Note, however, that official data on expenditure and consumption partially take into account economic activity outside the state sector, although they entirely exclude incomes from illegal activities.

15. The following discussion is meant to provide a framework for the analysis of basic empirical evidence on consumption behavior in the USSR; it does not provide a complete survey of the debate on the existence of repressed inflation in CPEs. For surveys of this debate, see Davis and Charemza (1989), Portes (1989), and van Brabant (1990).

16. As explained below, the possibility of adjusting labor supply in response to goods market disequilibrium has been one of the main theoretical counter-arguments to the hypothesis of macroeconomic disequilibrium. Note however, that a reduction in labor supply may reduce the supply of consumer goods as well as household incomes, and can therefore have an uncertain effect on repressed inflation. Let:

$$C^D = cNW,$$

be the demand for consumer goods, where c is the propensity to consume, N is the number of hours supplied and W is the hourly wage rate. The value of the production of consumer goods is given by:

$$C^S = PNqh,$$

where P is the price of consumer goods, q is the share of workers employed in the consumer goods industry (so that Nq is the total number of hours worked in the production of consumer goods) and h is average hourly labor productivity. Then the effect on rationing (i.e., on the percentage difference between C^D and C^S) of a change in N is given by (cw-hq)/CR, where CR is consumption in real terms and w(=W/P) is the real wage rate. This effect could in principle be positive or negative. Specifically, assuming that the average wage rate equals average labor productivity (w=h), then a decline in N would bring about a reduction of rationing if the propensity to consume were higher than the share of workers employed in the consumer goods industry (a likely condition). However, w is likely to be lower than h (remember that *average* values are being considered); and therefore no precise conclusion can be drawn with respect to the effect on rationing of changes in labor supply.

17. Kornai (1980), pp. 456-459, however, recalls that some saving is needed to increment the stock of money held for transaction purposes; moreover, in the absence of consumer credit, the purchase of durables requires prior accumulation of saving; as housing credit is also scarce,

a large share of housing investment has to be financed by prior saving; and a larger stock of wealth can help raise living standards above the basic level provided by the state. Finally, the existence of shortages at the micro level increases the precautionary demand for wealth (especially for monetary assets).

18. Kornai (1982), pp. 263-68, suggests a number of such indicators.

19. The meaningfulness of these indicators in assessing the existence of macroeconomic disequilibrium is also uncertain. For example, the enlargement of parallel markets and the possibility of speculation may inflate demand on the state market (thus lengthening the queues) even in the absence of macroeconomic disequilibrium.

20. Holzman (1960).

21. Indicators of this kind are widely used by Soviet sources as a signal of imbalances. As recalled by Nove (1986), pp.255-256: "Some Western authors deny that the increase in savings bank deposits is abnormal...But many Soviet sources regard some of this saving as forced, frustrated purchasing power."

22. See Howard (1976).

23. Ofer (1990).

24. The lack of consumer credit only increases saving if the population grows or the proportion of available goods that require prior accumulation of savings increases. In this respect the growth of consumer durables in the USSR in the last thirty years has been impressive; between 1960 and 1987 the number of washing machines per 100 families rose from 4 to 70, that of television sets from 8 to 100, that of cars from 1 to 16, that of refrigerators from 4 to 93 (Goskomstat (1987), p. 222). It must be added, however, that most of the improvement occurred in the 1960s and the 1970s and that little progress has occurred in the 1980s, with the exception of cars.

25. Data availability problems prevent the comparison of the wealth ratios in the USSR with those in countries having similar per capita incomes.

26. See Asselain (1981) and Portes (1989).

27. Given a consumption function of form $C=cY$, the equilibrium level of the wealth to income ratio (w) is given by: $w = s/g$, where $s=1-c$ and g is the growth rate of disposable income (Modigliani (1986)). Since w is inversely related to g, in periods of decelerating disposable income growth it is normal to observe an increase in w even if s remains constant.

28. Note, however, that constant rationing of consumption would imply a rising stock of undesired wealth.

29. See Pickersgill (1976, 1980 and 1983) for the USSR.

30. A similar approach is followed by Ofer and Pickersgill (1980) based on the estimation of a consumption function on cross-sectional data.

31. The use of these disequilibrium indicators follows the analysis of rationed markets pioneered by Fair and Jaffee (1974). Under the hypothesis of excess demand and of the usual min condition, the behavior of consumption is described by: $C = CD(.) - R$, where C is observed consumption, CD is desired consumption and R is the amount for which demand is rationed. R is not observed; however, if variables can be found which are related to R (Fair and Jaffee use the price change in the rationed market under the hypothesis that the price adjustment is proportional to the size of the disequilibrium), then the above equation (and specifically the parameters of the demand function) can be estimated with ordinary econometric techniques. In their econometric model of the Soviet economy, Green and Higgins (1977) also use disequilibrium indicators to estimate consumption demand.

32. In her 1980 paper, Pickersgill suggests that this break could be due to repressed inflation. A different approach, unfortunately not extended to the USSR, has applied disequilibrium econometrics techniques to the consumption goods market in CPEs (Portes and Winter (1980), Portes, Quandt and Yeo (1988) and Burkett (1988), for example). These techniques, pioneered by Maddala and Nelson (1974), imply the specification and estimation of both a demand and a supply function for consumer goods; all observations are assumed to be either on the demand or on the supply function. The maximum likelihood principle is used to assign each observation either to the demand or the supply equation and to estimate the two functions. These studies, in which again consumption is expressed mainly as a function of disposable income, tend to conclude that CPEs were not characterized by a state of chronic repressed inflation (with the consequent accumulation of involuntary saving); periods of excess supply and periods of excess demand alternated and, in some cases, excess supply was the dominant regime.

33. The application of this technique is simpler than the one based explicitly on disequilibrium econometrics. First, estimates can be performed with OLS; second there is no need to specify a supply function, whose form would inevitably be arbitrary in the absence of appropriate models of enterprise behavior in CPEs. Finally, the use of disequilibrium econometrics would have implied the separation of the sample between points on the supply and points on the demand function; this procedure seems inappropriate given the very limited number of observations available.

34. Of course, if the equation did not fit the data, this assumption would be called into question.

35. This is an approximation; in theory one would like to include in consumption only the value of the "services" obtained from the current stock of consumer durables; in this case wealth could be defined as inclusive of consumer durables. Lack of adequate data on consumer durables, difficulties in estimating the value of their services and uncertainty on the inclusion, especially in a country such as the USSR, of consumer durables as components of wealth, ruled out such an approach.

36. As detailed in the statistical notes at the end of the chapter, wealth is defined as the sum of financial wealth (currency, bank deposits, Government bonds and insurance policies net of households' borrowing), plus houses and other real wealth (mainly livestock and other property held by rural households).

37. Human wealth is defined by the present discounted value of disposable labor income; this has been computed by adding to a three-period centered moving average of current disposable labor income the discounted expected stream of income in the next 27 years. In this respect it has been assumed, for simplicity, that per capita real income is to grow at the constant annual rate of 2.5 percent (close to the average for the sample period 1965-85, considered in the estimates). The average interest rate on bank deposits was used as discount factor. The 27 year interval has been selected in the following way: the average expected life *at birth* of the population in the USSR has been close to 69 years throughout the sample period (Kingkade (1987b), p.11). Assuming an average expected life of 72 years for the population of age 18 (taken as the average starting year of working life), 27 (= (72-18)/2) is the average number of years for which a middle aged worker expects to receive labor income (including pension payments) in the rest of his/her life.

38. The Social Consumption Fund provides education and health services, grants, pensions and scholarships to the Soviet population. The benefit ratio was also computed using the *per capita* benefits (i.e., the benefits for each member of the population) without altering substantially the econometric results.

39. Note that this specification does not correspond completely to an error correction applied on equation 2 as the change in disposable income, instead of the change in total wealth, appears as the "impact variable" in (3). Equation (3) implies that changes in disposable income (and hence in human wealth), possibly in connection with liquidity effects, affect consumption faster than changes in nonhuman wealth.

40. Limiting the estimation period largely to the Brezhnev era may help in identifying stable behavior in the absence of regime shifts. On the other hand, we are forgoing the opportunity to explain the "jump" in the propensity to save that occurred between the first and second half of the 1960s. It must be added, however, that the reliability of the data declines rapidly the further back one goes; indeed, it cannot be ruled out that the jump in the saving ratio observed in the middle of the 1960s was influenced by statistical measurement problems, particularly the absence of a direct measurement of cash holdings (see the statistical notes). The use of OLS in the estimation of consumption functions has well-known drawbacks. The main problem is the endogeneity of income with respect to consumption demand; in the context of centrally-planned economies, however, this endogeneity should not be taken for granted as total income may be entirely supply determined. More serious may be the consequences of measurement errors affecting disposable income; as consumption is derived residually, errors in the measurement of disposable income may spuriously increase the correlation between income and consumption. Little can be done about this problem, given the difficulties in selecting good instrumental variables, unaffected by measurement errors.

41. As detailed in Table III.3.5, Tables III.3.2-III.3.4 report for all tests (with the exclusion of the DW test and of Harvey's Psi tests) the percentage of the appropriate test distribution lying *to the right* of the computed test statistic, under the null hypothesis of absence of misspecification. The null hypothesis cannot be rejected at the conventional 5 percent level if the value reported in the table is higher than 5 percent. Note that for most of the tests reported in the tables only the asymptotic distribution is known. In light of the limited number of degrees of freedom, it seems to be safe to accept the null hypothesis only when the value reported is "substantially" higher than 5 percent.

42. Attempts to reintroduce in this equation the variables previously excluded were unsuccessful, as these variables remained insignificant and often had the wrong sign.

43. The fit of equation E is slightly better than that of equation C; but choosing it as the "preferred equation" would imply that, apart from a temporary shock effect (DlogY), changes in human wealth, and hence in disposable income, have no permanent effect on consumption, a conclusion which is rather implausible.

44. Even in the United States, human wealth is estimated to be around 12 times nonhuman wealth (Jorgenson and Fraumeni(1989)); it is not surprising that in the USSR this ratio is around twice as high.

45. In a Chow test for the existence of a structural break in 1986, the F-statistics for the three equations were respectively 6.2, 5.8 and 5.5. The null hypothesis of structural stability can therefore be rejected at the 0.5 percent level. The interpretation of this result is that actual consumption was not at the desired level indicated by previous behavior.

46. The choice of 1983 as an alternative structural break point is to some extent arbitrary. Note, however, that in 1983 procurement prices were substantially raised without any increase in retail prices, which may have created an imbalance between income distributed and consumers' expenditure. In addition, it should be pointed out that over the period 1983-85 all estimated equations had negative errors (showing actual consumption below its fitted value). However,

the errors fall within the conventional range of two standard errors and therefore, strictly speaking, they do not appear as "anomalous".

47. This figure for 1982 has been estimated assuming a constant ratio between the chronic overhang and total household wealth at the level observed for 1985.

48. The range covered by Soviet estimates of the monetary overhang is fairly wide. According to Goskomstat, the overhang at the end of 1989 was rub 165 billion, a figure close to the one reported by the Soviet press in that period and that would exceed the estimates here for that date by almost 30 percent. Estimates made by the Ministry of Internal Trade for 1990 (rub 200 billion) also are higher. On the other hand, the estimate provided by the Gosbank for the end of 1989 is only rub 105 billion (22 percent *below* the estimate in this chapter). And, according to Braginski (1990) and Petrakov (1990) the overhang in 1989 was even smaller (rub 70 billion). Thus, the estimates derived here fall well within the range of figures presented by different Soviet sources and are indeed close to the average value of those estimates.

49. The data on consumption expenditure used here are derived as the difference between disposable income and saving; the latter is measured quite accurately but disposable income takes into account only partially the incomes generated outside the socialized sector.

50. It may be argued, for example, that expected inflation could increase consumption, by reducing the yield on noninterest-bearing (or fixed interest) money holdings.

51. For example, past prolonged shortages of food products are unlikely to give rise to an immediate expenditure.

52. As reported by Smith (1973) "although the downturn in individual home building may possibly be a reflection of deliberate restrictive policies, it is more likely the outcome of an increasingly stringent problem in providing building materials" (p. 413). Only recently has the Soviet Government enacted new legislation to favor "a reversal of the long-term decline of this 'private sector' over a 30-year period." (Andrusz (1990), p. 563.)

53. By comparison, financial wealth in G-7 countries ranges from 30 to 50 percent of households' total wealth.

54. Lottery bonds are Government bonds whose return (averaging 3 percent each year) is paid in the form of lottery winnings; although their maturity is formally rather long, they can be converted into cash upon presentation at the state-owned Savings Bank.

55. Before the 1987 reform, the funds deposited in different accounts by enterprises could be used only for specific purposes. Thus, certain types of expenditure required the previous accumulation of funds in specific accounts, even if other funds were available in other accounts. As the "liquidity services" of one unit of enterprise deposits increased, the demand for nominal monetary balances may have decreased.

56. Credit to enterprises declined, in nominal terms, by 5.0 percent in 1987, 6.8 percent in 1988, and 3.8 percent in 1989 (Table K.2, Appendix II-1).

57. This comparison is admittedly difficult because of the structural differences between the Soviet and Western economies. However, it can provide a broad yardstick against which enterprise liquidity can be evaluated.

58. Including, for the USSR, the investment funds of enterprises.

59. This assumption corresponds to the traditional assumption that the demand for real money balances is independent of the price level (though not the inflation rate). While this assumption is easily accepted for transaction balances, it is less so in the case of balances held as a store of wealth. The optimum stock of real wealth held by households in the steady state (i.e., for a constant real growth rate) should grow in line with households' real disposable income (or its "permanent" component) (Modigliani (1987)). As discussed below, the need to equilibrate

the flow of consumer goods to its demand in real terms (i.e., the need to avoid the creation of a new overhang), implies a decline in real disposable income in the short run. Moreover, the fact that, as a result of the move to a market economy, long-term prospects for income growth might improve, can further reduce the need to accumulate wealth. It is therefore possible that the desired amount of wealth would decline in real terms after the price liberalization.

60. This method of computing the equilibrium price index differs from a procedure, sometimes used in the analysis of inflation processes in CPEs, which instead focuses on the equilibrium condition in the goods market. In that approach, the percentage increase in the price level necessary to eliminate the monetary overhang is derived by dividing the overhang by the initial level of consumption spending. The two approaches can yield quite different results in the event that the initial ratio of consumption to wealth is different from unity. In general, price liberalization is likely to affect nominal money holdings—as the result of both increased consumer expenditure in nominal terms and possible increases in nominal wages as enterprise profits rise—as well as prices.

61. It is significant that all reform plans so far advanced have included wide recourse to wage indexation as a way to protect the incomes of the population against the effect of price increases.

62. At the end of 1990, enterprise money holdings (M2) were estimated to have been close to rub 198 billion, while desired money holdings were estimated at around rub 113 billion (see section 3.d); thus the price increase necessary to equal their actual and desired money holdings is around 75 percent (198/113=1.752).

63. The presidential guidelines, approved in October 1990 (see Chapter II.3), explicitly consider the potential conflict between the need to increase the production of consumer goods and the investment demand of enterprises. They suggest that "limits on enterprises' use of their own funds will have to be imposed for some time. This can be done through special taxes on investments." In the guidelines there seems to be no consideration of the effect that a reduced supply of investment goods, or an increase in their cost, might have on the demand for labor and on wages.

64. Data on the distribution of bank deposits by size were recently published by the Soviet press (see *Vechernaia moskva*, February 27, 1990, p. 2). Of course, it could be argued that, as the auction price of a Volga GAZ 24-10 automobile is close to rub 100,000, deposits of rub 5,000 and more are not excessive. Here, however, the point is not to show that bank deposits are large (it has indeed already been remarked that per capita total and financial wealth is low in the USSR by international standards), but that they are unevenly distributed.

65. Even if no adjustment is made for this distortionary effect, wealth concentration in the USSR appears to be not too far from that prevailing in market economies. Data derived from Wolff ((1987), p. 137 and p. 153) show that the percentage of wealth owned by the wealthiest 20 percent of the population in France, Belgium, United Kingdom, Denmark, Sweden, United States and Canada averaged 73 percent (at the middle of the 1970s), ranging from around 60 percent in the United States to 85 percent in the United Kingdom. In the USSR, 20 percent of the largest bank deposits account for 63 percent of total bank deposits of the population (Chart 6).

66. The conversion rates used in the 1947 reform were: 1:1 for coins and bank deposits below 3,000 old rubles; 2:3 for deposits between 3,000 and 10,000 old rubles, 1:2 for deposits above 10,000 rubles; and 1:10 for bank notes. The reform therefore penalized heavily large deposits and, particularly, cash holdings (excluding coins). A nonconfiscatory monetary reform (involv-

ing the introduction of a "heavy" ruble at a 1:10 ratio, with a corresponding change in all prices and incomes) was enacted at the beginning of 1961.

67. Milder measures than monetary conversion at unfavorable rates (such as conversion of liquid assets into long-term deposits or government bonds) could also be considered. Monetary conversion could also be seen as one of the steps in the process of transformation of state-owned enterprises into joint-stock companies (see McKinnon (1990)). A temporary freeze of around rub 50-60 billion of enterprise deposits has recently been considered by the Soviet Government as a possible way to reduce inflationary pressures.

68. For a detailed discussion of the problems of the housing sector, see Chapter V.9.

69. It has been suggested that the sale of houses even at token prices would be beneficial for the public deficit because, in many cases, rents do not even cover maintenance costs. However, the effects on saving could be adverse, to the extent that households might perceive their wealth to have risen, and increase their consumption accordingly.

70. The Italian experience of the 1970s and 1980s provides a case in point. As inflation reached two digit figures after the first oil shock, the traditional bond market was disrupted and the deficit had to rely almost entirely on monetary base financing, thus exacerbating the inflation problem. A return to a nonmonetary financing of the debt was obtained initially through the issue of short term Treasury Bills and, subsequently, through indexed bonds.

Table III.3.1. USSR: International Comparison of Wealth Ratios and Saving Rates

	Year	Total Net Wealth [1]	Financial Net Wealth [1]	Gross Saving [2]	Net Saving [2]
United States	1981	4.23	2.24	9.71	6.17
Japan	...	...	...	16.08	13.48
Germany	1988	...	2.07	8.00	8.92
France	1983 & 1988	4.39 (1983)	1.27 (1988)	7.57	...
Italy	1988	6.00	1.98	23.80	21.50
United Kingdom	1988	6.23	2.02	7.13	4.97
Canada	...	...	...	11.88	9.68
(Average G-7)	...	...	...	8.96	7.56 [3]
USSR	1955	0.70	0.19		
USSR	1985	1.09	1.09	5.70 [2]	5.64 [2]
USSR	1990	1.40 [4]	1.23 [4]		

1. As a ratio to households' consumption.
2. In percentage of households' disposable income. All saving rates refer to the 1980-87 average with the exception of Italy (1983-87) and the USSR (1980-85).
3. Excluding France.
4. Estimates.

407

Table III.3.2. USSR: Estimates of Households' Consumption (1)

(OLS; annual data: 1965-85; dependent variable DlogC)

Variables	Equation A	Equation B	Equation C	Equation D	Equation E
Constant	-0.33	-1.42	-1.39	2.10	0.68
	(-0.30)	(-2.76)	(-2.84)	(1.88)	(0.78)
$\log (W/C)_{-1}$	0.41	0.41	0.40	0.48	0.39
	(1.99)	(2.79)	(2.84)	(3.70)	(3.05)
$\log (1+H/W)_{-1}$	0.23	0.41	0.40	-0.38	-0.08
	(0.93)	(2.77)	(2.84)	(-1.41)	(-0.35)
Dependency ratio	-0.0021	—	—	-0.0024	—
	(-1.21)			(-1.98)	
Benefit ratio	-0.55	—	—	0.70	0.80
	(-1.55)			(1.69)	(1.91)
Real interest rate	0.055	—	—	0.29	—
	(0.16)			(1.20)	
IR1	-0.065	—	—	—	—
	(-0.58)				
IR2	—	—	—	-0.45	-0.38
				(-3.12)	(-2.66)
DlogY	0.80	0.88	0.91	0.86	0.96
	(3.56)	(6.74)	(12.58)	(5.23)	(7.62)
Adjusted R^2	0.88	0.89	0.89	0.93	0.92
Standard error	0.0080	0.0078	0.0076	0.0061	0.0065
Normality	63.1%	61.3%	61.8%	50.4%	78.4%
DW	1.90	1.51	1.47	2.21	1.90
MLM	93.5%	29.78%	24.3%	49.4%	62.8%
Ljung-Box	95.2%	33.0%	29.2%	42.6%	64.5%
Heteroskedasticity 1	58.8%	69.3%	78.8%	17.1%	60.7%
Heteroskedasticity 2	16.2%	45.1%	37.1%	5.6%	0.45%
Chow test	19.0%	50.0%	58.5%	58.1%	95.3%
Variance ratio test	20.3%	11.0%	20.3%	26.7%	3.9%
Generalized Chow test	15.3%	38.3%	60.5%	91.0%	87.4%
Harvey's Psi (forward)	-3.86	0.05	-0.78	-2.11	-0.32
Harvey's Psi (backward)	-0.26	-0.56	1.13	0.42	-0.72
F test on $a_1 = a_{-1}'$	—	—	76.4%	—	—

408

Table III.3.3. USSR: Estimates of Households' Consumption (2)

(OLS; annual data: 1965-85; dependent variable DlogC)

Variables	Equation A	Equation B	Equation C	Equation D
Constant	-0.27 (-1.19)	-1.48 (-2.73)	-1.27 (-2.70)	-0.71 (-0.50)
log (WFIN/C)$_{-1}$	0.26 (0.99)	0.42 (2.76)	0.37 (2.71)	0.30 (1.05)
log (1+H/WFIN)$_{-1}$	0.19 (0.57)	0.43 (2.74)	0.37 (2.71)	0.27 (0.80)
Dependency ratio	-0.0011 (-0.71)	—	—	-0.0010 (-0.62)
Benefit ratio	-0.58 (-1.07)	—	—	-0.32 (-0.44)
Real interest rate	0.015 (0.05)	—	—	-0.015 (-0.05)
IR1	0.09 (1.04)	—	—	—
IR2	—	—	—	0.01 (0.10)
DlogY	0.83 (3.58)	0.85 (6.49)	0.94 (12.64)	0.84 (3.45)
Adjusted R^2	0.87	0.89	0.89	0.86
Standard error	0.0083	0.0078	0.0077	0.0087
Normality	41.3%	63.3%	61.6%	53.5%
DW	1.71	1.54	1.46	1.74
MLM	51.3%	33.1%	23.8%	49.6%
Ljung-Box	63.8%	36.5%	27.5%	61.1%
Heteroskedasticity 1	77.6%	64.3%	83.7%	97.9%
Heteroskedasticity 2	3.1%	37.6%	44.8%	10.5%
Chow test	23.5%	47.0%	64.5%	20.9%
Variance ratio test	22.1%	9.6%	25.9%	2.8%
Generalized Chow test	32.3%	32.2%	70.3%	5.9%
Harvey's Psi (forward)	-2.58	0.17	-1.01	-1.22
Harvey's Psi (backward)	0.44	-0.79	1.34	1.32
F test on $a_1 = a_{-1}'$	—	—	43.6%	—

Table III.3.4. USSR: Estimates of Households' Consumption (3)

(OLS; annual data: 1965-85; dependent variable DlogC)

Variables	Equation A	Equation B	Equation C
Constant	0.10	-0.02	-1.13
	(0.58)	(-2.33)	(-1.25)
$\log (Y/C)_{-1}$	0.38	0.38	0.36
	(1.74)	(2.58)	(1.49)
Dependency ratio	-0.0010	—	-0.0008
	(-0.70)		(-0.20)
Benefit ratio	-0.12	—	-0.09
	(-0.95)		(-0.20)
Real interest rate	-0.04	—	—
	(-0.12)		
IR1	0.04	—	—
	(0.53)		
IR2	—	—	0.01
			(0.09)
DlogY	0.89	0.92	0.87
	(3.97)	(12.38)	(3.86)
Adjusted R^2	0.87	0.89	0.86
Standard error	0.0084	0.0078	0.0085
Normality	59.1%	63.5%	61.9%
DW	1.60	1.46	1.66
MLM	34.7%	23.0%	49.9%
Ljung-Box	41.5%	28.6%	46.9%
Heteroskedasticity 1	95.4%	77.9%	85.4%
Heteroskedasticity 2	23.7%	40.4%	27.6%
Chow test	15.4%	61.2%	20.6%
Variance ratio test	15.7%	22.1%	26.3%
Generalized Chow test	7.0%	64.1%	67.1%
Harvey's Psi (forward)	-1.83	-0.86	-0.57
Harvey's Psi (backward)	0.18	1.35	1.95

Table III.3.5. USSR: Estimates of Households' Consumption
Definitions

Variables

Y = households' disposable income (per capita in real terms)

W = total nonhuman wealth (per capita in real terms)

C = households' consumption (per capita in real terms)

H = human wealth (per capita in real terms)

WFIN = net financial wealth (per capita in real terms)

IR1 = Holzman's disequilibrium indicator (Chart 1, lower panel)

IR2 = relative kolkhoz prices (Chart 1, top panel)

Tests

Normality = Lagrange multiplier test of normality of residuals (Jarque and Bera (1980))

DW = Durbin-Watson test

MLM = Lagrange multiplier test of autocorrelation of residuals modified for small samples (Harvey (1981))

Ljung-Box = portmanteau test of autocorrelation of residuals (Ljung and Box (1978))

Heteroskedasticity1 = test of autoregressive conditional heteroskedasticity (Engle (1982))

Heteroskedasticity2 = test of linear dependence between residuals and regressors (Breusch and Pagan (1979))

Chow test = test of stability of equation parameters against the hypothesis of structural break in 1975

Variance ratio test = test of stability of residual variance against the hypothesis of structural break in 1975 (Phillips and McCabe (1983))

Generalized Chow test = Wald test of stability of equation parameters against the hypothesis of structural break in 1975 in the presence of instability of residual variance (Honda and Ohtani (1984))

Harvey's Psi (forward) = stability test based on recursive estimates (starting from the beginning of the sample period) (Harvey (1981))

Harvey's Psi (backward) = stability test based on recursive estimates (starting from the end of the sample period) (Harvey (1981))

Note: t statistics are reported in parentheses below the coefficient estimates. For all the above tests, with the exception of the DW and of Harvey's Psi test, the table reports the percentage of the appropriate test distribution lying on the right of the computed test statistic under the null hypothesis of absence of misspecification. The lower bound of the DW statistic (at the 5 percent level) is 0.637 in the equation with eight regressors and 1.026 in the equations with four regressors (including the constant). Harvey's Psi test has a t distribution with T-K-1 degrees of freedom.

Table III.3.6. USSR: Estimates of the Wealth Overhang of Households in 1990

(In billions of rubles)

	Based on Model Simulations	Judgmental Estimate of Chronic Overhang	Total Overhang
	(1986-90)		
Equation C (Table III.3.2)	100	59	159
Equation C (Table III.3.3)	103	59	162
Equation B (Table III.3.4)	104	59	163
	(1983-90)		
Equation C (Table III.3.2)	124	48	172
Equation C (Table III.3.3)	131	48	179
Equation B (Table III.3.4)	135	48	183

Table III.3.7. USSR: Composition of Households' Wealth and Saving

(Percentage shares)

	1955-59	1960-64	1965-69	1970-74	1975-79	1980-84	1985-89
Wealth [1]							
Net financial wealth	32.7	40.4	57.1	70.7	79.9	83.3	87.2
Houses	62.4	53.5	34.3	22.9	15.1	11.7	9.0
Other real assets	4.9	6.1	8.6	6.5	5.0	5.0	3.9
Total	100.0	100.0	100.0	100.0	100.0	100.0	100.0
Saving [2]							
Net financial wealth	66.7	65.8	84.9	89.8	93.0	90.4	91.9
Houses	28.8	29.8	9.4	5.9	3.7	4.9	6.1
Other real assets	4.5	4.4	5.7	4.3	3.3	4.7	2.0
Total	100.0	100.0	100.0	100.0	100.0	100.0	100.0

Sources: See statistical note.
1. Composition of wealth at the end of the period.
2. Average composition of saving during the period.

Table III.3.8. USSR: International Comparison of Enterprise Liquidity [1]

	M1 [2]	M2 [3]	Total Financial Assets	M1	M2	Total Financial Assets
	(in percentage of value added at factor cost) [4]			(in percentage of GDP)		
Germany	16.3	26.8	31.1	14.1	23.1	26.8
France	7.4	11.1	20.6	5.6	8.4	15.5
Italy	14.7	20.2	27.4	12.2	16.8	22.8
United Kingdom	6.3	19.0	19.8	4.6	13.8	14.4
USSR	18.8	22.7	22.7	16.7	20.1	20.1

1. Data refer to 1988 for all countries except for the USSR, for which projections for 1990 have been used.
2. Currency and demand deposits.
3. M1 plus time deposits and another short-term assets.
4. Excluding value added of public administration. For the USSR, NMP net of turnover tax but with depreciation added.

413

Chart 1. **USSR : PRICES ON COLLECTIVE FARM MARKETS, 1960-90**
(Relative to state prices)

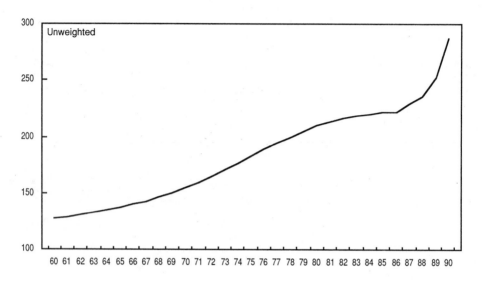

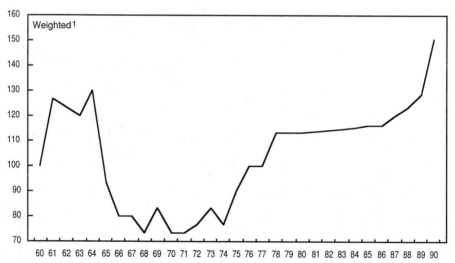

Sources: Dirkens (1981); Nuti (1989); Goskomstat (1989); Alexeev, Gaddy and Leitzel (1990).

1. Unweighted ratio multiplied for the share of output sold in the free market (1960 = 100).
(Holzman's rationing indicator).

Chart 2. **USSR : HOUSEHOLDS' WEALTH, 1955-90**

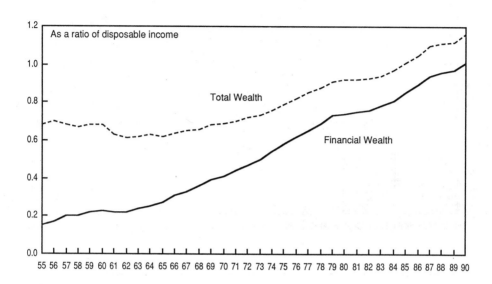

As a ratio of disposable income

Total Wealth

Financial Wealth

55 56 57 58 59 60 61 62 63 64 65 66 67 68 69 70 71 72 73 74 75 76 77 78 79 80 81 82 83 84 85 86 87 88 89 90

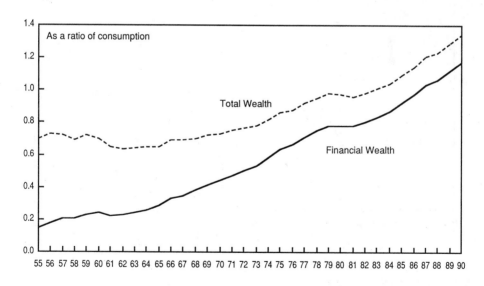

As a ratio of consumption

Total Wealth

Financial Wealth

55 56 57 58 59 60 61 62 63 64 65 66 67 68 69 70 71 72 73 74 75 76 77 78 79 80 81 82 83 84 85 86 87 88 89 90

Sources: See statistical note.

415

Chart 3. **USSR : HOUSEHOLDS' SAVINGS, 1955-90[1]**

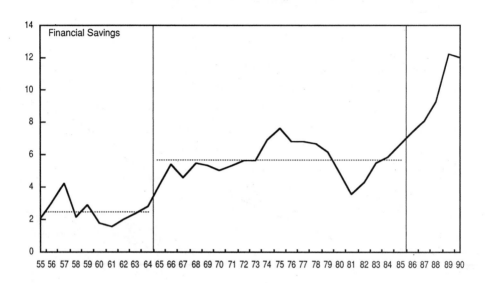

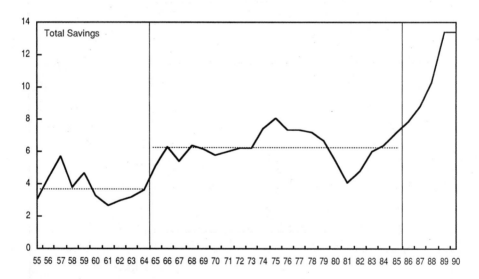

Sources: See statistical note.

1. In percent of disposable income.

Chart 4. **USSR : CONSUMPTION EQUATION**

(Equation C of Table III.3.2)

(Percentage growth rates)

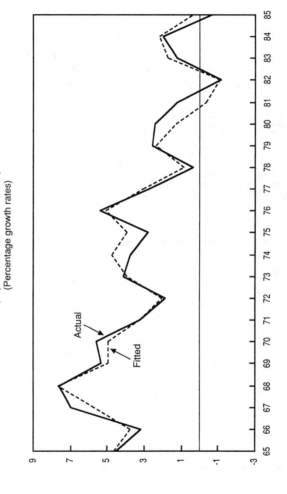

417

Chart 5. **USSR : ENTERPRISE LIQUIDITY**
(Percentage ratios)

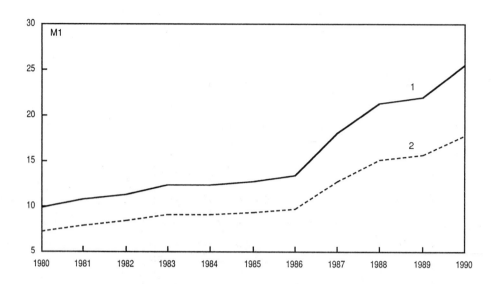

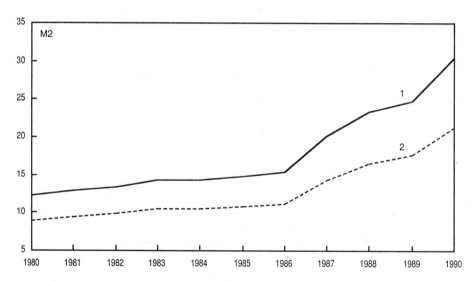

1. In relation to NMP.
2. In relation to GDP.

Chart 6. **USSR : DISTRIBUTION OF BANK DEPOSITS BY NUMBERS OF ACCOUNTS**

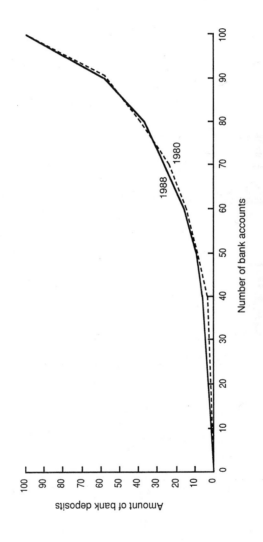

The Exchange and Trade Systems

1. INTRODUCTION AND OUTLOOK[1]

The exchange and trade system has continued to be largely shaped by central planning. Most trade and capital transactions are determined within the framework of the annual foreign exchange plan which has been derived from the state plan. Similarly, the policies governing external borrowing and reserves are specified in the foreign exchange plan and executed by the Vneshekonombank (VEB). In this system, the exchange rate has played only a minor role in the allocation of resources. For most products, differences between foreign and domestic prices at the prevailing exchange rate have continued to be compensated by so-called price equalization taxes or subsidies. Since 1986, however, several steps have been taken towards decentralizing trade and foreign exchange operations. Foreign trade has been partially liberalized, and enterprises have been allowed to borrow abroad against a license obtained from the VEB. So-called differentiated foreign exchange coefficients (DVKs) were established for many products in 1987 with the intention of making enterprises more sensitive to changes in foreign currency prices. Moreover, foreign exchange retention quotas were introduced in 1987, and foreign exchange auctions established in 1989.

The liberalization measures were accompanied by a relaxation of domestic financial policies leading to a sharp increase in imports and external borrowing by firms which were not in a position to honor their debt service obligations on a timely basis. Moreover, the official exchange rate was kept largely unchanged throughout this period at a level which did not reflect market conditions. As a result, excessive demand for foreign exchange has increased rapidly in recent years, as reflected in movements of the parallel market exchange rate. Moreover, frequent—and often ad hoc—changes in the trade and foreign exchange regulations have made the system highly complex and lacking in transparency, which has added to uncertainty among the rapidly growing number of foreign traders as well as foreign trading partners. By contrast to a number of other CMEA countries, however, the liberalization of the exchange system has not yet given rise to a substantial amount of foreign exchange deposits or foreign retention rights by enterprises and households (3.1 billion valuta rubles in October 1990), which tend to complicate the conduct of monetary policy.

Given the existence of the foreign exchange allocation system and multiple exchange rates, external transactions generally have not been guided by market signals or by efficiency considerations. For transactions in convertible currencies, several exchange rates have been in effect: the official exchange rate, the special exchange rate (mainly for tourist transactions), an auction rate (for a very limited number of transactions), and since November 1, 1990, a commercial exchange rate. In addition, the existence of the DVK system has effectively resulted in a multiplicity of exchange rates applying to different foreign trade transactions. For transactions with CMEA countries, special trade, pricing, and settlements provisions have been in place, with different exchange rates for commercial and noncommercial transactions which also have had little—if any—relation to market levels. These arrangements will change in 1991 with the dismantling of the CMEA system.

Under the presidential guidelines for reform, the ruble is to become convertible in time, but steps and a timetable for achieving this objective have not been described. Initial reforms were introduced in November 1990 with the introduction of a commercial exchange rate which was substantially depreciated compared with the official exchange rate. The commercial exchange rate would be used for export receipts surrendered and all capital inflows, as well as for imports for the use of government agencies or arranged on the basis of state orders, most business services and all government debt service in accordance with the foreign exchange allocation plan. At the same time, a number of other changes were made in the exchange and trade system. Specifically, the DVKs were eliminated, higher retention quotas were granted for some exports, import taxes were substantially reduced and export taxes were introduced for the main raw materials. The introduction of the commercial exchange rate at a sharply depreciated level compared with the previous official exchange rate and the simultaneous removal of DVKs would tend to promote a more efficient and transparent foreign exchange system. The overall impact of the reforms on competitiveness is, however, less clear. On balance, it is unlikely to be a major improvement.

The presidential guidelines also foresaw that some portion of the foreign exchange retained by enterprises, supplemented by official foreign exchange holdings, would be sold in the free market to economic entities wishing to import and make other payments not included in the foreign exchange allocation plan. Except for a small list of banned items, there would be no quota restrictions on imports. Exports of goods of national importance would be subject to quotas. According to the guidelines, state orders would continue to be in effect for basic export goods in 1991 and 1992 at a level sufficient to meet the country's minimum foreign exchange requirements.

If the objective of establishing convertibility of the ruble for current account transactions is to be achieved, several further steps of reform will be necessary. Export quotas would need to be liberalized and lifted in line with progress in domestic reforms. Similarly, payments for current invisibles would need to be liberalized progressively. At the same time, the different exchange rates would need to be unified. In particular, the commercial exchange rate and the free market rate, which together account for most of the foreign exchange transactions, should converge. The convergence would be facilitated by the elimination of the monetary overhang and the tightening of financial policies, which would tend to appreciate the free market exchange rate. More specific measures to achieve convergence would include the shifting of a progressively larger share of transactions, including imports by the government and those heretofore subject to state orders, toward the free market and the sale of official foreign exchange holdings in the free market (subject to the reserves objective). Exporters should also be required to tender to the foreign exchange market, within a set time, the foreign exchange they are allowed to retain, and not be allowed to hold balances indefinitely in retention accounts. In the context of price liberalization, the convergence of rates is also likely to require a further depreciation of the commercial exchange rate.

2. EXCHANGE RATE ARRANGEMENTS

Exchange rate arrangements in the USSR are complex, and responsibilities for setting and monitoring exchange rates are divided among several institutions. Given the derived nature of most exports and imports as part of the national production plan, exchange rates have until recently not played a significant role in stimulating foreign trade flows, the bulk of the latter instead being assured by state orders irrespective of profitability. The system of price equalization taxes and subsidies has been used to offset the profits or losses accruing to enterprises as a result of the differences between foreign currency prices for traded goods (converted at the official exchange rate) and domestic wholesale prices. Beginning in 1987, however, many products were assigned differentiated foreign exchange coefficients (DVKs). By keeping DVKs unchanged in a situation of changing foreign prices, importing or exporting enterprises would experience changes in their profits which might make them more responsive to changes in world market conditions. Responsibility for determining exchange rates with the convertible currency area is vested in Gosbank (the official rate, the commercial rate and the special exchange rate) and the Vneshekonombank (the auction rate and forward rates). For the nonconvertible area, both commercial and noncommercial exchange rates with the CMEA countries and other socialist countries are set by the Council of Ministers on the basis of intergovernmental agreements negotiated by the Ministry of Finance.

a. The official exchange rate

The official exchange rate of the ruble for transactions with nonsocialist countries[2] is derived on the basis of a peg to a basket of currencies (Table III.4.1). A change in the level of the peg requires a decision by the USSR Council of Ministers based on a proposal by the principal financial authorities, notably, the Ministry of Finance, Gosbank and the Vneshekonombank (VEB).[3] For a given level of the peg, the setting of official exchange rates for the ruble is entrusted to Gosbank in accordance with its statutes as approved by Decree No. 1061 of the USSR Council of Ministers of September 1, 1988. Because of the system of price equalization taxes and subsidies under the traditional system of central planning, the rubles converted at the official exchange rate (so-called valuta rubles) were simply accounting units. Historically, Soviet trade statistics have been published in terms of valuta rubles.

(1) Background

A decree of the USSR Council of Ministers of November 15, 1961 set the gold content of the ruble at 0.987412 grams of fine gold, yielding an official exchange rate of rub 0.90 per U.S. dollar. The exchange rates for other foreign currencies were also altered at that time in accordance with the ruble's new gold content and Gosbank was instructed to modify them subsequently in accordance with any changes in the gold content of these currencies. At the same time, the practice of establishing premia or discounts to the official exchange rates of freely convertible currencies for noncommercial transactions was discontinued and hence, from 1961 to November 1989, when a special exchange rate for foreign tourists and various noncommercial transactions was introduced, the USSR used the same exchange rate for both commercial and noncommercial operations in the currencies of nonsocialist countries.

The devaluation of the U.S. dollar in 1971 and its transition to floating in 1973 led to an adaptation of a new methodology for setting the exchange rates. From March 1973, the unweighted average percentage deviation of the current market exchange rates of 14 major freely convertible currencies from their settlement parities or central rates against the U.S. dollar was used to determine the exchange rates of these currencies against the ruble. Later, the current market exchange rates of the 14 foreign currencies, taken as the basis for calculating the rates against the ruble for the preceding month, replaced the settlement parities or central rates as the basis for determining the exchange rate.

A new method of exchange rate determination that was more appropriate to the changed conditions in international currency markets and to the pattern of the USSR's settlements with the nonsocialist countries was adopted in November 1977 pursuant to a decision of the Chairman of the Gosbank Board dated September 14, 1977. Since then, the value of the valuta ruble has been determined on the basis of a weighted basket of currencies. Under the new method, relative basket weights and base rates are used to calculate a foreign exchange component for each currency in the basket and then to compute a settlement rate against the ruble for one of the basket currencies, such as the U.S. dollar. Exchange rates for the other basket currencies are then derived from their current market exchange rates against the U.S dollar and the latter's rate against the ruble (Table III.4.2).

The original currency basket contained 14 currencies. Each of these currencies accounted for at least 0.5 percent of the USSR's external settlements and the basket covered the bulk of these settlements. Several changes, none of them fundamental in nature, have been made in the methodology since then. In particular, the structure of the basket and the relative weights of its constituent currencies have undergone certain revisions.

(2) Current method of calculation

On September 1, 1981, the number of currencies included in the basket was reduced from 14 to 6. While these currencies retain the same proportion to each other in the new basket as they had before, their relative weights were normalized to add up to 100 percent. Thus, the current basket composition is as follows: U.S. dollar - 42 percent; deutsche mark - 19 percent; pound sterling, French franc and Swiss franc - 10 percent; and Japanese yen - 9 percent. Changes have also been made in the base rates used for calculating the ruble rates against foreign currencies. Initially, the average of market exchange rates in the three months preceding the date of calculation had been used. In view of the sharp fluctuations of the cross rates of the other currencies against the U.S. dollar, the base rates were changed to the exchange rates set by Gosbank on the date immediately preceding the calculation.

Proposals to change the exchange rates for foreign currencies against the valuta ruble are prepared by Gosbank. At first, new rates were set at the beginning of each month, then on the first and sixteenth day of each month and—since September 1986—each week. Proposals to change the exchange rates of foreign currencies against the valuta ruble are made official through orders of Gosbank's Board, signed by its Chairman or his first deputy. Based on these orders, a foreign exchange bulletin—currently containing exchange rates for 35 currencies (including the ECU)—is issued at the beginning of each month and distributed to interested organizations in the USSR and abroad. Weekly changes in the exchange rates are published in *Izvestiia*. In addition, exchange rates for another 80 currencies (including the SDR) that are not officially quoted by Gosbank are published once a month for information purposes. This bulletin is sent to interested organizations.

The current practice in changing exchange rate quotations is as follows. For 17 currencies and the ECU the exchange rates are changed weekly.[4] For another six currencies the exchange rate is recalculated only once a month and a new rate is promulgated only if it deviates by more than 1 percent from the existing rate.[5] For the remaining 11 currencies, a new rate is set once a month provided that the new rate deviates by more than 5 percent from the existing one.[6] For six of the 34 currencies, banknotes and coins are not bought by Gosbank.[7] There are no prescribed commissions on the buying and selling of foreign exchange at the official rates and buying and selling rates are identical with the official ones.

Changes in the list of currencies included in the official bulletin are made from time to time. Thus, the currencies of Algeria, Guinea and Iraq were removed during 1987-88 and shifted to the list of currencies not officially quoted. This made it possible to appreciate the ruble against these currencies in an attempt to encourage the use of local currency balances accumulated in the accounts of Soviet organizations operating in those countries. Another change was the inclusion from November 1989 of a special exchange rate for 17 of the currencies in the official bulletin. The bulletin is expected to be revised shortly to reflect the introduction of the commercial exchange rate on November 1, 1990.

Since March 1988, Soviet enterprises and organizations have been offered forward exchange contracts to hedge against exchange rate risks. Forward exchange contracts can be arranged through the VEB for the principal 17 currencies and the ECU. Contracts offered range from 1 to 12 months. The volume of hedging operations has so far remained small. Alternatively, Soviet exporters or importers have been using foreign exchange reservations, often in SDRs and Swedish kronor.[8]

b. The commercial exchange rate

A new commercial exchange rate was introduced from November 1, 1990 at a rate of initially rub 1.6624 = US$1.[9] The commercial rate was to apply to the settlement of most current account transactions (other than those involving retained export earnings or imports not covered by the foreign exchange allocation plan), inward and outward capital investments, and nontrade transactions carried out by juridical persons. It was also to be used for most accounting and customs valuation purposes.[10] The rate was set at a level that was estimated to ensure that 90 percent of exports were profitable (in the sense that at this rate, the exporter's local currency proceeds were at least as high as the domestic wholesale price). As domestic prices were not adjusted to pass on the new exchange rate to consumers and industrial users, the so-called budget efficiency was reduced to a lower level.[11] Gosbank was to adjust the commercial rate, which is depreciated by two thirds in relation to the official rate, in line with the basket of the six currencies governing the official exchange rate.

c. Special exchange rates

Since November 1989 a special rate (equivalent to ten times the official rate) has been in effect for the purchase of foreign exchange from foreign tourists and various noncommercial transactions such as sales of foreign exchange to enterprises for business travel abroad—up to the amount of foreign exchange surrendered by these enterprises—and to natural persons for the purposes indicated in section 4.b below. This rate is quoted for the 17 exchange rates that are changed weekly.

Special foreign exchange rates also exist with a number of countries for the crediting of debt service payments to the USSR to special accounts that are used for payment for Soviet imports from those countries. In the case of India, ruble credits are repaid in rupees at a rate calculated by correcting the 1979 gold parity of rub 1 = Rs. 10 on the basis of daily calculations by the Reserve Bank of India of a 16 currency basket (the original SDR basket). As a result of this correction, the special rate was rub 1 = Rs. 21.22 (or about rub 4.71 = Rs. 100) in early September 1990, compared with a rate of rub 3.40 = Rs. 100 in effect for commercial transactions on September 5, 1990. In the case of Syria, the pre-1971 gold parity of the ruble and the pound sterling is adjusted monthly by the average of weekly calculations of the deviations of the exchange rates of 15 currencies against the pound sterling from their base period exchange rates. Similar arrangements exist with Algeria and Libya.

d. Market-determined exchange rates

Since November 1989, foreign currency auctions have been conducted on the basis of Decree No. 1,405 of the USSR Council of Ministers of December 2, 1988 (on Measures to Establish an All-Union Foreign Exchange Market).[12] The auctions, which were until recently conducted about once a month, are organized by the VEB and carried out by an auction committee composed of representatives of Gosplan, the Ministry of Finance, Gosbank and VEB.[13] The auctions are governed by the rules and regulations adopted for this purpose by these ministries and agencies. These rules and regulations have been modified as experience has been gained with the auctions.

The circle of parties authorized to participate in the auctions has grown over time to include state production and scientific production enterprises, associations and organizations; commercial associations established by these bodies; production enterprises of public organizations; design, research and development organizations operating on a self-financing basis; and state and collective farms and other organizations in the agro-industrial sector. Joint ventures and production cooperatives were admitted from October 25, 1990. Since April 1990, a single price (in terms of rubles per valuta ruble) has been established in each auction. As a result, all participants end up buying or selling foreign currency on the same

427

terms. The foreign exchange acquired in the auctions can be used without limitation except that only 25 percent of foreign exchange holdings can be used to purchase consumer goods for the workers of the organization.

Purchasers must pay an auction fee of rub 200 while sellers pay a commission of 1 percent (but not exceeding rub 1,000 per transaction) of the amount sold. With the introduction of the commercial exchange rate on November 1, 1990, the minimum amount for sales at auction was raised from 50,000 to 150,000 valuta rubles and the minimum amount for purchases was raised from 10,000 to 30,000 valuta rubles.

The amounts sold at auction to date have remained modest (about US$150 million, or about 0.3 percent of estimated 1990 convertible currency imports, in the 11 auctions held until November 15, 1990 (Table III.4.3)). The foreign exchange premium over the official rate rose steadily in the first seven auctions from 1,400 percent to 4,000 percent (from rub 15.2 to rub 41.2 per valuta ruble, or rub 9.5 to rub 24.2 per U.S. dollar), but stabilized in the eighth auction, which was the largest so far (some US$20 million) and included 60 sellers and 37 buyers. In October-November 1990, the exchange rate appreciated slightly.

The presidential decree that introduced the commercial exchange rate also called for the introduction of a free exchange market for juridical persons with effect from January 1, 1991 in the form of an interbank market, a trading floor for foreign exchange, an auction or in another form. The new arrangement would replace the VEB auctions. Only licensed commercial banks (which had hitherto been prevented from participation) and brokers would be able to trade in the auctions.

e. The black market exchange rate

Parallel market transactions are illegal and the purchase or sale of foreign exchange by individuals is punishable, e.g., under Article 88 of the penal code of the RSFSR. Available data indicate that the exchange rate for the U.S. dollar in mid-October 1990 was rub 15-16 (buying) and rub 18-20 (selling) in Moscow and rub 10.6 (buying) and rub 30.0 (selling) in Vienna (Table III.4.4). Apart from Moscow, major domestic black markets are in Leningrad, Klaipeda and resort towns with foreign visitors. The black market rates abroad appear to be more volatile than the domestic ones. Thus, the black market ruble in Vienna appreciated temporarily in July 1990 (by some 24 percent on a mid-point basis) after the Soviet authorities restricted travel to the Czech and Slovak Federal Republic, Hungary and Poland. Reported cross rates between the U.S. dollar and other foreign currencies are broadly consistent in the black markets, which testifies to their comparative efficiency. Nonetheless, buying-selling spreads remain large.

f. Exchange rates with the nonconvertible currency area

(1) The transferable ruble

Since 1964, commercial transactions with member countries of the CMEA have been conducted in terms of transferable rubles through accounts maintained by the International Bank for Economic Cooperation (IBEC). The official exchange rate of the transferable ruble (TR) in terms of the valuta ruble has been maintained at rub 1 = TR 1, except for a brief period in 1973-74 when it was set at rub 1.2 = TR 1. Other CMEA member countries also have set, and occasionally changed, the exchange rates of their currencies vis-à-vis the transferable ruble. Initially, the exchange rate between the transferable ruble and the U.S. dollar was determined on the basis of the gold content of the two currencies, with the gold content of the transferable ruble being identical to that of the ruble (TR 1 = 0.987412 grams of fine gold). Hence, the exchange rate was TR 0.9 = US$1. After the U.S. dollar began to float in 1973, the method of calculation for the transferable ruble was changed to an 11 currency basket and the U.S. dollar exchange rate for the transferable ruble reflected the unweighted average of deviations of the market exchange rates of the basket currencies from their settlement parities or central rates. In 1978, the transferable ruble was pegged to a basket of 12 currencies, each of which represents at least 1 percent of convertible currency settlements of CMEA member countries. The basket, which in principle is to be updated every year, has since January 1, 1988 had the following composition:

Currency	Weight in percent
U.S. dollar	49
Deutsche mark	18
French franc	6
Pound sterling	5
Austrian schilling	5
Italian lira	4
Japanese yen	3
Swiss franc	2
Dutch guilder	2
Belgian franc	2
Swedish krona	2
Canadian dollar	1

The base rate of the transferable ruble against the U.S. dollar was determined on the basis of the average exchange rates of the 11 other currencies in the basket during the three months preceding the changeover to the new basket. The IBEC recalculates the basket each day.[14] If the calculated exchange rate for the U.S. dollar deviates by more than 1 percent from the existing one, all of the posted exchange rates for the transferable ruble are changed. It should be noted that

429

non-dollar exchange rates are changed only if the threshold value for the U.S. dollar is exceeded.

The adoption of different weighting schemes for the determination of exchange rates of the valuta ruble and the transferable ruble for convertible currencies has produced cross rates between the ruble and the transferable ruble that deviate from parity. As in the case of exports paid in convertible currencies, there is a retention scheme for exports against transferable rubles. While no auctions of transferable rubles have been held so far, the VEB has arranged bilateral deals among enterprises and organizations.[15] The exchange rates agreed in these deals carried premia for the transferable ruble in the range of 30 to 100 percent.

(2) Other exchange rates for transactions with socialist countries

Bilaterally agreed exchange rates for commercial transactions settled in national currencies exist for the Bulgarian lev, the North Korean won, the Mongolian tugrik, the Polish zloty and the Czechoslovak koruna.

Decree No. 664 of the USSR Council of Ministers of April 9, 1984 empowers the Ministry of Finance to set the exchange rates of the socialist countries' currencies against the ruble for noncommercial transactions, as defined in a 1971 agreement among the participating socialist countries.[16] Under a methodology agreed among the socialist countries, the noncommercial exchange rates are to reflect the purchasing power of each currency. Initially, a basket representative of the living expenses of a diplomat's family of four was used. Later, allowance also was made for tourist expenditures. The basket currently used for these calculations distinguishes three groups: foodstuffs, durable consumer goods, and services. Both volumes and prices are agreed at the level of the CMEA. In principle, the purchasing power rates of the resulting matrix are not allowed to deviate by more than 20 percent (previously 10 percent) from the corresponding transferable ruble cross rates for each pair of countries. In fact, exchange rates have been set on a bilateral basis in recent years and have resulted in large breaks in cross rates (Table III.4.6).

The noncommercial transactions are settled through the central banks of the countries participating in the agreements of 1963 and 1971 (or banks authorized by the respective central banks). Accumulated balances in the interest-free accounts opened for this purpose are consolidated at the end of each year by applying a conversion coefficient which is designed to adjust for the difference between the average levels of CMEA prices (as reflected in the above described basket) and world market prices outside the CMEA area. Because of differing rates of inflation over time, the coefficient has been reduced from 3.4 in 1963 to 2.3 in 1971 and 1.6 now. The consolidated and converted balances are added to each pair of countries' accounts with IBEC. The USSR served notice that it wanted to terminate the arrangement for noncommercial transactions from November 1, 1990.

430

3. FOREIGN EXCHANGE ALLOCATION AND PAYMENTS

a. General principles of Soviet foreign exchange law

The authority to make basic changes in the foreign exchange control regulations lies with the Supreme Soviet. The President and the Council of Ministers may also regulate exchange control matters by way of decrees. The State Foreign Economic Commission (GVK), a standing body of the USSR Council of Ministers established in August 1986, coordinates all foreign economic relations and oversees the activities in this area of Gosplan, Gosbank, the Ministry of Finance, the Ministry of Foreign Economic Relations (MVES), the VEB, the Central Customs Office, Intourist, and other organizations dealing with foreign trade and economic relations. Implementing regulations in the exchange control area are prepared and issued by various central bodies, particularly the Ministry of Finance and the VEB. Responsibility for implementation of foreign exchange regulations is vested in the Ministry of Finance and the VEB.

Exchange control regulations differentiate between the treatment of juridical and natural persons. Except for some liberalization for natural persons initiated in July 1990, the regulations have remained highly centralized and restrictive. A draft foreign exchange control law that, *inter alia*, would introduce the internationally accepted distinction between residents and nonresidents, is before the Supreme Soviet of the USSR. Under the provisions of the draft law, the powers of Gosbank would be strengthened, in part at the expense of the VEB. Thus, it is foreseen that Gosbank would regulate the foreign exchange market and government indebtedness, and determine the criteria for permitting commercial banks to undertake foreign exchange operations and exercise general control over their activity.

All transactions in foreign exchange between juridical persons in the territory of the USSR must be made through the VEB or, with its permission, through other banks. In November 1990, six out of some 300 banking institutions had been licensed to carry out such transactions. All transactions between juridical persons in the territory of the USSR must be carried out on a noncash basis (i.e., by crediting and debiting accounts). All juridical persons established in the USSR must keep their foreign exchange in accounts maintained with the VEB. Funds may be kept in banks abroad only with the permission of the VEB. All transactions in the territory of the USSR between Soviet juridical persons and foreign companies have international character and must be made in foreign exchange, with the following two exceptions: the Ministry of Finance may allow transfers in rubles if they are up to rub 100,000 in the case of foreign companies from the convertible currency area, and up to rub 500,000 if they are from socialist countries. All payments between Soviet juridical persons in the territory of the USSR must be denominated in rubles except that (i) joint ventures can buy and sell against foreign exchange on the basis of agreed prices and currencies, and (ii) subcontractors can receive payment in foreign currency from a Soviet exporter up to the value of their own sale to the exporter.[17] Soviet juridical persons have the right to participate in foreign currency auctions at freely determined exchange rates. All Soviet juridical persons are eligible to obtain foreign currency credit through the VEB, except for joint ventures, which may get such credit from foreign banks with the permission of the VEB.

The following principles govern foreign exchange law for natural persons. All foreign exchange must be obtained from the VEB. Soviet law does not make a distinction between residents and nonresidents. However, for natural persons there is such a distinction in practice. Foreign citizens as well as stateless persons who have been given the right to reside in a foreign country or in the USSR may open accounts "A". Foreign exchange can be credited to accounts "A" without limitation and these accounts can be debited to make payments abroad or to other accounts "A" and, with the permission of the Ministry of Finance, to the accounts of Soviet citizens. The latter, as well as foreigners living permanently in the USSR ("residents"), may have either of two types of accounts: accounts "V"— denominated in valuta rubles—to accumulate foreign exchange from wages, grants, prize money, and honoraria from sports, cultural or literary events or accounts "B"—denominated in foreign exchange—for legacies, pensions and alimony receipts. Balances in either type of account can be (i) taken out of the country in the form of cash with a certification of withdrawal; (ii) transferred abroad with the permission of the Ministry of Finance; or (iii) spent in foreign currency stores. Special conversion coefficients are applied when funds in those accounts are spent in shops selling imported goods for rubles or when they are converted to rubles. With the introduction of the commercial exchange rate on November 1, 1990, the conversion rate for purchases in shops selling imported goods for rubles was changed from rub 4.6 to rub 1.53 per valuta ruble and the conversion rate for rubles was changed from rub 10 to rub 3.3 per valuta ruble.

The distinction between accounts "B" and "V" has been blurred since Soviet citizens and foreigners living permanently in the USSR were given the right, by a decree issued in July 1990,[18] to open foreign exchange accounts without disclosing the provenance of the funds deposited. In October 1990, balances held in accounts "A", "B" and "V" amounted to rub 0.5 billion.

b. Prescription of currency

Payments to and from countries with which the USSR maintains multilateral or bilateral payments agreements are made in the currencies and in accordance with the terms and procedures set forth in these agreements. If there are no specific agreements, or if transactions take place outside the scope of the agreements, settlement is made in convertible currency. Barter deals are generally discouraged (but see the discussion of licensing for barter deals in section 4.a.(2) below) and require the approval of the Council of Ministers.

(1) CMEA arrangements

Since its inception in 1964, the multilateral payments agreement managed by the IBEC under the aegis of the CMEA has been by far the predominant prescription of currency arrangement. The transferable ruble[19] is used widely in the economic and financial cooperation of CMEA member countries, in particular to express prices and denominate transactions and bilateral balances within IBEC. Transactions settled in transferable rubles include most intra-CMEA commodity trade, services, credits, consolidated and converted balances of past noncommercial transactions, and certain other transactions. Some transactions, including trade in the form of so-called currency goods, are carried out on the basis of bilateral agreements for goods expressed at world market prices. An example is an agreement between the USSR and Poland to channel about 15 percent (or some TR 800 million) of protocol trade in 1990 through bilateral accounts.[20] The bilateral transferable ruble accounts maintained by IBEC for CMEA members have no explicit limits. Efforts are made to avoid imbalances—and where they arise, to reverse them—through trade flow planning within the framework of five-year plans and annual protocols. However, in recent years deviations of annual results from plan indicators have become more sizeable as intra-CMEA trade has begun to move away from quotas and state orders intermediated by foreign trade organizations to nonquota trade conducted directly by producers and end-users in the USSR and/or some of the European CMEA member countries.

Payments deficits of individual CMEA countries are covered by IBEC credits to the authorized bank of the debtor country, the sources of which are the IBEC's own funds or transferable ruble assets of other member countries. Two types of credit are extended. First, transfer credits are granted automatically at an interest rate of 3.5 percent a year up to annually approved limits equivalent to 2 percent of the value of CMEA trade of the corresponding country in the preceding calendar year. These credits are automatically reduced by payments surpluses. Second, term credits are granted for a period of six months to three years at interest rates of 3.75 percent to 5 percent a year (Table III.4.8). They are extended on the basis of an annually approved credit plan, with general limits for individual countries, which is compiled on the basis of projections of receipts and payments during the year with a breakdown by countries and types of transaction. After the limits on transfer and term credits are exhausted, the authorized bank of the debtor country can turn to the IBEC with a detailed substantiation of the need for additional credit. Such credit can be granted with approval of the IBEC Council. In exceptional cases, when a member country has a persistent deficit, credits with terms in excess of three years can be negotiated bilaterally with surplus countries.

Specified noncommercial transactions are effected under a 1971 agreement. As described above, these transactions are effected at special exchange rates and the accumulated balances at year-end are converted to transferable rubles using

433

conversion coefficients and added to creditor and debtor positions vis-à-vis the IBEC.

(2) Bilateral payments agreements

Bilateral payments agreements exist with socialist countries that are not members of CMEA (Albania, Cambodia, China, Lao P.D.R., North Korea, and Yugoslavia) and, since 1990, Poland. Other bilateral payments agreements are in effect with Finland and a number of developing countries (Afghanistan, Egypt, Ethiopia, India, Iran, and Syria). The most important of these agreements in terms of turnover are those with Finland and India.

The first bilateral payments agreement with Finland was concluded in 1940. Since 1950, trade and payments agreements have been negotiated on a five-year cycle. Detailed commodity lists are agreed within annually negotiated protocols. Prices are based on cash world market prices prevailing at the time of delivery. These prices are converted to clearing rubles (the currency of the clearing accounts) at Gosbank's official exchange rate. With the recent introduction of the commercial exchange rate, new practices in this regard are being discussed. The present clearing arrangement with Finland is based on a five-year agreement covering 1986-90. Under its 1989 protocol, the USSR's exports and imports amounted to about US$2.8 billion and US$3.4 billion, respectively. About one fifth of these transactions were settled in convertible currency. In 1987, a special interest-bearing medium-term account, repayable in quarterly installments in convertible currency, was introduced to accommodate Finland's substantial claims beyond the swing limit (of currently rub 200 million). Since 1988, all claims beyond rub 100 million earn interest at prevailing international money market rates, and all balances beyond the swing limit are protected by an exchange rate guarantee. In October 1989, a new five-year agreement covering the period 1991-95 was signed. The new agreement envisaged that the clearing system would continue to serve as a basis for settling payments between the USSR and Finland. However, more extensive possibilities to settle commercial transactions in freely convertible currency were to be developed. In early December 1990, agreement was reportedly reached to settle bilateral trade in convertible currencies from 1991, although outstanding orders would be settled in an offsetting fashion.

The agreement with India has been in effect since 1953. Annual trade plans within the framework of five-year agreements have in recent years been drawn up in such a way as to permit India to service its debt arising from Soviet export credits for military equipment, technical services and the construction of industrial plants. Thus, data for the Indian fiscal year ended March 1990 indicate planned Soviet exports of US$1.7 billion and imports of US$2.5 billion. Actual trade values came close, with exports slightly exceeding, and imports slightly trailing, planned values. While prices may be quoted in third-country currencies (e.g., Soviet oil exports in U.S. dollars), accounts are maintained, and payments are

434

made, in Indian rupees. The USSR maintains working balances with commercial banks in India. Excess balances are transferred to a central account with the Reserve Bank of India, which invests them in Indian Treasury bills. When the USSR makes payments, the Reserve Bank discounts the bills and transfers Indian rupees to the designated commercial bank. If India has payments surpluses, a technical credit in rupees is provided to the USSR at an interest rate comparable to the Treasury bill rate. Outstanding balances are revalued whenever the value of the Indian rupee changes by more than 3 percent against the original SDR basket of 16 currencies.

From January 1, 1991, commercial transactions with Yugoslavia are also scheduled to be switched from clearing dollars to convertible currency. Under an agreement signed in October 1990, trade with China is to be conducted from January 1, 1991 in convertible currencies.[21]

4. TRADE IN GOODS AND SERVICES AND TRANSFERS

a. Exports and imports[22]

Recent years have witnessed considerable changes in the regulatory, organizational and incentive structures of foreign trade. As a result, the trade system has moved from one of strict state monopoly, which had been established as early as April 1918 and under which foreign transactions were tightly controlled through the annual plan and quarterly foreign exchange budgets, to a more decentralized one involving more than 20,000 registered agents with trading rights.

(1) Trading rights

While Gosplan and, since its creation in August 1986, the State Foreign Economic Commission (GVK) continue to be responsible for preparing the annual foreign trade plan, the Ministry for Foreign Economic Relations (MVES) has been the main executive body for the coordination of foreign trade since the beginning of 1988. Until then, this function had been discharged jointly by the State Committee for Foreign Economic Relations, which oversaw 12 specialized all-union Foreign Trade Organizations (FTOs), and the Ministry of Foreign Trade, which oversaw 30 FTOs. Separate trading rights had been enjoyed by the Ministries of Civil Aviation, Ocean Transportation, Railways, Communication, and Finance (for planned noncommercial operations), Intourist, Gosbank, and a few others. Also, in August 1986 the Government had decided to give trading rights to other organizations.[23] As a result, some 100 new trading organizations (many of them for machinery) had appeared by April 1, 1989 when all enterprises (including joint ventures), associations, production cooperatives, and other organizations whose products (works, services) were deemed competitive in foreign markets were allowed to register with the MVES to import or export any product contained in a list approved by the Council of Ministers.[24] By the second half of 1990, more than 20,000 firms had been registered, including 7,500 state enterprises, 3,500 cooperatives and 1,800 joint ventures. However, the number of firms actually engaged in foreign trade was significantly smaller (perhaps only one third as many).

MVES currently controls 25 FTOs, which account for some 70 percent and 50 percent of total exports and imports, respectively. The high share of these FTOs in foreign trade—it is higher still in trade with the convertible currency area—is due to the fact that they cover raw materials (ores and metals) and energy products (oil, gas, and coal). MVES is also responsible for the implementation of construction projects abroad (mostly in CMEA countries and countries with bilateral payments agreements), and those in the USSR that are based on government-to-government agreements. Other FTOs have been assigned to branch ministries and offices. In addition, republics, some local government bodies (Moscow and Leningrad) and various associations have formed their own specialized FTOs.

Enterprises can avail themselves of the services of existing FTOs or apply to the MVES for direct trading rights. To register, a firm must state the product or products in which it intends to trade and pay a one-time registration fee of rub 250. The registration process includes the following steps:[25] submission of the application form; assignment of a registration number that is to be used for customs purposes and license applications; entry into the official State Register of Participants in Foreign Economic Relations; issuance of a registration certificate; and notification on the part of the MVES of the appropriate government bodies. The registration process is to be completed within 30 days from the date the application is received. Registration of joint ventures is automatic with their authorization to operate by the Ministry of Finance.[26] There is a short list of prohibited items that includes precious stones and metals, drugs, nuclear materials and weapons. Also, the purchase of domestic goods for resale abroad or the import of goods for domestic resale or re-export is generally not permitted.

(2) Trade licensing

The MVES, with the approval of the State Foreign Economic Commission, is empowered to administer for specified time periods restrictions on exports and imports of certain goods and services and to certain countries or groups of countries, as required by balance of payments or other considerations, including in particular the regulation of supply and demand in the internal market, the compliance with export or import commitments, the achievement of advantageous understandings in commercial negotiations, and retaliation against discriminatory actions. The restrictions take the form of quantitative or value quotas. Exempt from the quotas are (i) commodities imported to service foreign loans extended by the USSR or needed for the construction of projects in the territory of the

USSR, and (ii) the imports and exports of joint ventures and international associations and organizations.

Trade falling under such restrictions as well as products (works, services) included in the list of goods of general state importance are subject to licensing. Licenses can also be required as a punitive measure for participants in foreign economic relations that have practiced dishonest competition or caused harm to the interests of the state. Licenses, which are nontransferable, can be issued as either general licenses for certain types of transactions with a validity period of, as a rule, up to one year or as one-time licenses for a specific transaction with a validity period limited to the time necessary to complete the transaction, but not to exceed one year. Where justified, the validity period of either type of license may be extended.

Licenses for exports or imports of goods of general state importance are issued by the appropriate government bodies in accordance with the responsibilities assigned to them in the lists of products (works, services) approved for 1989 and 1990 by the USSR Council of Ministers (Tables III.4.9 and III.4.10). Such licenses are issued for a specified quantity or value of deliveries (where necessary, with price recommendations). Specialized FTOs receive, as a rule, general licenses under the state planning targets to export or import the corresponding item. Enterprises, associations, production cooperatives, and other Soviet organizations receive one-time licenses.

Licenses for items subject to restriction are issued by the MVES for the quantity or value of delivery (where necessary, with price recommendations) for each separate transaction (one-time licenses). Preference in filling the quotas covering restricted items is given to specialized FTOs and exporters or importers that offer the best trading conditions.

A copy of the license must be attached to the customs declaration and serves as the basis for permission for the licensed freight to cross the USSR state border. Licensees must notify the issuing government body of the conclusion of the trade transaction. Licenses are generally issued within 7-10 days but must be approved or rejected with justifications within 30 days of the receipt of the application. There is a fee of rub 50 per license application.

MVES informs other issuing bodies regularly about adverse developments in trade relations with individual countries or groups of countries, market conditions for individual products (works, services), and other factors relevant for making decisions on the issuance of licenses. Thus, on October 15, 1990, licensing requirements were imposed on imports from the Czech and Slovak Federal Republic and Hungary in an effort to stem growing trade deficits with these countries by restricting imports above protocol limits.

In addition to general and one-time licenses which monitor foreign trade on a countrywide basis, a new type of license was introduced in 1990 to give effect to a December 1989 decision to give each republic the right to export on a barter

437

basis, mainly to stimulate border trade. The size of the barter quotas was limited to 1 percent of each republic's domestic market. Thus, the RSFSR was allowed a quota of rub 240 million for exports (other than foodstuffs, construction materials, and fertilizers) that can be withdrawn from that republic's market in 1990 and exchanged for an equal value of imports. By mid-1990, the RSFSR had obtained licenses equivalent to 22 percent of its quota. At the same time, rates of utilization ranged from 2 percent in Kazakhstan to 100 percent in Azerbaidzhan.

Altogether, in the period January 1-August 23, 1990, about 12,200 licenses for exports and imports had been issued, including about 9,000 by the MVES and about 100 by the republics. Within the overall total, about 700-1,000 were general licenses and the remainder, one-time licenses. Reflecting the primary objective of licenses to ensure domestic supplies, about 70 percent of exports were subject to license, compared with only 6 percent of imports.

(3) Trade taxation

The existing import tariff, which has zero rates for about one half of all items and very low ones for the remainder, is not being enforced. Since August 1990, with retroactive effect from July 1, 1990 and until the end of 1990, special import taxes ranging from 130 percent to 2,090 percent were applied to 95 groups of consumer goods.[27] Exempt from this tax, which for most products has lower rates for imports from CMEA countries, are temporary imports, imports for resale in foreign currency stores and imports representing capital subscriptions by foreign producers to joint ventures in the USSR. The Ministry of Finance, in consultation with Goskomtsen and the MVES, was empowered to adjust these tax rates in the light of changes in business conditions for the individual commodities in the external and domestic markets. With the introduction of the commercial exchange rate, the import tax rates were reduced to less than one third the previous level. A new import tariff, replacing the nomenclature of the CMEA's Unified Classification System with that of the Harmonized System, has been prepared for introduction at the beginning of 1991. The rates under discussion included MFN rates averaging 15-20 percent and maximum rates of 100 percent.

Exports of raw materials and fuels are subject to implicit (i.e., price equalization) taxes with an average rate of about 60 percent. From January 1, 1991, explicit export taxes were to be introduced for main raw materials (i.e., oil, gas, metals and wood) on the basis of the export value converted into rubles at the commercial exchange rate and ranging from 5-50 percent. These taxes were meant to tax away part of the windfall profits arising from the introduction of the commercial exchange rate.

(4) The system of differentiated foreign exchange coefficients

Through the end of 1986, domestic wholesale prices were insulated from movements in the foreign currency prices of exports and imports, with differences being effectively subsidized or taxed away through the mechanism of price equalization. As a result, there was no particular incentive for enterprises to produce for export since they received the same domestic wholesale price regardless of whether they sold to the domestic market or to an intermediary FTO. Similarly, end-users in general had no price advantage from using imported goods.

Decree No. 991 of the Council of Ministers of August 1986 established a system of differentiated foreign exchange coefficients (DVKs) that entered into effect on January 1, 1987. The coefficients, ranging initially from 0.1 (e.g., exports of ginseng to country group 2) to 15.9 (imports of yarn from country group 2), were applied multiplicatively to the valuta ruble value obtained from converting the foreign exchange surrendered or purchased at the official exchange rate. The original DVK system, which was administered by the Ministry of Finance, was rather complex with some 3,000 coefficients for exports and imports (virtually all items participating in foreign trade except oil, its derivatives and other energy products, which remained subject to classical price equalization) that differentiated by type of product and country group of origin or destination.[28] As mentioned above (section 2), this system was intended to make domestic enterprises more sensitive to fluctuations in foreign prices. But in practice DVKs were not kept unchanged if enterprise profits were curtailed, and the system degenerated into an *ad hoc* and nontransparent system of implicit taxation or subsidy.

Reflecting a decision in late 1988 by the Council of Ministers to phase out the DVKs, their number was reduced beginning in 1989 and by October 1990 they only applied to exports of machinery. Fewer imports than exports were covered; other imports, especially those outside the plan, were subject to import taxes. The dispersion of coefficients also was reduced, with DVKs ranging from 0.4 to 1.5 in late 1990. DVKs were withdrawn with the introduction of the commercial exchange rate on November 1, 1990.

(5) Foreign exchange retention

To encourage self-financing of foreign exchange transactions, a foreign exchange retention scheme was introduced in 1987,[29] thus effectively bringing to an end the state foreign exchange monopoly that had existed after the short-lived experiment with free foreign exchange trading in the 1920s. The retention scheme applied to exports settled in convertible currencies, transferable rubles, the currencies of other socialist countries and clearing currencies under bilateral agreements. With the introduction of the retention scheme, the centralized provision of foreign exchange through the foreign exchange allocation plan was reduced. In 1990, retention rates for convertible currency exports ranged from 0 percent to 100 percent of export value, with higher rates generally provided for more processed goods, e.g., timber, 25 percent; surgical equipment, 95 percent; and radio and television sets, 100 percent. Most raw materials and oil products received no retention rights, although exporters of crude oil, natural gas and coal were given retention rights of up to 20 percent during 1990 in an effort to stimulate production. Preferential arrangements existed for exports under economic cooperation agreements, border trade exports, and exports from the Far Eastern economic region. However, because of the exclusion of most raw materials and energy products, the average retention rate was only 7-8 percent. Rates are set at the enterprise level, which could result in two similar products produced by different enterprises obtaining vastly different retention rights.

The original retention scheme has been liberalized over time. Instead of repurchase rights (without exchange rate guarantee) that were carried as contingent liabilities of the VEB in valuta rubles (off-balance sheet), exporters were given the option to maintain accounts in foreign currency or in valuta rubles[30] with the VEB (on-balance sheet). In addition, off-balance sheet repurchase rights can now be converted at any time (e.g., at the time foreign exchange is surrendered) into outright ownership of foreign exchange in the form of interest-bearing accounts maintained with VEB. The requirement to service foreign currency loans from VEB out of retained amounts (rather than all export proceeds) was abolished. And since 1989, enterprises can use retained amounts immediately (rather than in the year following the receipt of payment from abroad, without interest compensation) and use a specified proportion of amounts retained for consumer goods, medicine and medical equipment for their workers (rather than exclusively for capital goods as previously). In December 1988, the proportion of retained convertible currency funds that could be spent for the benefit of workers was set at 10 percent but shortly thereafter it was raised to 25 percent. Retained balances in transferable rubles or the currencies of other socialist countries can be used for imports for the benefit of workers in their entirety while those under bilateral agreements can be used up to 10 percent for that purpose. Higher proportions can be used by entities in the Far Eastern economic region. Retained foreign exchange may also be used for business trips abroad (see section 4.b below). In October 1990, the VEB's on- and off-balance sheet obligations under the retention scheme amounted to 2.6 billion valuta rubles.

According to a presidential decree issued on November 2, 1990, foreign exchange receipts from exports are to be surrendered from January 1, 1991, at the commercial exchange rate, as follows. Forty percent are to be surrendered to a joint union-republic fund mainly for servicing the USSR's external debt. Retention quotas would then be applied to the remaining 60 percent. Of the 40 percent surrendered, 90 percent would be surrendered to the joint union-republic fund, without earmarking, and 10 percent, to republic, regional and local funds. A foreign exchange committee with union and republic representation and chaired by the USSR Prime Minister would develop and implement foreign exchange policy, including the disposition of the resources surrendered to the union-republic fund.

To make the retention scheme more consistent and transparent, efforts were underway to introduce new product-specific rates in early 1991 ranging from 20 percent to 80 percent of export proceeds (net of surrender for external debt servicing) in direct proportion to the amount of domestic processing (Table III.4.12). Because of the critical situation in the oil and coal mining sectors, relatively high retention rates were proposed for exports of crude oil and coal. For oil exports in excess of the agreed state procurement level of 61 million tons for 1991, the authorities intended to allow retention of 50 percent of the full value of export proceeds.

(6) Trade financing

To facilitate the increasing number of direct exporters' and importers' trade transactions and arrange financing, the VEB has been expanding its network of domestic branches. Trade in raw materials, energy products, and foodstuffs in convertible currencies is generally conducted on a cash basis. Thus, payment for oil exports is usually received within 30 days after shipment. Recently, under a German agricultural credit, some foodstuffs have been imported with payment terms of one year. Also, reflecting recent payment difficulties, foreign suppliers who used to deliver on open account now require documentary credits. The VEB, in turn, requires a full cash deposit at the time it opens an import letter of credit. Deposits held for commercial letters of credit issued in favor of foreign suppliers amounted to rub 0.5 billion in October 1990. Machinery and equipment are usually imported on the basis of bank credit and suppliers' credit. Guarantees are increasingly sought for such loans by the foreign lender.

b. Current invisibles

Payments for services and transfers in convertible currencies other than those related to merchandise imports are generally highly restricted. On the basis of a personal invitation from abroad, Soviet citizens are entitled to convert up to rub 2,000 a year into convertible currency at the special exchange rate for travel abroad.[31] Higher amounts are available for travel to socialist countries. However, travel to the Czech and Slovak Federal Republic, Hungary and Poland was restricted in July 1990. Insurance against commercial risk is being offered by Gosstrakh, an agency of the Ministry of Finance. Except for forward foreign exchange cover offered by the VEB, there is no insurance yet for other types of risk. As mentioned, enterprises can use their own foreign exchange to send employees on business trips abroad, including stays for training purposes. Receipts from foreign travelers for hotel accommodation, transportation, and certain other services are converted at the official exchange rate.[32]

Under a 1963 agreement among 12 socialist countries (including the GDR) and its 1971 amendment, payments for 22 listed types of services and personal transfers are channeled through bilateral accounts at special exchange rates. These services and transfers include, *inter alia,* diplomatic expenses, international passenger transport, educational and medical expenses, and personal transfers such as wages and salaries, pensions, honoraria, royalties, child support and savings. In July 1990, the USSR served notice that it intended to withdraw from the agreement with effect from November 1, 1990. The export or import of Soviet banknotes and coin is prohibited. Unspent ruble balances may be reconverted up to the amount exchanged at the special exchange rate. Foreign means of payment must be declared upon entry into the USSR. Foreign currency may be re-exported by foreign visitors up to the amounts declared upon entry.

5. CAPITAL TRANSACTIONS

a. Capital

(1) Foreign direct investment[33]

Apart from joint construction projects within the framework of the CMEA, inward investment has since January 1987 taken the form of joint ventures.[34] Investment must be in hard currency, but reinvestment of ruble profits is also permitted. The initial legislation was liberalized significantly in late 1988[35] by permitting majority foreign participation, and giving enterprises the freedom to appoint non-Soviet citizens as chief executive officer or chairman of the board and to hire and fire labor. Under a new investment law adopted in July 1990, the tax liabilities of joint ventures with no more than 30 percent foreign participation were set equal to those of state enterprises (e.g., 45 percent for the company profit tax). If foreign participation exceeds 30 percent, no profit tax is due for the first two calendar years after the first profit is recorded (exception: trading and fishing companies). Profit tax is 30 percent and there is an additional 15 percent for profits remitted abroad.[36]

The Ministry of Finance is responsible for issuing registration numbers for joint ventures, which then must register with the MVES.[37] The MVES must ensure that Soviet laws and regulations are complied with. There are no lines of economic activity that are proscribed for joint ventures. The foreign partners must be juridical persons and present documentation as to their financial solvency from a bank of their country of residence. As of early August 1990, 2,020 joint ventures had been registered, but the number of companies in operation was much smaller.

On October 26, 1990, a presidential decree was issued permitting foreign investors to buy Soviet securities and to acquire 100 percent ownership in Soviet companies. The decree also permitted the reinvestment or transfer abroad of profits realized by foreign investors in accordance with Soviet law and it guaranteed foreign investors treatment not less favorable than that accorded to Soviet enterprises. The decree anticipated the adoption by the Supreme Soviet of a new investment law with identical provisions.[38]

On the basis of a July 14, 1990 resolution of the RSFSR Supreme Soviet "On Setting Up Free Enterprise Zones in the Territory of Russia," the RSFSR Supreme Soviet decided in October 1990 to set up such a zone in the Far Eastern port of Nakhodka. Enterprises in the zone were to enjoy a five-year tax waiver on reinvested profits and a reduced tax rate of 10 percent on profits transferred abroad. Goods were to be imported into the zone duty free and measures to take foreign investments by force, such as nationalization, requisition, confiscation and other measures similar in their consequences, were declared inadmissable in the zone's territory.

Investment protection agreements have been signed (but not necessarily ratified) with several countries including Austria, Belgium, Canada, China, Finland, France, Germany, Italy, Netherlands, Spain and the United Kingdom. Agreements with several other countries are either ready to be signed or in the process of negotiation. Double taxation agreements exist with 25 countries. The most recent one, with China, was signed in July 1990.

Outward direct or portfolio investment is permitted in accordance with Decree No. 412 of the USSR Council of Ministers of July 1989 and requires a license from the VEB. The investment must be financed with the Soviet enterprise's own foreign exchange or a loan extended or authorized by the VEB. The VEB has full branches in Zürich and Cyprus and representative offices in 11 other countries, including the United States since 1989. Together with Gosbank, VEB also owns five banks in Paris, London, Vienna, Luxembourg and Frankfurt. Of these, the Moscow Narodny Bank in London in turn has a branch in Singapore.

(2) Loans

External loans are contracted in accordance with the annual plan. Financial loans may be contracted only by the VEB. Since 1988, bonds have also been issued in foreign markets. Subject to an overall ceiling, the VEB grants licenses for nonfinancial borrowing operations abroad. Most licenses issued are one-time licenses but a few large enterprises are given general licenses. Licenses are also required for suppliers' credits exceeding either the equivalent of rub 1 million or a maturity of one year. A brief examination of the borrower's dossier is made in the case of license applications for suppliers' credits. The granting of a license does not entail any responsibility of the VEB or the state vis-à-vis foreign suppliers or other creditors. There is no registration requirement for the amounts and terms of financing actually obtained.

The VEB also provides foreign currency loans to Soviet enterprises under a global annual ceiling and in accordance with policy guidelines established by the government.[39] Loans with a maturity of up to eight years can be extended for projects that generate foreign exchange earnings. Loans for current operations are limited to a maturity of two years. In either case, debt service is expected to be made from the borrower's enhanced foreign exchange flow. Both types of loans are granted on the basis of a thorough analysis of the borrower's creditworthiness and of the self-liquidating nature of the operation to be financed. The latter condition can be waived if the borrower is judged to be particularly creditworthy. In any case, adequate collateral or third-party guarantees must be provided in order for loans to be approved. In a break with past practice, the VEB can refuse to comply with requests by superior organs (e.g., branch ministries) to extend such loans. The outstanding volume of such foreign currency loans to state enterprises is about rub 1.5 billion. Loans to joint ventures may be made outside the annual global ceiling for foreign currency loans. VEB may also provide guarantees to these enterprises and license them to borrow abroad provided that the terms obtained do not deviate significantly from market conditions. As of January 1, 1990, joint ventures had received foreign currency credits amounting to rub 750 million. About rub 110 million of these credits (15 percent) had been extended by the VEB; the remainder had been received from foreign banks, including rub 180 million (27 percent) with the VEB's guarantee. The maturities of these loans ranged from several months to more than 10 years.

b. Gold

Soviet citizens may buy, sell and hold gold in any form. However, they may not take gold (except jewelry) abroad. Gold is exported exclusively on the basis of decisions by the Council of Ministers. As with other precious metals, the VEB acts as the broker in these transactions. Gold jewelry is exported by Glavalmazzoloto.

NOTES

1. Several issues related to the foreign exchange and trade system are discussed in greater detail in Chapter IV.3.

2. All countries except CMEA member countries, Albania, and the Democratic People's Republic of Korea, Lao, P.D.R., and Yugoslavia. In addition to the USSR, CMEA member countries in 1990 were Bulgaria, Cuba, the Czech and Slovak Federal Republic, the German Democratic Republic, Hungary, Mongolia, Poland, Romania, and Viet Nam.

3. Under a draft foreign exchange law currently before the Supreme Soviet, the level of the peg would be set by the Supreme Soviet of the USSR.

4. Australian dollars, Austrian schillings, pounds sterling, Belgian francs, deutsche marks, Dutch guilders, Danish kroner, Italian lire, Canadian dollars, Norwegian kroner, U.S. dollars, Finnish markka, French francs, Swedish kronor, Swiss francs, Yugoslav dinars, Japanese yen and the ECU.

5. Greek drachmas, Spanish pesetas, Kuwaiti dinars, Lebanese pounds, Portuguese escudos, and Turkish lira. No rate is being quoted for the Kuwaiti dinar for the time being.

6. Afghan afghanis, Egyptian pounds, Indian rupees, Iranian rials, Irish pounds, Icelandic kroner, YAR dinars, Malaysian ringgit, Persian rupees, Singapore dollars, and Sudanese pounds.

7. Egyptian pounds, Indian rupees, Iranian rials, Pakistan rupees, Sudanese pounds and Yemeni dinars.

8. Foreign exchange reservations are contract clauses insuring against foreign exchange risk by providing for a proportional adjustment in the contract price in the event that the exchange rate in question changes beyond established limits. As the basket compositions of the SDR and the Swedish krona are broadly similar to that of the ruble, this technique provides a high degree of stability for export and import prices in rubles.

9. Presidential decree of October 26, 1990. The decree mentioned a commercial exchange rate of rub 1.8 per U.S. dollar, but reflecting the cross rates of currencies of the basket at the time of its introduction, the actual exchange rate was slightly different.

10. The official exchange rate would remain in effect for ruble-denominated claims of the USSR on developing countries.

11. Budget efficiency results if a valuta ruble of imports yields more than one ruble upon domestic resale.

12. The legal basis for the establishment of a foreign exchange market was laid by a decree of the USSR Council of Ministers of September 1987.

13. The VEB began to hold the auctions twice a month in October 1990.

14. The calculation comprises the following steps: First, the moving five-day arithmetic average of the market exchange rates of the U.S. dollar against the 11 other currencies in the basket is calculated. Second, these average rates are divided by the base rates of the U.S. dollar against the 11 currencies. Third, the resulting 11 indices are multiplied with each currency's share in the basket to obtain a weighted average index. Fourth, the base exchange rate between the transferable ruble and the U.S. dollar is multiplied with the average index. Finally, exchange rates for the non-dollar currencies are derived by multiplying the U.S. dollar rates with their cross rates.

15. There were 50 such transactions from December 1989 to February 1990.

16. The 1971 agreement, which amended the original agreement of 1963, enumerates 22 groups of invisibles payments and personal transfers, including passenger transportation, medical and educational expenses, and wages, that are eligible for settlement at the special noncommercial exchange rates.

17. Under the draft foreign exchange law, only domestic banks would be authorized to make payments in foreign currency in the territory of the USSR.

18. Decree "On Improving Retail Trade and the Performance of Services for Foreign Currencies" of July 1990.

19. For a description of the CMEA trading arrangements see Appendix II.3 and Chapter IV.3.

20. On the Polish side, a more appreciated exchange rate (of Zl 7,500 instead of Zl 9,500 per US$1) was introduced for transactions channeled through this account. For the balance in the bilateral account as of mid-1990, see Table III.4.7.

21. As part of the agreement with China, the USSR's debts to that country are to be paid with exports of goods valued at world market prices.

22. The foreign trade regime is described and analyzed in greater detail in Chapter IV.3.

23. Decrees No. 991 and 992 of the Central Committee of the CPSU and of the USSR Council of Ministers of August 19, 1986.

24. Decree No. 1405 of the USSR Council of Ministers dated December 2, 1988.

25. The USSR Council of Ministers authorized the Baltic republics in the Spring of 1990 to register firms located in their territories. From January 1, 1991, all firms were scheduled to register with the appropriate republics.

26. In the case of infraction of rules, trading rights can be suspended or entities may become subject to stricter regulation of all their foreign trading operations, including the requirement of one-time licenses for each transaction.

27. Decree No. 815 of the USSR Council of Ministers of August 13, 1990.

28. There were five country groups. For an illustrative example of rates in effect in 1990, see Table III.4.11.

29. Decree No. 991 of the Central Committee of the CPSU and the USSR Council of Ministers dated August 19, 1986. The retention scheme was subsequently modified on the basis of Decree No. 1074 of the Central Committee of the CPSU and the USSR Council of Ministers dated September 17, 1987 and Decree No. 1405 of the USSR Council of Ministers dated December 2, 1988.

30. Valuta ruble accounts bear interest at a rate corresponding to the average of the interest rates of the six currencies in the basket used for valuing the ruble. Their value is stable vis-à-vis the basket of these currencies. Thus, when the commercial exchange rate was introduced on November 1, 1990, the amounts kept in valuta ruble accounts were increased threefold in order to maintain the foreign currency value of these accounts unchanged.

31. Foreign exchange at the special exchange rate is also made available for approved medical treatment abroad and for persons settling permanently abroad.

32. Since November 1, 1990, the commercial exchange rate is being used for conversion.

33. The regulations governing inward foreign direct investment are described in greater detail in Chapter IV.4.

34. Decree No. 49 of the USSR Council of Ministers dated January 13, 1987.

35. Decree No. 1405 of the USSR Council of Ministers dated December 2, 1988.

36. The remittance tax was lowered from 20 percent to 15 percent on July 1, 1990.

37. In anticipation of the transferral as of January 1, 1991 of registration procedures to the republics in which the respective firms are located, the Ministry of Finance ceased to accept documents from applicants on November 15, 1990.

38. The draft law goes further than the decree, however, in (i) allowing foreign investors to open ruble accounts and engage in economic activities involving Soviet currency, and (ii) protecting foreign investment against adverse shifts in subsequent Soviet legislation.

39. Under the provisions of Decree No. 1405 of the USSR Council of Ministers dated December 2, 1988, individual loans are not to exceed rub 5 million.

Table III.4.1. USSR: Exchange Rate of the Ruble
Against the U.S. Dollar, 1985-90

(In rubles per 100 U.S. dollars)

	1985	1986	1987	1988	1989	1990
			End of Period			
January	87.95	75.85	64.49	59.78	61.75	59.95
February	92.00	73.55	64.66	60.38	61.59	60.10
March	88.15	72.75	64.07	59.38	62.56	61.20
April	85.75	72.60	62.67	59.37	62.30	60.74
May	85.65	71.15	62.80	59.71	65.35	59.74
June	86.10	71.45	63.89	62.06	64.30	59.76
July	82.30	69.00	64.18	62.06	63.44	58.61
August	80.60	67.85	63.39	62.91	64.44	56.40
September	79.57	67.71	63.37	63.16	63.30	...
October	78.70	68.26	62.33	61.19	62.89	...
November	77.18	68.41	60.17	59.84	62.24	...
December	76.42	67.83	58.43	60.67	60.88	...
			Period Average			
January	87.47	75.55	65.69	59.14	61.44	60.68
February	89.90	73.20	64.80	60.36	62.12	60.00
March	90.32	71.95	64.48	59.73	62.13	60.96
April	86.15	72.41	63.39	59.23	62.60	60.76
May	86.12	70.45	62.71	59.49	64.12	59.96
June	85.87	71.13	63.64	60.68	64.97	59.97
July	83.80	69.63	64.17	62.38	63.72	59.08
August	81.12	68.25	64.32	63.05	63.82	57.55
September	81.80	67.76	63.13	62.86	64.45	56.92
October	78.54	67.44	63.01	62.23	63.00	...
November	77.60	68.43	60.75	60.32	62.74	...
December	76.42	67.80	59.26	60.08	61.60	...
First quarter	89.23	73.57	64.99	59.74	61.90	60.55
Second quarter	86.05	71.33	63.25	59.80	63.90	60.23
Third quarter	82.24	68.55	63.87	62.76	64.00	57.85
Fourth quarter	77.52	67.89	61.01	60.88	61.13	...
First half	87.64	72.45	64.12	59.77	62.90	60.39
Second half	79.88	68.22	62.44	61.82	62.57	...
Year [1]	83.76	70.34	63.28	60.80	62.74	...

Source: Gosbank.

1. There are small discrepancies with the annual average for the U.S. dollar given in Table III.4.2. For conversion purposes the average rates contained in Table III.4.2. have been used in this chapter.

447

Table III.4.2.   USSR: Average Annual Exchange Rates of the Ruble
Against Major Convertible Currencies, 1979-89

(In rubles per one hundred currency units) [1]

Year	U.S. dollar	Deutsche mark	Swiss franc	French franc	Pound sterling	Japanese yen
			(Average period)			
1979	65.49	35.80	39.47	15.40	140.07	2.99
1980	65.15	35.83	38.89	15.45	152.03	2.93
1981	72.02	32.12	36.80	13.43	145.46	3.29
1982	72.51	30.01	35.82	11.81	126.12	3.04
1983	74.25	29.28	35.48	9.84	112.57	3.12
1984	81.69	28.81	34.81	9.37	109.62	3.43
1985	83.70	28.50	34.25	9.34	108.04	3.52
1986	70.35	32.03	39.15	10.36	105.75	4.18
1987	63.34	35.19	42.41	10.51	103.38	4.37
1988	60.75	34.72	41.73	10.23	108.24	4.75
1989	63.00	33.55	38.60	9.88	103.35	4.58

Source: Gosbank.
1. 1,000 currency units in the case of the Japanese yen.

Table III.4.3.   USSR: Foreign Currency Auctions, 1989-90

Date	Amount Sold (In millions of valuta rubles)	Price [1] in Rubles per	
		Valuta ruble	U.S. dollar [2]
1989			
November 8	8.4	15.2	9.46
1990			
January 17	8.2	17.5	10.50
February 21	9.0	21.3	12.80
April 5	9.6	23.1	14.00
May 10	9.8	27.1	16.20
June 22	6.8	35.1	20.98
July 19	9.0	41.2	24.15
August 21	11.7	41.2	23.24
October 9	9.5	40.0	24.00
October 25	3.9	38.0	20.88
November 15	8.1	38.0	20.88
Total	94.0		

Source: Vneshekonombank; *Ekonomika i zhizn'*, various issues; and calculations.
1. Average of successful bids until April; uniform price thereafter.
2. Approximate, using end-of-month exchange rates.

Table III.4.4. USSR: Black Market Exchange Rates for the
Ruble in Moscow and Vienna, 1990

(In rubles per currency unit indicated)

In Moscow

Date	U.S. Dollar		Deutsche Mark		Cross Rate [1]
	Buying	Selling	Buying	Selling	
End January	10	14.5-15	7	7.7-8	1.67
End February	10	16-20	6.5-7.5	8.5-10	1.72
End March	10-11	16-20	7-7.5	9-10	1.70
End April	11-13	17-20	7.5-8.5	10-11.5	1.63
End May	11-13	17.8-20	8	10.5-11.5	1.63
End July	15	18-25	8-8.5	11.5-12	1.82
End August	17	19-23	9	12-13	1.77
Mid September	15-18	20-25	10-12	15-16	1.47
Mid October	15-16	18-20	8-9	10-11.5	1.79
End October	16	19-20	9	11-12	1.73

In Vienna

Date	U.S. Dollar			Deutsche Mark		
	Buying	Selling	Appreciation/Depreciation [2]	Buying	Selling	Appreciation/Depreciation [2]
End January	8.71	16.57	...	5.09	9.92	...
End February	8.75	16.64	-0.4	5.09	9.92	—
End March	10.25	23.40	-24.5	5.93	13.88	-24.2
End April	8.41	15.47	40.9	4.91	9.25	39.9
End May	9.80	21.18	-22.9	5.70	12.62	-22.7
End June	10.57	25.67	-14.5	6.19	15.41	-15.2
End July	9.28	20.00	23.8	5.70	12.62	17.9
End August	10.36	27.00	-21.6	6.47	17.34	-23.1
End September	10.86	30.86	-10.5	6.78	19.82	-10.5
Mid October	10.57	30.00	2.8	6.78	19.82	—

Sources: Kommersant, various issues; *Wiener Zeitung,* various issues.
1. DM per US$1; on a mid-point basis.
2. In percent, on a mid-point basis from the preceding date; appreciation (+).

Table III.4.5. USSR: Exchange Rate of the Transferable Ruble
Against the U.S. Dollar, 1985-90

(In transferable rubles per 100 U.S. dollars at end of period)

	1985	1986	1987	1988	1989	1990
January	82.66	74.55	64.90	61.76	64.27	63.68
February	85.19	73.20	64.53	62.31	64.72	63.09
March	84.81	71.81	64.90	62.10	65.16	63.67
April	81.28	71.60	64.49	61.48	65.57	63.75
May	82.57	71.44	64.17	61.50	67.55	62.68
June	82.28	71.19	64.42	63.43	67.84	62.86
July	80.91	70.29	65.05	64.78	66.48	62.20
August	79.52	68.80	64.93	65.60	66.75	61.68
September	80.45	68.33	64.77	65.47	67.12	...
October	77.70	67.71	64.88	64.27	66.27	...
November	77.64	68.52	62.11	63.05	65.57	...
December	76.09	68.07	61.22	63.04	64.31	...

Source: International Bank for Economic Cooperation (IBEC).

Table III.4.6. USSR: Exchange Rates of the Ruble Against CMEA Country Currencies for Noncommercial Transactions, 1985-90

(In rubles per number of national currency units indicated)

	Number of currency units	1985 Multi-lateral	1985 Bila-teral[1]	1986 Multi-lateral	1986 Bila-teral[1]	December 31, 1987 Multi-lateral	December 31, 1987 Bila-teral[1]	1988 Multi-lateral	1988 Bila-teral[1]	1989 Multi-lateral	1989 Bila-teral[1]	June 30, 1990 Bila-teral
Bulgarian lev	100	113.64	100.00	113.64	100.00	113.64	100.00	113.64	100.00	113.64	100.00	100.00
Cuban peso	100	90.00		90.00		90.00		90.00		90.00		90.00
Czechoslovak koruna	100	10.00		10.00		10.00		10.00		10.00	12.50	12.50
GDR mark	100	31.25		31.25		31.25		31.25		31.25		31.25
Hungarian forint	1,000	67.80	56.50	67.80	56.50	67.80	56.50	67.80	56.50	67.80	52.63[2]	52.36
Mongolian tugrik	100	23.92		23.92		23.92		23.92		23.92		23.92
Polish zloty	10,000	129.53		142.86	119.05	104.17		74.07	61.73	8.33	6.94	6.94
Romanian leu	100	12.05		12.05		12.05		12.05		12.05		12.05
Vietnamese dong	10,000	1,000.00	900.00	250.00	222.22	45.45	41.67	11.11	9.26	11.11	9.26	9.26

Source: Ministry of Finance.
1. Bilateral rate given only if different from multilateral rate.
2. Exceeds the 20 percent maximum deviation permitted under the multilateral agreement.

451

Table III.4.7.   USSR: Settlement Balances with Socialist Countries,[1] 1988-90

	December 31, 1988	December 31, 1989	June 30, 1990
	(In millions of transferable rubles)		
CMEA countries			
Bulgaria	289.3	-491.9	-452.4
Cuba	773.6	896.0	500.5
Czechoslovakia	-795.4	-666.4	-1,038.0
German Democratic Republic	70.5	-851.2	-2,576.4
Hungary	-180.9	-800.0	-887.7
Mongolia	37.8	7.1	86.8
Poland	539.2	-392.6	-2,613.1
Romania	-325.7	-240.2	140.9
Viet Nam	814.7	556.7	659.9
Subtotal [2]	1,223.1	-1,982.5	-6,179.5
Other operations [3]	-12.2	-36.8	-154.7
Total [2]	1,210.9	-2,019.3	-6,334.2
	(In millions of rubles)		
Other socialist countries			
China	-140.1	-51.0	-248.2
Kampuchea	95.0	94.7	57.4
Laos	6.9	7.5	14.2
North Korea	340.7	445.1	364.7
Yugoslavia	-1,005.6	-989.6	-1,174.6
Poland (clearing)	—	—	-91.1
Total [2]	-703.1	-493.3	-1,077.6

Source: Vneshekonombank.
1. Balance in favor of the USSR.
2. Subtotals and totals have been added for illustrative purposes only. Claims and liabilities cannot be netted against each other.
3. Represent transactions with international organizations (IBEC, IIB).

452

Table III.4.8. USSR: Financing Terms for IBEC Credits
to European CMEA Members[1], 1990

Type of Credit	Maximum Term	Interest Rate (In percent per year)
Transfer credit	automatic within calendar year	3.50
Term credit	6 months	3.75
	1 year	4.25
	2 years	4.50
	3 years	5.00

Source: Vneshekonombank.
1. Preferential interest rates are in effect for transfer and term credits to Cuba, Mongolia, and Viet Nam.

Table III.4.9. USSR: Imports Subject to Licensing in 1989-90

Name of Products (Works, Services)	Organizations Issuing Licenses
Medicines	USSR Ministry of Health
Chemical insecticides and herbicides	USSR Ministry of Mineral Fertilizer Production
Printed products and publication services in the Soviet Union	USSR State Committee for Publishing Houses
Film, video and audio production	USSR State Committee for Cinematography; USSR State Committee for Television and Radio Broadcasting; USSR State Committee for Publishing Houses; USSR Ministry of Culture; Councils of Ministers of Union Republics (for respective product list)
Services for construction of facilities on USSR territory with involvement of foreign firms through resources from central sources	USSR Ministry of Foreign Economic Relations
Employment of foreign labor	USSR State Committee for Labor and Social Problems
Theatrical, concert and other artistic activity	USSR Ministry of Culture
Operations to attract foreign currency resources in the form of credits, loans, deposits, investments, and in other forms	Vneshekonombank

Source: USSR Council of Ministers.

Table III.4.10. USSR: Exports Subject to Licensing in 1989-90

Name of Products (Works, Services)	Organizations Issuing Licenses
Crude oil, natural gas, gas condensate, petroleum products (gasoline, kerosene, jet fuel, diesel fuel, fuel oil, paraffin wax, lubricants)	USSR Ministry of Foreign Economic Relations
Ores and concentrates of ferrous metals, pig iron, ferrous metal rolled products, steel pipes, ferroalloys, vanadium pentoxide, ferrous metal scrap and waste products	USSR Ministry of Foreign Economic Relations
Ores, concentrates and industrial products of nonferrous metals, ores and concentrates of precious metals, nonferrous metals, including secondary metals, their alloys, powders, oxides, salts, solutions, semi-finished products, rolled products, nonferrous metal scrap and waste products	USSR Ministry of Foreign Economic Relations
Rare and rare-earth metals, their compounds and semiconductive materials	USSR Ministry of Foreign Economic Relations
Industrial products from precious metals	USSR Main Directorate for Diamonds and Gold
Apatite concentrate, ammonia, mineral fertilizers, sulphur, sulphuric acid, boron-containing raw materials and products made therefrom, acetic acid, acetic anhydride, cyclohexane, cyclohexanon, methanol, caprolactum, polyutheranes	
Benzene (other than crude, coal-bearing benzene) ...	USSR Ministry of Foreign Economic Relations
Phenol, styrenes, carbon black (industrial carbon) ...	USSR Ministry of the Petroleum Industry
Polyethylene, polypropylene, polystyrene, polyvinyl chloride resin, ion-exchange resins, plasticizers, dimethyl terephthalate, acrylonitrile, ethylene glycol, dies and semi-finished products for their production, chemical textile threads and fibers, plastic pipes, food industry ethyl alcohol	USSR Ministry of the Chemical Industry
Lumber and cellulose-paper products (other than low-grade wood and wood processing waste)	USSR Ministry of the Timber Industry
Waste paper	USSR Gossnab; Councils of Ministers of the union republics
Cement	USSR Ministry of Construction Materials
Gemstone raw materials, products made therefrom, collection materials, paleontological specimens ...	USSR Ministry of Geology; USSR Academy of Sciences (for corresponding product list)
Cotton (except for low grades), flax fiber, natural wool, fur and hides	USSR Ministry of Foreign Economic Relations
Grain (including groats), flour, feed concentrates, oil-yielding seed, vegetable oil, edible animal fats (including butter), sugar, meat and meat products, milk and milk products	USSR Ministry of Foreign Economic Relations
Fish and fish products (except for fish from inland waters, other than sturgeon)	USSR Ministry of the Fish Industry
Fish from inland waters, except for sturgeon	Councils of Ministers of the union republics

Table III.4.10 (Concluded). USSR: Exports Subject to Licensing in 1989-90

Name of Products (Works, Services)	Organizations Issuing Licenses
Liquor and vodka	State Agroindustrial Committee
Wine	Councils of Ministers of the union republics
Wild game and birds	Councils of Ministers of the union republics
Wild vegetation	Councils of Ministers of the union republics
Medicines (including medicinal plant raw materials)	Councils of Ministers of the union republics
Products of Tibetan medicine	Councils of Ministers of the union republics
Medical equipment	USSR Ministry of Health
Soviet inventions and other results of scientific and technical activity	USSR State Committee for Science and Technology
Theatrical, concert and other artistic activity	USSR Ministry of Culture
Operations to allocate foreign currency resources in the form of credit, loans, deposits, investments, and in other forms	Vneshekonombank

Source: USSR Council of Ministers.

455

Table III.4.11. USSR: Selected Foreign Trade Items Subject to Differentiated Foreign Exchange Coefficients[1], August 1990

Customs Classification	Item	Country Group[2]				
		I	II	III	IV	V
		Exports				
191	*Trucks and garage equipment* [3]	0.6	0.6	0.6	0.6	0.6
...	KamAz trucks	0.7	1.0	0.9	0.7	0.7
19103	Buses	0.8	0.8	1.2	—	—
192	*Ships and port equipment* [3]	0.8	1.6	1.2	1.0	0.6
19201	Passenger ships	0.4	0.4	—	—	—
19225	Boats	1.2	1.2	1.2	—	—
		Imports				
100	*Metal-cutting machine tools* [3]	0.9	1.3	1.1	1.0	0.9
10010	Lathes	1.0	—	1.2	—	—
101	*Presses* [3]	1.0	1.3	1.0	1.0	1.0
10117	Hydraulic presses for testing pipes .	0.9	—	1.0	—	—

Source: Ministry of Finance.
1. The coefficient scheme was abolished on November 1, 1990.
2. Group I: European CMEA member countries; group II: convertible currency settlements plus payments agreements with China, Finland, and India; group III: payments agreements with Egypt, Iran, and Yugoslavia; group IV: non-European CMEA members; group V: all other countries.
3. Unless otherwise specified.

Table III.4.12. USSR: Selected Foreign Exchange Retention Rates, 1990-91
(In percent)

	1990	1991[1]
Crude oil	5-20	60
Oil products	—	35
Coal	20	40
Gas, electric energy	3.5	20
Ferrous and non-ferrous metals	—	30
Information processing	...	70
Instruments	...	70
Transportation equipment	...	65
Machinery and equipment	...	60
Textiles and shoes	...	55

Source: State Foreign Economic Commission, USSR Council of Ministers.
1. Rates applicable after deduction of 40 percent of export proceeds for the servicing of external debt.

NOTES

NOTES

NOTES

NOTES

NOTES

NOTES